Praise for *ASP.NET 2.0 Illustrated*

"This book is a phenomenal start for someone new to ASP.NET, as well as a complete guide to the new features of version 2.0 for programmers familiar with an earlier version. The beginning chapters detail concepts using a hypothetical company, examining the myriad sorts of requests and situations often requested by clients. The authors deal with these in an eloquent, realistic manner. They have clearly worked in the industry and have faced real-world challenges that programmers encounter daily. The content covers everything from the most basic tasks to the most complex, and is a comprehensive collection of information on ASP.NET 2.0. Every topic is well-referenced for additional information, but contains clear examples that work. The content is technical but the clear writing makes it easy to understand. Difficult concepts are explained in such a way that this book will quickly become your favorite reference for ASP.NET!"

—*Ronda Pederson, consultant, Microsoft MVP Visual Developer, ASP/ASP.NET*

"As to be expected from two of today's leading technical authors, this book is a cracking guide to getting the most from the ASP 2.0 Framework. Detailed chapters, concise yet practical examples, and clear explanation provide the grounding and support necessary to leverage the new features that ASP 2.0 brings to the table—all explained with a logical, no-nonsense approach. This book will be borrowed by every developer you work with, so guard it wisely!"

—*John Timney, Microsoft MVP, senior Web services consultant, British Telecom*

"This book will absolutely change the way you view ASP.NET technology. Read it and your existing Web sites will suddenly appear to be underperforming."

—*Chris Carpenter, senior software engineer, L3 Communications, Inc.*

ASP.NET 2.0
Illustrated

Microsoft .NET Development Series

John Montgomery, *Series Advisor*
Don Box, *Series Advisor*
Martin Heller, *Series Editor*

The **Microsoft .NET Development Series** is supported and developed by the leaders and experts of Microsoft development technologies including Microsoft architects and DevelopMentor instructors. The books in this series provide a core resource of information and understanding every developer needs in order to write effective applications and managed code. Learn from the leaders how to maximize your use of the .NET Framework and its programming languages.

Titles in the Series

Brad Abrams, *.NET Framework Standard Library Annotated Reference Volume 1: Base Class Library and Extended Numerics Library*, 0-321-15489-4

Brad Abrams and Tamara Abrams, *.NET Framework Standard Library Annotated Reference, Volume 2: Networking Library, Reflection Library, and XML Library*, 0-321-19445-4

Keith Ballinger, *.NET Web Services: Architecture and Implementation*, 0-321-11359-4

Bob Beauchemin, Niels Berglund, Dan Sullivan, *A First Look at SQL Server 2005 for Developers*, 0-321-18059-3

Don Box with Chris Sells, *Essential .NET, Volume 1: The Common Language Runtime*, 0-201-73411-7

Keith Brown, *The .NET Developer's Guide to Windows Security*, 0-321-22835-9

Eric Carter and Eric Lippert, *Visual Studio Tools for Office: Using C# with Excel, Word, Outlook, and InfoPath*, 0-321-33488-4

Eric Carter and Eric Lippert, *Visual Studio Tools for Office: Using Visual Basic 2005 with Excel, Word, Outlook, and InfoPath*, 0-321-41175-7

Mahesh Chand, *Graphics Programming with GDI+*, 0-321-16077-0

Krzysztof Cwalina and Brad Abrams, *Framework Design Guidelines: Conventions, Idioms, and Patterns for Reusable .NET Libraries*, 0-321-24675-6

Anders Hejlsberg, Scott Wiltamuth, Peter Golde, *The C# Programming Language,* 0-321-15491-6

Alex Homer, Dave Sussman, Mark Fussell, *ADO.NET and System.Xml v. 2.0—The Beta Version,* 0-321-24712-4

Alex Homer, Dave Sussman, Rob Howard, *ASP.NET v. 2.0—The Beta Version,* 0-321-25727-8

James S. Miller and Susann Ragsdale, *The Common Language Infrastructure Annotated Standard,* 0-321-15493-2

Christian Nagel, *Enterprise Services with the .NET Framework: Developing Distributed Business Solutions with .NET Enterprise Services*, 0-321-24673-X

Brian Noyes, *Data Binding with Windows Forms 2.0: Programming Smart Client Data Applications with .NET*, 0-321-26892-X

Fritz Onion, *Essential ASP.NET with Examples in C#*, 0-201-76040-1

Fritz Onion, *Essential ASP.NET with Examples in Visual Basic .NET*, 0-201-76039-8

Ted Pattison and Dr. Joe Hummel, *Building Applications and Components with Visual Basic .NET*, 0-201-73495-8

Dr. Neil Roodyn, *eXtreme .NET: Introducing eXtreme Programming Techniques to .NET Developers*, 0-321-30363-6

Chris Sells, *Windows Forms Programming in C#*, 0-321-11620-8

Chris Sells and Justin Gehtland, *Windows Forms Programming in Visual Basic .NET*, 0-321-12519-3

Paul Vick, *The Visual Basic .NET Programming Language*, 0-321-16951-4

Damien Watkins, Mark Hammond, Brad Abrams, *Programming in the .NET Environment*, 0-201-77018-0

Shawn Wildermuth, *Pragmatic ADO.NET: Data Access for the Internet World*, 0-201-74568-2

Paul Yao and David Durant, *.NET Compact Framework Programming with C#*, 0-321-17403-8

Paul Yao and David Durant, *.NET Compact Framework Programming with Visual Basic .NET*, 0-321-17404-6

For more information go to www.awprofessional.com/msdotnetseries/

ASP.NET 2.0 Illustrated

- **Alex Homer**
- **Dave Sussman**

✦✦Addison-Wesley

Upper Saddle River, NJ • Boston • Indianapolis • San Francisco
New York • Toronto • Montreal • London • Munich • Paris • Madrid
Capetown • Sydney • Tokyo • Singapore • Mexico City

Many of the designations used by manufacturers and sellers to distinguish their products are claimed as trademarks. Where those designations appear in this book, and the publisher was aware of a trademark claim, the designations have been printed with initial capital letters or in all capitals.

The .NET logo is either a registered trademark or trademark of Microsoft Corporation in the United States and/or other countries and is used under license from Microsoft.

The authors and publisher have taken care in the preparation of this book, but make no expressed or implied warranty of any kind and assume no responsibility for errors or omissions. No liability is assumed for incidental or consequential damages in connection with or arising out of the use of the information or programs contained herein.

The publisher offers excellent discounts on this book when ordered in quantity for bulk purchases or special sales, which may include electronic versions and/or custom covers and content particular to your business, training goals, marketing focus, and branding interests. For more information, please contact:

U.S. Corporate and Government Sales
(800) 382-3419
corpsales@pearsontechgroup.com

For sales outside the United States please contact:

International Sales
International@pearsoned.com

This Book Is Safari Enabled

The Safari® Enabled icon on the cover of your favorite technology book means the book is available through Safari Bookshelf. When you buy this book, you get free access to the online edition for 45 days.

Safari Bookshelf is an electronic reference library that lets you easily search thousands of technical books, find code samples, download chapters, and access technical information whenever and wherever you need it.

To gain 45-day Safari Enabled access to this book:

- Go to http://www.awprofessional.com/safarienabled
- Complete the brief registration form
- Enter the coupon code 2WFE-69XG-ISGD-VBGC-VJRR

If you have difficulty registering on Safari Bookshelf or accessing the online edition, please e-mail customer-service@safaribooksonline.com.

Visit us on the Web: www.awprofessional.com

Library of Congress Cataloging-in-Publication Data:

Homer, Alex.
    ASP.NET 2.0 illustrated / Alex Homer and Dave Sussman.
        p. cm.
    Includes index.
    ISBN 0-321-41834-4 (pbk. : alk. paper)
1. Active server pages. 2. Web sites—Design. 3. Web site development.
4. Microsoft .NET. I. Sussman, David, II. Title.
    TK5105.8885.A26H65974 2006
    005.2'768—dc22

                                                  2006008002

ISBN 0-321-41834-4

Text printed in the United States on recycled paper at R.R. Donnelley in Crawfordsville, Indiana.

First printing, June 2006

Contents

Figures

Tables

Preface

IT WAS LATE in the afternoon on a cold and rainy day in 1996 as we sat in the office in Birmingham, England, staring at a blank page in Internet Explorer 3 and wondering when the old Gateway 386 server under the desk would finally finish grinding through a dbWeb query and produce some results. The e-mail, from a small offshoot of the IIS team at Microsoft, arrived as we waited, asking if we would be interested in looking at a new product ("still under development") called Denali. Why not? It seemed that the case study for the final chapter of our book on Web site and database integration was going nowhere.

So we installed Denali 0.9 and started to play with it. Somewhere about ten in the evening, blown away by what we were seeing, the decision was made. The final chapter of the book would be a preview of this amazing new technology—released to the public some months later as Active Server Pages. Little did we realize then that this one event would determine the direction of our future writing career, right up to the current day.

What is remarkable, comparing ASP 1.0 with the current ASP.NET 2.0 release, is how much has changed in the past ten years. Our first book about ASP included the history of the Internet, a comprehensive reference to HTML 3.2 and a new styling language called CSS, a full tutorial on VBScript, plus descriptions and examples of every object, method, and property of ASP and its associated database access technology, called ActiveX Data Objects. We even had room in the 1,000 or so pages to cover the SQL language, using MTS and MSMQ, building COM components, a few case studies, and a raft of appendices.

Now, with ASP.NET, we could fill 1,000 pages just describing server controls. ASP.NET has grown up to become a fully fledged, rich, and all-encompassing language-agnostic technology suitable for building any type of Web-based application. Covering all of ASP.NET 2.0 and the associated .NET Framework classes to the same level of detail as our first book on Active Server Pages would fill a whole shelf in your bookcase!

Instead, this book aims to provide you with the concise and detailed information on ASP.NET 2.0 that you need to build great Web sites and Web-based applications. We've attempted to share with you our passion for ASP.NET, our experience of working with it over many years, and our long and fruitful relationship with the team at Microsoft. We hope that you, too, will develop the same passion for ASP.NET as we have.

What Do I Need to Use This Book?

This book is aimed at developers who are reasonably familiar with the Web, HTML, CSS, JavaScript, and the C# language. We have tried to avoid using code or concepts that are obscure or unduly complex, instead concentrating on the techniques and technologies in ASP.NET 2.0.

The examples were developed in Visual Studio 2005, though you can use Visual Web Developer (VWD) if you only have this available. You will also need access to a database—either SQL Server 2005 or SQL Server Express Edition as installed with Visual Studio 2005 and VWD. You can download the examples, and run many of them online, from our server at http://www.daveandal.net/books/8344/. Alternatively, you can obtain the samples from the Addison-Wesley Web site at http://www.awprofessional.com/msdotnetseries.

Acknowledgments

OUR THANKS GO to all those people within and outside of Microsoft who have, not only for this book but over the years, provided so much support and assistance. We are proud to have been able to work with Scott Guthrie, the father of ASP, as he and his team have taken this technology from a page template-based scripting language into the comprehensive and efficient development language it is today. Our thanks also go, of course, to the entire editorial, production, marketing, and sales teams at Addison-Wesley. We offer a special thanks to Appan Annamalai, who contributed much of the material on localization for Chapter 14 of this book.

About the Authors

Alex Homer is a computer geek and Web developer with a passion for ASP.NET. Although he has to spend some time doing real work (a bit of consultancy and training, and the occasional conference session), most of his days are absorbed in playing with the latest Microsoft Web technology and then writing about it. Living in the picturesque wilderness of the Derbyshire Dales in England, he is well away from the demands of the real world—with only an Internet connection to maintain some distant representation of normality. But, hey, what else could you want from life? You can contact Alex through his own software company, Stonebroom Limited, at alex@stonebroom.com.

Dave Sussman has had proper jobs and reels at the thought of having to do so again. He spends most of his life immersed in alpha and beta technologies, learning all he can and writing and speaking about them. He is still convinced that .NET is the best thing Microsoft has ever released, and never ceases to be amazed at how much better it keeps getting. Like Alex, he lives in a quiet rural village—one of those people call quaint—and still hasn't finished decorating his house. But then it's only been four years. You can contact Dave though his company, ipona limited, at dave@ipona.com.

■1■

Technology, Tools, and Getting Started

W HEN MICROSOFT RELEASED the .NET Framework 1.0 Technology Preview in July 2000, it was immediately clear that Web development was going to change. The company's then-current technology, Active Server Pages 3.0 (ASP), was powerful and flexible, and it made the creation of dynamic Web sites easy. ASP spawned a whole series of books, articles, Web sites, and components, all to make the development process even easier. What ASP didn't have, however, was an application framework; it was never an enterprise development tool. Everything you did in ASP was code oriented—you just couldn't get away with not writing code.

ASP.NET was designed to counter this problem. One of its key design goals was to make programming easier and quicker by reducing the amount of code you have to create. Enter the declarative programming model, a rich server control hierarchy with events, a large class library, and support for development tools from the humble Notepad to the high-end Visual Studio .NET. All in all, ASP.NET was a huge leap forward.

Now, with the release of version 2.0, we've seen another giant step towards increased developer productivity. The feature set of ASP.NET has increased, with more server controls and APIs wrapping functionality, reducing the amount of code you need to write. The toolset has also improved, with Visual Studio 2005 having more features, a better designer, and greater support for standards and validation. Along with Visual Studio 2005, there is Visual Web Developer Express Edition, a cut-down (but not by much) version of Visual Studio that provides the same great development environment for an unbeatable price—it's free!

New Features of ASP.NET 2.0

This chapter isn't an in-depth look at any specific feature—instead, we are going to give you a taste of what's to come so you can see how much easier Web development is going to be. For this overview of new features, we've broken them down into rough end-to-end scenarios.

Templates for a Consistent Look and Feel

ASP.NET 1.x provides an easy way to develop Web sites, but one thing that has become apparent is the lack of an architecture for applying a consistent look and feel. Several workaround techniques emerged:

- Creating a custom class object that inherits from `Page` and having this custom page preload controls
- Creating a templated server control, where the templates provide the layout areas for each page, and using this control on every page
- Having User Controls for common areas of the site, such as headings, menus, and footers

Of these, the first two require knowledge of creating server controls, and while this is a topic most ASP.NET developers could master, it may not be one they've had experience with. Therefore, a solution using custom server controls tends to be avoided. The last option, though, is a simple solution, easy to create and implement. User Controls were created to provide reusable functionality, and this is a great use for them. However, to apply a consistent look and feel you need to first place the User Controls on each page and then ensure that they are placed in the same place on each page. In other words, you really need a page template, and in reality this manifests itself as an ASP.NET file that you simply copy for each new page. The danger of this approach is that it's too easy to modify a page and change the layout for that single page.

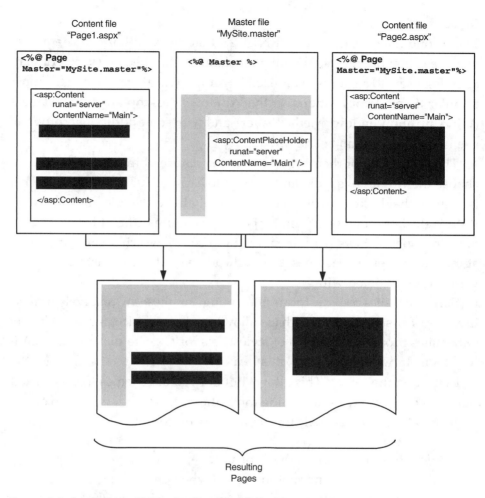

FIGURE 1.1: Combining a Master Page and a child page

To provide a templating solution, ASP.NET 2.0 has the concept of Master Pages, which provide a template for the look and feel of a page. A Master Page is an ASP.NET page that provides a template for other pages, giving shared page-level layout and functionality. The Master Page defines place-holders for the content, which can be overridden by child pages. The result-ant page is a combination of the Master Page and the child page, as shown in Figure 1.1.

Master Pages are covered in Chapter 9.

Styles for Controls

The second major feature of ASP.NET 2.0 that deals with the look and feel of a site is that of themes. Theming, or skinning, has become very popular, allowing users to create a customized look for applications. Two of the most popular themed applications on the Windows desktop are audio players (WinAmp and Windows Media Player), and with some additional software, even Windows XP can be themed.

The popularity of theming is due to the nature of humans—we like to choose the way things look, and we like to express our individuality. This is easy on the desktop, where users generally have a single machine each. With Web sites, however, theming becomes a more difficult issue because of the number of users. Tracking which users have which themes and managing those themes becomes an overhead that site administrators don't want to get involved with.

Some Web sites provide forms of theming, but these are relatively limited in terms of customization, perhaps allowing only a choice of color scheme. Other sites provide a selection of stylesheets for users to pick from, assuming their browsers support this feature, or alternatively change the stylesheet on the server. This allows not only color schemes to be selected but also complete styles, including fonts, the style of borders, and so on.

In ASP.NET 2.0, the goals for theming are quite simple.

- Allow customization of the appearance of a site or page using the same design tools and methods used when developing the page itself. This means there's no need to learn any special tools or techniques to add themes to a site.
- Allow themes to be applied to controls, pages, and even entire sites. For example, this allows users to customize parts of a site while ensuring that other parts (such as corporate identity) aren't customized.
- Allow all visual properties to be customized, thus ensuring that when themed, pages and controls can achieve a consistent style.

The implementation of this in ASP.NET 2.0 is built around two areas: skins and themes. A **skin** is a set of properties and templates that can be applied to controls. A **theme** is a set of skins and any other associated files (such as images or stylesheets). Skins are control-specific, so for a given theme there could be a separate skin for each control within that theme. Any controls without a skin inherit the default look. There are two types of themes.

- Customization themes override control definitions, thus changing the look and feel of controls. Customization themes are applied with the Theme attribute on the Page directive.
- Stylesheet themes don't override control definitions, thus allowing the control to use the theme properties or override them. Stylesheet themes are applied with the StylesheetTheme attribute on the Page directive.

The implementation is simple because a skin uses the same definition as the server control it is skinning, and themes are just a set of files in a directory under the application root. For example, consider this sample directory structure.

```
default.aspx
\Themes
  \MyTheme
    MySkin.skin
  \YourTheme
    YourSkin.skin
```

Each theme consists of a directory under the Themes directory. Within each theme there is a file with a .skin suffix, which contains the skin details for that theme. For example, MySkin.skin might contain:

```
<asp:Label SkinID="Normal" runat="server"
  Font-Bold="True" BackColor="#FFC080" />
<asp:Label SkinID="Comic" runat="server"
  Font-Italic="True" Font-Names="Comic Sans MS" />
```

This defines two skins for the Label control, each having different visual properties. The theme can be chosen by setting the appropriate page-level property, and the skin is chosen by setting a control-level property, as demonstrated in the following code snippets:

```
<%@ Page Theme="MyTheme" %>

<form runat="server">

  <asp:Label SkinID="Comic" Text="A Label" />

</form>
```

or

```
<%@ Page StylesheetTheme="MyTheme" %>

<form runat="server">

  <asp:Label SkinID="Comic" Text="A Label" />

</form>
```

Both of these can be set at runtime as well as design time, so this provides an extremely powerful solution, especially when connected with the new Personalization features.

Personalization and themes are covered in Chapter 12.

Securing Your Site

With the large amount of business being done on the Web, security is vitally important for protecting not only confidential information such as credit card numbers but also users' personal details and preferences. Thus, you have to build into your site features to authenticate users. This was easy to do in ASP.NET 1.x, although you still had to write code. Security was created by picking your preferred security mechanism (most often Forms Authentication) and then adding controls to your page to provide the login details—username, password, "remember me" checkbox, and so on. There was no built-in mechanism for storing personal details, so this was a roll-it-yourself affair.

With ASP.NET 2.0, the pain has been taken out of both areas. For login functionality, there is now:

- A Login control, providing complete functionality for logging into a site
- A LoginStatus control, which indicates the login status and can be configured to provide automatic links to login and logout pages
- A LoginName control to display the current (or anonymous) name
- A LoginView control, providing templated views depending on the login status

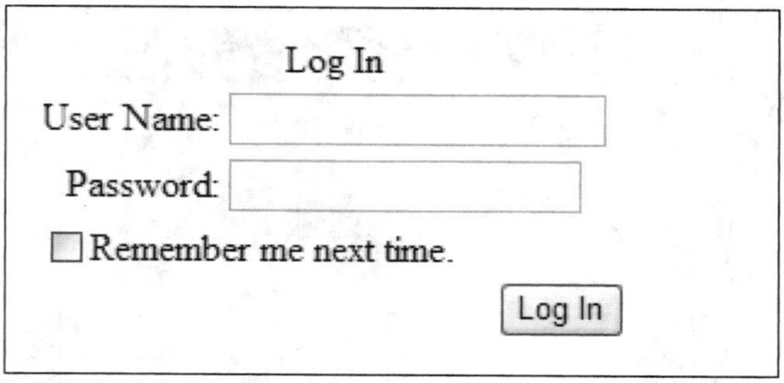

FIGURE 1.2: The Login control

- A `CreateUser` wizard, to allow simple creation of user accounts
- A `PasswordRecovery` control, encompassing the "I forgot my password" functionality

For example, to add login features to your page all you need to do is add the following code:

```
<form runat="server">
  <asp:Login runat="server" />
</form>
```

This gives us the simple interface shown in Figure 1.2.

This could be achieved easily in previous versions of ASP.NET, but not with such simplicity. You needed labels, text entry boxes, buttons, and validation, whereas now it's all rolled into one control. Sure it looks plain, but this is the basic unformatted version. Using Visual Studio 2005, you can auto-format this for a better look. You can also skin the interface, as shown in Figure 1.3, or even template it to provide your own customized look. Along with the other login controls, you get a complete solution for handling user logins.

The user interface isn't the only part of logging into a site; there's also the code needed to validate the user against a data store. With ASP.NET 1.x this required not only code to be written but also knowledge of what that data store was and how it stored data. ASP.NET 2.0 introduces a new Membership API, whose aim is to abstract the required membership functionality from the

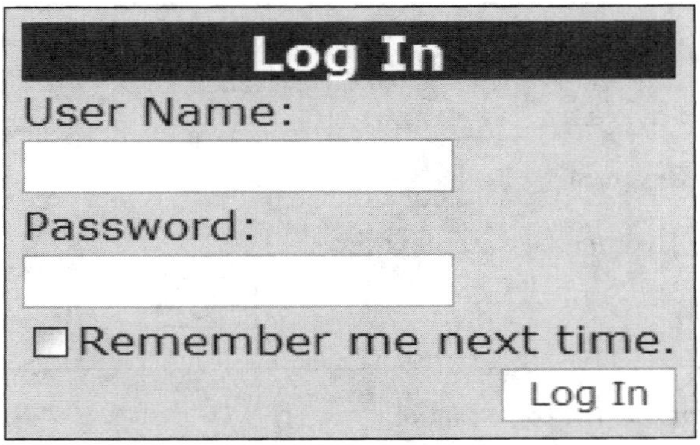

FIGURE 1.3: A skinned Login control

storage of the member information. For example, validation of user credentials can now be replaced with the code shown in Listing 1.1.

Listing 1.1. Validating User Credentials

```
If Membership.ValidateUser(Email.Text, Password.Text) Then
  ' user is valid
Else
  ' user is not valid
End If
```

What's better is that when using the Login control you don't even have to do this—the control handles it for you.

The great strength of the Membership API is that it is built on the idea of Membership Providers, with support for Microsoft SQL Server and Active Directory supplied by default. To integrate custom membership stores, you simply need to provide a component that inherits from the Membership interface and add the new provider details to the configuration file.

The Membership API has some simple goals.

- Offer an easy solution for authenticating and managing users, requiring no knowledge of the underlying storage mechanism.
- Provide support for multiple data providers, allowing data stored about users to come from different data stores.

- Provide comprehensive user management in a simple-to-use API, giving an easy way for developers to store and access user details.
- Give users a unique identity, allowing integration with other services such as the Personalization and Role Manager features.

Security, membership, and role management are covered in Chapter 11.

Personalizing Your Site

One of the areas driving changes on the Internet is that of communities. People like to belong, and the Internet is a big, lonely place. Community sites give you a home, a sense of belonging. Part of that comes from being in contact with like-minded people, and part comes from the features some of these sites offer. Our houses are decorated to our style, and many of us customize our Windows desktop, so why shouldn't our favorite Web sites offer the same opportunity?

Hand in hand with the Membership API lie the Personalization features. These provide a simple programming model for storing user details (including those of anonymous users), with easy customization. Like Membership, Personalization can be configured to work with multiple data providers and provides an easy way to define custom properties for each user. This leads to a user profile with strong types, allowing easy access within ASP.NET pages. For example, you can create a profile with Name, Address, and Theme as properties and a page that allows the user to update them, as shown in Listing 1.2.

The simplicity of this method means we only have to deal with the user profile. We don't need to know how it stores the data—we just deal with the properties each profile has. This personalization also allows us to easily use the theming capabilities, changing the theme when the page is created, as demonstrated here.

```
Sub Page_PreInit(Sender As Object, E As EventArgs)

  Me.Theme = Profile.Theme

End Sub
```

Listing 1.2. Using the Profile Custom Properties

```
<script runat="server">

  Sub Page_Load(Sender As Object, E As EventArgs)

    Name.Text = Profile.Name
    Address.Text = Profile.Address
    UserTheme.Text = Profile.Theme

  End Sub

  Sub Update_Click(Sender As Object, E As EventArgs)

    Profile.Name = Name.Text
    Profile.Address = Address.Text
    Profile.Theme = UserTheme.Text

  End Sub

</script>

<form runat="server">
  Name:    <asp:TextBox id="Name" runat="server" /> <br />
  Address: <asp:TextBox id="Address" runat="server" /> <br />
  Theme:   <asp:TextBox id="UserTheme" runat="server" /> <br />
  <asp:Button Text="Update" onClick="Update_Click" runat="server" />
</form>
```

To ensure that the theme customization is applied before the controls are created, we use the new `PreInit` event.

Personalization is covered in Chapter 12.

Creating Portals

As if customization of a site's look weren't enough, ASP.NET 2.0 also brings a way to alter the structure with its new portal framework.

The success of the ASP.NET IBuySpy portal application and its offshoots, such as DotNetNuke and Rainbow, shows that customized sites are popular. The issue has always been how to provide a consistent look while still allowing user customization, not only of the style but also of the content and placement of content. Microsoft has already implemented solutions to provide this functionality, including SharePoint Server and Outlook WebParts.

In ASP.NET 2.0, WebParts become the underlying technology for all Microsoft portal applications, providing a single easy-to-use, extensible framework. The concept revolves around two key sets of controls—a set of zone controls and a range of different `WebParts` controls. The zone identifies areas on the page in which the appearance or behavior of the content is consistent (e.g., the colors, styles, and layout orientation), and the `WebParts` identify the individual content areas or modules within each zone. There are different types of `WebPart` controls for different purposes, for example:

- Generic Web Parts, which are used to reference assemblies or user controls that contain the content that is normally visible on the page
- A range of catalog parts, which display parts that are not currently on the page but are available to be added
- A range of editor parts such as the `AppearanceEditorPart` and the `LayoutEditorPart`, which allow customization of the visible parts

For example, consider an intranet site that needs a selection of areas of content, such as contact information, stocks, weather, and so on. Figure 1.4 shows a sample page.

This page has two main areas of content—the left area containing details of employees, which is a user control, and the right area with weather details (a custom server control), and **Stocks** and **Canteen**, which are both user controls. Each of the two areas is a `WebPartZone` control, and the content within them is user controls or server controls within a `ZoneTemplate`. The code for the left `WebPartZone` control appears in Listing 1.3.

Listing 1.3. Sample Intranet Site Using WebParts

```
<asp:WebPartZone ID="LeftZone" runat="server" style="float:left;">
  <ZoneTemplate>
    <uc1:Contacts ID="Contacts1" runat="server" />
  </ZoneTemplate>
  <CloseVerb ImageUrl="~/Images/CloseVerb.gif"
    Description="Removes the WebPart from the page" />
  <MinimizeVerb ImageUrl="~/Images/MinimizeVerb.gif" />
  <RestoreVerb ImageUrl="~/Images/RestoreVerb.gif" />
  <EditVerb ImageUrl="~/Images/EditVerb.gif"
    Description="Edit the properties of the WebPart" />
  <ExportVerb Text="Export" />
  <SelectedPartChromeStyle BorderColor="#A7B756"
    BorderStyle="Dotted" BorderWidth="5px" />
</asp:WebPartZone>
```

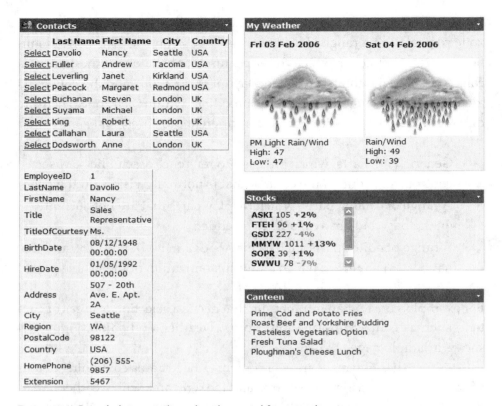

FIGURE 1.4: Sample intranet site using the portal framework

At first glance, this doesn't look like much improvement over existing layout methods such as user controls—in fact, it looks more complex. However, the framework on which WebParts is built is great for developers and users alike. Developers only have to drop user controls or server controls into a `ZoneTemplate` to automatically receive WebParts functionality.

For example, the Personalization features allow each Web part to be moved to another location within its zone or to a different zone. Moving a WebPart is simply a matter of drag and drop, as shown in Figure 1.5, where the **Stocks** section is being moved to the left zone.

Editing of `WebPart` controls is also part of the portal framework. You can use a control called the `WebPartPageMenu` to automatically provide a drop-down list where users can change the mode that the page is viewed in and then edit the properties of the individual WebParts. By default the user can alter a range of layout and appearance properties, such as the title, height, width, and orientation (see Figure 1.6).

The portal framework is covered in Chapter 13.

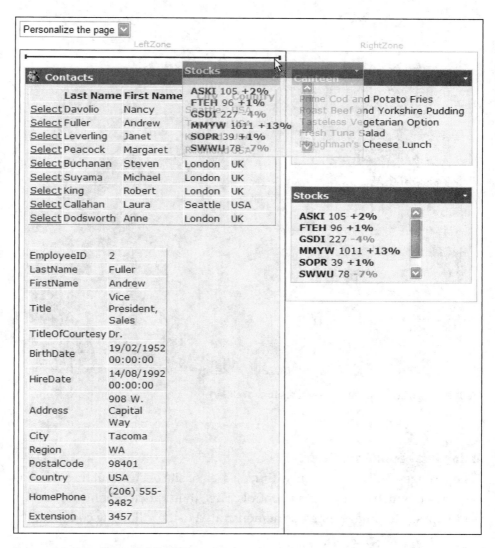

FIGURE 1.5: Dragging a WebPart to another location

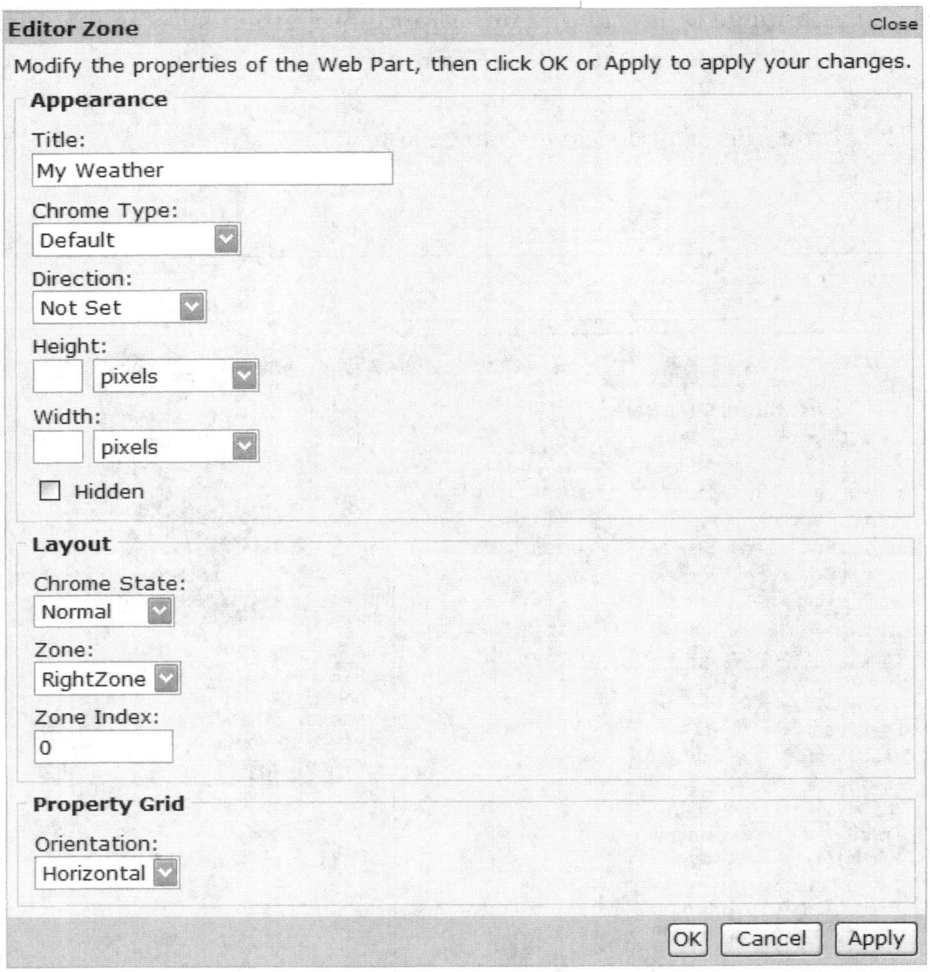

FIGURE 1.6: The built-in editing features for a WebPart

Using Images on Your Site

Using images isn't a particularly difficult area of site design, but their use has been eased with two new server controls. First, the ImageMap control provides easy support for image maps, as demonstrated in the following code sample.

```
<asp:ImageMap runat="server"
    onClick="Map_Click"
    ImageUrl="images/states.jpg">
  <asp:CircleHotSpot X="100" Y="100" Radius="25"
      PostBackValue="Other State" />
```

```
<asp:RectangleHotSpot Top="200" Left="150"
    Right="200" Bottom="150"
    PostBackValue="More State"/>
<asp:PolygonHotSpot Coordinates="3,4, 15,18, 45,18, 15,70, 3,4"
    PostBackValue="State 1" />
</asp:ImageMap>
```

The detection of the hot spot is handled in the postback event.

```
Sub Map_Click(Sender As Object, E As ImageMapEventArgs)

    Select Case e.PostBackValue
    Case "State 1"
      ' ...
    Case "Other State"
      ' ...
    Case "More States"
      ' ...
    End Select

End Sub
```

Images are covered in Chapter 11.

Using Data on Your Site

It's probably no exaggeration to say that most, if not all, Web sites use some form of data to drive them. Whether XML files, a database, or another dynamic form of storage, the data allows a site to respond to the user and to be up to date. ASP.NET 1.x provided some great data binding capabilities, but they always involved code, often the same code used over and over. One of the key goals of ASP.NET 2.0 is to reduce code and to ease the use of databases, especially for beginner programmers. To achieve this, a new set of data controls has been introduced, removing the need for in-depth knowledge of ADO.NET.

Data source controls provide a consistent and extensible method for declaratively accessing data from Web pages. There are several data source controls, including `AccessDataSource`, `SqlDataSource`, `XmlDataSource`, and `ObjectDataSource`. The use of data controls is simple, as shown here.

```
<asp:SqlDataSource id="ds1" runat="server"
  ConnectionString="server=.;database=pubs;Trusted_Connection=True"
  SelectCommand="SELECT * FROM authors"/>

<asp:DataGrid DataSourceId="ds1" runat="server" />
```

This just encapsulates the code everyone used to put in the `Page_Load` event—it connects to the database, fetches the data, and binds the grid. The contents of the `SelectCommand` can be a stored procedure as well as a SQL command, thus preserving the separation of data access from the page itself. There are commands for updating, inserting, and deleting.

This model is extended by use of a parameter collection, allowing parameters to be passed into the command from a variety of sources. For example, the code in Listing 1.4 automatically takes the value from the `TextBox` control `txtState` and feeds this into the parameter `@state`.

Listing 1.4. Using a ControlParameter

```
<asp:SqlDataSource id="ds1" runat="server"
  ConnectionString="server=.;database=pubs;Trusted_Connection=True"
  SelectCommand="SELECT * FROM authors WHERE state=@state">
  <SelectParameters>
    <asp:ControlParameter name="@state" ControlID="txtState"
      PropertyName="Text" />
  </SelectParameters>
</asp:SqlDataSource>

<asp:TextBox id="txtState" runat="server" />

<asp:DataGrid DataSourceId="ds1" runat="server" />
```

There are also other parameter types, allowing parameter information to be taken directly from Session variables, Cookies, the Request (QueryString), and the HTML Form.

Data Binding

Data binding in ASP.NET 1.x was simple, but it did cause confusion in some areas. For example, should you use early binding, for which you have to know the underlying data structure? Or should you take the development shortcut and use late binding, like this:

```
<%# DataBinder.Eval(Container.DataItem, "au_lname") %>
```

With ASP.NET 2.0, this syntax has been simplified.

```
<%# Eval("au_lname") %>
```

In addition, there is a `Bind` method, which provides two-way binding, allowing easy creation of pages that can update data. There is also an equivalent `XPath` syntax for XPath expressions when binding to XML documents.

```
<%# XPath("@au_lname") %>
```

Binding to Objects

One of the most requested features has been the ability to bind data directly to objects. Good design dictates that you separate your data access layer from your presentation layer, and this is often done as a set of classes. The new `ObjectDataSource` allows you to simply bind directly to existing objects, such as classes, thus allowing you to have a strongly typed data layer but still use the easy data binding that ASP.NET 2.0 brings.

Binding to Configuration Settings

A similar binding syntax is used to allow declarative access to certain configuration parameters, such as application settings, connection strings, and resources. Here is the syntax for these:

```
<%$ section: key %>
```

For example:

```
<%$ ConnectionStrings: pubs %>
```

Data source controls and data binding are covered in Chapters 3, 4, and 5.

Internationalization

Building Web sites that support multiple languages is important because Web sites are used by more and more people for whom English is a secondary language. In ASP.NET 2.0, support for multiple languages is extremely simple, based around global resources (sometimes called shared resources) and local page resources. Global resources live in the `Resources` folder underneath the application root and consist of XML-based resource files (`.resx`) containing keys and content for those keys. Global resources can be accessed by any page in the application. For example, consider a file called `shared.resx`, which among the meta-data might have a key like this:

```
<data name="SharedResource">
  <value>English Label from shared resource file</value>
</data>
```

There might also be a French language resource file, `shared.fr-fr.resx`.

```
<data name="SharedResource">
  <value>French shared resource</value>
</data
```

Binding to these resources declaratively can be done in the same way as binding to configuration resources, for example:

```
<asp:Label runat="server" id="MyLabel"
    Text="%<$ Resources: SharedResource %> />
```

At page compilation time the browser language is detected and the resource selected from the appropriate file.

Another way to fetch this resource is to use a meta-attribute on the label.

```
<asp:Label runat="server" id="MyLabel"
    meta:resourcekey="Shared:SharedResource"/>
```

In this case, the first part of the `meta` value identifies the name of the file, and the second part (after the colon) identifies the key.

Local resources are only accessible to individual pages. Like global resources, they are stored in `.resx` files, but this time under a `Local-Resources` directory, where the name of the resource file is the `ASP.NET` page with the `.resx` extension applied. Thus, for a page supporting two languages there would be two local resource files, `LocalResources\UsingResources.aspx.resx` and `LocalResources\UsingResources.aspx.fr-fr.resx`. Either of the binding formats works for local resources, but generally the meta one is used because Visual Studio 2005 can automatically process ASP.NET pages, adding the meta-attribute and building a resource file.

Resources are covered in Chapter 9.

Changes from Version 1.x

In addition to the large number of new features, there have been some APIs that have been made obsolete. The list is too long to include here, but you can find it on MSDN, where the APIs are broken down by namespace and assembly. The location of the list is http://msdn.microsoft.com/netframework/programming/obsoleteapi/default.aspx.

Obtaining and Installing .NET 2.0

The .NET 2.0 Framework is freely available, and can be downloaded either as a stand-alone package (354MB for the runtime and the SDK, or 22MB for the redistributable), or with the free tool, Visual Web Developer 2005 Express Edition (2MB installer). Both can be obtained from Microsoft at http://www.asp.net.

Visual Web Developer (VWD) is built from the same code base as the full Visual Studio 2005, so it provides many of the same features, such as the designer, editors, and so on, and is perfectly suitable for full Web site development. VWD also includes SQL Server Express Edition, a version of SQL Server 2005 designed for developer use, so together you have everything you need to develop Web sites.

Some features, such as support for automatic localization, testing, and source code control, are only available in Visual Studio 2005, and there are the following three versions:

- Visual Studio 2005 Standard Edition, which is the mainstream, entry-level suite aimed at occasional developers creating Windows, mobile, and Web applications. It includes all languages (VB, C#, C++, and J#).
- Visual Studio 2005 Professional Edition, aimed at professional developers, includes remote server development and debugging as well as remote SQL Server 2005 development (in addition to all of the features of the Standard Edition).
- Visual Studio Team System Editions, designed for corporate developers in teams, comes in three versions: for architects, for developers, and for testers. All features of the Professional Edition are included, as are features such as Microsoft Office development, code profiling and analysis, unit testing, and project management.

For a more detailed view of the differences between all of the versions, see the page on MSDN at **http://msdn.microsoft.com/vstudio/products/compare/default.aspx**.

Running Side-by-Side with 1.x

ASP.NET 2.0 runs side by side with versions 1.0 and 1.1 without any problems. Applications can continue to use 1.x while others use 2.1. If running on Windows Server 2003, you must first enable ASP.NET 2.0 as an extension, which can be done in Internet Information Services Manager (see Figure 1.7).

If you need to run both ASP.NET 1.x and 2.0 on IIS 6, then each version must have its own application pool (see Figure 1.8), and Web sites must be placed in the appropriate pool (see Figure 1.9).

If you mix ASP.NET 1.x and ASP.NET 2.0 applications within the same application pool, the applications may work for a while, but you will receive errors and the applications may shut down. If you experience unusual application failures, check the Event Log for errors, and check the application pools.

Security Accounts

You should be aware that on IIS 6, the default `ASP.NET` worker process identity is NT AUTHORITY/NETWORK SERVICE, rather than the ASPNET

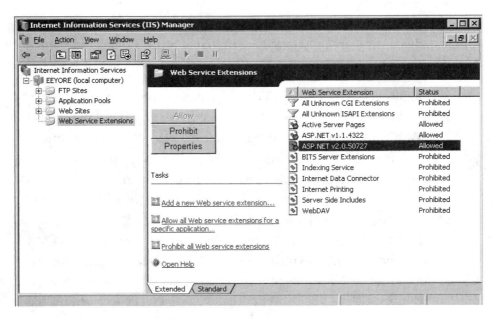

FIGURE 1.7: Enabling ASP.NET 2.0 in IIS

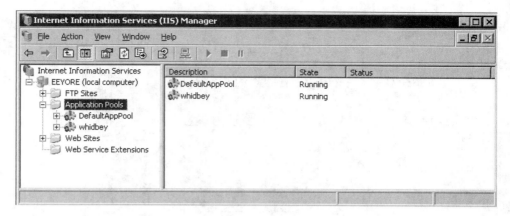

FIGURE 1.8: Creating a separate application pool

local machine account used in IIS 5 and IIS 5.1. This doesn't affect the general running of ASP.NET, but would affect database logins and permissions if using trusted connections.

Upgrading and Deploying Applications

The default installation of Visual Studio 2005 supports a different model than that supported in the previous version because it no longer uses a project system. A folder-based approach is used instead, where a Web project consists solely of the files in a folder. This has caused some problems with upgrading existing applications, so the migration wizard has been updated and is available as a separate download. Also available as add-ons to Visual Studio are Web Application projects, which bring back the project-based approach, making migration of projects easier to manage.

Deployment is also eased by another add-on, Web Deployment Projects. This add-on allows more control over the compilation and deployment process, such as the ability to have different configuration files for development and deployment.

All three of these don't change the base framework, and are simply add-ons for Visual Studio 2005. You can obtain them from http://www.asp.net/.

Installing the Samples

The samples used throughout this book are running live at the Dave and Al Web site, at http://daveandal.net/, where you'll also find a downloadable

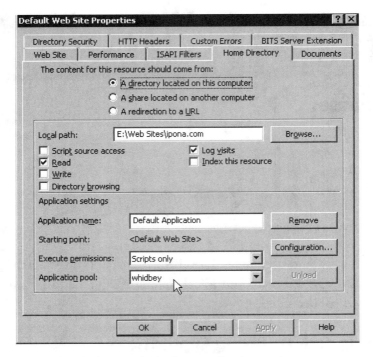

FIGURE 1.9: Placing a Web Site in an application pool

copy. There is also a full Read Me file detailing the steps required for installation available on the site.

SUMMARY

There are many changes within ASP.NET 2.0—too many to mention in this introduction, although some highlights were covered. You can see—even from just this quick overview—that there are a large number of great features that ease the development process.

The remainder of the book covers these changes (including items such as changes to existing controls, changes to page attributes, new controls, and so on) in detail.

▉ 2 ▪
Is It Really This Easy?

I N THE PREVIOUS CHAPTER, you saw how ASP.NET 2.0 contains a raft of new features that reduce the code you need to write and save you time and effort when building dynamic and interactive Web pages and applications. To further illustrate this, and so that you get a better feel for the way all these features combine to provide the overall ASP.NET 2.0 development experience, this chapter presents a scenario-based demonstration focused on a day in the life of a developer who is in the process of fulfilling the requirements of a fictional customer.

Although this may seem a contrived approach, it actually follows the general process of evolving your applications to meet the needs of the users. More than that, it shows you how all the various features in ASP.NET 2.0 fit together and interact to give you improved productivity and a simpler development process. Along the way, you will see the process steps required for:

- Using a data source control and `GridView` to display data
- Enabling sorting and paging for the rows
- Providing a row editing feature
- Adding filtering to select specific sets of rows
- Displaying single rows in a form for editing
- Working with data exposed through a business object
- Caching the data to reduce database access

- Using a master page to give a consistent look and feel
- Adding a menu and other navigation features

By the end of this chapter, you will have a good understanding of the main features in ASP.NET 2.0 that make your life as a developer much easier.

A Day in the Life of a Developer

It's nine-thirty in the morning, and your second cup of coffee is just starting to take effect when the phone rings. At the other end is Margaret, the CEO of AdventureWorks Trading Inc., and she is in no mood for light conversation. It seems that, although they love the new Web site you created for them, they just discovered that there is no page for their staff to view lists of products. So you commit to provide one, drain the remnants of the now cold coffee, and fire up Visual Studio 2005.

Using a Data Source Control and GridView to Display Data

To build almost all types of data access pages, you need to be able to get the data from the database and display it in a Web page. In previous versions of ASP and ASP.NET, you would already be thinking about creating a connection to the database, building a `Recordset` or filling a `DataSet`, and then either iterating through the rows to create an HTML table (in ASP 3.0) or taking advantage of server-side data binding in ASP.NET 1.*x*.

However, in ASP.NET 2.0, the process is much easier. You start by using the Server Explorer window (or the Database Explorer window in Visual Web Developer) to create a connection to the database (see Figure 2.1).

Now that you have access to the database, you need a new Web page. This will be part of the existing AdventureWorks Web site that you have already built, and so you must first open this site. Visual Studio 2005 and Visual Web Developer allow you to open an existing site using a range of techniques—including directly from the file system, from the local IIS folders via HTTP, or from a remote site via FTP or the Microsoft FrontPage Extensions (see Figure 2.2).

Next, you create a new Web Form, switch to Design view, and drag the **Product** table from the Server/Database Explorer window onto the new Web Form. This adds a `SqlDataSource` and a `GridView` control to the page

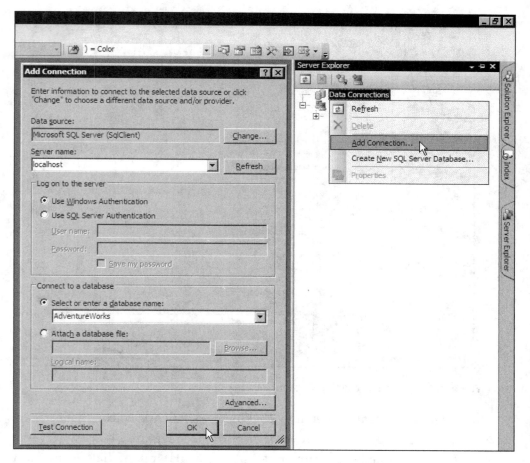

FIGURE 2.1: Connecting to a database

and you can run the page to see the results. OK, so it isn't very pretty and probably contains columns that you don't want to display, but it really does save you time in getting the basics of the page up and running—and you haven't written any code at all! (see Figure 2.3).

You can now fine-tune the page to provide just the features you want by removing columns, adding formatting to the values, and applying one of the predefined (Auto Format) styles to the GridView. The Visual Studio 2005 and Visual Web Developer page designers provide a "tasks" pane for many of the rich controls such as the GridView that makes it easy to complete all these tasks. The tasks pane appears when you first add a control to

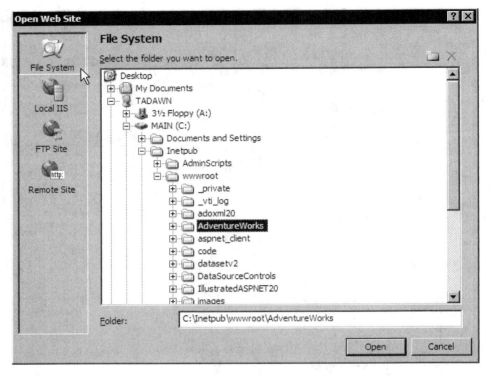

Figure 2.2: Opening an existing Web site

the page. You can also open it by clicking the small arrow icon that appears when you move the mouse over the control (see Figure 2.4).

The tasks panes contain a set of links that open dialogs or start Wizards—depending on the control type. For the GridView control, as you can see in Figure 2.4, the tasks include applying an Auto Format, selecting the appropriate data source control, enabling various features directly supported by the new GridView control in ASP.NET 2.0, and modifying the columns displayed by the GridView control. You only want to display the six most useful columns, so you can remove the rest from the list. Moreover, you want the StandardCost and ListPrice columns to display as currency values, so you can specify this in the DataFormatString property for these columns (see Figure 2.5).

Enabling Sorting and Paging for the Rows

The GridView control now displays the required columns from the database table, but it is not very easy for the user to find the rows they want to

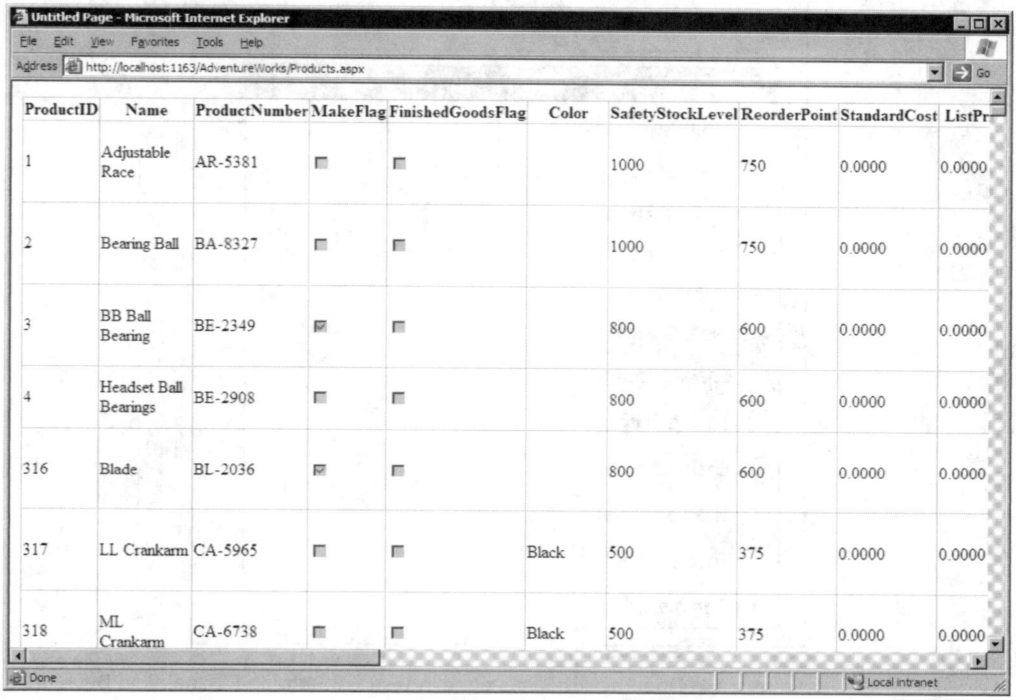

Untitled Page - Microsoft Internet Explorer

File   Edit   View   Favorites   Tools   Help

Address http://localhost:1163/AdventureWorks/Products.aspx   Go

ProductID	Name	ProductNumber	MakeFlag	FinishedGoodsFlag	Color	SafetyStockLevel	ReorderPoint	StandardCost	ListPr
1	Adjustable Race	AR-5381	☐	☐		1000	750	0.0000	0.0000
2	Bearing Ball	BA-8327	☐	☐		1000	750	0.0000	0.0000
3	BB Ball Bearing	BE-2349	☑	☐		800	600	0.0000	0.0000
4	Headset Ball Bearings	BE-2908	☐	☐		800	600	0.0000	0.0000
316	Blade	BL-2036	☑	☐		800	600	0.0000	0.0000
317	LL Crankarm	CA-5965	☐	☐	Black	500	375	0.0000	0.0000
318	ML Crankarm	CA-6738	☐	☐	Black	500	375	0.0000	0.0000

Done   Local intranet

FIGURE 2.3: Creating a data display page with drag and drop in Visual Studio 2005

view. All the rows appear in one long list sorted by product number. It would be helpful if users could sort the rows in a different order (perhaps by name when they don't know the product number), and it would also be nice to be able to limit the display to a specific number of rows and provide navigation controls so that they can see separate "pages" of rows.

Prior to ASP.NET 2.0, you would now be writing code to sort the source rowset into the required order, and then connecting this code up to controls in the page. In ASP.NET 2.0, it is all automatic. You just turn on sorting and paging with the checkboxes in the tasks pane (see Figure 2.6). The column headings become hyperlinks, and the paging controls appear at the foot of the grid.

Then you can make the page look nicer by selecting an appropriate **Auto Format** option from the list that appears when you click the link in the tasks pane, and the page is complete (see Figure 2.7).

You run the page to see the results. Clicking any one of the column heading hyperlinks sorts the rows in ascending order by that column value. Another click on the heading changes the sort order to descending. You've

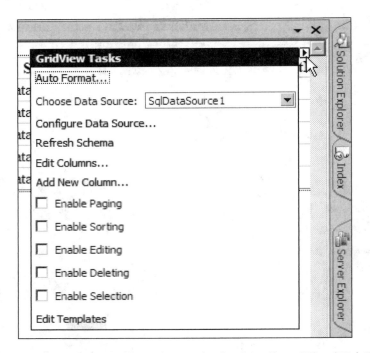

FIGURE 2.4: Opening the Tasks pane in Visual Studio and Visual Web Developer

created an extremely useful and usable page, and you have not written any code at all.

Providing a Row Editing Feature

While you have the tasks pane open for the `GridView` control, you might as well take advantage of some of the other features it offers. How about allowing users to edit the rows? This used to involve a lot of work writing code to handle the edit/update/cancel options that are part of the process for editing rows in a Web page, even in ASP.NET 1.*x*, and you still had to figure out how to push the changes back into the database by executing SQL `UPDATE` statements.

In ASP.NET 2.0, all of this goes away if you are happy to use the default parameterized SQL statement approach to updating the database table. You just select the **Enable Editing** and **Enable Deleting** options in the tasks pane for the `GridView` control. You will see the **Edit** and **Delete** links appear at the left-hand side of the grid (see Figure 2.8).

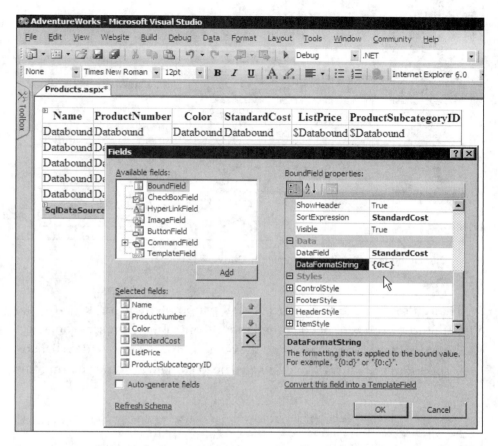

FIGURE 2.5: Modifying the columns displayed by the GridView control

Now users can edit any of the column values in individual rows (except for the primary key column) and persist these changes back to the database (see Figure 2.9), while you still have not written a single line of code!

Adding Filtering to Select Specific Sets of Rows

Just when you think you've satisfied Margaret the CEO at AdventureWorks Trading Inc. with a shiny new Web page for displaying product information, the phone rings again. It's Mike, the AdventureWorks sales manager, who says that his sales people from different divisions of the company will want to be able to filter the list by category, rather than just getting a list of all of the products. He would also like this implemented as soon as possible.

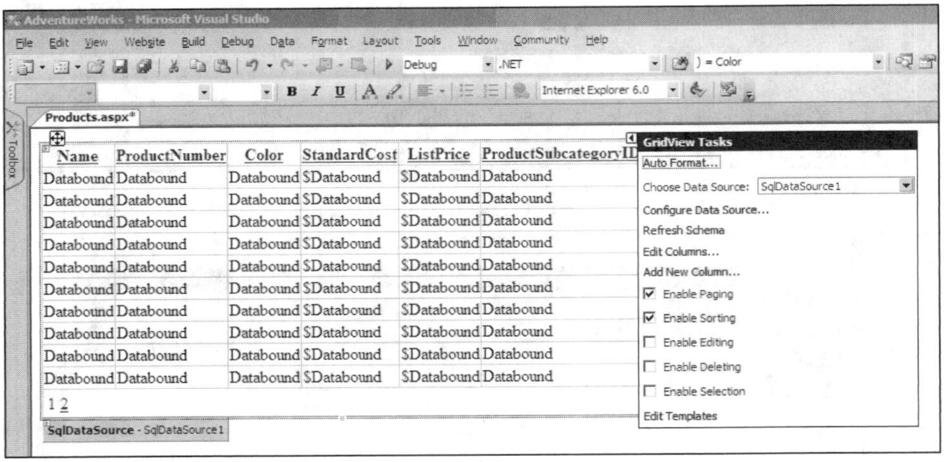

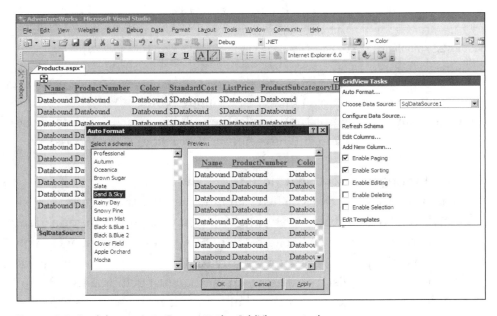

FIGURE 2.6: Enabling sorting and paging in the GridView tasks pane

Thoughts of a nice long lunch break evaporate, and back you go to Visual Studio. You will need some kind of control where users can select the category they want to view, and the obvious one is a drop-down list box (a `DropDownList` control). You will also need some way of populating this

FIGURE 2.7: Applying an Auto Format to the GridView control

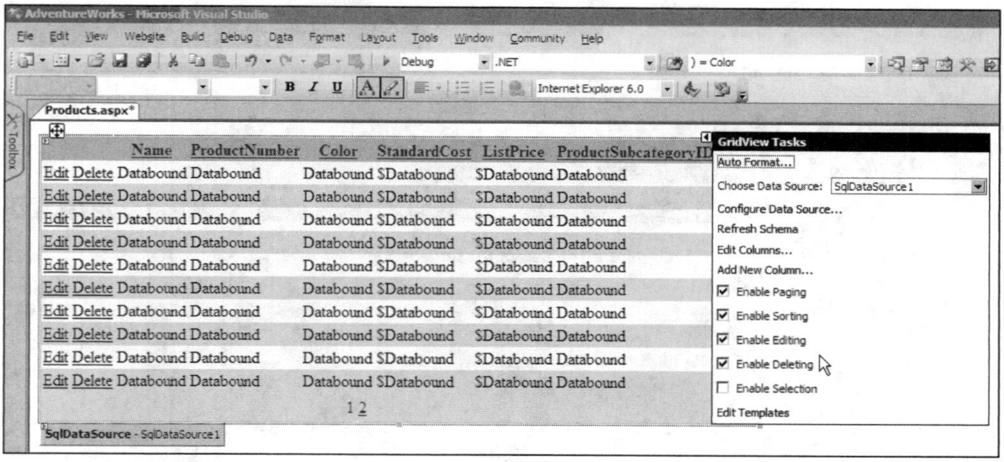

FIGURE 2.8: Enabling editing in the tasks pane of a GridView control

drop-down list with the available categories, taken from the database rows in the Products table. Therefore, step one is to drag another `SqlDataSource` control onto the page and click the **Configure Data Source** link in the tasks pane to start the Configure Data Source Wizard.

The first page of the Wizard specifies the connection string to use (you select the same one that was created for the previous `SqlDataSource` control from the list), and then you can specify the query to select the rows for the database. The table named `ProductSubcategory` contains the ID and name of each category for the items in the `Products` table (see Figure 2.10).

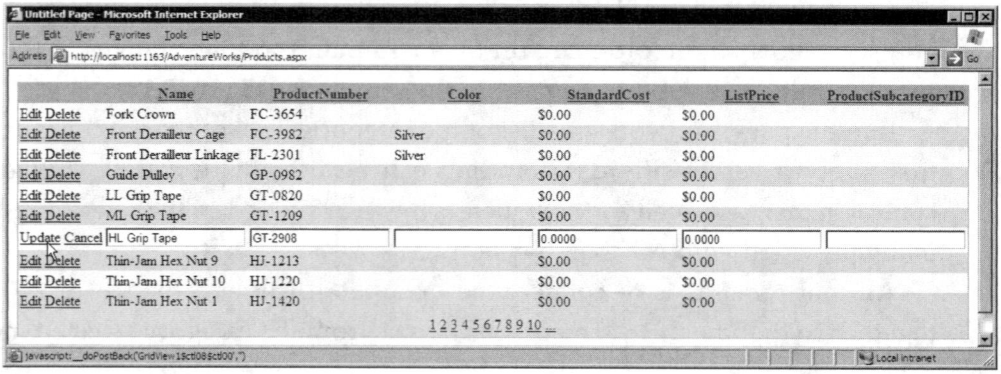

FIGURE 2.9: Editing the rows in the GridView control

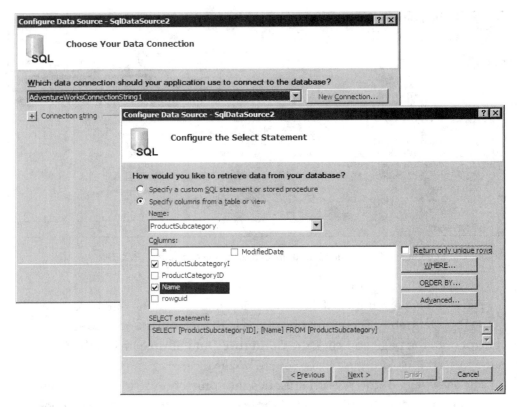

FIGURE 2.10: Setting the properties of the new SqlDataSource to select the category details

Now you can drag that DropDownList control onto the page and select the new SqlDataSource control as the source of the data. You specify that the DropDownList will show the name of the subcategory, while the value of each item in the list will be the ProductSubcategoryID. Also, make sure you set AutoPostback to True (in the tasks pane) so that changes to the selected value will submit the page to the server (see Figure 2.11).

Run the page, and you see a list of the categories. All of the list controls that support server-side data binding can be used with a data source control in this way, even controls such as the DropDownList that were originally provided with ASP.NET version 1.x.

All that remains is to connect the DropDownList and the GridView together so that the GridView displays rows from the category selected in

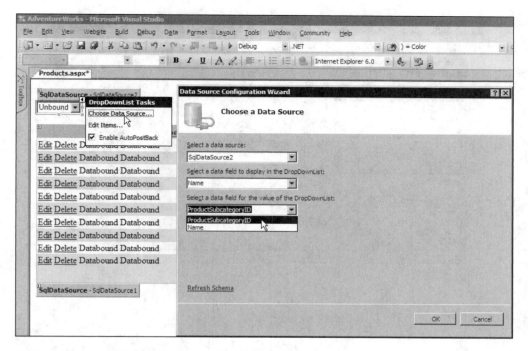

FIGURE 2.11: Setting the properties of the new DropDownList control

the `DropDownList`. How much code do you need to write for this? Perhaps you can guess that the answer is (still) none.

Select the `SqlDataSource` control that powers the `GridView` control and run the Configure Data Source Wizard again by selecting this option in the tasks pane. In the second page of the Wizard, click the **WHERE** button to open the Add WHERE Clause dialog. Here you specify the column to which the condition will apply; the comparison operator; and the source of the value to compare against the column value. This value is, of course, the value currently selected in the `DropDownList` control, and the dialog shows the SQL expression that will be added as the WHERE clause next to the **Add** button (see Figure 2.12).

This adds a WHERE clause to the SQL statement that includes a parameter for the category, and adds a `ControlParameter` to the declaration of the `SqlDataSource` control. If you switch to **Source** view in Visual Studio 2005 or Visual Web Developer, you will see the code for the `SqlDataSource` control

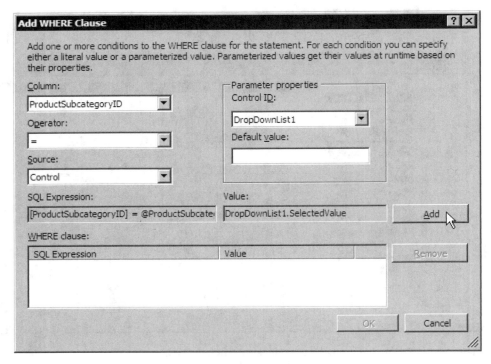

FIGURE 2.12: Adding a WHERE clause to select on subcategory

with this `ControlParameter` element nested in the `SelectParameters` section (see Listing 2.1).

Listing 2.1. The SqlDataSource Control and Its Nested ControlParameter

```
<asp:SqlDataSource ID="SqlDataSource1" runat="server" ... >
 <InsertParameters>
   ...
 </InsertParameters>
 <UpdateParameters>
   ...
 </UpdateParameters>
 <DeleteParameters>
   ...
 </DeleteParameters>
 <SelectParameters>
  <asp:ControlParameter ControlID="DropDownList1"
      Name="ProductSubcategoryID" PropertyName="SelectedValue"
      Type="Int16" />
 </SelectParameters>
 </asp:SqlDataSource>
```

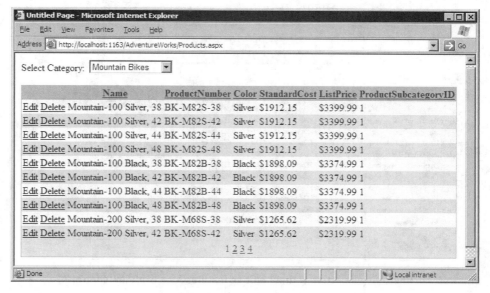

FIGURE 2.13: Filtering the rows by category using a DropDownList and ControlParameter

Now, as the page posts back each time the user makes a selection in the `DropDownList`, the original `SqlDataSource` control populates the parameter in the SQL statement with the `SelectedValue` property of the `DropDownList`, so that the `GridView` displays only rows from the selected category (see Figure 2.13).

Displaying Single Rows in a Form for Editing

The page now displays the rows from the database table, allows them to be sorted in almost any order, and displays them in separate pages. It also allows filtering by product category to be applied to the rows, and editing to be performed on all but the primary key column. However, this editing feature is not the most ideal of approaches, and it is not as intuitive as the traditional approach for editing the values in one row in a separate "form"-style page.

In ASP.NET 2.0, you can take advantage of a new control named `DetailsView` that provides a "one page at a time" view of the rows exposed by a data source control. Moreover, you can connect the `GridView` and `DetailsView` controls together so that viewing rows is easy in the grid, while editing is more intuitive in the "form" view.

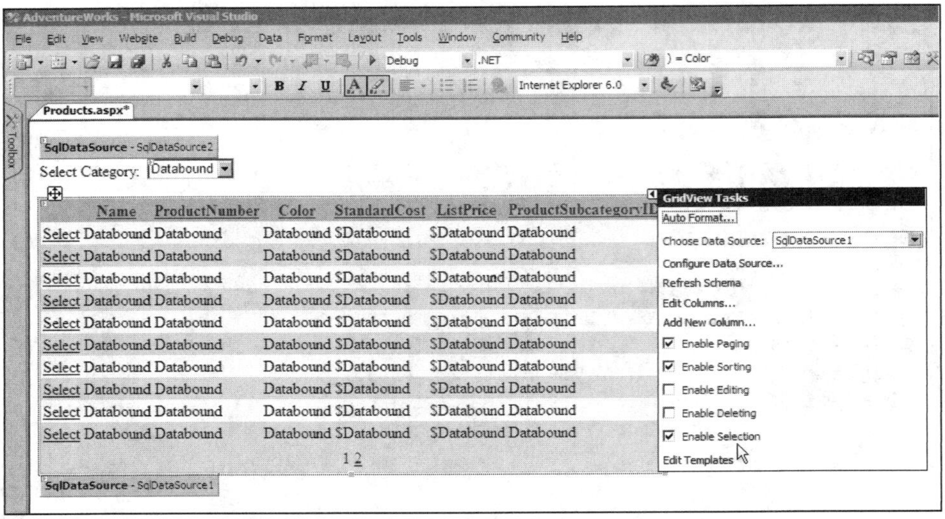

FIGURE 2.14: Specifying selection without editing features for a GridView control

The first step in this process is to turn off editing in the `GridView`, and enable selection so that users can select a row in the `GridView` control. Both of these tasks are performed simply by setting the checkboxes in the tasks pane for the `GridView` control (see Figure 2.14).

Now you drag another `SqlDataSource` control onto the page and click the **Configure Data Source** link in the tasks pane to start the Wizard. In the first page, you select the same connection string as before. In the second page of the Wizard, you specify that the query should include all except for the last two columns from the `Product` table. Then click the **WHERE** button to add a `ControlParameter` to the `SqlDataSource` control just as you did in the previous section. However, this time, specify the `SelectedValue` property of the `GridView` control so that—following a postback—this third `SqlDataSource` control will expose only the row selected in the `GridView` control (see Figure 2.15).

By default, the `SqlDataSource` does not provide for editing of rows. It only did so for the `SqlDataSource` that powers the main `GridView` control because you created this by dragging a table from the Server/Database Explorer window onto the page. When you add a `SqlDataSource` to a page from the Toolbox, you must specify if you want to be able to update

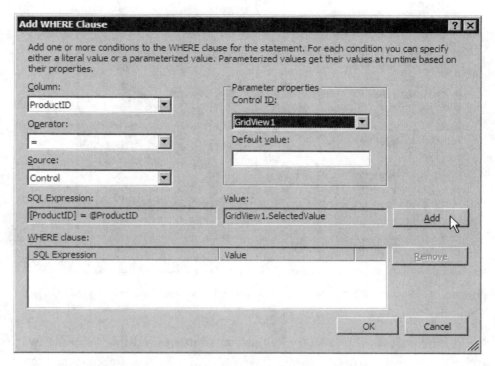

FIGURE 2.15: Creating a ControlParameter for the third SqlDataSource control

the rows (in most cases you will not, and so this default makes sense). You therefore remember to click the **Advanced** button in the second page of the Wizard and tick the options in the dialog that appears (see Figure 2.16).

Next, drag a DetailsView control onto the page and bind it to the new SqlDataSource control using the drop-down **Choose Data Source** list in the tasks pane. While you are there, use the options in the tasks pane for the DetailsView control to apply the same Auto Format as before, and turn on **Enable Inserting**, **Enable Editing**, and **EnableDeleting**. You then see the **Edit**, **Delete**, and **New** links appear at the bottom of the control (see Figure 2.17). You also adjust the width of the DetailsView control by dragging the right-hand border.

Now you can run the page to see the results. You discover that, as you select rows in the GridView, the DetailsView shows the values for that row. Moreover, using the links at the bottom of the DetailsView, all the

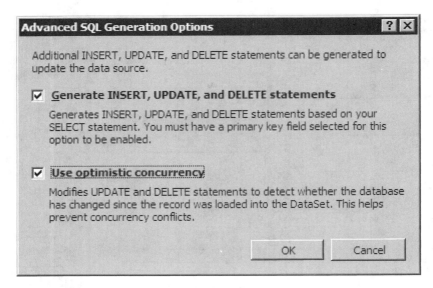

FIGURE 2.16: Specifying the options to allow row updates through controls linked to this SqlDataSource

values (except for the primary key) are available for editing. You can even insert new rows. It looks rather like a traditional executable data access application, yet you have built it in less than an hour—and you still have not had to write any code at all (see Figure 2.18)!

Working with Data Exposed through a Business Object

Just as you are leaning back and admiring your handiwork, the phone rings again. This time, it is the senior developer at AdventureWorks Trading Inc.—and he is not a happy fellow. His team has spent months building an object-oriented business and data access layer, and they do not approve of people using SQL statements to access the database directly. This *n*-tier architecture approach is a common scenario, and you probably should have known better at the start. The SqlDataSource can use stored procedures instead of SQL statements, but to use a data layer based on business objects means more significant changes are required.

However, all you actually need do is change the controls that expose the data (the SqlDataSource controls) for controls that can communicate with business objects. AdventureWorks can provide a .NET managed code assembly that implements their data access layer, so all you have to do is switch to using this in place of direct database access.

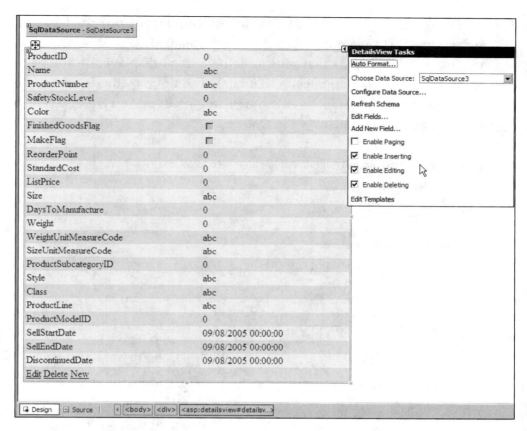

FIGURE 2.17: Setting the editing options for the DetailsView control

However, first, you must install the business object. As it is a .NET assembly, there is no registration required. A compiled DLL can just be dropped into the `bin` folder of the application, and then referenced in the pages. What happens if the code is not compiled? In that case, you can run the compiler from the command line, or use Visual Studio to compile it, and then deploy.

Even better, in ASP.NET 2.0, you can deploy the source code and leave it to ASP.NET to compile it and register it with the application at runtime. Files placed in the `App_Code` subfolder of the application root folder are compiled automatically as soon as the application starts (when the first hit is received), and the compiled code is stored on disk for use in subsequent hits. If you edit or update the source code file, it is automatically recompiled and the application restarts.

The (extremely simplified) data access component provided by the AdventureWorks team is a single `class` file named `DataLayer.cs` containing public methods that return the data to be displayed in the page (it does not support updates to the data). The three methods it exposes are named `GetProductsByCategory`, `GetProductByProductID`, and `GetCategoryList`—as shown in Listing 2.2.

Listing 2.2. The Data Access Component Implemented as a Class File

```
using System;
using System.Data;
using System.Data.SqlClient;
using System.Configuration;
public class DataLayer
{
  public DataSet GetProductsByCategory(Int32 category)
  {
    String connect = ConfigurationManager.ConnectionStrings[
          "AdventureWorksConnectionString1"].ConnectionString;
    String sql = "SELECT ProductID, Name, ProductNumber, Color, "
            + "StandardCost, ListPrice, ProductSubcategoryID "
            + "FROM AdventureWorks.Production.Product "
            + "WHERE ProductSubcategoryID = @Category";
    using (SqlConnection con = new SqlConnection(connect))
    {
      SqlDataAdapter da = new SqlDataAdapter(sql, con);
      da.SelectCommand.Parameters.AddWithValue("@Category", category);
      DataSet ds = new DataSet();
      da.Fill(ds, "Products");
      return ds;
    }
  }
  public DataSet GetProductByProductID(Int32 pid)
  {
    String connect = ConfigurationManager.ConnectionStrings[
          "AdventureWorksConnectionString1"].ConnectionString;
    String sql = "SELECT ProductID, Name, ProductNumber, "
            + "SafetyStockLevel, Color, FinishedGoodsFlag, "
            + "MakeFlag, ReorderPoint, StandardCost, ListPrice, "
            + "Size, DaysToManufacture, Weight, "
            + "WeightUnitMeasureCode, SizeUnitMeasureCode, "
            + "ProductSubcategoryID, Style, Class, ProductLine, "
            + "ProductModelID, SellStartDate, SellEndDate, "
            + "DiscontinuedDate "
            + "FROM AdventureWorks.Production.Product "
            + "WHERE ProductID = @ProductID";
    using (SqlConnection con = new SqlConnection(connect))
    {
```

```
        SqlDataAdapter da = new SqlDataAdapter(sql, con);
        da.SelectCommand.Parameters.AddWithValue("@ProductID", pid);
        DataSet ds = new DataSet();
        da.Fill(ds, "Products");
        return ds;
    }
}
public SqlDataReader GetCategoryList()
{
    String connect = ConfigurationManager.ConnectionStrings[
            "AdventureWorksConnectionString1"].ConnectionString;
    String sql = "SELECT ProductSubcategoryID, Name "
            + "FROM AdventureWorks.Production.ProductSubcategory";
    SqlConnection con = new SqlConnection(connect);
    try
    {
        con.Open();
        SqlCommand cmd = new SqlCommand(sql, con);
        return cmd.ExecuteReader(CommandBehavior.CloseConnection);
    }
    catch
    {
        return null;
    }
}
}
```

The data access class listed here is designed to be only a basic demonstration of using the `ObjectDataSource` control. A "real-world" example would generally contain a great deal more code, incorporate update methods, and use stored procedures rather than declarative SQL statements.

The ASP.NET page calls these methods, via the data source control, to fetch rows from the database table. Therefore, the next step after deploying the data access class file is to remove the `SqlDataSource` controls from the page and replace them with instances of the `ObjectDataSouce` control. Using the Configure Data Source Wizard for each one, you connect these controls to the data access layer so that they can expose the same rowsets as the `SqlDataSource` controls did. No changes are required to the UI of the page, and—besides the data-access layer class—there is still no code required!

Figure 2.19 shows the only two steps required to connect the `Object-DataSource` that populates the `DropDownList` of categories to the `GetCategoryList` method, because this method accepts no parameters. The `ObjectDataSource` for the `GridView` control requires a parameter, and this

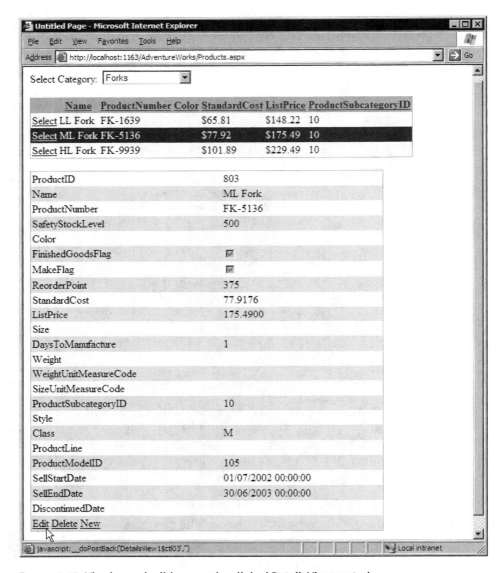

FIGURE 2.18: Viewing and editing rows in a linked DetailsView control

is specified in the third step of the Configure Data Source Wizard—it recognizes that a parameter is required, and you link it up to the SelectedValue property of the DropDownList just as you did when using a SqlDataSource control earlier (see Figure 2.20).

Having added a third ObjectDataSource control to replace the SqlDataSource that populates the DetailsView control, you just connect

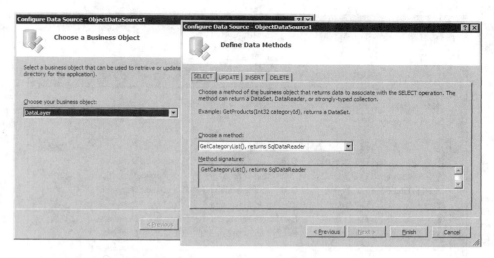

FIGURE 2.19: Configuring the ObjectDataSource for the DropDownList

the `DropDownList`, `GridView`, and `DetailsView` controls to the new data source controls using the tasks panes for each one. Because the data layer does not support editing, the tasks panes do not display the **Enable Editing** checkbox (see Figure 2.21).

Now you can run the page, and see that—with the exception of editing features—the results are the same (see Figure 2.22). This is just what you want and expect, because the UI has not changed. In addition, the work

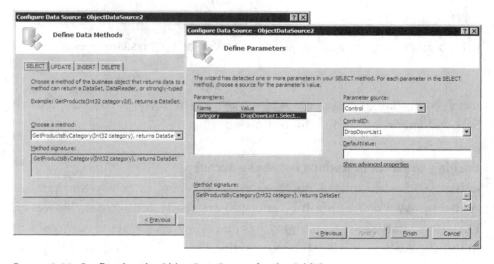

FIGURE 2.20: Configuring the ObjectDataSource for the GridView

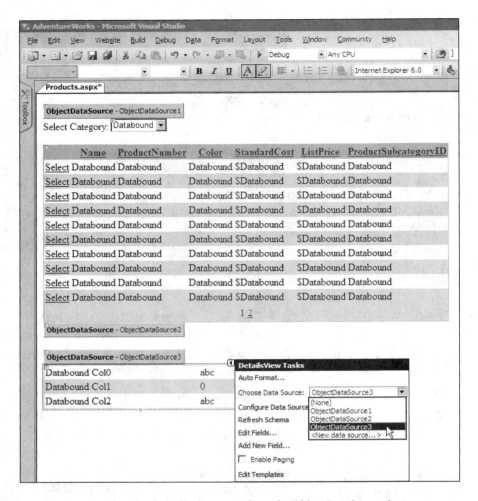

FIGURE 2.21: Connecting the data display controls to the ObjectDataSource instances

involved in changing to a data access/business object layer from declarative SQL statements is not difficult or time-consuming.

Caching the Data to Reduce Database Access

It has taken a couple of hours to build the new page for Margaret at AdventureWorks Trading Inc., and you are ready for a break. However, Lucy (the database administrator), has just been told about the new features in the application. It is her job to keep the database running smoothly and efficiently, and she is worried that you are going to slow things down. You

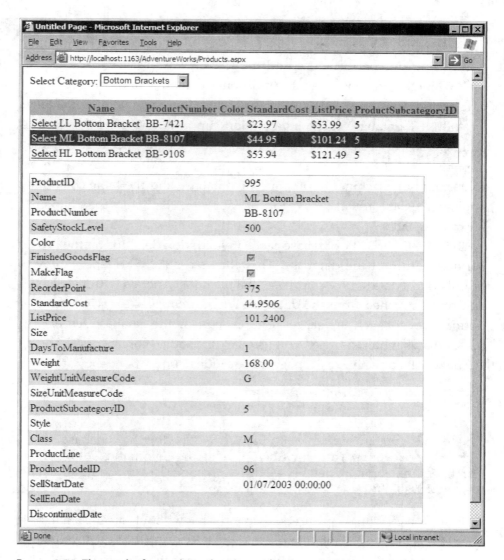

FIGURE 2.22: The results from using a data access/business logic layer

are generating constant hits on her database server for every postback as users sort, page, filter, select, and edit rows.

Lucy is a great believer in caching data where it does not change very often, and wants you to implement this in the new page. No, not next week, but now. It looks very much like the game of golf you were planning is not going to happen today.

AdventureWorks Trading Inc. uses the new SQL Server 2005 database, and so you can take advantage of a feature called database cache invalidation to improve performance and reduce database server loading. This makes much more sense than the traditional technique of caching for a specific period, based on a best guess as to how often the data might change.

ASP.NET database cache invalidation supports both SQL Server 2000 and SQL Server 2005. In SQL Server 2000, you use the special tool named `aspnet_regsql` (in the `%windir%\Microsoft.NET\Framework\[version]` folder of your machine) to prepare the database and the table containing your source data. You also have to edit your `Web.Config` file (see Chapter 11 for more details).

In SQL Server 2005, database cache invalidation depends on the Broker Service feature of the database. This allows a `SqlCacheDependency` to be linked to a data source control so that the data is cached within ASP.NET and only refreshed from the database when it changes (or when another notifiable event such as a server restart occurs on the database server).

All that is required, when you use the data source controls, is to add an `OutputCache` directive to the page that includes a `SqlDependency` attribute.

```
<%@OutputCache SqlDependency="CommandNotification"
             Duration="60" VaryByParam="*" %>
```

> Note that you must enable the Broker Service for the database, and grant the relevant permissions, before using the Command Notification architecture. For more details, see http://msdn.microsoft.com/library/enus/dnvs05/html/querynotification.asp.

Now you can run the page and then refresh it without causing a database query to occur (you can monitor database activity using the **SQL Profiler** tool that comes with SQL Server). However, if you open the source table in Visual Studio or Visual Web Developer and change one of the column values, you will see that the next time you refresh the page there is a hit on the database.

Using a Master Page to Give a Consistent Look and Feel

The styles you applied to the `GridView` and `DetailsView` controls, using the Auto Format feature, provide a reasonably attractive outcome. However, they say that beauty is in the eye of the beholder, and so it is no surprise to hear the phone ringing again. This time, Juan-Paul from the marketing department is "just calling to say" that they have a corporate design scheme from their Web site, and he would really appreciate your help to "facilitate an outward appearance of compatibility for reasons of enhanced staff resource utilization via familiarization with the infrastructure."

You take a wild guess that he means he wants the new page to follow the same style and layout as the existing pages. After promising Juan-Paul that you will "personally endeavor to push the envelope, drive the process, and aim skyward toward a satisfactory and visually coherent solution," you fire up Visual Studio again.

Luckily, you took advantage of the Master Pages feature of ASP.NET 2.0 when you built the AdventureWorks Web site. Therefore, fitting the new page into the existing site simply means converting it from a "normal" Web page into a Content Page and referencing the Master Page file. You did this because you realized marketing departments have a changeable attitude to life, and you may well be required to change the whole design and layout of the site at some time in the future. Figure 2.23 shows the Master Page, with

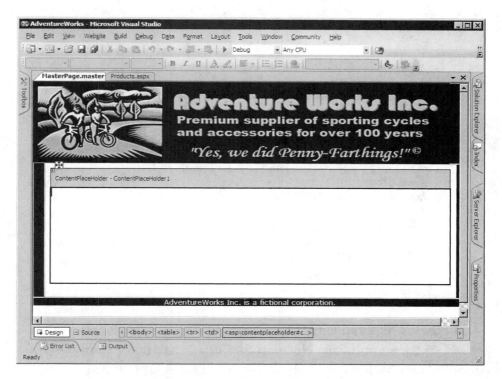

FIGURE 2.23: The AdventureWorks Master Page in Design View in Visual Studio

the `ContentPlaceHolder` control indicating the area occupied by the content from each of the Content Pages. The code that creates this page is shown in Listing 2.3, where you can see the `PlaceHolder` control within an HTML table.

Listing 2.3. The Source Code of the AdventureWorks Master Page

```
<%@ Master Language="C#" AutoEventWireup="true"
    CodeFile="MasterPage.master.cs" Inherits="MasterPage" %>
<!DOCTYPE html PUBLIC "-//W3C//DTD XHTML 1.1//EN"
        "http://www.w3.org/TR/xhtml11/DTD/xhtml11.dtd">
<html xmlns="http://www.w3.org/1999/xhtml" >
<head runat="server">
    <title>AdventureWorks Inc.</title>
    <link rel="Stylesheet" type="text/css"
        href="StyleSheet.css" title="Default" />
</head>
<body topmargin="0" leftmargin="0" rightmargin="0">
 <form id="form1" runat="server">
  <table width="100%" border="0" cellpadding="0" cellspacing="0">
   <tr>
    <td align="left" colspan="3" bgcolor="#000000">
     <img src="Images/header.jpg" border="0" vspace="0" />
    </td>
   </tr>
   <tr>
    <td bgcolor="#000000"> </td>
    <td style="padding:10px">
     <asp:ContentPlaceholder id="CP1" runat="server" />
    </td>
    <td bgcolor="#000000"> </td>
   </tr>
   <tr>
    <td align="center" colspan="3" bgcolor="#000000">
     <span class="footer">
      AdventureWorks Inc. is a fictional corporation.
     </span>
    </td>
   </tr>
  </table>
 </form>
</body>
</html>
```

All that is required is to strip out of the page all the `<html>`, `<body>`, `<head>`, `<form>`, and other elements that are not part of the display of rows from the new Web page. Then add the `MasterPageFile` attribute to the `Page` directive, and wrap the content in a `Content` control that specifies the

`ContentPlaceHolder` control on the Master Page that it will populate. Listing 2.4 shows how this looks in outline.

Listing 2.4. The Outline Structure of a Content Page

```
<%@ Page Language="C#" AutoEventWireup="true"
        CodeFile="Products.aspx.cs" Inherits="Products"
        MasterPageFile="~/MasterPage.master" %>
<asp:Content ContentPlaceHolderID="CP1" runat="server" ID="Content1">
   ... all page content goes here ...
</asp:Content>
```

Now, in Design view of the "product list" page, you can see how the new page fits into the Master Page (see Figure 2.24), with the Master Page itself grayed out and not available for editing unless you open it in a separate window. At runtime, the Master Page content merges into the content generated by the new page you have been building to give the combined result.

Adding a Menu and Other Navigation Features

One item missing from the site is a menu that makes it easy to navigate from one page to another. Again, ASP.NET 2.0 provides all you need to implement various navigation strategies, and the common and effective solution is often a dynamic fly-out or drop-down menu. The data to drive the `Menu` control comes from an XML file named `Web.sitemap`, which defines the items for the menu, their position within the hierarchical menu structure, the pop-up tool-tip for each item, and the target URL for navigation. With the new "products" page added to the XML file, the menu will automatically provide a link to this page.

You drag a `SiteMapDataSource` control from the Toolbox and drop it onto the page, using the Configure Data Source Wizard to select the `Web.sitemap` file. Then you drag a `Menu` control from the Toolbox and drop it onto the Master Page, select the new `SiteMapDataSource` control in the **Choose Data Source** list, and use the tasks pane to apply a suitable Auto Format (see Figure 2.25).

You also decide to make it easy for users to tell where they are in the site hierarchy by adding a `SiteMapPath` control to the Master Page as well, at the bottom of the right-hand section of the page below the `ContentPlaceHolder` control. This uses the same `Web.sitemap` file, and

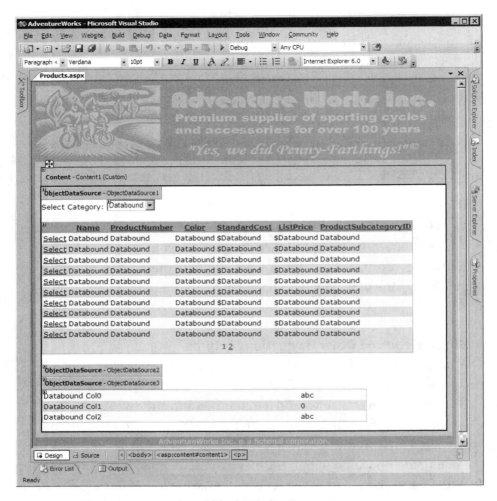

FIGURE 2.24: The new page running within the Master Page

automatically displays a "breadcrumb trail" for the current page (see Figure 2.26). In addition, like all the other features of ASP.NET 2.0 you have used so far, there is no code to write! It all just works…

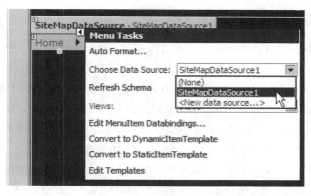

FIGURE 2.25: Adding a SiteMapDataSource and menu control to the Master Page

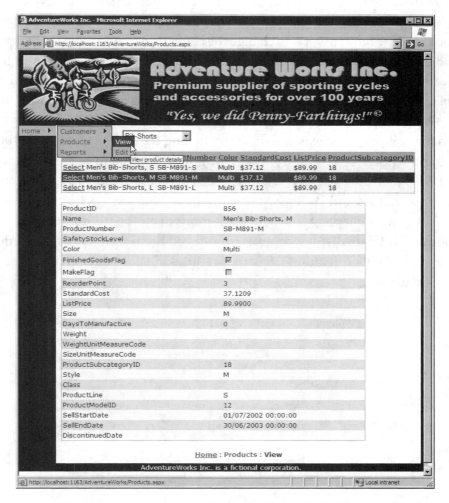

FIGURE 2.26: Adding a menu and a navigation trail to the Master Page

SUMMARY

Although this is a somewhat contrived scenario, this chapter has demonstrated just how powerful ASP.NET 2.0 is, and how it can considerably reduce development time while helping you to construct efficient and attractive Web sites and Web applications. One of the main goals of ASP.NET 2.0 is to reduce even further the amount of code you have to write to build dynamic and interactive pages, removing, in particular, the need for that repetitive code you seem to need for almost all of your projects! As you can see from this chapter, you can achieve remarkable results without writing any code at all.

In this chapter, you have seen how you can create and then evolve a data access page, starting with dragging a database table onto the editing window. You then saw how easy it is to change the content and appearance of the grid and then add features like sorting, paging, and editing. The next stage added a category selection capability, so that only specific sets of rows appear. Following this was implementation of a "form"-style view of the data.

Once the page provided the features required, you next saw how you can make it part of an existing site, by matching the overall style and layout using a Master Page and by integrating it with a menu and navigation system. All this was achieved within the visual design tool, using drag and drop techniques and Wizards, and without writing any code at all.

In the next chapter, you will work more deeply with the data source controls and data display controls introduced here, seeing how they offer a wide range of features to support all kinds of data management requirements.

■ 3 ■

Data Source and Data Display Controls

I N THE PREVIOUS CHAPTER, you saw how easy it can be to construct rich data-driven Web pages quickly, and integrate them into a site. The created pages have a great deal of functionality, but due to the nature of how they were designed, they have a fixed set of features and may have functionality that doesn't fit completely with your requirements. For example, the grids have sorting on the columns, but what if you don't want to allow sorting on all columns? Or what if you want to omit certain columns, change the formatting of others, or change the way editing can be performed on them? For these reasons, customization of the data controls is rich, and that's what this chapter will cover—how to get the best from the data source and grid controls.

Specifically, we're going to cover

- How to connect to databases, and where to store connection details
- How to use all of the data source controls, with detailed exploration of those for databases and XML data (Chapter 4 covers the `ObjectDataSource` in detail)
- How to use the data display controls, for both displaying and editing data

We will cover some data display controls in greater detail than others, because they are new to ASP.NET 2.0 and contain more functionality than the controls that existed in previous versions of ASP.NET. Let's start the exploration by examining databases and data connections.

Databases and Connections

Most Web sites will have some form of database behind them, whether to store a product catalog or just to manage user logins. This often requires a full installation of SQL Server on your development machine, but with ASP.NET 2.0 there is another option—SQL Server 2005 Express Edition (SSE). SSE is a cut-down version of SQL Server 2005, but has some interesting characteristics that make it especially suitable for the development environment. Two of these characteristics are automatic database attachment and user instancing.

Auto-Attached Databases

One problem with developing applications that use databases is the need to have SQL Server installed, where you need to attach a database, create a login to SQL Server, and add the login to the database. This would need to be done on each development machine unless the user is logged on as an Administrator, which is often the case but is not recommended.

SQL Server 2005 (both full and Express editions) supports automatic attachment of databases by adding the following into the connection string:

```
AttachDbFilename=db.mdf
```

With this in the connection string, SQL Server 2005 will automatically attach to the database when the application starts. You can also avoid explicit hard-coded paths to the database by using the new `App_Data` directory and a special feature to point to it. For example, consider the following connection string:

```
Data Source=.\SQLEXPRESS; AttachDbFilename=|DataDirectory|db.mdf
```

ASP.NET will replace the special string `|DataDirectory|` with the path to the `App_Data` directory, thus avoiding the need for a hard-coded path.

Even though databases can be dynamically attached, the problem of permissions still exists. How can a database be automatically attached if the user doesn't have permissions to attach databases? User Instancing is the solution to this problem, and it eliminates users having to be an Administrator.

User Instancing

To understand user instancing, you need to know how SQL Server instances work. By default, SQL Express will install with an instance name of SQLEXPRESS, which is why .\SQLEXPRESS is used in connections strings, because you are explicitly connecting to an instance. The default service account that SQL Express runs under is "NT AUTHORITY\NETWORK SERVICE"—this is the account that the instance will run under when the process starts. As it stands, this would still require explicit login and user creation.

User instancing solves this problem by creating an instance on demand, and instead of using the default service account, a user instance uses the user account as the service account. Thus, the process runs under the credentials of the user, so no explicit logins are required; because the process is running as the user, auto-attachment requires no additional permissions—the owner of the process automatically has full administrative rights to the database, even if the user is not an Administrator on the machine. All of this happens on demand, when the application starts, so there is no configuration required. The SQL Server process running the user instance stays active for 60 minutes after the last connection, although this can be configured with the `sp_configure` option "user instance timeout."

You can achieve user instancing by including the following in your connection string:

```
User Instance=True
```

User instancing only works with integrated security, so the full connection string will look like this:

```
Data Source=.\SQLEXPRESS;
AttachDbFilename=|DataDirectory|db.mdf;
User Instance=True;
Integrated Security=True;
```

User instancing is designed for the development scenario, to save configuration. As such there are limitations.

- Only local connections are allowed.
- Replication does not work with other user instances.
- Distributed queries do not work to remote databases.
- User instancing only works in SQL Server Express Edition.

The following common problems also arise because of user instancing:

- When using the Visual Studio 2005 or Visual Web Developer IDEs to connect to SQL Express, the SQL Express instance will run under the "NT AUTHORITY\NETWORK SERVICE" account, so this account requires write permissions on the MDF and LDF database files.
- ASP.NET pages run under the ASPNET user account, which means that an ASP.NET page that connects to a database with user instancing will result in the SQL Express process being owned by the ASPNET user. This means that the ASPNET user also requires write permissions on the database files.
- User instancing opens databases with exclusive access, to reduce the potential for data corruption due to multiple user instances with the same database name. Therefore, it is not possible to open the database in the IDE while it is still being used by the application. This is alleviated to a degree by the IDE, because running an application (via F5) will automatically close and detach the instance from the tool so that ASP.NET can open it. If you are running the application outside of the IDE, such as from a virtual root in IIS, then this will not be the case, and you may have to close the connection manually (use the Close Connection on the context menu).
- When connecting to a user instance database, you are connecting as an administrator. When deploying applications, you should connect as a lower-privileged account, so you will need to configure permissions on the database.

Connection String Placement

Connection strings are typically stored in `web.config`, and in version 1.*x* that usually meant the `appSettings` section. In ASP.NET 2.0, there is a new `connectionStrings` section, which provides a similar key/value pairing. For example:

```
<connectionStrings>
  <add name="AW"
    connectionString="Data Source=.\SQLEXPRESS; . . ."
    providerName="System.Data.SqlClient" />
</connectionStrings>
```

Although the `providerName` attribute isn't compulsory, connection strings won't appear in the Configure Data Source dialogs without a provider name being set.

Within applications, you can access these connection strings in two ways. In code, you use the `ConnectionStrings` property of the `ConfigurationManager` object. For example:

```
SqlConnection conn = new SqlConnection();
conn.ConnectionString =
    ConfigurationManager.ConnectionStrings["AW"].ConnectionString;
```

The `ConnectionStrings` property contains a collection of the connection strings from the section in `web.config`, so you use the `name` property as the index to the collection. The `ConnectionString` property then returns the actual connection string.

Within the markup of ASP.NET pages, you use an expression builder, which is a new feature of ASP.NET 2.0. Expression builders allow you to declaratively access features such as connection strings, application settings, and resources. For example, consider the following code:

```
<asp:SqlDataSource id="SqlDataSource1" runat="server"
  ConnectionString="<%$ ConnectionStrings:AW %> "
```

The expression builder uses a server side `<% %>` block, but when the first character within that block is a $ sign—this indicates an expression builder is to be used. Each expression builder has a known prefix, and for connection strings this is `ConnectionStrings`. In a similar method to code, you use the `name` attribute from the `web.config` section to identify the required connection string, using a : to separate the builder prefix from the name.

The beauty of these two methods is that from both code and markup you can use the centrally stored connection strings.

Visual Web Developer and Visual Studio 2005 Database Explorer

Both Visual Studio 2005 and Visual Web Developer have database management features, and although both are reached through different places, they act the same. In Visual Studio 2005, you use the Server Explorer, which by default is on the left of the screen, as shown in Figure 3.1. In Visual Web Developer, the Database Explorer is used, which by default is on the right of the screen, as shown in Figure 3.2. As you can see, their contents are the same, allowing access to the contents of the database from within the development tool.

Whichever tool you use, working with databases is simple. You can create and modify tables, stored procedures, views, and functions, and you can run ad-hoc queries. Throughout the book we'll refer to the Database

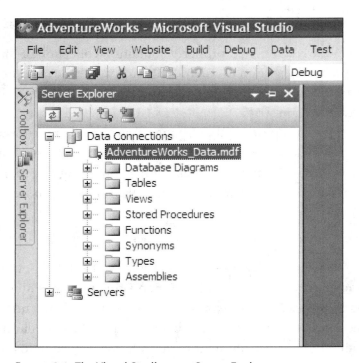

FIGURE 3.1: The Visual Studio 2005 Server Explorer

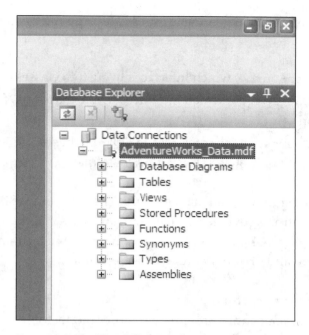

FIGURE 3.2: The Visual Web Developer Database Explorer

Explorer because it's more explicit; if you are using Visual Studio 2005, then use the Server Explorer to access the same functionality.

Data Source Controls

Chapter 2 showed how easy data source controls are to use, but there is more to them than their ease of use. Data source controls provide a declarative way to define not only the connection to a data store, but also the commands used to fetch and update data. Some data source controls don't interact directly with their data source, but interact by way of a provider. A provider abstracts the functionality of dealing with a data source and provides a consistent API for applications and controls to use. The providers are also pluggable, allowing you to replace the supplied providers with ones of your own.

The following four data source controls are supplied as standard with ASP.NET 2.0:

- `ObjectDataSource`, which interfaces to custom classes
- `SiteMapDataSource`, which interfaces to site map data, for site navigation
- `SqlDataSource`, which interfaces to SQL databases
- `XmlDataSource`, which interfaces to XML files

We're not going to cover all of these in this chapter, because the `Object-DataSource` control is covered in Chapter 4, and the `SiteMapDataSource` control is covered in Chapter 10. However, many of the techniques for the `SqlDataSource` and `ObjectDataSource` are similar.

The SqlDataSource Control

The `SqlDataSource` control provides a two-tier model for interacting with relational databases. It abstracts away from the developer the need to explicitly create connections and commands, leaving you free to concentrate on the data statements. When using the drag and drop functionality shown in the previous chapter, these statements default to explicit SQL, but you can also use stored procedures. There is no way to have stored procedures automatically created and used in the `SqlDataSource`, so you'll have to do this yourself. However, a quick solution is to use the drag-and-drop functionality, and then use the SQL statements as the SQL for your stored procedures.

To configure a `SqlDataSource` control, you can manually edit the properties, or use the smart task Configure Data Source option. The latter just walks you through selecting the connection (either from `web.config`, or creating a new one), selecting the tables and columns from which to fetch data, and optionally adding filtering and concurrency to the command. We'll look at these topics in the Filtering Data and Updating Data sections.

The `SqlDataSource` control has a number of properties that govern its behavior. The first of these is `DataSourceMode`, which can be set either to `DataSet` or `DataReader`, to identify how the data is to be fetched from the underlying data source. The default is `DataSet`, which provides two-way binding, while `DataReader` provides increased performance, but only allows read-only data.

To control how often the data is fetched, there are a number of properties specific to caching, allowing the control to cache data and only re-fetch it if it has changed since the last access. These will be covered in more detail in Chapter 6.

The properties that you will use most often relate to the commands used to fetch and modify data. For each type of data manipulation, there are two properties: a command to run, and a command type identifying if the command is inline SQL or a stored procedure.

Displaying Data with a GridView Control

At its simplest, the `SqlDataSource` control only requires that two properties be set to fetch data from a database: the `ConnectionString` and the `SelectCommand`. For example:

```
<asp:SqlDataSource ID="SqlDataSource1" runat="server"
  ConnectionString="<%$ ConnectionStrings:NorthwindConnectString %>"
  SelectCommand="SELECT * FROM Products" />
```

This simply fetches all rows from the **Products** table. To switch to stored procedures, you replace the inline **SQL** statement with the name of the stored procedure, and add the `SelectCommandType` attribute, setting its value to `StoredProcedure`.

```
<asp:SqlDataSource ID="SqlDataSource1" runat="server"
  ConnectionString="<%$ ConnectionStrings:NorthwindConnectString %>"
  SelectCommand="usp_Products"
  SelectCommandType="StoredProcedure" />
```

You can use this data source control by binding another control, such as a `GridView`, to it. For example:

```
<asp:GridView ID="GridView1" runat="server"
  DataSourceID="SqlDataSource1" />
```

This uses the `DataSourceID` property to identify the ID property of the data source control supplying the data, and is a common feature across the data source controls. By default the `GridView` displays all columns from the underlying data source, but this can be turned off by setting the `Auto-GenerateColumns` property to `False`, and by explicitly defining the columns. This will be covered in detail in the Customizing the GridView Control section.

Filtering and Selecting Data

One of the greatest features of the new data controls is the support for parameterized queries, which allows you to filter data dependent upon external criteria, such as another control, or a query string. You can filter data at the database by using `SelectParameters`, or in the Web page after the data has been fetched, by using `FilterParameters`. The difference is that `SelectParameters` and WHERE clauses are applied before the data is fetched, while `FilterParameters` fetch the data and then filter it. These are not mutually exclusive actions, and both can be performed if necessary. Selection is useful if the set of data being searched is large, because only a subset of the data is returned from the database to the page. Filtering is useful when the data is cached, because it reduces the overhead on the database.

Filter and Select Parameters

There are seven sources of data that can be applied to selects and filters.

- `ControlParameter`, which takes its data from an ASP.NET server control
- `CookieParameter`, which takes its data from a Cookie
- `FormParameter`, which takes its data from an HTML FORM control
- `Parameter`, which is the base class for the other parameters, and has no default source of data
- `ProfileParameter`, which takes its data from a Profile property
- `QueryStringParameter`, which takes its data from a query string value
- `SessionParameter`, which takes its data from a session value

These parameters provide a great deal of flexibility in filtering data in a declarative manner. All of these parameters support the properties shown in Table 3.1.

In addition to these properties, each parameter type has its own specific properties, as shown in Table 3.2.

TABLE 3.1: Common Properties of All Parameter Types

Property	Description
ConvertEmpty StringToNull	Indicates whether or not an empty value should be converted to NULL before being passed to SQL Server. The default value is True.
DefaultValue	Indicates the default value of the parameter, if one is not supplied by an external source.
Direction	Indicates the direction of data flow, and can be one of the `ParameterDirection` enumerations: • `Input`, for data transferred to SQL Server • `InputOutput`, for data transferred to and from SQLServer • `Output`, for data transferred from SQL Server • `ReturnValue`, for data transferred from SQL Server as the return value of a query
Name	The name of the parameter.
Size	The size of the parameter. Not required for fixed size types.
Type	The data type of the parameter. Can be one of the `TypeCode` enumerations: `Boolean, Byte, Char, DateTime, DBNull, Decimal, Double, Empty, Int16, Int32, Int64, Object, SByte, Single, String, UInt16, UInt32, UInt64`.

In action, all of these parameters work in the same way. The data to be used in the select or filter is taken from the location specified by the parameter. So for a `ControlParameter`, the ID identifies the control, and `PropertyName` identifies the property storing the data. For example, if a `TextBox` was used as the source of the parameter data, the `Text` property would be used as the `PropertyName`. Simple controls, such as a `TextBox`, aren't the only source of parameter data; a `GridView` could use the `SelectedValue` as the `PropertyName`, which would use the key field (from the `DataKeyNames` property) for the parameter value.

TABLE 3.2: Specific Parameter Type Properties

Parameter	Property	Description
ControlParameter	ControlID	The ID of the control supplying the parameter data.
	PropertyName	The name of the property on the control. For example, the Text property.
CookieParameter	CookieName	The name of the cookie supplying the parameter data.
FormField	FormParameter	The name of the form field supplying the parameter data.
ProfileProperty	PropertyName	The name of the Profile property supplying the parameter data.
QueryString Parameter	QueryString Field	The name of the query string field supplying the parameter data.
Session Parameter	SessionField	The name of the session field supplying the parameter data.

Configuring parameters can be done with the wizard, declaratively in source view (which is what the wizard generates), or in code.

Selecting Data Using the Configuration Wizard

The configuration wizard is extremely easy to use, but it's worth pointing out the key areas where query parameterization is affected by it. The first place (see Figure 3.3), shows the **WHERE** button, which will open a window allowing the parameters to be configured.

In Figure 3.4, you can see on the left side of the window that three pieces of key information are required:

* The Column, which is the column in the set of data that you filtering on. This is the column name added to the WHERE clause in the SQL

- The Operator, which gives different options for comparison, such as equals, greater than, and LIKE
- The source, which is the source of the value, and matches the parameter types

Figure 3.5 shows how to configure the source of the data for the filter. In this case, you can see that **TextBox1** is selected, and you can see the SQL Expression as it will be added to the code. Clicking **Add** will create the WHERE clause.

The wizard doesn't do anything more than provide a way to visually set the SelectParameters on the control, so you can also set these manually if desired.

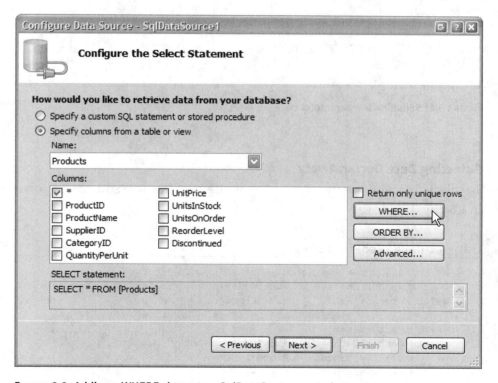

FIGURE 3.3: Adding a WHERE clause to a SqlDataSource control

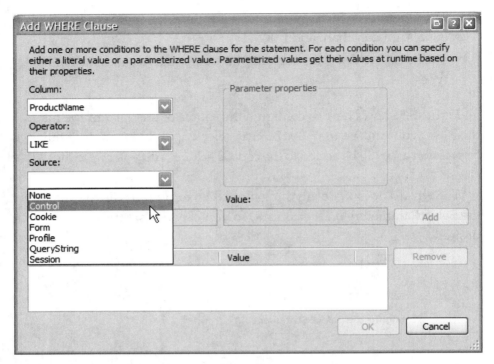

FIGURE 3.4: Selecting the parameter type

Selecting Data Declaratively

To select data, you use the `SelectParameters` of the data source, as shown in Listing 3.1.

Listing 3.1. Using SelectParameters

```
<asp:SqlDataSource ID="SqlDataSource1" runat="server"
  ConnectionString="<%$ ConnectionStrings:NorthwindConnectString %>"
  SelectCommand="SELECT * FROM [Products] WHERE
             ([ProductName] LIKE '%' + @ProductName + '%')">
  <SelectParameters>
    <asp:ControlParameter Name="ProductName" Type="String"
      ControlID="TextBox1" PropertyName="Text" />
  </SelectParameters>
</asp:SqlDataSource>
```

Listing 3.1 shows the results of configuring a `SqlDataSource` control with the wizard. Here the select command has had the WHERE clauses

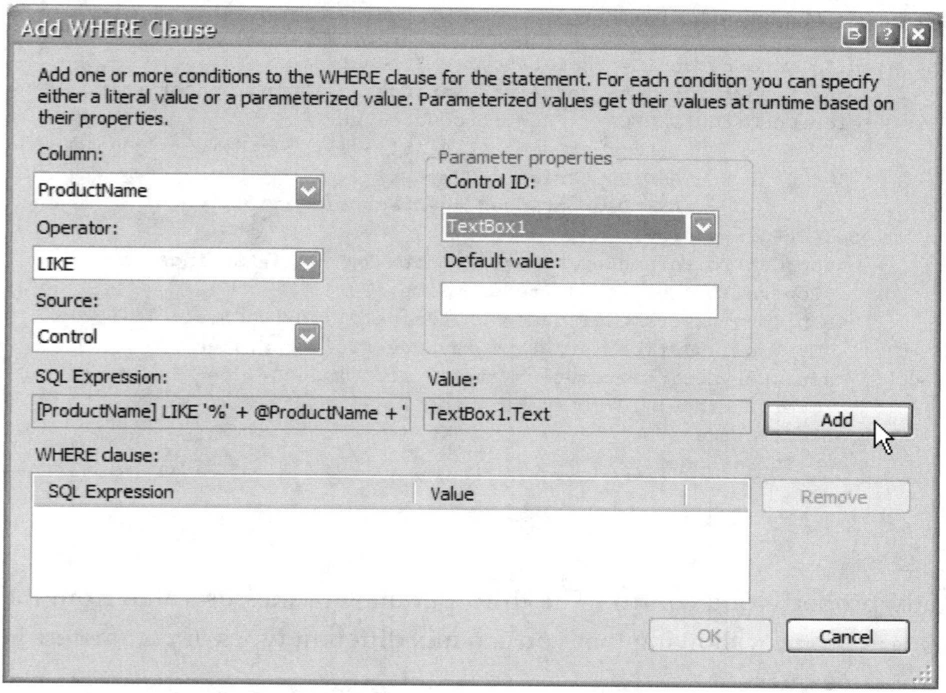

FIGURE 3.5: Selecting the source of the parameter data

added. Notice that the parameter in the WHERE clause is treated just like a standard SQL Server parameter, by preceding it with the @ character. Also notice that the Name property of the ControlParameter matches the parameter name in the query. You can use any value for the name of parameters, but it must match the actual parameter, and keeping it the same as the column name makes it easy to read.

Additional parameters can be added if necessary, as shown in Listing 3.2.

Here there are three parameters. This first is as shown earlier, while the second is matching only rows where the UnitPrice is below a certain value, and the third matches the discontinued column. The SelectCommand still follows the standard SQL format, but each parameter has an entry in the SelectParameters. The first two take their values from controls, the first from the Text property of a TextBox and the second from the SelectedValue of a list. This shows that you can take the value from

Listing 3.2. Multiple SelectParameters

```
<asp:SqlDataSource ID="SqlDataSource1" runat="server"
   ConnectionString="<%$ ConnectionStrings:NorthwindConnectString %>"
   SelectCommand="SELECT * FROM [Products] WHERE
                  ([ProductName] LIKE '%' + @ProductName + '%')
                  AND UnitPrice < @UnitPrice
                  AND Discontinued = @Discontinued">
   <SelectParameters>
     <asp:ControlParameter Name="ProductName" Type="String"
       ControlID="TextBox1" PropertyName="Text" />
     <asp:ControlParameter Name="UnitPrice" Type="Decimal"
       ControlID="PriceList" PropertyName="SelectedValue" />
     <asp:QueryStringParameter Name="Discontinued" Type="Boolean"
       QueryStringField="Discontinued" />
   </SelectParameters>
   </asp:SqlDataSource>
```

any property of a control. The third parameter takes its value from the `QueryString`, showing that you can mix different types of parameters in the same query.

Filtering is slightly different, in that the `SelectCommand` is not modified, but a `FilterExpression` property is added, and `FilterParameters` is used instead of `SelectParameters`, as shown in Listing 3.3.

Listing 3.3. Using FilterExpression and FilterParameters

```
<asp:SqlDataSource ID="SqlDataSource1" runat="server"
   ConnectionString="<%$ ConnectionStrings:NorthwindConnectString %>"
   SelectCommand="SELECT * FROM [Products]"
   FilterExpression="ProductName LIKE '{0}%'">
   <FilterParameters>
     <asp:ControlParameter Name="ProductName" Type="String"
       ControlID="TextBox1" PropertyName="Text" />
   </FilterParameters>
   </asp:SqlDataSource>
```

Notice that parameters in the `FilterExpression` aren't explicitly named—they are positional. So `{0}` refers to the first parameter in `FilterParameters`; subsequent parameters would be `{1}`, `{2}`, and so on.

Selecting Data in Code

When used declaratively, filtering and selecting requires no code, and provides a simple way to link data-bound controls to other controls, or other sources of filter data. You cannot directly filter or select from within code, although there are events that allow you to modify parameter values before an action takes place. The SqlDataSource control does have a Select method, but this only performs sorting or paging.

Updating Data

For data updates, the SqlDataSource control provides a similar model to that of selection, where there is a SelectCommand, a SelectCommandType, and SelectParameters. For modifying data, we have the properties shown in Table 3.3.

Like the select features, these can be configured manually or via the wizard. For the latter, you select the **Advanced** option when selecting your table or query, and the window that pops up (see Figure 3.6) allows you to have the data modification statements automatically added to the data source. You also have the option of adding optimistic concurrency, which adds a column check to each column being modified. This ensures that data is only updated if all of the columns are the same, thus preventing you from overwriting data that someone else has updated. This is covered in Chapter 5 in more detail.

Once configuration has finished, you'll find the commands and parameters set. For example, consider Listing 3.4. Here the data source has been configured with only three columns to make things easier to see.

Each of the commands is a normal SQL statement, and you can see how the parameters match up appropriately. For the DeleteCommand only a single parameter is needed, ProductID, because this uniquely identifies the row. This information is automatically taken from the key value fields from the database, so if you have a table whose unique key is multiple columns, you will require multiple DeleteParameters.

TABLE 3.3: Properties Used for Data Modification

Action	Property	Description
Adding new data	`InsertCommand`	The command to run to insert a single row into the database.
	`InsertCommand Type`	The type of command contained within the `InsertCommand` property. Can be one of the `SqlDataSource-CommandType` enumerations: `StoredProcedure` or `Text`.
	`Insert Parameters`	The collection of parameters containing data to insert.
Updating existing data	`UpdateCommand`	The command to run to update a single row in the database.
	`UpdateCommand Type`	The type of command contained within the `UpdateCommand` property. Can be one of the `SqlDataSourceCommandType` enumerations: `StoredProcedure` or `Text`.
	`Update Parameters`	The collection of parameters containing data to update.
Deleting data	`DeleteCommand`	The command to run to delete a single row in the database.
	`DeleteCommand Type`	The type of command contained within the `DeleteCommand` property. Can be one of the `SqlDataSource-CommandType` enumerations: `StoredProcedure` or `Text`.
	`Delete Parameters`	The collection of parameters containing data to delete.

Listing 3.4. A Fully Configured SqlDataSourceControl

```
<asp:SqlDataSource ID="SqlDataSource1" runat="server"
    ConnectionString="<%$ ConnectionStrings:NorthwindConnectString %>"
    SelectCommand="SELECT [ProductID], [ProductName], [UnitPrice]
             FROM [Products]
             WHERE ([ProductName] LIKE '%' + @ProductName + '%')"
    DeleteCommand="DELETE FROM [Products]
             WHERE [ProductID] = @ProductID"
```

```
    InsertCommand="INSERT INTO [Products] ([ProductName], [UnitPrice])
                VALUES (@ProductName, @UnitPrice)"
    UpdateCommand="UPDATE [Products]
                SET [ProductName] = @ProductName,
                    [UnitPrice] = @UnitPrice
                WHERE [ProductID] = @ProductID">
  <SelectParameters>
    <asp:ControlParameter ControlID="TextBox1"
      Name="ProductName" PropertyName="Text"
      Type="String" />
  </SelectParameters>
  <DeleteParameters>
    <asp:Parameter Name="ProductID" Type="Int32" />
  </DeleteParameters>
  <UpdateParameters>
    <asp:Parameter Name="ProductName" Type="String" />
    <asp:Parameter Name="UnitPrice" Type="Decimal" />
    <asp:Parameter Name="ProductID" Type="Int32" />
  </UpdateParameters>
  <InsertParameters>
    <asp:Parameter Name="ProductName" Type="String" />
    <asp:Parameter Name="UnitPrice" Type="Decimal" />
  </InsertParameters>
</asp:SqlDataSource>
```

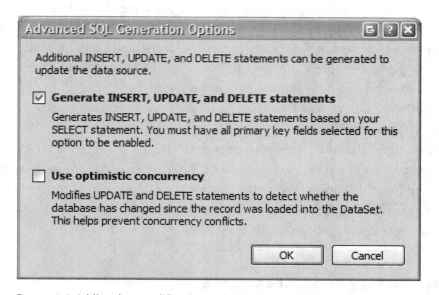

FIGURE 3.6: Adding data modification to the SqlDataSource control

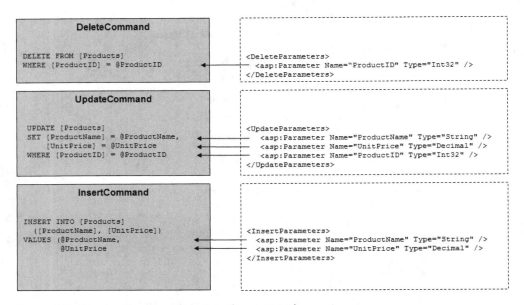

FIGURE 3.7: Mapping the parameters into the command

For the `UpdateCommand` there are three parameters: `ProductName` and `UnitPrice`, which are updated, and `ProductID`, which identifies the row to update. Notice that even though these take different actions in the command, the parameters within the `UpdateParameters` are defined in the same way.

For the `InsertCommand`, and the associated parameters, only two are required—the two defining the data to be inserted.

Figure 3.7 shows how the `<asp: Parameter/>` objects are mapped to the command parameters.

One thing to notice is that for data updates, the parameters created by the wizard are the base Parameter type, because the data comes from the underlying data source. When the control bound to the data source issues a command, the appropriate values are pushed from the control into the parameters and the command is executed.

Data Display and Edit Controls

In the previous chapter you saw how easy it was to configure a grid to use a data source control to not only display the data, but to also provide editing. These topics are worthy of discussion in more detail, and the following common scenarios will be covered:

- How to bind controls to sources of data
- Which controls to use to display data
- How to allow custom editing of the data
- How to customize the display controls

The methods of handling these questions are similar for many of the controls, so you'll find it easy to switch between them.

Data Binding to Data Source Controls

Along with the declarative style of setting the `SqlDataSource` control, the new grid and edit controls provide a `DataSourceID` property, which can be set to the `ID` of the data source. This automatically links the two controls, so that when the page is loaded, the data is fetched and displayed automatically. For example:

```
<asp:SqlDataSource ID="SqlDataSource1" runat="server"
  ...
</asp:SqlDataSource>

<asp:GridView ID="GridView1" runat="server"
  DataKeyNames="ProductID"
  DataSourceID="SqlDataSource1"></asp:GridView>
```

The `DataKeyNames` property identifies the unique key of the underlying data; it isn't required for displaying data, but it is required when you use the grid for updating data. The `GridView` will automatically display all columns supplied to it, but by default provides a read-only view. To enable modification, you can use the properties on the GridView Tasks pane, as shown in Figure 3.8.

Enabling editing and deleting adds a custom column to the grid.

```
<asp:GridView ID="GridView1" runat="server"
  DataKeyNames="ProductID"
  DataSourceID="SqlDataSource1">
  <Columns>
    <asp:CommandField ShowDeleteButton="True"
                      ShowEditButton="True" />
  </Columns>
</asp:GridView>
```

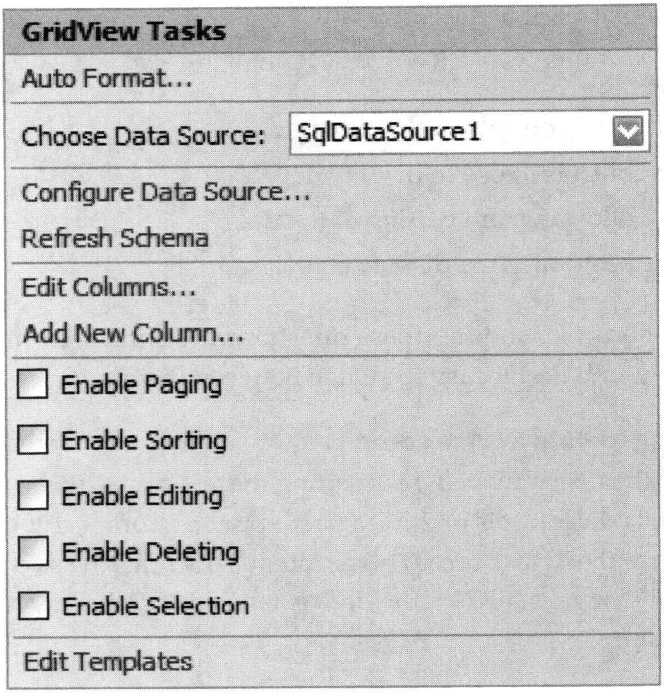

FIGURE 3.8: GridView Tasks pane

The common task doesn't have an option to enable new rows, and although there is a ShowInsertButton property, the grid itself doesn't support the notion of a new row; you don't get a blank row into which you can add your new data. There are ways to overcome this with the grid if required, but a far better solution is to use a DetailsView or FormView control, which is where the ShowInsertButton is primarily used. The DetailsView and FormView controls are covered later in the chapter.

Setting the ShowDeleteButton and ShowEditButton to True automatically gives edit and delete functionality, as shown in Figure 3.9. When the **Edit** button is selected, the row automatically switches to edit mode, with text boxes for editing the columns. Clicking **Update** automatically sends the changes back to the data source, which in turn sends them back to the SQL table.

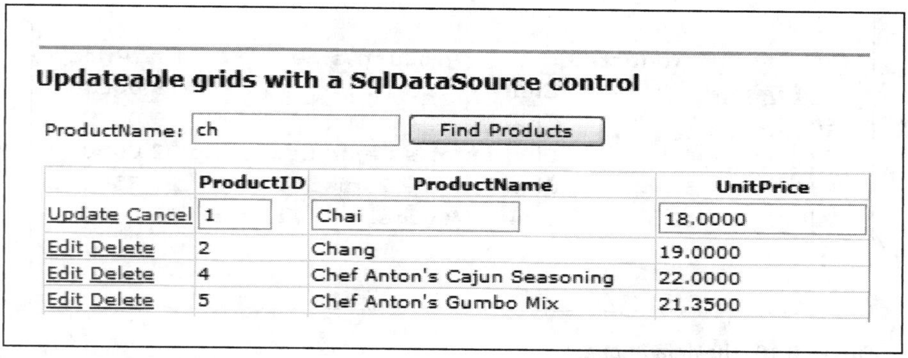

FIGURE 3.9: A GridView in edit mode

No code is required to enable editing and deleting within a grid. When the **Update** link is clicked, the column values are passed into the parameters of the `SqlDataSource` and the `UpdateCommand` is executed. If the **Cancel** link is clicked, the current values are ignored and the `Update-Command` is not run.

Customizing the GridView Control

The look shown in Figure 3.9 is the default look and behavior for a `GridView` control, but you can achieve complete flexibility by customizing the control.

Adding a Custom Pager

Screen real estate is always a problem, especially when displaying tables of data. This is solved by paging the data, so that a limited number of rows are shown at once. Paging is easily achieved by setting the `AllowPaging` property to `True`, and optionally the `PageSize` property to the number of rows to show (this defaults to 10). Adding paging will, by default, place an additional row at the bottom of the grid with the page numbers, as shown in Figure 3.10.

	ProductID	ProductName	UnitPrice
Edit Delete	1	Chai	18.0000
Edit Delete	2	Chang	19.0000
Edit Delete	4	Chef Anton's Cajun Seasoning	22.0000
Edit Delete	5	Chef Anton's Gumbo Mix	21.3500
Edit Delete	12	Queso Manchego La Pastora	38.0000
1 2 3			

FIGURE 3.10: The default pager

The pager can be customized in two ways. The first is to use the PagerSettings element, the general declaration of which is shown in Listing 3.5.

Listing 3.5. The PagerSettings Element

```
<PagerSettings
    FirstPageImageUrl="String"
    FirstPageText="String"
    LastPageImageUrl="String"
    LastPageText="String"
    Mode="NextPrevious|NextPreviousFirstLast|Numeric|NumericFirstLast"
    NextPageImageUrl="String"
    NextPageText="String"
    PageButtonCount="Integer"
    Position="Bottom|Top|TopAndBottom"
    PreviousPageImageUrl="String"
    PreviousPageText="String" />
```

The PageButtonCount property defines how many page numbers are shown, and if set to a value lower than the actual number of pages, ellipses are shown to indicate there are more pages.

The pager can be set to show text instead of page numbers by using the Mode property, and when done that way, the PageText properties define the text to show. These default to <<, <, >, and >>, but you can set them to any text you like, as shown in Listing 3.6.

Listing 3.6. Setting the Pager Text Links

```
<PageSettings
  Mode="NextPreviousFirstLast"
  FirstPageText="First"
  LastPageText="Last"
  NextPageText="Next"
  PreviousPageText="Previous" />
```

As an alternative, you can set the `ImageUrl` properties, which will display image links instead of text links.

You can perform further customization by templating the pager, by using the `PagerTemplate` subelement. Within the `PagerTemplate`, you can add any content, including server controls. For example, instead of page numbers of **Next/Previous** buttons, you could place a `DropDownList` containing the pages.

Defining Columns

If you don't want to accept the automatic generation of columns, you can set the `AutoGenerateColumns` property to `False` and use the `Columns` subelement to define your own. The advantage of this is that you can define how the columns appear in both display and edit modes, as opposed to the default types used by the grid. In default mode, labels are used for displaying data, and a `TextBox` is used in edit mode for strings, and a `CheckBox` for bit columns. Instead of using this default, you can use the following controls:

- `BoundField`, which acts like a default column, displaying text in display mode, and a `TextBox` in edit mode
- `ButtonField`, which displays a button in each row. The button can be a standard `Button`, a `LinkButton`, or an `ImageButton`
- `CheckBoxField`, which displays bit data as a `CheckBox`
- `CommandField`, which can display a text link, buttons, or image buttons to use for issuing commands on the grid. The commands can be standard ones to switch between display and edit mode, in which case the standard set of commands are displayed

(Select, Edit, Delete, Insert, and Cancel), or custom commands to perform custom actions in the button event handler

- `HyperLinkField`, which displays a `HyperLink` control
- `ImageField`, which displays an `Image` control
- `TemplateField`, which provides a custom area for content

There are different types of templates for different states, and these are covered in more detail in the Template Columns section.

The BoundField Control

The `BoundField` control displays as text in display mode, and as a `TextBox` in edit mode. The field to display is set with the `DataField` property, while the `DataFormatString` property can be used to format the value. For example, displaying a currency value can be done by setting `DataFormatString` to `{0:C}`. Listing 3.7 shows the outline syntax for the `BoundField` control.

Listing 3.7. Syntax of the BoundField Control

```
<asp:BoundField
   DataField="String"
   DataFormatString="String"
   ApplyFormatInEditMode="[True|False]"
   ConvertEmptyStringToNull="[True|False]"
   NullDisplayText="String"
   HtmlEncode="[True|False]"
   ReadOnly="[True|False]"
   Visible="[True|False]"
   InsertVisible="[True|False]"
   SortExpression="String"
   ShowHeader="[True|False]"
   HeaderText="String"
   AccessibleHeaderText="String"
   ControlStyle-[PropertyName]="[value]"
   HeaderStyle-[PropertyName]="[value]"
   HeaderImageUrl="String"
   ItemStyle-[PropertyName]="[value]"
   FooterText="String"
   FooterStyle-[PropertyName]="[value]" />
```

A description of these properties can be seen in Table 3.4.

The ButtonField Control

The `ButtonField` control is for when you need a button or link in the column to cause a page postback, perhaps to indicate that more details for the

TABLE 3.4: Properties of the BoundField Control

Property/Attribute	Description
DataField	Sets or returns a `String` that is the name of the column in the source rows that will provide the data to display in this column of the grid.
DataFormat String	Sets or returns a `String` that contains the formatting details for the value displayed in this column.
ApplyFormatIn EditMode	Sets or returns a Boolean value that indicates whether the formatting applied by the `DataFormatString` property when in "normal" mode will also be applied in "edit" mode; for example, displaying a currency symbol and trailing zeros in the text box in edit mode rather than just the numeric value.
ConvertEmpty StringToNull	Sets or returns a `Boolean` value that indicates whether an empty string in this column should be treated as null. This is useful when editing the data if the data source expects null values to be used when no value is present.
NullDisplay Text	Sets or returns a `String` that is the text to display in the grid for rows that have a null value in this column.
HtmlEncode	Sets or returns a `Boolean` value that indicates whether are the values in this column will be HTML-encoded before they inserted into the output generated by the `GridView` control.
ReadOnly	Sets or returns a `Boolean` value that indicates whether the values in this column can be edited. If True, the column will not display a text box in edit mode.
Visible	Sets or returns a `Boolean` value that indicates whether this column is visible within the output generated by the grid control.
Insert Visible	Sets or returns a `Boolean` value that indicates whether this column is visible when the grid is in insert mode.
Sort Expression	Sets or returns a `String` that defines the sort expression for this column, as a comma-delimited list of column names.
ShowHeader	Sets or returns a `Boolean` value that indicates whether the header for this column will be displayed.
HeaderText	Sets or returns a `String` that is the text to display in the header row for this column.

(Continued)

TABLE 3.4: (Continued)

Property/Attribute	Description
Accessible HeaderText	Sets or returns a `String` that sets the value of the HTML abbr attribute of the <th> elements that display the column headings when this column is rendered. Non-visual page reader applications and specialist user agents use the abbr attribute to assist in determining the layout of a table.
ControlStyle	Returns a reference to a `Style` instance that describes the style and formatting of any server controls displayed in the row.
HeaderStyle	Returns a reference to a `TableItemStyle` instance that describes the style and formatting of the header for this column.
Header ImageUrl	Sets or returns a `String` that is the relative or absolute URL of an image to display in the header row for this column.
ItemStyle	Returns a reference to a `TableItemStyle` instance that describes the style and formatting of the values in the data-bound rows in this column.
FooterText	Sets or returns a `String` that is the text to display in the footer row for this column.
FooterStyle	Returns a reference to a `TableItemStyle` instance that describes the style and formatting of the footer for this column.

row are to be shown, or to perform an action on the row, such as editing. A `ButtonField` control can be a standard button, a link button, or an image button. Listing 3.8 shows the outline syntax of the `ButtonField` control.

Listing 3.8. Syntax of the ButtonField Control

```
<asp:ButtonField
    ButtonType="[Button|Image|Link]"
    CommandName="String"
    DataTextField="String"
    DataTextFormatString="String"
    CausesValidation="[True|False]"
    ValidationGroup="String"
    Text="String"
    ImageUrl="String"
    ApplyFormatInEditMode="[True|False]"
    HtmlEncode="[True|False]"
    Visible="[True|False]"
    InsertVisible="[True|False]"
    SortExpression="String"
```

```
ShowHeader="[True|False]"
HeaderText="String"
AccessibleHeaderText="String"
ControlStyle-[PropertyName]="[value]"
HeaderStyle-[PropertyName]="[value]"
HeaderImageUrl="String"
ItemStyle-[PropertyName]="[value]"
FooterText="String"
FooterStyle-[PropertyName]="[value]" />
```

The properties in bold are specific to the `ButtonField` control and are described in Table 3.5, while the others are the same as for the `BoundField` control.

The CheckBoxField Control

The `CheckBoxField` control is used to display a checkbox, which reflects the Boolean value from the underlying data, such as a bit column from SQL Server. Listing 3.9 shows the outline syntax for the `CheckBoxField` control.

Listing 3.9. Syntax of the CheckBoxField Control

```
<asp:CheckBoxField
    DataField="String"
    DataFormatString="String"
    NullDisplayText="String"
    ReadOnly="[True|False]"
    Text="String"
    ApplyFormatInEditMode="[True|False]"
    HtmlEncode="[True|False]"
    InsertVisible="[True|False]"
    Visible="[True|False]"
    SortExpression="String"
    ShowHeader="[True|False]"
    AccessibleHeaderText="String"
    HeaderText="String"
    ControlStyle-[PropertyName]="[value]"
    HeaderStyle-[PropertyName]="[value]"
    HeaderImageUrl="String"
    ItemStyle-[PropertyName]="[value]"
    FooterText="String"
    FooterStyle-[PropertyName]="[value]" />
```

The property in bold is specific to the `CheckBoxField` control and is described in Table 3.6, while the others are the same as those for the `BoundField` control.

TABLE 3.5: Properties of the ButtonField Control

Property/Attribute	Description
ButtonType	Sets or returns a value from the ButtonType enumeration (Button, Image, or Link) that specifies the type of control to create in each row for this column. The default is Link.
CommandName	Sets or returns a String value that is the Command-Name property of the button in each row of the output.
DataTextField	Sets or returns a String that indicates the name of the column within the source data that will supply the value for the Text property of the control (the caption of a button or the text of a link).
DataTextFormatString	Sets or returns a String that contains the formatting information for the value in the row. Uses the same syntax as the DataFormatString property described for the BoundField control, using {0} as a placeholder.
CausesValidation	Sets or returns a Boolean value that indicates whether the button will cause any validation controls in the page to validate their values and report any errors. The default is True.
ValidationGroup	Sets or returns a String that is the name of the group of validation controls that this button will be a member of. See Chapter 9 for more details about validation groups.
Text	Sets or returns a String that will be used in place of DataTextField, in other words, the static value for the caption or text of the link that is the same for every row.
ImageUrl	Sets or returns a String that is the relative or absolute URL of the image to display when the ButtonType property is set to Image.

TABLE 3.6: Properties of the CheckBoxField Control

Property/Attribute	Description
Text	Sets or returns a String that will be used as the Text property of the CheckBox control.

The HyperLinkField Control

The `HyperLinkField` control is used to display a clickable link in each row using a standard HTML <a> element. The text and link reference can be set as static text or bound to columns from the underlying data. Listing 3.10 shows the outline syntax for the `HyperLinkField` control.

Listing 3.10. Syntax of the HyperLinkField Control

```
<asp:HyperLinkField
  DataTextField="String"
  DataTextFormatString="String"
  Text="String"
  DataNavigateUrlFields="String[,String]"
  DataNavigateUrlFormatString="String"
  NavigateUrl="String"
  Target="String"
  ApplyFormatInEditMode="[True|False]"
  HtmlEncode="[True|False]"
  Visible="[True|False]"
  SortExpression="String"
  ShowHeader="[True|False]"
  HeaderText="String"
  AccessibleHeaderText="String"
  ControlStyle-[PropertyName]="[value]"
  HeaderStyle-[PropertyName]="[value]"
  HeaderImageUrl="String"
  ItemStyle-[PropertyName]="[value]"
  FooterText="String"
  FooterStyle-[PropertyName]="[value]" />
```

The properties in bold are specific to the `HyperLinkField` control and are described in Table 3.7 while the others are the same as for the `Bound-Field` control.

Using the DataNavigateUrlFields Property

You can specify more than one column for the `DataNavigateUrlFields` property or attribute of a grid-type control. When the `GridView` binds a `HyperlinkField` to its source data, all the columns declared for the `DataNav-igateUrlFields` property can be used within the `DataTextFormatString`

TABLE 3.7: Properties of the HyperLinkField control

Property/Attribute	Description
DataTextField	Sets or returns a String that indicates the name of the column within the source data that will supply the value for the Text property of the control (the visible text of the link).
DataTextFormat String	Sets or returns a String that contains the formatting information for the bound value that is applied to the Text property of the link.
Text	Sets or returns a String that will be used in place of DataTextField, in other words, the static value for the text of the link that is the same for every row.
DataNavigateUrl Fields	Sets or returns a String Array that specifies the names of the columns within the source data that will supply values for the NavigateUrl property of the control (the href attribute of the resulting <a> element). Use a comma-delimited list of column names when declaring the control. This means that you can use values from different columns for hyperlinks. See the next section, Using the DataNavigateUrlFields Property.
DataNavigateUrl FormatString	Sets or returns a String that contains the formatting information for the bound values that will be applied to the NavigateUrl property.
NavigateUrl	Sets or returns a String that will be used in place of DataNavigateUrlFields, in other words, the static value for the href of the links that is the same for every row.
Target	Sets or returns a String that is the name of the target window for the link and will be used as the target attribute of the resulting <a> element.

property to provide more than one href value for the hyperlinks. For example, you can declare a HyperlinkField like this:

```
<asp:HyperLinkField DataTextField="ProductName"
   DataNavigateUrlFields="ProductID,ProductName"
   DataNavigateUrlFormatString=
      "http://www.mysite.com/products?product={0}" />
```

In this case, for a row containing the product named `Chang` with `ProductID` value 2, the `href` value will appear as:

```
http://www.mysite.com/products?product=2
```

However, you can also declare the `DataNavigateUrlFormatString` as:

```
DataNavigateUrlFormatString=
  "http://www.mysite.com/products?product={1}" />
```

In this case, the `href` value for the same row will appear as:

```
http://www.mysite.com/products?product=Chang
```

The same effect can be obtained, of course, by changing the value of the `DataNavigateUrlFormatString` property at runtime in the `Item-DataBound` event, just as you would with one of the v1.x grid or list controls.

However, the most useful feature of all, and one that was much requested by users, is that the `DataNavigateUrlFormatString` can now contain more than one placeholder, for example:

```
DataNavigateUrlFormatString=
  "http://www.mysite.com/products?product={0}&amp;name={1}" />
```

The `href` value for the same row will now appear as:

```
http://www.mysite.com/products?product=2&name=Chang
```

This gives you the opportunity to easily create `href` values that contain multiple query string parameters. Just remember to use the HTML-encoded ampersand (`&amp;`) to concatenate them together, as shown.

The ImageField Control

The `ImageField` control is used to display images, using the underlying data to provide the URL for the image. Listing 3.11 shows the outline syntax for the `ImageField` control.

The properties in bold are specific to the `ImageField` control and are described in Table 3.8, while the others are the same as those for the `BoundField` control.

Listing 3.11. Syntax of the ImageField Control

```
<asp:ImageField
  DataImageUrlField="[String]"
  DataImageUrlFormatString="[String]"
  DataImageTextField="[String]"
  DataImageTextFormatString="[String]"
  AlternateText="[String]"
  NullImageUrl="[String]"
  ApplyFormatInEditMode="[True|False]"
  HtmlEncode="[True|False]"
  Visible="[True|False]"
  SortExpression="String"
  ShowHeader="[True|False]"
  HeaderText="String"
  AccessibleHeaderText="String"
  HeaderStyle-[PropertyName]="[value]"
  HeaderImageUrl="String"
  ItemStyle-[PropertyName]="[value]"
  FooterText="String"
  FooterStyle-[PropertyName]="[value]" />
```

TABLE 3.8: Properties of the ImageField Control

Property/Attribute	Description
DataImageUrlField	Sets or returns a String that indicates the name of the column within the source data that will supply the value for the ImageUrl property of the image control.
DataImageUrl FormatString	Sets or returns a String that contains the formatting information for the bound value that is applied to the Url property of the image.
DataAlternate TextField	Sets or returns a String that indicates the name of the column within the source data that will supply the value for the AlternateText property of the image control.
DataAlternate TextFormatString	Sets or returns a String that contains the formatting information for the bound value that is applied to the AlternateText property of the image.
AlternateText	Sets or returns a String that contains the alternate text displayed for the image.
NullImageUrl	Sets or returns a String that contains the URL of the image to display if the data in the DataImageUrlField contains a null value.

Command Columns

Earlier in the chapter, you saw that a column can be added that can issue commands to the grid. These commands can take the form of selecting rows, deleting rows, switching between display and edit mode, or a custom command. To add these commands to a grid, you use a CommandField control, the outline syntax of which is shown in Listing 3.12.

Listing 3.12. Syntax of the CommandField Control

```
<asp:CommandField
    ButtonType="[Button|Image|Link]"
    UpdateText="String"
    UpdateImageUrl="String"
    ShowCancelButton="[True|False]"
    CancelText="String"
    CancelImageUrl="String"
    ShowSelectButton="[True|False]"
    SelectText="String"
    SelectImageUrl="String"
    ShowEditButton="[True|False]"
    EditText="String"
    EditImageUrl="String"
    ShowInsertButton="[True|False]"
    InsertText="String"
    InsertImageUrl="String"
    NewText="String"
    NewImageUrl="String"
    ShowDeleteButton="[True|False]"
    DeleteText="String"
    DeleteImageUrl="String"
    CausesValidation="[True|False]"
    ValidationGroup="String"
    Visible="[True|False]"
    SortExpression="String"
    ShowHeader="[True|False]"
    HeaderText="String"
    AccessibleHeaderText="String"
    ControlStyle-[PropertyName]="[value]"
    HeaderStyle-[PropertyName]="[value]"
    HeaderImageUrl="String"
    ItemStyle-[PropertyName]="[value]"
    FooterText="String"
    FooterStyle-[PropertyName]="[value]" />
```

The properties in bold are specific to the CommandField control and are described in Table 3.9, while the others are the same as those for the BoundField control.

TABLE 3.9: Properties of the CommandField Control

Property/Attribute	Description
ButtonType	Sets or returns a value from the ButtonType enumeration (Button, Image, or Link) that specifies the type of controls to create in each row of this column. The default is Link.
UpdateText	Sets or returns a String value that is the caption for the button that causes an update process to occur. The default is Update.
UpdateImage Url	Sets or returns a String that is the relative or absolute URL of the image to display in place of a text Update link.
ShowCancel Button	Sets or returns a Boolean value that indicates whether a **Cancel** button will be displayed in this column when the row is in edit mode.
CancelText	Sets or returns a String value that is the caption for the button that cancels an update process. The default is Cancel.
CancelImageUrl	Sets or returns a String that is the relative or absolute URL of the image to display in place of a text Cancel link.
ShowSelect Button	Sets or returns a Boolean value that indicates whether a **Select** button will be displayed in this column.
SelectText	Sets or returns a String value that is the caption for the button that causes the row to be shown in selected mode. The default is Select.
SelectImage Url	Sets or returns a String that is the relative or absolute URL of the image to display in place of a text Select link.
ShowEdit Button	Sets or returns a Boolean value that indicates whether an **Edit** button will be displayed in this column.
EditText	Sets or returns a String value that is the caption for the button that causes the row to be shown in edit mode. The default is Edit.
EditImageUrl	Sets or returns a String that is the relative or absolute URL of the image to display in place of a text Edit link.
ShowInsert Button	Sets or returns a Boolean value that indicates whether an **Insert** button will be displayed in this column. Inserting only has an effect in the DetailsView and FormView controls, and is not supported in the GridView control.

Property/Attribute	Description
InsertText	Sets or returns a String value that is the caption for the button that causes the row to be shown in insert mode. The default is Insert.
InsertImage Url	Sets or returns a String that is the relative or absolute URL of the image to display in place of a text Insert link.
NewText	Sets or returns a String value that is the caption for the button that causes the row to be shown in New mode. The default is New.
NewImageUrl	Sets or returns a String that is the relative or absolute URL of the image to display in place of a text New link.
ShowDelete Button	Sets or returns a Boolean value that indicates whether a **Delete** button will be displayed in this column.
DeleteText	Sets or returns a String value that is the caption for the button that deletes a row. The default is Delete.
DeleteImage Url	Sets or returns a String that is the relative or absolute URL of the image to display in place of a text Delete link.
Causes Validation	Sets or returns a Boolean value that indicates whether the button will cause any validation controls in the page to validate their values and report any errors. The default is True.
Validation Group	Sets or returns a String that is the name of the group of validation controls that this button will be a member of. See Chapter 9 for more details about validation groups.

You can use a CommandField control to provide automatic management of data editing. For example, setting the ShowEditButton property to True will display an **Edit** link in the column. Clicking this link will switch the row into edit mode, which automatically shows **Update** and **Cancel** links. The former will update the underlying data with your changes, while the latter will cancel your changes. Both return the row to display mode. The ShowDeleteButton property will show a **Delete** link, which deletes the underlying row with no user confirmation. Confirmation and events will be covered in the Using Events section later in the chapter.

Template Columns

If the column types presented here do not give enough control over the layout of your data, you can use templated columns, which work in much the same way as templates work on controls such as the `DataList` or `DataGrid`. You specify the output in one or more templates, and the control selects the appropriate template depending upon the status of the grid. Listing 3.13 shows the outline syntax for a `TemplateField` control.

Listing 3.13. Syntax of the TemplateField Control

```
<asp:TemplateField
  ApplyFormatInEditMode="[True|False]"
  HtmlEncode="[True|False]"
  Visible="[True|False]"
  SortExpression="String"
  ShowHeader="[True|False]"
  HeaderText="String"
  AccessibleHeaderText="String"
  HeaderStyle-[PropertyName]="[value]"
  HeaderImageUrl="String"
  ItemStyle-[PropertyName]="[value]"
  FooterText="String"
  FooterStyle-[PropertyName]="[value]" >

    <HeaderTemplate>...</HeaderTemplate>
    <ItemTemplate>...</ItemTemplate>
    <AlternatingItemTemplate>...</ AlternatingItemTemplate>
    <EditItemTemplate>...</EditItemTemplate>
    <FooterTemplate>...</FooterTemplate>

  <asp:TemplateField>
```

All the attributes of the control are the same as those listed for the `BoundField` control in Table 3.4. The five kinds of templates that you can specify, highlighted in Listing 3.13, are documented in Table 3.10.

When using template columns, you have to provide the binding directly, and for this you would use the `Eval` or `Bind` methods. The difference between these methods is that `Eval` provides read-only binding, while `Bind` provides read-write binding, and you'd generally use these in different templates. For example, consider Listing 3.14, where an `ItemTemplate` is used to display the price of a product, and the `EditItemTemplate` shows a `TextBox`, but also has a `RequiredFieldValidator` to ensure that a value is entered for the price.

TABLE 3.10: Templates of the TemplateField Control

Template	Description
HeaderTemplate	The markup, text, controls, and other content required to generate the entire content for the header of this column of the grid.
ItemTemplate	The markup, text, controls, and other content required to generate the entire content for this column in data-bound rows within the grid.
AlternatingItem Template	The markup, text, controls, and other content required to generate the entire content for this column in alternating data-bound rows within the grid.
EditItem Template	The markup, text, controls, and other content required to generate the entire content for this column in the row within the grid that is in edit mode.
FooterTemplate	The markup, text, controls, and other content required to generate the entire content for the footer of this column of the grid.

Listing 3.14. Two-Way Binding in a Template

```
<asp:TemplateField HeaderText="Price"  SortExpression="UnitPrice"
  ItemStyle-Font-Bold="True">
  <ItemTemplate>
    <asp:Label runat="server"
      Text='<%# Eval("UnitPrice", "${0:F2}") %>' />
  </ItemTemplate>
  <EditItemTemplate>
    <asp:TextBox ID="UnitPrice" runat="server"
      Text='<%#Bind("UnitPrice")%>' />
    <asp:RequiredFieldValidator ID="rfv1" runat="server"
      ControlToValidate="UnitPrice"
      Text="You must enter the price" />
  </EditItemTemplate>
</asp:TemplateField>
```

This technique is very useful when you want to use the data update features of the data source and grid controls, but also need custom content such as validation or drop-down lists when the user is editing data.

The use of Eval is a shortcut to the old syntax of DataBinder.Eval. Bind is new in version 2.0.

Styling Columns

You can style columns in a number of ways, either using properties on the columns themselves, or by setting general column properties in the grid, which can be done in two ways. The first way is to set the properties on the GridView declaration, like this:

```
<asp:GridView ID="grid1" runat="server" DataSourceID="ds1"
  RowStyle-BackColor="Aqua" HeaderStyle-Font-Bold="True"
```

Alternatively, you can set the styling as separate elements, like this:

```
<asp:GridView ID="grid1" runat="server" DataSourceID="ds1">
  <HeaderStyle Font-Bold="true" Font-Names="Verdana" />
  <RowStyle Font-Names="Verdana" />
</asp:GridView>
```

There is no practical difference between the two methods, although the latter style is easier to read and keeps the styling separate from the rest of the grid declaration. Styles can also be set on columns, like this:

```
<asp:HyperLinkField DataTextField="ProductName"
  ItemStyle-Font-Bold="True" ItemStyle-BackColor="Yellow" />
```

As well as using the individual style elements, you can use CSS to style elements by using the CssClass property.

```
<asp:HyperLinkField DataTextField="ProductName"

  CssClass="GridLink" />
```

The following eight style elements are available:

- AlternatingRowStyle, for alternating rows (RowStyle handles the others)
- EditRowStyle, for rows in edit mode
- EmptyDataRowStyle, for the row shown when there is no data to display
- FooterStyle, for the footer row
- HeaderStyle, for the header row
- PagerStyle, for the page row
- RowStyle, for all rows, unless AlternatingRowStyle is also set
- SelectedRowStyle, for rows selected by a select command

Styles used on individual columns override any styles set at the grid level.

Custom GridView Commands

You are not limited to using a `CommandField` to issue commands, because any button control (anything that causes a postback) can be set to emulate the standard commands. Each submit-style button has two properties, `CommandName` and `CommandArgument`, which can be set to a specific command. When an appropriately set button is clicked within the context of a grid row, the command is executed. For example, consider the following:

```
<asp:LinkButton id="LinkButton1" runat="server"
  CommandName="Edit" Text="Edit" />
```

If this is placed in a column, then clicking the link will execute the Edit command, switching the row into edit mode, exactly as it would be done through a standard edit **Command** button. You can set the `CommandName` property to any of the following: `Insert`, `Cancel`, `Delete`, `New`, or `Select`.

Putting it All Together—A Customized GridView Control

There is no limit to the way you can combine columns, and you can even leave the auto-generation of columns on and define columns within the `<Columns>` section. In this case, any columns you explicitly define are placed at the start of the grid, while automatic columns are placed afterwards. It's generally better to explicitly name the columns, because you then have control over how they appear. Figure 3.11 shows a grid with a variety of column types and formats.

Definition of this grid is as shown in Listing 3.15. Auto-generation of columns is disabled, and sorting and paging are enabled, with a style set for the header and each row.

Although not the best looking grid, you can see that the column types and styling give you a great deal of flexibility in the look and feel of grids. You can see that although editing is possible, when you come to edit more than one or two columns, the `GridView` could have limitations. For example, adding validation is possible, but validation errors might not fit within the grid cells. Or what if you have a column that accepts a large amount of text—a product description perhaps—where a cell within a grid would provide a restrictive way of both viewing and editing the data? A better editing solution, or for display of single rows of data, is to use either a `DetailsView` or `FormView` control.

Listing 3.15. The GridView Definition

```
<asp:GridView ID="grid1" runat="server" DataSourceID="ds1"
  DataKeyNames="ProductID"
  AutoGenerateColumns="False"
  AllowSorting="True" AllowPaging="True" PageSize="5">
  <HeaderStyle Font-Bold="True" Font-Names="Verdana" />
  <RowStyle Font-Names="Verdana" />
  <Columns>
    <asp:ButtonField ButtonType="Button" DataTextField="ProductID"
      SortExpression="ProductID" HeaderText="ID" />

    <asp:HyperLinkField DataTextField="ProductName"
      DataNavigateUrlFields="ProductID,ProductName"
      DataNavigateUrlFormatString="http://www.site-that-shows-more-
info.com/products?product={0}&amp;name={1}"
      SortExpression="ProductName" HeaderText="Product"
      ItemStyle-Font-Bold="True" ItemStyle-BackColor="Yellow" />

    <asp:BoundField DataField="QuantityPerUnit"
      HeaderText="Packaging"  />

    <asp:CheckBoxField DataField="Discontinued" HeaderText="N/A" >

    <asp:TemplateField HeaderText="Price"
      SortExpression="UnitPrice" ItemStyle-Font-Bold="True">
      <ItemTemplate>
        <asp:Label runat="server"
          Text='<%# Eval("UnitPrice", "${0:F2}") %>62;' />
      </ItemTemplate>
      <AlternatingItemTemplate>
        <asp:Label runat="server" ForeColor="DarkGray"
          Text='<%# Eval("UnitPrice", "${0:F2}") %>' />;
      </AlternatingItemTemplate>
      <EditItemTemplate>
        <asp:TextBox ID="UnitPrice" runat="server"
          Text='<%#Bind("UnitPrice")%>' />
        <asp:RequiredFieldValidator ID="rfv1" runat="server"
          ControlToValidate="UnitPrice"
          Text="You must enter the price" />
      </EditItemTemplate>
    </asp:TemplateField>

    <asp:CommandField ButtonType="Image" ShowCancelButton="True"
      ShowEditButton="True" ShowDeleteButton="True"
      CancelImageUrl="s.gif" EditImageUrl="q.gif"
      UpdateImageUrl="i.gif" DeleteImageUrl="x.gif"
      CancelText="Cancel this update" EditText="Edit this row"
      UpdateText="Apply these changes" DeleteText="Delete this row"/>

  </Columns>
</asp:GridView>
```

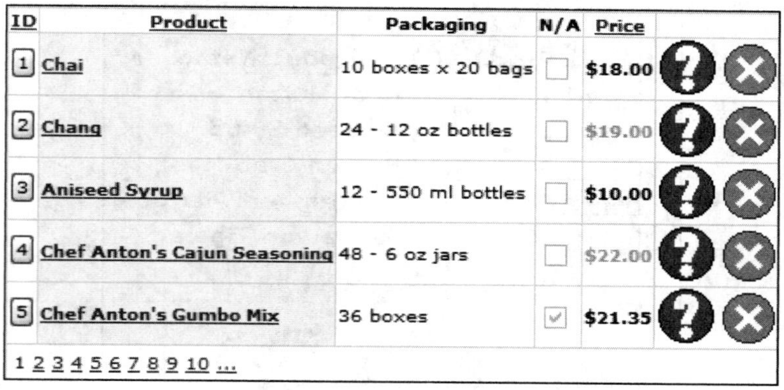

FIGURE 3.11: A GridView with a mixture of column types

The DetailsView Control

The DetailsView control provides a view of a single row of the data, in a form style rather than a grid style. The DetailsView can be used stand-alone, or in combination with a GridView, for showing and editing individual rows. This works well when combining the selection from a grid and a SelectParameters on a SqlDataSource control, as shown in Listing 3.16.

Listing 3.16. Using a DetailsView Control

```
<asp:SqlDataSource ID="SqlDataSource2" runat="server"
  ConnectionString="<%$ ConnectionStrings:NorthwindConnectString %>"
  DeleteCommand="..." InsertCommand="..." UpdateCommand="..."
  SelectCommand="SELECT * FROM Products
                 WHERE ProductID = @ProductID)">
  ...
  <SelectParameters>
    <asp:ControlParameter ControlID="GridView1"
      Name="ProductID" PropertyName="SelectedValue"
      Type="Int32" />
  </SelectParameters>
</asp:SqlDataSource>

<asp:DetailsView ID="DetailsView1" runat="server"
  DataKeyNames="ProductID" DataSourceID="SqlDataSource2">
</asp:DetailsView>
```

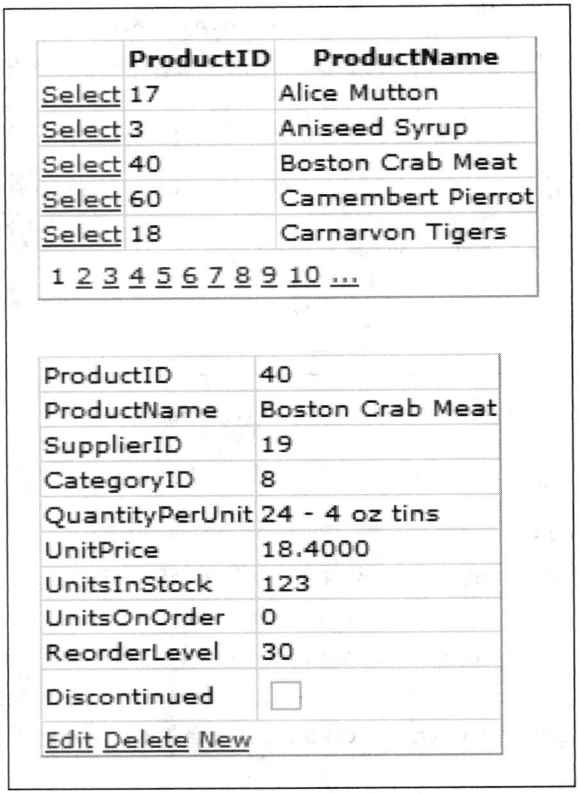

FIGURE 3.12: Showing a single row with a DetailsView control

Figure 3.12 shows the `DetailsView` displaying a row of data, with the row having been selected in a `GridView`.

By default the `DetailsView` does not show any edit commands, but these can be added in one of two ways. The first is by properties on the control itself, like this:

```
<asp:DetailsView ID="DetailsView1" runat="server"
  DataKeyNames="ProductID" DataSourceID="SqlDataSource2"
  AutoGenerateInsertButton="True"
  AutoGenerateDeleteButton="True"
  AutoGenerateEditButton="True">
```

This would add the commands at the bottom of the control, as shown in Figure 3.12. Alternatively, a `CommandField` can be explicitly defined, like this:

```
<asp:DetailsView ID="DetailsView1" runat="server"
  DataKeyNames="ProductID" DataSourceID="SqlDataSource2">
```

```
    <Fields>
      <asp:CommandField ShowDeleteButton="True" ShowEditButton="True"
        ShowInsertButton="True" />
    </Fields>
  </asp:DetailsView>
```

Like the `GridView`, the default behavior is suitable for both display and editing of data, but it does have the same limitations, such as how to display different controls to edit the data.

Defining Fields

The `DetailsView` automatically generates the fields based upon the underlying data. Like the `GridView` though, automatic generation of fields can be turned off and the fields specified directly. This is done with the `AutoGenerateRows` property and the `Fields` subelement, as shown in Listing 3.17.

Listing 3.17. Defining the Fields on a DetailsView

```
<Fields>
  <asp:BoundField DataField="ProductID"
    HeaderText="ProductID" InsertVisible="False"
    ReadOnly="True" SortExpression="ProductID" />
  <asp:BoundField DataField="ProductName"
    HeaderText="ProductName" SortExpression="ProductName" />
  <asp:BoundField DataField="SupplierID"
    HeaderText="SupplierID" SortExpression="SupplierID" />
  <asp:BoundField DataField="CategoryID"
    HeaderText="CategoryID" SortExpression="CategoryID" />
  <asp:BoundField DataField="QuantityPerUnit"
    HeaderText="QuantityPerUnit" SortExpression="QuantityPerUnit" />
  <asp:BoundField DataField="UnitPrice"
    HeaderText="UnitPrice" SortExpression="UnitPrice" />
  <asp:BoundField DataField="UnitsInStock"
    HeaderText="UnitsInStock" SortExpression="UnitsInStock" />
  <asp:BoundField DataField="UnitsOnOrder"
    HeaderText="UnitsOnOrder" SortExpression="UnitsOnOrder" />
  <asp:BoundField DataField="ReorderLevel"
    HeaderText="ReorderLevel" SortExpression="ReorderLevel" />
  <asp:CheckBoxField DataField="Discontinued"
    HeaderText="Discontinued" SortExpression="Discontinued" />
  <asp:CommandField ShowDeleteButton="True"
    ShowEditButton="True" ShowInsertButton="True" />
</Fields>
```

You can see that these are the same fields as used in the GridView, so you can use TemplateField controls to provide customization, such as displaying drop-down lists for supplier and category when editing data, as shown Listing 3.18 with the supplier.

Listing 3.18. Using TemplateField Controls

```
<asp:TemplateField HeaderText="Supplier">
  <ItemTemplate>
    <%#Eval("CompanyName") %>
  </ItemTemplate>
  <EditItemTemplate>
    <asp:SqlDataSource ID="Sds1" runat="server"
     ConnectionString="<%$ConnectionStrings:NorthwindConnectString%>"
      SelectCommand="SELECT SupplierID, CompanyName
                    FROM Suppliers ORDER BY CompanyName" />
    <asp:DropDownList ID="SupplierID" runat="server"
      DataSourceId="Sds1"
      DataValueField="SupplierID" DataTextField="CompanyName"
      SelectedValue='<%#Bind("SupplierID")%>' />
  </EditItemTemplate>
</asp:TemplateField>
```

You can see that the ItemTemplate simply displays the CompanyName, while the EditItemTemplate contains a SqlDataSource and a DropDownList. The data source fetches the ID and name of all suppliers, and the list binds to this data, as seen in Figure 3.13. The DataValueField holds the ID, while the DataTextField holds the display data. The key item here is the SelectedValue, which is set to a data-binding expression, using Bind to provide two-way binding to the SupplierID column. Because SelectedValue is used, whatever SupplierID the underlying row has is displayed as the currently selected item in the list, and because Bind is used, when the **Update** link is clicked, that new SupplierID is pushed back to the database through the data source control.

The DetailsView can be further customized with styling, in a similar way to the GridView. The DetailsView supports the following style elements:

- AlternatingRowStyle, for alternating rows (RowStyle handles the others)
- CommandRowStyle, for the row holding the commands (Edit, New, etc.)
- EditRowStyle, for rows in edit mode

- `EmptyDataRowStyle`, for the row shown when there is no data to display
- `FieldHeaderStyle`, for the row headers
- `FooterStyle`, for the footer row
- `HeaderStyle`, for the header row
- `InsertRowStyle`, for the row shown when in insert mode
- `PagerStyle`, for the page row
- `RowStyle`, for all rows, unless `AlternatingRowStyle` is also set

There are also other properties, such as `GridLines`, which sets the display borders, so you can remove the grid-like look this control has.

Using a Stand-Alone DetailsView

The `DetailsView` doesn't have to be used in conjunction with another control, displaying details for a selection, but can be used stand-alone. While it still only displays one row at a time, it can step through rows in a set of data, as shown in Figure 3.14, where three records have been stepped through. The navigation buttons are intelligent, so they only show when

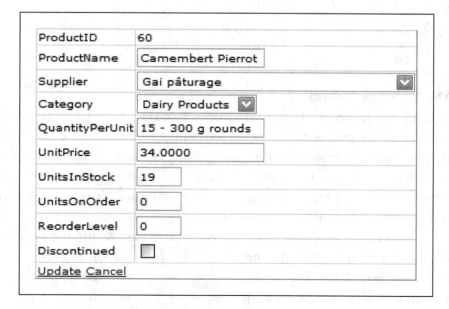

FIGURE 3.13: TemplateColumns with DropDownLists

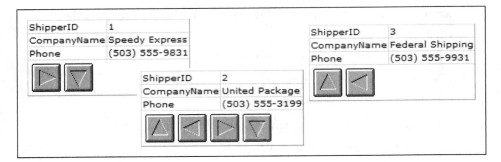

FIGURE 3.14: The DetailsView in standalone mode

required; for the first record, only the **Next** and **Last** buttons are visible, while for the last record on, the **First** and **Previous** buttons are visible.

Custom DetailsView Commands

Like the `GridView`, any button can emulate the standard button commands by use of the `CommandName` and `CommandArgument` properties. For the standard commands, the CommandName would be set to one of: `Insert`, `Cancel`, `Delete`, `New`, or `Select`. To emulate the paging buttons, you set the `CommandName` to `Page` and the `CommandArgument` to one of `First`, `Last`, `Prev`, or `Next`. For example:

```
<asp:LinkButton id="LinkButton1" runat="server"
   CommandName="Page" CommandArgument="First"
   Text="First" />
```

The FormView Control

If more flexibility is required than the `DetailsView` provides, then a `FormView` can be used. This is very similar in action to a `DetailsView`, displaying a single row at a time, but it provides no default user interface; you have to provide the entire interface via templates. Most of the properties and usage of the `FormView` are the same as for the `DetailsView`, but conceptually it differs in one major way. When using custom columns on the `DetailsView`, you define the fields, and then within the fields, you define the templates. With the `FormView`, because there is no default interface, you define the templates, and then within the templates, you put all of the content to be displayed when that template is visible. For example, consider Figure 3.15, which shows three states of a `FormView`.

The FormView declaration is shown in Listing 3.19.

Listing 3.19. The FormView Declaration

```
<asp:FormView id="FormView1" DataSourceID="dvs1" runat="server"
  DataKeyNames="ShipperID" AllowPaging="True"
  PagerSettings-Mode="Numeric">
```

Listing 3.20 shows the `ItemTemplate`, and you can see that the entire interface is detailed, including a table for layout, standard server controls using read-only binding, and `LinkButton` controls for the commands, which allow rows to be edited, deleted, and added.

Listing 3.20. The FormView ItemTemplate

```
<ItemTemplate>
  <table border="0" cellpadding="5">
  <tr>
    <td>
      <asp:Image ID="Image1" runat="server"
        Width="100" Height="123"
        ImageUrl='<%# Eval("ShipperID", "{0}.gif") %>'
        AlternateText='<%# Eval("CompanyName", "{0} Logo") %>' />
    </td>
    <td>
      <b><%# Eval("CompanyName") %></b><p />
      <%# Eval("Phone") %><p />
      <asp:LinkButton id="btnEdit" runat="server"
        CommandName="Edit" Text="Edit Details" /><br />
      <asp:LinkButton id="btnDelete" runat="server"
        CommandName="Delete" Text="Delete Shipper" /><br />
      <asp:LinkButton id="btnInsert" runat="server"
        CommandName="New" Text="Add New Shipper" />
    </td>
  </tr>
  </table>
</ItemTemplate>
```

Listing 3.21 shows the `EditItemTemplate`, with both read-only and read-write binding. The read-only binding is used for the `ShipperID`, the primary key column of the table, which cannot be edited. The `CompanyName` and `Phone` columns use `Bind` to allow the user-entered value to be pushed back to the database. Because this template is shown when editing data, the buttons have their commands set to `Update` and `Cancel`—the two actions that can be performed on a row in edit mode.

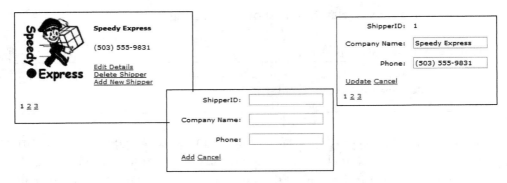

FIGURE 3.15: The FormView control in normal, insert, and edit modes

Listing 3.21. The FormView EditItemTemplate

```
<EditItemTemplate>
  <table border="0" cellpadding="5">
    <tr>
      <td align="right">ShipperID:</td>
      <td><%# Eval("ShipperID") %></td>
    </tr>
    <tr>
      <td align="right">Company Name:</td>
      <td>
        <asp:TextBox id="txtEditName" runat="server"
             Text='<%# Bind("CompanyName") %>' />
      </td>
    </tr>
    <tr>
      <td align="right">Phone:</td>
      <td>
        <asp:TextBox id="txtEditPhone" runat="server"
          Text='<%# Bind("Phone") %>' />
      </td>
    </tr>
    <tr>
      <td colspan="2">
        <asp:LinkButton id="btnUpdate" CommandName="Update"
          Text="Update" runat="server" />
        <asp:LinkButton id="btnCancel" CommandName="Cancel"
          Text="Cancel" runat="server" />
      </td>
    </tr>
  </table>
</EditItemTemplate>
```

Listing 3.22 shows the `InsertItemTemplate`, which uses `Bind` for read-write binding of the `ShipperID` and `Phone`; even though this is a new row, `Bind` is still used. Because this is a new row, the commands are set to `Add` and `Cancel`; `Add` will add the new row, calling the `InsertMethod`, while `Cancel` will cancel the insertion and return the row to display mode.

Listing 3.22. The FormView InsertItemTemplate

```
<InsertItemTemplate>
  <table border="0" cellpadding="5">
    <tr>
      <td align="right">ShipperID:</td>
      <td>
        <asp:TextBox id="txtInsertID" runat="server"
          Text='<%# Bind("ShipperID") %>' />
      </td>
    </tr>
    <tr>
      <td align="right">Company Name:</td>
      <td>
        <asp:TextBox id="txtInsertName" runat="server"
          Text='<%# Bind("CompanyName") %>' />
      </td>
    </tr>
    <tr>
      <td align="right">Phone:</td>
      <td>
        <asp:TextBox id="txtInsertPhone" runat="server"
          Text='<%# Bind("Phone") %>' />
      </td>
    </tr>
    <tr>
      <td colspan="2">
        <asp:LinkButton id="btnAdd" CommandName="Insert"
          Text="Add" runat="server" />
        <asp:LinkButton id="btnAbandon" CommandName="Cancel"
          Text="Cancel" runat="server" />
      </td>
    </tr>
  </table>
</InsertItemTemplate>
```

You can see that even though there is more source, there is still no requirement for code to provide data updates. The techniques for the `DetailsView` and `FormView` are very similar, and the whole use of commands is common to all of these data controls. The declarative nature of these controls makes them easy to use, but there are still occasions when code is required. The first is if you want to avoid the two-tier system of the `SqlDataSource`, such as using a separate data layer, which is covered in Chapter 4, and the second is when you require some advanced features of the data source and grid controls, which is covered in Chapter 5.

SUMMARY

In this chapter, we have looked at the basic features of the `SqlDataSource` and data editing controls: the `GridView`, `DetailsView`, and `FormView`. Together these provide a simple, declarative way of displaying and editing data, and with their rich customization they can provide a great deal of control over how that data is manipulated.

You saw that the `SqlDataSource` control provides commands for fetching data from the database and commands for sending data changes back to the database. The use of parameters allows the displayed data to be filtered according to external criteria, such as a user-selectable value, or stored values, such as those in the session.

The `GridView` utilizes the data features of the `SqlDatsSource` control to provide a grid with editing capabilities, while the `DetailsView` and `FormView` provide single-row display and editing. In the next chapter, you will see the `ObjectDataSource` control, which allows data to be accessed via custom classes. In Chapter 6, you will look at more advanced features of the data source and edit controls.

■4■
Data Binding to Business Objects

I N THE PREVIOUS CHAPTER, you saw how the `SqlDataSource` control provides a declarative way to access databases, allowing easy two-way data binding for controls. While this works well, and is acceptable in certain sites, many people wish to move all data access out of the ASP.NET pages. This is a fairly standard arrangement, as it leaves the ASP.NET pages containing just the user interface—those bits that the user sees. All data access code is moved into a set of classes, which makes development and maintenance easier, especially in large organizations with teams of developers.

In this chapter we're going to look at what features ASP.NET 2.0 provides to enable this scenario—the use of data and business layers to abstract logic away from the page. In particular, we are going to cover the following topics:

- How to create business and data layers
- How to use the `ObjectDataSource` control to provide declarative access to the business and data layers
- How to use Typed Data Sets as business objects

As we progress through this chapter, you'll see that many aspects of using the `ObjectDataSource` control are similar to the `SqlDataSource` control seen in the previous chapter.

Two- and Three-Tier Architecture

It the world of large business and enterprise applications, it is not surprising to hear talk of architecture, business layers, data layers, and so on. For single developers or small teams, however, the emphasis is more often on getting the job done quickly, and architectural decisions often get left behind. However, the use of tiers in application architecture is extremely simple to implement, and provides great benefits. You abstract all of the data logic into a single set of classes and provide a consistent interface from that set of classes. This means that should your underlying data storage change (perhaps from one database to another or just by adding features), any code that uses the data layer will continue to work.

The next benefit is in distribution of workload; people can be dedicated to particular areas of the application. This would enable a Web designer to work with the HTML and CSS, while the developer codes the other layers. This is an additional benefit if source code control is used (and it should be), because if the data layer is separated from the ASP.NET pages, they can be checked out of a source code control system separately and worked on by different people—there's no waiting for someone else to finish with the file.

It is important to understand that this talk of layers is purely a logical view. While there can be a physical separation between the layers, especially with the class files themselves, there doesn't have to be a physical separation between the deployment of those layers—they can all be hosted within the same Web site.

Business Layers, Data Layers, or Both?

Some questions that often get asked when a new development project starts are, "What sort of separation is required?" And, "Are multiple layers required, and how should they be split?" The answer, of course, is "it depends." It depends on how much business logic you have, and whether you want the extra overhead of an additional layer. Figure 4.1 shows the typical arrangement for three- and four-tier layers; with three tiers, the user interface calls the data layer directly; with four tiers, the interface calls the business layer, which in turn calls the data layer.

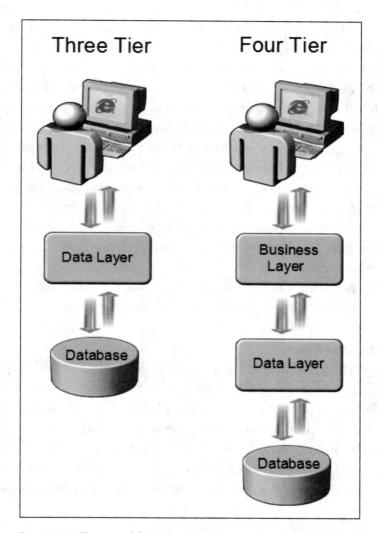

FIGURE 4.1: Three- and four-tier architectures

Object Data Mappers

With only a data layer, you will typically be returning `DataSet` or `DataTable` objects from your class methods. With an additional business layer, this approach can still be used—the data layer returns a `DataTable` to the business layer, which performs any necessary logic and passes the `DataTable` to the interface layer. This is a perfectly acceptable scenario; it reduces the amount of code required and performs well. One issue with this solution is that the interface needs to know how the data is stored—you are returning

`DataTable` objects, so the interface must know how to manipulate them, for binding purposes.

To alleviate the issue of the interface layer knowing about the actual storage mechanism, you can have the business layer expose the data in a different form, normally as a strongly typed business object. For example, you could expose the `Shippers` table as a `Shipper` object, with properties such as `ShipperID`, `CompanyName`, and `Phone`. Your interface then needs to know only about the objects, not where the data is stored or how it is fetched.

There are several ways of implementing a strongly typed business layer, one of which is typed data sets, which are covered later in the chapter. Others include object mappers and code generation tools, which take the database schema and create strongly typed code libraries that you can plug into your applications.

There are benefits to each solution, and for simplicity we're going to cover a simple data layer that the interface uses directly.

Creating a Data Layer

Creating a data layer is as simple as creating classes that expose public methods. These classes can be placed in the `App_Code` directory, a special directory where classes are automatically compiled. Next, you have to decide what goes into the class—typically there will be methods for each type of action you need to perform. For example, consider the actions required for a table: Get all rows, get a single row, insert a new row, update data in an existing row, and delete a row. There may be other actions, but these are core ones required.

Creating the Data Class

Let's consider these as individual methods of a class called `ShipperData-Layer`, starting with fetching all rows, as shown in Listing 4.1.

The first thing to notice is that this is a static method. This isn't a necessary part of data access classes, but reduces the need for calling routines to instantiate the class. Within the class a connection is made to the database, and a command is created using a SQL statement—in reality this should be a stored procedure, but has been left as SQL here so that you can see exactly what's being run. A `DataTable` object is then created, and the command executed, with the output of the command being loaded into the `DataTable` object, which is returned. The `using` statement ensures that the `SqlConnection`

Listing 4.1. Fetching All Shippers

```
public static DataTable GetShippers()
{
  using (SqlConnection conn = new SqlConnection(
    ConfigurationManager.ConnectionStrings["NorthwindConnectString"].
      ConnectionString))
  {
    conn.Open();

    SqlCommand cmd = new SqlCommand("SELECT * FROM Shippers", conn);

    DataTable tbl = new DataTable();
    tbl.Load(cmd.ExecuteReader(CommandBehavior.CloseConnection));

    return tbl;
  }
}
```

object is closed and freed from memory, allowing the connection to be reused
by another user.

A similar routine is shown in Listing 4.2, which shows the method to
fetch a single shipper. Here the method accepts a parameter which is the ID
of the shipper to fetch. The rest of the routine is similar, but this time
the SQL statement features a WHERE clause, and a parameter is added to the
command to contain the ShipperID value.

Listing 4.2. Fetching a Single Shipper

```
public static DataTable GetShipper(int ShipperID)
{
  using (SqlConnection conn = new SqlConnection(
    ConfigurationManager.ConnectionStrings["NorthwindConnectString"].
      ConnectionString))
  {
    conn.Open();

    SqlCommand cmd = new SqlCommand(
      "SELECT * FROM Shippers WHERE ShipperID=@ShipperID", conn);
    cmd.Parameters.Add("@ShipperID", SqlDbType.Int).Value =
      ShipperID;

    DataTable tbl = new DataTable();
    tbl.Load(cmd.ExecuteReader(CommandBehavior.CloseConnection));

    return tbl;
  }
}
```

Listing 4.3 shows the method to insert a new shipper, and it follows a familiar pattern. The parameters to the method are the columns of the table, but without the ID value—this is automatically generated by SQL Server, so isn't required.

Listing 4.3. Inserting a New Shipper

```
public static int Insert(string CompanyName, string Phone)
{
  using (SqlConnection conn = new SqlConnection(
    ConfigurationManager.ConnectionStrings["NorthwindConnectString"].
      ConnectionString))
  {
    conn.Open();

    SqlCommand cmd = new SqlCommand("INSERT INTO
          Shippers(CompanyName, Phone)
          VALUES(@CompanyName, @Phone)", conn);
    cmd.Parameters.Add("@CompanyName",
      SqlDbType.NVarChar, 40).Value = CompanyName;
    cmd.Parameters.Add("@Phone",
      SqlDbType.NVarChar, 24).Value = Phone;

    return cmd.ExecuteNonQuery();
  }
}
```

Within the `Insert` method, the parameters are used as the values for an `INSERT` statement, which is run using the `ExecuteNonQuery` method. This indicates that no rows of data are being returned.

Listing 4.4 shows the `Update` method, which will update an existing shipper. The parameters are the ID value, which will identify the shipper being updated, and the `CompanyName` and `Phone`, which are the values to update.

Within the `Update` method, a simple `UPDATE` statement is run, using the parameters passed into the method.

Listing 4.5 shows the `Delete` method, which takes a single parameter—the ID of the shipper to delete.

These classes are all that's required for a simple data access layer for a single table. One thing that you'll notice is that there's a lot of similar code, and you can see how this would increase the size of classes once you start creating layers for each table. One way around this is to use code generation tools to automatically create the code for you, or you can simply create some classes to streamline the data layer.

Listing 4.4. Updating a Shipper

```
public static int Update(int ShipperID, string CompanyName,
                         string Phone)
{
  using (SqlConnection conn = new SqlConnection(
    ConfigurationManager.ConnectionStrings["NorthwindConnectString"].
      ConnectionString))
  {
    conn.Open();

    SqlCommand cmd = new SqlCommand("UPDATE Shippers
          SET CompanyName=@CompanyName, Phone=@Phone
          WHERE ShipperID=@ShipperID", conn);
    cmd.Parameters.Add("@ShipperID",
      SqlDbType.Int).Value = ShipperID;
    cmd.Parameters.Add("@CompanyName",
      SqlDbType.NVarChar, 40).Value = CompanyName;
    cmd.Parameters.Add("@Phone",
      SqlDbType.NVarChar, 24).Value = Phone;

    return cmd.ExecuteNonQuery();
  }
}
```

Creating Helper Classes

We said earlier that a data layer performs the following five basic operations:

- Fetching all rows
- Fetching a single row
- Inserting a row
- Updating a row
- Deleting a row

Listing 4.5. Deleting a Shipper

```
public static int Delete(int ShipperID)
{
  using (SqlConnection conn = new SqlConnection(
    ConfigurationManager.ConnectionStrings["NorthwindConnectString"].
      ConnectionString))
  {
    conn.Open();

    SqlCommand cmd = new SqlCommand("DELETE FROM Shippers
          WHERE ShipperID=@ShipperID", conn);
    cmd.Parameters.Add("@ShipperID",
      SqlDbType.Int).Value = ShipperID;

    return cmd.ExecuteNonQuery();
  }
}
```

With these actions in mind, a helper class could be created, such as the one shown in Listing 4.6.

Listing 4.6. A Data Layer Helper Class

```
public static class DataLayerHelper
{
  public static DataTable Get(string cmdText)
  {
    using (SqlConnection conn = new SqlConnection(
    ConfigurationManager.ConnectionStrings["NorthwindConnectString"].
      ConnectionString))
    {
      conn.Open();
      SqlCommand cmd = new SqlCommand(proc, conn);
      DataTable tbl = new DataTable();
      tbl.Load(cmd.ExecuteReader(CommandBehavior.CloseConnection));
      return tbl;
    }
  }

  public static DataTable GetByID(string cmdText,
                                  string IDName, int IDValue)
  {
    using (SqlConnection conn = new SqlConnection(
    ConfigurationManager.ConnectionStrings["NorthwindConnectString"].
      ConnectionString))
    {
      conn.Open();
      SqlCommand cmd = new SqlCommand(cmdText, conn);
      cmd.Parameters.Add(IDName, SqlDbType.Int).Value = IDValue;
      DataTable tbl = new DataTable();
      tbl.Load(cmd.ExecuteReader(CommandBehavior.CloseConnection));
      return tbl;
    }
  }

  public static int ExecuteNonQuery(string cmdText,
    SqlParameter param)
  {
    using (SqlConnection conn = new SqlConnection(
    ConfigurationManager.ConnectionStrings["NorthwindConnectString"].
      ConnectionString))
    {
      conn.Open();
      SqlCommand cmd = new SqlCommand(cmdText, conn);
      cmd.Parameters.Add(param);
      return cmd.ExecuteNonQuery();
    }
  }

  public static int ExecuteNonQuery(string cmdText,
```

```
  ref SqlParameter[] sqlParams)
{
  using (SqlConnection conn = new SqlConnection(
  ConfigurationManager.ConnectionStrings["NorthwindConnectString"].
    ConnectionString))
  {
    conn.Open();
    SqlCommand cmd = new SqlCommand(cmdText, conn);
    cmd.Parameters.AddRange(sqlParams);
    return cmd.ExecuteNonQuery();
  }
}
}
```

The first parameter of each method is the command text to run; this is the SQL statement (or it could be a stored procedure name, although the commands would need to have their `CommandType` property set to `CommandType.StoredProcedure`). The `Get` method simply executes the statement and returns a `DataTable` containing the fetched rows. The `GetByID` accepts two additional parameters: `IDName` and `IDValue`, which hold the name of the ID column and the value to fetch. The remaining method, `ExecuteNonQuery`, is overloaded and can accept either a single `SqlParameter` object or an array of `SqlParameter` objects. The array of parameters is passed by reference, so that any output parameters can be passed back to the data layer (this will be covered in Chapter 5). These methods simply execute a statement using the supplied parameters.

The data layer class can now be simplified, as shown in Listing 4.7.

The job of the simplified classes is now to define the commands to be run and the parameters that these commands require. While this isn't a great benefit for a single data class, the helper can be used for all subsequent data classes, making them easier and quicker to create.

Now that the data layer is defined, it's time to see how they can be used in ASP.NET pages.

The ObjectDataSource Control

When dealing directly with SQL Server in two-tier architectures, you use the `SqlDataSource` to manage the flow of data between the database and the ASP.NET pages. When you need to use classes to manage the actual data handling, you can use an `ObjectDataSource` control. In use, this behaves in a similar manner to its SQL equivalent, but instead of specifying SQL

Listing 4.7. The Simplified Data Layer Class

```
public class ShipperDataLayer
{
  public static DataTable GetShippers()
  {
    return DataLayerHelper.Get("SELECT * FROM Shippers");
  }
  public static DataTable GetShipper(int ShipperID)
  {
    return DataLayerHelper.GetByID("SELECT * FROM Shippers
         WHERE ShipperID=@ShipperID", "ShipperID", ShipperID);
  }
  public static int Insert(string CompanyName, string Phone)
  {
    SqlParameter[] sqlParams = new SqlParameter[] {
      new SqlParameter("@CompanyName", SqlDbType.NVarChar, 40),
      new SqlParameter("@Phone", SqlDbType.NVarChar, 24)};

    sqlParams[0].Value = CompanyName;
    sqlParams[1].Value = Phone;

    return DataLayerHelper.ExecuteNonQuery("INSERT INTO
         Shippers(CompanyName, Phone)
         VALUES(@CompanyName, @Phone)", ref sqlParams);
  }
  public static int Update(int ShipperID, string CompanyName,
                       string Phone)
  {
    SqlParameter[] sqlParams = new SqlParameter[] {
      new SqlParameter("@ShipperID", SqlDbType.Int),
      new SqlParameter("@CompanyName", SqlDbType.NVarChar, 40),
      new SqlParameter("@Phone", SqlDbType.NVarChar, 24)};
    sqlParams[0].Value = ShipperID;
    sqlParams[1].Value = CompanyName;
    sqlParams[2].Value = Phone;

    return DataLayerHelper.ExecuteNonQuery("UPDATE Shippers
         SET CompanyName=@CompanyName, Phone=@Phone
         WHERE ShipperID=@ShipperID", ref sqlParams);
  }
  public static int Delete(int ShipperID)
  {
    SqlParameter param = new SqlParameter("@ShipperID",
      SqlDbType.Int);
    param.Value = ShipperID;

    return DataLayerHelper.ExecuteNonQuery("DELETE FROM Shippers
         WHERE ShipperID=@ShipperID", param);
  }
}
```

commands or stored procedures, you specify the class and methods. The outline syntax for the ObjectDataSource control is shown in Listing 4.8.

Table 4.1 provides details for the main properties of the ObjectDataSource control. There are others not described here, and some not shown in Listing 4.8, but they will be covered in Chapter 5 when we look at some of the advanced data features.

Listing 4.8. ObjectDataSource Syntax

```
<asp:ObjectDataSource id="String" runat="server"
  DataObjectTypeName="String"
  TypeName="String"
  SelectMethod="String"
  SelectCountMethod="String"
  UpdateMethod="String"
  InsertMethod="String"
  DeleteMethod="String"
  EnablePaging="[True|False]"
  StartRowIndexParameterName="String"
  MaximumRowsParameterName="String"
  FilterExpression="String"
  SortParameterName="String"
  OldValuesParameterFormatString="String"
  ConflictDetection="[OverwriteChanges|CompareAllValues]"
  ConvertNullToDbNull="[True|False]"
  EnableCaching="[True|False]"
  CacheDuration="Integer"
  CacheExpirationPolicy="[Absolute|Sliding]"
  CacheKeyDependency="String"
  SqlCacheDependency="String">

    <SelectParameters>
      [<System.Web.UI.WebControls.Parameter ...>]
    </SelectParameters>
    <UpdateParameters>
      [<System.Web.UI.WebControls.Parameter ...>]
    </UpdateParameters>
    <DeleteParameters>
      [<System.Web.UI.WebControls.Parameter ...>]
    </DeleteParameters>
    <InsertParameters>
      [<System.Web.UI.WebControls.Parameter ...>]
    </InsertParameters>
    <FilterParameters>
      [<System.Web.UI.WebControls.Parameter ...>]
    </FilterParameters>

</asp:ObjectDataSource>
```

TABLE 4.1: Properties of the ObjectDataSource Control

Property	Description
TypeName	A `String` that contains the type name of the object to create. This can be a partially qualified name such as `MyClass` or a fully qualified name such as `MyNamespace.MyClass`.
DataObjectTypeName	A `String` that contains the type name of the object to be used as the parameter type for the `Insert`, `Update`, and `Delete` methods.
SelectMethod	The method of the object to invoke for a `SELECT` operation. Any parameters required can be defined as the `SelectParameters` property or in the nested `SelectParameters` element of the control declaration.
SelectCountMethod	The method of the object to invoke to return a count of the total number of available objects. Selection and filtering can be applied in the usual way with parameters.
UpdateMethod	The method of the object to invoke for an `UPDATE` operation. Any parameters required can be defined as the `UpdateParameters` property or in the nested `UpdateParameters` element of the control declaration.
InsertMethod	The method of the object to invoke for an `INSERT` operation. Any parameters required can be defined as the `InsertParameters` property or in the nested `InsertParameters` element of the control declaration.
DeleteMethod	The method of the object to invoke for a `DELETE` operation. Any parameters required can be defined as the `DeleteParameters` property or in the nested `DeleteParameters` element of the control declaration.
EnablePaging	A `Boolean` value that specifies whether paging will be enabled within the control. When set to `True`, the `StartRowIndexParameterName` and `MaximumRowsParameterName` property values are used to specify the rows or objects retrieved.

Property	Description
`StartRowIndexParameter Name`	The name of the value in the `InputParameters` collection that defines the index of the first row or object to return when paging is enabled.
`MaximumRowsParameter Name`	The name of the value in the `InputParameters` collection that defines the maximum number of rows or objects to return when paging is enabled.

At its simplest, for displaying data, you only need to set two properties, and only three more for data updates.

Using the ObjectDataSource Control

The `ObjectDataSource` control supports configuration via a wizard, accessible from the Smart Tasks. The first screen, shown in Figure 4.2, allows

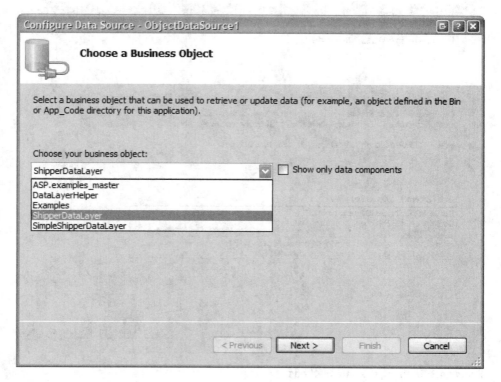

FIGURE 4.2: Choosing a business object

selection of the business object—the class that contains the methods that will handle the data.

The next screen, Figure 4.3, allows you to select the methods for each of the four core data access actions: selecting data, updating data, inserting data, and deleting data.

Once the configuration has been completed, the `ObjectDataSource` will look like Listing 4.9. You can see that the `TypeName` contains the class name, and the `SelectMethod`, `DeleteMethod`, `InsertMethod`, and `UpdateMethod` properties have been set to the method names within the class. You can also see that for each method, an appropriate set of parameters has been created, with a `Parameter` object for each parameter on the method. There are no `SelectParameters` because the `SelectMethod` doesn't have any—it fetches all rows from the data table.

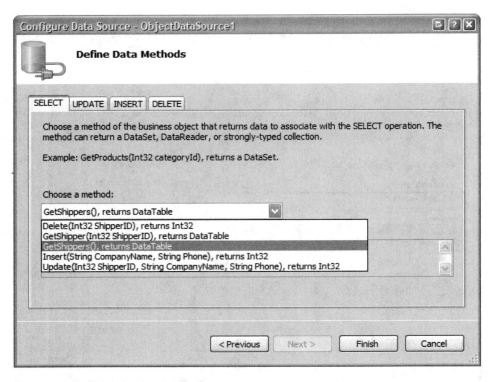

FIGURE 4.3: Defining the data methods

Listing 4.9. A Configured ObjectDataSource Control

```
<asp:ObjectDataSource ID="ObjectDataSource1" runat="server"
  TypeName="ShipperDataLayer"
  SelectMethod="GetShippers"
  DeleteMethod="Delete"
  InsertMethod="Insert"
  UpdateMethod="Update">
  <DeleteParameters>
    <asp:Parameter Name="ShipperID" Type="Int32" />
  </DeleteParameters>
  <UpdateParameters>
    <asp:Parameter Name="ShipperID" Type="Int32" />
    <asp:Parameter Name="CompanyName" Type="String" />
    <asp:Parameter Name="Phone" Type="String" />
  </UpdateParameters>
  <InsertParameters>
    <asp:Parameter Name="CompanyName" Type="String" />
    <asp:Parameter Name="Phone" Type="String" />
  </InsertParameters>
</asp:ObjectDataSource>
```

If you pick a select method that has parameters, then the parameter definition window will automatically display, allowing you to pick the source for the parameter data, as shown in Figure 4.4.

You use the ObjectDataSource in the same way as a SqlDataSource, by binding a control to it. For example, Listing 4.10 shows a DetailsView bound to the ObjectDataSource.

Like the SqlDataSource control, the ObjectDataSource control can be used in master details situations, as shown in Figure 4.5, where the top grid selects data and the bottom allows editing.

Listing 4.10. A DetailsView Bound to the ObjectDataSource

```
<asp:DetailsView ID="DetailsView1" runat="server"
  DataSourceID="ObjectDataSource2" DataKeyNames="ShipperID"
  AllowPaging="True" AutoGenerateRows="False">
  <Fields>
    <asp:BoundField HeaderText="Company Name"
      DataField="CompanyName" />
    <asp:BoundField HeaderText="Phone" DataField="Phone" />
    <asp:CommandField ShowDeleteButton="True"
      ShowEditButton="True" ShowInsertButton="True" />
  </Fields>
</asp:DetailsView>
```

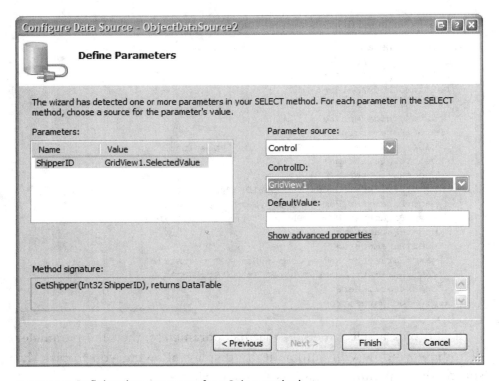

FIGURE 4.4: Defining the parameters for a Select method

Getting the Identity Value of an Inserted Row

A common feature of database tables is that they use an identity column as their unique key, meaning that SQL Server automatically creates the key value when the data is inserted. This key value is required when creating

FIGURE 4.5: Master Details using ObjectDataSource controls

master and detail rows, such as in an order and order details scenario. For example, the order details table would have a foreign key, OrderID, which is the primary key field in the orders table. To create a new order, you first have to insert the details into the orders table and then use the new key value for that order when you insert the details into the order details table.

When using a data class to insert the new row in the orders table, there are two ways in which the identity value can be returned: as a return value or as an output parameter. The return value is simplest, but a general rule is that return values are for the actual value returned by the execution method (ExecuteNonQuery). Also, you may want to return more than one value, in which case output parameters are more suitable.

To create output parameters, you simply add an additional parameter to the parameter list, but you set its value to -1 and its Direction property to ParameterDirection.Output. This tells the data code that the value is being output from the executing command. Once the command has been executed, the output parameter can be accessed via the parameter array, as seen in Listing 4.11.

Listing 4.11. Returning Output Parameters

```
public static int Insert(int CustomerID, int EmployeeID,
  ...
  ref int OrderID)
{
  SqlParameter[] sqlParams = new SqlParameter[] {
    new SqlParameter("@CustomerID", SqlDbType.Int),
    new SqlParameter("@EmployeeID", SqlDbType.Int),
    ...
    new SqlParameter("@OrderID", SqlDbType.Int)};

  sqlParams[0].Value = CustomerID;
  sqlParams[1].Value = EmployeeID;
  ...
  sqlParams[n].Value = -1;
  sqlParams[n].Direction = ParameterDirection.Output;

  int rv = DataLayerHelper.ExecuteNonQuery("INSERT INTO
      Orders(CustomerID, EmployeeID, ...)
      VALUES(@CustomerID, @EmployeeID, ...);
      SELECT @OrderID = SCOPE_IDENTITY()", ref sqlParams);

  OrderID = (int)sqlParams[n].Value;

  return rv;
}
```

With stored procedures, the output parameter is declared the same way as input parameters, but with the addition of OUTPUT after the data type. Chapter 5 will cover how to use the data source control's events to manipulate parameters, both before commands are executed and after.

Typed Data Sets

Typed data sets are a form of strongly typed business objects that fetch data from the database and expose it via a set of methods. They provide the main functionality of a business and data layer, with methods to fetch and modify data, so they save you from having to create your own layer. You create typed data sets by adding a new item to the App_Code folder, selecting the **DataSet** option from the Add New Item dialog (see Figure 4.6).

When a data set is created, the TableAdapter Configuration Wizard launches, the first screen of which (see Figure 4.7) allows you to define the SQL statement to fetch the data. The **Advanced Options** button shows another window (see Figure 4.8) allowing you to select whether data modification

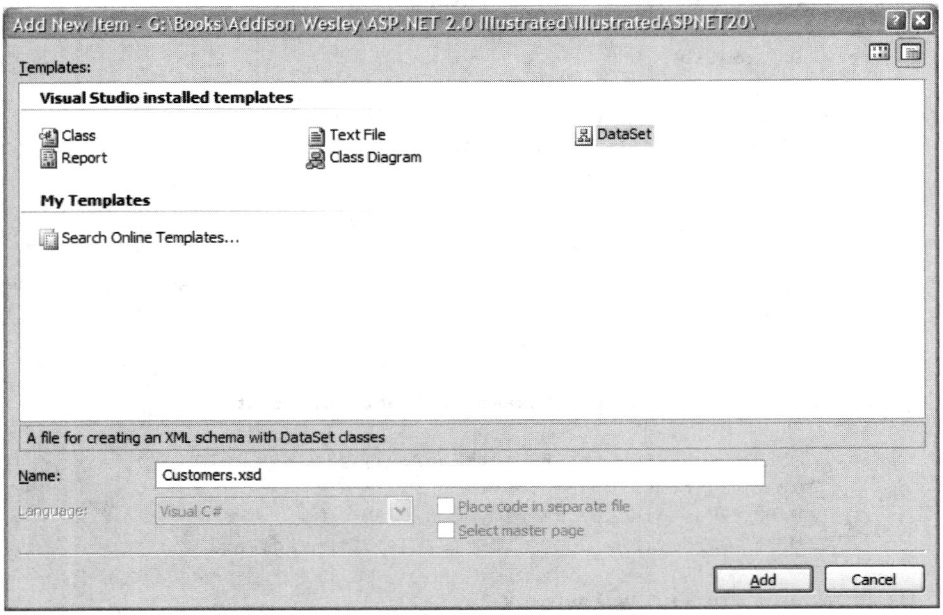

FIGURE 4.6: Adding a DataSet

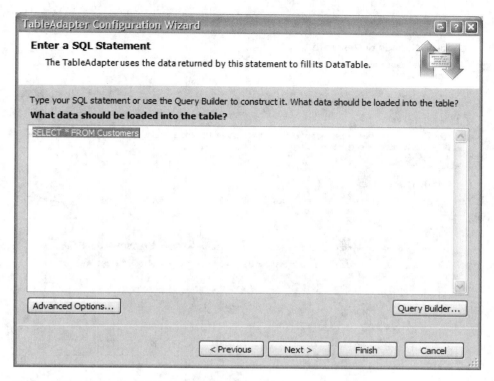

FIGURE 4.7: Defining the SQL statement for the DataSet

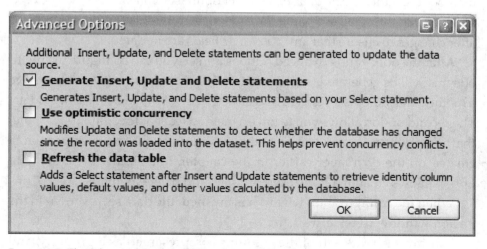

FIGURE 4.8: The Advanced Options of DataSet configuration

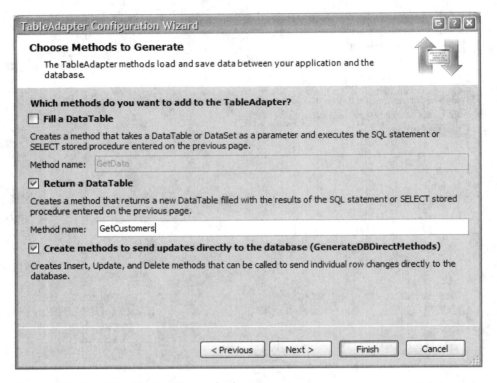

FIGURE 4.9: Generating the DataSet methods

methods are added to the dataset, whether optimistic concurrency will be used (covered in more detail in Chapter 5), and whether the data should be refreshed after changes to ensure that any IDENTITY fields are updated.

After the query and advanced options are set, you can configure the methods that will be generated (see Figure 4.9). The first option allows you to have a method that accepts a DataTable or DataSet object to be filled with data. The second option allows you to have a method (called GetCustomers, here) that returns a DataTable object—this is similar to the methods manually created on the data layer earlier in the chapter. In a similar vein, the final option allows creation of the insert, update, and delete methods.

When the configuration wizard has finished, the data set is shown in the design window (see Figure 4.10).

You can see that each of the columns is represented as a property, and that the GetCustomers method shows as a method of a subtype—CustomersTableAdapter. The typed data set doesn't generate a class, but

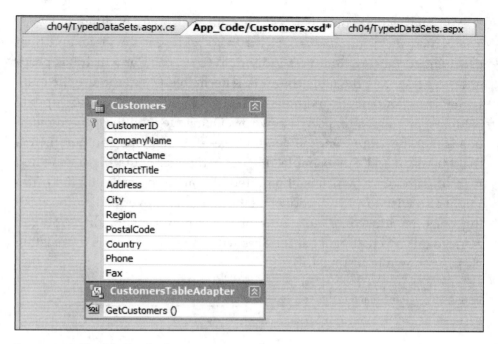

FIGURE 4.10: The DataSet Designer

instead generates an XML definition of what the class will contain; you can see this if you select **View Code** from the menu when viewing the data set. Since the data set is in the `App_Code` directory, the class is automatically generated from the XML at compile time.

You can use the data set objects directly in code, a shown in Listing 4.12.

Listing 4.12. Using a Typed DataSet from Code

```
CustomersTableAdapters.CustomersTableAdapter c =
  new CustomersTableAdapters.CustomersTableAdapter();

Customers.CustomersDataTable ct = c.GetCustomers();

Customers.CustomersRow cr = ct.Rows[0];

cr.CompanyName = "New Company name";
c.Update(cr);

c.Update(1, "New Company Name", "New Contact Name", ...);

c.Insert(10, "Another New Company Name",
           "Another New Contact Name", ...);
```

You can see that you can access the data at a variety of different levels. You can create a `CustomersDataTable` to represent the table, and then use a `CustomersRow` to access individual rows, each of which has properties representing the table columns. Alternatively, you can use the `CustomersTableAdapter` methods directly, calling `Update` to update columns, or `Insert` to insert a new row. One issue with the created methods is that they represent the default case—the methods and parameters that Microsoft add. For example, the first parameter of the `Insert` method is the `CustomerID`, which isn't required; it is an auto-generated field. You might also wish to add additional methods, perhaps overloading the existing ones, or add completely new ones for new functionality. You can achieve this by creating a partial class with the same name as the existing class, as shown in Listing 4.13.

Listing 4.13. Adding functionality to a Typed DataSet

```
namespace CustomersTableAdapters
{
  public partial class CustomersTableAdapter
  {
    public void Update(string NewCompanyName)
    {
    }

    public void MyMethod()
    {
    }
  }
}
```

Here the namespace and class match those of the generated class. The new `Update` and `MyMethod` methods would now appear on the class (even in IntelliSense). The use of a `partial class` means that the same class is split across multiple physical files, something that wasn't possible in previous versions of the framework. This means that your custom code is standalone, and will not be lost if you regenerate the data set, for example, by adding a new column to the table.

Using Typed DataSets with the ObjectDataSource Control

Using typed `DataSets` with the `ObjectDataSource` control is similar to using standard classes, except there are a couple of things to watch out for. You can use the `Configure DataSource` tasks, which will fill in the properties and set the parameters to pick the object and method, as shown in Listing 4.14.

Listing 4.14. An ObjectDataSource Using the Typed DataSet

```
<asp:ObjectDataSource ID="ObjectDataSource1" runat="server"
  TypeName="CustomersTableAdapters.CustomersTableAdapter"
  DeleteMethod="Delete" SelectMethod="GetCustomers"
  InsertMethod="Insert" UpdateMethod="Update"

  OldValuesParameterFormatString="original_{0}">
  <DeleteParameters>
    <asp:Parameter Name="Original_CustomerID" Type="String" />
  </DeleteParameters>
  <UpdateParameters>
    <asp:Parameter Name="CustomerID" Type="String" />
    <asp:Parameter Name="CompanyName" Type="String" />
    <asp:Parameter Name="ContactName" Type="String" />
    <asp:Parameter Name="ContactTitle" Type="String" />
    <asp:Parameter Name="Address" Type="String" />
    <asp:Parameter Name="City" Type="String" />
    <asp:Parameter Name="Region" Type="String" />
    <asp:Parameter Name="PostalCode" Type="String" />
    <asp:Parameter Name="Country" Type="String" />
    <asp:Parameter Name="Phone" Type="String" />
    <asp:Parameter Name="Fax" Type="String" />
    <asp:Parameter Name="Original_CustomerID" Type="String" />
  </UpdateParameters>
  <InsertParameters>
    <asp:Parameter Name="CustomerID" Type="String" />
    <asp:Parameter Name="CompanyName" Type="String" />
    <asp:Parameter Name="ContactName" Type="String" />
    <asp:Parameter Name="ContactTitle" Type="String" />
    <asp:Parameter Name="Address" Type="String" />
    <asp:Parameter Name="City" Type="String" />
    <asp:Parameter Name="Region" Type="String" />
    <asp:Parameter Name="PostalCode" Type="String" />
    <asp:Parameter Name="Country" Type="String" />
    <asp:Parameter Name="Phone" Type="String" />
    <asp:Parameter Name="Fax" Type="String" />
  </InsertParameters>
</asp:ObjectDataSource>
```

The one thing that is different from earlier examples is the use of the `OldValuesParameterFormatString` property, which defines the format of the parameter holding old values—i.e., the values that are not being updated. This is used most often when optimistic concurrency checking is in place, but in this example, the old value is the CustomerID—the ID value is auto-generated, so not updateable. Within the OldValuesParameterFormatString property, the {0} is a placeholder, and is replaced with the actual parameter name, which you can see in the DeleteParameters and for the last parameter in the UpdateParameters.

The problem with the way the ObjectDataSource is configured is when used in conjunction with a GridView. This is shown in Listing 4.15, which was generated by binding the GridView to the ObjectDataSource.

Listing 4.15. A GridView Bound to a Typed DataSet ObjectDataSource

```
<asp:GridView ID="GridView1" runat="server"
  AutoGenerateColumns="False" DataKeyNames="CustomerID"
  DataSourceID="ObjectDataSource1">
  <Columns>
    <asp:CommandField ShowDeleteButton="True"
      ShowEditButton="True" />
    <asp:BoundField DataField="CustomerID"
      HeaderText="CustomerID" ReadOnly="True"
      SortExpression="CustomerID" />
    <asp:BoundField DataField="CompanyName"
      HeaderText="CompanyName" SortExpression="CompanyName" />
    <asp:BoundField DataField="ContactName"
      HeaderText="ContactName" SortExpression="ContactName" />
    <asp:BoundField DataField="ContactTitle"
      HeaderText="ContactTitle" SortExpression="ContactTitle" />
    <asp:BoundField DataField="Address" HeaderText="Address"
      SortExpression="Address" />
    <asp:BoundField DataField="City" HeaderText="City"
      SortExpression="City" />
    <asp:BoundField DataField="Region" HeaderText="Region"
      SortExpression="Region" />
    <asp:BoundField DataField="PostalCode" HeaderText="PostalCode"
      SortExpression="PostalCode" />
    <asp:BoundField DataField="Country" HeaderText="Country"
      SortExpression="Country" />
    <asp:BoundField DataField="Phone" HeaderText="Phone"
      SortExpression="Phone" />
    <asp:BoundField DataField="Fax" HeaderText="Fax"
      SortExpression="Fax" />
  </Columns>
</asp:GridView>
```

The columns have been automatically generated, and the important column to note is the CustomerID, shown in bold. Notice that the ReadOnly property is set to True. The grid knows that this is auto-generated and thus marks it as read-only, but the typed DataSet expects CustomerID as the first parameter to the Update method; there's a bit of difference in the way the two objects work.

There are two ways around this problem. The first is to allow updates to the CustomerID field, which probably isn't the best solution, because updates would fail in the SQL Server when they tried to update the **IDENTITY** column. The second solution is to modify the SQL commands that the typed DataSet uses.

Changing the SQL for the typed DataSet can be done by first opening the XSD file, and selecting the **CustomersTableAdapter** (Figure 4.11), and viewing the properties. Then, because each of the commands can be

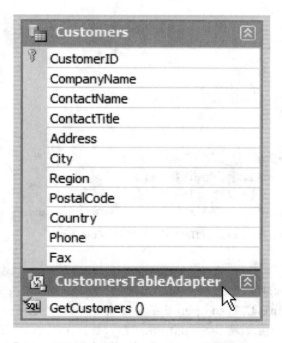

FIGURE 4.11: Selecting the CustomersTableAdapter

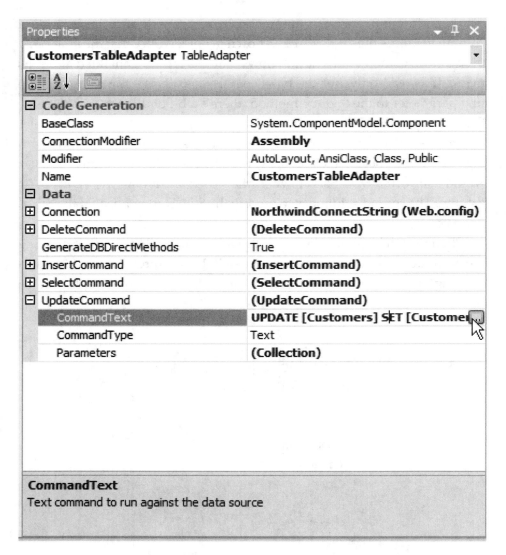

FIGURE 4.12: Viewing the CommandText of the UpdateCommand

modified, you can either edit the `CommandText` inline or click the small button (see Figure 4.12) to open the `QueryBuilder` (see Figure 4.13). Then you can simply remove the **CustomerID** column from the SQL statement.

Once you have changed, and saved, the typed `DataSet`, you can reconfigure the `ObjectDataSource` and grid, and the update command will now work. The same problem exists with the insert command, but that isn't

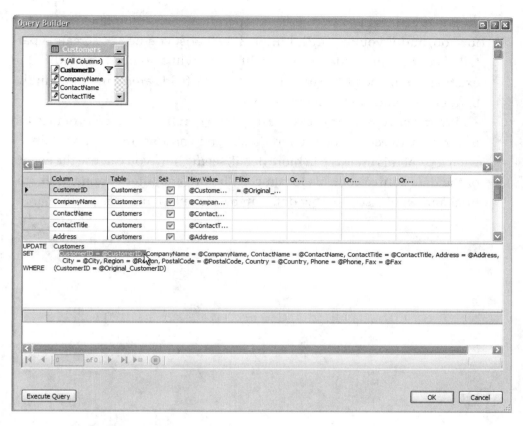

FIGURE 4.13: Using the Query Builder to modify commands

used with the GridView, but would need changing if you are using a DetailsView or FormView to perform your editing.

SUMMARY

In this chapter, we have looked at two ways of creating data and business layers: custom classes and typed DataSets. Both are created in the App_Code directory, means that they automatically get compiled by ASP.NET, so there is no need to create class libraries and deploy them to the application bin directory. For a custom class, you simply create methods to return data and methods to accept data to be modified. While the example in the chapter showed only the basic methods, there is no limit to the number and type you can create—it simply depends upon the requirement of your business object.

For typed `DataSets`, the basic operations are automatically created for you, and if you require additional methods, you need to create a partial class with the added functionality. You will also need to modify the existing commands to ensure that `IDENTITY` fields aren't modified in the `UpdateCommand` and `InsertCommand`.

Whatever type of object you use, the `ObjectDataSource` provides the interface between the object and databound controls. In the next chapter, we'll look at this interface in more detail, seeing how you can use the events of the data source controls to run code before and after command execution, and we'll also see how data can be cached to improve performance.

■ 5 ■
Advanced Data
and Page Techniques

I N CHAPTERS 3 AND 4, you saw how the data source controls provide an interface between the display controls, such as the `GridView` and `DetailsView`, and the underlying data store, whether that is direct SQL statements to a database or via a data or business layer. There are many times when the existing functionality meets requirements, but there are also times when you need more control over the process.

One of those times is when you need access to the parameters of commands, both before and after the command is executed. Another is when you need to trigger actions when the data has been modified, so that other controls can update their contents. Others times where you might need more control are concurrency errors, such as what happens if more than one person updates the same data at the same time. You might want to ensure that when saving a record, the user is notified if someone else has also changed that record.

SQL Server 2005 is not only an improved version of SQL Server 2000, but offers a really exciting new feature: .NET is built into the database. This means that a variety of things that were written in T-SQL, such as stored procedures and functions, can now be done with managed languages such as VB.NET or C#. We're not going to examine those directly, but one topic worth covering is the creation and use of user-defined types; these allow you to extend the existing type system so that custom types in your application code can be stored directly in the database.

When dealing with data, especially data fetched from remote locations, performance is always an issue. For example, consider the case where data is fetched from a Web Service, which either responds slowly, or perhaps doesn't respond at all. You not only slow the performance of an individual page while it waits for its data, but you also affect the scalability of the Web site. Asynchronous techniques allow you to solve the scalability issue. So in this chapter we are going to cover the following:

- The events of the data source controls
- The events of the data display and edit controls
- How to use pessimistic locking and handle concurrency errors
- How to use asynchronous Web pages to improve scalability
- How to create and use custom types in SQL Server 2005

All of these are great techniques that will help you interact with data you need to display and get the best out of your Web site.

DataSource Control Events

In the previous two chapters, you've seen the `SqlDataSource` and `Object-DataSource` controls in action, and you've seen how they can be used to fetch and modify data. A common requirement is to hook into that fetching and updating mechanism, perhaps to modify or access the parameters of the command, or perhaps to perform validation.

The data source controls provide events for the major operations: `select`, `insert`, `update`, and `delete`. Each operation has a pair of events, one that is raised before the operation, and one that is raised afterwards. These events are: `Selecting`, `Selected`, `Inserting`, `Inserted`, `Updating`, `Updated`, `Deleting`, and `Deleted`.

Modifying Parameters before Command Execution

The parameters of the data source control allow selection based upon a range of external criteria, but sometimes you need more than these can provide. For example, what if your Web site uses membership, and you want to filter a query based upon the login name? There's no parameter type to handle this explicitly, so you can use the `Selecting` event and dynamically add a parameter, as shown here.

```
protected void SqlDataSource1_Selecting(object sender,
                              SqlDataSourceSelectingEventArgs e)
{
  SqlParameter sp = new SqlParameter("UserName", User.Identity.Name);
  sp.Direction = ParameterDirection.Input;
  e.Command.Parameters.Add(sp);
}
```

Alternatively, you could declare the parameter as a standard `asp:Parameter` object and then just fill in the missing value. This is possibly more useful because it allows you to declaratively state the parameter order. For example, the `SelectParameters` could be declared as:

```
<SelectParameters>
  <asp:Parameter Name="UserName" Direction="input" Type="string"/>
  ...
</SelectParameters>
```

The event procedure would then be:

```
protected void SqlDataSource1_Selecting(object sender,
                              SqlDataSourceSelectingEventArgs e)
{
  e.Command.Parameters["UserName"].Value = User.Identity.Name;
}
```

These techniques give you complete control over the parameters before the query is executed.

For the data modification events, the event parameter is of type `SqlDataSourceCommandEventArgs`, which has two properties: `Cancel` and `Command`. If you set the `Cancel` property to `true` anywhere in the event procedure, then the event is cancelled and the command is not executed. This is a perfect scenario for validation; if you use `BoundColumn` fields, then you can't put validation onto them—you would have to use `TemplateColumn` fields and validation controls.

The `Command` property gives you access to the command being executed, so you can modify the command text or parameters.

Synchronizing DataSource Controls after Updates

One common use for the events is when you have linked controls, such as a GridView for display and a DetailsView for edit. When you modify data via the DetailsView, the GridView isn't updated, so the events can be used to refresh the data. For example, consider Listing 5.1, which has the OnDeleted, OnInserted, and OnUpdated properties set (these properties match to the events raised).

Listing 5.1. Using the Post-Execution Events of a SqlDataSource Control

```
<asp:SqlDataSource ID="SqlDataSource2" runat="server">
  <ConnectionString="<%$ ConnectionStrings:NorthwindConnectString %>"
  <SelectCommand="SELECT * FROM [Products]
                  WHERE ([ProductID] = @ProductID)">
  <OnDeleted="SqlDataSource2_Deleted">
  <OnInserted="SqlDataSource2_Inserted">
  <OnUpdated="SqlDataSource2_Updated">
  <SelectParameters>
    <asp:ControlParameter ControlID="GridView1" Name="ProductID"
      <PropertyName="SelectedValue" Type="Int32" />
  </SelectParameters>
</asp:SqlDataSource>
```

The code for these events is shown in Listing 5.2.

Listing 5.2. Handling the Post-Command Events

```
protected void SqlDataSource2_Inserted(object sender,
                          SqlDataSourceStatusEventArgs e)
{
  GridView1.DataBind();
}
protected void SqlDataSource2_Updated(object sender,
                          SqlDataSourceStatusEventArgs e)
{
  GridView1.DataBind();
}
protected void SqlDataSource2_Deleted(object sender,
                          SqlDataSourceStatusEventArgs e)
{
  GridView1.DataBind();
}
```

The code here is extremely easy, simply calling `DataBind` on the grid that is the filter for the data source control. Since these events run after the appropriate command has been executed, rebinding the grid will show the updated data. One thing to notice is that all of the events have a parameter of type `SqlDataSourceStatusEventArgs`, which contains details of the command just executed. The properties of this parameter allow access to the number of rows affected by the command, the command itself, and any exception details.

Accessing Output Parameters after Command Execution

One good use for the post command events is to access output parameters from commands, notably stored procedures. This is especially useful when you want to avoid having to return a rowset when only one or two values are required, such as the ID field from a newly inserted row. Returning values via parameters is faster than generating a rowset.

Let's consider a fairly typical stored procedure to insert a row into the Shippers table, as seen in Listing 5.3, which inserts a row with the supplied values and returns the new identity field.

Listing 5.3. The usp_InsertShippers Stored Procedure

```
CREATE PROCEDURE usp_InsertShippers
   @CompanyName   nvarchar(40),
   @Phone         nvarchar(24),
   @ShipperID     int OUTPUT
AS
   INSERT INTO Shippers(CompanyName, Phone)
   VALUES(@CompanyName, @Phone)

   SELECT @ShipperID = SCOPE_IDENTITY()
```

In the ASP.NET page, there would be a `SqlDataSource` control with a `DetailsView`, as shown in Listing 5.4. In this code, the `InsertCommand` is set to `usp_InsertShippers`, and there are three `InsertParameters`: two input parameters to hold the company name and phone number to be inserted, and an output parameter for the returned ID value. Notice that the `Direction` property on the `ShipperID` parameter is set to Output. There is also a label on the page for the display of the identity value.

Listing 5.4. A Page that Uses Output Parameters

```
<asp:SqlDataSource ID="SqlDataSource1" runat="server"
  ConnectionString="<%$ ConnectionStrings:NorthwindConnectString %>"
  InsertCommand="usp_InsertShippers"
  InsertCommandType="StoredProcedure"
  SelectCommand="SELECT * FROM Shippers"
  OnInserted="SqlDataSource1_Inserted">
  <InsertParameters>
    <asp:Parameter Name="CompanyName" Type="String"  />
    <asp:Parameter Name="Phone" Type="String" />
    <asp:Parameter Name="ShipperID" Type="Int32"
      Direction="Output" />
  </InsertParameters>
</asp:SqlDataSource>

<asp:DetailsView ID="DetailsView1" runat="server"
  DataKeyNames="ShipperID" DataSourceID="SqlDataSource1"
  AllowPaging="True" AutoGenerateRows="False"
  AutoGenerateInsertButton="True">
  <Fields>
    <asp:BoundField DataField="CompanyName"
      HeaderText="Company Name" />
    <asp:BoundField DataField="Phone"
      HeaderText="Phone Number" />
  </Fields>
</asp:DetailsView>

<br /><br />

Identity Value: <asp:Label ID="IdentityValue" runat="server" />
```

The `Inserted` event is shown in Listing 5.5, where you can see we simply index into the `Parameters` collection of the `Command`.

Listing 5.5. Extracting the Output Parameter

```
protected void SqlDataSource1_Inserted(object sender,
                              SqlDataSourceStatusEventArgs e)
{
  IdentityValue.Text =
    e.Command.Parameters["@ShipperID"].Value.ToString();
}
```

The results of this are shown in Figure 5.1—the new shipper has been added, with an ID value of 5.

Output Parameters with the ObjectDataSource Control

The technique of using output parameters is similar when using a data layer and the `ObjectDataSource` control, which supports the same set of

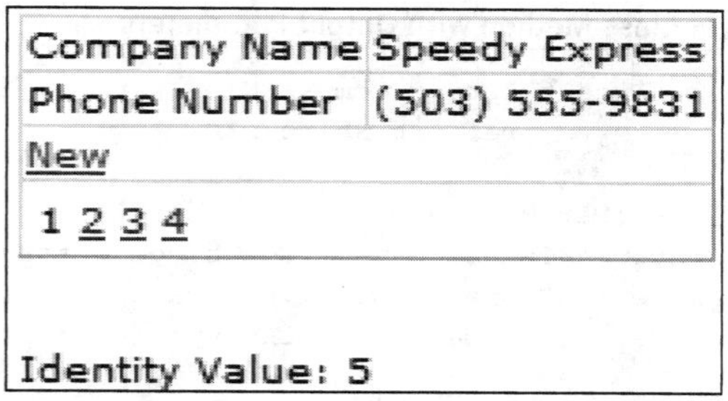

Company Name	Speedy Express
Phone Number	(503) 555-9831
New	

1 2 3 4

Identity Value: 5

FIGURE 5.1: The extracted Identity value

events as the `SqlDataSource` control. Output parameters appear as reference parameters in class methods, and should match with the parameters in the stored procedure. Listing 5.6 shows just such a stored procedure, with two parameters with data to be inserted, and the third declared as an `OUTPUT` parameter, which is set to the new inserted identity value.

Listing 5.6. The usp_InsertShippers Stored Procedure

```
CREATE PROCEDURE usp_InsertShippers
        @CompanyName        nvarchar(40),
        @Phone                  nvarchar(24),
        @ShipperID          int OUTPUT
AS
        INSERT INTO Shippers(CompanyName, Phone)
        VALUES(@CompanyName, @Phone)

        SELECT @ShipperID = SCOPE_IDENTITY()
```

The data layer class method that calls this procedure is shown in Listing 5.7.

This `Insert` method accepts three parameters, the first two being the values to be inserted. The third, `ShipperID`, is declared as `ref` and is the ID value of the newly created row to be returned to the user interface layer. Note that for the `SqlParameter` objects, this parameter has its `Direction` set to `ParameterDirection.Output`. After the procedure has been executed, the output parameter is accessed and its value used to set the value of `ShipperID`—the `ref` parameter of the method.

Listing 5.7. A Data Layer Class Method with Output Parameters

```
public static int Insert(string CompanyName, string Phone,
                    ref int ShipperID)
{
  SqlParameter[] sqlParams = new SqlParameter[] {
    new SqlParameter("@CompanyName", SqlDbType.NVarChar, 40),
    new SqlParameter("@Phone", SqlDbType.NVarChar, 24),
    new SqlParameter("@ShipperID", SqlDbType.Int)};

  sqlParams[0].Value = CompanyName;
  sqlParams[1].Value = Phone;
  sqlParams[2].Direction = ParameterDirection.Output;

  int rv = DataLayerHelper.ExecuteNonQuery("usp_InsertShippers",
            ref sqlParams, CommandType.StoredProcedure);

  ShipperID = (int)sqlParams[2].Value;

  return rv;
}
```

The parameters of the `ObjectDataSource` are similar, as seen in
Listing 5.8.

Listing 5.8. An ObjectDataSource with Output Parameters

```
<asp:ObjectDataSource ID="ObjectDataSource1" runat="server"
  InsertMethod="Insert" SelectMethod="GetShippers"
  TypeName="ShipperDataLayer"
  OnInserted="ObjectDataSource1_Inserted" >
  <InsertParameters>
    <asp:Parameter Name="CompanyName" Type="String" />
    <asp:Parameter Name="Phone" Type="String" />
    <asp:Parameter Name="ShipperID" Type="Int32"
      Direction="Output" />
  </InsertParameters>
</asp:ObjectDataSource>
```

Within the `Inserted` event (see Listing 5.9), the output parameters can
be accessed, but not in the same way as for the `SqlDataSource`. Although
the `ObjectDataSourceStatusEventArgs` has properties of the number of
rows affected and any exception details, it doesn't have a parameters collection. Instead, it has an explicit `OutputParameters` collection through
which you can access the output parameters from the underlying method.

Listing 5.9. The Inserted Event Procedure

```
protected void ObjectDataSource1_Inserted(object sender,
                         ObjectDataSourceStatusEventArgs e)
{
  IdentityValue.Text = e.OutputParameters["ShipperID"].ToString();
}
```

The `Inserted` event also has a `ReturnValue` property, allowing you to see the explicit return value from the method.

Custom Paging with an ObjectDataSource

If your data or business layer returns `DataSet` or `DataTable` objects, then the `ObjectDataSource` control automatically supports paging, but if you have a business layer that returns strongly typed objects, you have to manage the paging yourself. Paging revolves around the `ObjectDataSource` knowing the total number of rows in the underlying data, the number of rows in a page, and the item to start the page on.

To see this in action, consider the class in Listing 5.10. There's nothing special about this class; it simply represents an individual shipper.

Listing 5.10. The Shipper Class

```
public class Shipper
{
  private int _id;
  private string _companyName;
  private string _phone;

  public Shipper(int id, string companyName, string phone)
  {
    _id = id;
    _companyName = companyName;
    _phone = phone;
  }

  public int ID
  {
    get { return _id; }
    set { _id = value; }
  }

  public string CompanyName
  {
    get { return _companyName; }
    set { _companyName = value; }
  }

  public string Phone
  {
    get { return _phone; }
    set { _phone = value; }
  }
}
```

On its own, the `Shipper` class isn't much use alone and requires a class to represent a collection of shippers, as seen in Listing 5.11, which uses a Generic collection to represent the shippers.

Listing 5.11. The Shippers Class

```
public class Shippers
{
  public IList<Shipper> GetItems(int startIndex, int maxRows)
  {
    IList<Shipper> shippers = this.GetItemsInternal();
    IList<Shipper> pageShippers = new List<Shipper>();

    for (int i = startIndex; i < startIndex + maxRows; i++)
      pageShippers.Add(shippers[i]);

    return pageShippers;
  }

  public int GetShippersCount()
  {
    return this.GetItemsInternal().Count;
  }

  private IList<Shipper> GetItemsInternal()
  {
    IList<Shipper> shippers = new List<Shipper>();
    DataTable tbl = ShipperDataLayer.GetShippers();

    foreach (DataRow row in tbl.Rows)
      shippers.Add(new Shipper((int)row["ShipperID"],
        row["CompanyName"].ToString(),
        row["Phone"].ToString()));
    return shippers;
  }
}
```

The class has two public methods (methods for data updates have been omitted for brevity), and one private method. The private method, `GetItemsInternal`, calls the data layer to fetch a `DataTable` of shippers, and for each row in the table it creates a `Shipper` object, adding it to a collection. This method is the interface between the data layer and business layer.

The `ObjectDataSource` needs to know the total number of rows, so the `GetShippersCount` simply fetches the data and returns the number of items in the collection. This works as an example, but is not the best solution for real life, where you wouldn't want to fetch the entire set of records just to find the total number. In reality, you would probably perform a `SELECT COUNT(*)` statement, or call a method on the data layer that does this for you. In fact, if you are building a business layer like this, you may even want to remove the use of DataTable objects and use data readers directly in order to get the very best performance.

The GetItems method, which contains two parameters, is used to return the data to the ObjectDataSource. The first, startIndex, is the item number to start returning data from, and the second, maxRows, is the maximum number of rows to return. These can be used to selectively return the correct rows.

To use this class, the ObjectDataSource needs to know that paging is supported and which parameters the method defined in the SelectMethod uses for paging, as seen in Listing 5.12.

Listing 5.12. An ObjectDataSource Using Custom Paging

```
<asp:ObjectDataSource ID="ObjectDataSource1" runat="server"
  TypeName="Shippers" SelectMethod="GetItems"
  EnablePaging="true"
  StartRowIndexParameterName="startIndex"
  MaximumRowsParameterName="maxRows"
  SelectCountMethod="GetShippersCount">
</asp:ObjectDataSource>
```

The ObjectDataSource in Listing 5.12 has the EnablePaging property set to true, indicating that paging is enabled on the underlying class. The other properties are:

- StartRowIndexParameterName, which is set to the name of the parameter in the SelectMethod (GetItems) that identifies the index number to start the current page from.
- MaximumRowsParametername, which is set to the name of the parameter in the SelectMethod (GetItems) that identifies the maximum number of rows to return for a page.
- SelectCountMethod, which is set to the name of the method in the class (Shippers) that returns the total record count.

Use of this ObjectDataSource is exactly the same as when using a data source that doesn't use custom paging, as seen in Listing 5.13. Here the PageSize is set to 2, a value that is passed through to the maxRows parameter on the method that fetches the data. The BoundField columns have their DataField property set to the associated public properties on the business object.

Listing 5.13. A GridView Using a Custom Paged ObjectDataSource

```
<asp:GridView ID="GridView1" runat="server"
  AllowPaging="true" PageSize="2"
  AutoGenerateColumns="False"
  DataSourceID="ObjectDataSource1">
  <Columns>
   <asp:BoundField DataField="ID" HeaderText="ID" />
   <asp:BoundField DataField="CompanyName" HeaderText="CompanyName"/>
   <asp:BoundField DataField="Phone" HeaderText="Phone" />
  </Columns>
</asp:GridView>
```

To ensure that your business object works with an `ObjectDataSource` that isn't paging, you should also add a method that accepts no parameters to fetch the items, because the parameterized version will only be called if paging is enabled. You should also ensure that your method can accommodate situations in which paging is enabled on the data source but not on the display control, for example, a grid showing all rows. You can test for this by checking `maxRows`, which when 0 indicates all remaining rows from the `startIndex` are to be returned. If the display control isn't paging, `startIndex` will also be 0.

GridView and DetailsView Events

You've seen that the data source controls support events allowing you to hook into the data process, but the data display controls also support a variety of events. Some of these events are similar to those on the data source controls, and are for data modification. For example, the `GridView` control has `RowDeleting` and `RowDeleted` events, and the `DetailsView` has `ItemDeleting` and `ItemDeleted`. While it might seem odd that both the data source controls and the display controls have similar events, you have to remember that while these controls work together, they are not dependent upon each other. Data source controls are an interface to the data, allowing many controls to bind to them, while display controls don't have to fetch their data from the data source controls. For this reason, there are events on both types of controls that allow interaction with the data flow.

Handling GridView Update Events

For the `GridView` control, both the `Updating` and `Updated` events provide access to details being updated. The event procedure parameter has properties `Keys`, `OldValues`, and `NewValues`, which provide a way to access the data being sent back to the database. Prior to the command execution, you could examine the values, perform validation, and cancel the update if necessary, as shown in the code snippet here:

```
protected void GridView1_RowUpdating(object sender,
                        GridViewUpdateEventArgs e)
{
  if (!IsNumberic(e.NewValues("Price")))
  {
    e.Cancel = true;
    MessageLabel.Text = "Price must be a number";
  }
}
```

This checks the `RowIndex` that identifies the row being updated. If the row value for the `UnitPrice` column is not numeric, the update is cancelled. If you want to take the grid out of edit mode, you can set the `EditItemIndex` property of the grid to –1 (the same technique applies with selections using the SelectedIndex—setting it to –1 takes the grid out of select mode).

The `NewValues` property is a dictionary containing all of the new values being sent to the data store, and `OldValues` contains the old values.

Handling Data Editing Conflicts

One problem with data editing is the possibility of two people editing the same record at the same time. By default, the data source controls work on the last update principle, meaning that the last person to save changes wins—their values overwrite any previous changes. Essentially, the rows being edited or deleted are only matched by the row ID. The chances of a conflict happening depend upon your application type, but you may not want this default behavior.

To change to an optimistic model, you can set the `ConflictDetection` property of the data source to `CompareAllValues`, which adds all columns to the WHERE clause to uniquely identify the row. The values in the WHERE clause are the old values, before they were updated on the client, so the WHERE would only match if the row has not had any values changed. When configuring a data source, you can have these options set for you on the Advanced properties of the configuration, as shown in Figure 5.2.

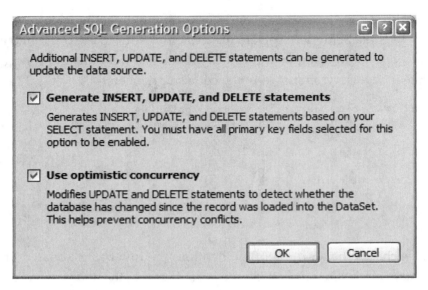

FIGURE 5.2: Configuring optimistic concurrency

Selecting optimistic concurrency for a SQL data source generates the code seen in Listing 5.14.

Listing 5.14. A SqlDataSource with Optimistic Concurrency

```
<asp:SqlDataSource ID="SqlDataSource1" runat="server"
  ConnectionString="<%$ ConnectionStrings:NorthwindConnectString %>"
  ConflictDetection="CompareAllValues"
  DeleteCommand="DELETE FROM [Shippers]
    WHERE [ShipperID] = @original_ShipperID
    AND [CompanyName] = @original_CompanyName
    AND [Phone] = @original_Phone"
  OldValuesParameterFormatString="original_{0}"
  SelectCommand="SELECT * FROM [Shippers]"
  UpdateCommand="UPDATE [Shippers]
    SET [CompanyName] = @CompanyName, [Phone] = @Phone
    WHERE [ShipperID] = @original_ShipperID
    AND [CompanyName] = @original_CompanyName
    AND [Phone] = @original_Phone">
  <DeleteParameters>
    <asp:Parameter Name="original_ShipperID" Type="Int32" />
    <asp:Parameter Name="original_CompanyName" Type="String" />
    <asp:Parameter Name="original_Phone" Type="String" />
  </DeleteParameters>
  <UpdateParameters>
    <asp:Parameter Name="CompanyName" Type="String" />
    <asp:Parameter Name="Phone" Type="String" />
    <asp:Parameter Name="original_ShipperID" Type="Int32" />
```

```
      <asp:Parameter Name="original_CompanyName" Type="String" />
      <asp:Parameter Name="original_Phone" Type="String" />
    </UpdateParameters>
  </asp:SqlDataSource>
```

The important points to note are the ConflictDetection property, and the WHERE clauses. Notice that each column is matched with a value called original_*Column*—this is the parameter that holds the original value. The OldValuesParameterFormatString method identifies the format these parameters are in, with {0} being a marker that is replaced by the column name. When the display control passes the values to the data source control, it passes both the newly updated values and the old values, and it's these old values that are placed into the original_ parameters.

When the update button is pressed, the update happens as normal and the Updated event of the data source is raised, at which point you can see whether there was a problem, as seen in Listing 5.15.

Listing 5.15. Detecting Errors in the SqlDataSource Control's Updated Event

```
protected void SqlDataSource1_Updated(object sender,
                              SqlDataSourceStatusEventArgs e)
{
  if (e.AffectedRows > 0)
    DisplayMessage.Text = "The record was updated sucessfully";
  else
  {
    if (e.Exception != null)
    {
      DisplayMessage.TemplateControl =
        "An error occurred updating the record.";
      ErrorMessage.Text = e.Exception.ToString();

      // You can stop the exception bubbling up by setting the
      //   ExceptionHandled property to true.
      //e.ExceptionHandled = true;
    }
    else
    {
      DisplayMessage.Text = "The record was not updated;
        no other database problem was reported so this may be
        because of a data conflict.";
    }
  }
}
```

The trouble you have with this event procedure is that you have no access to the data. You can see if any rows were affected, and whether an Exception was raised, and can make an assumption if no rows were updated. But since there is no access to the fields, that's about all you can do. A better solution is to use the RowUpdated event on the display control. For example, the GridView control not only sets the AffectedRows property, but gives you access to the OldValues and NewValues collections. This means that you could compare the values to see which are different, or just provide a way for the users to see all the values.

Listing 5.16 shows a sample event procedure to handle this type of conflict. Much is the same as in the event shown in Listing 5.15, but instead of just saying that a conflict may have occurred, it can offer much more information.

Listing 5.16. Detecting Errors in the GridView Control's Updated Event

```
protected void GridView1_RowUpdated(object sender,
                        GridViewUpdatedEventArgs e)
{
  if (e.AffectedRows > 0)
  {
    DisplayMessage.Text = "The record was updated sucessfully";
    ErrorPanel.Visible = false;
  }
  else
  {
   if (e.Exception != null)
    {
      DisplayMessage.Text = "An error occurred updating the record.";
      ErrorMessage.Text = e.Exception.ToString();

      // You can stop the exception bubbling up by setting the
      //   ExceptionHandled property to true.
      //e.ExceptionHandled = true;
    }
    else
    {
      e.KeepInEditMode = true;
      GridView1.DataBind();

      OriginalCompanyName.Text =
                        e.NewValues["CompanyName"].ToString();
      OriginalPhone.Text = e.NewValues["Phone"].ToString();

      DisplayMessage.Text = "The record was not updated; no other
          database problem was reported so this may be because of a
          data conflict.  Your values, which did not get written to
          the database, are shown below. If you Update this row now,
          your values will overwrite the current values. ";
    }
    ErrorPanel.Visible = true;
  }
}
```

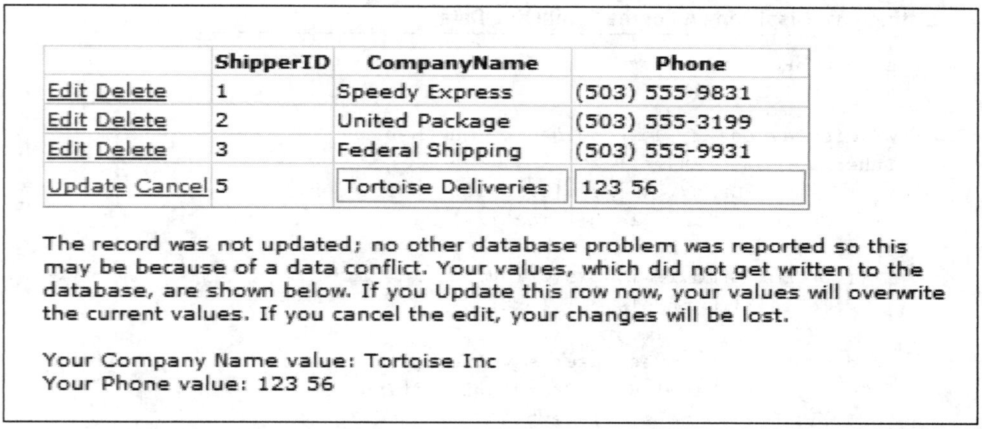

	ShipperID	CompanyName	Phone
Edit Delete	1	Speedy Express	(503) 555-9831
Edit Delete	2	United Package	(503) 555-3199
Edit Delete	3	Federal Shipping	(503) 555-9931
Update Cancel	5	Tortoise Deliveries	123 56

The record was not updated; no other database problem was reported so this may be because of a data conflict. Your values, which did not get written to the database, are shown below. If you Update this row now, your values will overwrite the current values. If you cancel the edit, your changes will be lost.

Your Company Name value: Tortoise Inc
Your Phone value: 123 56

FIGURE 5.3: An Edit page with conflict detection

The actions performed here are to first make sure that editing isn't finished by setting the KeepInEditMode property to true. Next, the GridView is rebound to the data, which ensures that the data shown now contains the values modified by the other user. This is important because the WHERE clauses are dependent upon this. Then the new values—those that the user on this page entered—are displayed in list boxes and an appropriate message is displayed. The results of this can be seen in Figure 5.3.

Another solution is to populate the row in edit mode with the new values and display the ones that the other user changed. This allows the user to simply click the **Update** button to save their changes rather than having to paste them back into the text box fields.

This code looks much more complex but is just as simple. After the grid hs been rebound to the fresh data, the values are extracted from the row being edited. Each cell in the row contains a TextBox control for data entry, so this is referenced and the Text property that contains the new value is extracted. If you were using template columns and using controls other than a TextBox, you would have to cast to the correct data type. These new values are displayed in labels on the page.

Next, the fresh values in the grid are overwritten with the new values—the values this user has just entered. Finally, the old values are displayed—these are the values that were in the grid when this user started editing. So now the

Listing 5.17. Displaying All of the Conflicting Data

```
e.KeepInEditMode = true;
GridView1.DataBind();

// display the values modified by another user
OtherUserCompanyName.Text =
    ((TextBox)GridView1.Rows[GridView1.EditIndex]
    .Cells[2].Controls[0]).Text;
OtherUserPhone.Text =
    ((TextBox)GridView1.Rows[GridView1.EditIndex]
    .Cells[3].Controls[0]).Text;

// overwrite the other user's values
((TextBox)GridView1.Rows[GridView1.EditIndex]
    .Cells[2].Controls[0]).Text =
        e.NewValues["CompanyName"].ToString();
((TextBox)GridView1.Rows[GridView1.EditIndex]
    .Cells[3].Controls[0]).Text =
        e.NewValues["Phone"].ToString();

// display the value before we edited it
OriginalCompanyName.Text = e.OldValues["CompanyName"].ToString();
OriginalPhone.Text = e.OldValues["Phone"].ToString();
```

user can see all three values and simply has to click the Update button to have his or her values overwrite the fresh ones, as seen in Figure 5.4.

Both of the techniques presented for conflict handling work just as well with the DetailsView and FormView controls, and the advantage of using the display controls is that you can use either the SqlDataSource or the ObjectDataSource controls for your data interface.

Asynchronous Pages and Data

The model for processing of ASP.NET pages is, by default, synchronous in nature. This means that there is a fixed flow to the page, with each page being processed by a thread; the thread isn't released until processing is finished. There are a limited number of threads available in the server thread pool, and once a server runs out of threads you start getting the dreaded "server unavailable" error. Even before that though, you'll see a performance loss as tasks wait for threads and memory use increases. So to improve performance, you want to not only process pages as fast as possible, but also release threads back to the thread pool as soon as you can. You

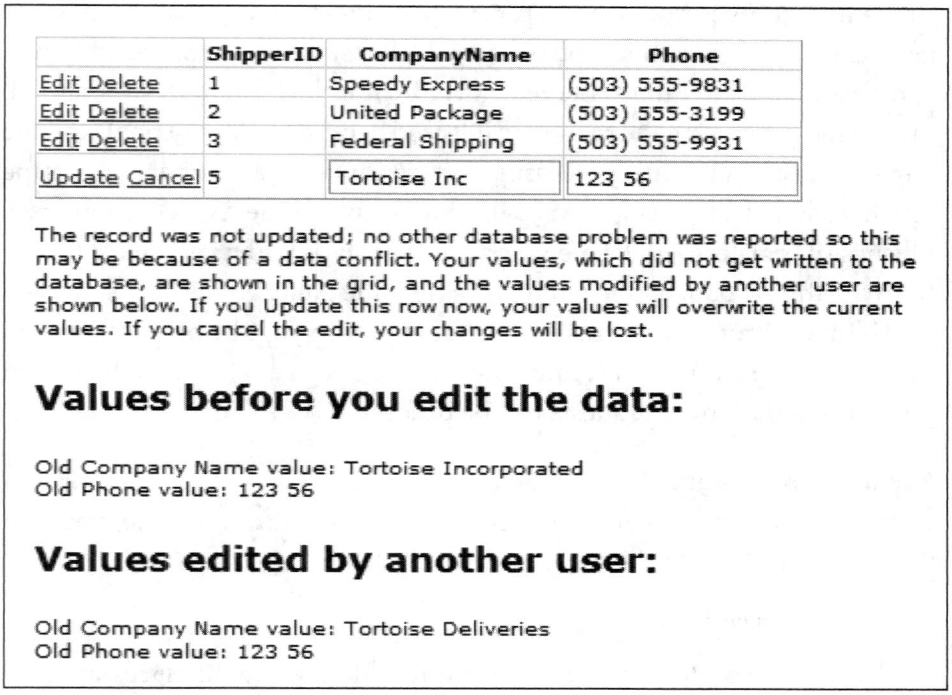

	ShipperID	CompanyName	Phone
Edit Delete	1	Speedy Express	(503) 555-9831
Edit Delete	2	United Package	(503) 555-3199
Edit Delete	3	Federal Shipping	(503) 555-9931
Update Cancel	5	Tortoise Inc	123 56

The record was not updated; no other database problem was reported so this may be because of a data conflict. Your values, which did not get written to the database, are shown in the grid, and the values modified by another user are shown below. If you Update this row now, your values will overwrite the current values. If you cancel the edit, your changes will be lost.

Values before you edit the data:

Old Company Name value: Tortoise Incorporated
Old Phone value: 123 56

Values edited by another user:

Old Company Name value: Tortoise Deliveries
Old Phone value: 123 56

FIGURE 5.4: An Edit page with improved conflict detection

generally don't have any explicit control over when to release the thread, but asynchronous processing can free up threads from long-running pages.

ASP.NET 2.0 introduces an easy model for asynchronous pages, but it's really important to understand exactly what asynchronous means in the context of Web pages. When a request is received from a client browser, the entire page has to be processed before the page can be returned to the browser. Asynchronous pages do not allow you to deliver pages in stages; you can buffer the output, but that's not the same thing. You can't deliver part of a page, run a task asynchronously, and then send more data back to the client.

The page is processed top to bottom by the same thread. That's the important point, because a single thread is taken up for the request. If the page stalls, perhaps accessing remote data via a Web Service, then the thread cannot be released back to the server until the request is finished. If this happens on lots of requests, it could be very simple for the server to run out of threads. Asynchronous pages allow you to remove the reliance upon a single thread if your page has a potentially long-running task as part of its normal processing routine. You dictate which tasks are to be processed asynchronously, and after the PreRender event, the asynchronous task is started. The thread processing the request is released back to the thread pool, and the page request waits until processing can continue; this happens when the asynchronous task finishes. ASP.NET knows when the asynchronous task finishes (it registers a delegate when the task starts), so it can take a thread from the thread pool and resume processing the page.

The asynchronous process is not about speeding up the processing of an individual page, but of the entire site. More threads available in the thread pool means that more requests can be processed.

Asynchronous Pages

To turn a page from a synchronous one to an asynchronous one, you add the Async attribute to the Page directive.

```
<%@ Page Async="true" . . . %>
```

You then need to register the event handlers that will start the asynchronous operation, and process the results once finished. For this you use the AddOnPreRenderCompleteAsync method, as shown in Listing 5.18.

Listing 5.18. The Code Behind an Asynchronous Page

```
public partial class AsyncPage : System.Web.UI.Page
{
  void Page_Load (object sender, EventArgs e)
  {
    AddOnPreRenderCompleteAsync (
      new BeginEventHandler(BeginAsyncOperation),
      new EndEventHandler (EndAsyncOperation)
    );
  }

  IAsyncResult BeginAsyncOperation (object sender, EventArgs e,
    AsyncCallback cb, object state)
  {
    // start long running task
  }
  void EndAsyncOperation (IAsyncResult ar)
  {
    // process results of long running task
  }
}
```

The task you perform needs to support the asynchronous model, and needs to have `Begin` and `End` methods; you call the `Begin` method in `BeginAsyncOperation` and the `End` method in `EndAsyncOperation`. You don't have to use the `Page_Load` event for the asynchronous registration; any event will do. For example, consider a Web page that shows a list of customers in a grid, and on selection more details for the customer are shown. Suppose you wish to fetch some data from a Web site, either by a Web Service or an RSS feed, to show some customer-related details—perhaps the weather in a customer's location, so that you know what sort of day it is when you call them, as seen in Figure 5.5.

This example uses the weather information provided by the Yahoo! Weather RSS feed at http://xml.weather.yahoo.com/rss/. The code for this (see Listing 5.19) shows three methods. The first is the `DataBound` method for the `DetailsView`, which is where the asynchronous registration takes place. This is only done if the `SelectedIndex` of the grid is not –1; this is if a row has actually been selected, which protects against the case where the data binding takes place but there is no selected row to bind against (which is how the data source controls work).

The next method, `BeginAsyncOperation`, is the start of the asynchronous operation, where the postal code of the selected customer is extracted from the `DetailsView`. The postal code is then used to define the location for the weather retrieval query. A `WebRequest` object is used to create an HTTP request to the query location, and the `GetBeginResponse` method is called—this starts the request asynchronously, and it's at this time that ASP.NET releases the thread back to the thread pool.

The third method, `EndAsyncOperation`, starts when the asynchronous operation tells ASP.NET it has finished. Here the `WebRequest` response is retrieved using a `WebResponse` object, and the data is read from that using a `StreamReader`. The `StreamReader` is passed into the `ReadXml` method of a `DataSet`, and the forecast table is bound to a `DataList`. There are several tables with different data in the XML returned, but the `forecast` one contains the three-day weather forecast.

	CompanyName	ContactName	Phone
Select	Gourmet Lanchonetes	André Fonseca	(11) 555-9482
Select	Great Lakes Food Market	Howard Snyder	(503) 555-7555
Select	GROSELLA-Restaurante	Manuel Pereira	(2) 283-2951
Select	Hanari Carnes	Mario Pontes	(21) 555-0091
Select	HILARION-Abastos	Carlos Hernández	(5) 555-1340

1 2 3 4 5 6 7 8 9 10 ...

CompanyName	Great Lakes Food Market
ContactName	Howard Snyder
ContactTitle	Marketing Manager
Address	2732 Baker Blvd.
City	Eugene
Region	OR
PostalCode	97403
Country	USA
Phone	(503) 555-7555
Fax	

Fri 16 Dec 2005	Sat 17 Dec 2005	Sun 18 Dec 2005
AM Clouds/PM Sun	PM Showers	Rain
High: 38	High: 40	High: 42
Low: 27	Low: 33	Low: 36

FIGURE 5.5: Capturing weather information asynchronously

Listing 5.19. Asynchronously Fetching Weather Information

```
protected void DetailsView1_DataBound(object sender, EventArgs e)
{
    if (GridView1.SelectedIndex != -1)
    {
        AddOnPreRenderCompleteAsync(
            new BeginEventHandler(BeginAsyncOperation),
            new EndEventHandler(EndAsyncOperation));
    }
}
```

```
IAsyncResult BeginAsyncOperation(object sender, EventArgs e,
  AsyncCallback cb, object state)
{
  string city = DetailsView1.Rows[6].Cells[1].Text;
  string qry =
    string.Format("http://xml.weather.yahoo.com/forecastrss?p={0}",
    city);

  _request = WebRequest.Create(qry);
  return _request.BeginGetResponse(cb, state);
}

void EndAsyncOperation(IAsyncResult ar)
{
  using (WebResponse response = _request.EndGetResponse(ar))
  {
    using (StreamReader reader =
      new StreamReader(response.GetResponseStream()))
    {
      DataSet ds = new DataSet();
      ds.ReadXml(reader);
      WeatherDisplay.DataSource = ds.Tables["forecast"];
      WeatherDisplay.DataBind();
    }
  }
}\
```

To display the weather, a simple `DataList` is used; as well as text details, the forecast data contains a code that represents the weather, and this is matched to an image in the `getWeatherIcon` method (see Listing 5.20).

While this example used `WebRequest` and `WebResponse` to perform the asynchronous data access, it would be equally simple to call a Web Service. You could also use this for a potentially long data operation, as seen in the example code in Listing 5.21. You can see that the pattern is exactly the same as for the previous example; it's just the action being performed that is different. Notice that `Dispose` is overridden to ensure that the connection object is disposed of as soon as it is not required. You can normally accomplish this with the `using` statement, but since the connection is required across multiple methods, that isn't possible, so disposal is done when the page is disposed of.

Listing 5.20. Binding to the Asynchronously Supplied Data

```
<asp:DataList ID="WeatherDisplay" runat="server"
  RepeatColumns="4" RepeatDirection="Horizontal" CellPadding="10">
  <ItemTemplate>
    <div style="font-weight:bold;">
      <%#Eval("day")%> <%#Eval("date")%></div>
    <br />
    <img src='<%# getWeatherIcon(DataBinder.Eval(
        Container.DataItem, "code"))%>'
      alt='<%#Eval("text", "Forecast image: {0}")%>>'
      style="height:100px; width:100px;"/><br />
    <%#Eval("text")%><br />
    <br />
    High: <%#Eval("high")%><br />
    Low: <%#Eval("low")%>
  </ItemTemplate>
</asp:DataList>
```

Listing 5.21. Asynchronous Data Binding

```
private SqlConnection _conn;
private SqlCommand _cmd;
private SqlDataReader _rdr;

protected void Page_Load(object sender, EventArgs e)
{
  if (!IsPostBack)
  {
    AddOnPreRenderCompleteAsync(
      new BeginEventHandler(BeginAsyncOperation),
      new EndEventHandler(EndAsyncOperation));
  }
}

IAsyncResult BeginAsyncOperation (object sender, EventArgs e,
  AsyncCallback cb, object state)
{
  string cstr = WebConfigurationManager.ConnectionStrings
    ["NorthwindConnectionString"].ConnectionString;
  _conn = new SqlConnection(cstr);
  _conn.Open();
  _cmd = new SqlCommand("long query", _conn);
  return _cmd.BeginExecuteReader(cb, state);
}
```

```
void EndAsyncOperation(IAsyncResult ar)
{
  _rdr = _command.EndExecuteReader(ar);
  GridView1.DataSource = _rdr;
  GridView1.DataBind();
}

public override void Dispose()
{
  if (_conn != null)
    _conn.Close();
  base.Dispose();
}
```

Notice that the `SqlCommand` uses `BeginExecuteReader` and `EndExecuteReader`—these are the asynchronous equivalent of `ExecuteReader`. This standard pattern will work for any object that supports asynchronous operation but should only be used where the operation is potentially lengthy and could tie up the thread.

If you are using ASP.NET 2.0 Web Service Proxies, then the pattern can change, because these proxies automatically support asynchronous operation with completion notification. Along with your Web method, the proxy generator creates a *methodAsync* to start the method asynchronously, and a *methodCompleted* event, for notification when the method has finished. If configured, the ASP.NET page will wait until the method has completed before finishing the page processing. For example, consider a Northwind Web Service, with the method shown in Listing 5.22, which simply returns a `DataSet` of products.

Listing 5.22. A Simple Web Service Method

```
[WebMethod]
public DataSet GetProducts()
{
  DataSet ds = new DataSet();
  ds.Merge(ProductsDataLayer.ReadCached());
  return ds;
}
```

If you create a Web Service Reference to this, called `localNorthwind-Service`, the proxy will be generated for you, allowing it to be used in an asynchronous manner, as shown in Listing 5.23.

Listing 5.23. Calling a Web Service Asynchronously

```
public partial class ch05_AsynchronousWebServices :
                        System.Web.UI.Page
{
  private localNorthwindService.NorthwindService _service;

  protected void Page_Load(object sender, EventArgs e)
  {
    if (!IsPostBack)
    {
      _service = new localNorthwindService.NorthwindService();
      _service.GetProductsCompleted +=
        new localNorthwindService.
            GetProductsCompletedEventHandler(
              _service_GetProductsCompleted);
      _service.GetProductsAsync();
    }
  }
  void _service_GetProductsCompleted(object sender,
      localNorthwindService.GetProductsCompletedEventArgs e)
  {
    GridView1.DataSource = e.Result;
    GridView1.DataBind();
  }
  public override void Dispose()
  {
    if (_service != null)
      _service.Dispose();
    base.Dispose();
  }
}
```

You can see that the pattern is different, and simpler. You first instantiate the Web Service and then set an event handler for the `GetProducts-Completed` event, which will be called when the Web Service call completes. Then the method is called asynchronously. In the completed event handler, the results from the Web Service are available as a property of one of the event parameters.

The advantage of this pattern over the `BeginAsyncOperation` and `EndAsyncOperation` is not only the cleaner code (which is more noticeable if you have several asynchronous Web Service calls), but the fact that it also allows impersonation, the culture, and the HTTP context to flow to the completed event handler.

Asynchronous Tasks

You've seen that there are two patterns for performing asynchronous tasks; one that uses `AddOnPreRenderCompleteAsync`, and one that uses asynchronous Web Service proxies. If you are not using Web Services, but need to have context information (such as impersonation or culture) flow with the asynchronous task, then the existing methods won't work. They also don't support any form of timeout so that you don't wait indefinitely; some tasks, such as the weather one shown earlier, aren't critical to the page operation, so it wouldn't be sensible for the page to fail just because the weather forecast wasn't available.

To solve these problems, you can use asynchronous tasks, which is similar in use to `AddOnPreRenderCompleteAsync` in that you have begin and end events. The difference lies in the way the asynchronous event is hooked up, as shown in Listing 5.24.

You can see that the begin and end methods are the same as in previous examples, but there is now a method for timeouts. All three methods are set up in a different way, this time by constructing a `PageAsyncTask` object, the constructor of which takes delegates to the asynchronous methods, and an object that is the context to flow through the events. The `PageAsyncTask` object is then registered using `RegisterAsyncTask`.

SQL Server 2005 User-Defined Types

SQL Server 2005 has the .NET Framework embedded within it, which allows the use of managed languages for creation of objects such as stored procedures, function, aggregates, and types. This book is not dedicated to SQL Server 2005, so most of these topics are not covered, but the use of user-defined types (UDTs) affects client applications such as ASP.NET pages, so is worthy of coverage here.

By "custom types," we mean any object defined within .NET. SQL Server already has support for native types, such as string, dates, numbers, and so on, but there may be other types you want to store. For example, you might

Listing 5.24. Using Asynchronous Tasks

```csharp
private WebRequest _request;

protected void DetailsView1_DataBound(object sender, EventArgs e)
{
  if (GridView1.SelectedIndex != -1)
  {

    PageAsyncTask task = new PageAsyncTask(
      new BeginEventHandler(BeginAsyncOperation),
      new EndEventHandler(EndAsyncOperation),
      new EndEventHandler(TimeoutAsyncOperation),
      null);
    RegisterAsyncTask(task);
  }
}

IAsyncResult BeginAsyncOperation(object sender, EventArgs e,
  AsyncCallback cb, object state)
{
  string city = DetailsView1.Rows[6].Cells[1].Text;
  string qry =
    string.Format("http://xml.weather.yahoo.com/forecastrss?p={0}",
    city);

  _request = WebRequest.Create(qry);
  return _request.BeginGetResponse(cb, state);
}

void EndAsyncOperation(IAsyncResult ar)
{
  using (WebResponse response = _request.EndGetResponse(ar))
  {
    using (StreamReader reader = new
      StreamReader(response.GetResponseStream()))
    {
      DataSet ds = new DataSet();
      ds.ReadXml(reader);
      WeatherDisplay.DataSource = ds.Tables["forecast"];
      WeatherDisplay.DataBind();
    }
  }
}
void TimeoutAsyncOperation(IAsyncResult ar)
{
  NoWeather.Visible = true;
}
```

want to store dates and times as separate columns, or perhaps you have a more complex object such as Longitude or Latitude for a mapping operation. You can create these UDTs as .NET structures and store them within SQL Server 2005 as a native type—so the column type is your custom type.

Let's take a look at location-based storage with Longitude and Latitude classes; with the increasing popularity of GPS systems, especially among sports enthusiasts (see http://www.expansys.com/p_sportsdo.asp for some cool PocketPC applications), and the uptake of free mapping services such as Virtual Earth, the storage of trip information can provide a great way to document your activities. Using SQL Server 2005, you can natively store the GPS details as a UDT, allowing them to be easily used in mapping applications.

A UDT is simply a structure in .NET that follows a set of rules:

- It is decorated with the `SqlUserDefinedType` attribute, to allow automatic type creation when deployed from Visual Studio 2005.
- The structure must implement the `INullable` interface, because SQL Server types can be null.
- You must implement the `Parse` method, which parses string values and converts them to the internal storage types.
- You must implement the `ToString` method, which converts the internal storage into a readable form.

Other properties and methods can be implemented, depending upon the requirements of the UDT. For the Latitude type, you could store the latitude in a decimal format, along with properties for Degrees, Minutes, Seconds, and the Hemisphere. This is shown in Listing 5.25, which details the minimum requirements for a SQL UDT. An equivalent UDT for Longitude is included in the downloadable samples, but is not discussed in depth; you'll see that it is very similar to the latitude.

Let's break this code down to see exactly what each section does, and why.

UDT Attributes

The first thing to notice is that the structure is attributed, first with `Serializable`; all UDTs must be serializable, because SQL Server serializes the data for storage internally in the database. The second attribute,

Listing 5.25. The Latitude User Defined Type

```
[Serializable]
[SqlUserDefinedType(Format.Native, IsByteOrdered = true)]
public struct Latitude : INullable
{
  internal float _latitude;
  internal short _degrees;
  internal short _minutes;
  internal short _seconds;
  internal bool _hemisphere;

  Latitude(float latitude)
  {
    _latitude = latitude;

    _degrees = (short)latitude;
    float m = (float)_latitude - _degrees;
    _minutes = (short)(m * 60);
    float s = (float)m - _minutes;
    _seconds = (short)(s * 60);
    _hemisphere = (latitude >= 0);
  }

  public static Latitude Parse(SqlString s)
  {
    string val = s.Value.Trim().ToLower();

    // if null string or the string "null" is
    // passed in the return a null Longitude instance
    if (s.IsNull || (val == "null"))
      return Null;

    float lat = float.Parse(val);

    if (lat < -90 || lat > 90)
      throw new ArgumentException("Latitude must be between
          -90 and 90");

    return new Latitude(lat);
  }
  public override string ToString()
  {

    return _latitude.ToString();
  }
  public bool IsNull
  {
    get {return _latitude == float.MinValue;}
  }
  public static Latitude Null
```

```
  {
    get {return new Latitude(float.MinValue);}
  }

  public short Degrees
  {
    get { return _degrees; }
  }

  public short Minutes
  {
    get { return _minutes; }
  }
  public short Seconds
  {
    get { return _seconds; }
  }
  public string Hemisphere
  {
    get { return _hemisphere ? "N" : "S"; }
  }
}
```

SqlUserDefinedType, does two things. First, it defines that this class is a UDT, which Visual Studio uses when deploying the assembly. Second, it defines characteristics of the type. The two in use here are Format. Native, which indicates that only native types are used and that SQL Server can perform the serialization, and IsByteOrdered, which indicates that the serialized data can be used for ordering and comparison.

The SqlUserDefinedType attribute supports the following properties:

- Format, which can be Native or UserDefined. If Native, SQL Server performs the serialization. For native serialization, all the fields must themselves be serializable types. If UserDefined is set, then you must implement IBinarySerialize and the Read and Write methods to serialize the fields yourself.

- IsByteOrdered, which when true allows SQL Server to use the serialized data for ordering and comparison, and to use the column for indexing.

- IsFixedLength, which when true indicates that all instances of the UDT have the length equal to MaxByteSize. This is only relevant when using UserDefined serialization.

- `MayByteSize` is the maximum size of the UDT instance when serialized. This is only relevant when using `UserDefined` serialization.

- Name, which indicates the name of the UDT and is only used by Visual Studio.

- `ValidationMethodName`, which is the name of the method used to validate instances of the UDT. This is used when the UDT has been deserialized from an untrusted source.

Serializable Types

One important point to notice is the types you can use as fields, which must be serializable types. This means that your fields must be one of the following types: `bool`, `byte`, `sbyte`, `short`, `ushort`, `int`, `uint`, `long`, `ulong`, `float`, `double`, `SqlByte`, `SqlInt16`, `SqlInt32`, `SqlInt64`, `SqlDateTime`, `SqlSingle`, `SqlDouble`, `SqlMoney`.

Take a look at the internal fields used in the UDT:

```
internal float _latitude;
internal short _degrees;
internal short _minutes;
internal short _seconds;
internal bool _hemisphere;
```

The degrees, minutes, and seconds are as expected—a `short`—because they only store small values. The value for latitude would perhaps be stored as a `decimal` type, but this isn't serializable, so `float` has been used. You could ignore this entirely, because the latitude can easily be recalculated from the other fields, but it's been included here to make the rest of the UDT simpler. The hemisphere (which would be N or S) is also an unexpected type—`bool` instead of `string` or `char`, because `string` and `char` are not serializable. Instead, a boolean flag is set to true for the Northern Hemisphere and false for the Southern Hemisphere.

Constructors

The constructor of a UDT is just like the constructor of any other type, and serves to initialize the type. In this example, a decimal (as in a description of the value, rather than the data type) latitude is used as the parameter, and the internal values are calculated from that.

```
Latitude(float latitude)
{
  _latitude = latitude;

  _degrees = (short)latitude;
  float m = (float)_latitude - _degrees;
  _minutes = (short)(m * 60);
  float s = (float)m - _minutes;
  _seconds = (short)(s * 60);
  _hemisphere = (latitude >= 0);
}
```

Multiple constructors are allowed, so it would be perfectly possible to have the following:

```
Latitude(short degrees, short minutes, short seconds,
         string hemisphere)
{
  _latitude = DMStoDecimal(degrees, minutes, seconds);
  _degrees = degrees;
  _minutes = minutes;
  _seconds = seconds;
  _hemisphere = (hemisphere == "N");
}
```

This is useful if the type is being used outside of SQL Server, but it is less useful within SQL because the constructor isn't used directly when values are created. Instead, the values are parsed.

Parsing Values

To enter values into the SQL table, you use the INSERT statement, and that doesn't change just because a column is a UDT. For UDT columns, the INSERT statement calls the Parse method of the UDT, passing into it a SqlString type of the value to be inserted. Parse must then break this string apart, converting it into the internal types.

```
public static Latitude Parse(SqlString s)
{
  string val = s.Value.Trim().ToLower();

  // if null string or the string "null" is
```

```
  // passed in the return a null Longitude instance
  if (s.IsNull || (val == "null"))
    return Null;

  float lat = float.Parse(val);

  if (lat < -90 || lat > 90)
    throw new ArgumentException("Latitude must be between
      -90 and 90");

  return new Latitude(lat);
}
```

It is important to remember that SQL types can be NULL, so you must plan for this. The Parse method just seen takes the string value, removes any white space, and converts it to lower case before checking for a null value on the string—SqlString is not a standard string, because it can be null. The string is then converted to a float and validated before being used to return a new instance of the UDT.

Outputting Values

To extract values from a UDT column, you specify the column name in SQL, which in turn calls the ToString method of the type. For the latitude type, this is simple—just returning a string value of the internal latitude.

```
public override string ToString()
{
  return _latitude.ToString();
}
```

You can, of course, output the value in any form you like, perhaps converting it to its individual degrees, minutes, and seconds.

Handling Null Values

SQL can store null values, so the UDT must cope with this, by having two properties with defined names. The first, IsNull, indicates whether the UDT is null; in the latitude UDT, this compares an internal _degrees field with a known value that is invalid for a legal value of degrees. You could easily store a flag to indicate the null status, but that requires an additional field, so an existing field is used.

The second property is Null, which returns a UDT instance, initialized with the value defined as our null value. Like IsNull, you could easily do this another way, perhaps having another constructor that takes a flag indicating that a null instance should be created.

```
public bool IsNull
{
  get { _latitude == float.MinValue;}
}
public static Latitude Null
{
  get {return new Latitude(float.MinValue);}
}
```

Adding Properties

Properties aren't a required part of creating a UDT, but they do allow flexibility in its use. Properties of a UDT are exactly the same as class properties.

```
public short Degrees
{
  get { return _degrees; }
}

public short Minutes
{
  get { return _minutes; }
}

public short Seconds
{
  get { return _seconds; }
}

public string Hemisphere
{
  get { return _hemisphere ? "N" : "S"; }
}
```

For example, when selecting a UDT column, the ToString method is used to return the value. For example, if Lat was a column of type Latitude, you could do the following:

```
SELECT Lat FROM TripDetails
```

If properties are supported in the UDT, these can be added directly to the column.

```
SELECT Lat.Degrees FROM TripDetails
```

SQL Server doesn't use these directly, but they are useful when accessing the UDT from client applications.

Additions to UDTs

There are plenty of additions you can make to UDTs to allow them to integrate with SQL Server and applications. Details of these are beyond the scope of this book, but it's worth pointing out areas that you might want to look at to enhance your usage of UDTs.

The first area is the addition of methods to provide extra functionality. For example, the latitude could have `ToDMS` and `FromDMS` methods to output and accept values stored in degrees, minutes, and seconds. This would be useful when creating client applications, because it would allow you to display and accept data in different formats. The downloadable samples implement these two methods so that you can see how they would work.

The second area is that of comparison of UDT instances. While native serialization allows automatic comparison, you can override this, if necessary, by implementing the Equals method and overriding the == and != operators. Within these, you can explicitly define how one instance of a UDT compares to another.

A more interesting issue is creating user-defined aggregates that extend the existing aggregates supported by SQL Server. For example, consider the latitude type; what does the MAX aggregate mean on a value that represents a latitude? MAX would, in fact, compare using internal values, so the North Pole would be the maximum value, as it has the highest latitude (90 degrees). What if you wanted to have the maximum per hemisphere? Aggregates like MAX and MIN make even less sense when applied to longitudes, where −180 is the minimum and 180 the maximum, with 0 being Greenwich in England. You could create aggregates called FurthestNorth and FurthestSouth, or FurthestEast and FurthestWest, which while providing similar results to MAX and MIN, make code much more readable. You could also create aggregates for TopLeft, TopRight, BottomLeft, and BottomRight, to provide bounds for a range of longitude and latitudes.

Creating a UDT in Visual Studio 2005

To create an SQL type in Visual Studio 2005, you select the SQL Server Project from the Database project types, as shown in Figure 5.6, where the

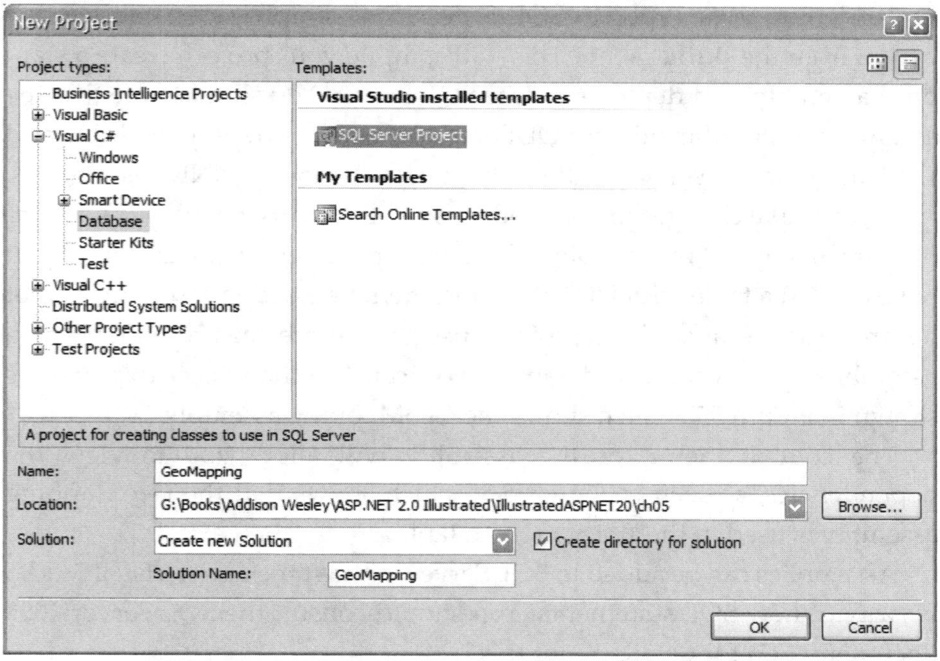

FIGURE 5.6: Creating a SQL Server project

project name is GeoAssembly—this will be the assembly name within SQL Server when the project is deployed. You can then add items to your project, and for a UDT, you pick User-Defined Type object, which creates a template for your UDT.

You can have multiple types within the same project and include other SQL Server objects such as stored procedures, aggregates, and functions. Compilation behaves in exactly the same way as with other projects.

Deploying the UDT to SQL Server 2005

Before deploying to SQL Server, you must make sure that the SQL Server CLR is enabled in the database, which it isn't by default. You can do this with the SQL Server Surface Area Configuration Tool or via the following SQL statements:

```
sp_configure 'clr enabled', '1'
GO
reconfigure
GO
```

To deploy your types to SQL Server, you simply select the **Deploy** option from the **Build** menu. This will compile your project, create a standard assembly, and deploy this into SQL Server. You should note that the assembly is stored inside of SQL Server, so you can deploy the MDF and LDF files to target servers without having to deploy any .NET assemblies.

If you make changes to your code, you will have to redeploy the assembly, which may not be possible if there are types in use. For example, if you have created a table with UDT columns, then the existing assembly cannot be dropped, because the type is in use. If you are unsure about which assemblies you have in a database, you can use the Object Explorer, as shown in Figure 5.7, which shows the GeoMapping assembly.

The context menu for the assembly will allow you to view the dependencies, as seen in Figure 5.8, which shows that the GeoMapping assembly is used in the `TripDetails` table.

Assemblies can be added to SQL Server without the use of Visual Studio by way of new SQL statements. You should consult the SQL Server 2005 documentation for details about this.

Creating Tables with UDT Columns

Once the assembly is deployed, you can use the UDTs as you would any other types, as shown in Figure 5.9, where the UDTs appear alongside the standard column types.

You can also use the UDTs in SQL to create tables, as shown in Listing 5.26 where `Longitude` and `Latitude` are used in the same way as other types.

Listing 5.26. Creating a Table with UDT Columns

```
CREATE TABLE [dbo].[TripDetails](
    [TripDetailID] [int] IDENTITY(1,1) NOT NULL,
    [TripID] [int] NOT NULL,
    [WaypointID] [smallint] NOT NULL,
    [Description] [nvarchar](255)
    COLLATE SQL_Latin1_General_CP1_CI_AS NOT NULL,
    [Lng] [dbo].[Longitude] NOT NULL,
    [Lat] [dbo].[Latitude] NOT NULL
) ON [PRIMARY]
```

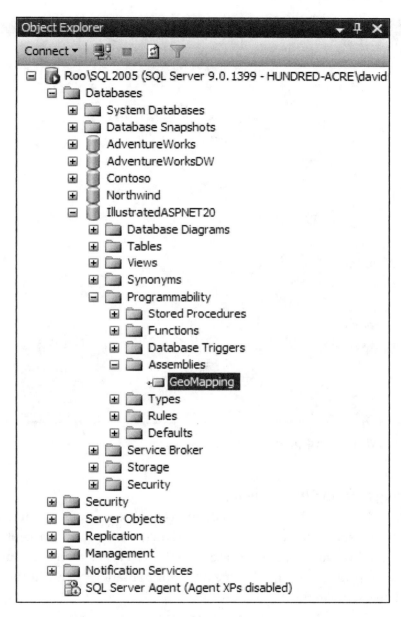

FIGURE 5.7: The SQL Server 2005 Object Explorer

This is actually an important point—UDTs are types, they aren't just a bolt-on extension. They are first-class types within SQL Server, and they can be used anywhere a standard type is used.

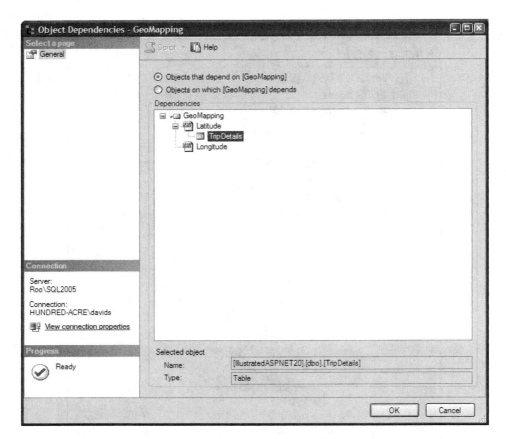

FIGURE 5.8: Viewing the dependencies for an assembly

Inserting Data into UDT Columns

Inserting data into a UDT column depends upon the `Parse` method of the UDT, because it is the `Parse` method that dictates the format accepted for the column insertion. In the latitude type shown earlier, the `Parse` method accepts a string containing the decimal representation of the latitude and would be used like this:

```
INSERT INTO TripDetails(TripID, WaypointID, Description, Lat, Lng)
VALUES(1, 1, 'Bellingham Harbour', '48.7566', '-122.4946')
```

You can see that there is nothing unusual about this statement—the longitude and latitude values are as expected. If the `Parse` method accepted, for example, a SqlDecimal type, the values could be inserted

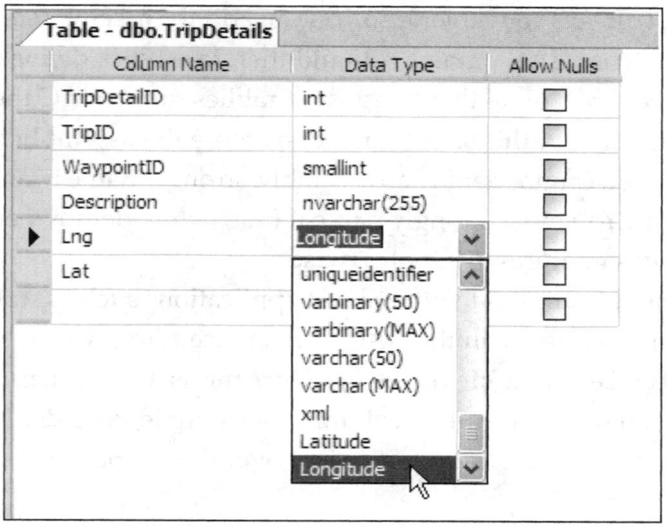

FIGURE 5.9: Adding a UDT column to a table

without quotes. If data was expected to be inserted in a different format, such as DDMMSSH, then the insert statement might be:

```
INSERT INTO TripDetails(TripID, WaypointID, Description, Lat, Lng)
VALUES(1, 1, 'Bellingham Harbour', '484523N', '1222940W')
```

You can implement multiple `Parse` methods to handle different type formats.

Accessing UDT Columns

Accessing UDT columns depends upon the client application knowing what the data type is. For example, in SQL Server Management Studio (SSMS), you cannot simply perform the following SQL query and get the results you expect:

```
SELECT * FROM TripDetails
```

The reason is that SSMS is a client application, and it doesn't know anything about the Longitude and Latitude types—these are embedded within the database itself. You can run the above query, but the UDT columns will come back in their binary format. To see the explicit values,. you have to do one of two things The first is to explicitly name the columns and use the `ToString` method:

```
SELECT Description Lng.ToString(), Lat.ToString() FROM TripDetails
```

This isn't always convenient, so you can add the assembly to the Global Assembly Cache (GAC), making it (and therefore types defined within it) globally accessible. Note that to add assemblies to the GAC they must be strongly signed, and this should be done before the assembly is added to SQL Server. You cannot deploy an assembly, strongly name it, and then add it to the GAC. You must strongly name it first, before deployment, because the assembly signatures differ otherwise.

The same rule applies to other client applications such as ASP.NET. The assembly must either be in the GAC or referenced from within your application project (i.e., in the bin directory). Once this is done, you can access the column as you would any other column. For example, consider Listing 5.27, which shows a `SqlDataReader` iterating over the `TripDetails`:

Listing 5.27. Using a UDT in Client Code

```
protected void Page_Load(object sender, EventArgs e)
{
using (SqlConnection conn = new
  SqlConnection(ConfigurationManager.ConnectionStrings[
  "IllustratedASPNET20ConnectionString"].ConnectionString))
{
  SqlCommand cmd = new SqlCommand("Select * from TripDetails", conn);
  conn.Open();

  SqlDataReader rdr =
            cmd.ExecuteReader(CommandBehavior.CloseConnection);
  Latitude lat;
  while (rdr.Read())
  {
    lat = (Latitude)rdr["Lat"];
    Response.Write(lat.ToString() + "<br />");
  }
  rdr.Close();
}
```

You can see that the column is accessed like non-UDT columns, and the `ToString` method is called to convert the internal value to text. You can use UDT columns directly in databound controls, as shown in Figure 5.10, which shows a grid bound to some details containing waypoints for a sailing trip. These are integrated with the `Microsoft Virtual Earth` control to allow the user to select the waypoint and the map to display the appropriate image. You can now see how you can build some really cool mapping applications using SQL Server 2005 as a store for custom mapping types.

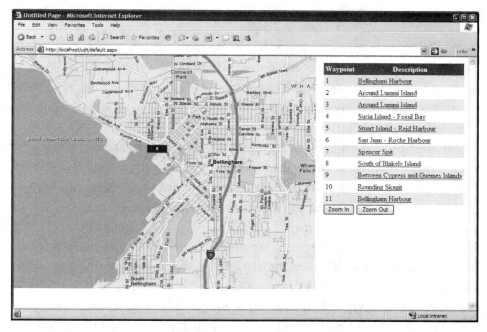

FIGURE 5.10: Databinding with UDT columns

If you wanted to insert data, perhaps using a stored procedure and parameters, then the parameter type should be defined as `SqlDbType.Udt` and the `UdtTtypeName` property set to the type of the UDT, as shown in Listing 5.28.

Listing 5.28. Using a UDT as a Parameter

```
SqlParameter param = new SqlParameter("@Lat", SqlDbType.Udt);
param.UdtTypeName = "dbo.Latitude";
param.Value = new Latitude(48.7566);
cmd.Parameters.Add(param);
```

This simply tells ADO.NET that the parameter is of a custom type, and defines what that type is.

Further Reading

If you'd like to find out more about SQL Server 2005 and the CLT integration, then you should consult the SQL Server and MSDN documentation. The SQL CLR team also have an excellent Weblog at http://blogs.msdn.com/sqlclr/, which contains some great samples.

SUMMARY

In this chapter, we have expanded on the data source control and data display control discussions of Chapters 3 and 4. We started by looking at some of the simple uses for the events of the data source controls, such as rebinding other display controls on the page and how to modify the parameters before a `SelectCommand` is executed.

We then moved on to output parameters and how to access values sent back from executed commands, such as the identity value of a newly inserted row. You saw that from within the event procedure, the way of accessing output parameters is the same whether using a `SqlDataSource` or `ObjectDataSource` control.

We then moved on to the `ObjectDataSource` using a strongly typed business class, and we showed how to implement custom paging so that the display controls can provide the same functionality that the `SqlDataSource` provides. The paging revolves around your business class supporting the use of the number of rows in a page and which row to start on, as well as knowing the total number of rows.

We then briefly saw an overview of the events for the `GridView` and `DetailsView` before moving into conflict detection and concurrency errors, detailing how to avoid the lost update problem. This section showed that events for the display controls are much more useful than the events on the data source controls, because the display control events provide access to all versions of the data being updated.

The second half of the chapter looked at one particular aspect of SQL Server CLR Integration, which is the use of custom types in database. We showed how to created a User-Defined Type to store mapping information, and then how that custom type can be used in client applications. You can see that this provides a simple way to create some exciting applications without having to worry about handling complex data, because the database and the UDT handle the data natively.

Now it's time to move into how to improve the performance of applications, so we'll take a look at caching.

▊ 6 ▪
Data and Output Caching

ACHING IS THE ACT of storing something for later retrieval, and in the Web world it is used to improve performance. There are many factors that affect the performance of Web sites, and two of these are the processing of ASP.NET pages and fetching data from databases. Once a Web site has been launched, the pages themselves generally stay fairly static, with only data changing, and even then that doesn't always change frequently. Fetching data from a database is relatively slow and uses resources (process, memory, etc.), so if that usage can be minimized, performance can be improved. Likewise, if a page doesn't change, why process it on every request?

Both of these problems can be solved with caching—storing data so that it doesn't have to be processed or fetched. The performance impact of reducing resource usage may not be noticeable on small sites, but for larger sites with many users you can achieve dramatic improvements. In this chapter we're going to look at various caching schemes and how they can be used to improve performance. In particular, we will cover the following topics:

- Using the application, session, HttpContext, and viewstate to store data
- How to use output caching to reduce processing overhead
- How to cache data to reduce SQL Server resource usage

- How to use cache notifications so that stale data is never shown
- How to use the cache API

Some of these techniques are simple, while others require a little more thought. All of them, however, are easy to code.

Application, Session, HttpContext, and ViewState Caching

Using the `Application`, `Session`, `HttpContext` and `ViewState` objects for caching data is not a new technique, and while extremely simple, it shouldn't be left out or ignored because of other techniques. All three objects provide simple key based collections for storage of data through the lifetime of the object. Since this lifetime is not persistent, you should only store data that is ephemeral in nature; anything that requires long-lived storage should use a database, or perhaps the Profile object for user-related data.

Using the Application State

The Application object exists for the lifetime of the application; that is, from the moment the first request to the application is received to the moment the application is shut down. Application shutdown can occur under different circumstances, and you should be aware that it can happen while the site is being used. ASP.NET is self-monitoring and can restart an application if, for example, memory demands exceed set limits. This means that you shouldn't rely on an item automatically being stored in the Application object; you should always check for a null value.

Using the Application object for state storage is as simple as indexing the Application object. For example:

```
Application["Start"] = DateTime.Now;
```

This will add the current date and time to the Application cache, indexed by `Start`. To extract the value, you use the same indexing scheme; but the application stores objects, so casting is required:

```
DateTime appStart = (DateTime)Application["Start"];
```

Because object storage is supported, you can store complex types, such as data. For example, a common caching pattern is to check to see if the data is in the cache (irrespective of which form of caching is used), and if it's present, return the data. If the data isn't present in the cache, it is fetched from its original location and stored in the cache. For example, consider some data from a database that is required in all pages, which could be stored in the application, as shown in Listing 6.1.

Listing 6.1. Storing Data in the Application

```
DataTable cachedData = (DataTable)Application["CommonData"];
if (cachedData == null)
{
  cachedData = DataLayer.FetchCommonData();
  Application["CommonData"] = cachedData;
}
```

Here the data is fetched from the `Application`, which returns `null` if the item isn't present, and if it isn't present, then it is fetched from the data layer and placed in the `Application` for subsequent requests. When using this form of caching, you have to balance the resource use (when storing the data in the application) against the time taken to fetch it from its original location. Performance and memory monitoring tools are useful in helping you make this decision.

If you know that every single page is going to use some cached data, you can use the `Application_Start` event to load the data, because this event runs once when the application starts. In this situation, you wouldn't need to check for the cached item, because you know it wouldn't be present when the application is just starting. If, however, only a selected number of pages use the cached data, or if use of the cached data is dependent upon user actions, you can use the code in Listing 6.1 to lazy load the data—that is, load it only when it is first requested and then cache it for later use.

Using the Session State

Session state is similar in use to Application state, but with one major exception: It is unique to each user of the site and is destroyed when the user leaves the site (after a timeout). Session state is therefore useful for storing data that a user would require throughout his or her use of the application. Bear in mind that Session state is intended for storage of transient data—data that doesn't need to be retained after the user leaves the site. For long-lived data, such as user preferences, you should use the Profile.

Listing 6.2 shows a common pattern for using the Session object for state storage.

Listing 6.2. Storing Data in the Session

```
DataTable cachedData = (DataTable)Session["UserData"];
if (cachedData == null)
{
  cachedData = DataLayer.FetchUserData();
  Session["UserData"] = cachedData;
}
```

Like the Application state, Session state takes resources, so you should examine your needs carefully. By default, Session state is enabled for applications and pages but can be turned off or disabled completely.

Disabling Session State

Disabling Session state is a performance optimization that you can perform at several levels. In pages, you can use the `EnableSessionState` attribute of the `Page` directive:

```
<% Page EnableSessionState="false" ... %>
```

Alternatively, if you require access to Session state but don't plan to update it, you can make it read-only for a page:

```
<% Page EnableSessionState="ReadOnly" ... %>
```

This ensures that you still have access, but don't go through the overhead of locking the state for update.

Configuring Session State

At the application level, you configure Session state in web.config, as seen in Listing 6.3.

The attributes are documented in Table 6.1.

You can see that there are a number of ways in which Session state can be stored. By default, the ASP.NET process stores the state, because this provides the fastest storage. However, because it is process-bound, Session state would not survive an application restart, which is where the state server and

Listing 6.3. Session State Configuration

```
<sessionState
  allowCustomSqlDatabase="[true|false]"
  cookieless="[AutoDetect|UseCookies|UseDeviceProfile|
              UseUri|true|false]"
  cookieName="String"
  customProvider="String"
  mode="[Custom|InProc|Off|StateServer|SQLServer|]"
  partitionResolverType="String"
  regenerateExpiredSessionId="[true|false]"
  sessionIdManagerType="String"
  sqlCommandTimeout="Integer"
  sqlConnectionString="String"
  stateConnectionString="String"
  stateNetworkTimeout="Integer"
  timeout="Integer"
  useHostingIdentity="[true|false]"
  >
  <providers>
    <clear />
    <add
      Name="String"
      Type="String"
      [providerSpecificConfiguration] />
  </providers>
</sessionState>
```

database options come in. The downsides of these, however, are that performance is slower than with the in-process method. For more detailed information on session state and performance, there is an excellent article in the MSDN Magazine, available online at **http://msdn.microsoft.com/msdnmag/issues/05/09/SessionState/default.aspx**.

> The SessionState configuration element should not be confused with the SessionPageState element, which is used to keep a history of view state and control state within the session.

Using HttpContext

If you don't need to store data across an entire session, but perhaps require data across multiple user controls within a page, then you can use the current context of the request. Each request has an associated HttpContext object associated with it, which provides access to many objects used within pages, such as the Request, Profile, and Trace. Also available on the context is an

TABLE 6.1: Attributes of SessionState Configuration

Attribute	Description
allowCustomSqlDatabase	Only relevant when mode is set to SQLServer, and indicates whether or not a custom database name can be specified in the Initial Catalog attribute of the SQL Server connection string. The default value is false, meaning the default ASP.NET session database is used.
cookieless	Indicates how cookies are used, and can be one of: AutoDetect, where ASP.NET determines whether the requesting device supports cookies. If so, then cookies are used; otherwise the query string is changed to include the session identifier. UseCookies, where cookies are always used. This is the default value. UseDeviceProfile, where ASP.NET uses the browser capabilities to determine whether cookies should be used. UseUri, where the query string is always used. true, which has the same effect as UseUri. false, which has the same effect as UseCookies.
cookieName	Defines the default cookie name used to store the session ID. The default value is ASP.NET_SessionId.
customProvider	Indicates the name of the provider when the mode is Custom. The name attribute should match one of the provider names declared in the <Providers/> section, and defaults to an empty string.
mode	Indicates how session state is being managed, and can be one of: Custom, which indicates that session state is stored in a custom manner. InProc, where session state is stored within the ASP.NET process. This is the default value. Off, where session state is turned off for the application. SQLServer, where session state is stored in a SQL Server database. StateServer, where session state is stored in a separate ASP.NET State Service.

Attribute	Description
partitionResolverType	Defines a type to be used to resolve the connection string for the request. Resolvers are used to enable session state to be partitioned to scale in Web Farm situations. If this attribute is set, the sqlConnectionString and stateConnectionString attributes are ignored. The default value is an empty string.
regenerateExpired-SessionId	Indicates whether or not the session identifier will be reissued when an invalid identifier is used by the client. The default value is true, where identifiers are only reissued when cookies aren't being used.
sqlCommandTimeout	Indicates, in seconds, the timeout for a SQL command when the mode is SQLServer. The default value is 30.
sqlConnectionString	Indicates the name of the connection string when using SQL Server to store session state. The default value is "data source=127.0.0.1; Integrated Security=SSPI", pointing at a local, trusted SQL Server database.
stateConnectionString	Required when mode is StateServer, and defines the server name/address and port where session state is stored. The default value is "127.0.0.1:42424".
stateNetworkTimeout	For when mode is StateServer, and defines the number of seconds to wait for the remote state server before the request is cancelled. The default value is 10 seconds.
timeout	Defines the number of minutes to wait after session activity (i.e., idle time) before the session is abandoned. The default value is 20 minutes.
useHostingIdentity	Indicates whether or not session state will revert to the hosting identity or use client impersonation. The default value is true, indicating that the identity of the hosting process (ASPNET on IIS5 or NETWORK SERVER on IIS6) or the identity specified in the process ‹identity› section is used. If false, the credentials of the current OS thread are used.

`Items` collection that can be used for storage and is particularly useful when you have multiple user controls on a page that need to share data. It is important to realize that this technique is only useful between controls within a single end-to-end request and that it does not apply between separate page requests.

For example, consider two grids that use the same data. You could use the data source controls and their built-in caching, but if you have an existing code library and need to bind in code, you might have the code shown in Listing 6.4 in both user controls:

Listing 6.4. Simple Binding to a Business Layer

```
protected void Page_Load(object sender, EventArgs e)
{
  if (!Page.IsPostBack)
  {
    GridView3.DataSource = Shippers.GetShippers();
    GridView3.DataBind();
  }
}
```

This code, if used in multiple user controls, would result in the same SQL command being run multiple times. There are several ways to cure this, and we'll look at others later in the chapter, but a simple solution would be for one control to read the data and cache it in the context. Rather than explicitly putting the code into your user control (which would limit the order of the controls on the page to ensure that the one that cached the data was executed first), you could create a central class, as shown in Listing 6.5.

Listing 6.5. A Caching Class Using the HttpContext

```
public static class Caching
{
  public static List<Shipper> GetShippers()
  {
    List<Shipper> ships =
        (List<Shipper>)HttpContext.Current.Items["Shippers"];
    if (ships == null)
    {
      ships = Shippers.GetItems();
      HttpContext.Current.Items["Shippers"] = ships;
    }
    return ships;
  }
}
```

This code is extremely simple and follows the by-now familiar pattern used in caching. It first fetches the data from the `Items` collection, and if it's not present in the cache, gets the data from the Shippers business class and stores it in the `Items` collection. Subsequent calls will fetch it from the collection.

Using ViewState

Another method of caching data is to use ViewState, although this does come with the warning that ViewState is transferred to and from the client on each request. The ViewState can be accessed just like other collections:

```
ViewState["CachedData"] = DateTime.Now;
```

You should generally try to use as little ViewState caching as possible in order to reduce overheads in transferring pages, but it does provide an alternative storage mechanism for small amounts of data. For best performance, you should turn off ViewState for controls and pages that don't require it. ASP.NET 2.0 supports a new feature for state storage, Control-State, which controls use to support the minimum state requirements for the control to operate. This allows ViewState to be turned off but for the control to still operate correctly.

Output Caching

The idea behind output caching is that if an ASP.NET page hasn't changed, why go through the process of recompilation and execution? Why not, after the page has been run for the first time, just store the HTML it generated, and when the page is requested again, just return the HTML? Less processing on the server means more pages can be served, and those people requesting cached pages get them quicker.

Of course, the issue you have is that pages are often dynamic; they contain server controls, user controls, and data, and maybe some part of the page changes with every request, meaning if it was cached, users would always see the same page they saw after the first request. A similar issue comes into play when pages contain data from a database, where you can cache the page, but what happens if the data changes? The users would see stale data.

All of these problems are solved by the ASP.NET caching framework, along with SQL Server (both 2000 and 2005) to help with the data side of things. The downside of caching is that it consumes memory, since the cache is memory-based, but a Least Recently Used (LRU) algorithm is used, meaning that items in the cache that are accessed infrequently can be removed from the cache. This ensures that the cache does not consume more memory than necessary.

The caching framework is flexible and has the notion of cache dependencies, where items in the cache can be dependent upon external conditions; when the conditions change, items can be removed from the cache. Items in the cache can be dependent upon:

- A time, so that after a certain time (either fixed or sliding) they can be removed from the cache
- A file, so if the file changes, the item can be removed from the cache
- A key, so if another item in the cache changes, the item can be removed from the cache
- A data query, so that if the underlying data the page is dependent upon changes, the item can be removed from the cache

Which method you use depends upon your requirements, but as a general rule, caching can bring huge improvements in performance and scalability.

Configuring Output Caching

The simplest caching solution is output caching, where the output of the page, or user control, is cached. The page output is the HTML that is sent back to the user, hence the term "output caching." Caching page output can be easily enabled by use of the OutputCache directive at the top of the page or user control:

```
<%@ OutputCache %>
```

The attributes that can be added to this directive are shown in Table 6.2.

TABLE 6.2: Attributes of the OutputCache Directive

Attribute	Description
CacheProfile	The page is cached depending upon the settings defined in the outputCacheSettings section of web.config. This attribute is not supported for user controls.
Duration	The time, in seconds, that the page is cached for. Once this time is exceeded, the page is evicted from the cache.
Location	The location where caching takes place. Can be one of the following `OutputCacheLocation` values: `Any`, indicating the output cache can be on the client browser, a proxy server, or on the ASP.NET server. `Client`, indicating the cache can be located on the client browser. `Downstream`, indicating the cache can be located on any HTTP 1.1 cache-capable server. `None`, indicating the output cache is disabled for the page. `Server`, indicating the cache is located on the ASP.NET server processing the request. `ServerAndClient`, indicating the cache can be located only at the client browser or the ASP.NET server.
NoStore	Indicates whether or not secondary cache stores cache sensitive information. This attribute is not supported for user controls.
Shared	Indicates whether or not user control output can be shared across multiple pages. The default is `False`.
SqlDependency	When using SQL Server 2005, a value of `CommandNotification` indicates that caching takes place until a notification is received from SQL Server 2005 indicating that the data set the page is based upon has changed. When using SQL Server 2000, this attribute contains a set of database and table names, indicating that caching takes place until any data in the named tables changes.

(Continued)

Table 6.2: (Continued)

Attribute	Description
VaryByControl	The page is cached depending upon a semicolon-separated list of control IDs representing the values upon which to cache. This attribute is only supported in user controls, and is required unless `VaryByParam` is used.
VaryByCustom	Indicates that the page is cached depending upon custom requirements. The custom requirements can be implemented by overriding the `Http-Application.GetVaryByCustomString` method in the global.asax file. A variation of custom requirements is if the string browser is used, in which case caching is depending upon the browser name and major version.
VaryByHeader	The page is cached depending upon a semicolon-separated list of HTTP headers. This affects HTTP 1.1 cache locations. This attribute is not supported in user controls.
VaryByParam	The page is cached according to a semicolon-separated list of query string or post values. This attribute is required, and to ignore any values use an empty string, or a * to cache on all values.

For example, consider a grid that shows categories, each of which has a link to another page to show more of the products for that category, perhaps identified with a link such as:

```
<asp:TemplateField>
  <ItemTemplate>
    <a href='<%#Eval("CategoryID",
       "ViewProducts.aspx?CategoryID={0}")%>'
       target="_blank">View Products</a>
  </ItemTemplate>
</asp:TemplateField>
```

The ViewProductsl.aspx page could cache its output depending upon the `CategoryID` passed in, so that multiple requests for the same product would be served from the cache:

```
<%@ Page Language = "C#" … %>
<%@ %@ OutputCache Duration = "30" VaryByParam="CategoryID" %>
```

The first time the page is processed, the output is cached. Subsequent requests with the same `CategoryID` would be served from the cache, but a different `CategoryID` would result in the page being rerun and the output also being cached. Now, there would be two items in the cache, and more would be added as different categories were viewed. You can easily test caching by adding a date and time at the top of the page, perhaps with the following line of code:

```
<% =DateTime.Now %>
```

Since this would only be executed once, when the page is first processed, subsequent requests for the page (such as simply refreshing the browser) would show the same time. If you wait until the duration is up, the page will be evicted from the cache, and the next request will reprocess the page, resulting in a new date and time.

One important point to note is that the more items you have in the cache, the more memory your Web server uses and the less memory is available for dynamic use, such as for surges in requests. While caching can improve performance, you have to balance that performance with the additional resources it requires.

Caching Portions of a Page

The problem with caching is that the entire contents of the page are cached. There are, however, circumstances when you would like to only cache portions of a page, and there are two ways in which you can achieve this. You can use Control caching, or fragment caching, as it is sometimes called, to cache portions of the page, or you can use post-cache substitution to cache the entire page but have portions of it dynamic upon each request.

Control Caching

You implement control caching by placing the portions of the page you wish to be cached into user controls. This allows you to help with the balance between caching and resource usage, because those parts of the page that are intensive to generate, such as data-bound grids or Web Service-based data, can be cached, while the remaining server controls and HTML can be generated each time. You exploit user controls for this by simply removing those portions of a page that you wish to cache and placing them into a user control. You can then add the OutputCache attribute to the user control, as shown in Listing 6.6.

Listing 6.6. A Cached User Control

```
<%@ Control Language="C#" AutoEventWireup="true"
    CodeFile="CachedUserControl.ascx.cs"
    Inherits="ch05_CachedUserControl" %>
<%@ OutputCache Duration="30" VaryByParam="none" %>

<h2>Cached User Control</h2>
<p>
  This user control was cached at <% =DateTime.Now %>
</p>
```

Although there is no real content in this user control, it works as a simple case to show caching. The control has the OutputCache directive, and the content is simply some text with the current date and time. Consider another user control, shown in Listing 6.7, which isn't cached, but also shows the current date and time.

Listing 6.7. A Non-Cached User Control

```
<%@ Control Language="C#" AutoEventWireup="true"
    CodeFile="NonCachedUserControl.ascx.cs"
    Inherits="ch05_NonCachedUserControl" %>

<h2>Non-cached User Control</h2>
<p>
  This user control was not cached at <% =DateTime.Now %>
</p>
```

For these to work, the user controls simply need to be included on a page, as shown in Listing 6.8.

The result of the control caching is shown in Figure 6.1.

You can see that the date on the page heading is the same as for the non-cached control, while the cached user control shows a different date—the date the page was first requested. Refresh was pressed a few times, showing that the control is cached, but not the rest of the contents. In the examples just presented, the page and control cache durations were the

Listing 6.8. Using Cached and Non-Cached User Controls

```
<%Page Language ="C#" AutoEventWireup="true"
    CodeFile="FragmentCaching.aspx.cs"
    Inherits="ch05_FragmentCaching" Title="Untitled Page" %>

<%Register Src="CachedUserControl.ascx"
    TagName="CachedUserControl" TagPrefix="uc1" %>
<%Register Src="NonCachedUserControl.ascx"
    TagName="NonCachedUserControl" TagPrefix="uc2" %>

<html>
<form runat="server">

  <h1>
    Page generated at <% = DateTime.Now %></h1>
    <uc1:CachedUserControl id="CachedUserControl1" runat="server" />

  <br /><br />

  <uc2:NonCachedUserControl ID="NonCachedUserControl1"
    runat="server" />

</form>
</html>
```

same, but there is no requirement for this to be the case; different values
are perfectly acceptable depending upon your caching requirements.

Post-Cache Substitution

For the opposite situation, you can use post-cache substitution, where most
of the page is cached but some portions aren't. A good example of this is

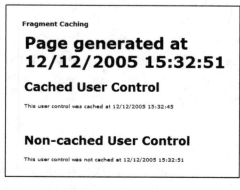

FIGURE 6.1: Control caching in action

advertisements, where each page request should show a new advertisement, even if the rest of the page is cached. This is in fact what the AdRotator control does.

Post-cache substitution is designed for use at the control level, where the control decides that its content should not be cached. It works like this: The control implements a dynamic rendering function in a callback that is registered with the response. The cached response keeps a marker to the content, which is replaced with your real content once the item is fetched from the cache and before it is sent to the client. This type of control caching is outside the scope of general caching techniques; for more information, see Nikhil Kothari's Weblog at http://www.nikhil.net/ -. Nikhil is a member of the ASP.NET team and has written a helper class that control developers can use to aid in post-cache substitution.

Disk Caching

We've mentioned that caching is always a compromise between speed of pages returned and resource usage of the server. Another form of caching is to cache the page output to disk, which reduces the memory overhead on the server. The trade-off here is that you don't have to go through the page regeneration, but you do still have file access.

Disk-based caching is not built in to ASP.NET 2.0, but there is a solution written by one of the members of the ASP.NET team that can improve performance if your request sizes are large. With memory-based caching, large requests would consume lots of memory, so as request size increases, disk caching becomes more viable.

Another great reason for disk caching is that the cache persists across restarts, which can reduce the time for pages to initially load.

Read more about disk caching on Dmitry's Weblog at http://blogs.msdn.com/dmitryr.

Configuring Caching

As well as configuring caching at the page level, you can also configure it globally in web.config, as shown in Listing 6.9, which details three sections. There is also a fourth section, SqlCacheDependency, which is covered in the section Configuring SQL Server 2000 Cache Invalidation in ASP.NET.

Listing 6.9. Cache Configuration

```
<caching>
  <cache
    disableExpiration="[true|false]"
    disableMemoryCollection ="[true|false]"
    percentagePhysicalMemoryUsedLimit="Integer"
    privateBytesLimit="Integer"
    privateBytesPollTime="Integer"
    />
  <outputCache
    enableFragmentCache="[true|false]"
    enableOutputCache="[true|false]"
    omitVaryStar="[true|false]"
    sendCacheControlHeader="[true|false]"
    />
  <outputCacheSettings>
    <outputCacheProfiles>
      <clear />
      <remove name="String" />
      <add enabled="[true|false]"
        name="String"
        duration="Integer"
        varyByControl="String"
        varyByHeader="String"
        sqlDependency="String"/>
    </outputCacheProfiles>
  </outputCacheSettings>
</caching>
```

The details for each of the elements and attributes are shown in Table 6.3, Table 6.4, and Table 6.5 respectively.

The cache section allows configuration of memory limits for caching, while the outputCache section allows configuration of output cache settings. Cache profiles are useful if you have common caching configurations that are used in multiple pages. To avoid having to modify every page with the same settings, you can configure a cache profile and use the CacheProfile attribute of the OutputCache page directive.

TABLE 6.3: Attributes for the Cache Element

Attribute	Description
disableMemoryCollection	When set to `true`, disables the collection of cache memory. The default value is `false`.
disableExpiration	When set to `true`, disables the expiration of items in the cache when memory pressure would normally expire them. The default value is `false`.
percentagePhysicalMemory-UsedLimit	Defines the maximum percentage of a machine's memory that will be used before expired items are flushed from the cache. The percentage includes the cache memory as well as application memory. The default value is 0, which allows ASP.NET to hueristically decide the value.
privateBytesLimit	Defines the maximum limit of an application's private memory before items are flushed from the cache. The default value is 0, which allows ASP.NET to hueristically decide the value.
privateBytesPollTime	Defines the time interval, as a TimeSpan, between polling for the applicaton's private memory usage.

TABLE 6.4: Attributes for the OutputCache Element

Attribute	Description
enableFragmentCache	Indicates whether or not fragment caching is enabled. The default value is `true`.
enableOutputCache	Indicates whether or not output caching is enabled. When disabled, the `OutputCache` page directive is ignored, and cache-control headers are added to the response to indicate that upstream proxies and clients should to cache the output. The default value is `true`.
omitVaryStar	Indicates whether or not an HTTP "`Vary: *`" header is added to the response. The default value is `false`.
sendCacheControlHeader	Indicates whether or not the "`cache-control:private`" header is added to the response. The default value is `false`.

TABLE 6.5: Attributes for the OutputCacheSettings Element

Attribute	Description
duration	Defines the amount of time in seconds that a page is stored in the cache.
enabled	Indicates whether or not the output cache is enabled for this profile.
location	Defines where the cached output can be stored. Can be one of: `Any`, `Client`, `Downstream`, `None`, `Server`, `ServerAndClient`.
name	Defines the name of the profile.
noStore	Indicates whether or not the `"Cache-control: no-store"` header is added to the response.
sqlDependency	Defines the SQL Dependency for the cache profile. SQL Dependencies are covered in the Data Caching section.
varyByControl	Defines the ID of the user control, or a semicolon-separated list containing IDs of multiple user controls, that is to be cached.
varyByHeader	Defines the semicolon-separated list of HTTP headers used to vary the cached output.
varyByCustom	Defines the custom function used to vary the cached output.
varyByParam	Defines the semicolon-separated list of parameters used to vary the cached output.

Data Caching

One of the greatest performance benefits can be achieved with caching of data, the fetching of which always involves some form of overhead. For XML files, this is the file system, and for databases, it is the connection and physical extraction of the data. Two types of data are generally displayed in Web pages: data that changes often, and data that doesn't change often. If the data doesn't change often, there is no point in going through the expensive operation of connecting to the database to get the data and using valuable database resources. A better solution would be to cache the data, thus saving the time and resources of the database server.

The problem with caching data, or even caching entire ASP.NET pages that have database-driven data on them, is what to do if the data changes. In fact, how do you even know if the data has changed? ASP.NET 2.0 provides features that allow its built-in cache to be invalidated when data changes so that the page is regenerated. This brings the best of both worlds—fresh data, but cached for increased performance.

The features of cache invalidation depend upon the database server, and both SQL Server 2000 and 2005 support this, although with different features.

SQL Cache Invalidation with SQL Server 2005

SQL Server 2005 supports notifications via a service broker—a feature that allows it to notify client applications when data has changed. This can be combined with ASP.NET's cache so that pages can be notified when the data they rely upon changes. When the data changes, SQL Server notifies ASP.NET, the page is evicted from the cache, and the next request will see the page regenerated with the fresh data.

Cache invalidation works with both SQL Server 2005 and the Express editions, but with the Express edition it will only work if user instancing is not used. That means that you cannot have the User Instance=true keywords in your connection string, and that you must have an attached database.

In operation, SQL Server cache invalidation is seamless, but it does require some initial setup.

Cache Invalidation Setup

The setup required depends upon how you connect to SQL Server and whether the user is a database owner (and hence has administrative rights in the database). Whatever permissions the user has, there is a one-time setup, involving ensuring that the database is at the correct version number and that the service broker endpoint is created.

For new databases, the version number will be correct, but for old databases that you have attached, it may not be. You can check this by issuing the sp_helpdb command in a new query, which will return a list of all

	name	db_size	compatibility_level	owner	dbid	created	status
1	AdventureWorks	165.94 MB	90	HUNDRED-ACRE\davids	5	Nov 29 2005	Status=ONLINE, Updateability=READ_WRITE, UserAcc...
2	FullServer	4.00 MB	90	HUNDRED-ACRE\davids	8	Dec 9 2005	Status=ONLINE, Updateability=READ_WRITE, UserAcc...
3	IllustratedASPNET20	5.50 MB	80	HUNDRED-ACRE\davids	6	Nov 30 2005	Status=ONLINE, Updateability=READ_WRITE, UserAcc...
4	master	5.25 MB	90	sa	1	Apr 8 2003	Status=ONLINE, Updateability=READ_WRITE, UserAcc...
5	model	3.19 MB	90	sa	3	Apr 8 2003	Status=ONLINE, Updateability=READ_WRITE, UserAcc...
6	msdb	7.44 MB	90	sa	4	Oct 14 2005	Status=ONLINE, Updateability=READ_WRITE, UserAcc...
7	Northwind	7.75 MB	90	HUNDRED-ACRE\davids	7	Nov 30 2005	Status=ONLINE, Updateability=READ_WRITE, UserAcc...
8	tempdb	9.56 MB	90	sa	2	Dec 7 2005	Status=ONLINE, Updateability=READ_WRITE, UserAcc...

FIGURE 6.2: The move toward managed execution

databases and associated details, as shown in Figure 6.2. Here you can see the list of databases; one of the columns is compatibility_level, which must be 90 for the service broker to work.

You can upgrade the compatibility level of a database by executing the following simple command:

```
exec sp_dbcmptlevel 'Northwind', '90'
```

You simply supply the database name and the level to upgrade to. When the version is correct, you can create the broker endpoint, using the script shown in Listing 6.10.

Listing 6.10. Creating a Broker Endpoint in SQL Server 2005

```
USE master
GO
CREATE ENDPOINT BrokerEndpoint
    STATE = STARTED
    AS TCP ( LISTENER_PORT = 4037 )
    FOR SERVICE_BROKER ( AUTHENTICATION = WINDOWS )
GO

ALTER DATABASE Northwind SET ENABLE_BROKER;
GO
```

This script is available as CreateAndEnableServiceBroker.sql in the databases directory of the downloadable samples.

If you are connecting to SQL Server as a trusted user, such as using integrated security, and that user has administrative rights, then this is all you require for the configuration. If you're not an administrative user, whether using integrated security or not, then you need to grant the database user additional permissions.

Cache Invalidation Setup for Non-Administrative Connections

For non-administrative users, the setup is also a one-time affair, but it is necessary to grant permissions so that the user can create the required objects. For this, you should run the script detailed in Listing 6.11.

Listing 6.11. Granting Permissions for SQL Notifications

```
— sql_dependencey_subscriber role in SQL Server
EXEC sp_addrole 'sql_dependency_subscriber'

— Permissions needed for users to use the Start method
GRANT CREATE PROCEDURE to startUser
GRANT CREATE QUEUE to startUser
GRANT CREATE SERVICE to startUser
GRANT REFERENCES on CONTRACT::
[http://schemas.microsoft.com/SQL/Notifications/PostQueryNotification]
to startUser
GRANT VIEW DEFINITION TO startUser

— Permissions needed for users to Execute
GRANT SELECT to executeUser
GRANT SUBSCRIBE QUERY NOTIFICATIONS TO executeUser
GRANT RECEIVE ON QueryNotificationErrorsQueue TO executeUser
GRANT REFERENCES on CONTRACT::
[http://schemas.microsoft.com/SQL/Notifications/PostQueryNotification]
to executeUser
EXEC sp_addrolemember 'sql_dependency_subscriber', 'executeUser'
```

This script is available as EnableServiceBrokerNonAdmin.sql in the databases directory of the downloadable samples.

Three sections appear in Listing 6.11. The first simply creates a new role for the subscriber of notifications. The second creates the permissions for the user to execute the Start method—this is something we'll be covering soon. The third section creates permissions for the user executing the database query. The *startUser* and *executeUser* can be the same user and can be a Windows user account (such as ASPNET) or an explicit SQL Server user account.

If the user doesn't have correct permissions, then you may see an error such as:

```
Cannot find the contract
'http://schemas.microsoft.com/SQL/Notifications/PostQueryNotification
', because it does not exist or you do not have permission.
Invalid object name 'SqlQueryNotificationService-d1963e55-3e62-4d54-
b9ca-b4c02c9e6291'.
```

Query Syntax

Once the database and permissions have been configured, you can start using SQL notifications, but one important point to note is that the syntax used for the query must follow certain conditions. The first is that you cannot use * to represent all columns—columns must be explicitly named. The second is that the table name must be qualified with its owner. For example:

```
SELECT ProductID, ProductName FROM dbo.Products
```

If you think you have everything configured correctly, but your pages don't seem to be evicted from the cache when you change the data, then you need to check the query as well as the database compatibility version (see Figure 6.2). Once permissions are correct, you will not see any exceptions regarding cached pages dependent upon SQL data, because failures happen silently.

Using SQL Server 2005 Cache Invalidation

Using the SQL Server 2005 cache invalidation is extremely simple, because you use the same features as you use for standard page caching, but this time you add the `SqlDependency` attribute:

```
<%@ OutputCache Duration="30" VaryByParam="none"
    SqlDependency="CommandNotification" %>
```

The page would now be output-cached, but a dependency would be created on any data commands within the page. Using `CommandNotification` means that the page is cached until notified by SQL server. For example, consider Listing 6.12, which has output caching enabled, based on SQL commands. The data source and grid controls contain no additions to take care of the caching, and were there more data controls with different queries, then a change to either data source would result in the page being evicted from the cache.

Listing 6.12. Caching Based on SQL Commands

```
<%@ Page Language="C#" … %>
<% OutputCache Duration="30" VaryByParam="none"
   SqlDependency="CommandNotification" %>

<html>
<form>

  <h1><%=DateTime.Now %></h1>

  <asp:SqlDataSource ID="SqlDataSource1" runat="server"
    ConnectionString="<%$ConnectionStrings:NorthwindConnectString%>"
    SelectCommand="SELECT [ProductID], [ProductName], [UnitsInStock],
                  [UnitsOnOrder] FROM [dbo].[Products]'>
  </asp:SqlDataSource>

  <asp:GridView ID="GridView1" runat="server"
    AutoGenerateColumns="False" DataKeyNames="ProductID"
    DataSourceID="SqlDataSource1" AllowPaging="True">
    <Columns>
      <asp:BoundField DataField="ProductID" HeaderText="ProductID"
        InsertVisible="False" ReadOnly="True" />
      <asp:BoundField DataField="ProductName"
        HeaderText="ProductName" SortExpression="ProductName" />
      <asp:BoundField DataField="UnitsInStock"
        HeaderText="UnitsInStock" SortExpression="UnitsInStock" />
      <asp:BoundField DataField="UnitsOnOrder"
        HeaderText="UnitsOnOrder" SortExpression="UnitsOnOrder" />
    </Columns>
  </asp:GridView>
</form>
</html>
```

This scenario can easily be tested by calling the page and clicking **Refresh**. The date should remain the same. But if you modify a row in the Products table and then click **Refresh**, the page will be updated with a new date. Because this query selects all rows, any change to the underlying data will result in the cache being invalidated. However, if the query had a WHERE clause, invalidation would only take place if the changed data was part of the set of rows returned by the query; changes to rows not part of the query have no effect upon the cache.

If you wish to cache only the data on a page, you have two options. You can wrap the data (data source and grid) up in a user control and use fragment caching, or you can add the caching dependency to the data source control directly and remove it from the page, as shown in Listing 6.13.

Listing 6.13. Adding Caching to the SqlDataSource Control

```
<asp:SqlDataSource ID="SqlDataSource1" runat="server"
  EnableCaching="true" SqlCacheDependency="CommandNotification"
  CacheDuration="30"
  ConnectionString="<%$ ConnectionStrings:NorthwindConnectString %>"
  SelectCommand="SELECT [ProductID], [ProductName], [UnitsInStock],
              [UnitsOnOrder] FROM [dbo].[Products]">
</asp:SqlDataSource>
```

In effect, this is similar to fragment caching for any controls on the page that are bound to the data source.

Caching Using Business and Data Layers

If you wish to use a business or data layer to abstract your data access code, caching can still be used, and there are two ways to achieve this. The first is to use output caching and have the page dependent upon the data, and the second is to only cache the data. For the first option, you use the same method as previously shown, adding the OutputCache directive to the page with the SqlCacheDependency attribute set to CommandNotification. An ObjectDataSource control can be used to fetch the data from the data layer, as shown in Listing 6.14.

Listing 6.14. Caching Using Data Layers

```
<%  Page Language="C#" … %>
<%  OutputCache Duration="30" VaryByParam="none"
    SqlDependency="CommandNotification" %>

<html>
<form>

  <h1><%=DateTime.Now %></h1>

  <asp:ObjectDataSource ID="ObjectDataSource1" runat="server"
      SelectMethod="Read" TypeName="ProductsDataLayer">
  </asp:ObjectDataSource>
  <asp:GridView ID="GridView1" runat="server"
    DataSourceID="ObjectDataSource1" AllowPaging="true" />

</form>
</html>
```

The data layer simply fetches the data, as shown in Listing 6.15.

Listing 6.15. A Data Class Used in a Cached Page

```
public static class ProductsDataLayer
{
  public static DataTable Read2()
  {
    using (SqlConnection conn = new
        SqlConnection(ConfigurationManager.ConnectionStrings[
        "NorthwindConnectString"].ConnectionString))
    {
      conn.Open();
      SqlCommand cmd = new SqlCommand("usp_GetProductsOrdered",
                                      conn);
      cmd.CommandType = CommandType.StoredProcedure;
      DataTable tbl = new DataTable();

      tbl.Load(cmd.ExecuteReader(CommandBehavior.CloseConnection));

      return tbl;
    }
  }
}
```

The query can be a SQL statement or a stored procedure, as long as the actual SQL statement follows the rules for query notifications—explicit column names and two-part table names. In addition, you should not use SET NOCOUNT ON in a stored procedure or the rowset will not be cacheable.

If you do not wish to place cache details within the page, it can be done programmatically by way of the SqlCacheDependencyClass and a method on the Response object. For example, consider Listing 6.16, which returns a DataTable, perhaps as a function within a page. Here the SqlCacheDependency object is created explicitly, with the SqlCommand object passed in as a parameter. This creates a dependency based upon the command. The dependency is then added to the list of dependencies of the ASP.NET cache using the AddCacheDependency method.

As well as adding items to the cache, the API also exposes other features. For example:

```
Response.Cache.SetExpires(DateTime.Now.AddSeconds(30));
Response.Cache.SetCacheability(HttpCacheability.Public) ;
Response.AddCacheDependency(dependency);
```

Listing 6.16. SqlCacheDependency from Code

```
using (SqlConnection conn = new
    SqlConnection(ConfigurationManager.ConnectionStrings[
    "NorthwindConnectString"].ConnectionString))
{
  conn.Open();
  SqlCommand cmd = new SqlCommand("usp_GetProductsOrdered", conn);
  cmd.CommandType = CommandType.StoredProcedure;
  DataTable tbl = new DataTable();

  SqlCacheDependency dependency = new SqlCacheDependency(cmd);

  tbl.Load(cmd.ExecuteReader(CommandBehavior.CloseConnection));
  Response.AddCacheDependency(dependency);

  return tbl;
}
```

If this code is in a class in the App_Code directory, the Response can be accessed with the HttpContext object:

```
HttpContext.Current.Response.AddCacheDependency(dependency);
```

This is not something you'd want to explicitly do in business or data layers though, because it ties the method to the interface, which could reduce reuse of this code for other scenarios.

Another method of caching is to cache only the data, leaving the page uncached. This works in a similar way to fragment caching, or adding the cache details to the data source control.

Listing 6.17 shows a standard pattern for caching using the Cache object of ASP.NET; the Cache object is the API into the underlying caching mechanism, so you can manipulate it directly as well as through page and control attributes.

In the ReadCached method, the first action is to check the Cache for an item; the cache provides a simple dictionary approach, so items can be accessed by a key value, Products in this case. If the item doesn't exist in the cache, the command is executed to fetch the data; note that a SqlDependency is explicitly created (and it has to be created before the command is executed). Once the data has been fetched, it is placed into the cache using the Insert method; the first parameter is the key, the second is the data being stored, and the third is the dependency. Once stored in the cache, the data is returned. The final code line will only execute if the item is already in the cache, so the Get method is used to fetch the item using its key value. The item is returned from the cache as an Object and thus has to be cast to its original data type, a DataTable.

Listing 6.17. Explicitly Caching Data

```
public static class ProductsDataLayer
{
  public static DataTable ReadCached()
  {
    if (HttpContext.Current.Cache["Products"] == null)
    {
      using (SqlConnection conn = new
        SqlConnection(ConfigurationManager.ConnectionStrings[
        "NorthwindConnectString"].ConnectionString))
      {
        conn.Open();
        SqlCommand cmd = new SqlCommand("usp_GetProductsOrdered",
                                        conn);
        cmd.CommandType = CommandType.StoredProcedure;
        DataTable tbl = new DataTable();

        SqlCacheDependency dependency = new SqlCacheDependency(cmd);

        tbl.Load(cmd.ExecuteReader(CommandBehavior.CloseConnection));

        HttpContext.Current.Cache.Insert("Products",
          tbl, dependency);

        return tbl;
      }
    }
    return (DataTable)HttpContext.Current.Cache.Get("Products");
  }
}
```

This code doesn't affect the page caching but uses the same mechanism. If the data changes, the cache receives notification from SQL Server, and the item is evicted from the cache.

SQL Cache Invalidation with SQL Server 2000

Caching using SQL Server 7 and 2000 uses many of the same constructs as for SQL Server 2005, but works in a different way. The first thing to note is that SQL Server 2000 does not use notifications, which means that caching is polling-based. The database isn't continuously polled, so there is no huge overhead. It works like this:

- You have to explicitly enable caching on a database and table level.
- A new table is created that has one entry for each table upon which cache dependencies exist. There is only one row per enabled table, so the number of rows in this table will never exceed the number of tables in the database.
- Triggers are added to tables enabled for caching, so that data changes result in an update to the notifications table.
- A background thread in ASP.NET polls the change notifications table for changes. If a row in the change notifications table has changed, then the page dependent upon this table is evicted from the cache.

The second point to note is that with SQL Server 2000, cache invalidation is based upon any changes to the entire table. So even changes to rows that are not part of the result set you are displaying will affect the page cache.

Enabling SQL Server 2000 for Cache Invalidation

To enable SQL Server 2000 for cache invalidation, you need to run a command line tool, aspnet_regsql, stored in the framework directory (\WINDOWS\Microsoft.NET\Framework\v2.0.50727). This tool has several uses, including adding application services such as membership and personalization to databases, and there are a number of command-line switches. The options for cache invalidation are shown in Table 6.6.

Enabling a Database for Cache Invalidation

Before a database table can participate in SQL cache invalidation, both the database and table must be enabled. To enable a database on a machine, use the following command:

```
aspnet_regsqlcache.exe -U [user] -P [password] -ed -d [database]
```

TABLE 6.6: Options for aspnet_regsql

Flag	Description
−?	Displays a help listing of the various flags supported by the tool.
−S	Names the SQL Server to connect to. This can be either the computer name or the IP address.
−U	Names the user to connect as when using SQL Server Authentication (e.g., the SQL Server administrator account, sa).
−P	Used in conjunction with the −U flag to specify the user's password.
−E	Connects to the SQL Server when using Windows Authentication and the current user has administrator capabilities on the database. The −U and −P flags are not needed when using −E.
−t	Specifies the table to apply necessary changes for SQL Server cache invalidation to.
−d	Specifies the database to apply changes for SQL Server cache invalidation to.
−ed	Enables a database for SQL cache dependency. This requires the −d option.
−dd	Disables a database for SQL cache dependency. This requires the −d option.
−et	Enables a table for SQL cache dependency. This requires the −t option.
−dt	Disables a table for SQL cache dependency. This requires the −t option.
−lt	Lists all tables enabled for SQL cache dependency.

If you have a separate database server and don't have ASP.NET 2.0 installed, then you can enable the database on any server and simply move the database files to the database server.

Figure 6.3 shows an example of enabling a SQL Server running on the local machine. The −E flag is used for Windows authentication. The −ed flag is used to enable the database, and the database is specified with the −d flag. This creates a new table named `AspNet_SqlCacheTables-ForChangeNotification`.

FIGURE 6.3: Enabling a database for SQL cache invalidation

This new table contains the columns shown in Table 6.7.

Now that the database is enabled for change notifications, you need to enlist tables that you wish to watch for changes.

Enabling a Table for Cache Invalidation

After you enable the database for change notifications, you need to enlist selected tables for change notifications, and for this you use the –et and –t flags:

```
aspnet_regsqlcache.exe -U [user] -P [password] -et -t [table] -d
[database]
```

For example, if you want to enable the **Products** tables in the **Northwind** database, you execute `aspnet_regsql` as shown in Figure 6.4.

TABLE 6.7: Columns of AspNet_SqlCacheTablesForChangeNotification

Column	Description
tableName	Stores the name of all tables in the current database capable of participating in change notifications.
notificationCreated	Sets the timestamp indicating when the table was enabled for notifications.
changeId	Sets the numeric change ID incremented when a table is changed.

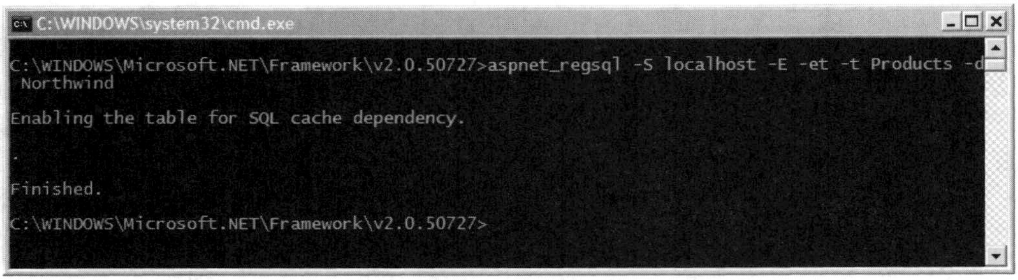

FIGURE 6.4: Enabling a table for SQL cache invalidation

This creates a trigger `Products_AspNet_SqlCacheNotification_ Trigger` on the `Products` table and also adds an entry into the `AspNet_ SqlCache TablesForChangeNotification` table for the `Products` table. Whenever data within the `Products` table is updated, inserted, or deleted, the trigger causes the `changeId` value stored in the `AspNet_SqlCache- TablesForChangeNotification` table to be incremented.

Configuring SQL Server 2000 Cache Invalidation in ASP.NET

When you use SQL Server 2000 cache invalidation, ASP.NET polls the database for changes. The information about the polling is defined in web.config, in the caching section, as shown in Listing 6.18.

Listing 6.18. SQL Server 2000 Cache Configuration

```
<caching>
  <sqlCacheDependency enabled="true" pollTime="10000">
    <databases>
      <add name="Northwind" connectionStringName="Northwind2000"
        pollTime="5000" />
    </databases>
  </sqlCacheDependency>
</caching>
```

The `SqlCacheDependency` section contains two attributes: `enabled`, to turn the feature on or off, and `pollTime`, which is the time in milliseconds between polls of the database. The `pollTime` defaults to `5000`. The databases sections details the databases upon which polling will take place, and follows the standard provider pattern of having add and remove elements. For add, the name is the key and doesn't have to correspond to the database being polled, although obviously a similar name makes sense. The `connectionStringName` identifies the connection string from the `connectionStrings` section, and `pollTime` specifies the polling time for this particular entry, overriding the `pollTime` set on the `sqlCacheDependency` element.

Using SQL Server 2000 Cache Invalidation in ASP.NET

The use of SQL Server 2000 for cache invalidation is similar to that for SQL Server 2005; the attributes and usage of controls is the same, but the dependency differs. For SQL Server 2000, instead of `CommandNotification`, you use the key name from the configuration and the table name, separated by a colon (:). For example:

```
<% OutputCache Duration="30" VaryByparam="note"
   SqlDependency="Northwind:Products" %>
```

In use, the page works exactly the same as for SQL Server 2005 notifications; upon first request, the page will be cached and will not be evicted from the cache until data has changed. Of course, the eviction doesn't happen immediately after the data changes but only after the poll time has elapsed.

The replacement of `CommandNotification` with the cache key and table applies to the API as well, when you create the `SqlCacheDependency`:

```
SqlCacheDependency dependency = new
   SqlCacheDependency("Northwind", "Products");
```

Here the first parameter is the key into the databases section of the caching configuration, and the second parameter is the table name.

How Polling Works

On the first poll, the list of notification-enabled tables is returned from the database. This list of tables is used to construct a cache entry for each table returned. Any dependencies requested through `SqlCacheDependency` are then made on this hidden cache entry. Thus, multiple `SqlCacheDependency` instances can be made for the same table, all dependent on one entry in the cache. When the table cache entry changes, it invalidates all dependent cache items.

The following is an example session (which assumes that the **Northwind** database and **Products** table are already configured for change notifications).

1. The user creates the page `default.aspx` and instructs the page to output to the cache and be dependent on the **Northwind** database's **Products** table.

2. The page is requested.

   a. `SqlCacheDependency` is created and polling begins.

   b. An entry in the cache is created for the **Products** table (e.g., `Products_Table`) by ASP.NET. This entry stores the `changeId` value returned from the database.

   c. The output-cached page is made dependent on the `Products_Table` cache entry.

3. The page is output cached and subsequent requests draw the page from the cache.

4. A sales manager updates the **Products** table for a new Web site special sale.

   a. The **Northwind Products** table changes and the `changeId` for this table is updated in the `AspNet_SqlCacheTablesForChangeNotification` table.

   b. The next poll by ASP.NET gets the new `changeId` value for the `Products` table.

   c. The `Products_Table` cache key is updated with the new `changeId` value, causing all dependent cache keys to be invalidated, including the `default.aspx` page.

5. The next request to the ASP.NET application causes the page to re-execute (because it is no longer in the output cache) and get added again.

The Cache API

Underpinning many of the caching features described in this chapter is the Cache API; it's the base set of caching classes that ASP.NET uses, which you can also use in your code. You'll find some of the concepts and patterns used here familiar, and some you've already seen in action, such as Listing 6.17. The Cache API revolves around two main objects, both from the System.Web.Caching namespace: `Cache` and `CacheDependency`.

At its simplest, the `Cache` can be used like other collection-based objects, because it has a default collection for its `Items` property, allowing items to be inserted and extracted by indexing into the collection. For example:

```
Cache["Shippers"] = Shippers.GetItems();

List<Shipper> = (List<Shipper>)Cache["Shippers"];
```

When adding items to the cache, you can also use the `Insert` method, which takes two parameters, the key and the object to cache. For example:

```
Cache.Insert("Shippers", Shippers.GetItems());
```

There is a `Get` method to fetch items, and a `Remove` method to delete items from the cache.

In use, the cache can follow the familiar pattern, and to see this in action, consider the `ShippersBusinessLayer` created in Chapter 5, which uses the `GetItemsInternal` method shown in Listing 6.19.

Listing 6.19. GetItemsInternal before Caching

```
private static List<Shipper> GetItemsInternal()
{
  List<Shipper> shippers = new List<Shipper>();
  DataTable tbl = ShipperDataLayer.GetShippers();

  foreach (DataRow row in tbl.Rows)
    shippers.Add(new Shipper((int)row["ShipperID"],
      row["CompanyName"].ToString(),
      row["Phone"].ToString()));

  return shippers;
}
```

Adding the basic level of caching into this would lead to Listing 6.20.

Listing 6.20. GetItemsInternal with Basic Caching

```
private static List<Shipper> GetItemsInternal()
{
  List<Shipper> shippers =
      List<Shipper>)HttpContext.Current.Cache["Shippers"]; ;
  DataTable tbl = ShipperDataLayer.GetShippers();
  if (shippers == null)
  {
    foreach (DataRow row in tbl.Rows)
      shippers.Add(new Shipper((int)row["ShipperID"],
        row["CompanyName"].ToString(),
        row["Phone"].ToString()));
    HttpContext.Current.Cache["Shippers"] = shippers;
  }

  return shippers;
}
```

Now the cache is checked for the shippers, and they are only fetched from the data layer if not in the cache.

Getting Items in the Cache to Expire

Items can be inserted into the cache and instructed to expire after a date or time has been reached. The date or time can be fixed, in which case the item is removed from the cache when the date and time arrives, or can be sliding, in which case the item is only removed from the cache if it hasn't been used for a given period of time. Both of these can be achieved using the `Insert` method, with the overloaded form having the following syntax:

```
Insert(Key, Item, Dependency, DateTime, TimeSpan)
```

The first two parameters are the same as shown previously—the cache key and the item to cache. The `Dependency` is a `CacheDependency` object, and we'll be coming to these later, but this can be `null` if no external dependency is required. The `DateTime` is the explicit date and time the cache entry is to expire, and `TimeSpan` is the date and time the cache entry is to expire, calculated from the last access of the item in the cache. These are mutually exclusive, so you can set one or the other to an enumeration to indicate which action is required. For example, to have absolute expiration, you could use the following:

```
Cache.Insert("Shippers", ships, null,
  DateTime.Now.AddSeconds(10),
  Cache.NoSlidingExpiration);
```

Here an explicit expiration point has been set at 10 seconds after the item was added to the cache; using `Cache.NoSlidingExpiration` means that the expiration time is absolute, irrespective of whether the item is being fetched from the cache frequently. Alternatively, you can specify a sliding expiration:

```
Cache.Insert("Shippers", ships, null,
  Cache.NoAbsoluteExpiration,
  TimeSpan.FromSeconds(10));
```

Here the absolute time is set to `Cache.NoAbsoluteExpiration`, to indicate a sliding expiration scheme is in use. The time span is set to 10 seconds from the last time the item was read from the cache. The advantage of sliding expiration is that it makes the most of caching, keeping items in the cache if they are frequently used, but evicting them if they are not.

The cache uses system memory, so there is always a trade-off in the performance it brings, and if you need to cache several items, you can specify additional parameters to indicate the priority of the cached item in relation to other cached items. For example:

```
Cache.Insert("Shippers", ships, null,
    Cache.NoAbsoluteExpiration,
    TimeSpan.FromSeconds(10),
    CacheItemPriority.AboveNormal, null);
```

Here an additional parameter indicates the priority of the item in the cache, and the value can be one of:

- AboveNormal, indicating items are less likely to be evicted than items with a Normal priority
- BelowNormal, indicating items are more likely to be evicted than items with a Normal priority
- Default, indicating the default priority for a cached item
- High, indicating items are least likely to be evicted
- Low, indicating items are most likely to be evicted
- Normal, indicating items are likely to be evicted after those with a Low or BelowNormal priority
- NotRemovable, indicating items will never be evicted from the cache

If you wish to use priorities, but don't wish to specify dates and times for eviction, then both the *DateTime* and *TimeSpan* parameters can be set to their respective enumeration values:

```
Cache.Insert("Shippers", ships, null,
    Cache.NoAbsoluteExpiration,
    Cache.NoSlidingExpiration,
    CacheItemPriority.AboveNormal, null);
```

The final parameter, which is null in the above code, is for a callback, allowing your code to be notified when an item is removed from the cache, which we'll look at later.

Making Cache Entries Depend upon External Factors

One problem with the code in Listing 6.20 is that since the items are cached, any changes to the underlying data won't get reflected in the data returned from the business layer—a problem you saw cured with the SQL Cache Dependencies object earlier in the chapter (Listing 6.16). This also affects other types of caching, where data comes from sources other than a database. XML files, for example, could be cached, but you'd want the item evicted from the cache when the file changes. Also, you may only want to cache items for a selected period of time, perhaps only while the item is being used, so that if it doesn't get used within a certain period of time it is evicted from the cache.

This is where cache dependencies come in, because you can make items in the cache dependent upon external factors such as files, times, or other items in the cache. For a cached item to be dependent upon something, you must use a `CacheDependency` object, which has a large number of over-loaded constructors. For example, to have a file-based dependency, you could use the code shown in Listing 6.21 to fetch an XML file.

Listing 6.21. File-Based Cache Dependency

```
public static DataSet GetXMLShippers()
{
  DataSet ships = (DataSet)HttpContext.Current.Cache["shippersXML"];
  if (ships == null)
  {
    string fileName =
          HttpContext.Current.Server.MapPath("shippers.xml");
    ships = new DataSet();
    ships.ReadXml(fileName);

    // create the dependency
    CacheDependency dep = new CacheDependency(fileName);
    HttpContext.Current.Cache.Insert("shippersXML", ships, dep);
  }

  return ships;
}
```

This uses the same `Insert` method to add an item to the cache but uses an overloaded form of Insert to pass a third parameter—the dependency. This is a `CacheDependency` object, created by passing in the filename that the item depends upon. When the item is inserted into the cache, the dependency keeps track of the file, and if the file changes, the item is evicted from the cache.

The CacheDependency object has a number of overloaded constructors, taking a variety of file names, dates, and other cache keys. For example, to have a dependency upon a file, you simply pass in the filename, or an array of filenames, for dependency upon more than one file):

```
CacheDependency dep = new CacheDependency(fileName);
```

Another form takes two string arrays; the first is an array of filenames, the second is an array of cache keys, so you can have a dependency upon multiple files, or other entries in the cache, thus chaining dependencies.

Multiple Cache Dependencies

Since the CacheDependency object has so many overloads for its constructor, a neater way to have multiple dependencies is to use the Aggregate-CacheDependency object, which allows you to package up the dependencies into a single aggregated object and then have the dependency based upon that. This aggregated class inherits from CacheDependency, so it just provides a way to have a single dependency to deal with and doesn't offer any features that CacheDependency doesn't have.

Being Notified When an Item in the Cache Expires

Removal notification allows you to identify when, and why, an item was removed from the cache, allowing you to perform a custom action, such as reloading the cached data if required. Within ASP.NET pages, this item isn't particularly useful, but it comes into its own when dealing with global data. For example, consider a Web site that displays a funny quote on each page, or a word of the day, the data of which is a sensible candidate for caching. You could load and cache this as the application starts, with a dependency, but how would you reload the data if it changed? The answer is a removal callback. For example, consider Listing 6.22, which depicts a simple static class to load word definitions into a string collection and to add new definitions to the file.

This could be loaded into the cache as the application starts, as shown in Listing 6.23. In the Application_Start event, the Words class is used to return the words, which are inserted into the cache with a dependency upon the file. The addition over earlier examples is the use of CacheItem-RemovedCallback, which defines the method to call when the item is removed from the cache. So, if the words file is updated, the string collection will be removed from the cache, and RefreshWords will be called.

Listing 6.22. The Words Class

```
public static class Words
{
  public static string WordsFile;

  static Words()
  {
    WordsFile =
      HttpContext.Current.Request.ServerVariables[
      "APPL_PHYSICAL_PATH"]
      + @"ch06\WordDefinitions.txt";
  }

  public static StringCollection ReadWords()
  {
    StringCollection words = new StringCollection();

    using (StreamReader rdr = new StreamReader(WordsFile))
    {
      string line;

      while ((line = rdr.ReadLine()) != null)
        words.Add(line);

      rdr.Close();
    }

    return words;
  }

  public static void Add(string word, string definition)
  {
    using (StreamWriter wrt = new StreamWriter(WordsFile, true))
    {
      wrt.WriteLine(word + ":" + definition);
      wrt.Close();
    }
  }
}
```

The signature of the callback, RefreshWords, must have the three parameters as defined here: the key of the item removed, the object removed, and the reason (which will be one of DependencyChanged, Expired, Removed, or Underused). Within RefreshWords the data is simply reloaded into the cache.

When to Use Caching

It's very difficult to provide concrete rules for when caching should be used, because it is very application-dependent. In general, any form of caching will have a benefit as long as your server has sufficient memory and if you don't try to cache everything. Perhaps the best rule to stick with

Listing 6.23. Using Cache Removal Callbacks

```
static HttpContext _ctx = null;

void Application_Start(object sender, EventArgs e)
{
  _ctx = Context;
  StringCollection words = Words.ReadWords();

  _ctx.Cache.Insert("Words", words,
    new CacheDependency(Words.WordsFile),
    Cache.NoAbsoluteExpiration, Cache.NoSlidingExpiration,
    CacheItemPriority.Normal,
    new CacheItemRemovedCallback(RefreshWords));
}

static void RefreshWords(string key, object item,
                      CacheItemRemovedReason reason)
{
  StringCollection words = Words.ReadWords();

  _ctx.Cache.Insert("Words", words,
    new CacheDependency(Words.WordsFile),
    Cache.NoAbsoluteExpiration, Cache.NoSlidingExpiration,
    CacheItemPriority.Normal,
    new CacheItemRemovedCallback(RefreshWords));
}
```

is to cache data that is frequently used and that costs a lot (in performance terms), which is often files and databases.

Since there are different types of caching, Table 6.8 gives a brief look at the technique use, where the cached data is visible, and the size of data the technique is useful for.

TABLE 6.8: When to Use Caching

Technique	Visibility	Optimum Data Size
Page ViewState	Page	Small
Data source controls	Page	Large
Page output caching	Page	Large
ASP Session	User	Small/Medium
ASP Application	Application	Medium
ASP.NET Cache	Application	Large
Disk file	Global	Large

You can see that because the cached data is stored in different places, its visibility is different, and this might dictate when the technique is used. When you investigate caching, it is important that you test the performance before and after caching has been done. You may think that a page is faster because it, or the data it relies upon, is being cached, but what if you have 500 simultaneous users, or 500 requests a second? How will the server cope with a large load? How can you fine-tune and find the optimum amount of data to cache, or the optimum time to cache it for, if you don't stress-test the application?

SUMMARY

This chapter has been all about performance, even though the topic is actually caching, because performance is the ultimate goal. You've seen a number of techniques for storing and accessing data, and you've seen common patterns in use.

We started with the Application, Session HttpContext, and ViewState, seeing their limitations, namely, that they are more suited to small amounts of data. We then moved on to output caching, which stores the HTML output by the processed page. This can provide a huge improvement in performance, especially when the page contains data sourced from a database or a file. Output caching can be finely controlled by caching pages, or parts of pages, using control caching or post-cache substitution. This allows you to only cache the parts of the page that are dependent on slow data.

To ensure that the data you cache is refreshed when changed, you can use cache invalidation by way of SQL Dependencies. These add items to the cache, including the output cache, and place a dependency upon them, allowing the item to be evicted from the cache when the data changes. This provides the best of both worlds: cached pages and up-to-date data.

Finally, you saw the Cache API, which is the underlying architecture behind much of the caching in the rest of the chapter. You saw that you can access the cache programmatically and set dependencies to ensure cached items are evicted when the data changes or when a certain time limit is up.

All of these techniques provide a simple way for you to improve the performance of your Web sites. Now it's time to look at another data topic in detail—XML.

■7■
Working with XML

W**E LOOKED AT A VARIETY** of topics relating to data and databases in Chapters 3, 4, and 5, but these aren't the only sources of data in modern applications. XML has increasingly become an important data format, not only for the storage of data, but also for the transfer of data. It is text-based, easily readable by both humans and machines, and provides a way for data to be validated. Because of this, XML has become the de facto standard in Web Services and the basis for real standards that define Web Service interoperability.

In this chapter, we're going to look at XML and its use within ASP.NET pages. We will not be covering the details of working with and creating XML documents using some of the explicit XML classes, because there are too many of them to cover here, but we'll provide introductions to the classes you'll find most useful. We'll also provide references to other material should you need to explore them in more detail.

In particular, we'll be looking at:

- Using Visual Studio to work with XML
- How to use data source controls to bind to XML data
- How to transform XML from one form into another
- How to update XML data
- How to deal with XML data stored in SQL Server 2005

In general, working with XML in ASP.NET is simple, but there are places where you need to consider how the XML is structured and how you are going to use it. Let's start with a look at how Visual Studio 2005 supports XML for the developer.

Working with XML in Visual Studio 2005

Creating an XML file in Visual Studio 2005 is as simple as picking the XML File option from the Add New Item window, which gives a standard editor, as seen in Figure 7.1.

Because this file doesn't contain a schema, you get no IntelliSense, but you can have Visual Studio 2005 create one for you, inferring the schema from the structure of the XML file. To create a schema, you use the Create Schema option from the XML menu. For example, the schema creation for the shippers XML file is shown in Figure 7.2. This file is not automatically added to the project, so you should make sure you save it. Schema editing does have IntelliSense, since the schema is a defined XML language.

The schema is created automatically in code view, but you can view this in the designer by selecting `View Designer` from the context menu; the

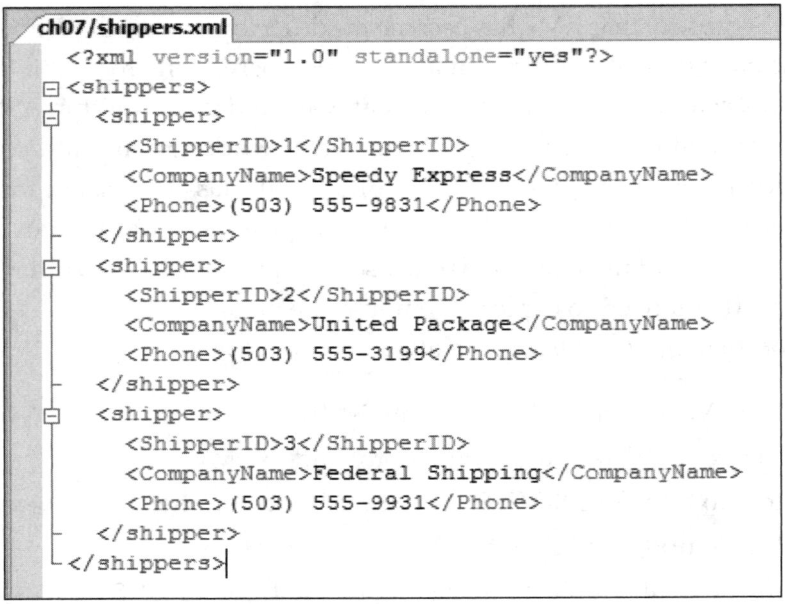

```
ch07/shippers.xml
   <?xml version="1.0" standalone="yes"?>
 <shippers>
   <shipper>
      <ShipperID>1</ShipperID>
      <CompanyName>Speedy Express</CompanyName>
      <Phone>(503) 555-9831</Phone>
   </shipper>
   <shipper>
      <ShipperID>2</ShipperID>
      <CompanyName>United Package</CompanyName>
      <Phone>(503) 555-3199</Phone>
   </shipper>
   <shipper>
      <ShipperID>3</ShipperID>
      <CompanyName>Federal Shipping</CompanyName>
      <Phone>(503) 555-9931</Phone>
   </shipper>
 </shippers>
```

FIGURE 7.1: Editing XML in Visual Studio 2005

```
shippers.xsd  ch07/shippers.xml
    <?xml version="1.0" encoding="utf-8"?>
  <xs:schema attributeFormDefault="unqualified" elementFormDefault="quali
    <xs:element name="shippers">
      <xs:complexType>
        <xs:sequence>
          <xs:element maxOccurs="unbounded" name="shipper">
            <xs:complexType>
              <xs:sequence>
                <xs:element name="ShipperID" type="xs:unsignedByte" />
                <xs:element name="CompanyName" type="xs:string" />
                <xs:element name="Phone" type="xs:string" />
              </xs:sequence>
            </xs:complexType>
          </xs:element>
        </xs:sequence>
      </xs:complexType>
    </xs:element>
  </xs:schema>
```

FIGURE 7.2: The Shippers schema

designer is the default view (see Figure 7.3). The schema designer provides a way to work with schemas without knowing the actual schema language.

To use this schema in the XML file, you add a namespace by use of the xmlns attribute. For example:

```
<shippers xmlns:s="shippers.xsd">
```

When adding a namespace, you get a drop-down list of public schemas to choose from, but you can just type in your own, and once added you get full IntelliSense, which allows easier editing of the XML data. This is the same schema editor that you use when working with typed data sets.

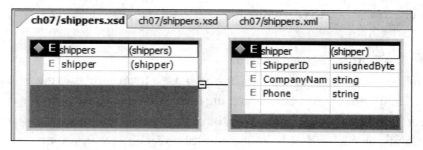

FIGURE 7.3: The schema designer

Databinding and Displaying XML Data

Databinding to XML data has been around for quite a long time—in fact, since Internet Explorer 4, which allowed binding to inline XML, launched. Within ASP.NET, binding is achieved either in code or with the `XmlDataSource` control, which works similarly to the other data source controls by providing an interface between the actual data and controls that display the data.

Manually Binding to XML Files

If you are not using an `XmlDataSource` control, and are using the `DataSource` property to set the binding, the simplest way to bind to XML data is to create a `DataSet`, read the XML into the `DataSet`, and bind to that, as seen in Listing 7.1.

Listing 7.1. Reading XML into a DataSet

```
DataSet ds = new DataSet();
ds.ReadXml(Server.MapPath("shippers.xml"));

GridView1.DataSource = ds.Tables[0].DefaultView;
GridView1.DataBind();
```

Here the `ReadXml` method of the `DataSet` is used to read the file into the data set. This will infer the schema and construct a table equivalent to the XML data (you can also use the `ReadXmlSchema` method to read in a pre-defined schema). There is also a `WriteXml` method to write the internal data out to an XML file; this is an excellent method of constructing XML files from SQL—just load it into the `DataSet` using normal commands, and then use `WriteXml` to create the file.

Using the XmlDataSource Control

To use the data source form of binding, you use a form similar to the SQL and Object data source controls, defining the control and using the `DataSourceID` property on the bound control. One thing that is different, though, is that the XmlDataSource is read-only, so it provides no facility for updating the data, nor does it provide a parameters collection for selection of data.

The XmlDataSource has three main properties for the loading and selection of data:

- `DataFile`, which is the XML file to load
- `TransformFile`, which is an XSLT stylesheet applied to the data before it is passed to any databound controls
- `XPath`, which applies an XPath expression to the data before it is passed to any databound controls

There are other properties, such as those that deal with caching, but these are the three that deal with the data files and selection. So at it's simplest, use of the control becomes:

```
<asp:XmlDataSource ID="XmlDataSource1" runat="server"
  DataFile="~/ch07/ShippersAttributes.xml" >
```

You can also specify the data inline, by use of the Data section:

```
<asp:XmlDataSource ID="XmlDataSource3" runat="server">
   <Data>
     <shippers>
       <shipper ShipperID="3" CompanyName="Speedy Express"
               Phone="(503) 555-9831" />
     </shippers>
   </Data>
</asp:XmlDataSource>
```

If both the `DataFile` property and the `Data` section are present, only the `DataFile` is used.

In use, you can use any of the controls that support databinding, but you have to be aware that some of these are designed for relational data, and XML is generally hierarchical. Thus, binding a grid to XML data might not be the best way to view the data, but using a hierarchical control such as a TreeView might be. For example:

```
<asp:XmlDataSource ID="XmlDataSource1" runat="server"
  DataFile="~/ch07/ShippersAttributes.xml" >
<asp:TreeView ID="TreeView1" runat="server"
  DataSourceID="XmlDataSource1">
```

However, this still may not give the results you expect, and what you do get depends upon how the XML is formatted. For example, consider the XML in Listing 7.2 and Listing 7.3. These represent the same data expressed in different ways; one uses elements and one uses attributes.

Listing 7.2. Shippers XML Using Elements

```
<shippers>
  <shipper>
    <ShipperID>1</ShipperID>
    <CompanyName>Speedy Express</CompanyName>
    <Phone>(503) 555-9831</Phone>
  </shipper>
  <shipper>
    <ShipperID>2</ShipperID>
    <CompanyName>United Package</CompanyName>
    <Phone>(503) 555-3199</Phone>
  </shipper>
  <shipper>
    <ShipperID>3</ShipperID>
    <CompanyName>Federal Shipping</CompanyName>
    <Phone>(503) 555-9931</Phone>
  </shipper>
</shippers>
```

Listing 7.3. Shippers XML Using Attributes

```
<shippers>
    <shipper ShipperID="1" CompanyName="Speedy Express"
    Phone="(503) 555-9831" />
    <shipper ShipperID="2" CompanyName="United Package"
    Phone="(503) 555-3199" />
    <shipper ShipperID="3" CompanyName="Federal Shipping"
    Phone="(503) 555-9931" />
</shippers>
```

When you bind a TreeView to these XML files, you might not get the results you expect, as Figure 7.4 shows.

The interesting thing to note here is that each nested element becomes a level in the TreeView. So for the element-based file, each element gets a level, while for the attributed file you only see two levels—the top and the secondary level for each shipper. What you also note is that the binding is automatically to the element name, not the contents or attributes. To change this behavior, you need to add explicit data bindings using the `DataBindings` section.

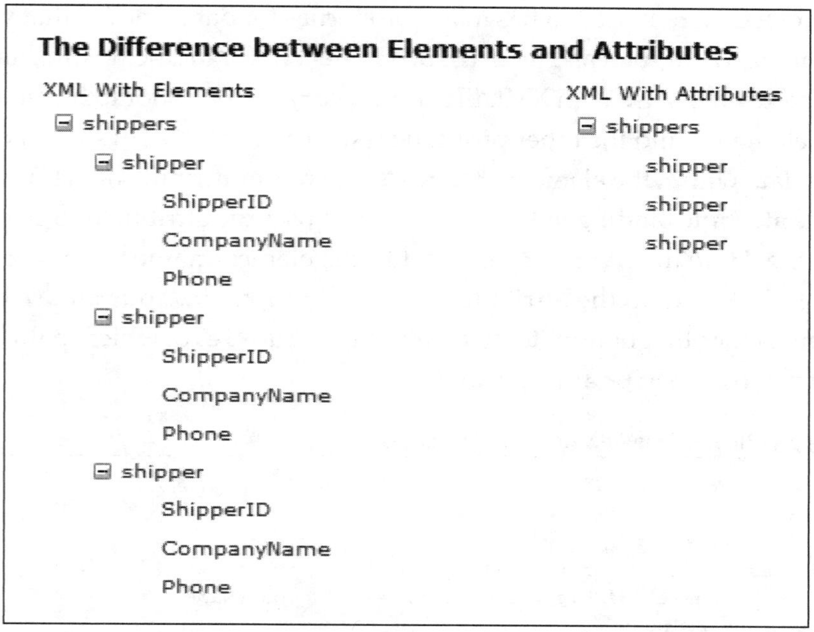

The Difference between Elements and Attributes

XML With Elements	XML With Attributes
⊟ shippers	⊟ shippers
⊟ shipper	shipper
ShipperID	shipper
CompanyName	shipper
Phone	
⊟ shipper	
ShipperID	
CompanyName	
Phone	
⊟ shipper	
ShipperID	
CompanyName	
Phone	

FIGURE 7.4: Binding a TreeView to XML files

Specifying TreeView Bindings

To bind TreeView nodes to the contents of elements rather than the element names, you use the `DataBindings` section of the TreeView and create a `TreeNodeBinding` for each element. You then specify the `DataMember` as the name of the element, and the `TextField` as `#InnerText`, which extracts the text from within the element, as seen in Listing 7.4.

Listing 7.4. Binding TreeView Nodes to Elements

```
<asp:TreeView ID="TreeView3" runat="server"
  DataSourceID="XmlDataSource1">
  <DataBindings>
    <asp:TreeNodeBinding DataMember="ShipperID"
      TextField="#InnerText" />
    <asp:TreeNodeBinding DataMember="CompanyName"
      TextField="#InnerText" />
    <asp:TreeNodeBinding DataMember="Phone"
      TextField="#InnerText" />
  </DataBindings>
</asp:TreeView>
```

The `TreeNodeBinding` has many properties for data binding that you'll be familiar with, such as `TextField`, `ValueField`, `FormatString`, and so on. The key to its use with XML files is that `DataMember` should be set to the XML elements, and the other properties (such as `TextField`) should be set to the data within the element (`#InnerText`) or the attribute name. You can see the attribute binding in Listing 7.5, which uses the attributed form of the XML file. Here the `DataMember` is set to the element name, `shipper`, and `TextField` is set to the attribute name, `CompanyName`. You can use other attributes for other bound items such as the `ValueField`, which in this case is bound to the `ShipperID` attribute.

Listing 7.5. Binding TreeView Nodes to Attributes

```
<asp:TreeView ID="TreeView4" runat="server"
  DataSourceID="XmlDataSource2">
  <DataBindings>
    <asp:TreeNodeBinding DataMember="shipper"
      ValueField="ShipperID" TextField="CompanyName" />
  </DataBindings>
</asp:TreeView>
```

Each `TreeNodeBinding` binds to a different level in the XML. The results of specifying the bindings can be seen in Figure 7.5.

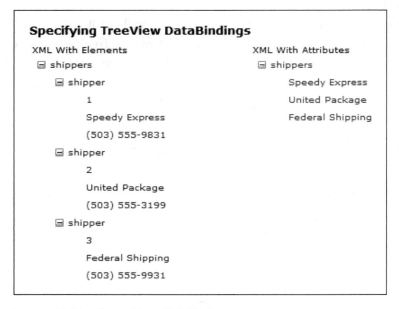

FIGURE 7.5: TreeView with explicit binding

Binding Expressions

If you are binding to XML but don't want to use the automatic binding, you can use binding expressions, in a similar way to binding to SQL data. For XML data, you use the XPath expression. For example:

```
<%# XPath("CompanyName") %>
```

This would bind to the CompanyName element, displaying the contents of the element. To bind to attributes, you precede the attribute name with an @ symbol.

```
<%# XPath("@Make") %>
```

You can use these binding expressions within any databound control, such as within templates of DataLists and Repeaters.

Applying Selections

When binding to SQL data, you can filter the data returned by adding a WHERE clause to the SQL statement. When dealing with XML data, you use XPath to provide the selection. XPath is a language designed for selecting data within XML documents, and while a full description is beyond the scope of this book, basic queries can be achieved with a few simple rules:

- Nodes are selected by their name.
- Nodes are separated by the forward slash character (/).
- Attributes are selected by preceding the attribute name with the at character (@).
- Filtering is done by enclosing the folder in square brackets.

To make this clear, let's look at a few examples, starting with the XML shown in Listing 7.6.

To select all of the Manufacturer nodes, you would use the following XPath query:

```
Automobiles/Manufacturer
```

To select only the Manufacturer node for Audi, you would use:

```
Automobiles/Manufacturer[@Make='Audi']
```

Listing 7.6. Cars XML File

```
<Automobiles>
  <Manufacturer Make="Audi" WebSite="http://www.audi.com/">
    <Car Model="A4" Id="02347">
      <Package Trim="Sport Package"/>
      <Package Trim="Luxury Package"/>
    </Car>
    <Car Model="A6" Id="02932">
      <Package Trim="Sport Package"/>
      <Package Trim="Luxury Package"/>
    </Car>
    <Car Model="A8"  Id="09381">
      <Package Trim="Sport Package"/>
      <Package Trim="Luxury Package"/>
    </Car>
  </Manufacturer>
  <Manufacturer Make="BMW" WebSite="http://www.bmw.com/">
    <Car Model="328i" Id="3675">
      <Package Trim="Sport Package"/>
      <Package Trim="Luxury Package"/>
      <Package Trim="Cold Weather Package"/>
    </Car>
    <Car Model="530d" Id="6784">
      <Package Trim="Sport Package"/>
      <Package Trim="Luxury Package"/>
      <Package Trim="Cold Weather Package"/>
    </Car>
  </Manufacturer>
  <Manufacturer Make="Porsche" WebSite="http://www.porsche.com/">
    <Car Model="928zx" Id="22476">
      <Package Trim="Sport Package"/>
      <Package Trim="Race Package"/>
    </Car>
    <Car Model="928i" Id="78954">
      <Package Trim="Sport Package"/>
      <Package Trim="Race Package"/>
    </Car>
  </Manufacturer>
</Automobiles>
```

To select the Car nodes for Audi, you would use:

```
Automobiles/Manufacturer[@Make='Audi']/Car
```

You can see that it's relatively straightforward to select nodes and attributes.

Using Binding Expressions and Selections

To make a filter appear at the data level, before the data is presented to the bound control, you use the XPath property of the XmlDataSource. The attribute values are shown using the XPath binding expression, as seen in Listing 7.7.

Listing 7.7. Selecting Nodes and Attributes

```
<asp:XmlDataSource ID="XmlDataSource4" runat="server"
  DataFile="~/ch07/cars.xml"
  XPath="Automobiles/Manufacturer"
  />
<asp:Repeater ID="Repeater1" runat="server"
  DataSourceID="XmlDataSource4">
  <ItemTemplate>
    <%# XPath("@Make")%>
  </ItemTemplate>
  <SeparatorTemplate>
    <br />
  </SeparatorTemplate>
</asp:Repeater>
```

Since XML data is hierarchical, you may need to display this hierarchy. With the SqlDataSource controls, you can use select parameters or filters, but these aren't supported on the XmlDataSource. Instead you use the XPathSelect binding expression to return a subset of the nodes, and this can be used as the data source for a control. Extending Listing 7.7 to show not only the make of car, but also the model, you get the code in Listing 7.8.

This shows a nested Repeater, with the inner repeater setting its Data-Source property to an XPathSelect expression, the parameter of which is a standard XPath expression. The outer Repeater binds to the manufacturer, and the inner one binds to the cars for that repeater, the results of which are shown in Figure 7.6.

Binding Expressions

Audi: A4 , A6 , A8
BMW: 328i , 530d
Porsche: 928zx , 928i

FIGURE 7.6: Nested binding with expressions

Listing 7.8. Binding to XML Hierarchies

```
<asp:XmlDataSource ID="XmlDataSource4" runat="server"
  DataFile="~/ch07/cars.xml"
  XPath="Automobiles/Manufacturer"
  />
<asp:Repeater ID="Repeater1" runat="server"
  DataSourceID="XmlDataSource4">
  <ItemTemplate>
    <%# XPath("@Make")%>:
    <asp:Repeater ID="Repeater2" runat="server"
      DataSource='<%#XPathSelect("Car") %>'>
      <ItemTemplate>
        <%# XPath("@Model") %>
      </ItemTemplate>
      <SeparatorTemplate>
        ,
      </SeparatorTemplate>
    </asp:Repeater>
  </ItemTemplate>
  <SeparatorTemplate>
    <br />
  </SeparatorTemplate>
</asp:Repeater>
```

Transforming XML

XSLT is one of the most successful and heavily used XML technologies, primarily due to the fact that it is a complete programming language for manipulating XML. In the world of data where XML is flowing between applications on a network, we need to process and reshape this data in accordance to some schema (whether explicitly through the use of an XML schema or DTD, or implicitly without a schema) so that people can share data.

In such a diverse world, no one is going to agree on a single data representation for a person, an invoice, or an address. This is where XSLT comes into its own by allowing different data representations to evolve independently, and then, through a transformation process, reshaping one XML structure into another. There are many reasons why XSLT is used; however, the reasons typically fall into one of the following categories:

- **Structural transformation:** Sometimes referred to as "fixed schema to fixed schema transformation," this is where you are transforming from one XML structure into another. For example, you may be transforming from your private schema into a public industry-agreed schema standard such as XML Business Reporting Language (XBRL). This is the most common usage scenario for XSLT and the one that people think of most often. Microsoft's BizTalk Server 2004 is an example of this type of transformation, where a schema mapping tool is used to generate an XSLT stylesheet.

- **Content publishing:** This is the separation of content from display information for the data. XSLT can generate more than just the XML outputs mentioned for structural transformation. It is also ideally suited for content publishing in the form of HTML, Scalable Vector Graphics (SVG), various wireless application protocols such as WAP, and—looking to the future—Microsoft's XML Application Markup Language (XAML), which is part of Windows Presentation Foundation, the UI model for Microsoft's future operating systems. Today, Microsoft's Office 2003 InfoPath application can be considered an example here because it uses XSLT to generate HTML pages for data publishing and retrieval.

- **Data-driven documents or sites:** Many large Web sites (e.g., MSN) must cope with issues such as globalization and personalization, and they cannot have an army of people continually editing sites to deal with the constant flow of new information. XSLT is ideally suited to building data-driven Web sites where the page's layout changes based on the type of content received. The Microsoft Office 2003 FrontPage application is an example, where—through the use of data connectors that map data into XML (e.g., relational data stored in a database)—it is possible to build Web sites that change automatically depending on the flow of information. This includes the ability to reorder, filter, sort, and group parts of a document or to display only the part that is relevant to a particular user's profile.

It is also worth understanding what makes XSLT such a powerful programming language. XSLT is described as a declarative language as opposed to most modern object-oriented programming languages such as C# and Visual Basic, which are procedural. Procedural languages have step-by-step operations, holding on to the previous state in order to execute the next statement. Declarative languages, on the other hand, are more like a set of rules or patterns that describe what should happen if a certain condition is matched. XSLT describes a set of rules for ways that the transformed document relates to the original document. The difficulty comes in that, due to human nature, training, or both, XSLT tends to be harder to grasp than object-oriented languages because you have to "see" the pattern matching as opposed to "reading" the code like sentences in a book. In reality, in application development, you end up using a combination of both procedural code, via XML APIs such as the `XmlDocument` (XML DOM), `XmlReader`, and `XmlWriter`, plus XSLT for the parts that need to be more flexible.

Luckily, the world of XSLT programming has been made significantly easier in Visual Studio 2005 with the introduction of an XSLT debugger that is integrated into the development environment.

As an example, suppose you have the shippers data shown in Listing 7.2 which uses elements, and you need it in attributed form (as shown in Listing 7.3). You could create an XSLT file to transform it, as shown in Listing 7.9.

A description of XSLT is outside the scope of this book (it's a book in itself), but for a quick explanation, it revolves around templates, where a template matches a target. A target is generally an element or attribute, and the code within the template dictates what the output is—elements or attributes, or even HTML. In the example just presented, each of the elements representing `ShipperID`, `CompanyName`, and `Phone` are converted to attributes of the shipper element. The new attributes have new names to make it clear that a transform is happening.

Debugging XSLT in Visual Studio 2005

XSLT can be a confusing language to work with, especially if you don't have much experience of recursion, but Visual Studio 2005 aids in this by

Listing 7.9. Transforming Shippers Elements to Attributes

```xml
<?xml version="1.0" encoding="utf-8"?>

<xsl:stylesheet version="1.0"
    xmlns:xsl="http://www.w3.org/1999/XSL/Transform">

    <xsl:template match="shippers">
    <shippers>
            <xsl:apply-templates select="shipper" />
        </shippers>
    </xsl:template>

    <xsl:template match="shipper">
        <xsl:element name="shipper">
            <xsl:apply-templates select="ShipperID" />
            <xsl:apply-templates select="CompanyName" />
            <xsl:apply-templates select="Phone" />
        </xsl:element>
    </xsl:template>

    <xsl:template match="ShipperID">
        <xsl:attribute name="id">
            <xsl:value-of select="."/>
        </xsl:attribute>
    </xsl:template>

    <xsl:template match="CompanyName">
        <xsl:attribute name="name">
            <xsl:value-of select="."/>
        </xsl:attribute>
    </xsl:template>

    <xsl:template match="Phone">
        <xsl:attribute name="phoneNumber">
            <xsl:value-of select="."/>
        </xsl:attribute>
    </xsl:template>

</xsl:stylesheet>
```

providing an XSLT debugger. To debug XSLT you need to specify the input file—the XML that is going to be transformed. You can do this by opening the XSLT file and setting the `Input` property to the file being transformed (see Figure 7.7).

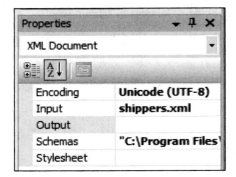

FIGURE 7.7: Setting the Input file for XSLT

Once the input file is defined, you can set breakpoints in the XSLT file, just like breakpoints in code files. To debug the file, you select Debug XSLT from the XML menu; you may receive a warning that the output file already exists, asking if you wish to overwrite it. This is because the output is written to a file, and if you have already run the XSLT, the temporary file already exists. Once running, the screen splits into two with the XSLT on the left and the output on the right. Breakpoints suspend processing (see Figure 7.8), and you can use the step over and step into debugging commands to step through the XSLT to see how it processes the file.

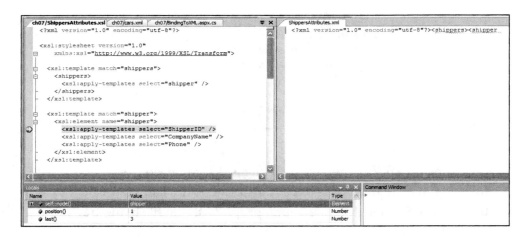

FIGURE 7.8: Debugging XSLT

Transforming with the XmlDataSource Control

To use and transform XML within ASP.NET pages, you can use the XmlDataSource control and its TransformFile property, which you set to the name of the XSLT file, as shown in Listing 7.10.

Listing 7.10. Transforming XML Using the XmlDataSource Control

```
<asp:XmlDataSource ID="XmlDataSource3" runat="server"
  DataFile="~/ch07/shippers.xml"
  TransformFile="~/ch07/ShippersAttributes.xsl" />

<asp:TreeView id="treeview5" runat="server"
  datasourceid="xmldatasource3">
  <databindings>
    <asp:treenodebinding datamember="shipper"
      valuefield="id" textfield="name" />
  </databindings>
</asp:TreeView>
```

In this example, the TransformFile is applied to the DataFile before the data is presented to bound controls. So the TreeView binds to the new attribute names rather than the old.

Transforming in Code

If you have a business or data layer that provides all data to the UI layer, you may not want to perform transforms within ASP.NET pages. Architecturally, a transform should really live in the data layer, so there is a full API for dealing with transforms; this is the XslCompiledTransform class, which lives in the System.Xml.Xsl namespace.

There are two simple methods on the XslCompiledTransform class. The first, Load, loads an XSLT file, while the second, Transform, performs the transformation. There are several overloaded forms of Transform, allowing a variety of output targets and parameters, such as the input and output file names. Listing 7.11 shows Transform with three parameters: the first is the file to transform, the second is a parameter list (in this case null), and the third is the output (in this case a StringWriter instance). The contents of the StringWriter are then displayed in a TextBox control.

Listing 7.11. Transforming XML in Code

```
StringWriter writer = new StringWriter();

XslCompiledTransform transform = new XslCompiledTransform();
transform.Load(Server.MapPath("ShippersAttributes.xsl"));
transform.Transform(Server.MapPath("shippers.xml"), null, writer);

transformedXML.Text = writer.ToString();
writer.Close();
```

The `XslCompiledTransform` class supports a number of advanced features, such as script support, parameters, and extension object, all of which are outside the scope of this discussion. If you'd like to learn more about this topic, there is a chapter on transforming XML in the Addison-Wesley book *ADO.NET and System.Xml v2.0—The Beta Version.* While aimed at beta 2 of .NET 2.0, most of the content is still suitable for the released product.

> The `XslCompiledTransform` class doesn't replace the `XslTransform` class but provides a number of additional features, one of which is vastly improved performance. If you are considering migrating applications to .NET 2.0, you should use the compiled class to achieve best results.

Working with Raw XML

The `XmlDataSource` control gives you a great way to display XML data, but there are times when you need to interact with XML documents. There are several classes you can use for working directly with XML, and which classes you use depends upon your requirements. There are generally two ways of working with XML: in-memory or streamed from a file, and these ways will dictate which classes you use. Whether you should use in-memory or streamed XML is also a question of your requirements, and certain scenarios naturally lead to one form or another. Typical scenarios where you *should* use in-memory XML stores include the following:

- **XSLT transformations:** Performing transformations naturally fits into memory usage, because nodes can be accessed in a random order.
- **Random access to a document that is being updated by a user:** For example, users often work on Microsoft Word documents over a

period of time. Performance here is not that critical, because a user's typing speed is typically the limiting factor.

- **Caching of configuration state or data that will be read many times in memory:** XML stores are best used in layered caching strategies in order to improve application responsiveness. Examples of this scenario include caching weather data for multiple page hits from different clients and working with an application configuration file that is loaded when the application starts and is read many times.

- **Application of business rules to a document to check its validity:** For example, e-commerce shopping carts may apply a discount to an order if a person buys more than five books. From an implementation perspective, this uses the node-level events that are fired when updates and changes occur to the document.

- **XML Digital Signatures (XMLDSig):** In some cases (but not all), in order to sign a document with an XML digital signature, the document has to be loaded into memory first. Streaming models for XMLDSig are also possible based on the `XmlReader`.

Typical scenarios where you *should not* use in-memory XML stores include the following:

- **When performance is critical:** Building a tree of nodes just to access a few elements within it is extremely costly and should be avoided.

- **When memory resource is critical:** Typically a UTF-8 encoded document will quadruple in memory compared to its file size, and a UTF-16 document will approximately double or treble in memory size. Thus your 1MB document jumps to 4MB in memory with the CLR garbage collector working overtime to recover the hundreds of strings allocated when the document is closed. Conversely, the `XmlReader` loads a 4K character buffer from the stream along with some additional state, and hence it is much less memory-intensive. Also, the `XmlReader` can read XML documents up to any size—hundreds of gigabytes, if necessary (there is no upper limit)—which is impossible with the memory-constrained `XmlDocument`.

- **When you have a "touch-once scenario:"** For example, in some low-volume XML messaging systems, the body of the message can simply be passed on to the relevant processing module once the message header has been read to determine the routing or action information. Message caching is still necessary in many cases to ensure message throughput, because you cannot rely on the application to stream the received XML messages fast enough.

Streaming XML

Streaming XML is a connected scenario, where you are navigating through an XML file. You use the XmlReader class for reading, and the XmlWriter class for writing. Typical scenarios where you will be streaming XML include the following:

- Reading and writing application XML configuration files
- Reading from URLs such as RSS feeds or writing the XML for the RSS feeds
- Validating an XML document with an XML schema to ensure that the document conforms to the schema and alternatively enforces business rules
- Combining the XmlReader and XmlWriter to perform simple data transformations. Consider this as an alternative to using XSLT, because this combination is often faster and uses less memory
- Pipelining XML processing. For example, you may have an XML document that is validated by a series of different XML schemas with business rules written in Visual Basic, C#, or XSLT that act on the data
- Accessing relational data as XML from a SQL Server database
- Implementing a custom XmlReader or XmlWriter in order to expose data not necessarily stored as XML as the XML data model. For example, you can implement an XmlReader over the file system to make it look like an XML document where the properties for the files, such as creation date and file size, are mapped to XML attributes. Equally, you can implement an XmlWriter that enables you to write to the file system as if it were an XML document

All of these scenarios can be achieved with the `XmlReader` and `XmlWriter` classes, both of which are simple to use, although you need to understand a bit about how XML documents are structured. This is best seen with an example.

Reading XML Documents

For example, consider Listing 7.12, which uses the `Create` method to create an `XmlReader` over the shippers file. Like the `SqlDataReader`, the `XmlReader` uses the `Read` method to read nodes from the underlying data, returning `false` if no more nodes can be read. The `Name` property returns the name of the element.

Listing 7.12. Using an XmlReader

```
using (XmlReader rdr =
  XmlReader.Create(Server.MapPath("Shippers.xml")))
{
  while (rdr.Read())
    Response.Write(rdr.Name + "<br/>");
  rdr.Close();
}
```

What's interesting about this code fragment is that it returns more than you'd first think.

```
shippers
shipper
ShipperID
ShipperID
CompanyName
CompanyName
Phone
...
shipper
shippers
```

What you notice is that the element names appear twice, which is because there are two of them in the XML file: the start and end parts of the element—each appear as separate nodes. There are also other nodes in the XML file; whitespace appears as a separate node as does the value of the element. This is what we mean when we said you must understand a bit about how XML documents are structured—they are node-based. So

Node Name	Node Type	Node Value
XmlDeclaration	xml	version="1.0" standalone="yes"
Whitespace		
Element	shippers	
Whitespace		
Element	shipper	
Whitespace		
Element	ShipperID	
Text		1
EndElement	ShipperID	
Whitespace		
Element	CompanyName	
Text		Speedy Express
EndElement	CompanyName	
Whitespace		
Element	Phone	
Text		(503) 555-9831
EndElement	Phone	
Whitespace		
EndElement	shipper	
Whitespace		
Element	shipper	
Whitespace		
Element	ShipperID	
Text		2

FIGURE 7.9: Nodes, types, and values of the Shippers document

everything within an XML document is a node, and you can see this in Figure 7.9, where even the white space in the document is a node. Compare this with Figure 7.10, where there are fewer nodes and no values, because the content is stored within attributes.

Node Name	Node Type	Node Value
XmlDeclaration	xml	version="1.0" encoding="utf-8"
Whitespace		
Element	shippers	
Whitespace		
Element	shipper	
Whitespace		
Element	shipper	
Whitespace		
Element	shipper	
Whitespace		
EndElement	shippers	

FIGURE 7.10: Nodes, types, and values for Shippers Attributes document

The most important point these figures show is that when navigating through documents with an XmlReader, you need to know the structure of the XML if you want to process it in an intelligent fashion. The XmlReader has plenty of methods to determine if the current node has a value, or has attributes, and what type of node it is so that you can build logic into the data reading.

Writing XML Documents

Writing XML documents is similar to reading them, in that you are dealing with nodes as they will appear in the output document. You have to remember that XML documents are hierarchical, and that nodes have a start point and an end point, and so you have to create the start and end of each node as you write the file. This is shown in Listing 7.13.

Listing 7.13. Writing XML Using the XmlWriter

```
StringBuilder bldr = new StringBuilder();

using (XmlWriter writer = XmlWriter.Create(bldr, null))
{
   writer.WriteStartDocument();
   writer.WriteComment("Generated automatically");
   writer.WriteStartElement("shipper");
   writer.WriteStartAttribute("shipperID");
   writer.WriteString("1");
   writer.WriteEndAttribute();
   writer.WriteStartAttribute("companyName");
   writer.WriteString("Speedy Express");
   writer.WriteEndAttribute();
   writer.WriteStartAttribute("phone");
   writer.WriteString("(503) 555-9831");
   writer.WriteEndAttribute();
   writer.WriteEndElement();
   writer.WriteEndDocument();
   writer.Close();
}

NewXML.Text = bldr.ToString();
```

This code uses the static Create method of the XmlWriter class to create the writer (ignore the null for the moment), writing into a StringBuilder. You can also write to streams and files, but the results of this example are output of the XML to a TextBox control. The writer is then used to write content, starting with the document—each XML must have a document

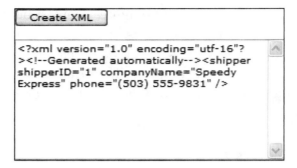

FIGURE 7.11: Unformatted XML

element (thats the `<?xml>` element) that indicates this is an XML document, its version, and the encoding scheme used. Next, `WriteComment` is used to write a simple text comment, and then the first element, shipper, is started with `WriteStateElement`, which writes `<shipper` to the string builder. Within this element, `WriteStartAttribute` is used to start an attribute, `WriteString` to write the value of the attribute, and `WriteEndAttribute` to write the closing `>` of the attribute. Other attributes can be added in the same manner before `WriteEndElement` is used to close the element, and `WriteEndDocument` is used to end the document. The results of this can be seen in Figure 7.11.

If you are supplying this XML to another program, this output is perfectly acceptable, with no white space, but it is slightly hard to read. The output can automatically be formatted by creating `XmlWriterSettings` and passing them into the `Create` method of the `XmlWriter` in place of the null shown in earlier code. Listing 7.14 shows this in action, using the `Indent` property of the `XmlWriterSettings` to indicate that indenting should be used for child elements and using `NewLineOnAttributes` to add a new line before an attribute. The results of this are shown in Figure 7.12.

Listing 7.14. Using XmlWriterSettings

```
XmlWriterSettings settings = new XmlWriterSettings();

settings.Indent = true;
settings.NewLineOnAttributes = true;
using (XmlWriter writer = XmlWriter.Create(bldr, settings))
```

```
Create XML

<?xml version="1.0" encoding="utf-16"?>
<!--Generated automatically-->
<shipper
  shipperID="1"
  companyName="Speedy Express"
  phone="(503) 555-9831" />
```

FIGURE 7.12: Formatted XML

Reading and writing XML using the XmlReader and XmlWriter classes is streaming-based, meaning that you have to deal with nodes in the order in which they appear in the document. If you need to deal with nodes in a more arbitrary manner, streaming is not the solution. Instead, you need to deal with an in-memory XML store.

Working with XML Documents in Memory

When working with XML in memory, you will use one of the XPathDocument, XmlDocument, or XmlDataDocument classes. The difference between them is summed up easily:

- The XPathDocument is read-only, and provides the best performance.
- The XmlDocument is read-write.
- The XmlDataDocument is read-write, and also provides XML in relational form.

All of these objects deal with an XML document in its entirety but don't provide a way to navigate around the nodes. For this, you use an XPathNavigator, which provides read (and write if the underlying object supports updates) access to the nodes in the document. The use of these is best seen with some examples.

Using the XPathDocument Object

The XPathDocument is really a way of providing a read-only document to an XPathNavigator, as it only has constructors and a single method— CreateNavigator. The constructors allow the document to be created

from a variety of sources, such as streams, text readers, and files, while the
`CreateNavigator` method returns an `XPathNavigator` that allows you to
navigate around the document. Listing 7.15 shows some examples of the
movement types, using `MoveToFirstChild` to move to the first child of the
current node; subsequent calls will move deeper into the hierarchy of
nodes. `MoveToFirstAttribute` allows you move to the first attribute for a
node, and there are equivalents for moving to the next node or attribute as
well as moving to previous nodes, the first node, selecting a range of nodes
with an XPath expression, and so on.

Listing 7.15. Using the XPathDocument and XPathNavigator

```
StringBuilder bldr = new StringBuilder();
XPathDocument doc = new XPathDocument(Server.MapPath("cars.xml"));
XPathNavigator nav = doc.CreateNavigator();

bldr.Append("Processing 'cars.xml' - editing allowed: " +
  nav.CanEdit.ToString() + "<br />");

nav.MoveToFirstChild();
string root = nav.Name;
bldr.Append("First child: " + root + "<br />");

nav.MoveToFirstChild();
string child = nav.Name;
bldr.Append("First child of '" + root + "': " + child + "<br />");
bldr.Append("Inner XML: " + nav.InnerXml + "<br />");

nav.MoveToFirstAttribute();
bldr.Append("First attribute of '" + child + "': " +
  nav.Name + "=" + nav.Value + "<br />");

nav.MoveToPrevious();
bldr.Append("Previous: " + nav.Name + "<br />");

nav.MoveToRoot();
nav.MoveToFirstChild();
bldr.Append("Reset: " + nav.Name + "<br />");

Label1.Text = bldr.ToString();
```

The output of this code is as follows:

```
Processing 'cars.xml' - editing allowed: False
First child: Automobiles
First child of 'Automobiles': Manufacturer
```

```
Inner XML: <Car Model="A4" Id="02347">
  <Package Trim="Sport Package" />
  <Package Trim="Luxury Package" />
</Car>
<Car Model="A6" Id="02932">
  <Package Trim="Sport Package" />
  <Package Trim="Luxury Package" />
</Car>
<Car Model="A8" Id="09381">
  <Package Trim="Sport Package" />
  <Package Trim="Luxury Package" />
</Car>
First attribute of 'Manufacturer': Make=Audi
Previous: Make
Reset: Automobiles
```

You can see that you can move forward and backward through the nodes, and you can access element and attribute values as well as the entire XML for the node. The limitation of the XPathDocument is that it is read-only, so for updates you need to consider the XmlDocument.

Using the XmlDocument Object

In use, XmlDocument can be similar to the XPathDocument in that you use an XPathNavigator to move through the document, but because the XPathDocument is read-write, you can use additional methods on the navigator to create new content, as seen in Listing 7.16.

Listing 7.16. Creating Nodes with an XmlDocument

```
XmlDocument doc = new XmlDocument();
doc.Load(Server.MapPath("cars.xml"));
XPathNavigator nav = doc.CreateNavigator();

Label1.Text = "Processing 'cars.xml' - editing allowed: " +
  nav.CanEdit.ToString() + "<br />";

nav.MoveToFirstChild();
nav.PrependChildElement(null, "Manufacturer", null, null);
nav.MoveToFirstChild();
nav.CreateAttribute(null, "Make", null, "Ferrari");
nav.CreateAttribute(null, "WebSite", null,
  "http://www.ferrari.com/");
nav.AppendChildElement(null, "Car", null, null);
nav.MoveToFirstChild();
nav.CreateAttribute(null, "Model", null, "F430");
nav.CreateAttribute(null, "Id", null, "00430");
```

Here a new manufacturer is created using the `PrependChildElement` method, which adds a new element, and `CreateAttribute` is used to create attributes on the new element. The output of this code is as follows:

```
<Automobiles>
  <Manufacturer Make="Ferrari" WebSite="http://www.ferrari.com/">
    <Car Model="F430" Id="00430" />
  </Manufacturer>
  <Manufacturer Make="Audi" WebSite="http://www.audi.com/">
    <Car Model="A4" Id="02347">
      <Package Trim="Sport Package" />
      <Package Trim="Luxury Package" />
```

The `XPathNavigator` offers many methods for creating content within the document it is navigating over, including appending elements, inserting before and after, replacing existing elements, and changing values of existing elements. What is interesting about this method of working with XML documents is that it offers great flexibility; you can work with existing content, add nodes individually, or, in conjunction with XmlReaders and XmlWriters, add content in bulk.

Using the XmlDataDocument Object

Many ASP.NET developers also sit in the database developer camp, having to do database design and administration. While knowledge of XML is also widespread, the use of the XML APIs described in this chapter isn't, and often the DataSet is used, because it has `ReadXML` and `WriteXML` methods to surface the relational data in XML form.

For the developer experienced with XML but not relational data, the `XmlDataDocument` is the solution. It is a subclass of the `XmlDocument` and provides one really important additional property, `DataSet`, which returns the XML data as a `DataSet` object. Before the `DataSet` can be exposed from the XML, a schema must be used so that the `DataSet` knows the structure of the underlying XML. Listing 7.17 shows this in action. First an `XmlDataDocument` is created, and the `DataSet` property is used to read the schema. The `DataSet` property is then used as the source for a grid, and because the `DataSet` property is simply just another view on the XML data, rows can be added to the `DataSet` and they are visible in the XML, as seen in Figure 7.13.

Listing 7.17. Using the XmlDataDocument

```
XmlDataDocument doc = new XmlDataDocument();
doc.DataSet.ReadXmlSchema(Server.MapPath("cars.xsd"));
doc.Load(Server.MapPath("cars.xml"));

GridView1.DataSource = doc.DataSet.Tables[0].DefaultView;
GridView1.DataMember = "Manufacturer";
GridView1.DataBind();

DataSet ds = doc.DataSet;
DataTable tbl = ds.Tables[0];

tbl.Rows.Add(new string[] {"Ferrari", "http://www.ferrari.com/"});
NewXML.Text = doc.OuterXml;
```

Converting between XML and Relational Data

As you've seen from the previous section, data can be exposed from a common source as both XML and relational, and there are a variety of ways in which this can be done. Figure 7.14 shows the interaction between the classes, showing how data can be accessed with different APIs. The advantage of this sort of flexibility is that developers can work with the API they are familiar with rather than having to learn new APIs.

FIGURE 7.13: Using the XmlDataDocument's DataSet

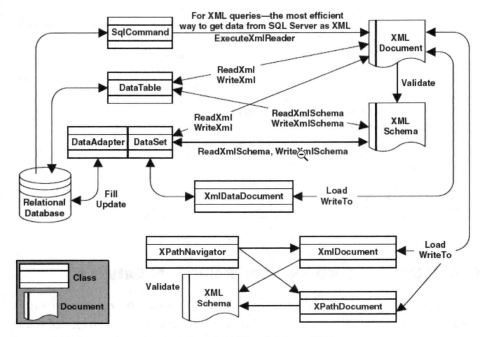

FIGURE 7.14: Access to and conversion of relational data as XML

Working with SQL Server 2005 XML Data

XML data isn't only sourced from documents, especially now that SQL Server 2005, which not only increases its general support for XML but also supports XML data as a native data type, allows you to do the following:

- Store XML in "typed" form, where a schema is registered with SQL Server and the XML must conform to this schema.
- Store XML in "untyped" form, where no schema is required and the XML just has to be well formed.
- Select the value from an `xml` column in SQL statements and stored procedures, just like any other column type.
- Query the XML in the column directly, using XPath and XQuery languages, to find and return specific values.

- Modify the XML in a column by adding or removing nodes or by changing the values of existing nodes.
- Bind XML to other SQL Server data types, allowing queries to access values in stored procedure variables and other non-xml columns.
- Access and return sets of node values, which resemble a single-column rowset.
- Create indexes on the xml columns to vastly improve performance when querying and updating the data.

There are two types of XML columns in SQL Server 2005: untyped and typed. Untyped columns have no schema, and data is stored in character format, complete with elements and attributes. Untyped columns are not validated, although they are checked for well-formed data. A typed column has a schema and therefore has validation applied when data is added or modified.

Creating XML Columns

Since the XML type is a standard type in SQL Server 2005, you simply use xml as a data type.

```
CREATE TABLE MyTable(MyIDColumn int, MyXmlColumn xml)
```

For a typed column, you must specify the schema when the table is created.

```
CREATE TABLE MyTable(MyIDColumn int, MyXmlColumn xml(MySchema))
```

The advantage of typed columns is that the data within them is converted to native types (int, char, etc.), allowing not only validation as data is inserted and modified but also querying within the XML.

Creating Schemas

Before you can create a typed column, you need to create a schema to define the structure of the XML that is allowable for the column. Schemas are stored within a **schema collection**, which can hold one or more schemas. To use a schema to define an xml data column, you must first create and register a schema collection that includes the schema with SQL Server using the CREATE XML SCHEMA COLLECTION statement. This statement takes a name that will be used to identify the schema collection after registration and a string-type parameter that contains or references the schema or schemas to be registered in that collection. In the simplest case, the code looks like this:

```
CREATE XML SCHEMA COLLECTION MySchema AS '<xsd:schema xmlns="...">
    ... schema content ...
</xsd:schema>'
```

After registration, the schema is identified by the name you specify (in this example, MyNewSchema). An alternative way to register a schema is to assign it to a variable and then use the variable in the CREATE XML SCHEMA COLLECTION statement. This approach is also useful when uploading schemas from the client because the schema itself can be sent as a parameter.

```
DECLARE @myschema nvarchar(1000)
SET @myschema = N'<xsd:schema xmlns="...">
    ... schema content ...
</xsd:schema>'
CREATE XML SCHEMA COLLECTION MyNewSchema @myschema
```

You can register more than one schema in a collection and have them all referenced with a single name by simply placing them in the string value you pass to the CREATE XML SCHEMA COLLECTION statement.

```
CREATE XML SCHEMA COLLECTION MyNewSchema '<xsd:schema xmlns="...">
    ... schema content ...
</xsd:schema>
<xsd:schema xmlns="...">
    ... schema content ...
</xsd:schema>
<xsd:schema xmlns="...">
    ... schema content ...
</xsd:schema>'
```

Within SQL Server Management Studio, you can apply a schema to an XML column in the table design, as seen in Figure 7.15.

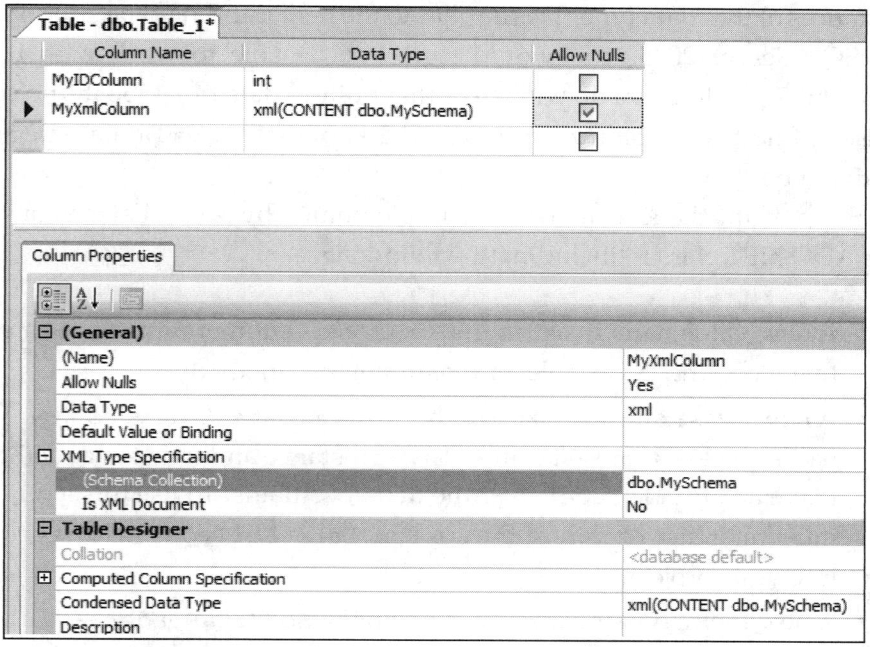

FIGURE 7.15: Specifying the schema for an XML column

Inserting Data into XML Columns

Inserting data is, as you'd expect, simply typing the XML into the INSERT statement.

```
INSERT INTO MyTable(MyIDColumn, MyXmlColumn)
VALUES(1, '<cars>... etc ...</cars>')
```

You can also cast the data as you insert it.

```
INSERT INTO MyTable(MyIDColumn, MyXmlColumn)
VALUES(1, CAST('<cars>... etc ...</cars>' AS xml)
```

Casting is also useful for enforcing the schema.

```
INSERT INTO MyTable(MyIDColumn, MyXmlColumn)
VALUES(1, CAST('<cars>... etc ...</cars>' AS xml(MySchema))
```

Accessing XML Columns from ADO.NET

For any particular data type to be of real use in applications, the client-side data access technology you use must be able to read, manipulate, and write instances of that data type. This applies to the new `xml` data type supported by SQL Server 2005. You would expect to be able to work with it in ADO.NET just like you do with any other built-in data types. So it's no surprise to find that version 2.0 of ADO.NET supports the `xml` data type as a native type.

Support for the `xml` data type is implemented by several extensions to the ADO.NET classes, including the following :

- A new value named `Xml` in the `SqlDbType` enumeration—Indicates that a column, a variable, or a parameter is an `xml` type.
- A new class named `SqlXml` in the `System.Data.SqlTypes` namespace—Represents an `xml` type instance and exposes a method to create an `XmlReader` over the data it contains. To use this, you must reference or import the `System.Data.SqlTypes` namespace into your project.
- A new method named `GetSqlXml` on the `SqlDataReader`— Returns a `SqlXml` instance for a specified column within a row. The column can be specified only by using its zero-based index within the row.
- A new property on the `DataAdapter`—Controls whether data is returned from any `xml`-typed columns in the database as a `String` or as a `SqlXml` instance. The property name is `UseProviderSpecific-Type`, and the value defaults to `false`, so you must set it to `true` before loading the data in order to access an `xml` column value as a `SqlXml` type.

These additions are used when accessing data in an `xml` column of SQL Server 2005 through a `DataSet` and a `DataReader`. For example, consider Listing 7.18, where a simple SELECT is performed over a table containing an XML column (`Instructions`). The column can be accessed like any other column, but untyped access like this returns the column data as a string.

Compare this with Listing 7.19, where the column is not accessed directly but instead the `GetSqlXml` method is used to return the column as

Listing 7.18. Streaming an XML Column

```
StringBuilder bldr = new StringBuilder();

using (SqlConnection conn = new
  SqlConnection(ConfigurationManager.ConnectionStrings[
  "AdventureWorks"].ConnectionString))
{
  conn.Open();

  SqlCommand cmd = new SqlCommand(
    @"select @BL:<@bl>n<@$p>        from Production.ProductModel
      WHERE Instructions IS NOT NULL", conn);
  SqlDataReader rdr = cmd.ExecuteReader();

  while (rdr.Read())
    bldr.Append(rdr["Instructions"].ToString() + "<br />");

  rdr.Close();
}
```

a `SqlXml` type. The `SqlXml` type has a `CreateReader` method which returns an `XmlReader`, which can be used to navigate over the XML.

If you are dealing with DataSets or DataTables, you can load the data as normal, but you must set the `ReturnProviderSpecificTypes` property to true, as seen in Listing 7.20, before loading the data, if you wish XML columns to be strongly typed.

This example loads the data twice, first with weak typing and then with strong typing. The output of this is:

```
Column type=System.String
Column type=System.Data.SqlTypes.SqlXml
```

The use of `ReturnProviderSpecificTypes` is an important consideration if you are building data layers that return XML columns. There is, of course, nothing stopping you from returning the XML as a string and then loading this into an `XmlDocument` using the `LoadXml` method, but it's an extra step you don't need to do with strongly typed data.

Listing 7.19. Streaming a Strongly Typed XML Column

```
SqlXml xml;
XmlReader xmlRdr;
StringBuilder bldr = new StringBuilder();

using (SqlConnection conn = new
  SqlConnection(ConfigurationManager.ConnectionStrings[
  "AdventureWorks"].ConnectionString))
{
  conn.Open();

  SqlCommand cmd = new SqlCommand(
    @"select @BL:<@bl>n<@$p>       from Production.ProductModel
      WHERE Instructions IS NOT NULL", conn);
  SqlDataReader rdr = cmd.ExecuteReader();

  while (rdr.Read())
  {
    xml = rdr.GetSqlXml(3);
    xmlRdr = xml.CreateReader();
    while (xmlRdr.Read())
    {
      switch (xmlRdr.NodeType)
      {
        case XmlNodeType.Element:
          bldr.Append("Element: " + xmlRdr.Name);
          break;
        case XmlNodeType.Text:
          bldr.Append("Text: " + xmlRdr.Value);
          break;
      }
    }
    bldr.Append("<br /><br />");
  }

  rdr.Close();
}
```

Listing 7.20. Loading Data into a DataTable

```
SqlXml xml;
StringBuilder bldr = new StringBuilder();

using (SqlConnection conn = new
  SqlConnection(ConfigurationManager.ConnectionStrings[
  "AdventureWorks"].ConnectionString))
{
```

```
SqlDataAdapter da = new SqlDataAdapter(
  @"select @BL:<@bl>n<@$p>        from Production.ProductModel
    WHERE Instructions IS NOT NULL", conn);
DataTable tbl = new DataTable();

da.Fill(tbl);
bldr.Append("Column type=" +
  tbl.Rows[0]["Instructions"].GetType().ToString() + "<br />");

da.ReturnProviderSpecificTypes = true ;
tbl = new DataTable();
da.Fill(tbl);
bldr.Append("Column type=" +
  tbl.Rows[0]["Instructions"].GetType().ToString());
}
```

SUMMARY

This chapter has not been an extensive look at XML, because the subject can easily take several chapters in its own right. What we've done is limit the topics to the most useful areas for ASP.NET developers, starting with Visual Studio 2005 and its support for XML and schemas.

We then moved on to displaying XML data through the use of data-bound controls and the XmlDataSource control. Here you saw the differences between binding to XML files with elements and XML files with attributes. One important point was the use of #InnerText as the TextField in bindings for nodes in a tree that bind to the data contained within elements, whereas for attributes, you can use the attribute name. You then saw the use of binding expressions and selections using XPath expressions, which are for use in templates of databound controls.

The next topic was transforming XML by using XSLT to transform XML from one form into another. You saw that XSLT can be a confusing language, but that the new XSLT Debugging features of Visual Studio 2005 allow XSLT to be stepped through just like other code. Transforming can be done with the XmlDataSoure control or with the XslCompiledTransform in code.

Next, you saw several ways of working with XML directly, either streaming the data with the XmlReader and XmlWriter objects or using in-memory XML stores such as the XmlDocument, XPathDocument, and

XmlDataDocument. The XPathNavigator provides a way of navigating over these in-memory stores, allowing you to move around the data, updating it if the underlying object allows it.

Finally, you saw how SQL Server 2005 allows XML to be stored as a native type, allowing validation and searching within the XML for each column. Accessing these XML columns can be done either as a string value or as a strongly typed SqlXml type.

Now it's time to move away from data and back into the world of ASP.NET forms and controls.

■ 8 ■
Building Interactive Web Forms

T RADITIONALLY, BUILDING WEB PAGES and Web applications has been unlike most other development scenarios. When you build an application in a language like Visual Basic, Pascal, C++, or any of the myriad other languages available, you are expected to know only two things: how to create the interface and how to write code. However, in the Web development arena, you have to master three topics: creating the interface (what the controls look like and do), understanding the underlying working of the environment (the HTML), and writing code. This is almost analogous to having to understand the microprocessor instructions when working in other high-level languages. Even the current leading-edge development tools like Visual Studio 2005 still offer three views of a Web page—Design view, Source view, and the server-side code itself.

In fact, Web developers have had a tough time over the years. It was fine to expect everyone to learn HTML and write their pages in a text editor in the early days, when the requirements for the pages were much simpler than they are today. In the intervening years, dynamic techniques for creating Web pages blossomed, yet all of them involved a low-level knowledge of the underlying instruction set—the HTML elements and their attributes.

Now, however, the level of complexity for even the most basic Web sites means that developers must be able to escape from the text editor approach and build pages from the same perspective, and using the same approaches, as when building traditional executable and Windows Forms applications.

In this chapter, we look at ASP.NET, and the controls and features it provides, from the point of view of an application developer rather than just a Web developer. You will see how—at last—the approach to building Web applications has moved away from the text editor and HTML guru to the use of a comprehensive development environment with a set of integrated and easy-to-understand controls. Of course, this approach is ideally suited to Web programming newcomers who may not have used earlier environments such as ASP 3.0, PHP, or even plain old HTML. The topics you will see in this chapter are:

- Understanding the control set for ASP.NET and choosing the right control
- Using the rich compound controls provided with ASP.NET
- Implementing validation in your pages
- Building Wizards with the Wizard control

To start with, you will explore the various types of controls that are available in ASP.NET 2.0 and how they relate to the postback architecture and event-driven environment of ASP.NET.

The ASP.NET Control Set

When building ASP.NET Web Form pages, it is vital to understand the range of controls that are available. You also need to know how the choice of controls affects the way that pages work and the way that you write code to implement the required server-side processes. The evolution of ASP.NET and Web programming in general means that often several different controls are available to implement a specific feature.

Standard HTML Server Controls

The standard HTML server controls generate the basic HTML elements, as reflected by the control names. In particular, this set of controls focuses on the HTML input-type controls—although there are many other types of controls in the 30 or so supplied in ASP.NET. This includes the `HtmlGenericControl` class, which ASP.NET uses if it encounters an HTML element with the `runat="server"` attribute that does not match any of the other HTML server controls.

The main advantage of the HTML server controls is that they are lightweight compared to the other ASP.NET controls. This might be a consideration if you build very complex pages, although in most cases the difference will only be noticeable when the server is under pressure or short of memory.

The HTML server controls expose properties named exactly as in the HTML declarations of the element. For example, the `HtmlInputText` control that implements a text box exposes the contents of the text box through the `Value` property, whereas all the other controls in the `System.Web.UI.WebControls` namespace use the more intuitive `Text` property.

> All of the standard HTML server controls are in the `System.Web.UI.HtmlControls` namespace. A full list and a description of each one is available at http://msdn2.microsoft.com/library/tct4wcsd(en-us,vs.80).aspx.

If you build your pages using Visual Studio 2005 or Visual Web Developer, you will find that the designer does not automatically add the `runat="server"` attribute to these controls when you place them on a page. This means that they are not, at this point, server controls—they are simply ordinary HTML elements that implement the controls in the browser. You must add the `runat="server"` attribute to the element yourself if you wish to interact with the control in your server-side code.

However, omitting it where server-side access is not required makes the page less resource-intensive. The browser will recognize and apply the attributes for these controls because they use the standard HTML attribute names. Therefore, the elements do not *have* to be server controls, and this is why Visual Studio omits the `runat="server"` attribute by default.

Text and Image Display Controls

ASP.NET provides a set of controls that display content without themselves being interactive. The most commonly used are the `Label` and `Image` controls, though there are other controls that you can use to display non-interactive content. Like all of the ASP.NET server controls, other than the HTML server controls described in the preceding section, the property names are consistent, and (in most cases) differ from the attribute names generated when the page renders to the browser. This is a perfect example of how ASP.NET brings Web programming more into line with normal application-style approaches by hiding the "third view" (the HTML) from developers and allowing them to concentrate on building the interface and then writing code.

Bear in mind that you do not *have* to use a control to display content. You can place text and normal declarative HTML elements in the page, just as Web developers have always done. When using a tool such as Visual Studio 2005, you can format and color this text without having to go into Source view and work directly with the HTML. You can also use the toolbar options to create bulleted and numbered lists, justify the text, and specify the font and text size. Table 8.1 shows the ASP.NET server controls for displaying text and images.

A list of all the ASP.NET Web Forms controls in the `System.Web.UI.` `WebControls` namespace is available at http://msdn2.microsoft.com/ library/8bhzsw6t(en-us,vs.80).aspx.

All Web Forms controls (server controls other than the standard HTML controls) are declared in the source of the page as elements with the prefix "asp" and must include the `runat="server"` attribute within the control declaration element. Visual Studio adds this automatically. Without it, processing of the element within the source of the page to generate the appropriate HTML content does not occur. Instead, the client receives only the element declaration itself, which the browser ignores because it does not recognize the "asp" namespace. If you find that controls are not appearing on a page when you expect them to be, use the **View | Source** option in your browser to see what the client is actually receiving.

There is not enough space in this chapter to demonstrate all of the ASP.NET controls, though you will see them all used in various ways throughout this book. However, in this chapter you will see how some of the more useful controls, and their specific features, can be used. For example, the next two sections demonstrate the basic ways you can use the `Panel` and the `Table` controls.

Example: Using the Panel Control

This example demonstrates how you can use a `Panel` control to create an area on the page for the display of text or other content. The `Panel` control

TABLE 8.1: Text and Image Display Server Controls

Control	Description
Image	Displays an image specified as the `ImageUrl` property. This can be a static image file (usually a GIF, PNG, or JPG image), or an animated GIF image.
Label	Displays a static text string specified as the `Text` property. This string can contain HTML markup, if required. At runtime, the control generates an HTML `<span>` element to contain the text.
Literal	Displays a static text string specified as the `Text` property. Unlike the `Label` control, however, the `Literal` control adds no HTML or other content of its own. It simply places the value of the `Text` property into the page at the location of the control. This value can contain HTML and other markup or content. It has a `Mode` property that specifies how the control translates or modifies the content at runtime. It can also remove unsupported elements depending on the current client type, and HTML-encode the content. A useful application of this control is the ability to show and hide blocks of content by setting the `Visible` property at runtime.
Panel	Generates either an HTML `<div>` element or a single-column single-cell HTML `<table>`, depending on the client type, and inserts the text or content specified as the `Text` property of the control. Setting the border and background color properties provides a useful technique for generating contrasting areas of content within a page. The `GroupingText` property allows a caption to appear at the top of the `Panel` content, and a fixed size `Panel` can display scrollbars.
Table	Generates an HTML `<table>` to which you dynamically add `TableHeaderRow`, `TableRow`, and `TableFooterRow` controls, each of which then contains a series of `TableHeaderCell` or `TableCell` controls. Use this control when you want to build tables dynamically and/or access the rows and cells in server-side code. In Visual Studio, for tables that do not require these features, use the `Table` HTML fragment available from the HTML section of the Toolbox, which does not generate the `runat="server"` attribute on the table, the rows, or the cells.

generates an HTML <div> element or a single-column single-row table, depending on the browser that accesses the page. Listing 8.1 shows the declarations of the control as they appear in Source view. You can, of course, set the properties of the Panel controls and enter the text content in Design view.

Listing 8.1. Using the Panel Control

```
<asp:Panel id="MyPanel1" Width="200" Height="100" ScrollBars="Vertical"
        BorderStyle="Solid" BorderWidth="1" runat="server">
  This is some test text for the Panel control to demonstrate ...
</asp:Panel>

<br /><br />

<asp:Panel id="MyPanel2" Width="200" Height="100"
        BorderStyle="Solid" BorderWidth="1" runat="server"
        Direction="RightToLeft" ScrollBars="Vertical">
  This is some test text for the Panel control to demonstrate ...
</asp:Panel>

<br /><br />

<asp:Panel id="MyPanel3" Wrap="false" Width="200" Height="100"
        BorderStyle="Solid" BorderWidth="1" runat="server"
        ScrollBars="Both">
  Scroll bars are useful when the text cannot<br />be wrapped ...
</asp:Panel>

<br /><br />

<asp:Panel id="MyPanel4" Width="200" runat="server"
        GroupingText="My Panel">
  This is some test text for the Panel control to demonstrate ...
</asp:Panel>
```

Notice how the Width and Height properties specify the size of the panel, and that you can also specify the addition of scroll bars and the text direction within the panel. The last panel demonstrates the use of the GroupingText property to generate an HTML <fieldset> and <legend> instead of the more usual <div> or HTML table. Figure 8.1 shows the example as it appears in Internet Explorer.

For more details about the Panel control, see: http://msdn2. microsoft.com/library/58dzaz0a(en-us,vs.80).aspx.

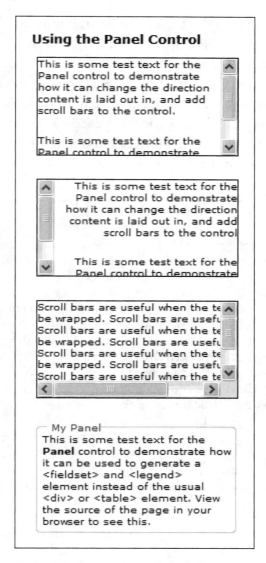

Figure 8.1: The Panel control example

Example: Using the Table Control and Associated Header Cells

This example demonstrates how you can generate HTML tables dynamically using the `Table`, `TableHeaderRow`, `TableRow`, `TableHeaderCell`, and `TableCell` controls. Each cell is added to the `Cells` collection of an appropriate row type, which is then added to the `Rows` collection of the `Table`.

The example also illustrates how you can improve the accessibility of your HTML tables using the new `AssociatedHeaderCellID` property of the ASP.NET `TableCell` class. The `AssociatedHeaderCellID` property accepts an array containing the ID of the row and column header cells that apply to the current cell, allowing non-visual user agents and specialized page readers to display the values in these header cells. This makes it much easier for users of these types of devices to assimilate the contents of a table without actually being able to see the layout.

> **■ NOTE**
>
> When a browser renders an HTML table, comprehending the information it contains is generally a matter of scanning the rows and columns and mentally relating them with the header descriptions for each row. Often the table is like a spreadsheet in design, where each cell value in the body relates to the description for the column and the row where it resides. For most users, this just involves looking at the header and the left-hand row to locate the desired descriptions, and then scanning down and across to the cell where they meet. However, for users of non-visual browsers and user-agents, this is hard to do. Their browser will usually iterate through the table row by row, and it is easy to lose track of which header description each cell in the row relates to. To assist such users, HTML 4.0 includes the `headers` attribute for a table cell, which should be set to a list of the header cell ID values for the header and row description that this cell relates to. This way, the browser can extract the header and row descriptions as it iterates through the cells in each row and present them to the user in a suitable manner.

The example page contains just an empty `Table` control, declared like this:

```
<asp:Table id="MyTable"  GridLines="Both" CellPadding="5"
           runat="server" />
```

Listing 8.2 shows the code in the `Page_Load` event handler that creates the table. Each header cell, including the first cell in each row (the header for the row), has an `ID` that is made up of the text "`HDesc`" and the column index, or "`RDesc`" and the row index. To make it easy to see the values of the `ID`, it is copied into the `ToolTip` property of these cells as well.

Listing 8.2. Creating the Table in the Page_Load Event Handler

```csharp
public void Page_Load()
{
  Int32 iRows = 4;
  Int32 iCols = 3;
  TableRow oRow;
  TableCell oCell;

  // create header row, setting ID of each cell
  oRow = new TableHeaderRow();
  for (Int32 iColCount = 0; iColCount <= iCols; iColCount++)
  {
    oCell = new TableHeaderCell();
    oCell.ID = "HDesc" + iColCount.ToString();
    oCell.Text = "Header" + iColCount.ToString();
    oCell.ToolTip = "ID = '" + oCell.ID  + "'";
    oRow.Cells.Add(oCell);
  }
  MyTable.Rows.Add(oRow);

  // create data rows
  for (Int32 iRowCount = 0; iRowCount < iRows; iRowCount++)
  {
    // first cell is a <th> "header" containing description of row
    oRow = new TableHeaderRow();
    oCell = new TableHeaderCell();
    oCell.ID = "RDesc" + iRowCount.ToString();
    oCell.Text = "RowDescription" + iRowCount.ToString();
    oCell.ToolTip = "ID = '" + oCell.ID + "'";
    oRow.Cells.Add(oCell);
    // remaining cells are data <td> elements
    for (Int32 iColCount = 1; iColCount <= iCols; iColCount++)
    {
      oCell = new TableCell();
      oCell.Text = "Row" + iRowCount.ToString() + " Col"
                 + iColCount.ToString();
      // add HTML "headers" attributes to cell
      oCell.AssociatedHeaderCellID = new String[2]
                             {"HDesc" + iColCount.ToString(),
                              "RDesc" + iRowCount.ToString()};
      // copy into tooltip so as to make visible in page
      oCell.ToolTip = "AssociatedHeaderCellID = '"
                    + oCell.AssociatedHeaderCellID[0] + " "
                    + oCell.AssociatedHeaderCellID[1] + "'";
      oRow.Cells.Add(oCell);
    }
    MyTable.Rows.Add(oRow);
  }
```

```
// create footer row
oRow = new TableFooterRow();
for (Int32 iColCount = 0; iColCount <= iCols; iColCount++)
{
  oCell = new TableCell();
  oCell.ID = "FDesc" + iColCount.ToString();
  oCell.Text = "Footer" + iColCount.ToString();
  // add HTML "headers" attributes to cell
  oCell.AssociatedHeaderCellID = new String[1]
                          { "HDesc" + iColCount.ToString() };
  // copy into tooltip so as to make visible in page
  oCell.ToolTip = "AssociatedHeaderCellID = '"
              + oCell.AssociatedHeaderCellID[0] + "'";
  oRow.Cells.Add(oCell);
}
MyTable.Rows.Add(oRow);
}
```

When creating the rows for the body of the table, the code creates a `String` array containing the column header ID and row header ID that apply to this cell, and then sets these on the cell using the `AssociatedHeaderCellID` property. Again, this is copied into the `ToolTip` property to make it easy to see the results when viewing the page. The `AssociatedHeaderCellID` property is also set for the footer cells, but this time it uses just the ID of the appropriate header cell.

Figure 8.2 shows the result. To see the way that the `AssociatedHeader-CellID` property adds attributes to the cells in a table, move your mouse pointer over the header, body, and footer rows to see the cell ID or the value of the `AssociatedHeaderCellID` property, or view the source for this page in your browser and look for the headers attributes.

> For more details about the `Table` control, see: http://msdn2.microsoft.com/library/sdw1fhcy(en-us,vs.80).aspx.

Hyperlink and Navigation Controls

An understanding of the specific behavior of different types of controls is vital. As an example, consider the situation where you need to implement a hyperlink in your page. You can generate a hyperlink using a normal HTML `<a>` element, an `<a>` element implemented as an `HtmlAnchor` server control, an ASP.NET `Hyperlink` server control, or a more complex control such as a `HyperLinkField` column in a list control or an `ImageMap` control. However,

```
Using the Table Control

┌──────────────┬─────────────┬─────────────┬─────────────┐
│   Header0    │   Header1   │   Header2   │   Header3   │
├──────────────┼─────────────┼─────────────┼─────────────┤
│ RowDescription0 │ Row0 Col1 │ Row0 Col2 │ Row0 Col3 │
├──────────────┼─────────────┼─────────────┼─────────────┤
│ RowDescription1 │ Row1 Col1 │ Row1 Col2 │ Row1 Col3 │
├──────────────┼─────────────┼─────────────┼─────────────┤
│ RowDescription2 │ Row2 Col1 │ Row2 Col2 │ Row2 Col3 │
├──────────────┤  AssociatedHeaderCellID = 'HDesc1 RDesc2'  │
│ RowDescription3 │ Row3 Col1 │ Row3 Col2 │ Row3 Col3 │
├──────────────┼─────────────┼─────────────┼─────────────┤
│   Footer0    │   Footer1   │   Footer2   │   Footer3   │
└──────────────┴─────────────┴─────────────┴─────────────┘
```

FIGURE 8.2: The dynamically generated Table control with the Headers attributes set on each cell

other controls such as a LinkButton, a CommandField column in a grid control, and several other rich controls such as the Menu and Wizard can also generate "normal" underlined hyperlinks in the page.

The difference is that the latter set of controls generates a postback to the same page when clicked, where the event-driven architecture of ASP.NET can produce the effect of a normal application form (hence, the name Web Forms). The former controls cause *navigation* (generally to a different page) rather than a *postback*, and so the type of control you choose is obviously vitally important. Later in this chapter, you will see more discussion about the postback architecture and the event-driven approach to Web programming in ASP.NET 2.0. Table 8.2 shows the ASP.NET Web Forms controls for creating clickable hyperlinks.

Bear in mind that many other controls can initiate a postback to the server. These include the various button controls, and the many interactive controls such as lists and checkboxes that have the AutoPostback property set to true. Even the BulletedList control (described in the section on list controls) can display the items in the list as hyperlinks.

Example: The ImageMap Control
This example demonstrates how you can use the ImageMap control to create a clickable image map on the client, based on a series of HotSpot control instances defined within the ImageMap control declaration.

Table 8.2: Hyperlink and Navigation Server Controls

Control	Description
HyperLink	Generates simple text hyperlink using an HTML `<a>` element, with the destination URL specified as the `NavigateUrl` property. You can display a clickable image instead of text by setting the `ImageUrl` property (the control automatically hides the image border in this case). Note, however, that the embedded image (an `<img>` element within the `<a>` element) is not a server control, and so you cannot interact with the `<img>` element server-side at runtime.
ImageButton	Generates an HTML `<input type="image">` element using the image specified as the `ImageUrl` property, and causes a postback to the server rather than navigation to another page. However, cross-page posting (posting of the form to a different page) is possible by specifying the destination URL as the `PostBackUrl` property of the control. Another useful feature is that the X and Y coordinates of the mouse-pointer within the image are available in the event handler that handles the `Click` event of this control.
ImageMap	A common navigation scenario is the use of a clickable image, where each region navigates to a different page. While this is achievable with an `ImageButton` control, it is not an ideal approach (in terms of its accessibility to all users or in terms of its provision of an intuitive interface) because the result of clicking an area is not determinable by the client. The `ImageMap` control takes advantage of the client-side capabilities and provides a better solution—one that most specialist browsers can accommodate and display information about in a useful way. A series of hotspot child controls (`CircleHotSpot`, `RectangleHotSpot`, and `PolygonHotSpot`) define the areas of the image and the target URL of each one. By default, the hotspot controls cause navigation to the URL specified as the `NavigateUrl` property. Alternatively, each hotspot can cause a postback to the URL specified as the `PostBackUrl` property, depending on the setting of the `HotSpotMode` property.
LinkButton	Generates a hyperlink `<a>` element, and so looks just like a normal hyperlink. However, the `href` attribute is set to a JavaScript function that calls the `submit` method of the server-side form in the page, causing a postback rather than navigation to another URL. Cross-page posting (posting of the form to a different page) is possible by specifying the destination URL as the `PostBackUrl` property of the control.

Control	Description
Menu	Generates a complete hierarchical menu, with dynamic drop-down or fly-out submenus, from an XML sitemap file. This includes the client-side code to implement the dynamic behavior, and the hyperlinks that cause navigation to the specified pages. For more details, see Chapter 10.
SiteMapPath	Generates a "breadcrumb trail" that indicates the location of the current page within the hierarchy of the site, as described in the sitemap file. For more details, see Chapter 10.
TreeView	Generates a complete tree view, including all client-side code required to implement dynamic behavior. The tree view can be static, or dynamic with collapsible nodes. Each node can be a hyperlink, a checkbox, or static text.

Listing 8.3 shows the declaration of the controls in this example, including several `PolygonHotSpot` controls and one `CircleHotSpot` control.

Listing 8.3. The Declaration of the ImageMap Control and HotSpot Controls

```
<asp:ImageMap id="UKMap" HotSpotMode="Postback" ImageUrl="UKMap.jpg"
          OnClick="MapClicked" runat="server">
  <asp:PolygonHotSpot PostBackValue="Northern Scotland"
        Coordinates="205,17,328,38,346,99,200,160,270,132,271,
                      130,268,132,270,130,201,159" />
  <asp:PolygonHotSpot PostBackValue="Southern Scotland"
        Coordinates="209,166,225,224,339,200,335,112" />
  ...
  <asp:CircleHotSpot PostBackValue="London"
        x="411" y="452" radius="11" />
  <asp:PolygonHotSpot PostBackValue="The Midlands"
        Coordinates="329,424,307,381,347,348,418,333,412,380,
                      407,429,399,439,358,428" />
  <asp:PolygonHotSpot PostBackValue="South East England"
        Coordinates="391,471,400,468,430,465,464,467,443,
                      494,411,506,394,494" />
</asp:ImageMap>
```

When you click a hotspot in this example, a postback occurs and the `Click` event is raised for the `ImageMap` control. This causes the routine named `MapClicked` (as specified in the declaration of the `ImageMap` control) to execute. It simply shows the `PostBackValue` property of that `HotSpot` control (see Listing 8.4).

Listing 8.4. Displaying the Value of the HotSpot That Was Clicked

```
public void MapClicked(Object sender, ImageMapEventArgs e)
{
    Message.Text = "You selected " + e.PostBackValue;
}
```

Figure 8.3 shows the result of running this example and clicking on the central area of the map. An alternative approach is to specify a URL for the

FIGURE 8.3: Using the ImageMap control to create a clickable image map

NavigateUrl property of each HotSpot control so that clicking on the map navigates directly to the target page.

You can also add HotSpot instances to an ImageMap control dynamically, as shown in Listing 8.5. This code adds five RectangleHotSpot controls to the ImageMap, each being 100 pixels square and arranged in a column at the left-hand side of the image. Each HotSpot will cause navigation to the page name MyPage.aspx, with the index of the HotSpot that was clicked as the area value in the query string. Notice that the code also adds an alt attribute to each HotSpot using the AlternateText property. This will appear on the client as a pop-up tooltip, and is useful in non-visual user agents to assist navigation.

Listing 8.5. Adding HotSpot Controls to an ImageMap Dynamically

```
// dynamically create hot spots for ImageMap control
HotSpotCollection hs = MyImageMap.HotSpots;
for (Int32 i = 0; i < 5; i++)
{
  RectangleHotSpot r = new RectangleHotSpot();
  r.Top = (i * 100);
  r.Left = 0;
  r.Bottom = r.Top + 99;
  r.Right = 99;
  r.HotSpotMode = HotSpotMode.Navigate;
  r.NavigateUrl = String.Format("~/MyPage.aspx?area={0}", i);
  r.AlternateText = String.Format("Go to area {0}", i);
  hs.Add(r);
}
```

For more details about the ImageMap control, see: http://msdn2. microsoft.com/library/7f9s61xx(en-us,vs.80).aspx.

Example: The TreeView Control

A common way to display hierarchical information is with a TreeView control. In Visual Studio, this control appears in the Navigation section of the Toobox, but it is useful for all kinds of tasks. This example demonstrates how you can use it to display information from an XML file exposed through an XmlDataSource control. The XML file contains a list of prestige vehicles, with several models and the various (fictional) trim packages for each one. Listing 8.6 shows the XML file with some repeating elements removed for clarity.

Listing 8.6. The XML Source File for the TreeView Example

```
<Automobiles>
  <Manufacturer Make="Audi" WebSite="http://www.audi.com/">
    <Car Model="A4" Id="02347">
      <Package Trim="Sport Package"/>
      <Package Trim="Luxury Package"/>
    </Car>
    <Car Model="A6" Id="02932">
      <Package Trim="Sport Package"/>
      <Package Trim="Luxury Package"/>
    </Car>
    <Car Model="A8"  Id="09381">
      <Package Trim="Sport Package"/>
      <Package Trim="Luxury Package"/>
    </Car>
  </Manufacturer>
  ... other manufacturers here ...
</Automobiles>
```

This is bound to an `XmlDataSource` control declared in the page, as shown in Listing 8.6. Below this you can see the declaration of the `TreeView` control, which specifies that the data will come from the `XmlDataSource` control by using the `DataSourceID` attribute. The `Expand-Depth` attribute specifies that the list is closed (with only the root node visible) by default, and the `ShowLines` attribute specifies that dotted lines will appear between each node when expanded. You can also set a wide range of properties that control the style and format of the tree items, and you can replace the default images used for the open and close buttons in the tree with your own if you wish. When the user clicks a node, the `TreeView` control raises the `SelectedNodeChanged` event and the routine named `ShowValue` will execute.

Nested inside the `TreeNode` declaration are the binding details for the XML file. By default, the `TreeView` displays the name of each node in the XML file, but you can use the `TreeNodeBinding` elements to specify how the binding to each node takes place. In this example, the first `TreeNodeBinding` element specifies that the `TreeView` should display the value of the `Make` attribute of the `Manufacturer` element as a hyperlink that navigates to the value of the `WebSite` attribute in the same element.

The remaining two `TreeNodeBinding` elements specify that the `TreeView` should just display the value of the `Model` attribute of the `Car` element and the

> **▪ NOTE**
>
> If you think of each element as a data row, the attributes are effectively the columns in the row and so it is similar to the techniques for creating `BoundField` controls in a `GridView` control when using a `SqlDataSource` control—as shown in Chapter 2.

Listing 8.7. The XmlDataSource Control and TreeView Control Declarations

```
<asp:XmlDataSource ID="XmlDataSource1" runat="server"
                   DataFile="~/ch08/XmlDataSource.xml" />
<asp:TreeView id="TreeView1" runat="server"
              DataSourceID="XmlDataSource1"
              ExpandDepth="0" ShowLines="true"
              OnSelectedNodeChanged="ShowValue">
  <DataBindings>
   <asp:TreeNodeBinding DataMember="Manufacturer" TextField="Make"
                        NavigateUrlField="WebSite" Target="_blank"
                        ToolTip="Visit this manufacturer's Web site" />
   <asp:TreeNodeBinding DataMember="Car" TextField="Model" />
   <asp:TreeNodeBinding DataMember="Package" TextField="Trim" />
  </DataBindings>
</asp:TreeView>
```

value of the `Trim` attribute of the `Package` element. Because there is no `NavigateUrlField` specified, these links cause a postback to the server. Figure 8.4 shows the example page, and you can see how the nodes in the XML file display as a clickable and expandable tree. You can also see the `ToolTip` for the `Car` element, and clicking this will open the appropriate manufacturer's Web site in a new browser window.

Listing 8.8 shows the code that handles the `SelectedNodeChanged` event, which runs when you click a node other than a `Car` node. The value of the clicked node is available directly from the `SelectedValue` property of the `TreeView` control. However, you can also get a reference to the node

Listing 8.8. Handling the SelectedNodeChanged Event

```
public void ShowValue(Object sender, EventArgs e)
{
  Label1.Text = "You selected:" + TreeView1.SelectedValue + "<br />";
  Label1.Text += "DataPath is:" + TreeView1.SelectedNode.DataPath
            + "<br />";
  Label1.Text += "ValuePath is:" + TreeView1.SelectedNode.ValuePath
            + "<br />";
}
```

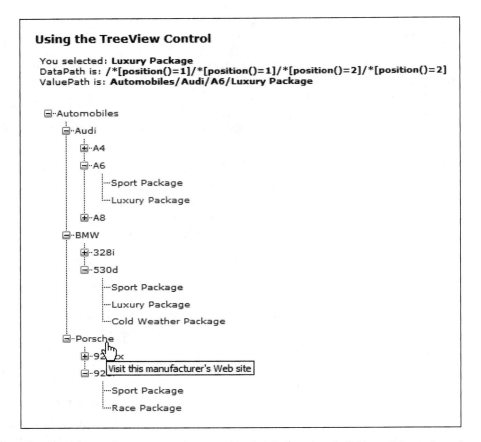

FIGURE 8.4: The TreeView example page showing the results of clicking a Trim node and then hovering over a Car node

itself using the `SelectedNode` property (this is similar to the way that most other list controls work, as you will see later in this chapter). The properties of the node include the `DataPath`, which returns the XPath expression the control uses to extract the value for the XML file, and the `ValuePath`, which is simply the path from the root node to the current node. All these values are visible at the top of Figure 8.4.

For more details about the TreeView control, see: http://msdn2. microsoft.com/library/f74eswe6(en-us,vs.80).aspx.

Input and Form Controls

ASP.NET 2.0 provides a set of controls that implement the range of interactive controls you see in a desktop application. These have the same names as the controls available in other environments such as VB.NET, and they provide features such as different types of button, various styles of text box, check boxes, and option (radio) buttons. They also all use a similar and standard set of property, method, and event names.

> This convergence of control types, combined with the design-led programming environment of tools like Visual Studio 2005 and Visual Web Developer, means that the differences between traditional application development and Web development have considerably narrowed. This is, of course, part of the process of moving toward a common display language that Windows Vista and operating systems even further down the line will use.

In addition, a set of special controls can easily perform client-side and server-side validation of the data submitted by the user. Table 8.3 summarizes all of these controls.

The next two sections demonstrate the `FileUpload` control, and show how the validation controls can be used to simplify validation of input values in your Web pages.

Example: The FileUpload Control

This example demonstrates use of the `FileUpload` control to upload files from the client to the server over HTTP. The `FileUpload` control generates the `TextBox` and `Browse` button you see in the example page (see Figure 8.5), and you just have to provide a button to start the process.

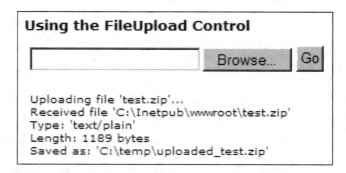

FIGURE 8.5: Displaying information about an uploaded file using the FileUpload control

TABLE 8.3: Input and Form server controls

Control	Description
Button	Generates a standard "submit" button in the page, with the caption provided by the Text property. Causes a postback, and raises a Click event that you handle in your server-side code. You can use the SubmitBehavior property to specify that a click on the button will cause a postback through the same mechanism as a LinkButton (calling the submit method of the form) instead of the browser's normal submit behavior. Cross-page posting (posting of the form to a different page) is possible by specifying the destination URL as the PostBackUrl property of the control.
CheckBox	Generates an <input type="checkbox"> element in the page, which implements a checkbox in the browser. The Text property sets the caption next to the checkbox, displayed in a <span> element that encloses the complete control. The Checked property indicates whether the checkbox is ticked, and there is no Value property (due to the way that the browser submits the setting of a checkbox control). If the AutoPostBack property is true, the browser submits the page when the user changes the setting of the checkbox. The InputAttributes and LabelAttributes properties give access to the collection of attributes on the <input> and <span> elements, respectively, allowing fine control over the appearance and formatting.
FileUpload	Generates an <input type="file"> element in the page, which implements a textbox and button in the browser that enables uploading of files to the server. There is no Text property, and server-side code cannot set the file name. Server-side access to the posted file is through the PostedFile property, and the properties HasFile, FileBytes, FileContent, and FileName provide information about the uploaded file. The file size limit is set in the maxRequestLength section of the server's Machine.Config or Web.Config file.
HiddenField	Creates a hidden control in the page that is useful for storing values sent to or returned from client-side code (such as JavaScript). The browser sends the value back to the server when the user submits the page; it becomes available to server-side code as the Value property.
RadioButton	Generates an <input type="radio"> element in the page, which implements an option button (or "radio" button) in the browser. The Text property sets the caption next to the button, displayed in a <span> element that encloses the complete control. The Checked property indicates whether the option is selected. This is the only control that allows use of the same value for the name attribute in more than one control, accessed through the GroupName property. If the AutoPostBack

Control	Description
	property is `true`, the browser submits the page when the user changes the setting of the option button. The `InputAttributes` and `LabelAttributes` properties give access to the collection of attributes on the `<input>` and `<span>` elements, respectively, allowing fine control over the appearance and formatting.
TextBox	Generates a text entry control in the page. The type depends on the setting of the `TextMode` property, which is a value from the `TextBoxMode` enumeration. This can be `SingleLine` to generate an `<input type="text">` element (a normal text box), `MultiLine` to generate a `<textarea>` element, or `Password` to generate an `<input type="password">` element (a password entry box that displays dots or asterisks instead of the typed text). The `Columns` property defines the width in characters. When `TextMode` is `SingleLine` or `Password`, the `MaxLength` property specifies the maximum input length. When `TextMode` is `MultiLine`, the `Rows` property specifies the number of rows of text to display and the `Wrap` property controls text wrapping within the text box. If the `AutoPostBack` property is `true`, the browser submits the page when the user changes the text and then moves the input focus to another control.
Compare Validator	Attached to an input control on the page, this control compares the value against that in another control, against a specifically declared value, or just checks that the control value is of the specified data type. If validation fails, the browser does not submit the page and an error message can be shown.
Custom Validator	Attached to an input control on the page, this control performs server-side and client-side validation of the value using custom functions that you provide. If validation fails, the browser does not submit the page and an error message can be shown.
Range Validator	Attached to an input control on the page, this control checks if the value of that control falls between two specifically declared values. If validation fails, the browser does not submit the page and an error message can be shown.
Regular Expression Validator	Attached to an input control on the page, this control checks if the value of that control matches a regular expression you specify. If validation fails, the browser does not submit the page and an error message can be shown.
Requiredfield Validator	Attached to an input control on the page, this control checks if that control contains a value. If not, the browser does not submit the page and an error message can be shown.
Validation Summary	Displays a list of the validation errors found in the page, or in the current validation group.

Listing 8.9 shows the declaration of the `FileUpload` control and a `Button` control for the user to start the upload process.

Listing 8.9. Declaring a FileUpload Control and Button to Start the Process

```
<asp:FileUpload id="MyFile" runat="server" />
<asp:Button id="btnUpload" Text="Go"
    OnClick="GetFile" runat="server" />
```

Listing 8.10 shows the code that runs when the Go button causes a postback to the server. Some details about the process are available as properties of the `FileUpload` control, and others are obtained from properties of the `Posted-File` instance exposed by the `FileUpload` control once upload is complete.

Listing 8.10. Handling an Uploaded File and Displaying Information About It

```
public void GetFile(Object sender, EventArgs e)
{
  if (MyFile.HasFile)
  {
    try
    {
      // get values from control
      lblResult.Text = "Uploading file '" + MyFile.FileName
                      + "'...<br />";
      // get values from PostedFile instance
      MyFile.SaveAs("C:\\temp\\uploaded_" + MyFile.FileName);
      lblResult.Text += "Received file '"
                      + MyFile.PostedFile.FileName + "'<br />"
                      + "Type: '" + MyFile.PostedFile.ContentType
                      + "'<br />Length: "
                      + MyFile.PostedFile.ContentLength.ToString()
                      + " bytes<br />"
                      + "Saved as: 'C:\\temp\\uploaded_"
                      + MyFile.FileName + "'";
    }
    catch (Exception ex)
    {
      lblResult.Text += "Cannot save uploaded file<br />" + ex.Message;
    }
  }
  else
  {
    lblResult.Text += "No file received";
  }
}
```

Remember that the default setting of the maximum file size to upload is 4096 bytes. You can change this, if necessary, by setting the maximum file (request headers) size you want to allow as the `maxRequestLength` attribute of the `<httpRuntime>` section of `machine.config` or `web.config`. Bear in mind that this might cause extended request times or open your server to denial-of-service attacks. For more details, see: http://msdn2.microsoft.com/library/w8fdw8xd(en-us,vs.80).aspx.

Example: The Validation Controls

One feature of building Web Form pages that collect data is ensuring that you validate data input by the user before you accept it. It is nice to do this client-side where possible, and avoid postbacks until the user fully completes the form. However, you must always validate (or re-validate) values on the server following a postback to protect your applications from spoofed pages or malformed requests.

The ASP.NET validation controls can perform client-side validation where the browser supports it, and always performs the same validation server-side afterwards. You can turn off client-side validation if you wish. The example we're using here demonstrates all of the validation controls listed in Table 8.3, with the exception of the `CustomValidator` control. Figure 8.6 shows the

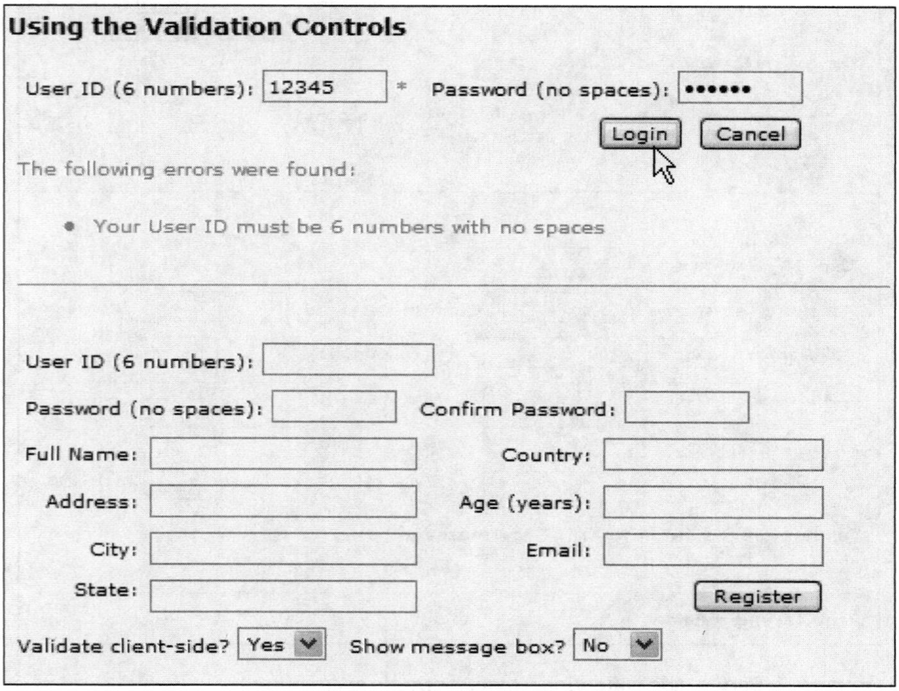

FIGURE 8.6: Client-side validation when an error is encountered

example page when you first open it and click the **Login** button without entering sufficient digits into the first text box.

In most modern browsers, the validation takes place client-side without causing a postback to the server. However, if you turn off client-side validation using the drop-down list box at the bottom left of the page and then click **Login** again, you will see that the page is submitted. This time, a message is shown at the bottom of the screen indicating that the `IsValid` property of the `Page` is `false`—in other words, validation failed for at least one control (see Figure 8.7). If you enter valid values for the top two controls in the page and click **Login**, you will see that `Page.IsValid` returns `true`.

The example page contains a great many controls declarations—too many to list in full here. However, Listing 8.11 shows the controls in the top

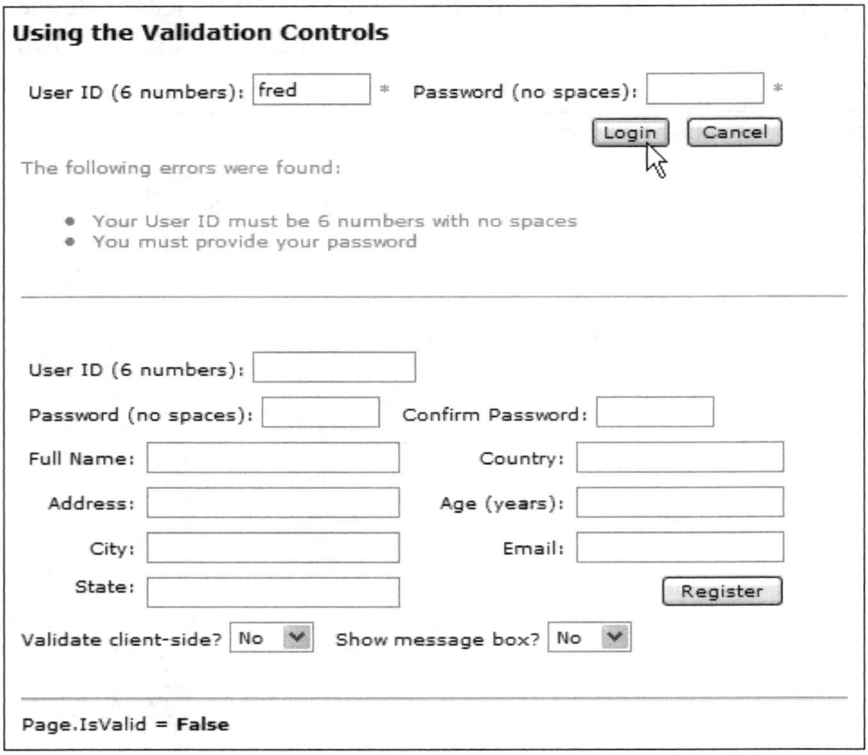

FIGURE 8.7: Server-side validation when an error is encountered

"Login" section of the page. Both TextBox controls have two validation controls attached. The RequiredFieldValidator checks that the TextBox contains a value, and the RegularExpressionValidator matches the value against a regular expression that signifies a valid value.

> **■ NOTE**
>
> With the exception of the RequiredFieldValidator, an empty control is considered as valid (although the CustomValidator will consider empty values as invalid if you set the ValidateEmptyText property of that control).

Listing 8.11. The Controls for the Login Section of the Example Page

```
User ID (6 numbers):
<asp:TextBox id="txtLogonUserID"
     TabIndex="1" Columns="10" runat="server"
     ToolTip="Must be 6 numbers, no spaces" />

<asp:RequiredFieldValidator id="valRequLogonUserID" runat="server"
     ValidationGroup="LoginGroup" ControlToValidate="txtLogonUserID"
     Display="Dynamic" ErrorMessage="You must provide a User ID">*
</asp:RequiredFieldValidator>

<asp:RegularExpressionValidator id="valRegexLogonUserID" runat="server"
     ValidationGroup="LoginGroup" ControlToValidate="txtLogonUserID"
     ValidationExpression="\d{6}" Display="Dynamic"
     ErrorMessage="Your User ID must be 6 numbers with no spaces">*
</asp:RegularExpressionValidator>

  Password (no spaces):
<asp:TextBox id="txtLogonPWord"
     TabIndex="2" TextMode="Password" Columns="10" runat="server"
     ToolTip="Must be between 4 and 8 characters, no spaces" />

<asp:RequiredFieldValidator id="valRequLogonPWord" runat="server"
     ValidationGroup="LoginGroup" ControlToValidate="txtLogonPWord"
     Display="Dynamic" ErrorMessage="You must provide a password">*
</asp:RequiredFieldValidator>

<asp:RegularExpressionValidator id="valRegexLogonPWord"
runat="server"
     ValidationGroup="LoginGroup" ControlToValidate="txtLogonPWord"
     ValidationExpression="\S{4,8}" Display="Dynamic"
     ErrorMessage="Your password must be between 4 and 8 ...">*
</asp:RegularExpressionValidator>

<asp:Button id="btnLogon" ValidationGroup="LoginGroup"
     Text="Login" OnClick="DoValidate" runat="server" /> 

<asp:Button id="btnCancel" CausesValidation="false"
     Text="Cancel" runat="server" />
```

Each validation control is attached to its source control (a `TextBox` in this example) through the `ControlToValidate` attribute, and declares an error message to display when validation fails. The "content" (the text between the opening and closing tags) of each validation control is displayed in the page at the point where the validation control is located when validation fails, and the example page uses the common approach of an asterisk. The `Display="Dynamic"` attribute indicates that this text is removed from the page when the value is valid and so does not take up space. When `Display="Static"`, the content is hidden, and a blank area shows in the page.

The `ValidationGroup` attribute allows you to have more than one set of validated controls on the same page. In the example, there is a "Login" section and a "Register" section, and the validation controls have a different value for the `ValidationGroup` attribute in each section. Only the validation controls within the validation group specified by the control that submits the page (a `Button` control in this example) carry out validation of their attached control values. If you only have one set of validation controls on a page, you can omit the `ValidationGroup` declaration and all the controls are then part of the default validation group.

Most controls that can submit a page (e.g., cause a postback) have the `ValidationGroup` property. They also have the `CausesValidation` property. By default, this is `true` so that validation takes place automatically on a postback. However, if you set it to `false` for a control, that control will not cause validation to occur—on either the client or the server. This is useful for **Cancel** buttons, which allow the user to "escape" from the page even when client-side validation is enabled. The example page also uses this attribute on the two drop-down list controls at the bottom of the page so that they can post back to the server without requiring the user to fill in the controls on the page with valid values first.

Each validation control also has properties specific to the type of control that indicate valid values. In the `RegularExpressionValidator`, this is the `ValidationExpression` property. For the `RangeValidator`, you set the `MaximumValue`, `MinimumValue`, and `Type` properties. For example:

```
MaximumValue="75" MinimumValue="18" Type="Integer"
```

For the `CompareValidator`, you can set either the `ControlToCompare` property to the ID of another control in order to compare the two control values (as in the "Confirm Password" section of the example page) or the `Value-`

`ToCompare` property to specify a fixed value. You also use the `Type` property to specify the comparison type (`Currency`, `Date`, `Double`, `Integer`, or `String`). You can also set the `Operator` property to `DataTypeCheck` if you just want to confirm that the control contains a valid value of a specific type.

The ValidationSummary Control

The validation controls are responsible for managing validation of the other controls in the page. The `ValidationSummary` control links to all the validation controls in the page to display a list of the error messages from each one where validation failed. By default, this list displays in red text at the point where the control is located. The declaration of a `Validation-Summary` control specifies the validation group that it belongs to (so the example page contains two `ValidationSummary` controls) and the text to display above the list of error messages:

```
<asp:ValidationSummary ValidationGroup="LoginGroup"
     id="valSummaryMessage" runat="server"
     HeaderText="The following errors were found:" />
```

Accessing the Validation Controls in Code

The validation controls do all the work for you, and all you have to do is check the `IsValid` property of the `Page` to see if validation succeeded or failed when a postback occurs. The code in the example page displays the value of this property each time the page loads, as shown in the `DoValidate` routine in Listing 8.12 (which runs when either the **Login** or **Register** button causes a postback).

The other two event handlers are attached to the `SelectedIndexChanged` events of the two drop-down lists at the bottom of the example page. The `SetClientValidation` routine executes when the user changes the setting for client-side validation (as shown in Figure 8.7), and demonstrates how you can iterate through the collection of validation controls on the page using the `Validators` collection of the `Page` object. Each validation control inherits from `BaseValidator`, so this is the ideal choice of type for the `for` loop.

The second drop-down list allows you to turn on display of a client-side message box for the two `ValidationSummary` controls. This routine just sets the `ShowMessageBox` property of these `ValidationSummary` controls on the page to `true`—though you can specify this as an attribute in the control declaration if you always want message boxes to be shown.

Listing 8.12. The Code to Handle the Events in the Validation Example Page

```
public void DoValidate(Object sender, EventArgs e)
{
   lblRegisterMsg.Text = "Page.IsValid = " + Page.IsValid.ToString()
}

public void SetClientValidation(Object sender, EventArgs e)
{
   Boolean bClientSide = (lstClientValidate.SelectedValue == "Yes");
   foreach (BaseValidator validator in Page.Validators)
   {
     validator.EnableClientScript = bClientSide;
   }
}

public void SetMessageBox(Object sender, EventArgs e)
{
   Boolean bMessageBox = (lstMessageBox.SelectedValue == "Yes");
   valSummaryMessage.ShowMessageBox = bMessageBox;
   valRegisterMessage.ShowMessageBox = bMessageBox;
}
```

Figure 8.8 shows the message box that appears when the ShowMessage-
Box property is true and there are invalid values in the controls in the current
validation group.

For more details on the validation controls, see:

CompareValidator: http://msdn2.microsoft.com/library/he3e5wby
(en-us,vs.80).aspx

CustomValidator: http://msdn2.microsoft.com/library/k40kfxx1(en-us,
vs.80).aspx

RangeValidator: http://msdn2.microsoft.com/library/afhtcss6(en-us,
vs.80).aspx

RegularExpressionValidator: http://msdn2.microsoft.com/library/
6a1dyf95(en-us,vs.80).aspx

RequiredFieldValidator: http://msdn2.microsoft.com/library/ycxs7t4x
(en-us,vs.80).aspx

ValidationSummary: http://msdn2.microsoft.com/library/2a9k273c
(en-us,vs.80).aspx

List and Grid Controls

Most Web applications deal with data—and one of the common ways to
display data is as a list. It may be a list of products for sale, a list of incoming
e-mail messages, a list of orders for a customer, or any other type of list.

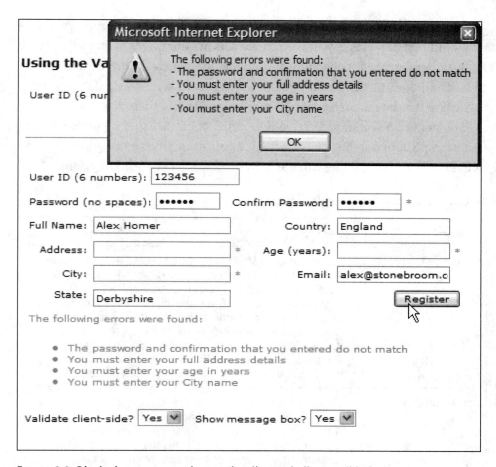

FIGURE 8.8: Displaying a message box on the client to indicate validation errors

ASP.NET provides a range of controls specifically aimed at generating lists of items and displaying each item is a specific way. For example, you can display items as a list of bullet points, in a grid or table, in a list box or drop-down list, as a set of checkboxes or option buttons, or in some custom repeating format of your own. The list controls also make it easy to manipulate the contents and get the user's selection(s) when the page is submitted.

Most simple list controls (such as `ListBox`, `DropDownList`, `CheckBoxList`, `RadioButtonList`, and `BulletedList`) can be populated using the `Items` collection, which exposes a collection of `ListItem` instances that have a `Text`, `Value`, `Selected`, and `Enabled` property. More complex list controls (such as `GridView` and `DetailsView`) can be populated using the `Fields` collection, which exposes a collection of objects to represent the rows in the control.

However, a fundamental feature of all list controls is support for server-side data binding. This makes it easy to create lists in your pages, using a database, XML document, or a collection of items as the source. More details on the GridView, DetailsView, and FormView controls, server-side data binding, and using the data source controls, is contained in Chapters 3, 4, and 5.

The next two sections describe two of the controls listed in Table 8.4. The first example looks at the BulletedList control, and the second looks at some of the ways you can work with the ListBox and DropDownList controls.

TABLE 8.4: The List and Grid Server Controls

Control	Description
BulletedList	Generates an HTML `<ol>` ordered list or `<ul>` unordered list containing one or more `<li>` list items. Properties such as BulletStyle, BulletImageUrl, and First-BulletNumber specify the appearance of the list items. The DisplayMode property specifies how the items provide any user interaction required (the items are displayed as a HyperLink, LinkButton, or plain text). Values are accessible through the Items collection, and the SelectedItem, SelectedValue, and SelectedIndex properties.
CheckBoxList	Generates a list of CheckBox controls, populated through either databinding or explicit addition of ListItem instances. The RepeatColumns, RepeatDirection, and Repeat-Layout properties specify whether the checkboxes appear in ordinary "flow" layout, or in the rows of an HTML table containing one or more columns. If the AutoPostBack property is true, the browser submits the page when the user selects a different item in the list. Values are accessible through the Items collection, and the SelectedItem, SelectedValue, and SelectedIndex properties.
DataList	Generates a single-column HTML table, with the data items inserted into each row. Templates can create the structure and content for each row, if required. This control is lighter than the GridView and DataGrid, but still supports selection and editing of rows. Each row is accessible as a DataListItem through the Items collection of the control.
DetailsView	Displays one row from a data source as a single page, with the column names and values laid out vertically—as in a paper form. The Rows collection provides access to the content. It supports automatic row deletes and updates, plus the inserting of new rows. Templates can create the structure and content for each row, if required.

Control	Description
DropDownList	Generates an HTML `<select size="1">... </select>` element in the page. Each `ListItem` instance in the source data generates a nested `<option>` element. If the `Auto-PostBack` property is `true`, the browser submits the page when the user selects a different item in the list. Values are accessible through the `Items` collection, and the `Selected Item`, `SelectedValue`, and `SelectedIndex` properties.
FormView	Displays one row from a data source as a single page, but without adding any layout or structure to display the values. Templates must be used to create the structure and content for each row. It supports automatic row deletes and updates, plus the inserting of new rows.
GridView	Displays multiple rows from a data source as a grid of columns and rows within an HTML table. Templates can create the structure and content for each column, if required. The `Columns` and `Rows` collections provide access to the content. It supports automatic row deletes and updates, and replaces the `DataGrid` control from earlier versions of ASP.NET (although this control is still available).
ListBox	Generates an HTML `<select>...</select>` element in the page with the number of rows visible specified as the `Rows` property. Each `ListItem` instance in the source data generates a nested `<option>` element. If the `AutoPost-Back` property is `true`, the browser submits the page when the user selects a different item in the list. Values are accessible through the `Items` collection, and the `Selected Item`, `SelectedValue`, and `SelectedIndex` properties.
RadioButtonList	Generates a list of `RadioButton` controls, populated through either data binding or explicit addition of `ListItem` instances. The `RepeatColumns`, `RepeatDirection`, and `RepeatLayout` properties specify whether the radio buttons appear in ordinary "flow" layout, or in the rows of an HTML table containing one or more columns. If the `AutoPostBack` property is `true`, the browser submits the page when the user selects a different item in the list. Values are accessible through the `Items` collection, and the `SelectedItem`, `SelectedValue`, and `SelectedIndex` properties.
Repeater	Generates repeated sections of content from a data source, but provides no structure or layout information. Templates must be used to create the structure and content for each row. The `Items` collection provides access to the content. This is a very light control, and provides best performance in situations where no data updates occur. Each row is accessible as a `DataListItem` through the `Items` collection of the control.

Example: The BulletedList Control

This example demonstrates use of the `BulletedList` control. This control renders the contents of the source data as a series of bullets that can contain text or hyperlinks. Figure 8.9 shows an example of the output generated by four `BulletedList` controls.

Listing 8.13 shows the declarations of the four controls in Figure 8.10. The top-left list (the first one in Listing 8.13) uses all the default values for the properties of the list. The `Text` to display for each item in the list is specified within the opening and closing tags of the `ListItem` controls declared within the `BulletedList` control.

The bottom-left list (the second one in Listing 8.13) specifies a numeric format (`BulletStyle="Numbered"`) and starts the list from the number 5 instead of the default of 1 (`FirstBulletNumber="5"`). It also uses server-side data binding to populate the list, by setting the `DataSource` property to a `String` array and calling the `DataBind` method. Alternatively, you can set the `DataSourceID` to the ID of a data source control to populate the list.

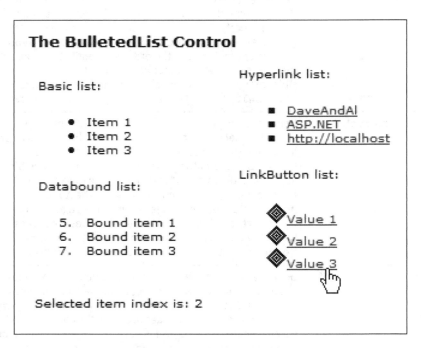

FIGURE 8.9: Examples of the output generated by the BulletedList control

The top-right list (the third one in Listing 8.13) uses square bullets (BulletStyle="Square") and displays the ListItem instances as hyperlinks (DisplayMode="Hyperlink"). The ListItem controls in this list also specify both a Text and a Value property for each item, and the Value property provides the URL to navigate to when the item is clicked.

The bottom-right list (the last one in Listing 8.13) displays each link using a LinkButton (DisplayMode="LinkButton") and a custom image (BulletStyle="CustomImage" and BulletImageUrl="bullet.gif"). Clicking on an item in this list initiates a postback to the server and runs the routine named ShowItem because the BulletedList control declaration includes OnClick="ShowItem". The Value property of the selected ListItem is available in the event handler.

Listing 8.13. The Declaration of the Four BulletedList Controls

```
Basic list:
<asp:BulletedList id="List1" runat="server">
  <asp:listitem>Item 1</asp:listitem>
  <asp:listitem>Item 2</asp:listitem>
  <asp:listitem>Item 3</asp:listitem>
</asp:BulletedList>

Databound list:
<asp:BulletedList id="List2" DisplayMode="Text"
    BulletStyle="Numbered" FirstBulletNumber="5" runat="server" />

Hyperlink list:
<asp:BulletedList id="List3" DisplayMode="Hyperlink"
    BulletStyle="Square" Target="_blank" runat="server">
<asp:ListItem Text="DaveAndAl" Value="http://www.daveandal.net" />
<asp:ListItem Text="ASP.NET" Value="http://www.asp.net" />
<asp:ListItem Text="http://localhost" />
</asp:BulletedList>

LinkButton list:
<asp:BulletedList id="List4" DisplayMode="LinkButton"
    BulletStyle="CustomImage" BulletImageUrl="bullet.gif"
    OnClick="ShowItem" runat="server">
<asp:ListItem Text="Value 1" />
<asp:ListItem Text="Value 2" />
<asp:ListItem Text="Value 3" />
</asp:BulletedList>
```

Listing 8.14 shows how the code in the page populates the second (data-bound) list, and how it reacts to a click on the fourth (LinkButton) list. In the `Page_Load` event handler, the code calls a routine named `GetListArray` that generates a simple single-dimension array of three `String` values and then binds this array to the `BulletedList` control. The `ShowItem` routine runs when a `LinkButton` in the fourth list is clicked, and simply retrieves the `SelectedIndex` of that item within the list from the `BulletedListEventArgs` instance passed to this routine.

Listing 8.14. The Server-Side Code in the BulletedList Example Page

```
public void Page_Load()
{
  if (!Page.IsPostBack)
  {
    List2.DataSource = GetListArray();
    Page.DataBind();
  }
}

public String[] GetListArray()
{
  String[] aList = new String[3];
  for (Int32 iLoop = 1; iLoop <= 3; iLoop++)
  {
    aList[iLoop - 1] = "Bound item " + iLoop.ToString();
  }
  return aList;

}
public void ShowItem(Object sender, BulletedListEventArgs e)
{
  lblResult.Text = "Selected item index is: " + e.Index;
}
```

For more details about the BulletedList control, see: http://msdn2. microsoft.com/library/k234932b(en-us,vs.80).aspx 7.

Example: The ListBox and DropDownList Controls

This example demonstrates some of the features of the `ListBox`, `DropDownList`, and `ListItem` controls. The `ListBox` and `DropDownList` controls are populated dynamically at runtime when the page first loads (in the `Page_Load` event handler) using some different approaches. The `DropDownList` then allows you to select and disable an entry in the `ListBox` control at the top of the page by setting the `Enabled` property of the appropriate `ListItem` to `false`. The properties of each `ListItem`, including the one that is disabled and therefore not visible (but still exists in the `Items` collection), are displayed below the `DropDownList` after you make a selection.

The values of the `SelectedIndex` and `SelectedValue` properties of the `ListBox` are also displayed, and you will see from experimentation that the disabled `ListItem` is still shown as selected, even if you disable it after selecting it. Figure 8.11 shows the example page after selecting `Item4` in the drop-down list. The techniques you see here are the same for all controls that contain a series of `ListItem` instances (a `ListItemCollection`), including `Check-BoxList`, `RadioButtonList`, `BulletedList`, `ListBox`, and `DropDownList`.

Listing 8.15 shows the declaration of the two list controls. There are no `<asp:ListItem>` elements in the declaration, because the lists are populated dynamically at runtime. However, the `DropDownList` uses the `AutoPostBack` property to specify that the page is submitted as soon as the user changes the selection and that the routine named `ShowValues` will execute when this postback occurs.

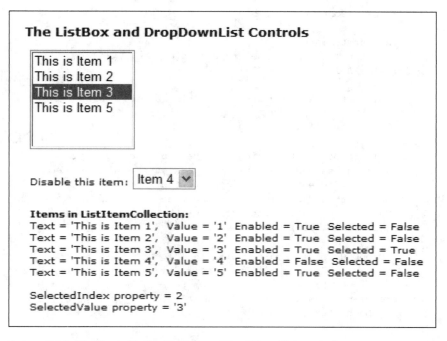

FIGURE 8.11: Working with the ListBox and DropDownList controls

Listing 8.15. The Declaration of the ListBox and DropDownList Controls

```
<asp:ListBox id="MyList" Rows="6" runat="server" />
<p />
Disable this item:
<asp:DropDownList id="MyDropDown" runat="server"
    AutoPostback="true" OnSelectedIndexChanged="ShowValues" />
```

Listing 8.16 shows the `Page_Load` event handler. This demonstrates several ways that you can populate list controls (besides server-side data binding). A `for` statement adds new `ListItem` instances to the lists, with each one specified as a new `ListItem` instance. This allows you to set the `Text` and `Value` properties. If you only want to set the `Text` property, you can use `MyList.Items.Add("My Text Value")` instead. You can also use the `Insert` method to add either a new `ListItem` or a text value, and access the items in the `ListItems` collection by index. You can see both of these techniques used in populating the `DropDownList` control in Listing 8.16.

Listing 8.16. Populating the ListBox and DropDownList Controls

```
public void Page_Load()
{
  if (!Page.IsPostBack)
  {
    // fill first ListBox
    // set the Text and Value properties of each ListItem
    for (Int32 i = 1; i <= 5; i++)
    {
      MyList.Items.Add(new ListItem("This is Item "
                                + i.ToString(), i.ToString()));
    }

    // fill DropDownList setting just text of each ListItem
    // start at second item then insert first item and set value
    // shows different ways to populate the Items collection
    // notice that Value must correspond to the index (and not the
    // Value property) of the items in the ListBox above
    for (Int32 i = 2; i <= 5; i++)
    {
      MyDropDown.Items.Add(new ListItem("Item "
                    + i.ToString(), (i - 1).ToString()));
    }
    MyDropDown.Items.Insert(0, "Item 1");
    MyDropDown.Items[0].Value = "0";
  }
}
```

Listing 8.17 shows how you can access the values in a list control, in this case following a postback, to display the user's selection and other information about the list (these are generic techniques for all simple list controls). The code first iterates through the ListItems collection for the ListBox enabling all the ListItem instances in the list, and then disables the item in the ListBox that is selected in the DropDownList. Next, the code iterates through the list again, displaying the four properties of each ListItem. Finally, it displays the value of the SelectedIndex and SelectedValue properties for the ListBox control.

Note that if a list control allows multiple selections to be made (usually a ListBox is used in this case with the SelectionMode="Multiple" attribute), the SelectedIndex and SelectedValue properties return the text and value of the *first* item in the list that is selected. Iterating the list is the only way that

Listing 8.17. Displaying Information About the List Controls

```
public void ShowValues(Object sender, EventArgs e)
{
  // start by making all items visible (i.e. enabled)
  foreach (ListItem item in MyList.Items)
  {
    item.Enabled = true;
  }

  // disable entry in first list that is specified in second list
  MyList.Items[Int32.Parse(MyDropDown.SelectedValue)].Enabled = false;

  // display details of Items collection
  lblList.Text = "<b>Items in ListItemCollection:</b><br />";
  foreach (ListItem item in MyList.Items)
  {
    lblList.Text += "Text = '" + item.Text
                + "',  Value = '" + item.Value
                + "'  Enabled = " + item.Enabled.ToString()
                + "  Selected = " + item.Selected.ToString()
                + "br />";
  }

  // display other properties of the first ListBox control
  lblList.Text += "<br />SelectedIndex property = "
              + MyList.SelectedIndex.ToString();
  lblList.Text += "<br />SelectedValue property = '"
              + MyList.SelectedValue + "'br />";
}
```

you can determine which items are selected when multiple selections are permitted.

For more details about the `ListBox` control, see: http://msdn2. microsoft.com/library/fe97eda3(en-us,vs.80).aspx.

For more details about the `DropDownList` control, see: http://msdn2. microsoft.com/library/7wfh8284(en-us,vs.80).aspx.

For more details about the `ListItem` control, see: http://msdn2. microsoft.com/library/6bf5ha6h(en-us,vs.80).aspx.

Rich Controls

While there is no real definition of what makes up a rich control, there are many controls in ASP.NET that do not directly relate to a specific type of form element or control. Examples are the `Wizard` control that provides a base for building multistep Wizards, or the `Calendar` control that implements a complete clickable calendar within a single control. Rich controls generally consist of a collection of other basic controls, and they can save a great deal of time and effort when constructing your Web pages.

Some rich controls also interface directly and automatically with the underlying ASP.NET system. For example, the `Login` control links to the membership and role management system automatically implemented by ASP.NET 2.0. Likewise, the WebParts controls that you can use to build portal-style pages integrate with the personalization system in ASP.NET 2.0. The Login controls (listed in Table 8.5) are discussed in more depth in Chapter 11. The WebParts controls (not listed here) are discussed in more depth in Chapter 13.

Example: The Calendar Control

This example demonstrates use of the `Calendar` control with the default appearance and formatting. The calendar rendered in the browser allows selection of single dates, whole weeks, and whole months because the declaration sets the `SelectionMode` to "DayWeekMonth" (see Listing 8.18).

TABLE 8.5: The Rich Controls and Login Controls

Control	Description
AdRotator	Generates an area on the page that contains a banner image. The banner is chosen in a semi-controllable random sequence from the banner details stored in an XML file specified for the `AdvertisementFile` property, or provided through server-side data binding. Values in the source data for each banner specify the navigation details and the relative weightings used to select the advertisement at runtime.
Calendar	Generates an interactive calendar that displays one month, and allows navigation between months and years. Dates are hyperlinks that cause a postback to the server, where the selected date, week, or month is available as the `SelectedDate` and `SelectedDates` properties.
MultiView	Provides a way to display one of a series of pages or views, each containing a selection of other controls. Each page or view is a `View` control instance, and navigation between the views is possible through `Button` controls that have specific `CommandName` values. The `Views` collection provides access to the collection of `View` instances, and the one currently displayed is set or read from the `ActiveViewIndex` property.
Wizard	This control also provides a series of pages or views, in a similar but more complex way than the `Multi-View` control. It automatically provides the navigation features as links or buttons and a sidebar containing a list of steps, and accepts templates for defining the content and style of sections of the control. Each step or page in the `Wizard` is a `WizardStep` instance, exposed through a collection as the `WizardSteps` property. The currently displayed step is set or read through the `ActiveStep` property.
Xml	Copies the contents of an XML file or a dynamic XML source specified through the `Document-Content` or `DocumentSource` properties into the page at the location of the control. An XSLT transformation can be applied to the XML first using a stylesheet specified as the `Transform` or `TransformSource` property.

(Continued)

TABLE 8.5: The Rich Controls and Login Controls (Continued)

Control	Description
Login	Generates the text boxes and button required to implement a login page, and optionally a checkbox to specify persistence for the login when Forms authentication is used.
LoginName	Generates output indicating the login name of the current user, or nothing if the user is anonymous (not logged in).
LoginStatus	Generates a hyperlink with the text "Login" when the current user is anonymous (not logged in), and "Logout" when the current user has been authenticated (is logged in).
LoginView	Provides three templates used to display data about the currently logged in user, or a message if there is no logged-in user.
ChangePassword	Provides the controls required for a page that allows users to change their password, as stored in the ASP.NET personalization system.
CreateUserWizard	Provides the controls required by users when they create a new account, as stored in the ASP.NET personalization system.
PasswordRecovery	Provides the controls required for users to specify the reminder details to have a lost or forgotten password e-mailed to them.

Listing 8.18. The Declaration of the Calendar Control

```
<asp:Calendar id="MyCal" runat="server"
    SelectionMode="DayWeekMonth"
    OnVisibleMonthChanged="MyCal_VisibleMonthChanged"
    OnSelectionChanged="MyCal_SelectionChanged" /><p />
```

The Calendar control declaration also specifies that code in the page should handle the VisibleMonthChanged and SelectionChanged events to display the date(s) selected, or the current and the previously selected months when the user navigates from one month to another (see Figure 8.12).

Listing 8.19 shows the code of the event handlers for the Visible-MonthChanged and SelectionChanged events. It is easy to extract the values of the previous and current months in the VisibleMonthChanged

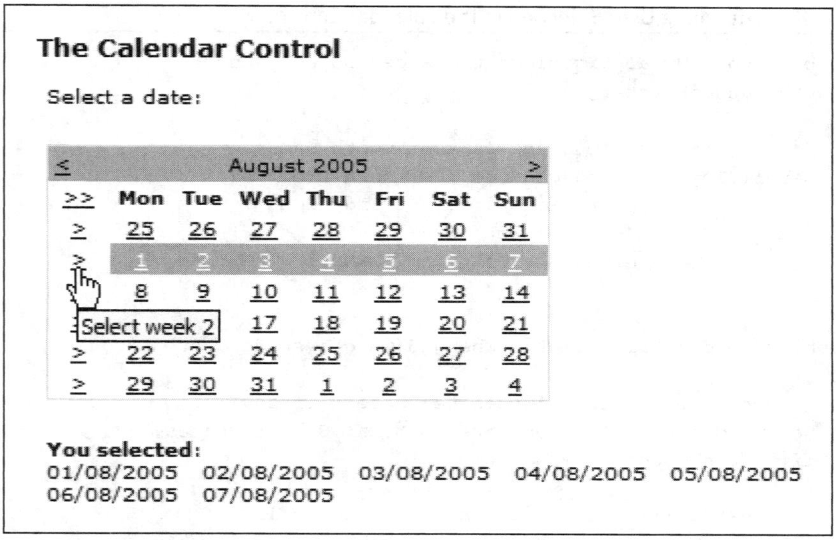

FIGURE 8.12: The Calendar control with a full week selected

event, because they are properties of the MonthChangedEventArgs instance passed to the event handler. The code formats these to display just the month name.

The code that handles the SelectionChanged event is a little more complicated. It queries the SelectedDates property to see if more than one date was selected. If so, it uses the SelectedDatesCollection that is available from the SelectedDates property to display a list of these. If only one date is selected, the code queries the SelectedDate property instead.

> For more details about the Calendar control, see: http://msdn2. microsoft.com/library/yzb6d7wx(en-us,vs.80).aspx 9.

Example: The Wizard Control

The final example in this chapter is the Wizard control. This control enables easy construction of multistep task-based data collection routines, just like the Wizards you are used to seeing in other types of applications and operating systems. The Wizard control looks after all the plumbing required to implement navigation between the individual Wizard steps, displaying the appropriate **Previous, Next, Finish**, and **Cancel** buttons, and optionally showing a list of steps in a "sidebar" next to the main Wizard area.

Listing 8.19. Handling User Selection in the Calendar Control

```
public void MyCal_VisibleMonthChanged(Object sender,
MonthChangedEventArgs e)
{
  // show the previous and current month names
  Label1.Text += "You changed the month from <b>"
              + e.PreviousDate.ToString("MMMM")
              + "</b> to <b>"
              + e.NewDate.ToString("MMMM") + "</b>";
}

public void MyCal_SelectionChanged(Object sender, EventArgs e)
{
  // get a collection of selected dates (if any)
  SelectedDatesCollection dates = MyCal.SelectedDates;
  if (dates.Count > 1)
  {
    // get a list of all dates in the selection
    Label1.Text += "<b>You selected</b>:<br />";
    foreach (DateTime dt in dates)
    {
      Label1.Text += dt.ToShortDateString() + "   ";
    }
  }
  else
  {
    // just get and display the selected date
    Label1.Text += "<b>You selected</b>: "
                + MyCal.SelectedDate.ToShortDateString();
  }
}
```

The Wizard control is almost infinitely configurable—you can show or hide various sections, such as the navigation button area, the sidebar, and the header. You can populate it using templates, replace the interface elements with your own images, and specify style information for all the items. The Visual Studio designer also shows each step individually using a drop-down menu, so that you can build your Wizard in Design view.

The Wizard is a container control that holds individual WizardStep controls. You can declare these in your page, or generate them dynamically at runtime and add them to the WizardSteps collection of the Wizard control. Likewise, you can access the existing steps in code though this collection. Figure 8.13 shows a simple Wizard. As you move from one step to

ActiveViewChanged event. ActiveStep is 'Step2' - Title is 'Second Step'

Step history:
Step4 Title: 'Final Step'
Step3 Title: 'Third Step'
Step2 Title: 'Second Step'
Step1 Title: 'First Step'
Control values:
'Step One Text'
'Step Two Text'
'Step Three Text'
'Step Four Text'

ActiveViewChanged event. ActiveStep is 'Step4' - Title is 'Final Step'

FIGURE 8.13: An example of using the Wizard control

another, the `ActiveViewChanged` event occurs, and you can access the current `WizardStep` instance from the `ActiveStep` property to display details. You can see in Figure 8.13 that the code in the example displays the `ID` and `Title` properties of the current step.

The example Wizard has four steps, and the current one is automatically highlighted in the sidebar (although Figure 8.13 only shows three of these steps). Clicking the **Finish** button in step four hides the Wizard and displays the step history (in reverse order starting from the most recent step viewed) and the values of the controls in all of the steps. As you can see, this makes it easy to use the full set of values once the user completes the Wizard, rather than having to concern yourself with how you will store them between pages when you build your own Wizard equivalents.

Listing 8.20 shows the declaration of the `Wizard` control in the example page, with some of the `WizardStep` elements removed for clarity. Notice how the attributes of the `Wizard` element wire up the events to the event handlers—the example page handles the `CancelButtonClick`, `FinishButtonClick`, and `ActiveStepChanged` events. After the style declarations for the sidebar and navigation sections comes the `Wizard-Steps` element that contains the individual `WizardStep` elements.

Listing 8.20. The Declaration of the Wizard Control

```
<asp:Wizard id="MyWizard" runat="server"
    DisplaySideBar="true" DisplayCancelButton="true"
    OnCancelButtonClick="WizardCancel"
    OnFinishButtonClick="WizardFinish"
    OnActiveStepChanged="StepChanged"
    Backcolor="White" CellPadding="10" BorderColor="Black"
    BorderStyle="Ridge" BorderWidth="3" ActiveStepIndex="0">

<SideBarStyle BackColor="#FFFFC0" VerticalAlign="Top" />
<NavigationStyle BackColor="LightBlue" BorderStyle="None" />

<WizardSteps>

  <asp:WizardStep id="Step1" Title="First Step" runat="server">
    <asp:Image runat="server" id="Image1"
              Width="110px" Height="110px" AlternateText="Step 1"
              ImageUrl="~/ch08/step1.gif" ImageAlign="Left"
              style="margin-right: 20px; padding-bottom: 10px;" />
    This is step 1<br />
    <asp:TextBox id="txtStep1" Text="Step One Text" runat="server" />
  </asp:WizardStep>

  ... more WizardStep declarations here ...

  <asp:WizardStep StepType="Finish" id="Step4" Title="Final Step"
              runat="server">
    <asp:Image runat="server" id="Image4"
              Width="110px" Height="110px" AlternateText="Step 4"
              ImageUrl="~/ch08/step4.gif" ImageAlign="Left"
              style="margin-right: 20px; padding-bottom: 10px;" />
    This is step 4<br />
    <asp:TextBox id="txtStep4" Text="Step Four Text" runat="server" />
  </asp:WizardStep>

</WizardSteps>

</asp:Wizard>
```

Each step in the example Wizard contains an image, the step number, and a text box containing some default text. The final step is declared as a "Finish" step (and so will contain the **Finish** button) by virtue of the StepType= "Finish" attribute. The equivalent StepType="Start" attribute could be included in the first WizardStep declaration, to ensure that it does not contain a **Previous** button. However, if these attributes are omitted, the Wizard control assumes that the first and last ones within the WizardSteps element are, respectively, StepType="Start" and StepType="Finish".

Listing 8.21 shows the code in the example page that handles the three events. The `StepChanged` routine runs when the active step changes and simply outputs the `ID` and `Title` properties of the current step. The `ActiveStep` property returns a `WizardStepBase` instance (from which the `WizardStep` type inherits).

Clicking the **Finish** button runs the `WizardFinish` routine, which extracts the step history as an `ArrayList` from the `Wizard` control using the `GetHistory` method, and iterates through. It then accesses the `TextBox` controls to extract the values from each step, and hides the `Wizard` control.

Listing 8.21. The Code to Handle the Events in the Wizard Example

```
public void StepChanged(Object sender, EventArgs e)
{
  // display details of current step
  WizardStep wstep = (WizardStep)MyWizard.ActiveStep;
  lblMessage.Text = "ActiveViewChanged event. ActiveStep is '"
              + wstep.ID + "' - Title is '" + wstep.Title + "'";
}

public void WizardFinish(Object sender, WizardNavigationEventArgs e)
{
  // display history of steps (stored in reverse order)
  lblMessage.Text = "Step history:</b><br />";
  ArrayList steps = (ArrayList)MyWizard.GetHistory();
  foreach (WizardStep wstep in steps)
  {
    lblMessage.Text += wstep.ID + " Title: '" + wstep.Title + "'br />";
  }

  // display values in text boxes
  lblMessage.Text += "Control values:</b><br />'"
              + txtStep1.Text + "'br />'"
              + txtStep2.Text + "'br />'"
              + txtStep3.Text + "'br />'"
              + txtStep4.Text + "'br />";

  // hide the Wizard
  MyWizard.Visible = false;
}

public void WizardCancel(Object sender, EventArgs e)
{
  // display message and hide Wizard
  lblMessage.Text = "Canceled";
  MyWizard.Visible = false;
}
```

Finally, clicking the Cancel button runs the `WizardCancel` routine, which just hides the Wizard control.

Container Controls

Some controls in ASP.NET do not generate any user interface or content within the rendered page. These include the `PlaceHolder` control that is useful when you want to allocate a place on the page for sets of controls that you generate dynamically within your server-side code. There are also two controls, the `ContentPlaceHolder` and `Content` controls, used when you take advantage of the Master Page feature built into ASP.NET 2.0. Master Pages are discussed in more detail in Chapter 9.

However, bear in mind that many ASP.NET controls can also act as containers. Programmatically, most controls expose a collection named `Controls`, which contains references to all the ("child") controls that are contained within that control. You can use this collection, as you will see in examples throughout the book, to work with these child controls. The most common scenario is use of the `Find` method of the `Controls` collection, which returns a reference to a control you specify using its `ID` value. Table 8.6 lists and describes the specialist container controls.

Mobile Controls

The final group of controls has a specific purpose outside building Web pages aimed at normal desktop Web browsers such as Internet Explorer and Mozilla Firefox. Increasingly, people use small-screen devices such as PocketPCs, Personal Digital Assistants (PDAs), and mobile cell phones to access the Internet. These devices may not support the full feature set of HTML, and—in fact—may not support HTML at all. Many cell phones only understand languages such as Wireless Markup Language (WML).

The Mobile Controls, originally added to ASP.NET version 1.0 as the Mobile Internet Toolkit, is a set of controls specially tailored to provide output that works on all kinds of devices and user agents. A full list of these controls, which reside in the `System.Web.UI.MobileControls` namespace, is available at http://msdn2.microsoft.com/library/361h4hy6 (en-us,vs.80).aspx. You will see that there are some familiar controls such as `TextBox`, `Label`, and `Panel` as well as the validation controls. Most of the other controls are specialized for cell phones or designed to generate output that works well on small-screen devices.

TABLE 8.6: Specialist Container Controls in ASP.NET

Control	Description
Content	Defines an area on a page whose content (text, HTML, controls, etc.) is inserted into a `ContentPlaceHolder` control on a Master Page at runtime. A page can contain more than one `Content` control, each specifying the `ID` of the target `ContentPlaceHolder` control. The Master Page file is defined in the `Page` directive, and the page can contain no other content.
ContentPlaceHolder	Defines an area on a Master Page where the content from a `Content` control will appear. Any existing content within the `ContentPlace-Holder` control is replaced by the `Content` control's content. If no `Content` control matches this `ContentPlaceHolder`, any existing content within the `ContentPlaceHolder` control is displayed.
PlaceHolder	Generates no output, and simply reserves a place on the page where code can dynamically add content at runtime by inserting child controls (of any type) into the `Controls` collection of the `PlaceHolder` control.
Substitution	Defines an area on the page that is never cached when output caching is defined for that page. ASP.NET always regenerates the content of the `Substitution` control, even if the remainder of the page is served from the output cache.

Like the standard ASP.NET controls, the Mobile Controls use a series of device descriptions stored in configuration files within the `Browsers` subfolder of the usual .NET Framework folder (at `%windir%/Microsoft.NET/Framework/[version]/CONFIG/Browsers/`). These descriptions include a great deal of detail about each device, including things like the markup languages it supports, the screen resolution, and the font styles as well as whether support is available for cookies, images, or tables.

However, the Mobile Controls make much more use of these feature lists, by changing almost every aspect of the output they generate—right down to the markup language itself. This means that you can build your site to give the appearance and include the content you want, and then leave it to the controls to generate automatically the appropriate output for each device that visits.

You may now have decided just to use the Mobile Controls for all of your pages, so that the site is compatible with all types of visiting devices. However, this is not generally practical. The range of controls in the Mobile Controls set is limited, and many do not provide the interactivity of the standard controls or the same opportunities for changing the appearance. They are also more processing-intensive because of the detection and format translation they must perform.

However, the main reason that a single page containing the Mobile Controls is not practical for all of your visitors is that you really do have to design your pages to suit either a large desktop screen or a small screen. It is very difficult—if not impossible—to get optimum results in both using the same selection of controls and content. Instead, you should consider building two sets of pages. The good news is that the Mobile Controls expose similar interfaces to the standard controls, using the same property names where this is possible, and so you can use most of your existing server-side code, components, and business logic for both sets of pages.

Chapter 14 looks in more detail at the issues of building pages that work on multiple devices, that can be read by different types of specialist user agents, and that are localized for different cultures and languages.

Layout Approaches—Tables and Stylesheets

The traditional technique for laying out items on a Web page, other than the default "flow layout" where each item just follows the preceding one, is the use of HTML tables. These have some advantages, being easy to construct and automatically adapting themselves to the browser window size. However, their use today is regularly discouraged in favor of Cascading Style Sheets (CSS). These allow separation of content from display and layout information, and allow specialized user agents (such as page readers for visually impaired users) to disregard the style and layout information in order to better present the content to the user.

ASP.NET provides support for both approaches, and—in some cases—makes its own choice on whether tables or CSS are used to render content. Controls such as the `GridView`, `DataList`, `Panel`, and `Login` always generate HTML tables. However, all controls expose properties that allow you to specify styling information. You can set the `Style` property of a control using the appropriate set of CSS selectors (style values), or you can set the

`CssClass` property to the name of a style defined in your CSS stylesheets. Visual Studio 2005 and Visual Web developer also provide excellent support for generating stylesheets and control-level style information through a stylesheet editor and `Style` property dialogs.

Choosing the Appropriate Control Type

As you can see from the preceding sections, there are a great many different controls you can choose from when building Web pages. Deciding which one to use involves some knowledge of their capabilities and specific features, which you will accumulate over time. However, there are some general rules that are useful:

- When you will not access the element or control in the page from within your server-side code, you should consider using a standard HTML element *without* the `runat="server"` attribute. This avoids ASP.NET creating an instance of the control within the control tree and allows it simply to render the HTML in the source of the page direct to the client.

- If you are accessing the properties, methods, or events of a control in client-side script only (for example in JavaScript, DHTML/CSS, or for interaction with an ActiveX control or Java applet) you do not need to create them as server controls. Again, they can be standard HTML elements *without* the `runat="server"` attribute.

- If the element is a hyperlink opening the same or (more likely) a different page or URL, and you do not need to pre-process the element attributes (for example, you do not need to dynamically set the URL), you can use standard HTML elements *without* the `runat="server"` attribute.

- If all your server-side code is in the `Page_Load` event handler and you have no event handlers for other controls, you can use a standard HTML `<input type="submit">` element or an `<input type="image">` element *without* the `runat="server"` attribute to submit the page to the server.

In most other cases, you will require server controls that contain the `runat="server"` attribute. However, bear in mind that sometimes it is useful simply to add this attribute to the HTML element to convert it to a server control, rather than using the ASP.NET Web Forms controls (the controls with the `"asp"` prefix). This can produce a lighter-weight page with less processing requirements in situations where you have many controls on the page.

The ASP.NET Page and Postback Model

ASP.NET provides a Web page execution model that differs considerably from the approaches taken previously. Instead of executing chunks of code at the appropriate stages of sending the page to the client, ASP.NET treats the page as a `Class` (in code terms) and compiles it into Microsoft Intermediate Language code (MSIL). This code is stored on disk and then executed by the .NET Framework Just-In-Time (JIT) runtime system when requested by a user. This provides fast and efficient performance, but it also enables the use of new (in terms of Web development) programming techniques.

Differentiating between Postback and Navigate

One of the fundamental actions in a Web page is the user clicking a link or button that performs some action. Traditionally, this would take them to a different page. This page might handle the values submitted by the user if they clicked a **Submit** button, or it may just be the next page of content that they wish to view. However, as you saw in the section Hyperlink and Navigation Controls, ASP.NET differentiates between these two types of actions—called postback and navigation.

A postback occurs when the link, button, or some other control on the page causes reloading of the same page, unless you use the cross-page postback feature (described in Chapter 10). This is the default action when you place controls on a Web Form page, because it contains an HTML `<form>` element that always posts its content back to the same page when submitted—you cannot change this behavior unless you add some client-side script to change the form attributes after the page loads (and this is strongly discouraged).

The ASP.NET Event-Driven Architecture

The result of a postback is that ASP.NET can, using the viewstate information that it inserts into the page, recreate the same series of objects as a `Class` and re-execute it. By taking into account the values of the controls that are sent with the request when the user submits the page, ASP.NET can figure out if any values in the controls have changed. It can also tell which control caused the postback and whether the postback is, in fact, from the same page (providing some rudimentary security against spoofing by users who create malicious pages that post to your application). From this information, ASP.NET can then raise events within the class, such as the `Click` event for a `Button` control or the `TextChanged` event for a `TextBox` control. Your code can handle these events, just as you would in a normal executable application built in other languages.

In addition, the values of all the controls (including the values of properties other than the value itself) are available within the page. The view-state of the page (an encoded string placed into a hidden control in the page when sent to the client) contains these values as well as a representation of the original control tree. This means that ASP.NET automatically maintains the user's selections in lists, text they typed into text boxes, and settings of checkboxes and option buttons, between each postback. This makes a lot of sense—in a normal application users do not expect to see all the controls in a window return to their default values each time they click a button. The good news is that, unlike most other Web development environments, there is no need for you to write code to do this in ASP.NET.

Request and Response Information

Just because ASP.NET handles all the manipulation of the values submitted by the client for you does not mean that you lose control. If you have worked with other Web technologies, you will have used the `Request` and `Response` objects (or their equivalents) to get at the values submitted from an HTML form. In ASP.NET, these objects are available, though you will generally have no need to query them for control values.

Instead, however, they provide a range of properties that provide other information about the user's request and the response sent by the server. The `Request` object allows you to discover information about the user, such as their public IP address, and about the page or file that they requested—such as the physical path on your server or the individual parts of the URL they provided. The `Response` object allows you to set specific values for the server's response, such as the content type and encoding and to inject content into the `Stream` returned to the client.

A full list of the properties, methods, and events for the HttpRequest class, an instance of which implements the ASP.NET Request object, is at http://msdn2.microsoft.com/library/ha0633cx(en-us,vs.80).aspx. The equivalent for the HttpResponse class, which implements the ASP.NET Response object, is at http://msdn2.microsoft.com/library/wfa24xy1 (enus,vs.80).aspx. You will see the Request and Response objects used throughout this book, including in the next chapter, where you will explore more features of the ASP.NET page architecture and the design of interactive Web Form pages.

SUMMARY

In this chapter, you have seen a list of the controls that are part of ASP.NET and how they fall into categories based not only on their use, but also on the way that you work with them and write code to interact with them. A good example of this is the common approach used to access and manipulate the contents of the simple list controls such as ListBox, DropDownList, and BulletedList.

You will have come across many of the controls in earlier, more task-focused chapters, and you will see them all again many times throughout the remainder of this book. However, you should now have a better grasp of why there are different sets of controls and how they differ.

Another important issue covered in this chapter is how you choose the appropriate control when building your pages. There appear to be several controls that do the same thing, such as HtmlAnchor, Hyperlink, ImageMap, and ImageButton. In this chapter, you saw how to make a decision about which type of server control to choose—and, in fact, when not to use a server control at all.

The chapter finished with a brief overview of the underlying architecture of ASP.NET, discussing the event-driven model and the way that it relies on request and response information. In the next chapter, you will explore this topic in more detail as you look at the Page class that implements the ASP.NET page object, and see the features it provides for streamlining your page operation. This includes ways of presenting a uniform appearance across multiple pages.

9

The Page Class and Master Pages

IN THE PREVIOUS CHAPTER, you saw the controls provided with ASP.NET and how many of the more useful of these controls are used. You also saw some discussion of the ASP.NET page architecture and event mechanism. In this chapter, you will see more details about the fundamentals of the ASP.NET `Page` object and the HTTP context within which your pages execute.

Several objects are available that you can access when building interactive Web pages and classes that integrate with ASP.NET. However, much of the core functionality of ASP.NET comes from the `Page` class, which exposes a range of properties, methods, and events. The ASP.NET controls use these events, and your code can access them as well. This chapter looks at the life cycle of the ASP.NET page, and a range of the features it provides.

Another major area where ASP.NET version 2.0 provides a huge advance over previous versions of ASP (and many other interactive Web programming environments) is in its provision of Master Pages. These allow you to easily and quickly create a consistent look and feel for your site—and change it when required.

This chapter concentrates on:

- The `HttpRequest`, `HttpResponse`, `HttpServerUtility`, and `HttpContext` classes
- The ASP.NET `Page` class

- Client-side scripting features
- Sub-classing the `Page` object
- Working with Master Pages

To start, you will see how the fundamental objects exposed by ASP.NET provide interaction with the underlying HTTP request and response model.

The HttpRequest, HttpResponse, HttpServerUtility, and HttpContext Classes

In most Web programming environments, you access all of the data about a user's request to your Web site, or the response you send back, on the server using the HTTP `Request` and `Response` objects. In ASP.NET, these are available (as you saw in the previous chapter) through the `HttpRequest` and `HttpResponse` classes. These two classes are accessible through properties of the `HttpContext` class, and—since the current context is always available in an ASP.NET page—you can access them simply by using the property names `Request` and `Response`:

```
sClientsIPAddress = Request.UserHostAddress;
Response.ContentType = "image/png";
```

Using the HttpRequest Class

The `HttpRequest` class provides a series of properties that allow you to access things like the URL and path of the resource requested, the public IP address of the requesting client, the user logon details if the site requires authentication, and the physical location of the resource on your server. It also provides the following four collections, each of the specialized type `NameValueCollection`, that contain values sent along with the request:

- The `Request.Form` collection contains all the values sent from the controls in a `<form>` section of the page when the `method` attribute of the form is `"POST"` (the default in ASP.NET).
- The `Request.QueryString` collection contains all the values sent from the controls in a `<form>` section of the page when the `method` attribute of the form is `"GET"`.

- The `Request.Cookies` collection contains the values of all the cookies sent by the client with the request.
- The `Request.ServerVariables` collection contains the values of all the HTTP headers sent by the client with the request, plus details about the resource location, the client, and the request type (these are used by ASP.NET to populate the many properties of the `Request` class).

You can even query for a value across all the collections using just `Request["value-key"]`, rather than specifying a particular collection—such as `Request.Form["value-key"]`. The example for the `HttpResponse` class that you will see shortly demonstrates some of the ways you can use the `HttpRequest` object to get information about a user's request.

A full list of the properties, methods, and events for the `HttpRequest` class, which implements the ASP.NET `Request` object, is at http:// msdn2.microsoft.com/library/ha0633cx(en-us,vs.80).aspx.

Using the HttpResponse Class

The `HttpResponse` class provides a series of properties that are useful if you want to directly manipulate the response sent back to the client. The many properties and methods available include those that manipulate the HTTP headers of the response, manage buffering and caching, set the status values, and provide access to the response stream so that you can inject custom content such as the contents of a disk file. Like the `Request` object, the `Response` object also exposes a `Cookies` collection that contains the values of all the cookies sent to the client for storage on its machine.

A full list of the properties, methods, and events for the `HttpResponse` class, which implements the ASP.NET `Response` object, is at http://msdn2.microsoft.com/library/wfa24xy1(en-us,vs.80).aspx.

The example here demonstrates some of the ways you can use the `HttpRequest` and `HttpResponse` objects to get information about the request and manipulate the response sent to the client. The main body of the page shows the values of some of the `Request` properties and the contents of the `Request` collections.

To read the `Form`, `QueryString`, and `ServerVariables` collections, the example uses a simple routine, shown in Listing 9.1, to iterate through the `AllKeys` array of the collection passed to it. For each key in the collection, it extracts the value using the indexer `nv[key]`, and adds it to a `StringBuilder`. After processing all the keys and values, it returns the contents of the `StringBuilder`.

Listing 9.1. Reading the Contents of a Generic Request Collection

```
String GetCollectionContents(NameValueCollection nv)
{
  StringBuilder sb = new StringBuilder();
  // iterate through all the keys in the collection
  foreach (String key in nv.AllKeys)
  {
    // get value of this key for display
    sb.Append(key + "='"+ nv[key] + "'<br />");
  }
  return sb.ToString();
}
```

The `Page_Load` event handler calls this routine three times, with the appropriate `Request` collection specified and the results inserted into `Label` controls on the page (see Listing 9.2).

Listing 9.2. Populating the Page with the Contents of the Request Collections

```
// display the values in the Request collections
lblForm.Text = GetCollectionContents(Request.Form);
lblQueryString.Text = GetCollectionContents(Request.QueryString);
lblCookies.Text = GetCookiesCollectionContents(Request.Cookies);
lblServerVariables.Text = GetCollectionContents(
                              Request.ServerVariables);
```

However, notice that the `Cookies` collection requires a different routine, named `GetCookiesCollectionContents`, in order to display all the values correctly. Listing 9.3 shows this routine.

In the case of the `Cookies` collection, each value is an `HttpCookie` instance, which implements a range of properties such as the `Path`, `Expiry`, and `Secure` properties. More importantly, each cookie can contain more than one value—each named `HttpCookie` instance within the `Cookies` collection has a `Values` property that returns a `NameValue Collection` containing the subkey names and values for this cookie.

Listing 9.3. Displaying the Values in the Cookies Collection

```
String GetCookiesCollectionContents(HttpCookieCollection cc)
{
  StringBuilder sb = new StringBuilder();
  // iterate through all the cookies in the collection
  foreach (String key in cc.AllKeys)
  {
    // iterate through all the values (subkeys) in this cookie
    foreach (String subkey in cc[key].Values)
    {
      // get value of this subkey for display
      sb.Append(key + "["+ subkey + "] ='"+ cc[key][subkey]
                + "'<br />");
    }
  }
  return sb.ToString();
}
```

Therefore, as you can see in Listing 9.3, the code has to iterate through both the `AllKeys` array of the collection itself, and then through the `Values` collection for each cookie. If you are sure that a cookie only contains one value, however, you can just query the `Value` property of that cookie.

Figure 9.1 shows the example page, and you can see the contents of the `Request` properties and collections. The screenshot shows the results after adding a multivalue cookie to the response—you can see the values of the form controls in `Request.Form` collection—and the value of the query string used to load this example is visible in the `Request.QueryString` collection. The `Request.Cookies` collection shows the values in the cookie named TestCookie, and you will see how to add cookies to the response shortly.

At the bottom of the page are a few values extracted from the `Response` object, showing things like the character set, encoding, and expiry details of the response (see Figure 9.2).

Adding Cookies to the Response

The example page shown in Figure 9.1 demonstrates how you can easily create and add cookies to the response sent to the client. When you click the **Add cookie** button at the top of the page, an event handler named `btnCookie_Click` executes. Listing 9.4 shows this routine. It starts by checking if a cookie with the specified name is already present in the `Cookies` collection, using the `Get` method of the `HttpCookieCollection`

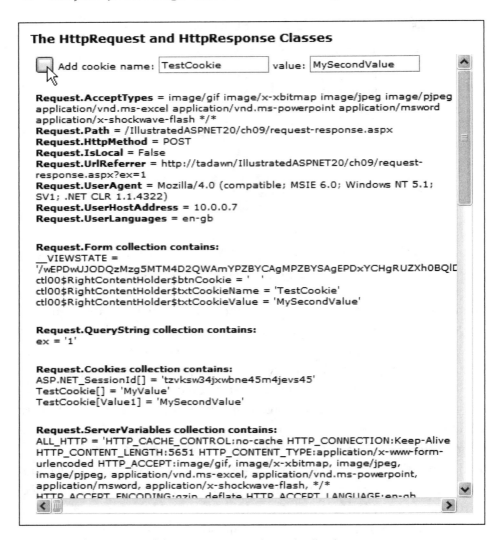

FIGURE 9.1: The contents of the Request properties and collections

class. If it does not exist, the Add method adds a new cookie to the collection and automatically makes it part of the response for this page.

If the cookie already exists, the code gets a reference to it as an Http-Cookie instance and checks how many values it already has (the number of items in the Values collection). Then it adds a new value to this collection by incrementing the name and then setting the value from the text box on the page. The important point to remember, then, is to add the cookie to the Response, because it is not automatically added in this case.

```
SERVER_PROTOCOL = 'HTTP/1.1'
SERVER_SOFTWARE = 'Microsoft-IIS/6.0'
URL = '/IllustratedASPNET20/ch09/request-response.aspx'
HTTP_CACHE_CONTROL = 'no-cache'
HTTP_CONNECTION = 'Keep-Alive'
HTTP_CONTENT_LENGTH = '5651'
HTTP_CONTENT_TYPE = 'application/x-www-form-urlencoded'
HTTP_ACCEPT = 'image/gif, image/x-xbitmap, image/jpeg, image/pjpeg,
application/vnd.ms-excel, application/vnd.ms-powerpoint, application/msword,
application/x-shockwave-flash, */*'
HTTP_ACCEPT_ENCODING = 'gzip, deflate'
HTTP_ACCEPT_LANGUAGE = 'en-gb'
HTTP_COOKIE = 'ASP.NET_SessionId=tzvksw34jxwbne45m4jevs45;
TestCookie=MyValue&Value1=MySecondValue'
HTTP_HOST = 'tadawn'
HTTP_REFERER = 'http://tadawn/IllustratedASPNET20/ch09/request-
response.aspx?ex=1'
HTTP_USER_AGENT = 'Mozilla/4.0 (compatible; MSIE 6.0; Windows NT 5.1;
SV1; .NET CLR 1.1.4322)'

Response.Charset = 'utf-8'
Response.ContentEncoding = 'System.Text.UTF8Encoding'
Response.ContentType = 'text/html'
Response.Expires = '0'
Response.ExpiresAbsolute = '01/01/0001 00:00:00'
```

FIGURE 9.2: Some of the Response properties shown at the bottom of the example page

Listing 9.4. Adding or Modifying a Cookie in the Response

```csharp
void btnCookie_Click(Object sender, EventArgs e)
// handle click on "Add cookie" button
{
  // see if cookie already exists with this name
  if (Request.Cookies.Get(txtCookieName.Text) == null)
  {
    // not found so add a new cookie
    Response.Cookies.Add(new HttpCookie(
                   txtCookieName.Text, txtCookieValue.Text));
  }
  else
  {
    // get the existing cookie and count existing subkeys
    HttpCookie cookie = Request.Cookies[txtCookieName.Text];
    Int32 vals = cookie.Values.Count;
    // add another subkey with new value
    cookie.Values["Value" + vals.ToString()] = txtCookieValue.Text;
    // remember to add the cookie to the Request
    Response.Cookies.Add(cookie);
  }
}
```

When you use the example page, bear in mind that you have to cause the page to post back again after adding a new cookie before it appears in the `Request.Cookies` collection. Adding the cookie causes it to be stored on the client's machine, and it is only when the next request occurs that the browser sends the new cookie to the server.

Using the HttpServerUtility Class

The `HttpServerUtility` class provides features that you can use in your code to interact with the current request and response. These features are specific to the low-level actions often required when handling URLs and managing the execution cycle. They include the following:

- Accessing the server's name (`Server.MachineName`)
- Reading and setting the execution timeout (`Server.ScriptTimeout`)
- Translating virtual to physical paths (`Server.MapPath`)
- Getting information about the most recent error (`Server.GetLastError`)
- Encoding and decoding functions for HTML- and URL-encoded strings, including decoding just the path, and for URL tokens, the to/from byte arrays.
- Executing another page or transferring execution to another page. You will see these topics discussed in the next Chapter 10.

A full list of the properties, methods, and events for the `HttpServerUtility` class, which implements the ASP.NET `Server` object, is at http://msdn2.microsoft.com/library/z45t6hhk(en-us,vs.80).aspx.

This example demonstrates some of the ways you can use the `HttpServerUtility` object to work with requests and responses. It declares two `String` values; the first is a string that includes characters not valid in HTML, and the second is a fictional URL containing characters that are not valid in a URL (see Listing 9.5). Then the code creates an encoded version of each one using the appropriate method (`HtmlEncode` and `UrlEncode`).

Listing 9.5. Working with the HttpServerUtility Class

```
// declare two strings to encode and decode
String sSomeHTML
  = "This is some'<TEST TEXT>' to encode & decode";
String sSomeURL
  = "http://somesite.com/test page.aspx?text=1+2&value=3";
String sEncodedHTML = Server.HtmlEncode(sSomeHTML);
String sEncodedURL = Server.UrlEncode(sSomeURL);

StringBuilder sb = new StringBuilder();
// display actual strings HTMLEncode the first one for display
sb.Append("HTML String is:'<b>"+ sEncodedHTML + "'</b><br />");
sb.Append("URL String is:'<b>"+ sSomeURL + "'</b><p />");

// display encoded and decoded values
sb.Append("Server.HtmlEncode(HTML String) is:"
  + "<xmp style='font-size:small'>"+ Server.HtmlEncode(sSomeHTML)
  + "</xmp>");
sb.Append("Server.HtmlDecode(HTML String) is:"
  + "<xmp style='font-size:small'>"+ Server.HtmlDecode(sEncodedHTML)
  + "</xmp>");
sb.Append("Server.UrlEncode(URL String) is:"
  + "<xmp style='font-size:small'>"+ Server.UrlEncode(sSomeURL)
  + "</xmp>");
sb.Append("Server.UrlDecode(URL String) is:"
  + "<xmp style='font-size:small'>"+ Server.UrlDecode(sEncodedURL)
  + "</xmp>");
sb.Append("Server.UrlPathEncode(URL String) is:"
  + "<xmp style='font-size:small'>"+ Server.UrlPathEncode(sSomeURL)
  + "</xmp>");
lblResult.Text = sb.ToString();
```

Now a `StringBuilder` creates a `String` to display in a Label control on the page. First, the code displays the existing values of the two strings—although in order for the HTML string to display in the page, the code has to use the `HtmlEncoded` version. If it does not, the angle brackets would not be visible. Next, a series of `<xmp>` elements hold the results of applying the various methods of the `HttpServerUtility` class to the two strings.

Figure 9.3 shows the result. You can see that the `HtmlEncode` method encodes the angle brackets and the ampersand in the HTML string. For the URL string, the `UrlEncode` method replaces the slashes, spaces, and all other delimiters with the encoded equivalents. This allows the complete

```
Using the HttpServerUtility Class

HTML String is: 'This is some '<TEST TEXT>' to encode & decode'
URL String is: 'http://somesite.com/test page.aspx?text=1+2&value=3'

Server.HtmlEncode(HTML String) is:

This is some '&lt;TEST TEXT&gt;' to encode &amp; decode

Server.HtmlDecode(HTML String) is:

This is some '<TEST TEXT>' to encode & decode

Server.UrlEncode(URL String) is:

http%3a%2f%2fsomesite.com%2ftest+page.aspx%3ftext%3d1%2b2%26value%3d3

Server.UrlDecode(URL String) is:

http://somesite.com/test page.aspx?text=1+2&value=3

Server.UrlPathEncode(URL String) is:

http://somesite.com/test%20page.aspx?text=1+2&value=3
```

FIGURE 9.3: Using the encoding and decoding methods of the HttpServerUtility class

URL string to be passed to another page within (as a parameter of) the URL of the target page without error.

However, often you will only want to encode the URL to remove any characters that are not valid when using this string as the URL to load another page, without encoding all the characters. In this case, the `UrlPathEncode` method gives the required result.

Using the HttpContext Class

The `HttpContext` class exposes all of the HTTP data about the current request and response. This includes references to the current `HttpRequest`, `HttpResponse`, and `HttpServerUtility` instances (accessed through the `Context.Request`, `Content.Response`, and `Context.Server` properties). It also provides access to the current `TraceContext` for writing trace messages, the `HttpSessionState` and `HttpApplicationState` objects to read and set session-level and application-level values, and access for reading configuration and error details.

In an ASP.NET page, you do not have to specify this object when you access its properties or methods. For example, you can write to the current `TraceContext` using just:

```
Trace.Write("Warnings", "MyTraceValue");
```

Inside a component or assembly class, however, you must get a reference to the current context before you can interact with the HTTP request or response. This simply involves querying the `Current` property of the `HttpContext`:

```
sClientsIPAddress = HttpContext.Current.Request.UserHostAddress;
```

A full list of the properties, methods, and events for the `HttpContext` class, which implements the ASP.NET `Context` object, is at http://msdn2.microsoft.com/library/b99k0b4w(en-us,vs.80).aspx.

The ASP.NET Page Class

Much of the code you write interacts with the ASP.NET page through the `Page` object. The `Page` acts as a container for the controls you place on your Web Form. It also provides properties and methods that integrate with the controls and the underlying ASP.NET execution cycle. In fact, there are 15 events, around 50 methods, and over 60 properties for the `Page` object—though in reality, only a few are regularly used.

A full list of the properties, methods, and events for the `Page` class is at http://msdn2.microsoft.com/library/68987swh(en-us,vs.80).aspx.

To help you get a feel for the features of the `Page` class, the following sections demonstrate some of the more useful techniques:

- General Methods and Properties of the `Page` Class
- Accessing the Intrinsic ASP.NET Objects
- Finding Controls on a Page
- Writing Trace Information
- Skins and Themes
- User Input Validation
- The Page-level Events

The `Page` class also exposes the `IsCrossPagePostBack` and `PreviousPage` properties, which are useful when you take advantage of cross-page posting techniques (posting a form to a different ASP.NET page instead of using a postback). The next chapter discusses these, when you look in more detail at navigation techniques in ASP.NET. There are also two properties, `Master` and `MasterPageFile`, concerned with the use of Master Pages. You will see this topic discussed toward the end of this chapter.

General Methods and Properties of the Page Class

The `Page` object exposes information about the current page and the current request, and allows you to set various parameters of the response. The read-only properties available include:

- `IsPostBack`, which indicates whether the page execution is in response to a client postback, or if this is the first access
- `ClientQueryString`, which returns the query string portion of the URL requested by the client
- `Form`, which gets a reference to the server-side `<form>` on this page
- `Header`, which gets a reference to the document `<head>` section of this page
- `Title`, which gets a reference to the `<title>` section of this page

The write-only properties that specify features of the response are:

- `CodePage`, which sets the code page identifier for this page
- `ContentType`, which sets the HTTP MIME type for this page
- `Culture`, which sets the execution culture ID for this page
- `UICulture`, which sets the user interface culture ID for this page
- `LCID`, which sets the locale identifier for this page
- `Buffer`, which specifies whether the page output is buffered by IIS before being sent to the client (`true`), or is sent to the client as it is created (`false`)
- `ResponseEncoding`, which sets the encoding language for this page

This example shows how you can use several of these properties, along with some you will come across later in this section of the chapter. In the

`Page_Load` event, the code (see Listing 9.6) first sets the `ClientTarget` property of the page to the value selected in the drop-down list box. This list has the `AutoPostBack` property set to `true` so that a postback occurs whenever you change the selected value. Then the code creates a `StringBuilder`, appends the text to display by querying the properties of the `Page` class, and dumps the content into a `Label` control on the page. Notice how you can use the `IsLocal` property to ensure that remote users cannot see the path to this page on your site.

Listing 9.6. Using the Properties of the Page Class

```
// set the ClientTarget type from drop-down listbox
Page.ClientTarget = lstClientTarget.SelectedValue;

// get property values for display
StringBuilder sb = new StringBuilder();
sb.Append("Page.IsPostBack ='"+ Page.IsPostBack.ToString());
sb.Append("Page.ClientQueryString ='"+ Page.ClientQueryString);
sb.Append("Page.ClientTarget ='"+ Page.ClientTarget);
sb.Append("Page.Form.Method ='"+ Page.Form.Method);
sb.Append("Page.Title ='"+ Page.Title);
sb.Append("Page.CodePageID ='"+ Page.CodePage);
sb.Append("Page.ContentType ='"+ Page.ContentType);
sb.Append("Page.Culture ='"+ Page.Culture);
sb.Append("Page.UICulture ='"+ Page.UICulture);
sb.Append("Page.LCID ='"+ Page.LCID);
sb.Append("Page.Buffer ='"+ Page.Buffer.ToString());
sb.Append("Page.ResponseEncoding ='"+ Page.ResponseEncoding);
sb.Append("(Page.Header as HtmlHead).TagName ='"
                    + (Page.Header as HtmlHead).TagName);
if (Request.IsLocal)
{
  sb.Append("Page.MapPath(Request.Path) ='"
          + Page.MapPath(Request.Path) );
}
else
{
  sb.Append("Page.MapPath(Request.Path) is only displayed "
          + "for the local machine");
}
lblResult.Text = sb.ToString();
```

The example shows how you can get the title of a page (even though the `<title>` element is not declared as a server control), plus the `<head>` element and its contents. In the example, the `Header` is cast to an `HtmlHead` instance,

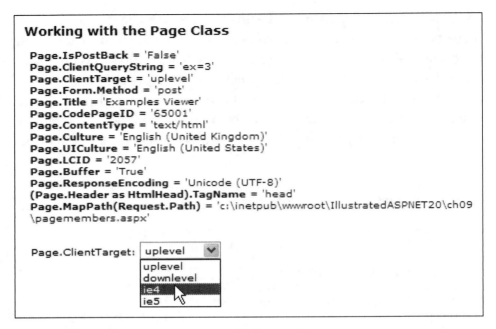

Working with the Page Class

```
Page.IsPostBack = 'False'
Page.ClientQueryString = 'ex=3'
Page.ClientTarget = 'uplevel'
Page.Form.Method = 'post'
Page.Title = 'Examples Viewer'
Page.CodePageID = '65001'
Page.ContentType = 'text/html'
Page.Culture = 'English (United Kingdom)'
Page.UICulture = 'English (United States)'
Page.LCID = '2057'
Page.Buffer = 'True'
Page.ResponseEncoding = 'Unicode (UTF-8)'
(Page.Header as HtmlHead).TagName = 'head'
Page.MapPath(Request.Path) = 'c:\inetpub\wwwroot\IllustratedASPNET20\ch09
\pagemembers.aspx'


Page.ClientTarget: uplevel
                   uplevel
                   downlevel
                   ie4
                   ie5
```

FIGURE 9.4: Querying and setting some properties of the Page class

and then the properties of this element can be displayed—such as the element (tag) name. Figure 9.4 shows this example page in action. Remember that many of the properties (in fact, all those you see here except for IsPostBack, ClientQueryString, Form, and Title) are read/write—so you can set the values of these as well as just querying them as in this example.

Specifying the Client Target

There is a read/write property on the Page class named ClientTarget, which allows you to override the automatic detection of browser capabilities. ASP.NET automatically tailors the output it generates to suit the browser type (where possible). For example, it generates CSS style information only for browsers that support this, and uses <font> elements for other browsers. You can specify the values "ie5" (Internet Explorer 5.5 and later), "ie4" or "uplevel" (Internet Explorer 4.0 and later), or "downlevel" (other browsers) to control the output rendering type. Alternatively, you can specify any of the `alias` values defined in the `<clientTarget>` sections of your `Web.Config` or `Machine.Config` file, or a specific user agent string.

Managing ViewState

ASP.NET pages use a hidden control within the server-side `<form>` section to store encrypted data between postbacks that is required for recreating the correct page and control tree with the previous values. This data is the *viewstate*, discussed towards the end of the previous chapter. You can enable and disable the storage of viewstate using the `EnableViewState` property for the page, and you can specify if authentication of the encrypted viewstate takes place on postback by using the `EnableViewStateMac` property.

You can also assign an identifier to the viewstate for each individual user of the site by setting the `ViewStateUserKey` property and then checking this on postback to identify individual users. Finally, you can specify if viewstate encryption takes place by setting the `ViewStateEncryptionMode` property. See the next section, Accessing the Intrinsic ASP.NET Objects, which describes how you can store and retrieve values from the viewstate.

Handling Errors

When an error occurs, ASP.NET raises an exception. If you do not handle the exception in your code, it causes the default error page to display. Instead of the default error page, you can set the `ErrorPage` property of the `Page` instance to a page name or URL so that browser redirection will occur if an unhandled page exception occurs.

Translating URLs

The `Page` class exposes the `MapPath` method, which you can use to resolve a virtual relative or absolute URL path to the equivalent physical file path on your server. The example for the section General Methods and Properties of the Page Class (earlier in this chapter) demonstrates this method.

Accessing the Intrinsic ASP.NET Objects

You saw earlier in this chapter how you access and use the intrinsic ASP.NET objects by accessing the `Request`, `Response`, and `Server` properties of the current page context in your code. You can also work with several other intrinsic objects:

- `Application`, which provides a global name/value dictionary for storing values that are accessible from any page, and by any user, within the current ASP.NET application (the current application virtual root).

- `Session`, which provides a name/value dictionary for storing values that are accessible only to the current client, and only until the current session times out after a default value of 20 minutes with no further page access. This timeout is set in the `Machine.Config` or `Web.Config` file. See Chapter 16 for more details about configuring session state storage.

- `ViewState`, which provides access to the name/value dictionary stored in a hidden control within the page. This is useful for storing small items of data and is accessible only across postbacks from this page.

- `Cache`, which provides a global name/value dictionary for storing values that are accessible from any page, and by any user, within the current ASP.NET application (the current application virtual root). Unlike `Application`, however, `Cache` provides methods that exert more control over when and how items are expired from the cache and how caching behaves when memory constraints affect the application. Chapter 6 looks in detail at caching techniques in ASP.NET.

- `User`, which provides access to the current user instance. When the application denies anonymous access using any of the available types of authentication, the `User` property of the `Page` contains a reference to an object that implements the `IPrinciple` interface—through which you can get access to details about the current user. Chapter 11 contains more information on the security features in ASP.NET.

You access the `Application`, `Session`, and `Viewstate` objects in the same way—with a key name that identifies the value you want to read or store. For example, you can store a value (which can be a simple value-type converted to a `String` or an object type that can self-serialize, such as a `DataSet` or `DataTable`) like this:

```
Application["MyString"] = "Value for my string";
Session["MyData"] = myDataSet;
ViewState["MyInteger"] = iMyValue.ToString();
```

To retrieve values, you access them using the key name and cast the result to the appropriate type:

```
sMyString = Application["MyString"];
myDataSet = Session["MyData"] as DataSet;
iMyValue = (Int32)ViewState["MyInteger"];
```

Finding Controls on a Page

One of the common tasks when writing code is getting references to controls on the page, or the child controls of another control. Every "container"control (a control such as a table or form that can contain child controls) has a `Controls` property that provides a reference to a collection of any child controls. This applies to the `Page` itself, and to all the container controls in the `Page.Controls` collection. Thus, the "control tree"for the page is in fact a hierarchical tree-like structure.

All container controls, such as `Page`, have methods that help you locate a specific control when you do not know the control ID value, or when it is located within a repeating container control. The `HasControls` methods returns `true` if there are any child controls, or `false` if the `Controls` collection is empty. It is useful if you are iterating through the controls on a page looking for some specific control type or property value. The example here demonstrates how you can achieve this.

Iterating through the control tree is of necessity a recursive process, so the example page contains a routine named `ShowControlTree` (see Listing 9.7) that takes a control as a parameter, plus a reference to a node in the `TreeView` control declared elsewhere on the page. It sets the text value of this node to a string containing the type name of the control passed in (after removing the `System.Web.UI` prefix), plus the value of the `ID` property of the control.

Then the code iterates through all the child controls in the `Controls` collection of the current control. For each one, it creates a new `TreeNode`

node within the current node, specifies it is to be displayed as plain text (not as a hyperlink), and adds it to the `TreeView` control. Finally, it calls itself recursively with references to the current child control and the new `Tree-Node`. This causes the routine to repeat the process for that control and all its child controls.

Listing 9.7. Iterating through the Controls in a Page and Adding Them to a TreeView

```
void ShowControlTree(Control ctrl, TreeNode node)
{
  // set text of the current node to show type and ID of control
  node.Text = ctrl.ToString().Replace("System.Web.UI." , String.Empty)
            + "[id='"+ ctrl.ID + "']";
  // iterate through the Controls collection of this control
  foreach (Control child in ctrl.Controls)
  {
    TreeNode nextnode = new TreeNode();
    nextnode.SelectAction = TreeNodeSelectAction.None;
    node.ChildNodes.Add(nextnode);
    // recursively call this routine for all child controls
    ShowControlTree(child, nextnode);
  }
}
```

To start the process off, the `Page_Load` event handler (see Listing 9.8) just has to create a new root node in the `TreeView`, specify the `SelectAction`, and add it to the `TreeView` in the same way as for the child controls in

Listing 9.8. The Page_Load Event Handler That Populates the TreeView and Page

```
void Page_Load()
{
  // add a root node to the TreeView for the Page class
  TreeNode node = new TreeNode();
  node.SelectAction = TreeNodeSelectAction.None;
  trvResult.Nodes.Add(node);
  // call a recursive routine to populate this node and
  // then iterate the child nodes doing the same thing
  ShowControlTree(Page, node);

  // search for all controls of type Label on this page
  // using a similar recursive routine
  StringBuilder sb = new StringBuilder(
                  "<b>List of all Label controls</b>:<br />");
  FindLabelControls(Page.Controls, sb);
  lblResult.Text = sb.ToString();
}
```

the ShowControlTree routine you just looked at. Then it can call the ShowControlTree routine with the Page as the root control and the new TreeView node. Figure 9.5 shows the results from this section of code, and you can clearly see the hierarchy of controls on the page.

Finding and Listing the Controls on a Page

```
⊟ ASP.find_controls_aspx [id='__Page']
   ⊟ ASP.Examples_master [id='']
      ⋯ LiteralControl [id='']
      ⊟ HtmlControls.HtmlHead [id='Head1']
         ⋯ HtmlControls.HtmlTitle [id='']
         ⋯ HtmlControls.HtmlLink [id='']
      ⋯ ResourceBasedLiteralControl [id='']
      ⊟ HtmlControls.HtmlForm [id='form1']
         ⋯ ResourceBasedLiteralControl [id='']
         ⋯ WebControls.Label [id='TopLineLeft']
         ⋯ LiteralControl [id='']
         ⋯ WebControls.Image [id='PageDiv']
         ⋯ ResourceBasedLiteralControl [id='']
         ⋯ WebControls.Label [id='TopLineRight']
         ⋯ LiteralControl [id='']
         ⋯ WebControls.ImageMap [id='TabImageMap']
         ⋯ LiteralControl [id='']
         ⋯ WebControls.Label [id='HeadingLeft']
         ⋯ LiteralControl [id='']
         ⋯ WebControls.Label [id='HeadingRight']
         ⋯ LiteralControl [id='']
         ⊟ WebControls.ContentPlaceHolder [id='LeftContentHolder']
            ⋯ ResourceBasedLiteralControl [id='']
         ⋯ LiteralControl [id='']
         ⊞ WebControls.ContentPlaceHolder [id='RightContentHolder']
```

FIGURE 9.5: Listing the controls in the page with a TreeView control

Searching for Specific Control Types

The second section of code in the Page_Load event handler in Listing 9.8 starts a process of searching through the page's control tree to find all Label controls. After creating a StringBuilder to store the results, it calls another recursive routine named FindLabelControls, passing in a reference to the Controls collection of the Page and the StringBuilder. The result is then placed in another Label control declared in the HTML section of the page.

Listing 9.9 shows the FindLabelControls routine, and you can see that it is also a recursive routine. It starts by iterating through the Controls collection passed to it. For each control in the collection, it checks if it is a Label control—and, if so, displays the value of the ID property. Then the code casts the reference to a Control instance into a Label instance so that the type-specific properties are available. In this case, the value of the EnableViewState property is extracted and displayed.

Listing 9.9. Searching for Label Controls in the Page's Control Tree

```
void FindLabelControls(ControlCollection cc, StringBuilder sb)
{
  // iterate through the Controls collection
  foreach (Control ctrl in cc)
  {
    // see if it is a Label control
    if (ctrl is Label)
    {
      sb.Append("ID ='"+ ctrl.ID + "'   ");
      // must cast Control to a specific type to get non-base
      // properties such as EnableViewState
      sb.Append("EnableViewState = "
        + (ctrl as Label).EnableViewState.ToString() + "<br />");
    }
    // see if it has any child controls
    if (ctrl.HasControls())
    {
      // recursively call this routine on the Controls
      // collection of this child control
      FindLabelControls(ctrl.Controls, sb);
    }
  }
}
```

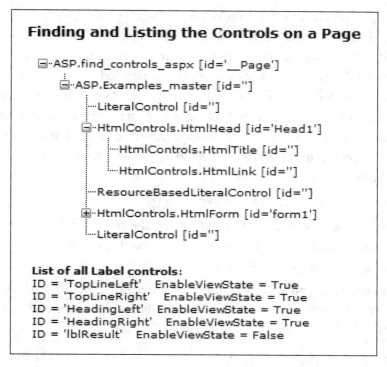

Finding and Listing the Controls on a Page

```
⊟··ASP.find_controls_aspx [id='__Page']
   ⊟··ASP.Examples_master [id='']
      ┊···LiteralControl [id='']
      ⊟··HtmlControls.HtmlHead [id='Head1']
      ┊  ┊···HtmlControls.HtmlTitle [id='']
      ┊  ┊···HtmlControls.HtmlLink [id='']
      ┊···ResourceBasedLiteralControl [id='']
      ⊞··HtmlControls.HtmlForm [id='form1']
      ┊···LiteralControl [id='']
```

List of all Label controls:
```
ID = 'TopLineLeft'   EnableViewState = True
ID = 'TopLineRight'   EnableViewState = True
ID = 'HeadingLeft'   EnableViewState = True
ID = 'HeadingRight'   EnableViewState = True
ID = 'lblResult'   EnableViewState = False
```

FIGURE 9.6: A list of all the Label controls within the page's control tree

Finally, after checking that the Controls collection of the current control contains at least one control using the HasControls method, the code calls itself recursively. It passes in the Controls collection of the current control and the StringBuilder, so that all the child controls of the current control are processed.

Figure 9.6 shows the section of the page that the code in Listing 9.9 generates. The first four Label controls are actually declared in the Master Page, but they are part of the current control tree when the page executes. The last Label control is the one that displays the results—the one containing the text you are looking at.

The FindControl Method

When a control is located within a repeating container control, such as the GridView, the actual ID value allocated to the control at runtime depends on the container(s) that hold the control. The ID value (visible if you select **View | Source** in your browser when viewing such a page) is a concatenation of the ID values of all the controls that contain this control, with the ID you specify for the control at design time appended.

The `FindControl` methods takes a control ID value and searches for a server control with the specified ID value within the current container, even if the actual ID of the control contains other concatenated control IDs. For example, you can find a control with the ID value `MyCtrl` anywhere on the page using:

```
Control ctrl = Page.FindControl("MyCtrl");
```

However, you will usually need to cast the control reference returned to the specific control type if you want to access its properties. For example:

```
TextBox txt = Page.FindControl("MyCtrl") as TextBox;
```

Be aware that you will get a `null` reference returned if the `FindControl` method cannot locate the control. The equivalent code in Visual Basic.NET is this:

```
Dim txt As TextBox = CType(Page.FindControl("MyCtrl"), TextBox)
```

Writing Trace Information

One of the great features in ASP.NET is the ability to write out trace information from your code, allowing you to more easily see and debug problem areas without having to resort to writing the information into the page. The `TraceContext` instance for the current page, accessed through the `Trace` property of the `Page`, provides the `Write` and `Warn` methods for writing trace information.

This information appears at the end of the page when you set the `Trace="true"` attribute in the @`Page` directive or in a `Web.Config` file (the `Warn` method generates information that is displayed in red text). You can specify a value that acts as a category type for the first parameter, and the value to write for the second one, as follows:

```
Trace.Write("Loading", "MyValue=" + MyObject.MyValue.ToString());
```

Or you can omit the category:

```
Trace.Write("Load Completed");
```

You can also specify an `Exception` instance (or one of its descendent class instances) as the third parameter, so that the error details display as well. You can also test if tracing is currently enabled using the `TraceEnabled` property (perhaps to avoid complex calculation of values if tracing is turned off), and you can specify the mode in which trace information is written using the `TraceModeValue` property (sorted by time or by category). You will see tracing used in the example in a later section, Page-Level Events.

Skins and Themes

ASP.NET allows you to change the appearance of your pages and site using Themes. A Theme is a set of style declarations (usually called skins) that apply to specific controls. Themes can set the CSS style properties, images, colors, and other features. Like all visual controls that support Themes, the `Page` class exposes four properties that you can use. These are:

- The `SkinID` property, which gets or sets the skin to apply to the control.
- The `StyleSheetTheme` property, which gets or sets the name of the style sheet applied to this page.
- The `Theme` property, which gets or sets the name of the page theme.

Chapter 12 looks in detail at the use of Themes along with the Personalization capabilities of ASP.NET.

Validation

The `Page` object interacts with all of the validation controls on a page (the previous chapter discussed the ASP.NET validation controls). During a postback, the `Page.IsValid` property indicates if any of the validation controls encountered an invalid value. You can get a reference to a collection of all the validation controls on the page from the `Page.Validators` property, or just the validation controls within a specified validation group using the `Page.GetValidators` method. Finally, you can cause all the validation controls to validate their values using the `Page.Validate` method.

Page-Level Events

The `Page` class exposes events that are raised as the request passes through the ASP.NET request pipeline (a series of modules that perform various operations including initialization and execution of the page), and you can handle these events in your code if you need to interact with the generation of the page. The first series of events occur on initialization, before the control tree is constructed. The three events are `PreInit`, `Init`, and `InitComplete`. The main use of the `Init` event is to set the Theme or Master Page for the page and to load details from the Personalization system.

The next step is the loading of the page, complete with the populated control tree and the values assigned to the controls. The three events are `PreLoad` (occurs before postback data is loaded into the controls on the page), `Load` (where you can interact with the fully populated controls), and `LoadComplete`. The `Load` event is the one you will use most of the time.

The final stage of sending the page content to the client is the series of -render events. These are `PreRender` and `PreRenderComplete`. In general, you will not have to use these two events in page-level code. They are more suited to use in custom controls that you create, where you use the `PreRender`, `Render`, and `PreRenderComplete` events to generate output from the control.

There are also events that occur during the execution of a page that are not part of the page's own event sequence. These include the following:

- `AbortTransaction`, which occurs when a user aborts a transaction
- `CommitTransaction`, which occurs when a transaction completes
- `DataBinding`, which occurs when the server control binds to a data source
- `Error`, which occurs when code or a control throws an unhandled exception. This event is useful for catching errors and displaying a custom message, although you can achieve the same effect by configuring the `customErrors` section of the `Web.Config` file for the site

This example demonstrates how you can handle some of the page-level events. It handles the `PreInit`, `Init`, `InitComplete`, `PreLoad`, `Load`, `PreRender`, and `PreRenderComplete` events described earlier. For each one, there is an event handler declared in the page for that event. For example, Listing 9.10 shows the event handler for the `LoadComplete` event, and you can see that it writes to both the current `TraceContext` instance and to a `Label` control on the page.

Listing 9.10. The Event Handler for the LoadComplete Event

```
protected void Page_LoadComplete(object sender, EventArgs e)
{
  Trace.Write("My Event Trace", "Page_LoadComplete event occurred.");
  lblResult.Text += "Page_LoadComplete event occurred.<br />";
}
```

However, not all events are automatically wired up in the `Page` class, and so the handler for the first event to occur (`PreInit`) also attaches the handlers for the other events that require this—as you can see in Listing 9.11.

Listing 9.11. Wiring Up Event Handlers in the PreInit Event Handler

```
protected void Page_PreInit(object sender, EventArgs e)
{
  // display details of event
  Trace.Write("My Event Trace", "Page_PreInit event occurred.");
  lblResult.Text += "Page_PreInit event occurred.<br />";

  // must attach some of the other events manually
  // these are not wired up automatically for Page
  Page.InitComplete += new EventHandler(Page_InitComplete);
  Page.PreLoad += new EventHandler(Page_PreLoad);
  Page.LoadComplete += new EventHandler(Page_LoadComplete);
  Page.PreRenderComplete +=new EventHandler(Page_PreRenderComplete);
}
```

In Visual Basic.NET, the syntax for wiring up an event handler is:
`AddHandler Page.InitComplete, New EventHandler (Page_InitComplete)`

One final feature of the example is that it handles the `AbortTransaction` event. For this to be possible, the page must specify that a transaction is required (here it uses the `Transaction` attribute of the `Page` directive), and it must import the `System.EnterpriseServices` namespace so that it can reference the `ContextUtil` class:

```
<%@ Page Language="C#" Trace="true" Transaction="RequiresNew" %>
<%@ Import Namespace="System.EnterpriseServices" %>
```

Listing 9.12 shows the event handler for the `Page_Load` event. It displays the same messages as all the other event handlers, and then calls the `SetAbort` method of the `ContextUtil` class that represents the current transaction context. This raises the `AbortTransaction` event, which the second event handler in Listing 9.12 handles. It simply writes to the Trace-Context, because the Page is now in the Render stage and so the contents of the Label control cannot be changed.

Listing 9.12. The Load and AbortTransaction Event Handlers for the Page

```
protected void Page_Load(object sender, EventArgs e)
{
  Trace.Write("My Event Trace", "Page_Load event occurred.");
  lblResult.Text += "Page_Load event occurred.<br />";

  // force ASP.NET to raise the AbortTransaction event
  // uses the COM+ utility classes, so the page requires
  // declaration of the System.EnterpriseServices namespace
  ContextUtil.SetAbort();
}
...
...
protected void Page_AbortTransaction(object sender, EventArgs e)
{
  // display message using Warn instead of Write
  Trace.Warn("My Event Trace", "Page_AbortTransaction occurred.");
}
```

Figure 9.7 shows the results of this example. You can see the text inserted into the Label control at the top of the page, followed by the trace information that ASP.NET generates automatically when tracing is enabled for the page. In the Trace Information section, you can see the messages created by the event handlers. The entry for the AbortTransaction event is in red because the code uses the Warn method instead of the Write method for this one.

Client-Side Scripting Features

ASP.NET attempts to provide a browser-based environment that is—with respect to usability and feedback—as close as possible to that of a traditional executable application. However, to achieve this requires client-side script to run in the browser. Almost all the modern browsers support client-side JavaScript, and ASP.NET is designed (where possible) to provide a fallback model that works for browsers that do not support client-side script.

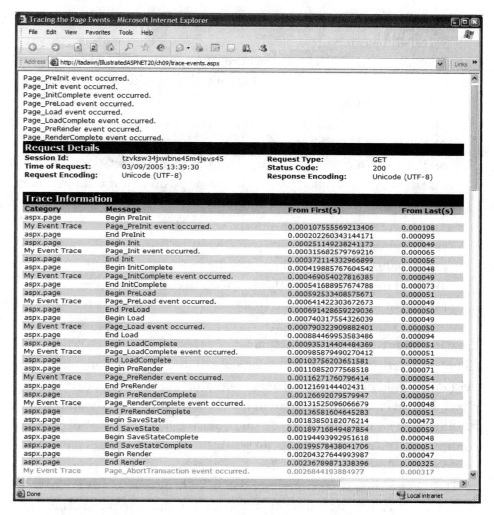

FIGURE 9.7: The trace output showing the messages created by the event handlers

You can set the following four properties to control how the rendered page behaves in the client's browser:

- The `FocusControl` method, which is mainly called directly on an individual control, rather than on the `Page` itself and which sets the input focus or cursor to that control when the page is rendered in the client's browser

- The `SetFocus` method on the current `Page` instance, which sets the input focus or cursor to a specific control when the page is rendered in the client's browser

- The `MaintainScrollPositionOnPostBack` property of the `Page` class, which when set to `true`, causes ASP.NET to attempt to set the input focus to the control that the user interacted with last, so that the page is scrolled back to the same position if it is longer than the browser window can accommodate

- The `SmartNavigation` property, which determines if ASP.NET should attempt to generate a page that uses background requests to repopulate sections that change as the user interacts with the page. You will not normally set this property in code, but you can set it instead in the `@Page` directive

Creating Client-Side Script Sections

Client-side script, or `<script>` elements that reference client-side script held in separate files, can be included verbatim in the page you send to the client. However, it is often useful to inject client-side script dynamically at runtime. One issue is that, if you do this from a custom user control or server control, you must be sure that only one instance of the script is injected—irrespective of the number of instances of that control on the page.

The `ClientScript` property of the `Page` instance returns an instance of the `ClientScriptManager` class for the current page. This class exposes a series of methods that you can use to access and modify individual script sections, including getting references to various objects in the scripts and the page, checking if scripts are registered, and adding new scripts and hidden controls. These are some of the more useful methods of the `ClientScriptManager` class:

- The `RegisterClientScriptBlock` method, which causes ASP.NET to emit the client-side script block defined within a `String` and to register it with the page using the unique name you provide

- The `IsClientScriptBlockRegistered` method, which indicates if a client-side script block, identified by a unique name that you specify, is currently registered in this page
- The `RegisterStartupScript` method, which causes ASP.NET to emit the client-side start-up script defined within a `String` and to register it with the page using the unique name you provide. A start-up script is code that runs as the page loads, and is located at the end of the `<form>` section of the page
- The `IsStartupScriptRegistered` method, which indicates if a client-side startup script, identified by a unique name that you specify, is currently registered in this page
- The `RegisterClientScriptInclude` method, which causes ASP.NET to emit a `<script>` element that loads a separate client-side script file and to register it with the page using the unique name you provide
- The `IsClientScriptIncludeRegistered` method, which indicates if a `<script>` element that loads a separate client-side script file, identified by a unique name that you specify, is currently registered in this page
- The `RegisterOnSubmitStatement` method, which causes ASP.NET to emit a client-side script function that executes before a postback submits the page and to register it with the page using the unique name you provide
- The `IsOnSubmitStatementRegistered` method, which indicates if a client-side script function that executes before a postback submits the page, identified by a unique name that you specify, is currently registered in this page
- The `RegisterHiddenField` method, which creates an `<input type="hidden">` control in the page that can be used by other controls or client-side code to submit values to the server during a postback

A full list of the methods for the `ClientScriptManager` class is at http://msdn2.microsoft.com/library/asxkek04(en-us,vs.80).aspx.

Asynchronous Page Callbacks

One of the features of client-side Web programming that was popular some years ago, but then seemed to die away in the quest for universal browser compatibility, has recently started to become more useful. This is because modern browsers support an increasingly wide and useful set of universal standards that allow the creation of client-side code that runs on all these browsers.

Currently, much of the focus is on an environment called Ajax (available from http://ajax.schwarz-interactive.de/csharpsample/default.aspx), which implements asynchronous client-side callbacks to the server from client-side script running in the browser, without requiring a page reload. A good example of this approach is the GoogleMaps site at http://maps.google.co.uk/.

Microsoft is also developing (at the time of writing) a client-side script library and integrated server-side system called Atlas, which will provide a range of features to enable asynchronous page operations (see http://atlas.asp.net/).

You can write your own custom code or use the Atlas or Ajax library. However, ASP.NET contains some built-in support for asynchronous callbacks. This includes the `IsCallback` property exposed by the `Page` object, which indicates if the current request for the page is from a client-side callback.

This simple example shows how you can create client-side asynchronous callbacks using the built-in features of ASP.NET. The example displays a single button that, when clicked, fetches the current time from the server and displays it below the button—and all without causing a postback to the server (see Figure 9.8).

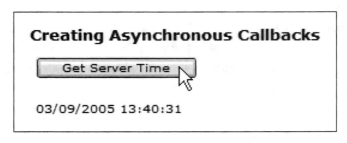

FIGURE 9.8: Fetching the time from the server asynchronously

The example page contains the following declaration of a button control. Notice that it is not a server control, and does not cause a postback—it simply calls a client-side JavaScript function named `getServerTime`. Alternatively, you can use any event that occurs in the client (even an interval timer event) to initiate the background request:

```
<input type="button" onclick="getServerTime();"
       value="Get Server Time"/>
```

There is a `<div>` element below the button that displays the result of the callback. Again, this is not a server control:

```
<div id="divTime"> </div>
```

Implementing the Server-side Callback Code

Most of the work in implementing the callbacks occurs on the server. The first step is to set up the page to accept callbacks and provide the required features to support them. This means implementing the `ICallbackEventHandler` interface, which you declare with an `Implements` directive at the start of the page:

```
<%@ Implements Interface="System.Web.UI.ICallbackEventHandler" %>
```

Now you can create the routine that executes when a callback occurs. The only requirement (and the only member of the `ICallbackEventHandler` interface) is an event handler named `RaiseCallbackEvent` that accepts a `String` and returns a `String` as the result. In the example page, the routine just returns the current date and time, as shown in Listing 9.13.

Listing 9.13. The Routine That Executes When a Callback Occurs

```
public String RaiseCallbackEvent(String arg)
{
  return DateTime.Now.ToString();
}
```

The next step is to generate the client-side function that the button on the page executes. This function must initiate the callback to the server. To build a suitable statement to achieve this, you can use the

GetCallbackEventReference method of the ClientScriptManager instance for the Page. This creates a String like this:

```
WebForm_DoCallback('__Page',arg,showServerTime,context,null,true);
```

The arguments are, in order, the following:

- The object that will receive the callback event
- Any arguments to be passed to it
- The name of the client-side function that the server will call to return the results
- Any context (such as a control name) that you want to provide to the callback method on the server
- The name of the client-side script function to execute if an error occurs (not specified in this example)
- Either true for asynchronous background requests or false otherwise

The current ClientScriptManager instance is accessible through the ClientScript property of the Page. The ClientScriptManager class also provides a method named GetPostbackEventReference that does much the same as the GetCallbackEventReference method, but it generates a client-side JavaScript statement that causes a postback to the server rather than a background request.

Listing 9.14 shows the entire Page_Load event handler in the example page. The first line of code generates the client-side callback statement you just saw. The next line creates the client-side code that includes two functions. The first is the getServerTime function that is executed by the button on the page. It includes the statement (generated in the previous line) that causes the callback, so that clicking the button will start the callback to the server.

The second function, named showServerTime (and specified in the call to the GetCallbackEventReference method), is the one that executes after the server-side RaiseCallbackEvent code that generates the result is complete. It gets a reference to the <div> element on the page and inserts the value returned by the server. Finally, the IsClientScriptBlockRegistered method of the ClientScriptManager is executed to see if this client-side script block is already registered with the page (in fact, it never will be because the script block is only ever inserted once on each `Page_Load` event, but it demonstrates the technique). Providing that it is not already registered, the code then calls the `RegisterClientScriptBlock` to insert the script block.

Listing 9.14. The Server-Side Page_Load Routine

```
void Page_Load()
{
  // generate the client-side script statement that will cause an
  // asynchronous server callback to occur. showServerTime is the
  // name of the client-side function that will be executed to
  // return the values from the server to the client.
  String generatedCallback
      = Page.ClientScript.GetCallbackEventReference(Page, "arg",
                              "showServerTime", "context", true);

  // create a String containing the client-side code to insert into
  // the page. getServerTime is the routine that will be executed
  // when the button on the page is clicked, and it uses the
  // callback statement generated in the previous line of code.
  // the function showServerTime simply inserts the return value
  // into a <div> control on the page.
  String clientCallFunction = "function getServerTime(arg, context)\n"
      + "{\n"
      + " "+ generatedCallback + ";\n"
      + "}\n"
      + "function showServerTime(result, context)\n"
      + "{\n"
      + " document.getElementById('divTime').innerText = result;\n"
      + "}\n";

  // check if the a script block with this name has
  // already been registered with the page
  if (! Page.ClientScript.IsClientScriptBlockRegistered(
                              "ServerTimeCallbackScript"))
  {
    // if not, insert the client-side script block just created
    Page.ClientScript.RegisterClientScriptBlock(this.GetType(),
        "ServerTimeCallbackScript", clientCallFunction, true);
  }
}
```

Listing 9.15 shows what the JavaScript code that is generated looks like in the page, for example, when you select **View | Source** in your browser. This more clearly demonstrates how the callbacks work. Clicking the button on the page executes the `getServerTime` function, which calls other server-side script routines inserted into the page automatically by ASP.NET. These routines instantiate the `XmlHttp` object (supported by most modern browsers) and use it to send a request to the server. ASP.NET executes the page up to the PreRender stage and returns only the result of the server-side callback function (named RaiseCallbackEvent). More client-side code then takes this returned value and calls the function you created as a callback (in this example showServerTime), passing to it the result obtained from the server.

Listing 9.15. The Client-Side Script That Is Sent to the Client

```
<script type="text/javascript">
<!--
function getServerTime(arg, context)
{
  WebForm_DoCallback('__Page',arg,showServerTime,context,null,true);
}
function showServerTime(result, context)
{
  document.getElementById('divTime').innerText = result;
}
// -->
</script>
```

All the client-side code required to achieve this, and hidden from you, is available because ASP.NET automatically adds a script include reference to the page, like this:

```
<script src="/IllustratedASPNET20/WebResource.axd?d=n8...23"
        type="text/javascript"></script>
```

It also inserts a start-up script section at the end of the <form> section of the page that initializes the whole process, including making the URL of the current page available to the client-side code and initializing the XmlHttp object (see Listing 9.16).

Listing 9.16. The Client-Side Start-up Script Inserted Automatically by ASP.NET

```
<script type="text/javascript">
<!--
var pageUrl='/IllustratedASPNET20/ch09/async-callback.aspx?ex=6';
WebForm_InitCallback();
// -->
</script>
```

Even though the client-side callback process looks complicated, it is relatively easy to implement—as you have seen in this example. It can provide much more usable and interactive interfaces, and you will find many uses for it in your applications. A good example is the MSDN Web site, as referenced throughout this book, where the left-hand tree view section is populated using client-side callbacks without requiring a page reload each time you make a selection in the tree.

Sub-Classing the Page Object

The Page class is the base class you will generally use directly in your Web Forms pages and ASP.NET Web applications. However, you can extend the standard Page class if you wish—perhaps by adding new methods or just changing the default settings of some properties to better suit your own requirements.

For example, Listing 9.17 shows the declaration of a class named MyBasePage that inherits from the standard ASP.NET Page class. It sets the ErrorPage property to a specific value and adds a new custom read/write property named MyProperty to the class. It also handles the PreInit event and looks for a value in the current user's profile to see if a Theme was specified by the user. If so, it sets this theme on the page using the Page.Theme property. Notice that the code first calls the OnPreInit method of the base Page instance.

Listing 9.17. The Base Class for Pages, Based on the Existing Page Class

```
public class MyBasePage : System.Web.UI.Page
{
  // set an existing property for all pages
  ErrorPage = "MyErrorPage.aspx"

  // add new property to all pages
  protected string _myProperty;
  public string MyProperty
  {
    get { return _myProperty; }
    set { _myProperty = value; }
  }

  // force all pages to use current theme
  protected override void OnPreInit(EventArgs e)
  {
    base.OnPreInit(e);
    if (HttpContext.Current.Profile.GetPropertyValue("Theme") != null)
      Page.Theme = HttpContext.Current.Profile.GetPropertyValue(
                                    "Theme").ToString();
  }
}
```

Now, other pages can inherit from this new base page. In the @Page directive, when using the code-behind model, the pages will specify a partial class file that implements the code for the page; for example, this declaration specifies a file named Default.aspx.cs that implements a partial class named _Default:

```
<%@ Page Language="C#" AutoEventWireup="true"
        CodeFile="Default.aspx.cs" Inherits="_Default" %>
```

Listing 9.18 shows how the code in the file Default.aspx.cs can access the new custom property named MyProperty just as it would access any other property of the Page class.

Listing 9.18. Specifying the Base Class and Setting the Custom Property

```
public partial class _Default : MyBasePage
{
    protected void Page_Load(object sender, EventArgs e)
    {
        MyProperty = "Some new value";
    }
}
```

Working with Master Pages

The final section of this chapter looks at a specific feature you can take advantage of when building Web pages and Web sites. You can create a Master Page that contains the boilerplate content for the site and then use this Master Page as the "container" for other pages. These other pages, generally referred to as Content Pages, display within the Master Page. You can have more than one Master Page in your site, though a Content Page can only specify one Master Page. You can also nest Master Pages so that a Content Page can specify a Master Page that in turn specifies another Master Page.

However, bear in mind that Visual Studio will not be able to create a Design View representation if you use a nested Master Page. You may find it is easier to build pages that use only a single Master Page, and then—once ready to deploy your site—add the directives that include nesting inside the parent Master Page. You can always remove them again for editing, and reinstate them for redeployment.

You saw a Master Page used to create the overall design of the fictional Adventure Works Web site in Chapter 2.

The two properties of the `Page` class that support Master Pages are:

- `Master`, which returns a reference to the Master Page for the current Content Page or Master Page
- `MasterPageFile`, which sets or returns the file name of the Master Page for the current Content Page or Master Page

You can also specify the Master Page for a complete Web site, or for specific folders within the site, by setting the `masterPageFile` attribute of the `<pages>` element in the `<system.web>` section of `Machine.Config` or `Web.Config`.

Simple Master Pages

Master Pages are a good way to produce a consistent look and feel for a site, and make it easy to update the appearance of the complete site simply by editing or changing the Master Page. Figure 9.9 shows how a Master Page file (`MySite.master`) that defines content such as the page header and left-hand navigation menu also contains a `ContentPlaceHolder` control. The two Content Pages (`Page1.aspx` and `Page2.aspx`) reference this Master Page through the `MasterPageFile` attribute of the `@Page` directive (this sets the `MasterPageFile` property).

In Content Pages, the only content permitted is one or more ASP.NET `Content` controls, each of which uses the `ContentPlaceHolderID` attribute to specify the `ContentPlaceHolder` where it displays. In Figure 9.9, only one `ContentPlaceHolder` control occurs on the Master Page, and there is one `Content` control on each Content Page. You can use more than one provided that they have matching `ID` and `ContentPlaceHolderID` values. If you do not provide a `Content` control in a Content Page for a `ContentPlaceHolder` control that exists in the Master Page, any content declared within the `ContentPlaceHolder` control (called default content) displays instead.

Nested Master Pages

For more complex sites and requirements, you can use more than one Master Page and specify which Master Page each Content Page will use. In Figure 9.10, there is a single root Master Page (`BigCorp.master`) and two other

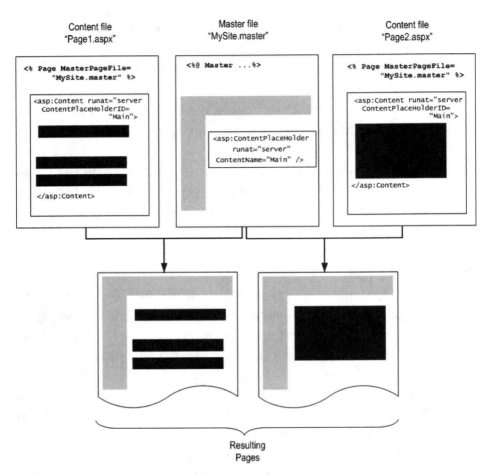

FIGURE 9.9: Using a single Master Page and two Content Pages

Master Pages (`Sales.master` and `Research.master`). However, the latter are nested Master Pages. They contain the `@Master` directive (instead of the `@Page` directive), specify the file `BigCorp.master` as their Master Page, and have a `ContentPlaceHolder` control for other Content Pages to populate. However, this `ContentPlaceHolder` control is within a `Content` control that references the `ContentPlaceHolder` control in the `BigCorp.master` Master Page.

The three Content Pages (in the third row of Figure 9.10) specify which Master Page they use and contain a `Content` control that points to the `ContentPlaceHolder` control on the Master Page they will populate. The

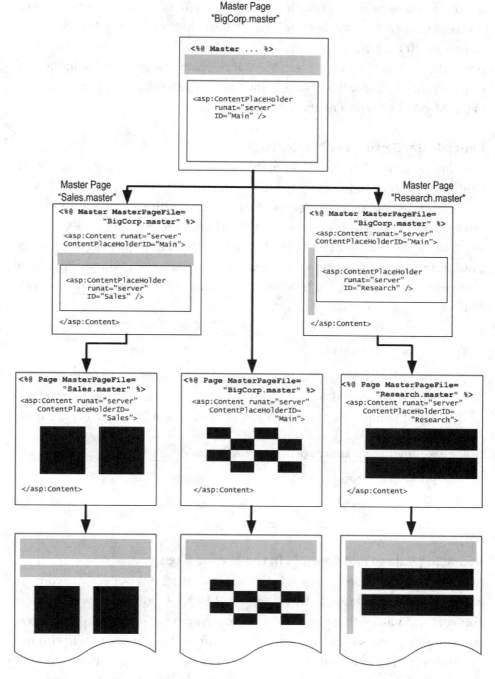

FIGURE 9.10: Using multiple nested Master Pages

left-hand and right-hand Content Pages populate the `ContentPlaceHolder` control in the two nested Master Pages. These `ContentPlaceHolder` controls are within a `Content` control on that Master Page, which is then used to populate the "root" Master page (`BigCorp.master`). You can see in the last row in Figure 9.10 how this results in the final output containing a combination of the Master Page content and Content Page content.

Dynamically Setting the Master Page

Another feature of Master Pages is the ability to choose one dynamically at runtime. One approach is to specify different Master Pages for different types of browsers or user agents. You just prefix the `MasterPageFile` attribute in the `@Page` directive with the alias of the browser type that you want to use this Master Page (providing that there is an alias in the configuration for this browser type). For example, if you have a Master Page you want used only for Mozilla browsers, while other browsers use the default Master Page, you would use:

```
<@Page MasterPageFile="Standard.master"
       mozilla:MasterPageFile="Mozilla.master"... />
```

Another way is to set the `MasterPageFile` property of the page in code. However, you must do this in the `PreInit` event of the `Page` class, as shown in Listing 9.19, and not in any later events such as the `Load` event.

Listing 9.19. Selecting a Master Page Dynamically at Runtime

```
protected void Page_PreInit(object sender, EventArgs e)
{
    Page.MasterPageFile = "~/MyNewMasterPage.master";
}
```

Accessing Values and Controls in the Master Page

Master Pages provide a great solution to separating out boilerplate content and page-specific content. However, the Master Page is likely to contain controls and values that you need to access from within the Content Pages. An example is the samples viewer that we provide to allow you to run the examples available for this book. As you load each example page, code in the Master Page changes the display of the colored tabs at the right-hand side of the page to reflect the current chapter number. This means that the Master Page needs to know the current chapter number each time the user loads a page.

Every page you see in the samples viewer specifies the Master Page file named `Examples.master` in the root folder of the site. Listing 9.20 shows a section of the partial code-behind class (`Examples.master.cs`) that implements the Master Page. You can see that it declares a public property named `CurrentChapter`.

Listing 9.20. The CurrentChapter Property Exposed by the Master Page

```
public partial class Examples : System.Web.UI.MasterPage
{
  // public property
  Int32 mCurrentChapter;
  public Int32 CurrentChapter
  {
    get { return mCurrentChapter; }
    set { mCurrentChapter = value; }
  }
  ...
```

Listing 9.21 shows the `@Page` directive for the page `Default.aspx`, and you can see the `MasterPageFile` attribute that specifies the Master page `Examples.master`. Notice that a `@MasterType` directive also specifies this Master Page file.

Listing 9.21. The @Page Directive Specifies the Master Page File

```
<%@ Page Language="C#"MasterPageFile="/Examples.master"
        AutoEventWireup="true"CodeFile="Default.aspx.cs"
        Inherits="_Default"%>
<%@ MasterType VirtualPath="~/Examples.master"%>
```

The code in the `Default.aspx` page, implemented as a partial code-behind class in the file `Default.aspx.cs`, looks for a "current chapter" value in the query string as the page loads. If it finds one, it sets the `CurrentChapter` property in the Master Page to this value by referencing it through the `Master` property of the `Page` class (see Listing 9.22).

Listing 9.22. Setting the CurrentChapter Property in the Master Page

```
protected void Page_Load(Object sender, EventArgs e)
{
  // update chapter number in master page
  // through the public property it exposes
  CurrentChapter = 0;
  if (Request.QueryString["ch"] != String.Empty)
  {
    try
    {
      CurrentChapter = Int32.Parse(Request.QueryString["ch"]);
      Master.CurrentChapter = CurrentChapter;
    }
    catch { }
  }
...
```

One point to watch out for is that some objects that are properties of the page are not actually available in the `Page_Load` or other events of the Master Page. For example, the current `User` object instance object is not attached to the page until construction of the Master Page is complete, and so cannot be accessed directly from the Master Page. However, you can usually get a reference to objects in code within the Master Page through the current ASP.NET context; for example, you can get the current user name like this:

```
String name = HttpContext.Current.User.Identity.Name;
```

If you want to access a control on a Master Page from a Content Page, you can expose a reference to the control as a property of the Master Page, as shown in Listing 9.23. Then, in the Content Page, you can set the text in the label control using `Master.MyLabelCtrl.Text = "My new value";`.

Listing 9.23. Exposing a Control as a Property in a Master Page

```
// public property to access control named MyLabelCtrl
public Label MyLabelCtrl
{
  get { return TheLabelControl; }
}
```

An alternative approach is to use the `FindControl` method of the `Page` class to search the `Controls` collection of the Master Page. This is a late-binding technique, which is not as efficient as the early-binding approach you just saw. However, it does mean that you do not have to expose the controls as properties in the Master Page. As an example, you could access the `Label` control in the Master Page that has ID value `MyLabel` from a Content Page using:

```
Label ctl = Master.FindControl("MyLabel") as Label;
```

Remember that controls in a `Content` region of a Content Page replace controls in the associated `ContentPlaceHolder` region on the Master Page. Therefore, if both the `Content` and `ContentPlaceHolder` controls contain a `Label` control, accessing that `Label` from server code in the Content Page will actually access the `Label` from the Content Page, and not that of the Master Page.

SUMMARY

In this chapter, you have seen a range of features of the `Page` class that implements the ASP.NET Web Forms page. You first examined the basic objects that form the basis for HTTP communication and Web server operation: the `HttpRequest`, `HttpResponse`, and `HttpServerUtility` classes. Each has a series of properties and methods appropriate to its position in the Web page request cycle; for example, `HttpRequest` provides details of the values submitted by the client, while `HttpResponse` allows you to access and interact with the response sent back to the client. The `HttpServerUtility` class provides methods that control page execution and makes tasks such as translating URL-encoded and HTML-encoded strings easier.

The `HttpRequest`, `HttpResponse`, and `HttpServerUtility` classes are all available from the current context, implemented by the `HttpContext` class that also provides features to assist you in creating Web pages and applications—an example being the ability to generate trace information for debugging and optimizing your code.

Like the `Page` class, all these objects are available to your code within the current context. The `Page` class itself, however, is the most complex of the classes you have seen in this chapter. With dozens of properties, methods, and events available, it provides many features that you will find useful in your ASP.NET pages. This chapter looks at many of these features, including accessing the intrinsic objects such as `Application` and `Session`, working with viewstate, finding controls on a `page`, writing trace information, and using the page-level events.

The chapter then briefly considered how you can subclass the `Page` class to add custom properties, pre-set existing properties, and use events to initialize features you want to be set on every page.

Finally, you saw how you can make creating and managing the appearance and layout of your site much easier using Master Pages. You also saw how you can use nested Master Pages, device-specific Master Pages, and set the Master Page dynamically at runtime. Finally, you examined techniques for accessing values and controls in the Master Page from a Content Page.

In the next chapter, you will look in more detail at the features of ASP.NET connected with navigation, site menus, and other features related to linking the pages within your Web sites.

10

Web Site Navigation Techniques

TWO COMMON APPROACHES FOR linking Web pages together were part of the original specifications for HTML. You can use a hyperlink, implemented as a `<a>` element, or a `<form>` section that posts its contents to another page. It became common in recent years, with the rise in interactive scripting techniques, to use a `<form>` section to post the values back to the *same* page—rather than a separate one that handles the posted values. This became known as the *postback* approach, which was discussed in previous chapters when you looked at the design of Web Forms in ASP.NET and the use of server controls.

As you saw, ASP.NET not only supports a postback architecture; it actually requires it for many of the features, such as maintaining control values, implementing an event-driven architecture, and supporting many of the interactive server controls. However, Web sites and Web applications rarely consist of just one page, and so other approaches to linking pages together are obviously required as well.

This chapter deals with Web site navigation topics and demonstrates many of the ways that you can link pages together using a range of server controls and non-server controls—some of which you have already seen in action in previous chapters. In fact, it is surprising when you come to look at a list of the approaches that are available to see how many different ways of implementing navigation ASP.NET supports.

The topics you will see in this chapter are the following:

- Simple navigation with hyperlinks
- Navigation with `LinkButton` controls
- Navigation through browser redirection
- Navigation through server-side redirection
- Cross-page posting of form contents
- Site maps, menu, and navigation path controls

The chapter begins with a brief overview of the use of hyperlinks in ASP.NET.

Simple Navigation with Hyperlinks

The simplest way to link two pages together is with a hyperlink. In ASP.NET, you have several choices for creating a hyperlink, including the following:

- As a non-server control using an HTML <a> element
- As a server control by adding the `runat="server"` attribute to an HTML <a> element
- Using an ASP.NET `Hyperlink` control
- Using an ASP.NET `LinkButton` control
- Using one of the more complex ASP.NET server controls that creates links

The important distinction between the various approaches is whether HTML that performs navigation or postback is generated. The first three approaches in the list just presented generate the familiar <a> element, such as:

```
<a href="next page">link text here</a>
```

For the first two approaches, you specify the attributes in your page using the standard HTML attribute names, such as `href`, `target`, and `title`. If you use the second approach, you can also set the link text for the element using the `InnerText` or `InnerHtml` properties, because the element is implemented on the server using the `HtmlAnchor` class. To implement a hyperlink that acts as an anchor at a specific position within the page, you use the `Name` property, as shown in Listing 10.1.

Listing 10.1. Creating a Hyperlink and Anchor using the HtmlAnchor Control

```
<a id="MyHyperlink" runat="server" href="#para1"
   title="Go to paragraph 1">Paragraph 1</a>
...
...
<a id="MyAnchor" runat="server" name="para1">This is Paragraph 1</a>
```

If the target anchor is within another page, you simply include the URL of that page in the `href` attribute:

```
<a id="MyHyperlink" runat="server" href="page2.aspx#para1">...</a>
```

You can place other controls within the `<a>` element. For example, you can create a clickable image that causes navigation to another page (or to an anchor in the same page), as shown in Listing 10.2.

Listing 10.2. Creating a Clickable Image Using the HtmlAnchor Control

```
<a id="MyHyperlink" runat="server" href="page2.aspx"
   title="Go to page 2">
  <img src="mypicture.gif" alt="Go to page 2" border="0"/>
</a>
```

This uses the `<img>` element directly, and not a server control. However, if you want to interact with the image (perhaps to specify the filename at runtime) you can replace it with an `HtmlImage` server control by adding the `runat="server"` attribute, or use an ASP.NET `Image` server control instead.

> Details of the `HtmlAnchor` class are at http://msdn2.microsoft.com/en-us/library/9ssczfkc(en-US,VS.80).aspx. Details of the `HtmlImage` control are at http://msdn2.microsoft.com/en-us/library/ky66zc99 (en-US,VS.80).aspx.

The ASP.NET Hyperlink Control

ASP.NET includes the `Hyperlink` control, which provides a much more structured and simpler approach to generating hyperlinks of all kinds. It can generate text links or clickable images, and it provides a wide range of properties that conform to the standard naming convention for server controls. To generate a simple hyperlink, you just need this:

```
<asp:Hyperlink id="MyLink" runat="server"
    NavigateUrl="mypage.aspx" Text="Click here" />
```

Like many server controls, you can also declare the content within the element tags, like this:

```
<asp:Hyperlink id="MyLink" runat="server"
    NavigateUrl="mypage.aspx">Click here</asp:Hyperlink>
```

To create a clickable image, you specify the `ImageUrl` property instead of the `Text` property, and ASP.NET automatically creates an `<a>` element with an embedded `<img>` element. It even turns off the display of the border of the image automatically by including the `border="0"` attribute. The `Target` property specifies the name of the browser window in which to open the page if you do not want it to show in the same window. The `ToolTip` property sets the `title` attribute of the `<a>` element and `<img>` element, and many other properties are available for specifying the style and appearance of the link.

Details of the `Hyperlink server` control are at http://msdn2.microsoft.com/en-us/library/1076w1hx(en-US,VS.80). aspx.

Using Access Keys

Many of the interactive server controls in ASP.NET provide the `AccessKey` property, which you can use to implement shortcut or hot-key access to that control. You set the `AccessKey` property to a single-character string that is the key the user will press in conjunction with the Alt key to move the input focus to that control. For example, this declares a `Hyperlink` control that receives the input focus if the user presses Alt+N when the page is displayed:

```
<asp:Hyperlink id="MyLink" runat="server"
    AccessKey="N" NavigateUrl="mypage.aspx" Text="Click here" />
```

Other Controls That Create Hyperlinks

Many other controls in ASP.NET generate normal HTML hyperlinks. For example, the `BulletedList` control you saw in Chapter 8 has a `DisplayMode` property that, when set to `Hyperlink`, causes the control to generate a list of text bullets that are wrapped in an `<a>` element (see Listing 10.3).

Listing 10.3. Creating a List of Hyperlinks Using the BulletedList Control

```
<asp:BulletedList id="MyList" runat="server" DisplayMode="Hyperlink">
  <asp:ListItem Text="DaveAndAl" Value="http://www.daveandal.net" />
  <asp:ListItem Text="ASP.NET" Value="http://www.asp.net"/>
  <asp:ListItem Text="Local Web site" Value="http://localhost" />
</asp:BulletedList>
```

In a similar way, the `TreeView` control described in Chapter 9 provides pure navigation capabilities. Each node in the tree is a `TreeNode` instance that exposes the `NavigateUrl` and `Target` properties. To generate an `<a>` hyperlink element for a node, set the `NavigateUrl` to anything other than an empty string (which is the default).

Many of the more complex server controls also create hyperlinks behind the scenes. The `TreeView` and `Menu` controls generate "skip links" allowing non-visual user agents to navigate past the control to the content of the page that follows. For example, the `TreeView` example in Chapter 9 generates this hyperlink located in the page just before the control's output:

```
<a href="#ctl00_RightContentHolder_trvResult_SkipLink">
  <img alt="Skip Navigation Links." src="..path to resource file.."
       width="0" height="0" style="border-width:0px;"
</a>
```

Then, after the control's output:

```
<a id="ctl00_RightContentHolder_trvResult_SkipLink"></a>
```

Other controls that create hyperlinks include the `AdRotator` control, the `ImageMap` control (described in Chapter 8), the `Menu` control (described later in this chapter), and the various types of hyperlink column that you can use in the `GridView` and `DetailsView` list controls (described in Chapters 3 and 4).

Navigation with LinkButton Controls

So far, you have seen the controls that generate standard clickable hyperlinks to navigate directly to another page or resource. However, the LinkButton and several other control types implement navigation using the postback architecture instead. They create a text link or clickable image that causes the server-side form on which they reside to post back to the server. ASP.NET automatically injects a client-side JavaScript function named __doPostBack into the page. This function takes two parameters: the control that called the function, and an argument to pass to the server-side code. It places these two values into hidden controls within the form, and then calls the client-side submit method of the form to cause the postback to occur.

To call the __doPostBack function, ASP.NET uses the capability of a hyperlink to execute JavaScript code by preceding the function name with the string "javascript:". For example, this hyperlink causes a postback to the server, with the form contents including the values MyLink and 42:

```
<a href="javascript:__doPostBack('MyLink','42')">Click here</a>
```

This is how the LinkButton control works, and many other features of the ASP.NET architecture depend on this technique as well. For example, setting the AutoPostBack property of a ListBox or TextBox control to true invokes this mechanism by adding a client-side event handler attribute to the control. For a ListBox, the client-side onchange event executes the __doPostBack function. For a TextBox, the client-side onblur event (which occurs when you move the input focus to a different control) executes the __doPostBack function.

Other controls can also cause a postback directly. These include the standard Button control, and the ImageButton control that generates a clickable image in the browser.

Using the LinkButton Control

The LinkButton looks like a hyperlink, but actually behaves like other button-style controls such as Button. When clicked, it causes a postback to the server, which raises an event you can handle in your server-side code. This means, of course, that the LinkButton is not limited to causing navigation. It can execute any server-side code you wish. An example is in the various grid-style controls such as GridView and FormView (described in Chapters 4 and 5). The `Select`, `Edit`, `Update`, and `Cancel` links automatically generated when you include a `CommandField` in the grid are `LinkButton` controls.

Many other complex controls such as the `BulletedList`, `Wizard`, and `Calendar` also generate `LinkButton` controls as part of their user interface, allowing you to handle the events generated as the user interacts with the control. Listing 10.4 shows a `BulletedList` control configured to create `LinkButton` controls, with the `DisplayMode` property set to "LinkButton". The `OnClick` attribute defines the server-side event handler invoked when the user clicks a link and, in this example, it just displays the index within the list of the clicked item.

Listing 10.4. Creating LinkButton Controls in a BulletedList Control

```
<asp:BulletedList id="List4" runat="server"
    DisplayMode="LinkButton" OnClick="ShowItem"
<asp:ListItem Text="Value 1" />
<asp:ListItem Text="Value 2" />
<asp:ListItem Text="Value 3" />
</asp:BulletedList>
...
...
public void ShowItem(Object sender, BulletedListEventArgs e)
{
  lblResult.Text = "Selected item index is: " + e.Index;
}
```

Of course, you can create your own `LinkButton` controls directly from the Toolbox in Visual Studio or by typing the element declaration:

```
<asp:LinkButton id="MyLink" runat="server" OnClick="DoSomething" />
```

The `LinkButton` is useful when you require a list of links on a page where some cause navigation and some cause a postback. Rather than mixing `HyperLink` and `Button` controls, which produces a rather untidy display, you can use `LinkButton` controls instead of `Button` controls. The `LinkButton` control is similar in underlying operation to the `Button` control (they both implement the `IButtonControl` interface), and so provides most of the features of `Button` as well—as you will see in the next sections.

Details of the `LinkButton` class are at http://msdn2.microsoft.com/en-us/library/73523y55(en-US,VS.80).aspx. Details of the `Button` class are at http://msdn2.microsoft.com/enus/library/b72c2ah5(enUS,VS.80).aspx.

The CommandName and CommandArgument Properties

If you use several LinkButton controls on a page, you can arrange for the same event handler to execute for any of the buttons. You can wire up as many controls as you want to the same event handler. The LinkButton (and other button controls) expose the CommandName and CommandArgument properties, which you can set to any String value you wish. The event handler can figure out which of the buttons the user clicked by examining the CommandName property value. If you want to pass in additional data to the event handler, you can set the CommandArgument property and read this for the button that caused the event.

For example, you can access the CommandName and CommandArgument property values in the Click event handler for a LinkButton as shown in Listing 10.5.

Listing 10.5. Accessing the CommandName and CommandArgument Properties

```
protected void MyLinkButton_Click(Object sender, EventArgs e)
{
  LinkButton linkbtn = sender as LinkButton;
  cmdName = linkbtn.CommandName;
  cmdArg = linkbtn.CommandArgument;
}
```

This capability is useful in controls such as the GridView, where multiple rows cause invocation of the same event handler. You set the CommandName to one of the values that initiates a specific action in the GridView, such as "Delete", "Update", or "Page", to cause the related actions. However, in the RowCommand event of the GridView, you can read the CommandName of the control that initiated the event, allowing you to add other controls to every row and react to the events they raise.

As an example, Listing 10.6 shows a GridView control that displays some rows from a database table—the columns are auto-generated because there is no AutoGenerateColumns="False" attribute. However, the <Columns> section also adds three columns declaratively. There are two ButtonField columns and a TemplateField column. The first ButtonField column generates a normal Button control in every row, because it has the ButtonType="Button" attribute. The second Button-Field column, which does not contain this attribute, generates the default of a LinkButton in every row. Notice that the ButtonField column exposes a CommandName property, declared as "SendButtonField" for the first column and "CopyButtonField" for the second column.

The TemplateField column contains both a Button and a LinkButton control, with the CommandName properties set to DetailsButton and DetailsLinkButton, respectively. However, when declaring individual button-type controls, you can also set the CommandArgument property (you cannot set this for a ButtonField for reasons you will see shortly). In this example, the CommandArgument for both buttons is the value of the CategoryName and CategoryID columns of the current row, generated using Eval data-binding statements.

Listing 10.6. Using a ButtonColumn, LinkButton, and Button in a GridView control

```
<asp:GridView ID="GridView1" runat="server"
    DataSourceID="SqlDataSource1" DataKeyNames="CategoryName"
    OnRowCommand="GridView1_RowCommand">
  <Columns>
    <asp:ButtonField HeaderText="ButtonField" Text="Send"
        CommandName="SendButtonField" ButtonType="Button" />
    <asp:ButtonField HeaderText="ButtonField" Text="Copy"
        CommandName="CopyButtonField" />
    <asp:TemplateField HeaderText="TemplateField">
      <ItemTemplate>
        <asp:Button runat="server" ID="Button1"
            Text="Details" CommandName="DetailsButton"
            CommandArgument='<%# Eval("CategoryName")
                + " [" + Eval("CategoryID") + "]" %>' />
        <asp:LinkButton runat="server" ID="Button2"
            Text="Details" CommandName="DetailsLinkButton"
            CommandArgument='<%# Eval("CategoryName")
                + " [" + Eval("CategoryID") + "]" %>' />
      </ItemTemplate>
    </asp:TemplateField>
  </Columns>
</asp:GridView>
```

Figure 10.1 shows this example running in the browser. You can see the effect of the ButtonType property in the first two columns, and the Button and LinkButton controls in the third column. Clicking the Details button in the second row of the TemplateField column displays the CommandName and CommandArgument properties of the Button control, plus the string value of the CommandSource property (which is a reference to the control that raised the event) so that you can see what type of control ASP.NET generates.

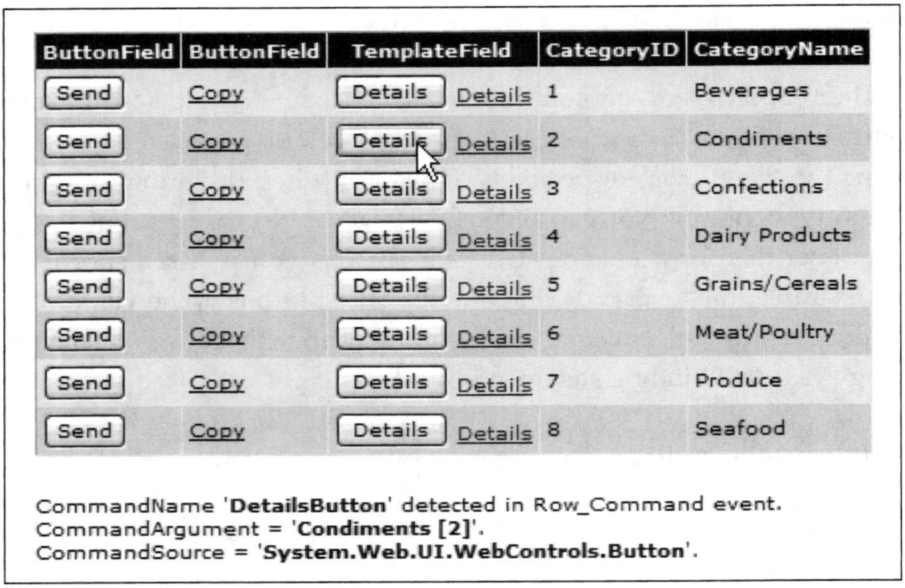

ButtonField	ButtonField	TemplateField		CategoryID	CategoryName
Send	Copy	Details	Details	1	Beverages
Send	Copy	Details	Details	2	Condiments
Send	Copy	Details	Details	3	Confections
Send	Copy	Details	Details	4	Dairy Products
Send	Copy	Details	Details	5	Grains/Cereals
Send	Copy	Details	Details	6	Meat/Poultry
Send	Copy	Details	Details	7	Produce
Send	Copy	Details	Details	8	Seafood

CommandName 'DetailsButton' detected in Row_Command event.
CommandArgument = 'Condiments [2]'.
CommandSource = 'System.Web.UI.WebControls.Button'.

FIGURE 10.1: Displaying the CommandName and CommandArgument in the RowCommand event of the GridView

The CommandArgument property contains the name of the category for this row, followed by the value of the ID.

Listing 10.7 shows the first part of the routine that handles the RowCommand event of the GridView control. The GridViewCommandEventArgs instance passed to the event handler exposes the CommandName, CommandArgument, and CommandSource of the control that raised the event.

Listing 10.7. Using a ButtonColumn, LinkButton, and Button in a GridView Control

```
protected void GridView1_RowCommand(Object sender,
                            GridViewCommandEventArgs e)
{
  Label1.Text = "CommandName '<b>" + e.CommandName
            + "</b>' detected in Row_Command event. <br/>";
  Label1.Text += "CommandArgument is '<b>" + e.CommandArgument
            + "</b>'.<br/>";
  Label1.Text += "CommandSource is '<b>"
            + e.CommandSource.ToString() + "</b>'.";
  . . .
}
```

What is interesting is the result of clicking one of the buttons or links in the ButtonField column. In this case, ASP.NET automatically wires up the `CommandArgument` of the buttons to the `RowIndex` of each row in the `GridView` control. This means that you can extract the row index and use it to access the rows or the other properties of the `GridView`. For example, the code in Listing 10.8 sets the `DataKeyNames` property of the `GridView` to the `CategoryName` column through the attribute `DataKey-Names="CategoryName"`. This means that you can access the value of the `DataKey` for the current row using the index returned in the `Command-Argument` property—as shown in Listing 10.8.

Listing 10.8. Using the CommandArgument to Access the DataKeys of a GridView

```
protected void GridView1_RowCommand(Object sender,
                                    GridViewCommandEventArgs e)
{
  ...
  if (e.CommandName.IndexOf("ButtonField") > 0)
  {
    Int32 rowIndex = Int32.Parse(e.CommandArgument.ToString());
    Label1.Text += "DataKeys[0] = '<b>"
                 + GridView1.DataKeys[rowIndex].Value + "</br>'.";
  }
}
```

Figure 10.2 shows the result. You can see the `CommandArgument` value, and the value of the `DataKey` for that row.

Other places that the `LinkButton` occurs are in the `Wizard` control, which reads the `CommandName` property of any `LinkButton` or `Button` elements in the steps (pages) of the Wizard and automatically moves to the next step if the user clicks a button that has the `CommandName` value "MoveNext". Likewise, the `MultiView` control moves to the next view when the user clicks a button with the `CommandName` value "NextView".

Initiating Client-Side Events

The button-type controls `Button`, `LinkButton`, and `ImageButton` expose a property named `OnClientClick` as well as `OnClick`. As the name suggests, the `OnClientClick` property initiates a client-side event rather than the server-side event initiated by the `OnClick` event. You write a client-side function and then assign the name to the `OnClientClick` property of your chosen button-type control. You can also write the usual server-side `OnClick` event routine as well.

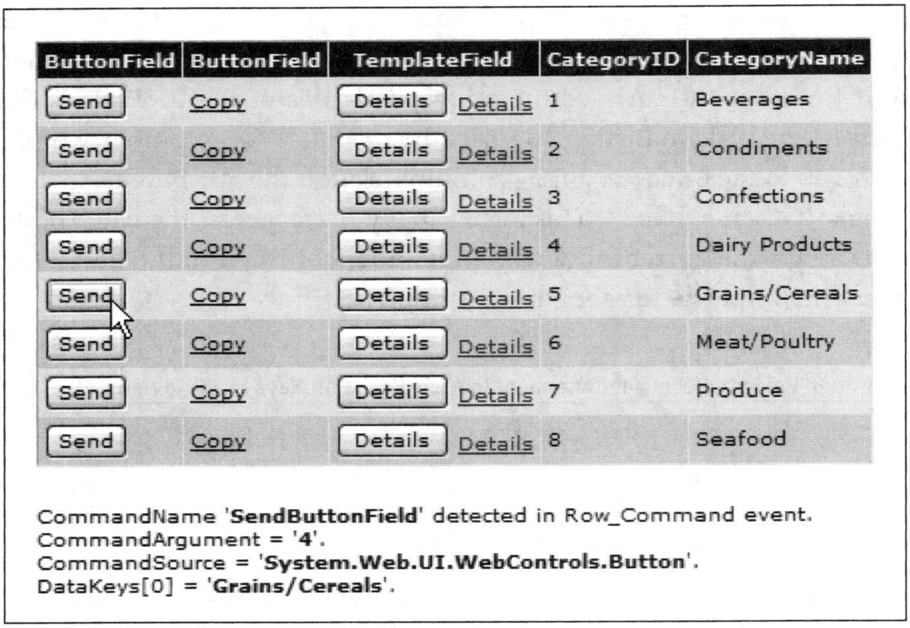

FIGURE 10.2: Using the CommandArgument property of a ButtonField in the RowCommand event of the GridView

Listing 10.9 shows the declaration of a `LinkButton` control with both the `OnClick` and `OnClientClick` attributes. By default, as you will expect, clicking the button causes the specified client-side code routine to execute first, followed by a postback that executes the server-side event handler.

Listing 10.9. Using the OnClick and OnClientClick Events with a LinkButton Control

```
<asp:LinkButton id="LinkButton1" runat="server" Text="Click me"
    OnClick="DoServerSideCode"
    OnClientClick="return DoClientSideCode()" />
```

For this example, the server-side code is a one-line routine that displays a message in a `Label` control elsewhere on the page, indicating that a post-back occurred and that the server-side event handler executed. You can see this code at the start of Listing 10.10, which also contains the client-side JavaScript function referenced in the `OnClientClick` attribute of the `LinkButton`. This routine first clears any text from the `Label` control on the page by getting a reference to it through the CSS2 `getElementById` function and setting the `innerText` property to an empty string. Then it displays a client-side JavaScript `confirm` dialog, and returns the result.

Listing 10.10. Handling the OnClick and OnClientClick Events

```
<script runat="server">
  protected void DoServerSideCode(object sender, EventArgs e)
  {
    Label1.Text = "Server-side code was executed.";
  }
</script>

<script language="javascript">
<!--
function DoClientSideCode()
{
  document.getElementById('Label1').innerText = '';
  return confirm('Client-side code is executing.\n'
                 + 'Run server-side code?');
}
//-->
</script>
```

The important point here is that, unless you cancel the client-side `click` event in your client-side code, a postback will occur. To cancel a client-side event, you must return `false` from the function that the control executes. If you look back at Listing 10.9, you will see that the declaration of the `LinkButton` includes `OnClientClick="return DoClientSideCode()"`. This means that whatever value the function named `DoClientSideCode` returns will be returned to the `LinkButton` control itself. If this value is `false`, the `LinkButton` will not cause a postback—which is exactly what will occur if the user clicks Cancel in the `confirm` dialog.

Therefore, as you can see in Figure 10.3, the client-side code runs first and displays the `confirm` dialog. If you select OK, the client-side function returns `true` and server-side code executes. If you click `Cancel`, the client-side function returns `false` and server-side code does not execute. This approach is useful for many features in a Web page; for example, getting users to confirm that they want to delete a row from the database or perform some other nonreversible action.

All of this discussion on the `LinkButton` and `Button` controls that cause a postback does not appear to relate to navigation issues—the topic of this

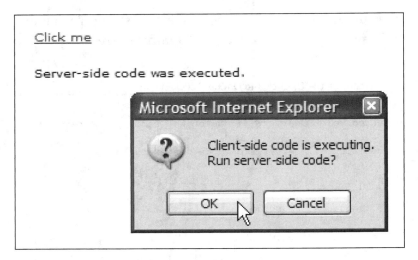

FIGURE 10.3: Using the OnClientClick property of a LinkButton control

chapter. In fact, you will see how they relate in the next section when you look at navigation through browser redirection.

Details of the OnClientClick property are at http://msdn2.microsoft.com/en-us/library/1c9t9zkk.

Navigation through Browser Redirection

Navigation consists of pointing the browser to a specific page in response to user interaction. The `Hyperlink` control, and various other complex controls that generate hyperlinks, cause the browser to load the specified page when the user clicks that link. However, you can force the browser to load a different page by sending back an "Object Moved" HTTP header that contains the new URL of the requested resource.

The simplest way to achieve this is through the `Redirect` method of the `HttpResponse` class. This method takes the URL of the page to load, and the browser will load that page instead of the current one. A limitation is that you must execute the `Redirect` method *before* you send any other output to the client. Once the headers are written and the main body of the page is being sent to the client, a call to the `Redirect` method will produce a runtime error.

A common approach is to clear the response buffer first, and then call the `Redirect` method. If you do not want your code to continue to execute after issuing the redirection to the client, you can call the `End()` method of the `HttpResponse` class.

```
Response.Clear();
Response.Redirect("http://www.mysite.com/newpage.aspx");
Response.End();
```

Alternatively, you can use the second overload of the `Redirect` method, and specify `true` for the second parameter to force ASP.NET to terminate execution.

```
Response.Clear();
Response.Redirect("http://www.mysite.com/newpage.aspx", true);
```

This technique is useful if you want to perform redirection only after executing some server-side code, perhaps to update a database or calculate the target URL dynamically based on some value provided by the user or the environment. For example, as shown in Listing 10.11, you might redirect the browser to a country-specific site using a value selected in a drop-down list on the page.

Listing 10.11. Using the Response.Redirect Method for Dynamic Redirection

```
void Page_Load()
{
  String newURL = String.Empty;
  switch (MyDropDownList.SelectedValue)
  {
    case "us":
      newURL = "http://mysite.com/";
      break;
    case "uk":
      newURL = "http://mysite.com/uk/";
      break;
    case "de":
      newURL = "http://mysite.de/";
      break;
    case default:
      newURL = "http://mysite.com/countrylist.aspx";
  }
  Response.Redirect(newURL, true);
}
```

The `CommandName` example, shown earlier in this chapter, is another prime candidate for the `Response.Redirect` method. While you can use a `HyperlinkField` in a `GridView` or other data display control to generate hyperlinks, you may need to interact with the value before performing the redirection. For example, if the value may be something that might be found on the Internet (perhaps it contains the word "web"), you could redirect to a search engine to get a listing of matching pages. Otherwise, you would display some data you had stored locally (see Listing 10.12).

Listing 10.12. Redirecting to a Search Engine with Response.Redirect

```
protected void GridView1_RowCommand(Object sender,
                                    GridViewCommandEventArgs e)
{
  String details = e.CommandArgument.ToString();
  if (details.IndexOf("web") > 0)
  {
    Response.Clear();
    Response.Redirect("http://google.com/search?q=" + details, true);
  }
  else
  {
    ... just display local data ...
  }
}
```

> You can also use the StatusCode, StatusDescription, and RedirectLocation properties of the Response class to cause a browser redirect, which is equivalent to using the Response.Redirect method. See http://msdn2.microsoft.com/en-us/library/y1hzy13b for more details.

Redirection with Client-Side Script

An alternative navigation approach is to perform client-side redirection using client-side script that runs in the browser. Extending the example shown in Figure 10.3 illustrates how it is easy to perform client-side redirection in response to any client-side event. All that is required is to set the `window.location.href` property in client-side script to the required URL, as shown in Listing 10.13, and the browser automatically loads from that URL. Just remember to return `false` from the client-side function to ensure that no postback occurs.

Listing 10.13. Client-Side Redirection with JavaScript Code

```javascript
<script language="javascript"
<!-
function DoClientSideCode()
{
  window.location.href = 'thenewpage.aspx';
  return false;
}
//-->
</script>

<asp:Button id="Button1" runat="server" Text="Redirect"
    OnClientClick="return DoClientSideCode()" />
```

Details of the client-side scripting object model are at http://msdn.microsoft.com/workshop/author/dhtml/reference/dhtml_reference_entry.asp.

Navigation through Server-Side Redirection

Another way to display a different page from the one the user requested is through server-side redirection. In fact, this is not truly navigation, because the user does not see a different URL in the browser and it appears to them that the page they requested is loaded. Server-side, ASP.NET loads a different page and sends the output back to the client as though it were coming from the page they requested.

You can perform two types of server-side redirection: transfer to another page (where execution ends at the end of that page), or execution of another page (where control returns to the original page when the second page completes its execution). ASP.NET provides two methods to support this feature. The `Transfer` method of the `HttpServerUtility` class performs transfer to another page, and the `Execute` method causes execution of the second page.

The HttpServerUtility.Transfer Method

The `Transfer` method has three overloads. The first simply takes the URL of the page to execute.

```
Server.Transfer("url")
```

By default, the contents of the Form and `QueryString` collections are available in the target page of the transfer. However, you can clear these collections first by using the second overload of the `Transfer` method. It takes an additional `Boolean` parameter that determines if the Request collections are preserved (set it to `False` to clear the collections).

```
Server.Transfer("url", [true | false])
```

Finally, you can also execute a class that implements the `IHttpHandler` interface, which is useful if you write your own HTTP handler. This overload also takes a second parameter that determines if the `Request` collections are preserved.

```
Server.Transfer(handler-class, [true | false])
```

Details of the HttpServerUtility.Transfer method are at http://msdn2. microsoft.com/en-us/library/y0w8173d.

The HttpServerUtility.Execute Method

The `Execute` method has five overloads. The simplest of these takes just the URL of the page to execute.

```
Server.Execute("url")
```

Like the `Transfer` method, an overload allows you to specify whether the `Request` collections are preserved.

```
Server.Execute("url", [true | false])
```

The `Execute` method has another useful feature. Unlike the `Transfer` method, which streams the output of the target page or handler into the response and sends it to the client, you can capture the output of the target when using the Execute method as a `TextWriter` instance.

```
Server.Execute("url", TextWriter)
```

In addition, an overload allows you to preserve or clear the `Request` collections.

```
Server.Execute("url", TextWriter, [true | false])
```

Finally, you can specify the target as a class that implements the `IHttpHandler` interface and preserve or clear the `Request` collections.

```
Server.Execute(handler-class, TextWriter, [true | false])
```

> Details of the HttpServerUtility.Execute method are at http://msdn2. microsoft.com/en-us/library/yw97w238.

Using the Transfer and Execute Methods

This example shows how you can use the `Transfer` and `Execute` methods. The initial page contains a `TextBox` and a `DropDownList` with values to pass to the target page, plus two buttons that initiate either the `Transfer` or the `Execute` method. For both of these, you can specify whether the contents of the `Request` collections are preserved using the drop-down lists.

Below the buttons is another drop-down list that takes effect only for the Execute method and allows you to specify if the results should be HTML-encoded (so that you can see the target page content as HTML) or just rendered in the usual way.

Executing the Target Page

The `Execute` method calls a target page named `catch-execute.aspx`, which first displays the values of two useful properties of the `Request`— the `FilePath` and the `CurrentExecutionFilePath`. These allow you to determine in code if the page was loaded directly by the browser (in which case they are the same), or whether it is running in response to an `Execute` or `Transfer` call (whereupon they are different).

Next are the values of the properties exposed by the initial (original) page. These properties are the `Text` value of the `TextBox` and a reference to the `DropDownList` control. The page displays the `DropDownList` control type and then accesses its `SelectedValue` through the control reference. Finally, the page displays the contents of the `Request.Form` collection.

Figure 10.4 shows the results of the Execute method for this example. The output generated by the target page displays between the two horizontal rules and is rendered by the browser because it is not HTML-encoded.

If you turn on the HTML-encode option, the results show the HTML generated by the target page. This is because the `Execute` method sends the output to a `TextWriter` instead of directly to the browser, and code can

FIGURE 10.4: Using the HttpServerUtility.Execute method to execute another page

therefore extract the content and apply the `Server.HtmlEncode` method to it for display. Figure 10.5 shows the result of selecting the HTML-encode option.

Transferring to the Target Page

The second button in the example initiates the `Transfer` method, causing the server to switch execution to the page named `catch-transfer.aspx`. This page opens in the browser and displays the same contents as the page you saw for the Execute method. The main difference is that it contains a button that allows you to return to the initial page (see Figure 10.6).

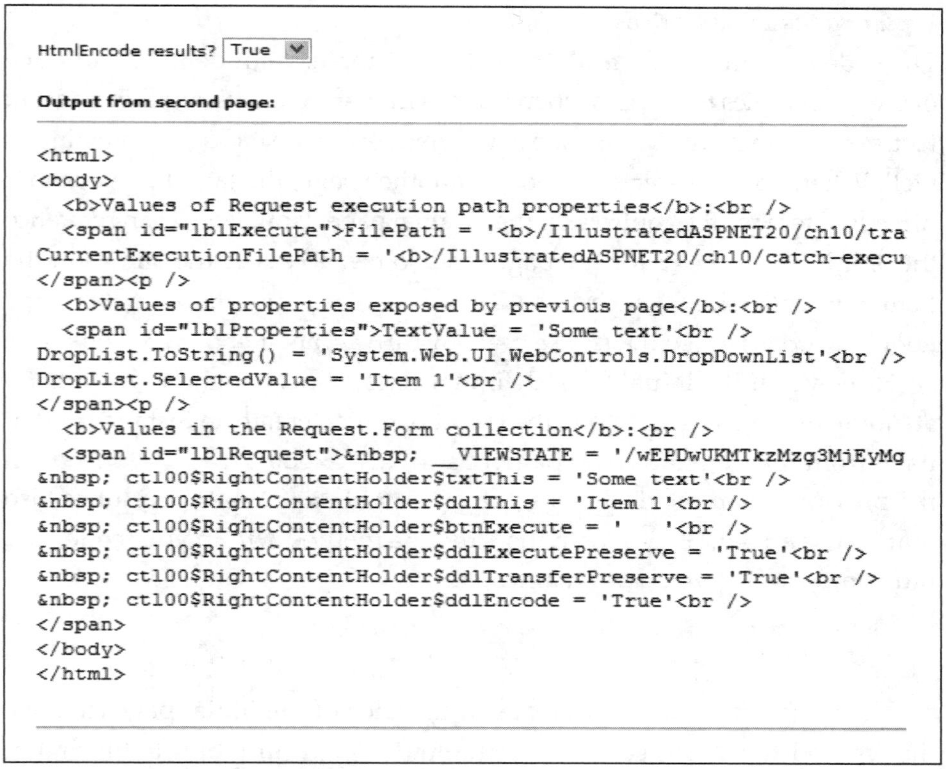

```
HtmlEncode results? True ▼

Output from second page:
_____

<html>
<body>
  <b>Values of Request execution path properties</b>:<br />
  <span id="lblExecute">FilePath = '<b>/IllustratedASPNET20/ch10/tra
CurrentExecutionFilePath = '<b>/IllustratedASPNET20/ch10/catch-execu
</span><p />
  <b>Values of properties exposed by previous page</b>:<br />
  <span id="lblProperties">TextValue = 'Some text'<br />
DropList.ToString() = 'System.Web.UI.WebControls.DropDownList'<br />
DropList.SelectedValue = 'Item 1'<br />
</span><p />
  <b>Values in the Request.Form collection</b>:<br />
  <span id="lblRequest">  __VIEWSTATE = '/wEPDwUKMTkzMzg3MjEyMg
  ctl00$RightContentHolder$txtThis = 'Some text'<br />
  ctl00$RightContentHolder$ddlThis = 'Item 1'<br />
  ctl00$RightContentHolder$btnExecute = '     '<br />
  ctl00$RightContentHolder$ddlExecutePreserve = 'True'<br />
  ctl00$RightContentHolder$ddlTransferPreserve = 'True'<br />
  ctl00$RightContentHolder$ddlEncode = 'True'<br />
</span>
</body>
</html>
```

FIGURE 10.5: Displaying the HTML content of the target page

```
Values of Request execution path properties:
FilePath = '/IllustratedASPNET20/ch10/transfer-execute.aspx'
CurrentExecutionFilePath = '/IllustratedASPNET20/ch10/catch-transfer.aspx'

Values of properties exposed by previous page:
TextValue = 'Some text'
DropList.ToString() = 'System.Web.UI.WebControls.DropDownList'
DropList.SelectedValue = 'Item 1'

Values in the Request.Form collection:
    __VIEWSTATE =
'/wEPDwUKMTkzMzg3MjEyMg9kFgJmD2QWAgIDD2QWEgIBDw8WAh4EVGV4dAUXRVh
  ctl00$RightContentHolder$txtThis = 'Some text'
  ctl00$RightContentHolder$ddlThis = 'Item 1'
  ctl00$RightContentHolder$ddlExecutePreserve = 'True'
  ctl00$RightContentHolder$btnTransfer = '   '
  ctl00$RightContentHolder$ddlTransferPreserve = 'True'
  ctl00$RightContentHolder$ddlEncode = 'True'

[ Back ]
```

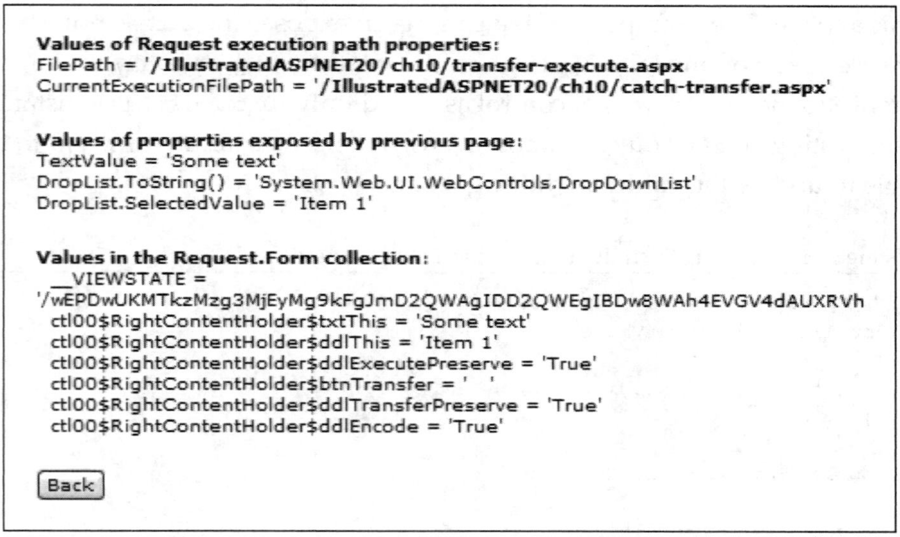

FIGURE 10.6: Displaying the HTML-encoded content of the target page

Exploring the Example Code

The code used in this example is relatively simple, yet it demonstrates one of the main topics that arises when transferring or executing another page. In fact, you will meet the same issue in the next section on cross-page posting as well. When you transfer execution to another page, the target page cannot directly reference the controls on the original page. However, it can reference the ASP.NET Context for the page, and so has access to the values in the Context collections (such as Request.Form, Request.QueryString, Request.Cookies, Request.ServerVariables, and Response.Cookies).

However, if the initial form defines a class name, using the ClassName attribute of the Page directive, the target page can create an instance of that page from the Context. The page transfer-execute.aspx you saw in the previous example declares a ClassName of ExecutePage. Notice also that, to use a TextWriter with the Execute method within your code, you must import the System.IO namespace:

```
<%@Page Language="C#"  ClassName="ExecutePage"  %>
<%@Import Namespace="System.IO"  %>
```

The target page can now create an instance of the initial page (the one that caused the Transfer or Execute method to run), but it still cannot directly access the controls on the page. The usual solution is to expose whatever you need to access in the target page as public properties of the initial page. The example you have just seen exposes the Text property of the TextBox on the initial page as a read-only String property, and a reference to the drop-down list control as a read-only DropDownList instance (see Listing 10.14). You can expose read/write properties if you want to be able to update the values in the target page.

Listing 10.14. Exposing Controls and Values as Public Properties

```
// public properties exposed to other pages
public String TextValue
{
  get { return txtThis.Text; }
}

public DropDownList DropList
{
  get { return ddlThis; }
}
```

The remaining code in the initial page consists of two routines that handle the `Click` events of the two buttons in the page. The `DoExecute` handler creates a new `StringWriter` and passes it to the `Execute` method, along with `True` or `False` as the third parameter—depending on the setting of the drop-down list box for this operation. The code then checks to see if HTML-encoding is required and places the results in a `Label` control on the initial page.

The `DoTransfer` handler is much simpler. It just executes the `Transfer` method, passing in `True` or `False` as the third parameter—depending on the setting of the drop-down list box for this operation (see Listing 10.15).

Listing 10.15. Handling the Button Clicks in the Initial Page

```
protected void DoExecute(Object sender, EventArgs e)
// execute next page when Execute button is clicked
{
  // create StringWriter and use it when executing target page
  StringWriter writer = new StringWriter();
  Server.Execute("catch-execute.aspx?somekey=thisvalue", writer,
               (ddlExecutePreserve.SelectedValue == "True"));

  // see if result should be HTML-encoded
  if (ddlEncode.SelectedValue == "True")
  {
    lblResult.Text = "<pre style='font-size:small'"
      + Server.HtmlEncode(writer.ToString()) + "</pre>";
  }
  else
  {
    lblResult.Text = writer.ToString();
  }
}

protected void DoTransfer(Object sender, EventArgs e)
// transfer to next page when Transfer button is clicked
{
  Server.Transfer("catch-transfer.aspx",
               (ddlTransferPreserve.SelectedValue == "True"));
}
```

The Code in the Target Page

In a page that is executed in response to the `Transfer` or `Execute` method, or through cross-page posting (as you will see in the next section), you can only access the controls in the initial page by exposing them as `public` properties or by using the `FindControl` method in the target page. The better solution is the use of `public` properties.

The two example target pages, `catch-execute.aspx` and `catch-execute.aspx`, include a `@Reference` directive that links them to the initial page:

```
<%@Reference Page=" transfer-execute.aspx" %>
```

The remaining code consists of a `Page_Load` event handler, shown in Listing 10.16. This code creates an instance of the initial page as the class

Listing 10.16. Displaying the Property Values in the Target Page

```
protected void Page_Load()
{
  if (!Page.IsPostBack)
  {
    try
    {
      // get a reference to the previous page
      ExecutePage refPage = (ExecutePage)Context.Handler, ExecutePage;

      // display the property values from the previous page
      lblProperties.Text = "TextValue = '" + refPage.TextValue
        + "'<br />nDROPLIST.oString() = ' "
        + refPage.DropList.ToString() + "'<br />\n"
        + "DropList.SelectedValue = '"
        + refPage.DropList.SelectedValue + "'<br />\n";
    }
    catch (Exception e)
    {
      lblProperties.Text = "ERROR: Cannot reference previous page"
                + e.Message;
    }

    // display the values in the Request.Form collection
    foreach (String val in Request.Form)
    {
    lblRequest.Text += "  " + val + " = '"
      + Request.Form[val] + "'<br />\n";
    }
  }

  // display the values of the Request execution path properties
  lblExecute.Text += "FilePath = '<b>" + Request.FilePath
            + "<br />\n";
  lblExecute.Text += "CurrentExecutionFilePath = '<b>"
            + Request.CurrentExecutionFilePath + "</br>'\n";
}
```

type specified in that page's @Page directive, and then accesses the public properties of that class. The reference to the DropDownList control in the initial page allows the SelectedIndex value to be obtained. Then the code iterates through the Request.Form collection to display the contents and queries the Request.FilePath and Request.CurrentExecutionFile-Path properties to get the execution path values.

The Transfer and Execute methods therefore allow you to separate features in your Web site to allow common functionality to be available on demand to any pages that require it. Remember that, as well as an ASPX page, you can transfer to or execute any class that implements the IHttpHandler interface.

Cross-Page Posting of Form Contents

As you saw at the start of this chapter, ASP.NET depends on the postback architecture, where pages containing a <form> section post back to themselves. However, there are cases when you may want to post the contents of a form to another page. For example, you may need to generate sections of the page using ASP.NET server-side code but post the form to another page, or have multiple submit buttons that post to different pages.

To support this, most of the controls that can cause a postback, such as the Button and LinkButton, expose the PostBackUrl property. You can set this to the URL of a page that will handle the posted form contents. Inside the target page, you can access the original page and read values from it—in much the same way as you saw when looking at the Server.Transfer and Server.Execute methods in the previous section of this chapter.

> Usually, the target page will be within the same ASP.NET application as the originating page. You can post to a page in another application, but in this case you will only be able to extract the contents of the Request collections (Form, QueryString, Cookies, and Server Variables). You will not be able to access the viewstate or properties of the originating page.

An Example of Cross-Page Posting

As a simple example of cross-page posting, Listing 10.17 shows the controls on a page that cause both a standard postback to the same page and a cross-page postback to another page. The source page contains a drop-down list named `Country`. A `Label` control is included to show the properties of the page when a standard postback occurs.

Listing 10.17. The Controls in the Page That Cause a Cross-Page Postback

```
<b>This is the first page</b><p />
Please select a country:
<asp:DropDownList id="Country" runat="server">
  <asp:ListItem text="USA" value="0" />
  <asp:ListItem text="Canada" value="1" />
  <asp:ListItem text="UK" value="2" />
</asp:DropDownList>
<p />
<asp:Button id="Button1" runat="server" Text="   "
         OnClick="Button1_Click" />
Cause a postback to the same page
<p />
<asp:Button id="Button2" runat="server" Text="   "
         PostBackUrl="~/ch10/catch-cross-page.aspx" />
Cause a postback to a different page
<p />
<asp:Label ID="Label1" runat="server" />
```

This source page also contains a server-side script section, shown in Listing 10.18. This code exposes a public property for the page, just as you saw in the `Server.Transfer` example earlier in this chapter. In this case, the property named `SelectedCountry` returns a reference to the drop-down list control on this page.

Listing 10.18. The Code in the Page That Causes a Cross-Page Postback

```
// public property exposed to next page
public DropDownList SelectedCountry
{
  get { return Country; }
}

void Button1_Click(Object sender, EventArgs e)
{
  Label1.Text = "Page posted back to itself.<br />"
    + "Page URL = " + Request.Url.LocalPath + "<br />"
    + "Page.IsPostBack = " + Page.IsPostBack.ToString() + "<br />"
    + "Page.IsCrossPagePostBack = "
    + Page.IsCrossPagePostBack.To String();
}
```

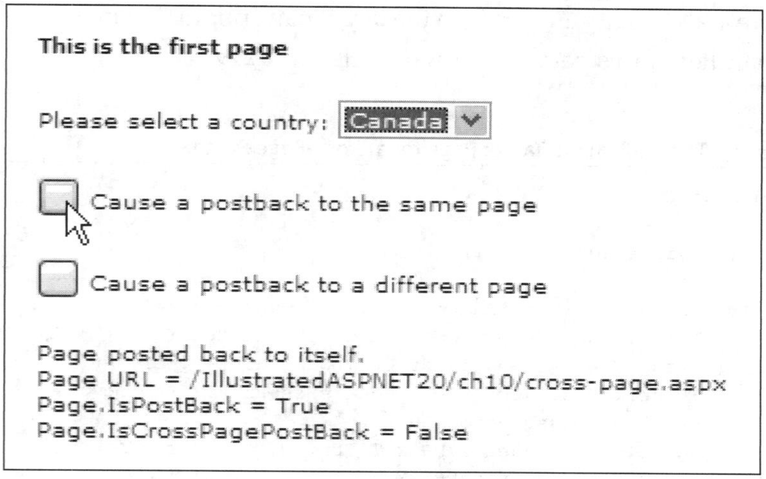

```
This is the first page

Please select a country:  Canada  ∨

☐  Cause a postback to the same page

☐  Cause a postback to a different page

Page posted back to itself.
Page URL = /IllustratedASPNET20/ch10/cross-page.aspx
Page.IsPostBack = True
Page.IsCrossPagePostBack = False
```

FIGURE 10.7: The result of a standard postback

The remaining code is an event handler for the first button on this page, which causes a standard postback. This event handler displays a message containing the URL of the current page and the value of the `IsPostBack` and `IsCrossPagePostBack` properties of the `Page` object.

Figure 10.7 shows the result of clicking the button that causes a standard postback. As you would expect, the `IsPostBack` property returns `True`, while the `IsCrossPagePostback` property returns `False`.

The second button in the source page, `Button2` in Listing 10.17, has the attribute `PostBackUrl="~/ch10/catch-cross-page.aspx"`, so when it is clicked, it will cause a postback to the target page `catch-cross-page.aspx` rather than to the source page. This target page contains the `PreviousPageType` directive, which points to the original source page:

```
<%@ PreviousPageType VirtualPath="~/ch10/cross-page.aspx" %>
```

An alternative approach is to declare a class type name in the source page:

```
<%@ Page ClassName="MySourcePage"...%>
```

Then you can specify this type name in the `PreviousPageType` directive:

```
<%@ PreviousPageType TypeName="MySourcePage"%>
```

There is also a `Label` control on the target page populated in the `Page_Load` event handler of this page, as shown in Listing 10.19.

Listing 10.19. The Code in the Target Page for a Cross-Page Postback

```
void Page_Load()
{
  if (PreviousPage != null)
  {
    PrevMessage.Text = "On the previous page you selected <b>"
      + PreviousPage.SelectedCountry.SelectedItem.Text + "</b>.<br />"
      + "Page URL = " + Request.Url.LocalPath + "<br />"
      + "Page.IsPostBack = " + Page.IsPostBack.ToString() + "<br />"
      + "Page.IsCrossPagePostBack = "
      + Page.IsCrossPagePostBack.ToString() + "<br />"
      + "PreviousPage.IsPostBack = "
      + PreviousPage.IsPostBack.ToString() + "<br />"
      + "PreviousPage.IsCrossPagePostBack = "
      + PreviousPage.IsCrossPagePostBack.ToString();
  }
  else
  {
    PrevMessage.Text = "Not a cross-page postback.";
  }
}
```

This code first checks that the page is loading in response to a cross-page post, where the `PreviousPage` property will be a reference to the page that causes the cross-page postback. If the page is loaded directly, the `PreviousPage` property will be `null`, and so the code will display an error message in this case.

Providing that there is a reference available to the previous page, the code then continues by displaying the `Text` property of the `SelectedItem` of the `Country` drop-down list on the previous page. It can obtain this control reference from the public property exposed by the source page through the `PreviousPage` property. Then the code displays the URL of this (target) page, followed by the `IsPostBack` and `IsCrossPagePostBack` properties. Finally, it accesses the previous (source) page again to display the value of its `IsPostBack` and `IsCrossPagePostBack` properties. Figure 10.8 shows the results.

What is happening is that the target page instantiates the source page in order to access its properties, causing the source page to execute right

```
This is the second page

On the previous page you selected Canada.
Page URL = /IllustratedASPNET20/ch10/catch-cross-page.aspx
Page.IsPostBack = False
Page.IsCrossPagePostBack = False
PreviousPage.IsPostBack = True
PreviousPage.IsCrossPagePostBack = True


[ Back ]
```

FIGURE 10.8: The result of a cross-page postback

up to the OnLoadComplete event. This causes the viewstate to be loaded and the control tree populated in both the source and the target page, so you should bear in mind the extra processing this involves.

For more information on the cross-page posting features of ASP.NET, see http://msdn2.microsoft.com/en-us/library/ms178139.

Site Maps, Menus, and Navigation Path Controls

ASP.NET 2.0 includes several features that make it easy to implement a central system for navigation within your Web sites and Web applications. There are several server controls, combined with an XML-format configuration file, that provide a way to define site structure and display navigation information.

Like the rest of ASP.NET, the architecture for navigation has been broken down into logical parts, allowing customization. First, there is a configurable provider supplying the site map information, and a set of controls that can take advantage of the data supplied by the provider. The provider not only exposes the site structure to other controls, but also keeps track of the current location—allowing each page to identify where in the hierarchy of the site it is located.

You can expose the entire structure and the current page details to users by binding controls to the provider. This pluggable architecture means that data defining the structure of a site can come from any data source—the site map provider is the link between the data and the navigation within a site.

Site Map Providers

A site map provider exposes the site structure by way of a set interface, and the details of the site map providers are stored in the `<system.web>` section of the `Web.Config` file. The default is the `XmlSiteMapProvider`, which uses a site navigation structure stored in an XML file. However, you can create your own providers if you wish, perhaps to read the site structure from a database, by inheriting from the abstract class `SiteMapProvider`. A discussion of this is outside the scope of the book, but the documentation for the .NET Framework contains more details.

Site Map Configuration Files

Listing 10.20 shows an example of a site map file. This file named `Web.sitemap` resides in the root of the ASP.NET application. You can see that the structure consists of a single `<sitemap>` root element, which contains a single `<siteMapNode>` element. This `<siteMapNode>` is the "base" location for

Listing 10.20. An Example Site Map File

```xml
<?xml version="1.0" encoding="utf-8" ?>
<sitemap xmlns="http://schemas.microsoft.com/AspNet/SiteMap-File-1.0">
  <siteMapNode title="Home" url="home.aspx">
    <siteMapNode title="Books" url="books.aspx"
                 description="List of all books">
      <siteMapNode title="ASP.NET" url="books.aspx?cat=asp"
                   description="Books about ASP.NET" />
      <siteMapNode title="ADO.NET" url="books.aspx?cat=ado"
                   description="Books about ADO.NET" />
      <siteMapNode title="System.Xml" url="books.aspx?cat=xml"
                   description="Books about System.Xml" />
    </siteMapNode>
    <siteMapNode title="Articles" url="articles.aspx">
                 description="List of all articles">
      <siteMapNode title="Recent" url="newarts.aspx"
                   description="Recent articles" />
      <siteMapNode title="Archive" url="oldarts.aspx"
                   description="Older aticles" />
    </siteMapNode>
    <siteMapNode title="Admin" url="admin\admin.aspx"
                 description="Site administration"
                 roles="webadmin,manager,siteadmin" />
  </siteMapNode>
</siteMap>
```

the site, and traditionally will be your site's Home page. Inside this "base" node is a hierarchical set of nodes that represent the other pages in your site.

Note that the structure does not reflect the actual physical folder structure of the site but only the relationship and grouping of the pages. For example, in the file shown in Listing 10.20, all of the pages except for the Admin page are in the root folder of the site, even though the file implements a nested structure to the pages. Also note that all the URLs you declare within the site map file must be unique, because this is how the control knows where it is within the hierarchy.

The "Admin" link shown in the last `<siteMapNode>` element in Listing 10.20 contains the `roles` attribute. This comes into effect when you enable the membership and security features of ASP.NET and means that only users who are accessing the site within that role will be able to view this link. For example, if you enable Forms authentication and specify a list of Windows Account Groups that can access your pages (such as Users\JohnSmith), the items in the site map with the corresponding `roles` attribute value will only be visible when the specified users access the page. You will see how the membership features work in the next chapter.

The `siteMapNode` element can also take other attributes not shown in Listing 10.20. The `SiteMapFile` attribute can be set to the name of an external file containing additional site map nodes, while the `Provider` attribute can be set to the name of a site map provider that will supply additional nodes. You can also add custom ("extended") attributes to the elements in a site map file, and access these in your code. For an example, see the section Reacting to Events in the Menu, TreeView, and SiteMapPath Controls later in this chapter.

> For more details about the way that ASP.NET uses site map files, see http://msdn2.microsoft.com/en-us/library/yy2ykkab.

Using a Site Map File

Having defined the structure of your site in a site map file, you can use it as the input to a `SiteMapDataSource` control. This works much like the other data source controls you saw in Chapters 3 and 4. It reacts to events in the page to load the data and exposes it in a structured way that other controls can use. Then you simply drag a `Menu` control onto the page and

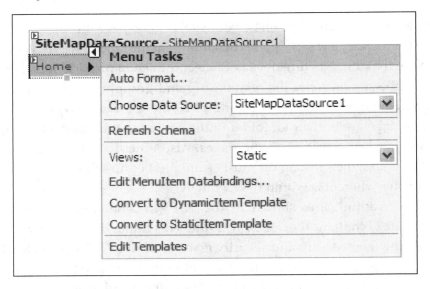

FIGURE 10.9: Using a SiteMapDataSource and Menu control in Visual Studio 2005

set the `DataSourceID` property to the ID of the `SiteMapDataSource` control, as shown in Figure 10.9.

When you view the page, you will see that the Menu control is extremely powerful. It automatically creates by default a dynamic "fly-out" menu structure, which—if you apply an auto-format using the Menu Tasks pane—gives an attractive result with almost no effort. Of course, you can customize the appearance using the many style properties of the control, if you wish.

You can also specify that the Menu control will provide a static display or a combination of static and dynamic modes. Only the first node is static by default and always appears on the page. All other nodes are dynamic and appear as fly-out or drop-down items. However, the `StaticDisplayLevels` property defines the number of levels that appear as static nodes, indented so the hierarchical structure is still visible. To support this mixed mode of operation, there are style elements for the static and dynamic portions of the menu as well as for the individual items that appear on those menus.

Another option is to change the direction of the menu to a drop-down style by setting the `Orientation` property to "Horizontal", though you must also set the `StaticDisplayLevels` property to 2 so that the menu items at this level are laid out horizontally. Figure 10.10 shows the results of a vertical and horizontal menu.

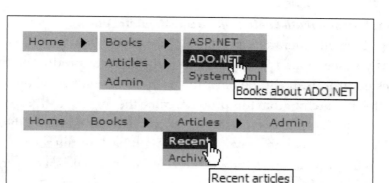

FIGURE 10.10: The Menu control in both horizontal and vertical modes

Using a TreeView Control with a SiteMapDataSource

You can use a `SiteMapDataSource` to power different types of controls, but the hierarchical nature of the data means that is it best suited to the special navigation controls. The `Menu` control you have just seen is an obvious example, but you can also use a `TreeView` control if you prefer an expandable display rather than the fly-out or drop-down style of the `Menu` control. Figure 10.11 shows a `TreeView` control with the "Windows Help File" auto-format (as provided in Visual Studio 2005) applied. Chapter 8 also looks at the `TreeView` control.

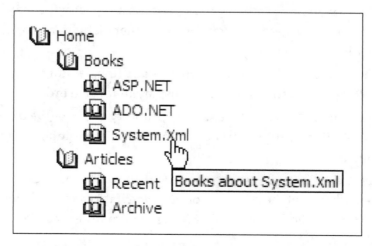

FIGURE 10.11: The TreeView control with an auto-format applied

Using a NavigationPath Control with a SiteMapDataSource

When a Web site hierarchy becomes much more than three levels deep, such as you see in many sites that categorize links or products into multiple nested groups, it can be hard for users to remember where they are within the hierarchy. From this problem came the concept of a "breadcrumb trail" consisting of a list of the parent and ancestor categories of the current page—effectively laying down a trail or path back to the root of the site.

ASP.NET provides the SiteMapPath control that makes it easy to implement this feature from a site map file. You do not even need a SiteMapDataSource control (though you will probably have one to power the other navigation controls on your pages), because the SiteMapPath control works directly with the site map provider and the Web.sitemap file.

The current page name (taken from the title attribute in the site map file) appears as simple text, and parent and ancestor page names appear as hyperlinks, allowing easy navigation back up the page hierarchy. The pop-up tool-tip text comes from the description attribute of the elements in the site map file.

The SiteMapPath control is highly configurable. As well as applying styles in the usual way, using the wide range of properties it exposes, you can do the following:

- Use the PathSeparator property to specify the string displayed between each link. The default is " : ".

- Set the ParentLevelsDisplayed property to specify the maximum number of levels before the current level that displays as you go deeper into the hierarchy.

- Set the PathDirection to CurrentToRoot (the default is RootToCurrent) so that the links display in reverse order.

- Set the RenderCurrentNodeAsLink property to True (the default is False) to display the current page name as a hyperlink instead of plain text.

- Set the ShowToolTips property to False (the default is True) to prevent display of the pop-up tool-tips even if they are still in the Web.sitemap file for use in other navigation controls. See Figure 10.12.

One other technique for styling the SiteMapPath control is through templates. You can template the complete control or just the separator between

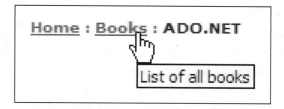

FIGURE 10.12: The SiteMapPath control in action

the links. For example, you can replace the separators with custom images using the `PathSeparatorTemplate` section as shown in Listing 10.21.

Listing 10.21. Using an Image as the Path Separator in a SiteMapPath Control

```
<asp:SiteMapPath ID="SiteMapPath1" runat="server"
  <PathSeparatorTemplate>
      <asp:Image runat="server" ImageUrl="arrow.gif"/>
  </PathSeparatorTemplate>
</asp:SiteMapPath>
```

Figure 10.13 shows the result.

For more information on the `SiteMapDataSource` control see http://msdn2.microsoft.com/en-us/library/y4575aw7(en-US,VS.80).aspx.

For more information on the `Menu` control see http://msdn2.microsoft.com/en-us/library/9c43aab8(en-US,VS.80).aspx.

For more information on the `TreeView` control see http://msdn2.microsoft.com/en-us/library/f74eswe6(en-US,VS.80).aspx.

For more information on the `SiteMapPath` control see http://msdn2.microsoft.com/en-us/library/8w8dksw3(en-US,VS.80).aspx.

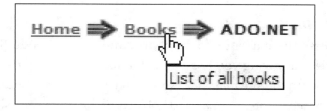

FIGURE 10.13: A SiteMapPath control using an image as the separator

Site Maps in Depth

The previous sections looked at the basic techniques for using the navigation controls in ASP.NET. However, there is a lot more you can do with them. You can use the properties of the `SiteMapDataSource` control to change the nodes displayed or set the current node. You can also write code to access the site map directly, and to react to the events exposed by the various navigation controls, in much the same way as with the data source controls you saw earlier in the book.

Using the Properties of the SiteMapDataSource Control

Four properties of the `SiteMapDataSource` control allow you to specify which nodes are visible to the user. You can set these properties at design time using attributes, or at runtime in code, as follows:

- The `ShowStartingNode` property, which specifies if the starting node (the "base" or Home node) is visible. The default is `True`. When set to `False`, only the first-level nodes and their descendants are visible.

- The `StartFromCurrentNode` property (default `False`), which indicates whether the current node is visible. Bear in mind that you will have to provide alternative navigation back to pages lower in the hierarchy if you set this property to `True`.

- The `StartingNodeOffset` property, which defines the offset from the starting node for which nodes are visible. It can be a positive number to hide nodes below the start node, or a negative number (when the `StartFromCurrentNode` property is also `True`) to show nodes above the starting node.

- The `StartingNodeUrl` property, which allows you to set the starting point of the nodes to be visible using the URL of a page rather than the numeric value equivalent to the level within the navigation hierarchy.

Accessing the SiteMap in Code

You can access the current site map structure in your code through the `SiteMap` object, allowing you to get information about the current page and the other nodes in the site map. The `RootNode` and `CurrentNode` properties return a reference to the `SiteMapNode` objects at the root of the site map and for the current page, respectively. For example, you can get the path of the current page using:

```
sCurrentPath = SiteMap.CurrentNode.Url
```

The `SiteMapNode` exposes a series of properties that allow you to navigate the site map hierarchy in code, including the following:

- `ChildNodes`, which returns a `SiteMapNodeCollection` containing all the child nodes of the current node, or null if no child nodes exist
- `ParentNode`, which returns the parent node of the current node, or `null` if no parent node exists
- `RootNode`, which returns the root node
- `NextSibling` and `PreviousSibling`, which return the next or previous node at the same level in the hierarchy, or `null` if a next or previous node does not exist
- `Title`, `Url`, `Description`, and `Roles`, which return the individual properties of the node as defined in the site map file

> For a full list of the members of the SiteMapNode class, see http://msdn2.microsoft.com/en-us/library/7wcs23wf(en-US,VS.80).aspx.

As a simple example of using these properties, you could provide a link to navigate to the previous level in the hierarchy using this code in your `Page_Load` event handler to set the `NavigateUrl` of a hyperlink control on the page:

```
MyLink.NavigateUrl = SiteMap.CurrentNode.ParentNode.Url
```

Reacting to Events in the Menu, TreeView, and SiteMapPath Controls

The `Menu`, `TreeView`, and `SiteMapPath` controls dynamically generate their UI from the data held in the underlying site map provider. As they traverse the node hierarchy from the root, adding each item in the path, they raise events that you can handle to manage and change the output. There are many events available, and they vary depending on the type of control.

For the `Menu` control, the most useful is the `OnMenuItemDataBound` event, while the `TreeView` control provides the `OnTreeNodeDataBound` event. The `SiteMapPath` control exposes the `OnItemCreated` and

`OnItemDataBound` events. You can also handle the `OnMenuItemClick` event for the `Menu` control to react to the user navigating through the site.

The example page shown in Figure 10.10 to Figure 10.13 handles these events. The first `Menu` control contains the attribute `OnMenuItemData-Bound="MenuDataBound"`, which causes the event handler shown in Listing 10.22 to execute. This code checks if the node currently binding to the control has the text "Admin." If so, it changes the node properties so that the node is not selectable, has the text "Not Available," and has no tool-tip.

Listing 10.22. Handling the MenuItemDataBound event of the Menu Control

```
void MenuDataBound(Object sender, MenuEventArgs e)
{
  if (e.Item.Text == "Admin")
  {
    // make the Admin node non-selectable and change the text
    e.Item.Selectable = false;
    e.Item.Text = "Not available";
    e.Item.ToolTip = "";
  }
}
```

An alternative approach is to use an extended property in the site map file. For example, you could add an `enabled` attribute to the "Admin" node of the site map file like this:

```
<siteMapNode title="Admin" url="admin\admin.aspx"
             description="Site administration"
             enabled="false" />
```

Then, in the handler for the `MenuItemDataBound` event of the `Menu` control, you can access this extended property and hide the node, as shown in Listing 10.23. You get a reference to the attribute through the `DataItem` property of the item currently being bound to the menu control (cast to a `SiteMapNode` instance), and from this the `enabled` attribute. If the attribute exists (it may not exist on every node), and is set to `false`, you hide the node in the same way as in Listing 10.22.

Back in the example page, the `TreeView` control in the example page contains the attribute `OnTreeNodeDataBound="TreeDataBound"`, and so executes the event handler named `TreeDataBound` as each node is bound

Listing 10.23. Accessing an Extended Property in a Site Map File

```
void MenuDataBound(Object sender, MenuEventArgs e)
{
   string enabledAttr = ((SiteMapNode)e.Item.DataItem)["enabled"];
   if (enabledAttr != null && !Boolean.Parse(enabledAttr))
   {
      // make the Admin node non-selectable and change the text
      e.Item.Selectable = false;
      e.Item.Text = "Not available";
      e.Item.ToolTip = "";
   }
}
```

to the control. The event handler, shown in Listing 10.24, checks if this is the "Admin" node. Notice in this case that you check the `Node` property of the `TreeNodeEventArgs` argument passed to the handler, rather than the `Item` property of the `MenuEventArgs` object passed to the `MenuItemDataBound` event handler in Listing 10.22.

If this is the "Admin" node, the code removes it from the `TreeView` by accessing the parent of the current node, and from this the collection of child nodes that contains this node. Then it uses the `Remove` method of the `ChildNodes` collection to remove the current node.

Listing 10.24. Handling the TreeNodeDataBound Event of the TreeView Control

```
void TreeDataBound(Object sender, TreeNodeEventArgs e)
{
   if (e.Node.Text == "Admin")
   {
      // remove the Admin node from the tree
      e.Node.Parent.ChildNodes.Remove(e.Node);
   }
}
```

Finally, the `SiteMapPath` control at the foot of the example page contains the attribute `OnItemDataBound="SiteMapPathDataBound"`, so that the event handler shown in Listing 10.25 executes as each node binds to the `SiteMapPath` control. In this case, the code just changes the color of the "Admin" link to red. Notice that you can get the current node from the `SiteMap` object directly.

Listing 10.25. Handling the OnItemDataBound Event of the SiteMapPath Control

```
void SiteMapPathDataBound(object sender, SiteMapNodeItemEventArgs e)
{
  if (SiteMap.CurrentNode.Title == "Admin")
  {
    // change forecolor of Admin link
    e.Item.ForeColor = System.Drawing.Color.Red;
  }
}
```

Figure 10.14 shows the results of these three event handlers when you select the "Admin" link using the second Menu control (the only one where you can select it). You can see the effects on the other Menu control, the Tree-View control, and the SiteMapPath control (the monochrome screenshot

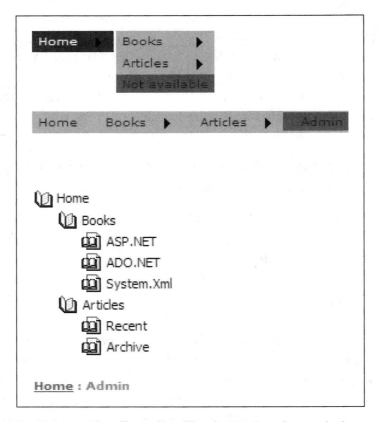

FIGURE 10.14: The effects of handling the DataBound events in the navigation controls

does not, however, show the red color of the text "Admin" in the `SiteMap-Path` control!).

Extending the SiteMap

It is worth bearing in mind that you can also extend the capabilities of the site map system by adding custom attributes to the `Web.sitemap` file. For example, you can add an attribute containing the URL of an image to display for each item, or an attribute containing some custom value you will use in your code. If your site map file contains nodes of this form:

```
<siteMapNode url="mypage.aspx" title="sometitle"
             imageUrl="~/images/myimage.gif" />
```

you can use the value in the `MenuItemDataBound` event handler like this:

```
e.Item.ImageUrl = (e.Item.DataItem as SiteMapNode)["imageUrl"];
```

SUMMARY

In this chapter, you have looked at the many ways of implementing navigation within your Web sites and Web applications. You saw how to create simple navigation with hyperlinks using the various HTML and ASP.NET server controls, including the `HtmlAnchor`, `Hyperlink`, and various list controls such as `BulletedList` and `TreeView`.

The difference between navigation and postback affects the way that you implement navigation and the appearance and behavior of the links you provide. This chapter examined the use of the `LinkButton` and similar controls, both individually and as part of more complex controls, where the default behavior is to cause a postback to the server rather than direct navigation.

Using a postback enables navigation through browser redirection, and there are several techniques for accomplishing this—including the `Response.Redirect` method and the use of client-side code. The converse is also possible, where you implement server-side redirection. In this case, the browser does not reflect the fact that a different page is executing. It also allows you to access the page originally requested, and it may prove useful for modularizing or reusing code in your applications.

The chapter next looked at the rather more specialist technique of cross-page posting form values. In most cases, you will take advantage of the postback architecture of ASP.NET to maintain viewstate and react to page events. However, you can post a form to another page instead and still be able to access the values and controls in the previous page.

Finally, this chapter looked at the specialist navigation features in ASP.NET. Using an XML file to define a site map allows controls such as the `Menu`, `TreeView`, and `SiteMapPath` to automatically create the navigation UI for your site. This offers a huge savings on development effort and provides an attractive and usable fly-out, drop-down, or collapsible menu system with a breadcrumb-trail indication of the current page position within the hierarchy of your site.

In the next chapter, you will see how many of these controls also integrate with the security and membership features in ASP.NET.

∎ 11 ∎
Security and Membership

A SP.NET CONTAINS A RANGE of features that make it easy to create areas of a Web site or Web application that are not universally available to anonymous visitors. This is a common requirement in many sites—perhaps an area where you provide premium content that you want to charge people to view or download, or where you simply want to monitor who is accessing that area of the site. While this has long been part of Web sites created in all kinds of programming and scripting languages, ASP.NET removes the need to create and maintain the basic code and processes that this requires. Instead, a set of intelligent server controls and built-in request handling features do most of the groundwork and simplify development.

Once you have a system of identifying visitors through a "login" feature such as that provided by ASP.NET, you can take the next step—maintaining useful information about visitors and presenting them with personalized content. For example, you may want to allow each user to specify the color or layout of the pages they visit, or their options when reading messages in a Web forum.

The following chapter looks in detail at personalization and the associated topics of themes and different appearances for the pages. This chapter, however, concentrates on the features that enable personalization and other possibilities, and shows how you can implement security, user identification, and login pages for visitors using the features built into ASP.NET.

The topics for this chapter are the following:

- Preventing anonymous access to Web sites and Web pages
- Membership and Roles in ASP.NET
- The ASP.NET Web Site Administration Tool
- The ASP.NET server controls that support the security features
- Accessing the Membership and Roles features in code

The chapter starts by looking at how you can secure all or part of your Web site, and how to provide login features.

Preventing Anonymous Access to Web Sites

By default in an ASP.NET Web site, visitors can browse the site anonymously, load pages, and download the content you provide. They do not have to provide any credentials—for example, by logging in to the site. For most Web sites, of course, this is just what you want. However, there are occasions, depending on the type of content you provide, when you want to force users to identify themselves before they access the content. This might be as soon as they arrive at the site, or it might be at some point such as a checkout, when they are buying goods, or just so that you can allocate forum posts this visitor makes to them.

The ASP.NET Configuration Files

Most of the default configuration settings for ASP.NET and the Web sites you create are in the `web.config` and `machine.config` files stored in the folder `[%WINDIR%]\Microsoft.NET\Framework\[version]\CONFIG\` of your machine. For example, if you installed Windows XP or Windows Server 2003 in the default location, the path for version 2.0 of ASP.NET is:

```
C:\WINDOWS\Microsoft.NET\Framework\v2.0.50727\CONFIG\
```

You can override most of these settings simply by placing a `web.config` file in the folders of your site or application. Visual Studio 2005 and Visual Web Developer can automatically create these files to enable debugging of pages as you build your site.

The `<system.web>` section of the `web.config` file can contain a section named `<authorization>` that controls access to the site and to individual subfolders with the site's virtual root. If there is no `<authorization>` in the local or default `web.config` file, the equivalent section in the configuration file for the machine, `machine.config`, provides the settings. Listing 11.1 shows the settings for the `<authorization>` section in the default `web.config` file. This allows all users to access your sites anonymously.

Listing 11.1. The Default Security Settings for Web Sites

```
<system.web>
  ...
  <authorization>
    <allow users="*" />
  </authorization>
  ....
</system.web>
```

However, you do not generally have to edit this file directly. The Web Site Administration Tool in ASP.NET (see Figure 11.1) provides a graphical interface that you can use to specify a wide range of settings for your Web sites. Of course, there is nothing to stop you from editing the file manually, as you will need to do if you want to store user details within it, but using the

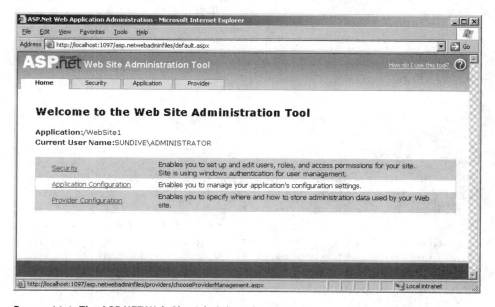

FIGURE 11.1: The ASP.NET Web Site Administration Tool

administration tool helps prevent errors, increases security, and simplifies the process considerably.

You will see the Web Site Administration Tool in detail shortly, but this section of the chapter explains the fundamental features of the ASP.NET security model. Understanding this will help you to make the right decisions about how you configure your site and will make using the tools and Wizards easier for you, because you will be aware of what they are actually doing.

Security and Access Control Settings in IIS and ASP.NET

By default, any visitor to your Web site can access it and view the content. This is because the default settings in Internet Information Server (IIS) are to execute anonymous visitors' requests under the context of a machine-level account named "IUSR_[*machine-name*]." This is a limited privilege account that only allows READ access to the folders and files within the WWWRoot folder of your machine. You can, of course, grant this account other permissions if you want to allow users to access other folders (for example, if you locate a Web site on a different drive), or if they require WRITE permission to upload or generate files. Figure 11.2 shows the default settings in Windows 2003 Server for the Default Web Site.

However, once IIS has authenticated visitors, it passes requests for ASP.NET pages and resources to ASP.NET for processing. ASP.NET then executes the request under a separate account. Depending on the operating system and the installed services and configuration, this account is either "ASPNET" or "NETWORK SERVICE."

■ NOTE

ASP.NET does not process resources that are not mapped to it, such as images, PDFs, ZIP files, and other types of documents. For these, you must set up security in the Authentication Methods dialog shown in Figure 11.2. An alternative is to map them to ASP.NET, which will simply pass them on to the client; however, this incurs a processing overload that is usually not acceptable. You can view or change the mappings between file types and ASP.NET for any Web site or virtual application directory in the Mappings page of the Application Configuration dialog that opens when you click Configure in the Properties dialog for that site or directory.

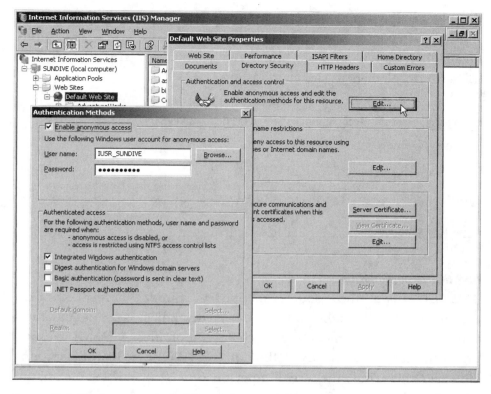

FIGURE 11.2: The Access control settings in Internet Information Server

Specifying the Account Used by ASP.NET

You can specify which account ASP.NET uses in your `machine.config` or `web.config` file, in the `<identity>` element in the `<system.web>` section. You can also enable or disable impersonation here. Listing 11.2 shows the settings available for the `<identity>` element.

Listing 11.2. The <identity> Element in an ASP.NET Configuration File

```
<system.web>
  ...
  <identity impersonate="true|false"
          userName="domain\username" password="password"/>
  ...
</system.web>
```

When you specify a different account from the default, using the `<identity>` element, you can store the user name and password in the file directly, as shown in Listing 11.2. Alternatively, you can encrypt them and store them in your machine registry using the `aspnet_setreg.exe` utility (available to download from **http://www.asp.net**). Then you change the `<identity>` element as shown in Listing 11.3.

Listing 11.3. Accessing Account Details Stored in Windows Registry

```
<system.web>
  ...
  <identity impersonate="false"
           userName="registry:HKLM\Software\AspNetIdentity,Name"
           password="registry:HKLM\Software\AspNetIdentity,Password"
  ...
  </system.web>
```

ASP.NET Impersonation

ASP.NET runs all the resources mapped to it under the context of the account you specify in the `<identity>` element. If, as is the default, there is no `<identity>` element in your configuration files, ASP.NET executes under the context of the "ASPNET" or "NETWORK SERVICE" account. However, this is only the case if impersonation is not enabled (again, this is the default).

If you enable impersonation in the `<identity>` element by setting `impersonate="true"`, ASP.NET will execute under the context of the account that IIS uses to authenticate each visitor. By default, IIS uses the "IUSR_[machine-name]" account when anonymous access is enabled. However, if you look back at Figure 11.2, you can see that it is possible to configure IIS to block anonymous requests and force users to authenticate using one of the available techniques (Integrated, Basic, Digest, or Passport).

ASP.NET will then execute and process its content under the context of the account that the user was authenticated with by IIS. In this case, you can also omit the username and password from the `<identity>` element.

However, in most cases, you will find that the default settings for ASP.NET, running under the "ASPNET" or "NETWORK SERVICE" account with impersonation disabled, will be the best approach for your Web sites and Web applications.

For more details of impersonation and the `<identity>` element,
http://msdn2.microsoft.com/en-us/library/72wdk8cc.aspx.

ASP.NET Authentication and Authorization

The previous sections of this chapter explained some of the basic concepts of
the way that ASP.NET and IIS relate in terms of securing your Web sites, and
how they interact to authenticate the users and execute ASP.NET resources
under specific accounts. However, once ASP.NET starts to process the
request received from IIS, it does so using its own configuration and security
settings. These are wholly contained in the `machine.config` file and—more
specifically—the various `web.config` files in the root and subfolders of your
Web site and application directories.

These are the settings the ASP.NET Web Administration Tool is specifically designed to manage. In this section of the chapter, you will see a brief
overview of these settings and the effect they have on your site. You will
see:

- The Authentication methods available
- How Authorization settings are specified
- How ASP.NET supports Roles and Membership

You will then be in a better position to get the most from the security features available in ASP.NET, and from features such as the Web Administration Tool.

ASP.NET Authentication Settings

The `<authentication>` element can appear in a `web.config` file in the root
of your Web site or a virtual application root folder. It specifies the type of
authentication ASP.NET uses, the specific settings for this authentication
process and, optionally, the accounts that have access to ASP.NET resources.
Listing 11.4 shows the format and content available for the `<authentica-
tion>` element.

Listing 11.4. The <authentication> Section in web.config

```
<system.web>
  ...
  <authentication mode="Windows|Forms|Passport|None">
    <forms name="name"
           path="/"
           domain="domain name"
           loginUrl="url"
           defaultUrl="url"
           protection="All|None|Encryption|Validation"
           timeout="30"
           slidingExpiration="true|false"
           requireSSL="true|false"
           cookieless="UseCookie|UseUri|UseDeviceProfile|AutoDetect"
           enableCrossAppRedirects="[true|false]">
      <credentials passwordFormat="Clear|SHA1|MD5">
        <user name="username" password="password"/>
      </credentials>
    </forms>
    <passport redirectUrl="internal"/>
  </authentication>
  ...
</system.web>
```

The mode attribute specifies the type of authentication process. The three types are:

- Windows. In this mode, ASP.NET authenticates users against the list of Windows accounts and groups specified for the machine or the domain within which the machine resides. When using this type of authentication, you do not include the <forms> or <passport> elements within your <authentication> element. Windows authentication is ideal for intranet usage, where users can authenticate in IIS using their Windows logon credentials.
- Forms. In this mode, ASP.NET stores a cookie on the user's machine that contains encoded authentication information. If this cookie is not present, for example, when they first visit the site, ASP.NET redirects them to a login page where they provide their username and password. The <forms> element, described in more detail in the next section, specifies the parameters and, optionally, the login credentials applied. When using this type of authentication, you do not include the <passport> element within your <authentication> element.

- `Passport`. In this mode, ASP.NET redirects users to the Microsoft Passport Web site where they enter their login credentials for authentication. The Passport site then redirects them to your site after placing a suitable cookie on their machine that identifies them. The `<passport>` element defines the URL for the Passport site, and you must sign up with Microsoft Passport (and pay a fee) to use this service. When using this type of authentication, you do not include the `<forms>` element within your `<authentication>` element.

Using Forms Authentication

The most common authentication approach for public Web sites and Web applications is Forms authentication. This does not rely on any specific network protocols and works through firewalls and proxy servers as well as over the Internet. It is, in fact, similar to the custom techniques that Web site developers have used for many years. However, ASP.NET makes it easy to program and, in most cases, a lot more secure than customer techniques.

The `<forms>` element contains the following series of attributes that define the behavior of the authentication process:

- `name`. This attribute defines the name of your application and identifies the cookie sent to the client. The default, if omitted, is .ASPXAUTH. If you run multiple applications on the same machine, you should provide each one with a unique name.
- `path`. This attribute defines the path to which the authentication cookie applies. In general, you will use "/" so that it applies to the complete site. This avoids issues such as repeated login redirects as users navigate different sections of the site.
- `domain`. This optional attribute can be used to change the name of the domain in the authentication cookie.
- `loginUrl`. This attribute specifies the URL of the login page where ASP.NET redirects visitors who do not have a valid cookie present.
- `defaultUrl`. This optional attribute specifies the URL that the Forms authentication system will redirect the user to once authentication is complete. The default value if omitted is "default.aspx".
- `protection`. This attribute defines if ASP.NET will apply encryption and/or validation to the cookie. The validation algorithm uses the

value of the `<machineKey>` element in `machine.config`. The encryption method is Triple-DES (3DES) if available and the key 48 bytes or more, or DES otherwise. You should generally specify `All` for maximum security.

- `timeout` and `slidingExpiration`. This attribute defines the number of minutes before the cookie expires, and hence the user has to log in again. Each page request resets the timer by creating a new cookie, unless you set the `slidingExpiration` attribute to `true`. The default for the `slidingExpiration` attribute is `false`.

- `requiresSSL`. This attribute specifies if requests to the login page (defined in the `loginUrl` attribute) must be over a secure connection using SSL. You should endeavor to always use SSL for your login pages, with the possible exception of applications where security is non-critical (such as when used only for page personalization).

- `cookieless`. This attribute specifies if cookies are used to maintain authentication between requests, or if the information should be encoded into the URL. The `"AutoDetect"` setting causes ASP.NET to use cookies where the browser supports them and they are enabled. The `"UseDeviceProfile"` setting specifies that ASP.NET should use cookies whenever the browser information stored in the browser capabilities files suggests that cookies are supported, without checking if the user has disabled them.

- `enableCrossAppRedirects`. This optional attribute, when set to `"true"`, allows code to redirect users to different ASP.NET applications while preserving the authentication state. In this case, you must specify the same `name`, `protection`, and `path` attribute values in both applications and the same specific keys for the `<machineKey>` sections of the `web.config` files.

The `<credentials>` Element

Both Windows and Passport authentication techniques maintain a list of valid users, outside of your ASP.NET application. Windows stores its accounts details in an internal secure database on the server or the domain controller. The Microsoft Passport site stores user details centrally, and it does not expose them to your ASP.NET applications.

However, when you use Forms authentication, you must provide the list of valid users so that ASP.NET can validate logon requests. One way is to include the list of users in your `web.config` file in the `<credentials>` element. For each `user`, you include a `<user>` element that specifies the user name and password. To avoid storing plain text passwords, you can encrypt them using the delightfully named `HashPasswordForStoringInConfigFile` method of the `System.Web.Security.FormsAuthentication` class. You then specify the encryption type you used in the `passwordFormat` attribute of the `<credentials>` element.

> For details of the `FormsAuthentication` class, see http://msdn2. microsoft.com/library/k3fc21xw(en-US,VS.80).aspx.

Cookie-less Sessions and Cookie-less Forms Authentication

One issue that you might come across when using Forms authentication is that it depends on the client's browser accepting and then returning the special cookie that indicates they were authenticated. For clients that do not support cookies, or who have disabled them in their browser options, Forms authentication (together with session support and other features of ASP.NET) will fail to work correctly, because ASP.NET cannot then recognize users when they make a subsequent request.

To get around this, you can use cookie-less sessions and cookie-less Forms authentication methods. When you enable cookie-less sessions, ASP.NET inserts the session ID into the URL so that it recognizes the user on the next request. The `<sessionState>` element in the `<system.web>` section of `web.config` can specify that ASP.NET should use cookie-less sessions:

```
<sessionState cookieless="true" />
```

You specify cookie-less Forms authentication using the `cookieless` attribute of the `<forms>` element, as shown at the beginning of this current section. The `FormsAuthentication` class exposes the static `CookiesSupported` and `CookieMode` properties that provide information about the current configuration or the current user's cookie support.

ASP.NET Authorization Settings

Having specified the type of authentication you will use, you now have a technique that allows ASP.NET to identify visitors to the site, or to a specific subsection of the site. However, you also have to provide ASP.NET with information on what permissions and privileges each user should have. In other words, having identified a user, should ASP.NET allow that user to access a specific folder or resource?

Listing 11.5 shows the format of the <authorization> element. It allows you to specify a list of users, roles, and verbs that you wish to either permit or deny access to the folder or resource. Note, however, that the roles defined here apply to Windows account groups, and are used only with Windows authentication. The techniques for managing roles in Forms authentication under the control of ASP.NET do not use the roles attribute.

Listing 11.5. The <authorization> Section in web.config

```
<system.web>
  ...
  <authorization>
    <allow users="comma-separated list of users"
           roles="comma-separated list of roles"
           verbs="comma-separated list of verbs"/>

    <deny users="comma-separated list of users"
          roles="comma-separated list of roles"
          verbs="comma-separated list of verbs"/>
  </authorization>
  ...
</system.web>
```

There are two specific characters you can use in the users attribute of the <allow> and <deny> elements:

- The asterisk (*) means "all users"
- The question mark (?) means "anonymous users," in other words, users that have been authenticated by IIS within the context of the "IUSR_[machine-name]" account

The verbs attribute refers to specific types of HTTP request; the types recognized by ASP.NET are GET, HEAD, POST, and DEBUG. This means that you can allow or deny access based on the type of request. For example, you can allow specific users (or all users) to access pages only by using values in the query string (GET) and not when posting values from a <form>.

The most stringent rules take precedence, so that (when using Windows authentication) you can deny access to a Windows account group in the <deny> element but then allow access to a specific account within that group using the <allow> element.

You use the <authorization> element in a web.config file placed in the secured target folder of your site—in other words, in the folder(s) where you want to limit access to specific authenticated users. These folders must be within the virtual application to which the <authentication> element applies. Alternatively, you can use the <location> element to target parts of a web.config file at a specific folder or resource, as shown in Listing 11.6.

Listing 11.6. Using a <location> Element in web.config

```
<configuration>
  ...
  <system.web>
    ...
    <authentication mode="Forms">
      <forms name="myapp" path="/" loginUrl="login.aspx"
          protection="All" requireSSL="true"
          timeout="30" slidingExpiration=" false">
        <credentials passwordFormat="Clear|SHA1|MD5">
          <user name="alex" password="56&FEw%x2K"/>
        </credentials>
      </forms>
    </authentication>
    ...
  </system.web>
  <location path="SecureArea"
    <system.web>
      <authorization>
        <allow users="?"/>
      </authorization>
    </system.web>
  </location>
  ...
</configuration>
```

The complete ASP.NET settings schema guide is available at http:// msdn2. microsoft.com/en-us/library/b5ysx397.

You will find a useful Microsoft patterns & practices guide to Windows Authentication in ASP.NET 2.0 at http://msdn.microsoft.com/library/ default.asp?url=/library/en-us/dnpag2/html/paght000025.asp.

ASP.NET Membership Provider and Role Manager

In the previous section, you saw how one approach for maintaining lists of valid users for an application when using Forms authentication is to store the details in the web.config file. However, doing this has the following disadvantages:

- It is not very secure, though you can encrypt the passwords to improve security. Visitors to the site cannot view web.config files, but anyone with access to the server directly or through the local network might be able to access and view these files.
- It is not very flexible, because you can only define users, and not roles or groups of users to which you want to grant permissions, in one operation. Instead, you must list and configure access for each user individually, and the options available for this are limited.
- It is not very easy to maintain. You have to edit the file directly whenever you want to change the list of users or just update their passwords.

A better approach is to use a database to store details of each user. You can implement this yourself (the FormsAuthentication class has methods and properties that make this easier) and validate users in your own custom code routines. You could even implement your own system of account groups or roles this way.

However, ASP.NET provides all the features you need to use a database to store all kinds of security, user, and role membership details. It also provides a series of server controls that help you build the pages that users need and that administrators require to create accounts, change passwords, and maintain the login information and role membership for each user. The two features of ASP.NET that support this are:

- The membership provider and the associated database tables and procedures
- The role manager and its associated database tables and procedures

The ASP.NET Web Site Administration Tool supports most of the actions you need to take when managing users and roles. However, some configuration tasks are required first. In this section of the chapter, you will see how ASP.NET integrates the membership provider and role manager, and the options available for specifying the provider settings that are necessary before you start using the Web Site Administration Tool.

The ASP.NET Application Database

As you will have realized from the previous section, ASP.NET uses a database to store membership and roles information for your applications. Figure 11.3

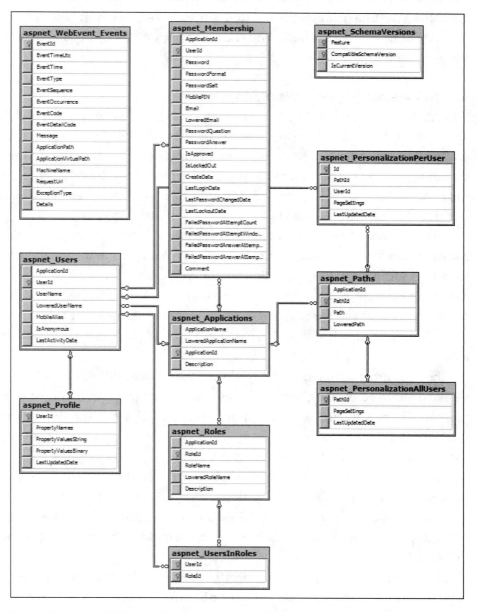

FIGURE 11.3: The ASP.NET Application Database schema

shows the complete schema for this database. You can see from the table names that it stores much more than just user and role details—it also holds personalization details, application details, and information about events that occur as ASP.NET executes.

Part of the configuration task that you must perform involves creating this database, and you will see how to do that later in this chapter in The ASP.NET Web Site Administration Tool section. First, however, you will see how ASP.NET knows where to find the database and the options you have for using different database servers and database locations.

ASP.NET Membership Provider Configuration

The ASP.NET membership provider manages the tables in the ASP.NET application database that store details of the users you define for that application or Web site. The <membership> section of web.config defines the configuration of the membership provider, including the connection to the database shown in Figure 11.3. Listing 11.7 shows the <membership> element (located within the <system.web> section) and the content.

The <membership> element consists of a series of one or more <add> elements within the <providers> section, each of which defines the parameters for a provider that will be available for the membership system to use. By default, it includes just the first one shown in Listing 11.7, named AspNet-SqlMembershipProvider. We have added two more to the list to demonstrate how you can choose a different configuration for your providers, if required.

The type attribute refers to the .NET class that implements the provider—we have removed the long version information string from the listing so that you can see the structure of the file more easily. In all three cases, the type in use is the default SqlMembershipProvider class that is provided as part of the ASP.NET framework.

The connectionStringName attribute refers to a value in the <connectionStrings> section of this web.config file, or a value defined in a web.config file nearer the root folder of this application. You will see more details of the <connectionStrings> section in the next section of this chapter.

The remaining attributes set specific properties of the provider that control how ASP.NET pages and controls can interact with it. Most are

Listing 11.7. The <membership> Section of web.config

```
<system.web>
  ...
  <membership>
    <providers>
      <add name="AspNetSqlMembershipProvider"
           type="System.Web.Security.SqlMembershipProvider, ..."
           connectionStringName="LocalSqlServer"
           applicationName="/"
           enablePasswordRetrieval="false"
           enablePasswordReset="true"
           requiresQuestionAndAnswer="true"
           requiresUniqueEmail="false"
           passwordFormat="Hashed"
           maxInvalidPasswordAttempts="5"
           minRequiredPasswordLength="7"
           minRequiredNonalphanumericCharacters="1"
           passwordAttemptWindow="10"
           passwordStrengthRegularExpression="" />

      <!-- following added to use SQL Server 2005 database -->
      <add name="Sql2005MembershipProvider"
           type="System.Web.Security.SqlMembershipProvider, ..."
           connectionStringName="SqlServer2005"
           ... />

      <!-- following uses remote SQL Server attached database -->
      <add name="Sql2005RemoteMembershipProvider"
           type="System.Web.Security.SqlMembershipProvider, ..."
           connectionStringName="Sql2005Remote"
           ... />

    </providers>
  </membership>
  ...
</system.web>
```

self-explanatory, and you will see how they relate to the ASP.NET server controls that manipulate the membership information toward the end of this chapter.

Notice that the three <add> elements in Listing 11.7 have unique names, even though they use the same built-in provider class. They also use different connectionStringName values. The listing intentionally omits the remaining attributes for the last two <add> elements to aid clarity; however, they exist in the file and are the same as the first <add> element.

Using a remote server allows you to centralize the membership and other information across multiple servers and use a failover database system for high-availability scenarios, if you wish.

Specifying the Database Connection Strings

The <add> elements in the <membership> section of web.config correspond to values defined in the <connectionStrings> section. Listing 11.8 shows an example <connectionStrings> section that contains three connection string definitions. These are, in order:

- A connection to the local SQL Server Express Edition database that is an optional component you can install with Visual Studio 2005. SQL Server 2005 and SQL Server Express Edition can auto-attach an .mdf database file as they connect. The AttachDBFilename and User Instance properties of the connection string specify that this will occur, and they provide the required location and instance information.
- A connection to a local instance of SQL Server 2005 using the database auto-attach feature.
- A connection to a remote SQL Server that has the database already attached, specifying the login details required to connect to this database.

Notice that all specify the database named aspnetdb in the file named aspnetdb.mdf. This is the default database name, though you can specify a different name if you wish when you create the database. The physical location, when using the auto-attach feature, is the App_Data subfolder within the root of the Web site or Web application virtual directory.

Note that the <connectionStrings> element does *not* reside within the <system.web> section, because it stores connection strings for all other types of applications (such as Windows Forms applications) as well as Web Forms pages.

Creating and Using Custom Providers

It should be clear from the preceding discussion that the provider model for membership (and for role management, as you will see shortly) is completely

Listing 11.8. The <connectionStrings> Section of web.config

```
<connectionStrings>
  <add name="LocalSqlServer"
      connectionString="data source=.\SQLEXPRESS;
                        Integrated Security=SSPI;
                        AttachDBFilename=|DataDirectory|aspnetdb.mdf;
                        User Instance=true"
      providerName="System.Data.SqlClient" />

  <!-- following added to use SQL Server 2005 database -->
  <add name="SqlServer2005"
      connectionString="data source=localhost;
                        Integrated Security=SSPI;
                        AttachDBFilename=|DataDirectory|aspnetdb.mdf;
                        User Instance=true"
      providerName="System.Data.SqlClient" />

  <!-- following added to use remote SQL Server attached database -->
  <add name="Sql2005Remote"
      connectionString="data source=myremoteserver;
                        Initial Catalog=aspnetdb;
                        User ID=myusername;
                        Password=secret"
      providerName="System.Data.SqlClient" />

</connectionStrings>
```

pluggable and extensible—you can replace the default ASP.NET providers with your own custom providers, or with third-party providers, to take information from any data source and in any format. There is not sufficient room in this book to cover building custom providers, but Microsoft provides plenty of information and resources to help if you decide to take that approach. The article "Building Custom Providers for ASP.NET 2.0 Membership" describes the process in detail and contains a sample Active Directory provider. You can find this article at **http://msdn.microsoft.com/library/en-us/dnaspp/html/bucupro.asp**.

The ASP.NET Provider Toolkit, developed by the ASP.NET team, is also available. This explains the provider design pattern and contains custom site map providers and Access database providers. You can find the toolkit at **http://msdn.microsoft.com/ASP.NET/downloads/providers/**.

ASP.NET Role Manager Configuration

Having looked at the configuration of the built-in membership provider in ASP.NET, you will not be surprised to discover that the built-in role provider follows much the same pattern. The `<roleManager>` section of `web.config` defines a list of providers that are available. It contains, by default, two providers:

- The `SqlRoleProvider` uses the same database as the membership provider to hold details of the roles and role membership, and you can configure the roles and members using the ASP.NET Web Site Administration Tool.
- The `WindowsTokenRoleProvider` is a read-only provider, and exposes information about roles for a specific Windows user account. It takes this information from the account groups held in Active Directory or on your server or local machine, depending on the configuration. You cannot create, add, or delete roles with this provider.

Listing 11.9 shows the `<roleManager>` section of an example `web.config` file that contains the two default role manager providers. It also contains two more entries that use the `SqlRoleProvider`, but this time connecting to a local and a remote instance of SQL Server 2005, and using auto-attach and a pre-attached database. In fact, the connection details are, as you would expect, stored in the `<connectionStrings>` section and referenced just as the membership providers you saw in the previous sections of this chapter were referenced.

> You will find a useful Microsoft patterns & practices guide to using role manager in ASP.NET 2.0 at http://msdn.microsoft.com/library/default. asp?url=/library/en-us/dnpag2/html/paght000013.asp.

The ASP.NET Web Site Administration Tool

Now that you have an understanding of the security, membership, and role management features in ASP.NET, it is time to look at how you enable and configure these on your server. The first step is to create the ASP.NET application database, whose schema you saw back in Figure 11.3. ASP.NET includes a utility to generate the database, which you must run before you start to configure membership and roles in your application.

Listing 11.9. The <roleManager> Section of web.config

```
<system.web>
   ...
   <roleManager>
     <providers>

       <add name="AspNetSqlRoleProvider"
            type="System.Web.Security.SqlRoleProvider ..."
            connectionStringName="LocalSqlServer"
            applicationName="/" />
       <add name="AspNetWindowsTokenRoleProvider"
            type="System.Web.Security.WindowsTokenRoleProvider, ..."
            applicationName="/" />

       <!-- following added to use SQL Server 2005 database -->
       <add name="Sql2005RoleProvider"
            type="System.Web.Security.SqlRoleProvider, ..."
            connectionStringName="SqlServer2005"
            applicationName="/" />

       <!-- following uses remote SQL Server attached database -->
       <add name="Sql2005RemoteRoleProvider"
            type="System.Web.Security.SqlRoleProvider, ..."
            connectionStringName="Sql2005Remote"
            applicationName="/" />

     </providers>
   </roleManager>
   ...
</system.web>
```

Creating the ASP.NET Application Database

To create the database, which you only need to do once on your server for each database server system you want to access, you use the `aspnet_regsql.exe` utility. This utility is located in the folder `[%WINDIR%]\Microsoft.NET\Framework\[version]\` of your machine. For example, if you installed Windows XP or Windows Server 2003 in the default location, the path for version 2.0 of ASP.NET is this:

```
C:\WINDOWS\Microsoft.NET\Framework\v2.0.50727\aspnet_regsql.exe
```

This utility performs a range of functions, including creating and configuring the ASP.NET application database, preparing a database to support cache dependencies (see Chapter 6), and creating the database and tables for SQL Server-based session state storage.

The `aspnet_regsql.exe` utility supports a multitude of command-line parameter options (run it with the `/?` parameter to see a list), but you can simply run it with no parameters to start it in graphical Wizard mode. This mode allows you to specify all the required information, and it then creates the application database with all the features you will require to support membership, roles, profiles, personalization, and event tracking.

The first page just describes the features of the utility. When you click **Next**, the second page allows you to configure a new or existing database, or to remove the application features from a database (see Figure 11.4).

Click **Next**, and the third page allows you to specify the database server where the ASP.NET application database will reside, the logon method and details for connecting to the database, and the name of the database (see Figure 11.5). The string `.\SQLExpress` specifies the local SQL Server Express Edition database installed with Visual Studio 2005. However, you can specify any other database server (local or remote) here. Leaving the

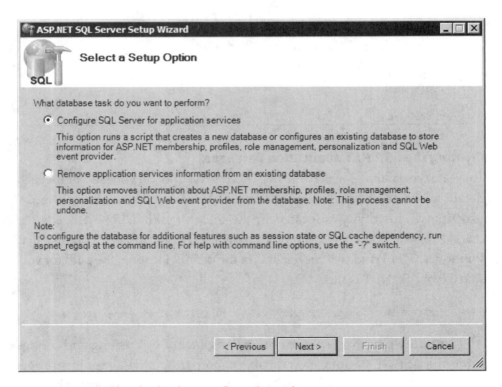

FIGURE 11.4: Selecting the database configuration option

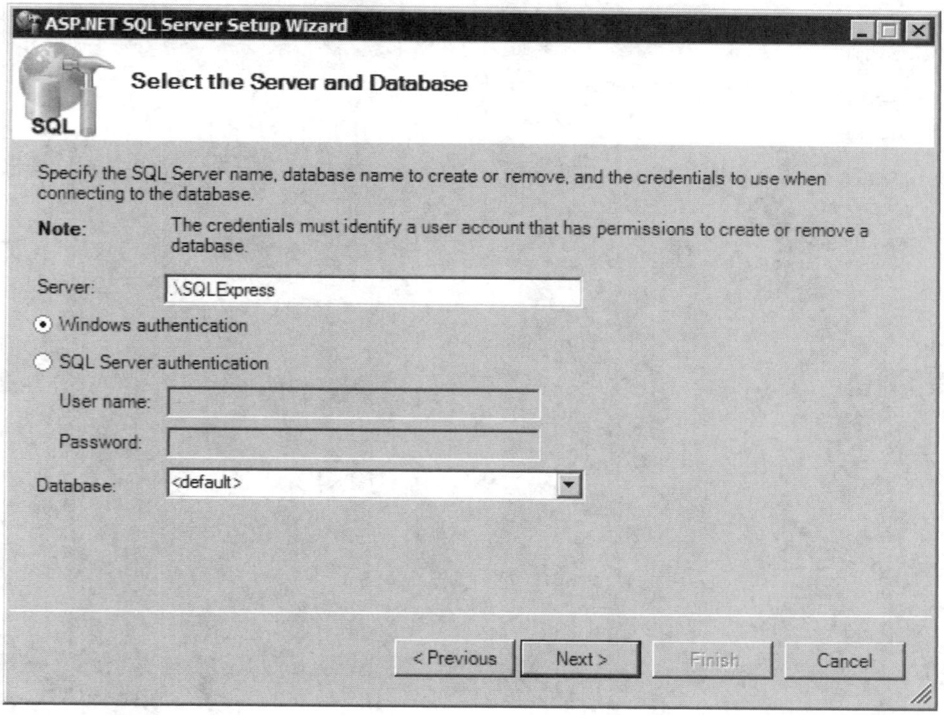

FIGURE 11.5: Specifying the database server location, authentication, and name

Database drop-down list set to `<default>` means that the Wizard will use the default name "aspnetdb."

Click **Next**, and the fourth page shows a summary of the details you entered (see Figure 11.6). When you click **Next** again, the Wizard creates and configures the database. Once complete, the final page displays a message indicating the result of the process.

You will find the database in the default database folder of your SQL Server installation. If you only have one instance of SQL Server 2005/SQL Server Express installed, the default path is `C:\Program Files\Microsoft SQL Server\MSSQL.1\MSSQL\Data\`. If you have more than one, the subfolders are named `MSSQL.1`, `MSSQ.2`, and so on.

As you create ASP.NET applications and enable the membership and role management features, the ASP.NET Web Site Administration Tool places a copy of this database in the `App_Data` subfolder of your application automatically.

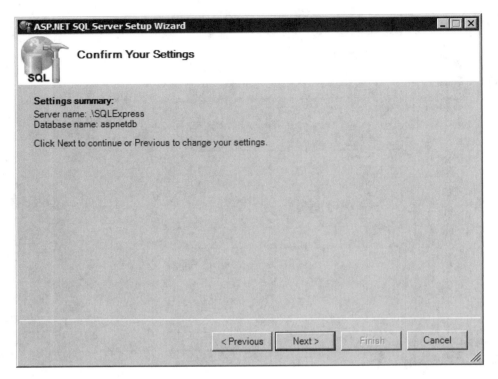

FIGURE 11.6: Confirming your settings

Using a Pre-Attached Database

If you prefer to use a database pre-attached to your SQL Server, you can - simply run SQL Server Management Studio and attach the database. Right-click the **Databases** entry in **Object Explorer**, and then select **Attach**. Click **Add**, browse to the `aspnetdb.mdf` file (or the file you want to attach if you used a different name), select it, and click **OK**. Then, in the **Attach Databases** dialog, click **OK** to complete the process.

You can attach the database in the `App_Data` subfolder if you wish, though it is better to place a copy of the database in a central location, using a unique name, so that you can attach databases for multiple applications. Of course, you will have to modify the connection strings as shown earlier in this chapter to connect to the database.

Troubleshooting ASP.NET Application Database Issues

There are some issues that you may come across when running the `aspnet_regsql.exe` utility, or when you first run the ASP.NET Web

Site Administration Tool. To avoid potential problems, you can do the following:

- Make sure you log on to the server as local Administrator, or that you use a local (machine) account that has full administrative permissions.

- Make sure that the account you are using, and the account that the Visual Studio built-in Web Server uses, have READ and MODIFY permission for the App_Data folder. You can try enabling these permissions for the Users group, which contains all the machine accounts, while setting up your application for the first time if you encounter problems.

- Make sure that the aspnetdb.mdf database is not in use by any other application.

- If you are using a remote server or a pre-attached database, grant access to this database for the "ASPNET" and "NETWORK SERVICE" accounts. Create a SQL Server login for each one, grant them login access to the database, and add this login to the aspnet_Membership_FullAccess database role.

Creating and Managing Users and Roles

With the ASP.NET application database configured, you can now create your Web application, create a new Web site, or open an existing Web site in Visual Studio 2005 or Visual Web Developer Express Edition. Once you are ready to add membership and roles support, select **ASP.NET Configuration** from the **Website** menu to start the ASP.NET Web Site Administration Tool (see Figure 11.7).

In the ASP.NET Web Site Administration Tool, you must first select the providers you will use, and you can test that your application can connect to them. You then run the Security Wizard to create roles and users, and configure access control for each one. Alternatively, you can manage the roles and users separately using the other options in the Security page. Once you have configured the roles and users, you can add each user to the appropriate role(s). Finally, you can set up other application options you require, including the facility to send e-mail messages to users when they create an account, or change their password.

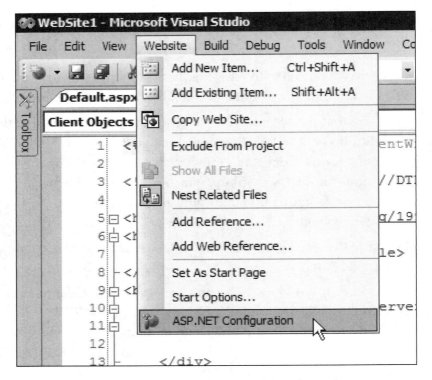

FIGURE 11.7: Starting the ASP.NET Web Site Administration Tool

The following sections cover these topics:

- Selecting the Providers
- Running the Security Wizard
- Managing Users, Roles, and Access Controls
- Adding Users to Roles
- Setting the SMTP E-mail Options

Selecting the Providers

Figure 11.8 shows the opening page of the Web Site Administration Tool. The **Application Configuration** option allows you to set and change values stored in the <appSettings> section of the web.config file, such as application-specific configuration values, constant values, and other specific information your application requires. You also use this page to take

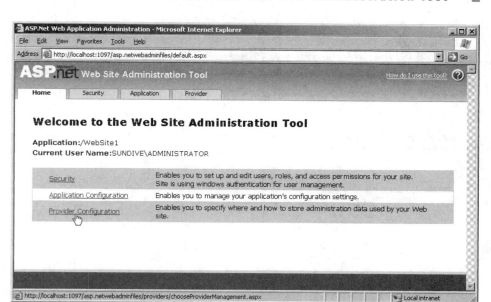

FIGURE 11.8: Selecting the Provider Configuration page

the application offline and online, turn on and off debugging and tracing, and specify the settings for your e-mail server.

However, what is of interest here is the security and provider settings. If this is the first time you have run the Web Site Administration Tool, the Security page contains just a message that you must specify the providers to use. Therefore, the first stop (see Figure 11.8) is the Provider Configuration page.

The Provider Configuration page first asks you whether you want to use a single provider for all your membership and roles information, or separate providers (see Figure 11.9). This means that you can store membership information and roles information in separate databases if you wish. For example, you could store the roles information on a separate shared remote server and access it from more than one application while maintaining user information in a separate database for each application.

The next page shows a list of all the installed providers for membership and role management. In Figure 11.10, you can see that we have set up providers for SQL Server 2005 as well as the default SQL Server Express Edition providers. By selecting the second option in the previous page, we

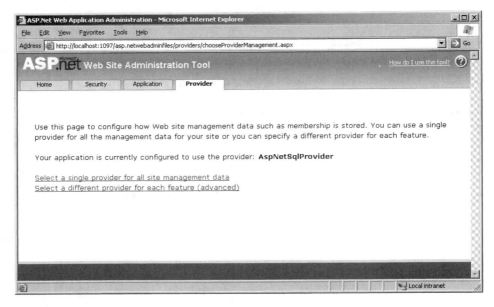

FIGURE 11.9: Specifying single or multiple providers

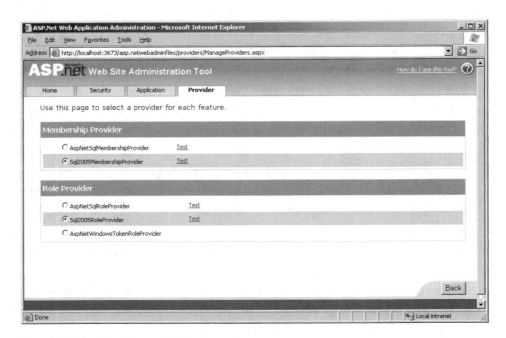

FIGURE 11.10: Selecting an installed provider

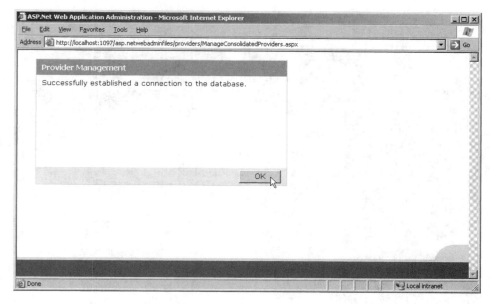

FIGURE 11.11: Verifying the provider database connection

can select a different provider for the membership and role management functions in this page.

Click the **Test** link after selecting the providers (there will only be one shown if you have not installed or configured other providers) to make sure that ASP.NET can connect to the provider database. Repeat this for both of the providers if you are specifying a different provider for the membership and role management functions. The result, as shown in Figure 11.11, should be a successful connection. If you get an error message, check the topics in the section Troubleshooting ASP.NET Application Database Issues, which appears earlier in this section of the chapter.

Running the Security Wizard

Now that you have selected and tested the provider(s) you are using, you can begin creating and configuring the users and roles for your application. The easiest way to get started is to use the Security Wizard. On the Security page of the Web Site Administration Tool, you will find a link to start this Wizard. The first page, shown in Figure 11.12, describes the features of the Wizard. Usefully, it contains a sidebar that shows the seven

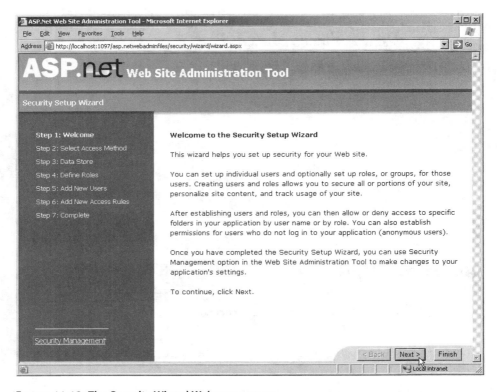

FIGURE 11.12: The Security Wizard Welcome screen

numbered steps you will work through and indicates the current step in bold text.

Click **Next** to get to the Select Access Method page. You specify here the type of authentication you will use. **From the internet** configures your application to use Forms authentication. **From a local area network** configures it to use Windows Authentication. The steps that follow are much the same, except that you cannot define and manage roles when using Windows authentication. In this walkthrough, we are using Forms authentication (see Figure 11.13).

The next page in the Wizard, shown in Figure 11.14, indicates whether you selected different providers for membership and roles (advanced provider settings), or a single provider for both.

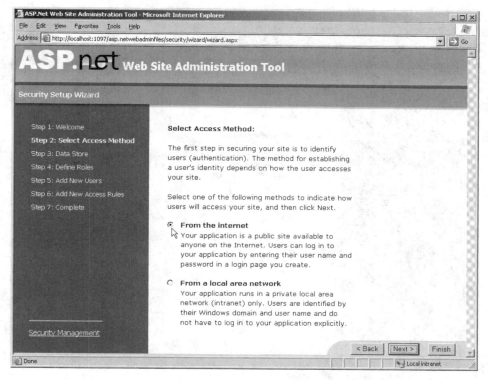

FIGURE 11.13: Selecting the access method

Clicking **Next** takes you to the Define Roles page. If you are using Forms authentication, you will see a checkbox that allows you to enable roles for this Web site (see Figure 11.15).

The next page provides the controls to create new roles. Simply enter the name of the role and click **Add Role** (see Figure 11.16).

As you create roles, the page shows them together with a **Delete** link that you can use to delete a role if you make a mistake or change your mind (see Figure 11.17). You should make your role names meaningful, so that you can easily tell what they mean later on. The name of each role must be unique irrespective of letter case (in other words, the all-lower-case equivalent of the role name must be unique), even though they are stored in the database with a GUID to identify them.

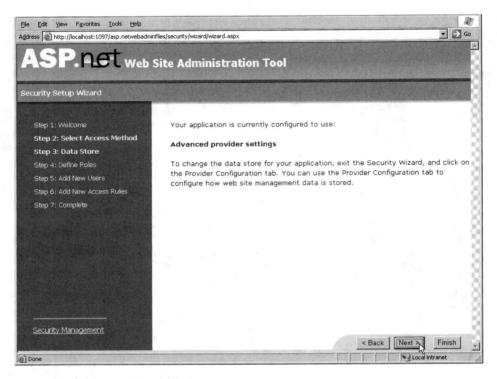

FIGURE 11.14: The provider settings screen

Once you are finished creating roles, click **Next** to go to the Add New Users page shown in Figure 11.18. You can sign up here for a new account. By default, you must specify a unique user name, a password that contains at least one non-alphanumeric character, an e-mail address, and a security question and answer.

The rules applied when creating accounts depend on the settings in your web.config file. If you look back at the <membership> element shown in Listing 11.7, you will see that the attributes for the <add> element allow you to:

- Turn on and off the security question and answer feature using the requiresQuestionAndAnswer="true|false" attribute.
- Specify whether the e-mail address for each user must be unique, or whether the same user can create multiple accounts with the same

e-mail address, using the `requiresUniqueEmail="true|false"` attribute.

- Specify the minimum length of a password using the `minRequired PasswordLength="`*n*`"` attribute.

- Specify the minimum number of non-alphanumeric characters in the password (the `minRequiredNonalphanumericCharacters="`*n*`"` attribute) or a regular expression that the password must validate against (the `passwordStrengthRegularExpression="`*expression*`"` attribute).

- Turn password retrieval and password reset on and off (e.g., generate a new random password) using the `enablePassword Retrieval="true|false"` and `enablePasswordReset ="true|false"` attributes.

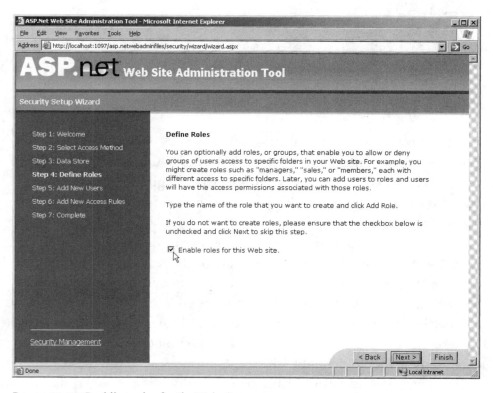

FIGURE 11.15: Enabling roles for the Web site

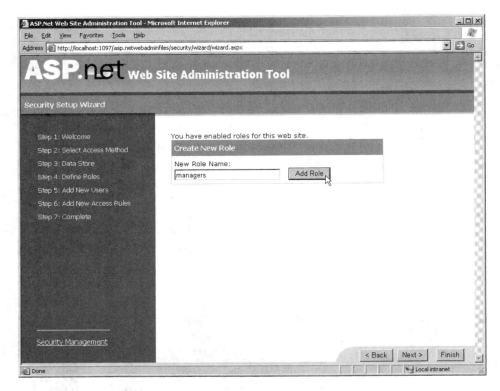

FIGURE 11.16: Adding a new role

The Wizard checks the values you enter to ensure they meet the rules specified in the membership provider configuration. If everything's acceptable, the Wizard displays a message (see Figure 11.19) and you can click **Continue** to create another account, or **Next** to continue to the next stage of the Wizard.

The next step is to set the access controls for the users and roles you created. The Add New Roles page allows you to select a folder within your site and apply rules for users and roles that apply to this folder. Any subfolders within the selected folder inherit these rules. The table at the bottom of the Wizard page shown in Figure 11.20 lists all the rules for the selected folder—you can see that the `SecureArea` folder inherits the `Allow [all]` rule from the root folder of the site.

However, you can apply rules to the subfolders that override those inherited. At runtime, ASP.NET applies the rules specific to each folder in

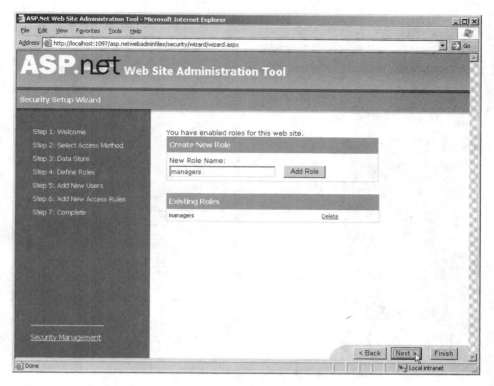

FIGURE 11.17: Viewing new and existing roles

the order they are listed in the table, though you can easily change the order when you come to manage the access rules using the Web Site Administration Tool later on. Figure 11.20 shows how you can grant access to the `SecureArea` folder for the "managers" role.

You can also set access control rules for specific users. These override the rules for the role of which the user is a member. Figure 11.21 shows how you can grant a specific user access to a folder, irrespective of whether they belong to a role or not. If you have not enabled roles in your application, you must allocate all access rules directly to users in this way.

To prevent users from accessing the selected folder, you select the **Deny** option in the **Permission** section (see Figure 11.22). The **Rule applies to** section allows you to select a role, a specific user, **All Users**, or **Anonymous Users**. The **All Users** option places a rule in the `<authorization>` section

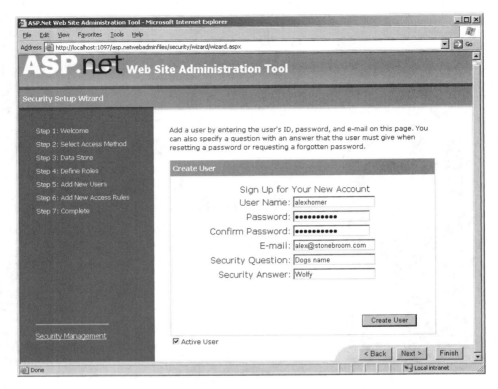

FIGURE 11.18: Signing up for a new user account

of `web.config` that uses the "`*`" character, which allows only the roles and users for which you specifically create **Allow** access rules to view pages in this folder. The **Anonymous Users** option uses the "`?`" character, which allows any user that has been authenticated to access the folder. If you just want to ensure that users log on before accessing a folder, and you are not concerned about which user it is, you just have to create a **Deny** rule that specifies **Anonymous Users**.

Figure 11.22 shows the result of creating a rule that denies all users access to the `SecureArea` folder. Notice how the table listing the access control rules differentiates users and roles with slightly different icons.

Once you have finished adding access rules, click **Next** to complete the Wizard. The final page provides confirmation that you have successfully completed the tasks, and you can click **Finish** to go back to the Web Site Administration Tool.

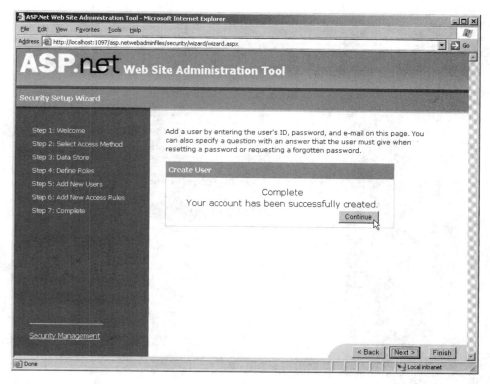

FIGURE 11.19: The account created screen

Managing Users, Roles, and Access Controls

So far, you have created the roles and users that you need for your Web site. You can see the number of each in the Security page of the Web Site Administration Tool (see Figure 11.23). In this example, we created two users, named "alex" and "dave," and two roles named "managers" and "visitors."

While you can always run the Security Wizard again to enable roles, and to modify users and roles, the Security page provides links to the individual tasks that make the process of managing users and roles much easier. The **Manage users** link displays a list of the users you have defined—you can select them using the first letter of their user name, search (with wildcards) to find specific users by name or e-mail address, or click the **All** link to show all users, as seen in Figure 11.24. For each one, you can edit the user

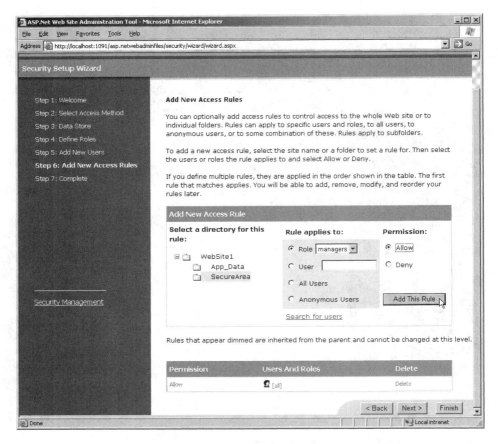

FIGURE 11.20: Allowing access for specific roles

details, delete the user, or manage the roles of which they are members (you will see how to allocate users to roles in the next section of this chapter).

The **Create or Manage Roles** link in the Security page provides a list of the existing roles configured for the application and allows you to manage or delete this role (see Figure 11.25). You can also add a new role in this page. The **Manage** link provides another route for allocating users to roles, as you will see in the next section of this chapter.

Finally, the **Manage Access Rules** link in the Security page takes you to a page where you can select a folder and see all the access rules applied to that folder. For each one, you can delete this rule or change the order in

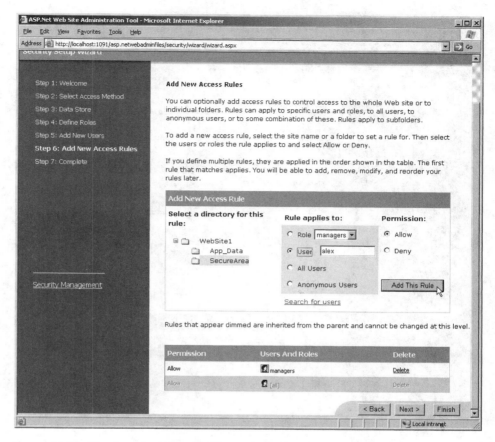

FIGURE 11.21: Allowing access for specific users

which rules are applied. The order is important, and you should ensure that the rules allowing users and roles come before those that deny all other users (see Figure 11.26). To reorder the rules, click on the **user** or **role** icon to select that row, and then use the **Move Up** and **Move Down** buttons.

To understand what the Security Wizard has done, look at the contents of the web.config files that it generates and modifies as you work through the Wizard and the other pages of the Web Site Administration Tool. In Listing 11.10, you can see all that is required is a <roleManager> element that enables roles for the application, and an <authentication> element with the mode set to "Forms." ASP.NET uses the setting in parent

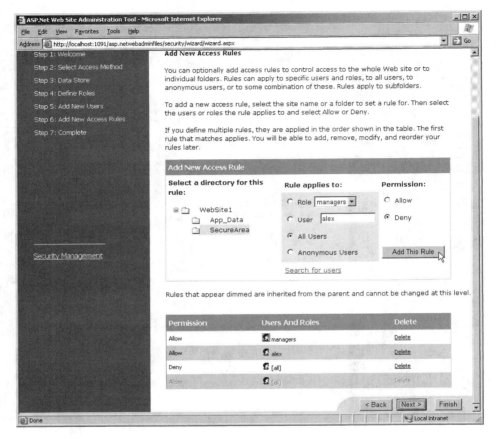

FIGURE 11.22: Denying all users access to a folder

`web.config` files and the `machine.config` file, and other settings that it generates at runtime.

Listing 11.10. The config.web File in the Root of the Application

```
<system.web>
  <roleManager enabled="true"/>
  <authentication mode="Forms"/>
  <compilation debug="true"/>
  ...
</system.web>
```

Listing 11.11 shows the `web.config` file created in the `SecureArea` sub-folder. It contains just an `<authentication>` element that specifies the access rules created by the Security Wizard. It allows access for members

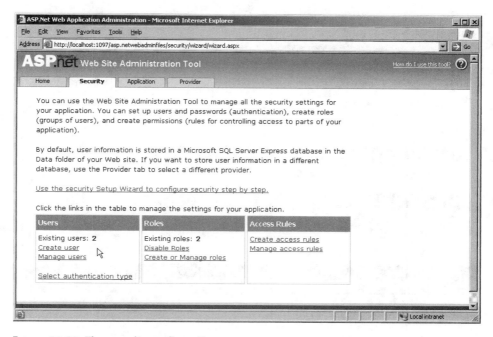

FIGURE 11.23: The security configuration page

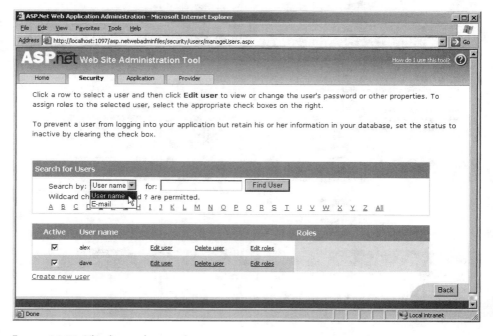

FIGURE 11.24: Viewing and managing users

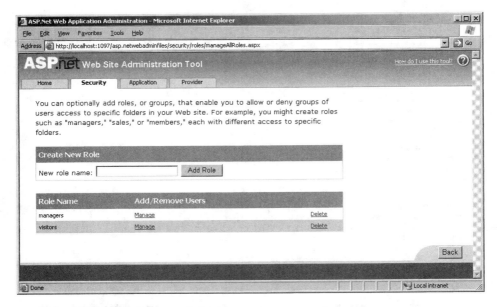

FIGURE 11.25: Viewing and managing roles

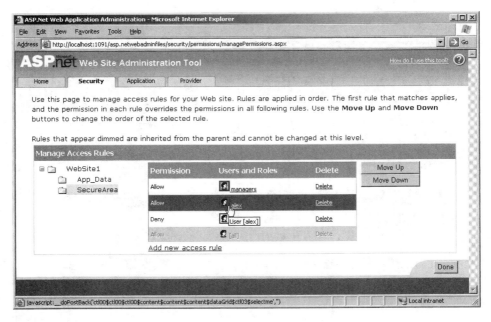

FIGURE 11.26: Viewing and managing access control settings

of the "managers" role and the user named "alex," and denies access to all others.

Listing 11.11. The config.web File in the SecureArea Subfolder

```
<system.web>
  <authorization>
    <allow roles="managers"/>
    <allow users="alex"/>
    <deny users="*"
  </authorization>
</system.web>
```

Adding Users to Roles

What you have not done so far is allocate the users to their respective roles. The Security Wizard you used earlier does not provide this feature. Instead, you use the Web Site Administration Tool. In the main Security page, click **Create or Manage Roles** as shown in Figure 11.27.

In the list of roles that appears, click **Manage** for the role you want to add users to (see Figure 11.28). You also follow this route to remove users from a role.

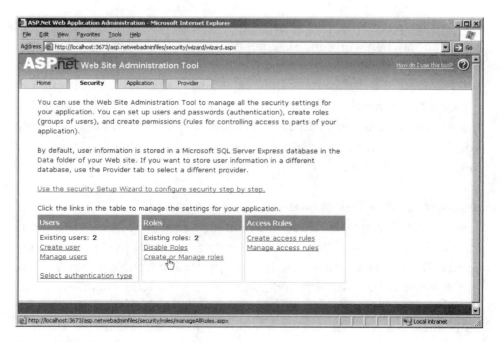

FIGURE 11.27: Creating and managing roles

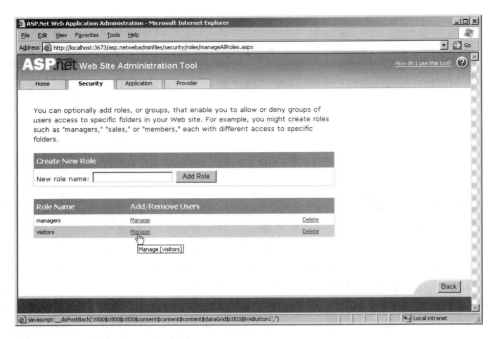

FIGURE 11.28: Selecting a role to manage

Now the page shows the selected role name (see Figure 11.29) followed by a section where you can list some or all of the users already defined for this application.

Once you find the user(s) you want to add to this role, you simply tick the **User Is In Role** checkbox as shown in Figure 11.30. Then you can repeat the search for users and add them to or remove them from this role until you have selected all those users you require. To continue, click the **Back** button to return to the main Security page.

Setting the SMTP E-mail Options

The membership system can send e-mail messages to users when they create an account or request a password. By default, it uses the local Windows Server SMTP Service. However, in the Application Configuration page of the Web Site Administration Tool, you can specify details of another mail server that will route the messages. You will generally have to provide authentication details if you use a remote mail server (see Figure 11.31).

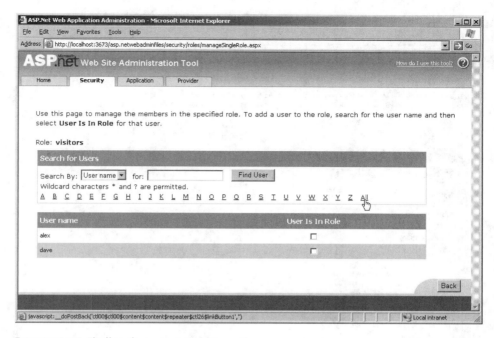

FIGURE 11.29: Finding the users to add to a role

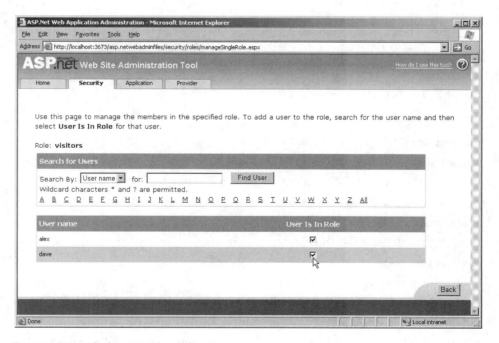

FIGURE 11.30: Placing users in a role

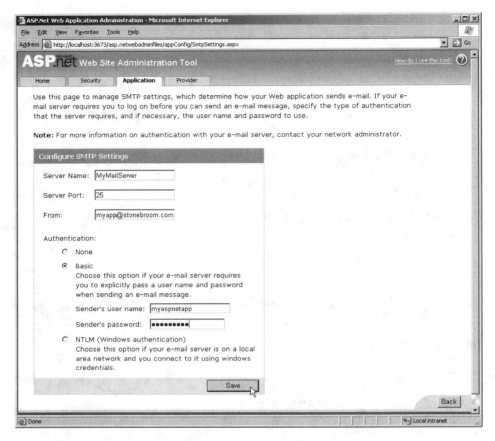

FIGURE 11.31: Specifying mail server details

Viewing the ASP.NET Database Contents

Visual Studio 2005 and Visual Web Developer (VWD) Express Edition allow you to view and modify the contents of a database. To see what the membership and roles data looks like, click **Server Explorer** (Visual Studio) or **Database Explorer** (VWD) on the **View** menu, or—even easier—double-click the ASPNETDB.MDF file that appears in the App_Data folder in the Solution Explorer window.

In the Server Explorer or Database Explorer window, open the **Tables** entry and you will see all the tables in your ASP.NET application database. Select a table, right-click, and select **Show Table Data** to see the contents. In Figure 11.32, you can see the rows in the **aspnet_Users** and **aspnet_Roles** tables containing the two users and two roles created in the previous sections of this chapter. Open the **aspnet_Membership** table to see full details

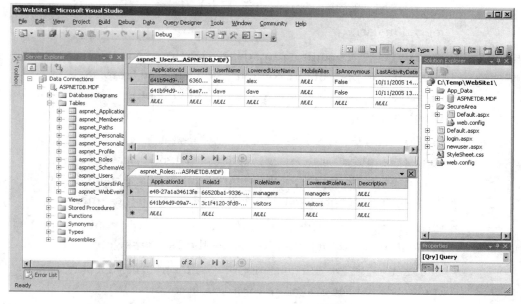

FIGURE 11.32: Viewing the contents of the application database

of each user, including their e-mail address, encrypted password, security question and encrypted answer, and last login date and time.

The ASP.NET Security Server Controls

A great deal of the effort of using the built-in membership and roles system in ASP.NET is the creation and configuration of the providers, the application database, and the roles and users. The good news is that, once these tasks are complete, building pages that use the membership and roles features is made a great deal easier by the range of built-in security server controls. This section of the chapter demonstrates how you can use these controls.

The Available Control Set

The following controls are provided with ASP.NET for managing users, security, and logins:

- `Login`. This control generates the HTML controls and content required for a user to log in to your site.

- `LoginStatus`. This control displays a "Login" or "Logout" link that indicates if the user is logged in or not and allows the user to go the login page or log out of the site.

- `LoginName`. This control displays the user name of the currently logged in user.

- `LoginView`. This control provides two template views that you can customize to present any content you wish. One template is displayed when the user is logged in, and the other when the user is not logged in.

- `PasswordRecovery`. This control provides the HTML controls and content required for the user to request that the password be sent via e-mail. It can prompt with the security question and validate the answer, and then it displays a message indicating the e-mail was sent.

- `ChangePassword`. This control provides the HTML controls and content required for a user to change the user password.

- `CreateUserWizard`. This control provides the HTML controls and content for a user to sign up for a new account.

All these controls integrate automatically with the membership and role providers so that you can offer all these features without having to write any code at all. They are all highly customizable. You can change the prompts, text messages and responses, button images, validation rules, and—in some cases—the individual controls they contain. You can also interact with them in your code to set most of the properties at runtime.

The security server controls are all located in the Login section of the Visual Studio Toolbox, as shown in Figure 11.33, and you can drag them onto a page in both Design and Source view just like any other ASP.NET server control.

Using the Security Server Controls

In this section of the chapter, you will see a simple demonstration that uses all of the security server controls. It consists of four pages:

- A Home page, default.aspx, which is the default page for the application.

- A Login page that allows users to enter their login credentials or request a forgotten password to be e-mailed to them.

- A Secure Area page, located in the secured folder, which displays details of the user and allows users to change their password.
- A New User page where visitors can sign up for a new account.

Each of these pages is examined in the following sections.

The Home Page

This page, shown in Design view in Figure 11.34, contains a LoginView control that has a simple text message in each template. The screenshot shows the LoggedInTemplate, indicating that the user is logged in. The AnonymousTemplate contains a message asking the user to login. Listing 11.12 shows the code that Visual Studio generates, and the text content we entered.

Listing 11.12. The LoginView Control in the Home Page

```
<asp:LoginView ID="LoginView1" runat="server"
  <LoggedInTemplate>
    Hi, you are logged in and are welcome to visit our
    secure area whenever you wish.
  </LoggedInTemplate>
  <AnonymousTemplate>
    Welcome to our site. Please log in if you wish to
    visit the secure area.
  </AnonymousTemplate>
</asp:LoginView>
```

Below the LoginView control is a LoginStatus and a LoginName control, both with all their default property settings. The final two controls are normal Hyperlink controls that point to the Secure Area page and the New User page.

Opening this page when you are not logged in displays the contents of the AnonymousTemplate in the LoginView control. Below that, the LoginStatus control displays the text "Login" and the LoginName control displays nothing (see Figure 11.35). If you click the **Go to Secure Area** link, you are immediately redirected to login.aspx, which is the page defined by default for the LoginUrl property of the Forms authentication system.

The Login Page

This page (see Figure 11.36) contains a Login control and a Password Recovery control. Both are styled in Design view, as are the security

FIGURE 11.33: The security server controls in the Visual Studio Toolbox

controls in the other pages you will see later, using the **Auto Format** option in task panes for the controls. Below them is a normal `Hyperlink` control that points to the Home page. There is no executable code in this page.

When the Login page loads in response to a user request, or following automatic redirection when the user requests a page in the secured folder, that user can enter the appropriate credentials to log in to the site (see Figure 11.37). The `Login` control contains, by default, a checkbox that allows the user to

FIGURE 11.34: The Home page containing LoginView, LoginStatus,
and LoginName controls

specify a persistent login (ASP.NET will automatically log the user in on
future visits), and you can preset the value of this feature or remove it from the
control if you prefer by setting the RememberMeSet and DisplayRememberMe
properties.

The Login control validates the contents of the User Name and Password text boxes, and displays messages and the usual red asterisk "*" next

FIGURE 11.35: Viewing the Home page when not logged in

to the text box if it is empty, or if the value does not comply with the length or regular expression criteria defined in the `<authentication>` element of `machine.config`.

The `PasswordRecovery` control provides a single text box for the user name. When a user provides the user name and clicks **Submit**, the control automatically displays the security question and prompts for the answer (unless you have disabled this feature in `web.config`). The control then creates a new random password for this user, displays confirmation that the password has been reset, and sends it to the user in an e-mail (see Figure 11.38).

If you have changed the default value in the `<authentication>` element in `machine.config` by setting `enablePasswordRetrieval ="true"`, ASP.NET just sends the user the current password.

The Secure Area Page

This page (see Figure 11.39) contains a `LoginStatus` and a `LoginView` control, just as in the Home page, plus a `ChangePassword` control and a `Hyperlink` pointing back to the Home page. Again, you can customize the

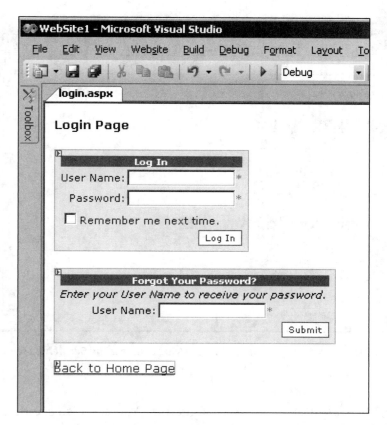

FIGURE 11.36: The Login page containing a Login and PasswordRecovery control

ChangePassword control extensively by setting properties that define the prompts, text, and messages it generates.

Viewing this page in the browser (see Figure 11.40), which is only possible after a successful login, you can see that the LoginStatus control now displays "Logout," and the LogonName control displays the user name ("alex"). If you enter your existing password and a new password, the ChangePassword control will change the password in the membership system and display a message indicating success or failure.

If you now go back to the Home page, as shown in Figure 11.41, you will see that the LoginStatus and LogonName controls now display "Logout"

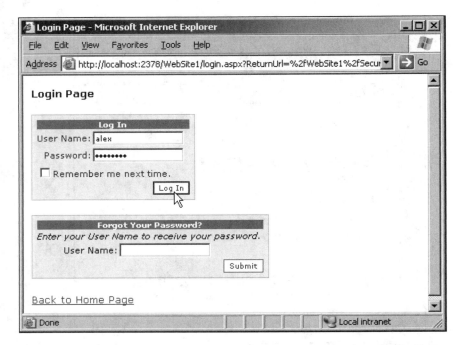

FIGURE 11.37: The Login page displayed when trying to access the SecureArea folder

and "alex," because this user is still logged in. You can also see that the `LoginView` control displays the contents of its `LoggedInTemplate` section.

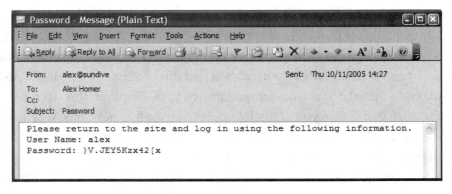

FIGURE 11.38: A password reminder e-mail

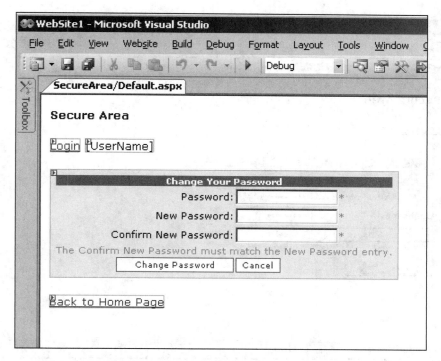

FIGURE 11.39: The SecureArea containing LoginStatus, LoginName, and ChangePassword controls

The New User Page

The fourth and final page in this example, shown in Design view in Figure 11.42, allows a user to sign up for a new account. Again, there is no code to write—you just drag a `CreateUserWizard` control onto the page. It is styled using the **Auto Format** option in the tasks pane for the control. As with the other controls, you can change almost all the visual aspects by setting properties at design time or runtime.

When you view this page using the link in the Home page, you can fill in the details required and ASP.NET automatically creates a new account within the membership system (see Figure 11.43). If the access control settings for a secured folder just deny access to anonymous users, this user will be able to log in and access that folder immediately. However, if you deny all users access to a secured folder, you must use the Security page of the Web

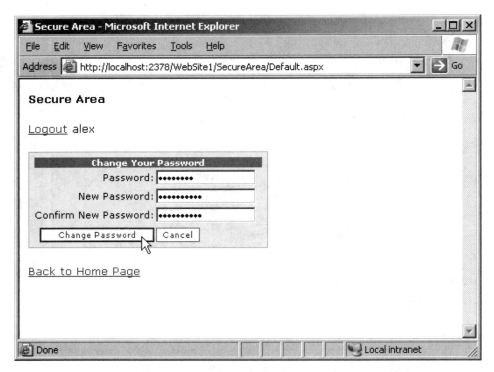

FIGURE 11.40: Changing your password in the SecureArea page after a successful login

Site Administration Tool to allocate this user to a role that does have access to the secure folder, or you can allocate access directly to this user.

> Remember that ASP.NET does not prevent access to resources other than ASP.NET pages and Web Services. Forms authentication does not protect other files, such as images, PDFs, ZIP files, and other types of documents. See the section Security and Access Control Settings in IIS and ASP.NET earlier in this chapter for more details.

Accessing the Membership and Roles Features in Code

The membership and roles system is implemented through a series of classes within the .NET Framework, and you can access these classes to read and set properties, and to call methods, in your code if you need to bypass

FIGURE 11.41: The Home page when the user is logged in

or complement the built-in membership and role features of ASP.NET. The following are the three main classes:

- Membership
- MembershipUser
- Roles

We will briefly look at the members of each class to give you an idea of the kind of things you can accomplish in your code.

The Membership Class

The Membership class exposes a set of static properties that refer to the currently logged in user. The properties equate to those you saw in machine.config that control how the membership system behaves. It includes properties such as EnablePasswordReset, EnablePassword Retrieval, MinRequiredPasswordLength, and RequiresQuestionAnd Answer.

The Membership Methods

There is a range of methods that allow you to get information about and manipulate the current user, and to find and get information about other users.

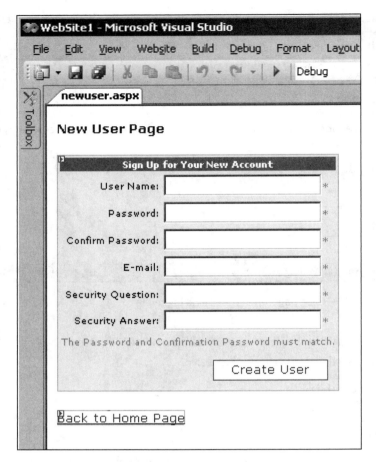

FIGURE 11.42: The New User page containing a CreateUserWizard control

Create and Delete a User

You can create and delete users with `CreateUser` and `DeleteUser` methods, which provide several overloads. These are the most commonly used:

```
Membership.CreateUser(user-name, password)
Membership.CreateUser(user-name, password, email)
Membership.DeleteUser(name)
```

Get a Reference to a User

You can get a reference to a single user as a `MembershipUser` instance using one of the overloads of the `GetUser` method. Setting the *is-online* parameter

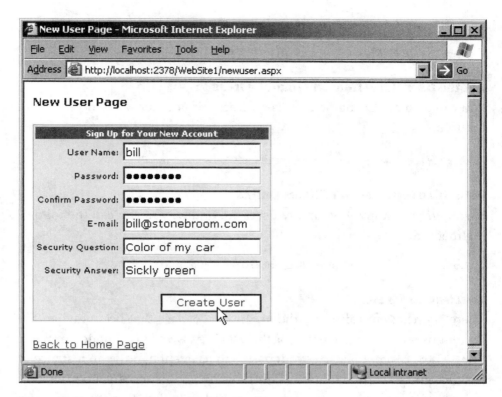

FIGURE 11.43: Signing up for an account in the New User page

to `true` means that the `LastActivity` property is updated in the membership system as well:

```
MembershipUser thisUser = Membership.GetUser()
MembershipUser thisUser = Membership.GetUser(user-name)
MembershipUser thisUser = Membership.GetUser(is-online)
MembershipUser thisUser = Membership.GetUser(user-name, is-online)
```

Find or Get a List of Users

To find users by name or e-mail address, or to get a list of all users, you use one of the following methods. All return a `MembershipUser Collection` instance, which you can iterate through to get a reference to each `MembershipUser` instance, or bind directly to a list control to display the user details.

```
MembershipUserCollection list = Membership.FindUsersByName(user-name)
MembershipUserCollection list = Membership.FindUsersByEmail(email)
MembershipUserCollection list = Membership.GetAllUsers()
```

Get the User Name from an E-mail Address

You can also get the name of a user directly if you know the user's email address:

```
String user-name = Membership.GetUserNameByEmail(email)
```

Determine the Number of Users Online

If you want to know how many users are online, you can call the following method:

```
Int32 count = Membership.GetNumberOfUsersOnline()
```

The Membership Event

There is one event raised by the `Membership` class that occurs when the current user account is created or the user's password is changed or reset. The `ValidatingPassword` event passes to its event handler an instance of the `ValidatePasswordEventArgs` class, which exposes properties that indicate the user name, the new password, whether this is a new user account, information on why the update failed if it did, and a `Cancel` parameter that you can set to `true` to prevent the update taking place.

Validating a User

As a simple example of using the `Membership` class, the code fragment shown in Listing 11.13 checks if the user name and password are valid, and if so calls the `RedirectFromLoginPage` method of the `FormsAuthentication` class to redirect the user to the next page. If authentication fails, the code displays a message.

A full list of the properties and methods of the Membership class is available at http://msdn2.microsoft.com/library/system.web.security. membership_members.

For details of the `FormsAuthentication` class, see http://msdn2. microsoft.com/library/k3fc21xw(en-US,VS.80).aspx.

Listing 11.13. A Simple Example of Validating a User in Code

```
if (Membership.ValidateUser(user-name, password))
{
  FormsAuthentication.RedirectFromLoginPage(user-name, false);
}
else
{
  MyLabel.Text = "Authentication failed";
}
```

The MembershipUser Class

The MembershipUser class represents a single user within the ASP.NET membership system, obtained from one of the Find or Get methods of the Membership class. It exposes properties that you can read or set to update this user. The property names are self-explanatory, and include LastLogin Date, CreationDate, LastActivityDate, LastPasswordChangedDate, Email, IsApproved, PasswordQuestion, and UserName.

After you update any of these properties, you must call the static UpdateUser method of the Membership class to push the changes back into the membership system. This approach means that updating several properties only requires one call to the database to perform the update.

```
Membership.UpdateUser(this-user)
```

The MembershipUser Methods

The following methods are available.

Get Password

To get the password for a user, so that you can perform custom validation, use one of the overloads of the GetPassword method—depending on whether the membership system is configured to require users to provide a security question and answer:

```
String password = this-user.GetPassword()
String password = this-user.GetPassword(answer)
```

Change Password

To change the password of a user, call the ChangePassword method:

```
Boolean worked = this-user.ChangePassword(oldPassword, newPassword)
```

Change Security Q/A

There is also a method to change the security question and answer for a user:

```
Boolean worked = this-user.ChangePasswordQuestionAndAnswer(password,
                                                           question, answer)
```

Reset Password

Finally, to reset the password when it cannot be retrieved (when `EnablePasswordReset` is `true` and `EnablePasswordRetrieval` is `false`) use the ResetPassword method. This returns the newly generated random password:

```
String newPassword = this-user.ResetPassword()
String newPassword = this-user.ResetPassword(answer)
```

> A full list of the properties and methods of the MembershipUser class is available at http://msdn2.microsoft.com/library/system.web. security.membershipuser_members.

The Roles Class

The `Roles` class provides methods that you can use to modify the roles in your application, get information about which users are in a role, add users to a role, and remove them from a role.

Create/Delete Roles

To create or delete roles, you use the `CreateRole` and `DeleteRole` methods:

```
Roles.CreateRole(role-name)
Roles.DeleteRole(role-name)
```

Get Role Names Lists

You use several different methods and overloads to get lists of role names as a `String` array. If you do not specify a user name for the `GetRoles-ForUser` method, it assumes the current user:

```
String[] role-names = Roles.GetAllRoles()
String[] role-names = Roles.GetRolesForUser()
String[] role-names = Roles.GetRolesForUser(user-name)
String[] user-names = Roles.GetUsersInRole(role-name)
String[] user-names = Roles.FindUsersInRole(role-name, user-name)
```

Check if User Is in Role

To check if a user is in a role, you use the `IsUserInRole` method. Again, if you do not specify a user name, the method assumes the current user:

```
Boolean result = Roles.IsUserInRole(role-name)
Boolean result = Roles.IsUserInRole(user-name, role-name)
```

Add Users to Roles

You can add users to roles with one of the overloads of the `Add User(s)ToRole(s)` methods. The relationship between users and roles is many-to-many, in that a user can be in more than one role, and a role contains more than one user. Therefore, there are methods that take single and an array of user names and/or role names:

```
Roles.AddUserToRole(user-name, role-name)
Roles.AddUserToRoles(user-name, role-names[])
Roles.AddUsersToRole(user-names[], role-name)
Roles.AddUsersToRoles(user-names[], role-names[])
```

Remove Users from Roles

To remove users from roles, you use one of the equivalent overloads of the `RemoveUser(s)FromRole` method:

```
Roles.RemoveUserFromRole(user-name, role-name)
Roles.RemoveUserFromRoles(user-name, role-names[])
Roles.RemoveUsersFromRole(user-names[], role-name)
Roles.RemoveUsersFromRoles(user-names[], role-names[])
```

A full list of the properties and methods of the Roles class is available at http://msdn2.microsoft.com/library/system.web.security.roles_members.

SUMMARY

This rather long chapter introduced you to the theory and practice of securing all or part of your Web site or Web application so that visitors must identify themselves before they can view these pages. As you saw, ASP.NET provides a membership and roles management system that when set up is almost transparent in operation. It keeps track of users, roles, and the membership of each role. It also interfaces with the security server controls, such as the `Login`, `CreateUserWizard`, and `PasswordRecovery` controls, so that you do not have to write any code at all to implement a complete secured access system in your sites and applications.

ASP.NET includes default membership and roles providers, though you can create your own or use third-party versions if you prefer. The providers also expose an API that you can access in your code so that you can automate processes, add extensions you require for your sites, or tailor the way the system works.

The membership and role systems support both Forms authentication and Windows authentication, and so you can choose the approach that best suits your network and your requirements. Forms authentication works fine on any type of network and with devices that do not support cookies, whereas Windows authentication tends to be limited to intranets where the server can access Windows credentials for users and the account groups defined within Windows.

A large section of this chapter was devoted to walking through the processes of creating the database required for membership and roles management, creating and configuring users and roles, and understanding how the processes relate to the underlying workings of IIS and ASP.NET and the contents of the `machine.config` and `web.config` files. By now, you should have a more thorough understanding of the principles and practice of security and membership in ASP.NET. This understanding will be useful in the following chapter as well, where you see how ASP.NET also supports user-based personalization features.

▛ 12 ▪

Profiles, Personalization, and Themes

I N THE PREVIOUS CHAPTER, you saw how easy it is to implement security features and membership in your Web sites and Web applications with ASP.NET. The built-in membership and roles providers use a database to maintain lists of users and roles (user groups), and the ASP.NET Web Site Administration Tool allows you to configure the security system, add and manage users and roles, and link users to the appropriate roles. Meanwhile, the intelligent server controls such as `Login`, `CreateUserWizard`, `PasswordRecovery`, and `ChangePassword` make it easy to take advantage of the lists of users and roles in your pages.

The provider model that supports membership and roles in ASP.NET also provides the core features required for adding profiles and personalization features to your sites. You can configure a site to recognize users as they log in, and then apply specific properties to the pages they view and the other features of your site or application. You can even arrange for a site to recognize users that have not logged on and are otherwise browsing the site or using the application anonymously.

In this chapter, you will see how the profiles and personalization features in ASP.NET work, how to configure them, and how you can use profiles in your applications. You will generally only use the personalization features with Web Parts, as you will see in the next chapter. Therefore, the topics for this chapter are the following:

- Configuring profiles and personalization
- Enabling profiles and declaring profile properties
- Using the profile system to store dynamic data for users
- Implementing a simple Web site that uses a profile-based shopping cart
- Providing visual personalization using themes

The chapter begins with a walkthrough on setting up the profiles and personalization system for your site.

Configuring Profiles and Personalization

The profiles and personalization features in ASP.NET are closely allied to the membership and roles management features you saw in the previous chapter. They use the same database as the membership and roles features to store personalized data for each user. They also build on a provider model that allows you to extend or replace the underlying profiles or personalization system if you wish.

Specifying the Profiles and Personalization Providers

ASP.NET supplies default profile and personalization providers called `Sql ProfileProvider` (from the `System.Web.Profile` namespace) and `Sql PersonalizationProvider` (from the `System.Web.UI.WebControls. WebParts` namespace). The default contents of the `machine.config` file specify `SqlProfileProvider` as the default provider for profiles, using SQL Server Express Edition as the database system and the **aspnetdb** database generated in the previous chapter.

You can see this provider declaration in Listing 12.1, together with a second declaration that uses the same provider but specifies a remote SQL

Server database system with a pre-attached copy of the `aspnetdb` database. The `type` attribute for each provider refers to the .NET class that implements the provider—we have removed the long version information string from the listing so that you can see the structure of the file more easily.

Listing 12.1. The <profile> Section of machine.config

```
<system.web>
  ...
  <profile>

    <providers>

      <add name="AspNetSqlProfileProvider"
           connectionStringName="LocalSqlServer"
           applicationName="/"
           type="System.Web.Profile.SqlProfileProvider, ..." />

      <!-- following added to use SQL Server attached database -->
      <add name="Sql2005RemoteProfile"
           connectionStringName="Sql2005Remote"
           applicationName="/"
           type="System.Web.Profile.SqlProfileProvider, ..." />

    </providers>

  </profile>
  ...
</system.web>
```

The default provider for the personalization system is specified in the root `web.config` file, located in the same folder as `machine.config`. The `web.config` file contains only settings that are specific to ASP.NET, whereas the `machine.config` file contains settings for all parts of the .NET Framework. The `<webParts>` section of `web.config` contains several settings, but Listing 12.2 shows those that are of interest when configuring personalization.

As with the membership and roles providers, the `connectionString-Name` attribute refers to a connection string declared in the `<connection-Strings>` section of `machine.config`. Listing 12.3 shows the two entries that relate to the provider declarations in Listing 12.1 and Listing 12.2.

Listing 12.2. The <personalization> Section of the Root web.config File

```
<system.web>
  ...
  <webParts>
    <personalization>
      <providers>

        <add name="AspNetSqlPersonalizationProvider"
            connectionStringName="LocalSqlServer"
            type="System.Web...WebParts.SqlPersonalizationProvider,
            ... />

        <!-- following added to use SQL Server attached database -->
        <add name="Sql2005RemotePersonalization"
            connectionStringName="Sql2005Remote"
            applicationName="/"
            type="System.Web.Profile.SqlPersonalizationProvider,
            ..." />

      </providers>
    </personalization>
  </webParts>
  ...
</system.web>
```

For details about building custom providers, including a custom profile provider, see http://msdn.microsoft.com/library/enus/dnaspp/html/ASPNETProvMod_Prt8.asp.

Listing 12.3. The <connectionStrings> Section of machine.config

```
<connectionStrings>

  <add name="LocalSqlServer"
      connectionString="data source=.\SQLEXPRESS;
                  Integrated Security=SSPI;
                  AttachDBFilename=|DataDirectory|aspnetdb.mdf;
                  User Instance=true"
      providerName="System.Data.SqlClient" />

  <!-- following added to use remote SQL Server attached database -->
  <add name="Sql2005Remote"
      connectionString="data source=myremoteserver;
                  Initial Catalog=aspnetdb;
                  User ID=myusername;
                  Password=secret"
      providerName="System.Data.SqlClient" />

</connectionStrings>
```

Creating and Modifying the ASP.NET Application Database

Once you have specified the providers for the profiles and personalization systems, or if you are happy to use the defaults, you must create or configure the `aspnetdb` database to store and manipulate the data. If you used the ASP.NET SQL Server Setup Wizard described in the previous chapter to configure the database for membership and roles, it will also have created the tables and procedures required in the database for the profiles and personalization system (see Figure 12.1).

> For more information about using the ASP.NET SQL Server Setup Wizard, see the section Creating the ASP.NET Application Database in the previous chapter.

Alternatively, you can use the `aspnet_regsql.exe` utility to add (or remove) the profiles and personalization features from `aspnetdb`. The utility, which you run in a Command window, is located at:

```
C:\WINDOWS\Microsoft.NET\Framework\v2.0.50727\aspnet_regsql.exe
```

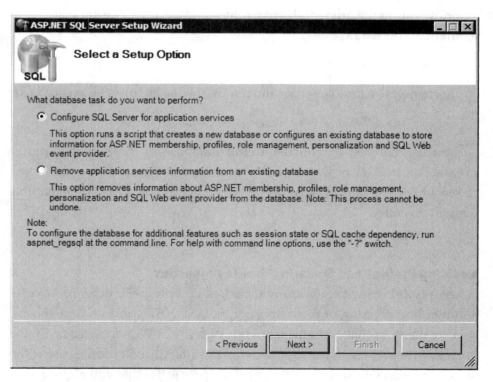

FIGURE 12.1: The ASP.NET SQL Server Setup Wizard

You must specify the database connection details using the server name (-S) and either the user name (-U) and password (-P), or integrated authentication using your current Windows credentials (-E). You also specify the feature you want to add (-A) or remove (-R). The feature identifiers are the following:

- all: All features
- m: Membership
- r: Role manager
- p: Profiles
- c: Personalization
- w: SQL Web event provider

Optionally, you can specify the name of the database using the -d argument. If omitted, the utility assumes the default name **aspnetdb**. As an example, to connect to the local SQL Server Express Edition database using Windows authentication and add profiles and personalization features to **aspnetdb**, you would enter:

```
aspnet_regsql -S.\SQLExpress -E -Apc
```

To connect to a remote server and remove all the features, you would use:

```
aspnet_regsql -Sservername -Uuserid -Ppassword -Rall
```

You can connect to your **aspnetdb** database in the Server Explorer (Visual Studio 2005) or Database Explorer (Visual Web Developer) window to see what tables are in place, giving you a good indication of the features actually installed.

Enabling Profiles and Declaring Profile Properties

After specifying the profiles provider(s), or accepting the default provider settings, and creating or reconfiguring the ASP.NET application database, you are ready to enable profiles for your Web site or Web application. In the local web.config file in the root folder of the site, turn on profiles using the <profile> element, and specify any profile properties that you require to be available to your visitors and application code.

> **■ NOTE**
>
> In the early beta releases of ASP.NET 2.0, the Web Site Administration Tool provided features to enable and configure profiles and profile properties. This feature is not available in the release version, and you must perform all configuration and management by editing the `machine.config` and `web.config` files directly.

Listing 12.4 shows the syntax and structure of the `<profile>` element. The attributes allow you to enable or disable this profile, specify the provider to use by default, optionally enable or disable automatic saving of profile values, and optionally specify the name of a custom class you want to use to manage the profile data.

Listing 12.4. Enabling Profiles and Specifying Profile Properties in web.config

```
<system.web>
  ...
  <profile enabled="true|false"
           defaultProvider="provider-identifier"
           automaticSaveEnabled="true|false"
           inherits="class-name">

    <properties>

      <clear />

      <add name="property-name"
           type="data-type-name"
           defaultValue="value"
           serializeAs="String|Binary|Xml|ProviderSpecific"
           readOnly="true|false"
           provider="provider-identifier"
           customProviderData="string-value"
           allowAnonymous="true|false"

      <remove name="property-name" />

      <group name="group-name">
        <add name="property-name" ... />
        <remove name="property-name" />
      </group>

    </properties>

  </profile>
  ...
</system.web>
```

Usually, when using the ASP.NET `SqlProfileProvider` class, you will just include the `enabled` and `defaultProvider` attributes. The default value for the `automaticSaveEnabled` attribute, if omitted, is `true`, so that the profile system saves any changes to profile properties back to the database when page execution ends. The system does not save the values of profile properties that have not changed, which reduces the processing overhead required.

The list of profile properties in the `<properties>` section defines the values available in your pages and stored in the database. You can clear the list (removing any properties added by `web.config` files in parent folders), remove individual properties, and add new ones. You specify the behavior and type of each property using the following series of attributes:

- `name`. Required—The name of the property.
- `type`. Optional—The .NET data type name, such as `String` (the default), `Int32`, `Boolean`, and so on.
- `defaultValue`. Optional—The value of the property until another value is assigned to it.
- `serializeAs`. Optional—The serialization format. The default is `String`, though you can specify other types depending on the way that the class implementing the property can serialize its value(s).
- `readOnly`. Optional—Specifies if this property can only be read and not updated. Usually you will provide a default value in this case.
- `provider`. Optional—The name of the provider to handle this property if it does not use the default provider specified in the `<profile>` element.
- `customProviderData`. Optional—A string value placed in the property's `Attributes` collection under the key "Custom-ProviderData".
- `allowAnonymous`. Optional—Specifies if this property is accessible to users that have not logged in to the site or application.

Profile Property Groups

You can define groups of properties that you will access in code as subsets of the profile for each user. This provides a more structured set of profile data and can make it easier to manage the information in your code.

Listing 12.5 shows an example profile for a Web site; the profile includes several properties that are `String` and `Int32` types, a read-only profile property with a default value, and a profile property group named "`Address`". Remember that the default type for a profile property, if not specified, is `String`.

Listing 12.5. A Simple Profile Configuration Example in web.config

```
<system.web>
  ...
  <profile enabled="true" defaultProvider="AspNetSqlProfileProvider">
    <properties>
      <add name="FirstName" type="String" />
      <add name="LastName" type="String" />
      <add name="Age" type="Int32" />
      <group name="Address">
        <add name="Street" />
        <add name="City" />
        <add name="ZipCode" />
        <add name="Country" />
      </group>
      <add name="TextSize" type="String" allowAnonymous="true"
          defaultValue="small" />
      <add name="SiteName" type="String" allowAnonymous="true"
          defaultValue="Demo" readOnly="true" />
    </properties>
  </profile>
  ...
</system.web>
```

Custom Profile Property Types

It is also possible to store profile properties that are more complex data types. For example, Listing 12.6 shows a class that implements a simple shopping cart. It exposes three properties; the `UserID` property is a `String`, the `CartItems` property is a `System.Data.DataTable` instance that contains a row for each item in the cart, and the `TotalValue` property is the total value of all the items in the cart as a `Double`.

There are also two public methods; the `AddItem` method takes the name, quantity, and value of an item to add, and the `Clear` method empties the cart. Obviously, a "real-world" cart would require extra features, such as a method to remove individual items, but this example will suffice to demonstrate the use of the profiles in ASP.NET.

Listing 12.6. A Simple ShoppingCart Class

```csharp
using System;
using System.Data;

namespace DemoShoppingCart
{

  public class ShoppingCart
  {

    // internal member variables
    private String user;
    private DataTable items;
    private Double total;

    // public properties
    public String UserID
    {
      get { return user; }
      set { user = value; }
    }

    public DataTable CartItems
    {
      get { return items; }
      set { items = value; }
    }

    public Double TotalValue
    {
      get { return total; }
      set { total = value; }
    }

    // default constructor
    public ShoppingCart()
    {
      // create an empty shopping cart
      user = String.Empty;
      // create an empty DataTable to hold the cart items
      items = new DataTable("Items");
      items.Columns.Add(new DataColumn("ItemName",
                    Type.GetType("System.String")));
      items.Columns.Add(new DataColumn("Qty",
                    Type.GetType("System.Int32")));
      items.Columns.Add(new DataColumn("Value",
                    Type.GetType("System.Double")));
      // set total value of the new cart to zero
      total = 0;
```

```
    }

    // add an item to the cart
    public void AddItem(String ItemName, Int32 ItemQty,
                        Double ItemValue)
    {
      // create new DataTable row and populate with values
      DataRow row = items.NewRow();
      row["ItemName"] = ItemName;
      row["Qty"] = ItemQty;
      row["Value"] = ItemValue;
      // add row to DataTable and update total value
      items.Rows.Add(row);
      total += (ItemQty * ItemValue);
    }

    // empty the cart by clearing the DataTable
    public void Clear()
    {
      items.Rows.Clear();
      total = 0;
    }

  }

}
```

You can obtain a useful starter kit for building e-commerce applications from the ASP.NET Web site. Called the PayPal-enabled eCommerce Starter Kit, you can download it from http://www.asp.net/default. aspx?tabindex=5&tabid=41.

You simply place the code file shown in Listing 12.6 that implements the class in the App_Code subfolder of your Web site and ASP.NET will compile it at runtime. You then add a using directive to the page to make it available to code in that page:

```
using DemoShoppingCart;
```

It is now possible to use this custom type as a profile property. In the web.config file for the site, you add it to the <properties> section; specifying the type as the *namespace.classname* for the class—as shown in Listing 12.7. You will see how to access instances of this class, along with the other profile properties, in the section Storing and Using Dynamic Profile Data, later in this chapter.

Listing 12.7. Adding the ShoppingCart Class as a Profile Property to web.config

```
<system.web>
  <profile enabled="true" defaultProvider="AspNetSqlProfileProvider">
    <properties>
      ...
      <add name="Cart" type="DemoShoppingCart.ShoppingCart"
          allowAnonymous="true" />
    </properties>
  </profile>
</system.web>
```

Anonymous Profiles

Several of the examples in the code listings earlier in this chapter include the `allowAnonymous="true"` attribute in the `<properties>` section of the `<profile>` element in the `web.config` files. This is a useful feature of the profiles system, and means that you can store information for users who have not logged into the site. However, you should use it with care, because it does mean that you can end up storing many rows of profile data in your application database as anonymous visitors browse the site, and ASP.NET does not remove these rows at the end of their useful life.

Anonymous profiles depend on a cookie stored on the user's machine, which ASP.NET generates when you enable anonymous profiles. When they visit the site again, the anonymous user ID stored in this cookie allows ASP.NET to reconnect visitors to their stored profile data. However, users may delete cookies, or just never visit your site again, and so the profile data rows remain in the `aspnet_Profile` table of the application database.

Therefore, if you use anonymous profiles, you should consider creating a stored procedure or other code routine that purges old rows from the database, based on the `LastUpdated` value that is stored in each row.

For this reason, anonymous profiles are not enabled by default. To enable them, you add the `<anonymousIdentification>` element to the `<system.web>` section of your `web.config` file, with the attribute `enabled="true"`:

```
<anonymousIdentification enabled="true" />
```

In fact, several features of ASP.NET use anonymous identification, not just profiles. You can use several attributes in this element to control how the anonymous identification process works, as shown in Listing 12.8.

Listing 12.8. The <anonymousIdentification> Element Syntax and Structure

```
<anonymousIdentification enabled="true|false"
    cookieName="cookie-name"
    cookiePath="path"
    domain="validity-domain-path"
    cookieTimeout="minutes"
    cookieSlidingExpiration="true|false"
    cookieProtection="All|None|Encryption|Validation"
    cookieRequireSSL="true|false"
    cookieless="UseCookie|UseUri|UseDeviceProfile|AutoDetect"
/>
```

The cookiePath, domain, cookieTimeout, cookieSlidingExpiration, cookieProtection, cookieRequiresSSL, and cookieless attributes all work in the same way as the equivalents in the <forms> element of the <authentication> element that you saw in the section ASP.NET Authentication and Authorization, in the previous chapter. All these attributes are optional. If they are omitted, the cookie name is ".ASPXANONYMOUS" with a timeout of 100000 minutes (around 69 days). It uses only Validation protection without SSL, and it applies to the whole site.

Storing and Using Dynamic Profile Data

Profiles provide a very useful way to store data related to each user, including anonymous users. Previously, in earlier versions of ASP.NET or in other Web site programming languages, you would have to create and manage a database to persist values that you can store in the profiles systems in ASP.NET 2.0. The profiles system provides a full set of features for managing the data it holds, including tasks such as migrating values from an anonymous profile to a known user's profile when that user logs in to the site, and automatically serializing and deserializing the stored data from complex data structures, such as a shopping cart.

The profiles system exposes all its features through static properties and methods of the Profile class that ASP.NET generates automatically at run-time for your application, based on the settings in your web.config files. Accessing a user's profile information is as simple as reading and writing the values of properties of the Profile object.

Profiles have several advantages over other built-in persistence features such as Session state. Because the values are stored in a database, they persist beyond the end of a user's session. Therefore, they are ideal for storing long-term data such as a visitor's name and address, visual site customization preferences, and other information that must survive over long periods.

Another major advantage of the profiles system is that the values it stores are typed (including complex user-defined types), rather than just being `String` values (as you would store in the ASP.NET `Session`, `Application`, or `ViewState`). This means that there is no need to cast, convert, or parse values to the appropriate type at runtime when reading them, or to cast/convert them to a `String` when writing them. Moreover, you are working with strongly typed instances when you access the `Profile` object, and so you get Intellisense and statement completion when writing code in Visual Studio and Visual Web Developer.

Reading Profile Data

All access to profile data is through the static `Profile` class. Therefore, given the properties defined in the `web.config` file shown in Listing 12.5 and Listing 12.7, you could read the stored profile data using code like that in Listing 12.9. Notice that the code checks to see if the current user is logged in or not, by accessing the `IsAuthenticated` property of the current `User.Identity` instance. This is required, because only the `TextSize`, `SiteName`, and `Cart` profile property declarations contain the `allowAnonymous="true"` attribute. Trying to access those that do not contain this attribute for an anonymous visitor raises an exception at runtime.

The code creates the output string containing the user's profile data in a `StringBuilder` and displays the contents in a `Label` control on the page. Notice how the code accesses the properties in the `"Address"` profile properties group using the group name. Finally, the code accesses the cart contents (properties) for the `Cart` profile property (the profile system will create a new empty cart automatically for each visitor), and binds the `DataTable` returned from the `CartItems` property to a `GridView` control to display the items in the cart.

Storing (Writing) Profile Data

Writing profile properties is just as easy as reading them. The properties are strongly typed, and so there is no need to cast or convert the values to

Listing 12.9. Accessing Stored Profile Data

```
StringBuilder builder = new StringBuilder();
if (User.Identity.IsAuthenticated)
{

  // read normal profile properties
  builder.Append(String.Format("Name: {0}, {1}",
               Profile.FirstName, Profile.LastName));
  builder.Append(String.Format("Age: {0}", Profile.Age));

  // read profile properties from Address profile group
  builder.Append(String.Format("Address: {0}, {1}, {2}, {3}",
               Profile.Address.Street, Profile.Address.City,
               Profile.Address.ZipCode, Profile.Address.Country));
}

// read anonymous profile properties
builder.Append(String.Format("TextSize: {0}", Profile.TextSize));
builder.Append(String.Format("SiteName: {0}", Profile.SiteName));

// read property values from shopping cart
builder.Append(String.Format("ShoppingCart: UserID: {0} "
             + "TotalValue: {1}", Profile.Cart.UserID,
               Profile.Cart.TotalValue));

// display DataTable of cart items in GridView control
gridCartItems.DataSource = Profile.Cart.CartItems;
gridCartItems.DataBind()

// display string of other property values in Label control
lblProfileData.Text = builder.ToString();
```

`String` instances first. However, bear in mind that you cannot (obviously) write to read-only properties, and that you cannot write to properties that are *not* declared as `allowAnonymous="true"` if the user is not logged in.

Listing 12.10 shows an example of updating the profile properties declared in Listing 12.5 and Listing 12.7. You can see that the code checks the `IsAuthenticated` property of the current `User.Identity` instance before writing to the non-anonymous properties. Again, the code accesses the profile group properties using the group name `"Address"`.

The code then (somewhat unrealistically in a "real-world" scenario) empties this visitor's shopping cart before adding some items to it.

Listing 12.10. Updating Stored Profile Data

```
if (User.Identity.IsAuthenticated)
{

  // update the normal profile properties
  Profile.FirstName = "Alex";
  Profile.LastName = "Homer";
  Profile.Age = 21;

  // update the profile properties in the Address group
  Profile.Address.Street = "123 High Road";
  Profile.Address.City = "UpperLittleVille";
  Profile.Address.ZipCode = "123456-789";
  Profile.Address.Country = "England";
}

// update the anonymous profile property
Profile.TextSize = "small";

// update the shopping cart, empty it first
Profile.Cart.Clear();
Profile.Cart.UserID = Profile.UserName;
Profile.Cart.AddItem("Small Green Thing", 1, 25.75);
Profile.Cart.AddItem("Excitingly Large and Loud Thing", 1, 45.00);
Profile.Cart.AddItem("Tiny But Interesting Flat Thing", 2, 3.95);
```

The example in the next section of this chapter combines the profile features you have seen so far to allow users to add items to a new or an existing cart, and to save the cart between visits to the site.

A Simple Example of Using a Shopping Cart

This example shows how you can use the profiles feature of ASP.NET to maintain information for users between visits to your site. It stores the same profile information you saw in previous sections of this chapter, but allows new users to input the information on their first visit and modify it during subsequent visits. The example also allows users to add items to their shopping cart, empty the cart, and view the current cart contents. Finally, it shows how you can migrate a shopping cart created by an anonymous visitor to a logged-in user's profile.

This last point is important. Visitors to online stores generally dislike having to log in or create a new account just to be able to browse the products available. Most online stores avoid this by allowing anonymous visitors to browse, add items to their shopping cart, and then log in only when they want to place an order. Therefore, being able to migrate an existing shopping cart from anonymous to logged-in users is a requirement in most situations.

The example shown here is a new section added to the example you saw in the previous chapter that allows users to register, create a new account, and then log in using this new account. An extra link on the Home page takes them to the Shopping Cart page, shown in Figure 12.2.

Figure 12.2 shows the page as it appears to a new anonymous visitor. You can see their **User name** (UserID property), as well as the read-only **Site name** that is also exposed to anonymous visitors. The LastUpdatedDate property of the Profile class shows the date and time that the profile was last updated—this value is maintained and exposed by the profile system.

Below this is a drop-down list where visitors can choose the text size they prefer. This is another anonymous property, saved in the profile when the visitor clicks the **Update** button. It is used to select the appropriate stylesheet each time the page loads. Finally, below this, are details of this visitor's

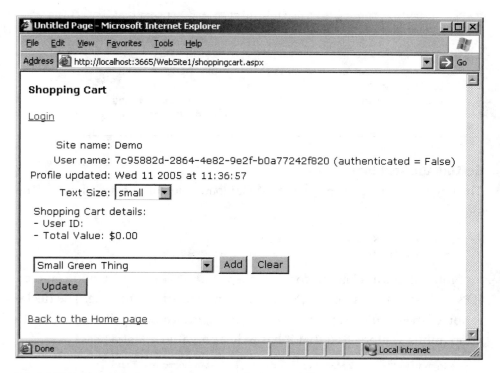

FIGURE 12.2: The shopping cart page as seen by a new visitor

shopping cart. Because this is their first visit, and they have not added any-thing to the cart, it is empty and there is no UserID property set for it.

The code in the Page_Load event handler calls a routine that displays the profile property values the first time that the page loads. Listing 12.11 shows the Page_Load event handler and the first section of the ShowProfileValues routine that it calls. Other than formatting the strongly typed values returned from the profile, the code works in the same way as you saw when reading profile information in the previous sections of this chapter.

Listing 12.11. Showing the Profile Properties When the Page Loads

```
protected void Page_Load(Object sender, EventArgs e)
{
  if (! Page.IsPostBack)
  {
    ShowProfileValues();
  }
}

protected void ShowProfileValues()
{
  // display user name stored in profile and authentication status
  lblUserName.Text = Profile.UserName + "(authenticated = "
                  + User.Identity.IsAuthenticated.ToString() + ")";

  // display read-only property value and last updated date
  lblSiteName.Text = Profile.SiteName;
  lblLastUpdated.Text = Profile.LastUpdatedDate.ToString(
                              "ddd d MM yyyy \\a\\t hh:mm:ss");
  ...
```

Setting the Text Size

The page contains a <link> element that loads the default stylesheet for the site:

```
<link id="lnkStylesheet" runat="server" type="text/css"
    rel="stylesheet" href="StyleSheet.css" />
```

Notice that this element contains the runat="server" attribute and an ID value, so server-side ASP.NET code can access it at runtime. The decla-ration of the profile property in web.config indicates that it is available to anonymous visitors, and that it has a default value of "small":

```
<add name="TextSize" type="String" allowAnonymous="true"
        defaultValue="small" />
```

In the `ShowProfileValues` routine, code can extract the value of this property for the current user, set the drop-down list to this value, and create a suitable stylesheet name to insert into the `<link>` element as the `href` attribute. This forces the browser to use the corresponding stylesheet, which sets the selected text size for the page:

```
lstTextSize.SelectedValue = Profile.TextSize;
lnkStylesheet.Href = "Style-" + Profile.TextSize + ".css";
```

You can see the effect of selecting a large text size in Figure 12.3. This approach can be used to change almost any aspect of the page style or appearance, and will persist between visits by this user.

Displaying the Shopping Cart and Adding Items

The `ShowProfileValues` routine calls another routine named `ShowShoppingCart` (see Listing 12.12), which accesses the `Cart` profile property and displays the `UserID` and `TotalValue` property values in `Label` controls on the page. Then, as in earlier examples, it binds the `DataTable` returned from the `CartItems` property to a `GridView` control on the page.

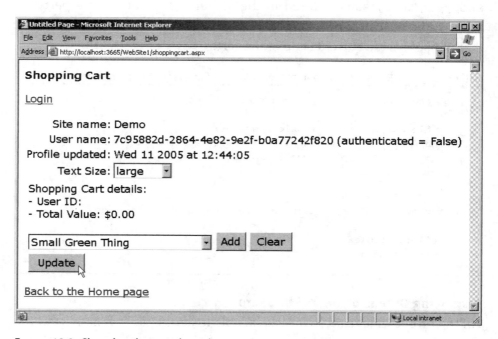

FIGURE 12.3: Changing the text size using an anonymous profile property

Listing 12.12. Displaying Details of the Shopping Cart for This Visitor

```
protected void ShowShoppingCart()
{
  if (Profile.Cart != null)
  {
    lblCartUserID.Text = Profile.Cart.UserID;
    lblCartValue.Text = Profile.Cart.TotalValue.ToString("F2");
    gridCartItems.DataSource = Profile.Cart.CartItems;
    gridCartItems.DataBind();
  }
}
```

The page has a drop-down list containing the items available to add to the cart, an **Add** button to add the selected item, and a Clear button to empty the cart (see Figure 12.4).

Listing 12.13 shows the code that runs when you click the **Add** or **Clear** button. The AddToShoppingCart routine takes the name and value of the item selected in the drop-down list and passes it to the AddItem method of the ShoppingCart instance stored in the visitor's Cart profile property. Notice that the code must convert the value to the correct data type (a Double) first.

The code to clear the shopping cart simply calls the Clear method of the ShoppingCart instance stored in the visitor's Cart profile property. In both routines, a call to the ShowShoppingCart routine updates the page so that it displays the current state of the cart.

Listing 12.13. The Routines to Add Items To and Clear (Empty) the Shopping Cart

```
protected void AddToShoppingCart(Object sender, EventArgs e)
{
  Profile.Cart.UserID = Profile.UserName;
  Profile.Cart.AddItem(lstAddToCart.SelectedItem.Text, 1,
            Double.Parse(lstAddToCart.SelectedItem.Value));
  ShowShoppingCart();
}

protected void EmptyShoppingCart(Object sender, EventArgs e)
{
  Profile.Cart.Clear();
  ShowShoppingCart();
}
```

Displaying Details of Logged In Users

All the profile data used so far is available to anonymous visitors, and the screenshots show it accessed by a visitor who has not yet logged in. This is obvious from the long user ID string, which is a unique auto-generated ID

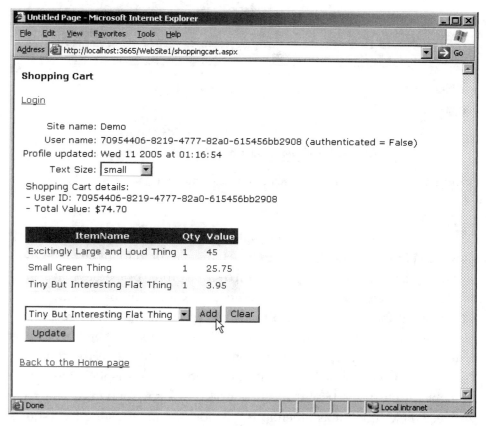

FIGURE 12.4: Adding items anonymously to the shopping cart

stored in their anonymous profile cookie. You can see this in Figure 12.5, together with the value of the `User.Identity.IsAuthenticated` property appended to the end of the ID. This part of the code you saw in Listing 12.11 generates this value:

```
lblUserName.Text = Profile.UserName + "(authenticated = "
        + User.Identity.IsAuthenticated.ToString() + ")";
```

However, the page also contains a `LoginStatus` and a `LoginView` control, just as in the Home page you saw in the previous chapter. When there is no logged-in user, the `LoginStatus` control displays the text "`Login`" and the `LoginView` control displays an empty string. You can see this in Figure 12.5.

FIGURE 12.5: The Login link and User name for a visitor not yet logged in

Once a visitor logs in and returns to this page, by following the **Login** link shown in Figure 12.5 or by going to the Home page and following the **Login** link there, the Shopping Cart page can access the profile properties that are not available to anonymous visitors. The Shopping Cart page contains an HTML table that has the `runat="server"` attribute and contains the controls to display and allow updates to the stored profile information. Therefore, as part of the `ShowProfileValues` routine you saw in Listing 12.11, the code first determines if the visitor is authenticated, and—if so—displays the values from the profile properties in `Label` controls on the page and makes the table visible. If the visitor is not authenticated, it hides the table. Listing 12.14 shows this section of code.

Listing 12.14. Displaying the Profile Property Values for Authenticated Users

```
if (User.Identity.IsAuthenticated)
{
  txtFirstName.Text = Profile.FirstName;
  txtLastName.Text = Profile.LastName;
  txtAge.Text = Profile.Age.ToString();
  txtStreet.Text = Profile.Address.Street;
  txtCity.Text = Profile.Address.City;
  txtZip.Text = Profile.Address.ZipCode;
  txtCountry.Text = Profile.Address.Country;
  tblUserDetails.Visible = true;
}
else
{
  tblUserDetails.Visible = false;
}
```

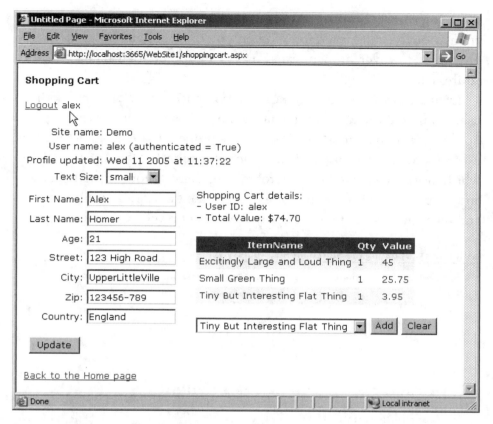

FIGURE 12.6: Displaying details of an authenticated user

You can see the result after logging on in Figure 12.6. Now text boxes display the name and address details of the authenticated user, drawn from the profile property values saved the last time this user visited the site. You can see the value of the `Profile.LastUpdatedDate` property as well as the user name and an indication that this is an authenticated user. The `LoginStatus` and a `LoginView` control at the top of the page now display the text "`Logout`" and the user name.

Updating the Profile Properties

Both authenticated and anonymous visitors can update their profile information at any time using the **Update** button at the foot of the page. The code in the page that you saw in Listing 12.13 automatically updates the shopping cart within their profile as they add items to it or empty it. For anonymous visitors, therefore, the only item to update is the `TextSize` property. However, authenticated users can update their name, age, and address details as well.

Listing 12.15 shows the routine that accomplishes this. It first checks if the user is authenticated, and if so, takes the values from the text boxes and updates the profile properties. Because the properties are strongly typed, an exception will occur for a non-numeric value found in the **Age** text box, in which case the code displays an error message. Finally, for both authenticated and anonymous visitors, the code updates the `TextSize` profile property and then calls the routine to display the current profile values in the page.

Listing 12.15. Updating the Stored Profile Property Values

```
protected void UpdateProfileValues(Object sender, EventArgs e)
{
  if (User.Identity.IsAuthenticated)
  {
    Profile.FirstName = txtFirstName.Text;
    Profile.LastName = txtLastName.Text;
    try
    {
      Profile.Age = Int32.Parse(txtAge.Text);
    }
    catch (Exception ex)
    {
      lblMessage.Text = "<p>Error: Cannot update Age -"
                        + ex.Message + "</p>";
    }
    Profile.Address.Street = txtStreet.Text;
    Profile.Address.City = txtCity.Text;
    Profile.Address.ZipCode = txtZip.Text;
    Profile.Address.Country = txtCountry.Text;
  }
  Profile.TextSize = lstTextSize.SelectedValue;
  ShowProfileValues();
}
```

Migrating Anonymous Users

The one remaining task in this example is to migrate the values for an anonymous user to an authenticated profile for the user when that user logs on to the site. While this is often a time-consuming process in other Web development environments, ASP.NET makes it easy. The integrated membership, profiles, and personalization system includes methods and events that allow you to interact with the authentication process to perform this kind of operation.

The profile system exposes an event named `OnMigrateAnonymous` that you can handle within the `global.asax` file for your site or application. It is raised when a user logs on, after successful authentication, and exposes a `ProfileMigrateEventArgs` instance that contains the anonymous user ID.

The underlying profiles system automatically exposes the set of profile property values for the current user as a `ProfileCommon` class instance, which is created as the application starts up based on the properties you declare in the `<profile>` section of `web.config`. The set of property values stored in the `ProfileCommon` instance are those of the current user, anonymous or authenticated. As a user logs on and is successfully authenticated, the `ProfileCommon` instance switches to expose the values of the logged on user.

However, the `Profile` class exposes a method called `GetProfile` that accepts a user ID as a parameter and returns a `ProfileCommon` instance containing the profile properties for that user. Therefore, you can use the anonymous user ID saved in the `ProfileMigrateEventArgs` instance to fetch the profile properties that were active for this user before he or she logged on and apply them to this user's current profile.

Listing 12.16 shows the complete `global.asax` file that the example uses to migrate a user's profile as he or she logs on to the site. The first stage fetches the anonymous profile that the visitor had before logging on using the `GetProfile` method. Then the code can apply the values to the current profile. However, you must consider how you want this process to behave in your specific application scenarios. For example, here the user's profile may have a saved shopping cart, and so the code only migrates the anonymous shopping cart if it contains some items. If the user has not added anything to the shopping cart before logging in, it does not overwrite the existing shopping cart with the anonymous one.

Listing 12.16. Migrating the Anonymous Profile to the Authenticated Profile

```
<%@ Application Language="C#" %>

<script runat="server">

  public void Profile_OnMigrateAnonymous(Object sender,
                                      ProfileMigrateEventArgs e)
  {
    // get profile data from anonymous profile
    ProfileCommon anonProfile = Profile.GetProfile(e.AnonymousID);

    // apply to authenticated profile - only need to do this
    // for the TextSize and Cart properties because these are
    // the only anonymous profile properties available
    Profile.TextSize = anonProfile.TextSize;
    // if nothing in "anonymous" cart, no need to copy
    // this means any previous cart will still be available
    if (anonProfile.Cart.TotalValue > 0)
    {
      Profile.Cart = anonProfile.Cart;
    }

    // because User name is stored in Cart must update this as well
    Profile.Cart.UserID = Profile.UserName;

    // delete the anonymous profile and remove the cookie
    ProfileManager.DeleteProfile(e.AnonymousID);
    AnonymousIdentificationModule.ClearAnonymousIdentifier();
  }

</script>
```

Once all the anonymous profile properties have been migrated to the current profile, the code deletes the anonymous profile (freeing up database space) and removes the anonymous cookie from the browser. Of course, this means that the user's saved anonymous profile values will not be visible to the user until he or she logs on to the site.

You may decide to leave the anonymous profile and cookie in place so that the user reconnects to the anonymous profile on his or her next visit. Just bear in mind that any changes the user makes to his or her profile after logging on will not be reflected in the anonymous profile that the user sees before logging on again the next time the user returns to the site. This may be confusing for users, and so in general it is better to remove the anonymous profile values and cookie.

> **NOTE**
>
> Whether you migrate a shopping cart (or any other property) or not depends on the business rules for your site. You may decide to abandon the shopping cart if the user leaves the site without going through the "checkout and order" stage. In this case, you will just migrate the anonymous shopping cart and other properties every time. This is what the example does with the `TextSize` profile property. Remember that the anonymous cookie sent to the user's browser should reconnect the user to his or her existing profile so that any values stored there will appear even before the user logs in—and will be persisted. However, if the user removes the cookie or logs in from a different machine, ASP.NET cannot reconnect that user to his or her stored profile. In this case, the default anonymous profile will overwrite the stored profile.

Figure 12.7 shows a page where the visitor has added items to the shopping cart and changed the text size while anonymous, and is now about to log in.

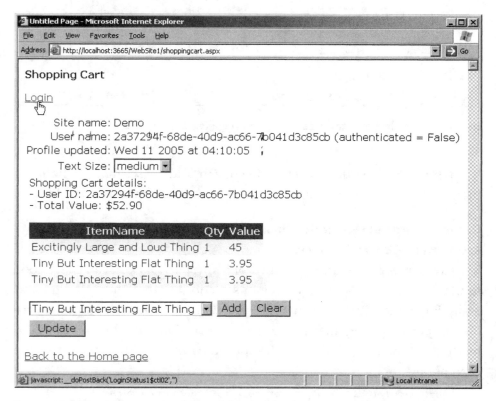

FIGURE 12.7: Shopping anonymously and then logging in

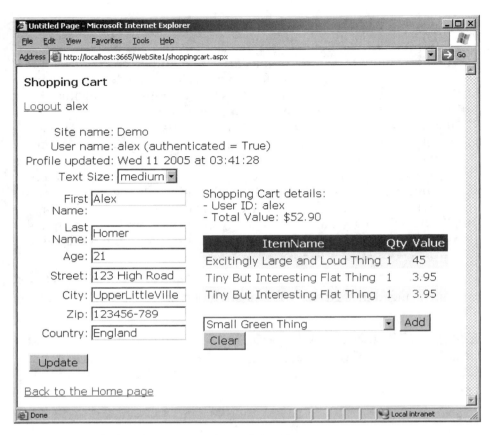

FIGURE 12.8: The migrated text size setting and shopping cart contents

Figure 12.8 shows the result after logging in. You can see that the shopping cart and text size are both migrated to the current authenticated profile.

Other Features of the Profile Class

Access Profile Properties Values

You saw some of the features of the profiles system that you can use in code to manipulate profiles in the previous section. Rather than reading and assigning values directly using indexers, you can access the values of profile properties using the `GetPropertyValue` and `SetPropertyValue` methods of the `ProfileBase` class exposed by the `Profile` property of the current page:

```
Object property-value = myProfile.GetPropertyValue(property-name)
myProfile.SetPropertyValue(property-name, property-value)
```

Access Profile Property Group

You can access a profile property group and its members using the methods of the `ProfileGroupBase` class, an instance of which is returned from the `GetProfileGroup` method of the `ProfileBase` class:

```
ProfileGroupBase group = myProfile.GetProfileGroup(group-name)
Object property-value = group.GetPropertyValue(property-name)
group.SetPropertyValue(property-name, property-value)
```

Push Values into the Database

You can force the profile provider to push updated profile property values into the database using the `Save` method:

```
myProfile.Save()
```

Create New ProfileBase Instance

You can create a new `ProfileBase` instance to store a new user profile using the static `Create` method:

```
Profile.Create(user-name)
Profile.Create(user-name, is-authenticated)
```

You can also access other properties of the `ProfileBase` class that you have not seen so far in this chapter to provide information about the current profile. These include the self-explanatory `IsAnonymous`, `IsDirty`, and `LastActivityDate`; `Context` (returns a reference to the current ASP.NET context), `PropertyValues` (returns a collection of the profile property values), and `Providers` (returns a collection of the available providers).

> For a full list of the members of the ProfileBase class, see http://msdn2. microsoft.com/en-us/library/system.web.profile.profilebase_members. aspx. For a full list of the members of the ProfileGroupBase class, see http://msdn2.microsoft.com/en-us/library/ms151849(en-US,VS.80). aspx.

Using Themes to Personalize Your Site

The profiles feature you have seen in this chapter provides a simple way to store information specific to each user, and to persist this information between visits. You saw how you could also use this feature to change the visual appearance of a site by, for example, changing the stylesheet depending on a user's profile information. In the example, this simply changed the size of the text in the page, but it can have a much more pronounced effect on the appearance of the pages.

Such an effect is becoming more important as users increasingly encounter applications that offer a customized "look and feel." The problem is that it takes a great deal of work to design the appearance you want, and to then implement it in each page and for each control or visual feature. Instead, in ASP.NET, you can use a new feature called themes that provides a way to customize the look and feel of your site, including graphics, CSS styles, properties, and so on.

Not only does this provide a way for you, the developer, to provide a consistent style, but it also allows the users to select the style. While this may not be required in every Web site, using themes does allow for consistency among pages and controls, and provides an easy way to change the look of the site.

Incorporating themes requires very few changes to the ASP.NET pages, because themes are stored external to the pages themselves. This means that, from the development perspective, the work involved is minimal. Once theme support is included in a site or a page, the addition, change, or removal of themes is simple. Alternatively, you can disable and prevent the use of themes at both the page and the control level, if required.

What Are Themes and Skins?

The themes feature uses two distinct terms to refer to its components:

- A skin is the visual style applied to an individual control, usually as a set of stylesheet attributes, images, colors, and so on.
- A theme is a collection of skins, and applies to an ASP.NET page rather than an individual control.

Each theme can have a default look that does not specify a skin, or there can be multiple skins within each theme. This means you can have a theme that itself provides differing appearances; for example, a theme called Pastel may have within it skins called Pink and Blue.

A theme does not have to provide a skin for every server control. Controls that do not have a skin defined within the theme file will have the default appearance that depends on the usual features such as the browser and stylesheet in use. For consistency, however, it looks better if you provide a skin for every control you use.

Default and Named Skins

A unique `SkinID` property can optionally identify each skin in a theme. This allows you to define multiple skins for the same control within one theme, as long as they have different `SkinID` values.

Within a theme file, skins that contain a `SkinID` are called named skins and are not applied automatically to controls of that type. You must apply these skins specifically to controls on the page by setting their `SkinID` property to that of the skin. Bear in mind, however, that an exception is raised if the specified skin cannot be found at runtime.

Skins that do not have a `SkinID` property are called default skins, and ASP.NET automatically applies these to controls of the matching type when the theme is set for the page.

Global Themes and Page Themes

The themes for a single Web site are stored within the `App_Themes` subfolder of the application root folder, with each theme in a separate folder. Within each theme folder is the `.skin` file that implements the theme and contains the skin details for each control, any CSS stylesheets required by the theme, and any images required for controls (for example, the expand/contract images for the `TreeView` control). Figure 12.9 shows the structure of three themes (provided with the examples for this book) as they appear in the `App_Themes` subfolder in Visual Studio.

Themes defined like this within the Web site `App_Themes` subfolder are called page themes, and they only apply to that site. Alternatively, you can create global themes that are available to any Web site on the machine. You simply place the complete theme files folder structure within the `aspnet_client\system_web\`[version]`\Themes` folder of your default Web site directory. For example, in version 2.0 where your default Web site is on drive C, you would place the files in the folder:

```
C:\Inetpub\wwwroot\aspnet_client\system_web\2_0_50727\Themes\
```

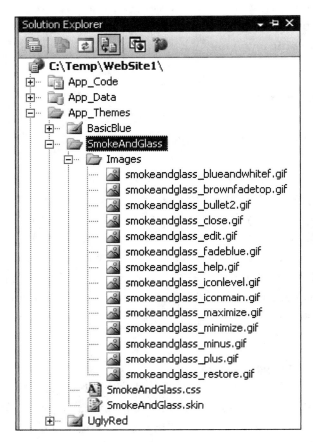

FIGURE 12.9: The structure of a theme in the App_Themes subfolder

There are no themes provided with ASP.NET. However, it is likely that packs of themes will be available as add-ons to the Framework, and you will find sample themes created by other developers available on the Web. Try http://www.dotnettreats.com/samplethemes/, or search for "download ASP.NET themes".

Creating Themes and Skins

Simple theming of controls requires only a declaration of that control in the .skin file, just as you would declare the control in an ASP.NET page but omitting the `ID` attribute. Listing 12.17 shows a simple skin definition for the `TextBox` control, taken from the example "Smoke and Glass" theme.

Listing 12.17. The Skin Definition for a Textbox in the Smoke and Glass Theme

```
<asp:TextBox runat="server"
    BackColor="#FFFFFF" ForeColor="#585880"
    BorderStyle="Solid" BorderWidth="1pt" BorderColor="#585880"
    Font-Size="0.9em" Font-Names="Verdana" />
```

Using CSS Stylesheets in a Theme

You can include a CSS stylesheet in your theme, as well as a `.skin` file, and use the selectors it contains to add styles to the controls and the page to which you apply the theme. The declarations in the stylesheet are exactly the same as a stylesheet you would specify using a `<link>` element in your pages, and can contain element-specific selectors that apply to the page as a whole as well as named selectors that you apply individually to controls. For example, your stylesheet can contain a declaration that sets the body text appearance like this:

```
body {font-family:Verdana,Arial,Helvetica,sans-serif;
    font-size:.9 em; line-height:110%; color:#35354D;}
```

It can also include named selectors, such as this one that specifies an image included in the `images` folder of the theme as the background of the elements to which this selector is specifically applied:

```
.theme_header {background-image :url(images/fade.gif);}
```

Using Images in a Theme

As well as specifying images included in a theme for the background of controls, such as you just saw in a CSS stylesheet, you can use them directly in properties of the control skin declarations. For example, Listing 12.18 shows the declaration of the skin for the `BulletedList` control in the "Smoke and Glass" sample theme. You can see that the `BulletImageUrl` property is set to an image within the themes folders (using a relative path based on the location of the `.skin` file), and the `BulletStyle` is "CustomImage". This causes any `BulletedList` control on a themed page to use the specified image for the bullets in the list.

Listing 12.18. The Skin Definition for a BulletedList in the Smoke and Glass Theme

```
<asp:BulletedList runat="server"
    Font-Names="Verdana"
    BulletImageUrl="images/smokeandglass_bullet2.gif"
    BulletStyle="CustomImage"
    BackColor="transparent" ForeColor="#585880" />
```

As another example, Listing 12.19 shows the declaration of the `GridView` control skin in the "Smoke and Glass" theme. Here, you can see how the properties for each section of the grid are set to match the theme, and that some (such as the `HeaderStyle`, `SelectedRowStyle`, `EditRowStyle`, and `FooterStyle` sections) use named style selectors to specify the CSS style to apply to that section.

Listing 12.19. The Skin Definition for a GridView in the Smoke and Glass Theme

```
<asp:GridView runat="server"
    ForeColor="#585880" CellPadding="5" GridLines="None"
    BorderStyle="Double" BorderColor="#E7E5DB" BorderWidth="2pt"
    Font-Size=".9em" Font-Names="Verdana"
  <HeaderStyle ForeColor="#585880" BorderColor="#CCCCCC"
    BorderWidth="1pt" CssClass="theme_header" />
  <RowStyle ForeColor="#585880" BackColor="#FFFFFF" />
  <AlternatingRowStyle ForeColor="#585880" BackColor="#F8F7F4" / >
  <SelectedRowStyle ForeColor="#585880" BorderStyle="solid"
    BorderWidth="2pt" BorderColor="585880"
    CssClass="theme_highlighted" />
  <EditRowStyle ForeColor="#585880" Font-Bold="True"
    BorderWidth="1pt" BorderStyle="Solid"
    CssClass="theme_highlighted" />
  <PagerStyle ForeColor="#585880" BackColor="#E7E5DB" />
  <FooterStyle ForeColor="#585880" CssClass="theme_header" />
</asp:GridView>
```

Figure 12.10 shows the result of the three control declarations in Listing 12.17, Listing 12.18, and Listing 12.19, including the effects of the CSS styles defined in the stylesheet that is part of this theme.

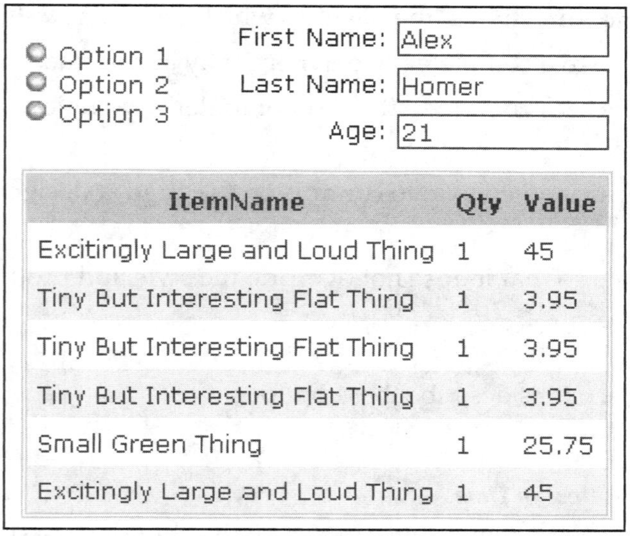

FIGURE 12.10: The effects of the Smoke and Glass example theme

One way to create a set of skins for a theme is to build a page containing the controls you want to generate skins for and style them as required by setting their properties. Then copy the control declarations into your `.skin` file and remove the control ID attributes. Remember that you can only have one default skin for each type of control in your .skin file. If you need more than one skin for a specific control type, you must create named skins by adding a unique SkinID attribute to all except the default skin declaration.

> Note that themes only apply to controls from the `System.Web.UI.WebControls` namespace and associated namespaces such as `System.Web.UI.WebControls.WebParts`.

Applying Themes and Skins

After creating and/or installing your themes, you can apply them to your pages and controls in the following ways, depending on whether you want to apply them at design time or runtime, and the scope that you want them to have:

- Use the <pages> section of the web.config file to specify the theme that applies to a complete site or section of a site.

- Use the @Page directive in the pages to which the theme will apply.
- Apply a theme to a complete page dynamically at runtime.
- Apply a theme to a complete site or set of folders dynamically at runtime.
- Apply a specific named skin to controls on the page at design time or runtime.
- Apply a theme so that it does not override the style and property settings on a control.

The following sections describe these options.

Applying a Theme at Design Time

You can set the theme for all the pages in a site or a subfolder of a site in the <pages> element of the <system.web> section of web.config. All pages in this folder and its subfolders will use the specified theme, unless overridden by another web.config file that specifies a different theme:

```
<system.web>
  <pages theme="SmokeAndGlass" ... />
</system.web>
```

To apply a theme to a specific page, you can declare it in the @Page directive:

```
<%@ page Language= "c#" Theme= "SmokeAndGlass" %>
```

You cannot declare a theme in a master page, though you can do so in the @Page directive of a content page.

Applying a Theme Dynamically at Runtime

If you want to apply a theme at runtime, you must do so in the Page_PreInit event handler for the page. You cannot use the Page_Load event handler, because at this stage ASP.NET has already set the properties for the controls in the page. Listing 12.20 shows a Page_PreInit event handler that sets the theme for the page to the "Smoke and Glass" theme as the page is executing.

Listing 12.20. Setting the Theme for a Page at Runtime

```
protected void Page_PreInit(Object sender, EventArgs e)
{
  Page.Theme = "SmokeAndGlass";
}
```

One problem with this approach is that you cannot change the theme in response to a postback in the usual way, because the values of the controls in the page are not available in the `PreInit` event. However, you can extract a value directly from the `Request` collections (`Form` or `QueryString`) in the `PreInit` event handler and use these to set the theme for the page.

An alternative approach is to apply the theme centrally at runtime using an HTTP handler module. You will see this approach in the example toward the end of this chapter, in the section Using an HTTP Module to Set the Theme, where the theme set depends on a value in the user's profile.

Applying a Named Theme at Design Time or Runtime

To apply a named theme to a control, you specify the `SkinID` of the skin as the `SkinID` property or attribute of the control. For example, to set the theme for a `Textbox` to the skin with SkinID "`MyTextboxSkin`", you would declare the `Textbox` control as:

```
<asp:Textbox runat=server SkinID="MyTextboxSkinID" ... />
```

All other `Textbox` controls on the page that do not specify a `SkinID` property will use the default theme skin (if a theme applies to the page). To set the `SkinID` dynamically, you must do so in the `Page_PreInit` event (see Listing 12.21)—as you do when setting the theme for a page dynamically.

Listing 12.21. Setting the SkinID of a Control at Runtime

```
protected void Page_PreInit(Object sender, EventArgs e)
{
  ThisTextbox.SkinID = "MyTextboxSkin";
}
```

Applying a Theme that Does Not Override Existing Styles and Property Values

By default, when you apply a theme using the Theme property of a page, in web.config, in the @Page directive, or by specifying a SkinID property on a control, the styles in the theme override the settings on the controls so that the theme can provide a consistent appearance over all the controls. If a control defines a property value also defined by the theme, the theme's value overrides the control's property setting.

Themes declared in a @Page directive, or set as the Theme property of a page at runtime, override any conflicting values set in a web.config file. Likewise, any settings in a skin specifically applied using the SkinID property override all other conflicting theme property values.

However, you can apply a theme in such as way that it does not override the existing properties and settings of the controls on a page. To achieve this, set the StyleSheetTheme property instead of the Theme property of the page, either dynamically at runtime or in the @Page directive:

```
<@Page Language="C#" StyleSheetTheme="SmokeAndGlass" ... />
```

If you want to set the StyleSheetTheme of a page dynamically at run-time, you must override the StyeSheetTheme property, as shown in Listing 12.22. You can access the Request collections to extract the required theme name, if required.

Listing 12.22. Setting the StylesheetTheme Property of a Page at Runtime

```
public override String StyleSheetTheme
{
  get { return "SmokeAndGlass"; }
}
```

Preventing the Use of Themes and Skins

Themes are not applied to pages or controls that contain the Enable-Theming="False" attribute, or which set the EnableTheming property to false. This means that you can set the theme for a page or a complete site and then prevent individual controls from using the theme.

If you build custom controls, you can prevent theming of the complete control, or just specific properties, using attributes in the class file that implements the control. To prevent a control or a property of the control from being themed, add the [Themable(false)] attribute to the class or member declaration. Listing 12.23 shows how this attribute can be applied to both the control class and a property of the class. Of course, if the control itself prevents theming, then you do not need the attribute on the individual members of the control.

Listing 12.23. Preventing Theming of a Customer Control with the Themable Attribute

```
[Themable(false)]
public class MyCustomControl : System.Web.UI.WebControl
{
  [Themable(false)]
  public String MyCustomProperty
  {
    get {...}
    set {...}
  }
  ...
}
```

An Example of Using Themes

As an example of how you can use themes, the membership and profiles example you saw in the previous chapter and earlier in this chapter also allows visitors to specify a theme for the site, and it persists this theme in their user profile. The Shopping Cart page in this version of the example contains an extra drop-down list that allows the selection of one of three themes, or "-none-" to remove the current theme. Figure 12.11 shows the page with the "Smoke and Glass" theme applied.

To achieve this, the first step is to add a property to the profile, in the <properties> section of the <profile> element in web.config (see Listing 12.24). Notice that this is an anonymous profile property, so that visitors can specify their preferred theme without having to log in first.

Listing 12.24. Adding the Profile Property for the User's Selected Theme

```
<profile enabled="true" defaultProvider="Sql2005ProfileProvider">
  <properties>
    ...
    <add name="PageTheme" allowAnonymous="true" />
  </properties>
</profile>
```

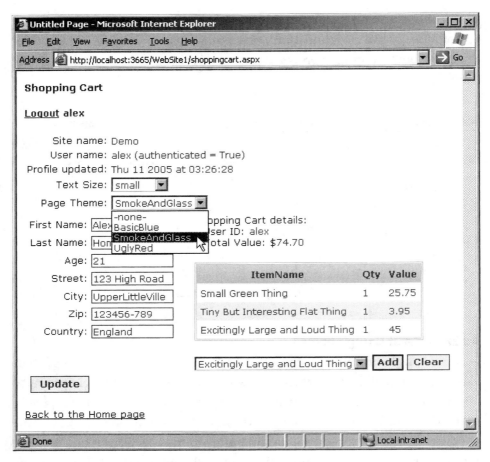

FIGURE 12.11: The Shopping Cart page with a theme applied

Next, a `DropDownList` control on the page allows visitors to select a theme (see Listing 12.25). The value `"-none-"` allows the user to remove the current theme.

Listing 12.25. A Drop-Down List for Selecting a Theme

```
<asp:DropDownList ID="lstPageTheme" runat="server">
  <asp:ListItem Text="-none-" />
  <asp:ListItem Text="BasicBlue" />
  <asp:ListItem Text="SmokeAndGlass" />
  <asp:ListItem Text="UglyRed" />
</asp:DropDownList>
```

Saving and Loading the Theme Profile Value

The code in the page must save the value selected in the drop-down list in the visitor's profile, and must extract it when the page loads to select the appropriate entry in the drop-down list. In the ShowProfileValues routine, which displays the visitor's profile values in the page, this extra line of code sets the drop-down list to the value stored in his or her profile. If there is no value stored there, it remains set to the first item "-none-":

```
lstPageTheme.SelectedValue = Profile.PageTheme;
```

In the UpdateProfileValues routine, which runs when a visitor clicks the **Update** button to save his or her profile settings, this line of code saves the selected theme name (or "-none-") in their profile:

```
Profile.PageTheme = lstPageTheme.SelectedValue;
```

Then it is just a matter of setting the Theme property of the page to the theme value stored in the current visitor's profile. As you saw earlier in this chapter, you can only do this in the Page_PreInit event. Listing 12.26 shows the code for the Page_PreInit event handler. This extracts the name of the theme from the Request.Form collection using the ID of the drop-down list control, checks that it is not an empty string or the value "-none-", and applies it to the Theme property of the Page.

Listing 12.26. Setting the Page Theme at Runtime in the Page_PreInit Event Handler

```
protected void Page_PreInit()
{
  String pagetheme = Request.Form["lstPageTheme"];
  if ((pagetheme != String.Empty) && (pagetheme != "-none-"))
  {
    Page.Theme = pagetheme;
  }
}
```

However, there is a problem with this approach in that the order of events means that changing the theme in the page using the drop-down list and **Update** button only changes the stored profile value after the Page_PreInit event has completed. Therefore, ASP.NET does not apply the new theme until the next page load.

In addition, if you want the theme to apply to more than one page, as is likely to be the case when visitors select the "look and feel" they want, you must include a `Page_PreInit` event handler in every page. A far better approach to use instead is a central method for applying themes to all the pages within a site or a specific set of subfolders.

Using an HTTP Module to Set the Theme

ASP.NET chains requests for Web pages and the corresponding responses through a series of HTTP modules that carry out various stages of the processing of the request and response, such as authentication, setting profiles, and rendering the page. You can tap into this chain and add your own modules if you wish. You must create a class that implements the `IHttpModule` interface, and then add it to your `web.config` file so that ASP.NET executes it as part of the request process. Listing 12.27 shows the HTTP module used in this example. The class `ApplyProfileToPage`, declared within the `ThemeModule` namespace in Listing 12.27, implements the three methods of the `IHttpModule` interface:

- The `Init` method receives a reference to the current ASP.NET application context. It adds an event handler named `MyPreRequest Handler` to the `PreRequestHandlerExecute` event of the context so that, when ASP.NET raises the `PreRequestHandlerExecute` event just before executing the page, it will call the `MyPreRequest Handler` event handler declared in this module.

- The `Dispose` method is where you would dispose of any non-.NET resources you use in your module, such as database connections and file handles, before the module is destroyed. The example module here has no resources to dispose.

- The `MyPreRequestHandler` routine is the event handler called when ASP.NET raises the `PreRequestHandlerExecute` event. In this routine, the code can access the page being executed and the current user's profile through the current `HttpContext`, extract the value of the `PageTheme` profile property, and apply it to the current page by setting its `Theme` property.

Listing 12.27. An HTTP Module to Set the Theme Property of All Pages

```csharp
using System;
using System.Web;
using System.Web.UI;

namespace ThemeModule
{

  public class ApplyProfileToPage : IHttpModule
  {

    public void Init(HttpApplication context)
    {
      context.PreRequestHandlerExecute += MyPreRequestHandler;
    }

    public void Dispose()
    {
      // do nothing
    }

    private void MyPreRequestHandler(Object sender, EventArgs e)
    {
      // get a reference to the current page
      Page p = HttpContext.Current.Handler as Page;

      if (p != null)
      {
        // get current profile as a ProfileCommon instance
        ProfileCommon pc = (ProfileCommon)HttpContext.Current.Profile;

        // set the Theme property of the page to the value
        // in the current user's profile PageTheme property
        p.Theme = pc.PageTheme;
      }
    }

  }

}
```

The result is that, when ASP.NET executes any page where this module is loaded into the application, the Theme property will already be set to the name of the theme stored in the current user's profile. Therefore, the only thing that remains is to arrange for ASP.NET to load this module as part of the application. This just requires an entry in the <httpModules> section of the web.config file for the application, as shown in Listing 12.28.

Listing 12.28. Adding the HTTP Module to web.config

```
<system.web>
  ...
  <httpModules>
    <add name="myThemeModule" type="ThemeModule.ApplyProfileToPage" />
  </httpModules>
  ...
</system.web>
```

There are two minor changes required to the Shopping Cart page to accommodate the new HTTP module. First, because the module simply applies the value of the PageTheme profile property to the page, the code in the Update ProfileValues routine that sets the value of this profile property when the user clicks the **Update** button must look for the value "-none-" and set the profile property value to an empty string in this case.

Second, because the HTTP module executes before the page itself, changing the profile value in the UpdateProfileValues routine will not cause the new theme to apply until the following page load. Therefore, when the user does change and save the value of the theme he or she wants to use, the UpdateProfileValues routine must cause another postback so that ASP.NET applies the newly selected theme. Listing 12.29 shows the corresponding section of the UpdateProfileValues routine with these changes implemented.

Listing 12.29. Changes to the UpdateProfileValues Routine to Set the Selected Theme

```
...
// update the page theme if it has changed
String oldTheme = Page.Theme;
String newTheme = lstPageTheme.SelectedValue;
if (newTheme == "-none-")
{
  newTheme = String.Empty;
}
if (newTheme != oldTheme)
{
  Profile.PageTheme = newTheme;
  // need to reload page to pick up new theme
  Response.Redirect(Request.Path, true);
}
...
```

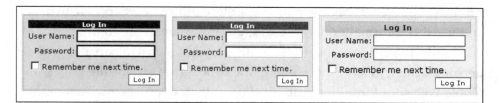

FIGURE 12.12: The effects of the three themes on the Login page

Because the screenshots in this book are not printed in color, it is difficult to see the detailed differences in appearance of the controls in the pages of the example. However, Figure 12.12 shows the Login control on the Login page of the site with the effects of the three themes in this example. This page is unchanged from the previous versions of the example, and yet by applying a theme across the entire site through an HTTP module, it changes to reflect the user's selected theme. This is a good indication of the power of themes for customizing your applications.

SUMMARY

This chapter closely follows the previous chapter in that it continues the discussion and demonstrates the usage of the security, membership, roles, profiles, and personalization features of ASP.NET. In the previous chapter, you saw how to set up, manage, and use membership and roles to control access to all or parts of your Web sites and Web applications. In this chapter, you saw how the underlying user identity and authentication features support other high-level capabilities such as profiles and personalization.

This chapter looked specifically at profiles and their usage for "personalization" in its most generic sense—allowing anonymous visitors and registered users to change the appearance and behavior of a site. However, personalization in its more exact definition in ASP.NET refers to a specific set of features that apply generally only to Web Parts. You will see more about this in the next chapter.

What you have seen here, however, is how you enable and configure both profiles and personalization. After that, the chapter concentrated on the profile features of ASP.NET by demonstrating how you create a set of profile properties, apply them to users, store information specific to users, and use this information when users revisit the site in the future.

Finally, the chapter concluded with a look at a specific area of general personalization in terms of changing the appearance of controls, pages, and whole Web sites through the application of themes and skins. Themes and skins are not specifically part of the profile or personalization features of ASP.NET, because you can use them just to create the desired appearance for your site or application without implementing any of the other features in this or the previous chapter. However, they do work well as part of the profiles system by allowing visitors to choose the look and feel they want.

■ 13 ■
Building Web Portals

C USTOMIZATION IS A BIG TOPIC in application development. Users like to be able to change the layout, appearance, and behavior of their applications—fine-tuning them to better suit their business practices and working preferences. However, while this customization capability has become common in mainstream applications such as Microsoft Office and Windows itself, Web sites that support this type of feature are still quite rare, although sites such as MSN and the Microsoft Live site (http://www.live.com/) are using customization heavily.

But all that changes in ASP.NET 2.0, as you've seen with the personalization features in the previous chapter. In this chapter, you'll see even more ways that users can customize their views of your Web applications and Web pages, using the Microsoft Portal Framework and the technology underlying it, WebParts. We'll be looking at:

- The portal framework that is now a fundamental part of ASP.NET 2.0
- What WebParts are and how you can use them in your pages
- How you can control the WebParts
- How you can allow the user to customize WebParts
- How you can connect WebParts together

We start with a look at what WebParts and the portal framework actually are and how they relate to building portal-style applications with ASP.NET 2.0 (and on different software platforms as well).

The ASP.NET 2.0 Portal Framework

In reality, the home page of any Web site or Web application is a "portal" to that site or application. In general, the home page carries things like news, information, and of course links to the other pages that make up the content of the site or application. However, the term "portal" has increasingly become associated with pages that offer a modularized view of information. This is one of the main aims of Microsoft SharePoint and other similar content management systems.

The ASP.NET 2.0 WebParts technology is designed to make this kind of page and application easy to build, often without requiring the developer to write any code.

The Goals of the Portal Framework

WebParts is not a brand-new technology, and in some ways it combines existing development efforts in an attempt to provide a general solution. The goals for the technology are to:

- Provide a robust framework for Web pages and applications that support modular content and can be customized by end users.
- Expose a programming model that is easy to understand and use, that requires no code to be written for most types of pages, and that is capable of providing support for more complex scenarios as well.
- Provide a rich user experience where this is supported by the client's software, plus safe fallback support for other clients.
- Be easy to configure for individual users and groups of users, and easy to tie in with the underlying personalization features of ASP.NET 2.0.
- Support the growth in WebParts technology that is happening outside ASP.NET, for example, in SharePoint, Content Management Server, and Office 2003, by establishing a foundation of a single portal technology for use across all Microsoft applications.
- Provide full support and integration for third-party WebParts and assemblies to be used, expose backward compatibility as far as possible, and offer a migration path for other existing technologies.

- Meet the performance demands of portal applications, which often experience bursts of high usage (such as when a group of users all start work at the same time).

Integration with SharePoint and Office WebParts

One important aim of the new ASP.NET WebParts technology is to allow it to be extended within SharePoint and other Microsoft applications, as well as to provide support for existing WebParts. WebParts have been around for a few years, in products like the Digital Dashboard and Content Management Server, and in the future, the ASP.NET 2.0 WebPart Framework will become the foundation of the next version of SharePoint, providing a great opportunity for WebParts to be shared among applications.

Customization and Personalization

The WebParts technology provides built-in capabilities for customizing the display. This is integrated with the ASP.NET personalization features so that the settings are persisted on a per-user or shared basis and automatically retrieved the next time that user logs in again. Whether personalization is stored on a per-user basis, or shared among all users, is termed the scope.

As an example of the customization features, the screenshot in Figure 13.1 shows how a rich client (Internet Explorer 6) allows the user to enter design mode and change the layout of the modules on the page by simply dragging them from one place to another.

WebParts technology implements all the customization processes automatically and many other features as well. You can minimize or "roll up" a WebPart so that only the title bar is visible. And, as you'll see in the example page shown in this chapter, you can easily expose features that allow the user to edit the appearance and behavior of individual WebParts, open dedicated Help windows for each one, close or hide individual Web-Parts, and add new WebParts to the page.

It all looks like a complex process, and it certainly does produce a page containing features that would take considerable developer effort to achieve from scratch. Yet the example in Figure 13.1, which we'll discuss in more depth shortly, contains only declarative content (ASP.NET server controls) and requires almost no server-side code to be written.

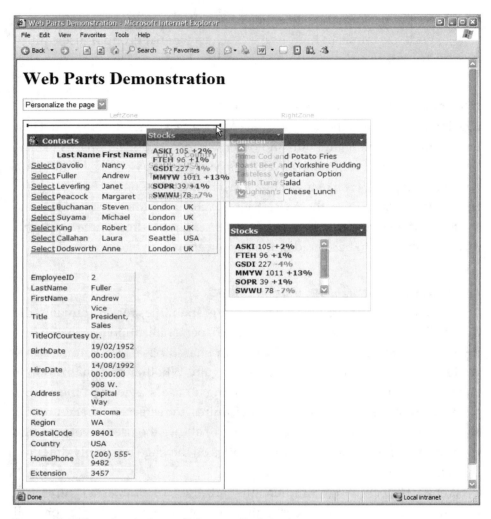

FIGURE 13.1: Changing the layout in Internet Explorer 6

About the WebParts Framework

The WebParts technology is exposed through a series of ASP.NET server controls. In combination, they work together to generate the kind of output and feature set you saw in the previous screenshot. Underneath, the source for the page builds up a structured hierarchy of objects from the server control declarations. Figure 13.2 shows that structure.

We'll be looking at each of these objects in detail as we progress through the chapter, seeing how they fit into the overall design of portals.

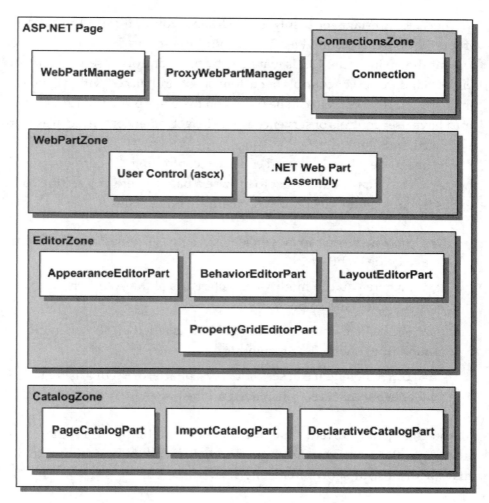

FIGURE 13.2: The object structure for a WebParts portal page

The WebPart Manager

The WebPartManager object is the operation controller for all WebParts on a page, and any page that has WebParts must have a WebPartManager. You place a single instance on the page, and the manager will maintain a list of WebParts and zones, manage the page state and personalization, and manage the communication between WebParts. At it's simplest you just have to add the control to the page:

```
<asp:WebPartManager ID="WebPartManager1" runat="server" />
```

The WebPartManager displays no UI, and you don't need to set any properties; it manages the WebParts behind the scenes for you. All of the content shown in Figure 13.1 is managed by user controls or server controls (either standard server controls or custom ones), and placed within "zones" on the page. Other content can be placed on the page, but within zones you must have user controls or server controls (in fact, other content such as text is allowed, but ignored).

The one place where you need code is in controlling the current state of the page. The default state is just to browse a page, where you see the content as is, but to allow customization there are other states:

- `Design`, where you can move WebParts between zones, and minimize or even hide WebParts.

- `Edit`, where you can modify characteristics of the WebParts, such as borders, titles, and so on.

- `Connect`, where you can connect WebParts together, allowing information from one to flow to another.

- `Catalog`, where you can see hidden WebParts, or WebParts that are available but that aren't displayed on the page.

You change the current state of the page by setting the `DisplayMode` property of the `WebPartManager` to a set value, and the easiest way to do this is with a list, as shown in Listing 13.1.

Listing 13.1. A WebPart Page Customization Menu

```
<asp:DropDownList ID="WebPartMenu" runat="server"
AutoPostBack="true" OnSelectedIndexChanged="MenuChanged">
<asp:ListItem value="EditDisplayMode"
  Text="Personalize the page" />
<asp:ListItem value="BrowseDisplayMode"
  Text="Browse the page" Selected="true" />
<asp:ListItem value="CatalogDisplayMode"
  Text="Show Catalog" />
<asp:ListItem Value="ConnectDisplayMode"
  Text="Connect WebParts" />
<asp:ListItem Value="DesignDisplayMode"
  Text="Design the page" />
</asp:DropDownList>
```

Within the postback event, you set the `DisplayMode` property, as seen in Listing 13.2.

Listing 13.2. Setting the DisplayMode of the Page

```
protected void MenuChanged(object sender, EventArgs e)
{
  switch (WebPartMenu.SelectedValue)
  {
  case "DesignDisplayMode":
    WebPartManager1.DisplayMode = WebPartManager.DesignDisplayMode;
    break;
  case "EditDisplayMode":
    WebPartManager1.DisplayMode = WebPartManager.EditDisplayMode;
    break;
  case "BrowseDisplayMode":
    WebPartManager1.DisplayMode = WebPartManager.BrowseDisplayMode;
    break;
  case "CatalogDisplayMode":
    WebPartManager1.DisplayMode = WebPartManager.CatalogDisplayMode;
    break;
  case "ConnectDisplayMode":
    WebPartManager1.DisplayMode = WebPartManager.ConnectDisplayMode;
    break;
  }
}
```

What is interesting about this is that the `DisplayMode` isn't an enumeration; instead the values you use are public static fields of the `WebPartManager`, of type `WebPartDisplayMode`. This allows the mode to set dif-ferent properties depending upon its needs.

You may wish to add intelligence into a menuing system, so that not all options are shown all of the time, or perhaps only certain options are available to certain users. This is important, since personalization is only allowed for authenticated users, so you could easily combine the menu with a `LoginView` control, or even construct the menu in code, using more advanced features of the WebParts to indicate which modes are allowed. For example, consider Listing 13.3, which constructs a menu dynamically.

The `GetCurrentWebPartManager` static method is used to get a reference to the `WebPartManager` on the page. While you can access the `WebPart-Manager` directly, this method proves useful if using a custom server control or a User Control for the menu. The `WebPartManager` has a property called

Listing 13.3. Constructing a WebPart Menu Dynamically

```
_manager = WebPartManager.GetCurrentWebPartManager(Page);
String browseModeName = WebPartManager.BrowseDisplayMode.Name;

// Fill the dropdown with the names of supported display modes.
foreach (WebPartDisplayMode mode in _manager.SupportedDisplayModes)
{
  String modeName = mode.Name;
  // Make sure a mode is enabled before adding it.
  if (mode.IsEnabled(_manager))
  {
    ListItem item = new ListItem(modeName + " Mode", modeName);
    DisplayModeDropdown.Items.Add(item);
  }
}
```

SupportedDisplayModes that contains a collection of modes currently supported, and this takes into account whether the user is authenticated (and if not, then only browse mode is supported). The Name property of each supported mode is then used to construct a ListItem for the menu.

Listing 13.4 shows how the WebPartDisplayMode property can be used to simplify the setting of the DisplayMode, removing the switch statement.

Listing 13.4. Changing the DisplayMode from the Dynamic Menu

```
protected void DisplayModeDropdown_SelectedIndexChanged(
  object sender, EventArgs e)
{
  String selectedMode = DisplayModeDropdown.SelectedValue;

  WebPartDisplayMode mode =
    _manager.SupportedDisplayModes[selectedMode];
  if (mode != null)
    _manager.DisplayMode = mode;

}
```

The approach shown in Listings 13.3 and 13.4 not only simplifies your code, but also abstracts the menu handling into a neat package.

WebParts and Authorization

By default, all users can browse pages with WebParts, but to customize a page, the user must be authenticated. Changing the DisplayMode of the WebPartManager, therefore, is only possible when the user is logged in; an error otherwise occurs. You can protect against this in several ways, including using `User.Identity.IsAuthenticated` before changing the `DisplayMode`.

Authorization for WebPart customization is done in the same way as other authorization, by modifying `web.config`. For example, consider Listing 13.5, which shows the `webParts` section, with subsections for `personalization` and `authorization`. The `authorization` section has the standard `allow` and `deny` elements allowing selection of `users` and `roles` to determine the authorization in place. When specifying `users` or `roles` you also need to specify the `verbs`, which can be one of, or both of, `enterSharedScope` or `modifyState`. You set `enterSharedScope` to indicate if a user or role can enter shared scope—that is, if personalization is shared between users, and `modifyState` if a user or role can modify personalization. In Listing 13.5, only users in the `Admin` roles are allowed to modify the personalization state of the page, and all other users are denied this right.

Listing 13.5. Configuring WebPart Authorization

```
<webParts>
  <personalization>
    <authorization>
      <allow roles="Admin" verbs="modifyState" />
      <deny users="*" verbs="modifyState" />
    </authorization>
  </personalization>
</webParts>
```

This can be used in conjunction with the Authorization Filter and custom code to indicate whether a certain WebPart is valid for the current user. This is discussed more in the Authorization Filter section later in the chapter.

Zones and WebParts

Once you have a menu, you need to decide upon the zones the page will have. A zone is a templated control that references all the WebParts for the current zone and synchronizes the layout, appearance, and colors of these WebParts. An ASP.NET page can contain more than one `WebPartZone`, as seen in Figure 13.3.

Web Parts Demonstration

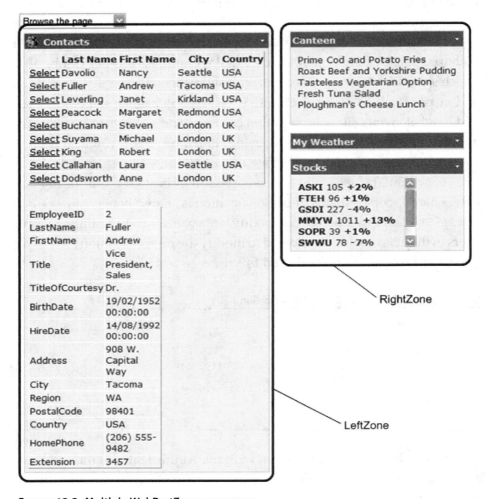

FIGURE 13.3: Multiple WebPartZones on a page

You cannot see the zones when browsing a page, but with any of the other page states, the zones are shown. For example, Figure 13.4, shows a page being designed, and the WebPart Framework shows the zones so that you can easily see where the drag and drop points are.

A `WebPartZone` declaration follows the same principles as most other familiar templated controls. It accepts attributes that define the behavior of the

FIGURE 13.4: Zones shown when designing a page

zone and all of the WebParts within the zone, elements that define the style of specific sections of the output, and a `ZoneTemplate` that contains the declaration of the WebParts that will appear in this zone by default (see Listing 13.6).

Listing 13.6. Outline of a Simple WebPartZone Control Declaration

```
<asp:WebPartZone ID="LeftZone" runat="server"
  BorderColor="#CCCCCC" Font-Names="Verdana" Padding="6">
  <PartChromeStyle BackColor="#F7F6F3" BorderColor="#E2DED6"
    Font-Names="Verdana" ForeColor="White" />
  <MenuLabelHoverStyle ForeColor="#E2DED6" />
  <EmptyZoneTextStyle Font-Size="0.8em" />
  <MenuLabelStyle ForeColor="White" />
  <MenuVerbHoverStyle BackColor="#F7F6F3" BorderColor="#CCCCCC"
    BorderStyle="Solid" BorderWidth="1px" ForeColor="#333333" />
  <HeaderStyle Font-Size="0.7em" ForeColor="#CCCCCC"
    HorizontalAlign="Center" />
  <MenuVerbStyle BorderColor="#5D7B9D" BorderStyle="Solid"
    BorderWidth="1px" ForeColor="White" />
  <PartStyle Font-Size="0.8em" ForeColor="#333333" />
  <TitleBarVerbStyle Font-Size="0.6em" Font-Underline="False"
    ForeColor="White" />
  <MenuPopupStyle BackColor="#5D7B9D" BorderColor="#CCCCCC"
    BorderWidth="1px" Font-Names="Verdana" Font-Size="0.6em" />
  <PartTitleStyle BackColor="#5D7B9D" Font-Bold="True"
    Font-Size="0.8em" ForeColor="White" />
  <ZoneTemplate>
    ... WebParts for this zone are referenced here ...
  </ZoneTemplate>
</asp:WebPartZone>
```

Bear in mind that the layout of the WebParts in the page may be different when the page is actually displayed. If this is a postback, and editing of the page layout is enabled, the user may have moved WebParts from one zone to another. Likewise, if personalization is enabled for the page, WebParts may appear in a different zone from the original location.

WebParts

As mentioned earlier, you can only have two kinds of controls within a `WebPartZone`:

- Standard ASP.NET User Controls (referenced through a `Register` directive in the page), which can contain HTML, markup, dynamic content, or any other content available for use in a Web page
- Compiled .NET assemblies (referenced through a `Register` directive in the page), which generate the same kinds of content as a User Control or Web page

The controls are placed within the zones just like they would be on any other page. For example, consider Listing 13.7, which shows two zones with a variety of controls. The `Contacts`, `Canteen`, and `Stocks` are User Controls, while the `MSNWeatherWebPart` is a custom server control, from code in the `App_Code` folder.

The design time experience of WebParts is excellent, as seen in Figure 13.5, where the zones appear as containers and can be placed anywhere on the page (those in the figure have CSS styling applied for their layout). Within the zones, the WebParts can be placed using tables, CSS, or just in straight flow mode.

By just placing these controls within the zone, they automatically become WebParts. This means that they automatically inherit the functionality of WebParts, such as having a title bar, the minimize, close, and editing buttons (depending upon the page mode). Each WebPart within a zone can be moved around either within the zone or to other zones, or minimized or closed (assuming the WebPart allows it). One thing you may notice is that in Source view of the page, the User Controls for the Canteen and Stocks show a validation warning on their `Title` attribute. This is because a User Control doesn't have a `Title` attribute, but at runtime any control placed within a

Listing 13.7. Placing Controls within a WebPartZone

```
<%@ Page Language="C#" ... %>

<%@ Register Src="canteen.ascx" TagName="canteen" TagPrefix="uc2" %>
<%@ Register Src="stocks.ascx" TagName="stocks" TagPrefix="uc3" %>
<%@ Register Src="Contacts.ascx" TagName="ctcs" TagPrefix="uc1" %>
<%@ Register tagprefix="sample" namespace="Sample.Web.UI" %>
...

  <asp:WebPartZone ID="LeftZone" runat="server">
    <ZoneTemplate>
      <uc1:ctcs ID="Contacts1" runat="server" />
    </ZoneTemplate>
  </asp:WebPartZone>

  <asp:WebPartZone ID="RightZone" runat="server">
    <ZoneTemplate>
      <uc2:canteen ID="Canteen1" runat="server" Title="Canteen" />
      <uc3:stocks ID="Stocks1" runat="server" Title="Stocks" />
      <sample:MSNWeatherWebPart runat="server" ID="mWeatherWebPart"
        Title="MSN Weather" />
    </ZoneTemplate>
  </asp:WebPartZone>
```

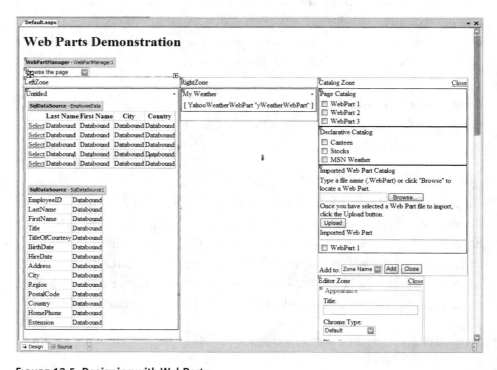

FIGURE 13.5: Designing with WebParts

`WebPartZone` automatically inherits properties of a `WebPart`, one of which is `Title`. So at design time you get a warning, but at runtime the `Title` property is part of the User Control.

Another feature that WebParts automatically get is the user experience when users design a page. Any WebPart can be moved around the page, as seen in Figure 13.1. When the page is in design mode, you simply drag the title bar of a WebPart and drop it into its new location. In design mode, the zones are shown and an insert mark is dynamically placed, showing you where the WebPart would be placed when you drop it. You don't have to provide any code or functionality for this to work because it's provided by the WebParts framework.

Implementing WebParts

User Controls make excellent WebParts, but you may find you need more control over how the control is displayed in a zone. Or perhaps you wish to deploy a WebPart to multiple applications, or even to third parties, in which case you will probably consider writing a custom server control. Or perhaps you simply want to avoid the validation warning, or would like control over the default properties of a WebPart. If so, then you can implement the `IWebPart` interface and set the properties yourself, either within User Controls or custom server controls.

User Controls as WebParts

For a User Control, you can implement `IWebPart` by modifying the code-behind class, like this:

```
public partial class Contacts : System.Web.UI.UserControl, IWebPart
```

You then need to implement the properties defined by the interface. You can do this manually or have Visual Studio implement defaults for you. When you have typed `IWebPart`, a small `SmallTask` appears just underneath the `I`, allowing you to select from one of two implementation methods (see Figure 13.6); selecting one will add the stub properties and methods that the interface requires. For the `IWebPart` interface, there are only properties, which are:

- `CatalogIconImageUrl`, defines the URL of an image that identifies the WebPart in a catalog (more on catalogs later)

- `Description`, defines the description for the WebPart
- `Subtitle`, defines the subtitle for the WebPart. The subtitle is concatenated with the `Title` property
- `Title`, defines the title of the WebPart
- `TitleIconImageUrl`, defines the URL of the image that appears in the WebPart's title bar
- `TitleUrl`, defines the URL that identifies additional information about the WebPart

Listing 13.8 shows the implemented properties for the Contacts user control. These simply define the default values for this WebPart, and users can change them if they personalize the page.

Implementing the `IWebPart` interface isn't required for user controls but does give you a greater degree of control over the default values for properties.

Custom Controls as WebParts

The other way of implementing WebParts is to write a custom server control, and in this case you inherit from `WebPart`, which provides the base implementation for WebParts. The MSN Weather WebPart is extremely simple, because it simply writes out some controls and client script that fetches the weather from MSN. The code is shown in Listing 13.9.

This code shows a standard server control, which renders out some content that just happens to consist of HTML and JavaScript. The `ZipCode` property identifies the region to show the weather for; later in the chapter you'll see how this property can be replaced by a connection to other WebParts so that the `ZipCode` is automatically supplied.

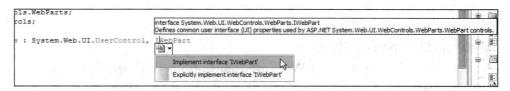

FIGURE 13.6: Automatically implementing interfaces

Listing 13.8. The Contacts User Control WebPart Properties

```csharp
private string _catalogIconImageUrl = "~/images/contact.gif";
private string _description = string.Empty;
private string _subtitle = string.Empty;
private string _title = "Contacts";
private string _titleIconImageUrl = "~/images/contact.gif";
private string _titleUrl = string.Empty;

public string CatalogIconImageUrl
{
  get { return _catalogIconImageUrl; }
  set { _catalogIconImageUrl = value; }
}

public string Description
{
  get { return _description; }
  set { _description = value; }
}

public string Subtitle
{
  get { return _subtitle; }
}

public string Title
{
  get { return _title; }
  set { _title = value; }
}

public string TitleIconImageUrl
{
  get { return _titleIconImageUrl; }
  set { _titleIconImageUrl = value; }
}

public string TitleUrl
{
  get { return _titleUrl; }
  set { _titleUrl = value; }
}
```

WebPart Chrome and Style

The non-content areas of a WebPart (the border, title bar, open/close/ minimize buttons, and so on) are together referred to as the chrome of the window. The individual buttons and command links on the title bar of a

Listing 13.9. The MSN Weather WebPart

```
public class MSNWeatherWebPart : WebPart
{
  private const string HtmlFormat = @"
          <div id=""weatherView""></div>
          <script id=""weatherScript""
            language=""javascript""></script>
          <script language=""javascript"">
          function CreateWeather(sAcid) {{
            var oData = window['weatherScript'];
            if (sAcid != '') {{
                    oData.onreadystatechange = ShowWeather;
                    oData.src =
  'http://www.msnbc.com/m/chnk/d/weather_d_src.asp?acid='
  + sAcid;
            }}
          }}

          function ShowWeather() {{
              if (typeof(makeWeatherObj) != 'undefined') {{
                          var oWea = new makeWeatherObj();
              var sTmp =
  '<b>Current Weather Conditions</b><hr size=1>' +
  '<table cellpadding=2 cellspacing=0 border=0><tr>' +
  '<td valign=""middle"">' +
  '<img src=""http://www.msnbc.com/m/wea/i/36/' + oWea.swCIcon +
  '.gif"" align=absmiddle></td>' +
  '<td>'+ oWea.swCity + ', ' + oWea.swSubDiv + '<br>' +
  oWea.swTemp + '&#176;F</td></tr></table>' +
  '<a href=""http://www.weather.com"">More weather information</a>';
  document.all['weatherView'].innerHTML = sTmp;
              }}
          }}

          CreateWeather('{0}');
          </script>
          ";

  private string _zipCode;
  public string ZipCode
  {
    get {return _zipCode;}
    set {_zipCode = value;}
  }

  protected override void Render(System.Web.UI.HtmlTextWriter writer)
  {
    writer.Write(String.Format(HtmlFormat, _zipCode));
  }
}
```

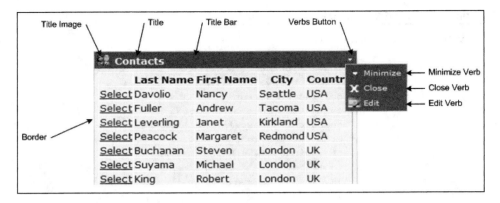

FIGURE 13.7: WebPart chrome and style

WebPart, and the links available in a drop-down list from the title bar of each WebPart, execute actions that are implemented by the WebParts technology. These buttons or links, their appearance, and the actions they execute are defined as a series of individual verbs, as shown in Figure 13.7.

The chrome for a WebPart can be changed, either within the WebPart itself, or in the zone, in which case all WebParts inherit the same chrome. For example, consider Listing 13.10, which shows the definition for a zone. There are elements allowing definitions for the various verbs—the actions that can take place on the WebParts in the zone. In this example, each verb defines an image to show alongside the title, and to set a description for the verb, which shows as a tooltip. Each verb also has an associated style, allowing the look to be altered.

Listing 13.10. Changing the Chrome of WebParts

```
<asp:WebPartZone ID="LeftZone" runat="server" style="float:left;">
  <ZoneTemplate>
    <uc1:Contacts ID="Contacts1" runat="server" />
  </ZoneTemplate>
  <CloseVerb ImageUrl="~/Images/CloseVerb.gif"
    Description="Removes the WebPart from the page" />
  <MinimizeVerb ImageUrl="~/Images/MinimizeVerb.gif" />
  <RestoreVerb ImageUrl="~/Images/RestoreVerb.gif" />
  <EditVerb ImageUrl="~/Images/EditVerb.gif"
    Description="Edit the properties of the WebPart" />
  <MenuVerbStyle BorderColor="#5D7B9D" BorderStyle="Solid"
    BorderWidth="1px" ForeColor="White" />
</asp:WebPartZone>
```

The chrome can be set in each page, on each zone, or by way of themes (see Chapter 12 for more on themes), allowing you to remove the presentation of the WebParts from the page that includes them. This allows the pages to remain clear and easy to read, so that you don't get bogged down by lots of styling.

Styling can be performed either in code or using the **AutoFormat** option in Design view. There are many styles, covering the WebPart as a whole, the chrome, the verb menu, the individual items on a verb menu, and so on.

WebPart Verbs

As seen, there are verbs that identify the actions allowable for a WebPart. Not all verbs are available all of the time, because availability depends upon the state of the page. For example, `minimize` isn't visible when the WebPart is already minimized. The allowable verbs are:

- `Close`, to close a WebPart, removing it from the current page and moving it to the page catalog
- `Connect`, to connect the WebPart to another WebPart
- `Delete`, to remove the WebPart from the page; it is not moved to the catalog
- `Edit`, to edit the appearance and layout of the WebPart
- `Export`, to export he properties of a WebPart to a file
- `Help`, to display the help for a WebPart
- `Minimize`, to minimize the WebPart so that only the title is displayed
- `Restore`, to restore a WebPart from its minimized state

Each of these verbs can have their properties set individually, such as the title or an image, and they may cause zones to appear, depending upon the verb selected. Since the verbs are added to WebParts automatically, you don't have to code anything, although if building WebParts as custom server controls, you can interact directly with the verbs and even create your own verbs.

Catalog Zones

By default, users can remove WebParts from a page by clicking the Close link. The closed WebPart can be added back into a page by using a catalog. The catalog holds two sets of WebParts: those that the user has removed from the page (the Page Catalog) and those that are available for use on the page, but weren't declared within a zone (the Declarative Catalog). A catalog is a zone, and it can be placed anywhere on the page. For example, consider Listing 13.11, which shows a `CatalogZone`.

Listing 13.11. Declaring a CatalogZone

```
<asp:CatalogZone ID="CatalogZone1" runat="server">
  <ZoneTemplate>
    <asp:PageCatalogPart ID="PageCatalogPart1" runat="server" />
    <asp:DeclarativeCatalogPart ID="DeclarativeCatalogPart1"
      runat="server">
      <WebPartsTemplate>
        <uc2:canteen ID="Canteen1" runat="server" Title="Canteen" />
        <uc3:stocks ID="Stocks1" runat="server" Title="Stocks" />
        <sample:MSNWeatherWebPart runat="server"
          ID="mWeatherWebPart" Title="MSN Weather" />
      </WebPartsTemplate>
    </asp:DeclarativeCatalogPart>
  </ZoneTemplate>
</asp:CatalogZone>
```

Within the `ZoneTemplate` of the `CatalogZone`, there are two catalog Web-Parts: the `PageCatalogPart` and the `DeclarativeCatalogPart`. The `Page-CatalogPart` shows WebParts that have been removed from the page by the user, and therefore has no other content. The `DeclarativeCatalogPart` shows the parts that are available but that weren't put on the page when it was designed.

The `CatalogZone` only appears when the page is placed into catalog mode, which is when the `DisplayMode` of the `WebPartManager` is set to `WebPartManager.CatalogDisplayMode`. Figure 13.8 shows the Catalog Zone in action. On the left, the Page Catalog is selected, showing the WebParts that the user has removed from the page—in this case, the MSN Weather WebPart. On the right, the Declarative Catalog is selected, where there are three WebParts: Canteen, Stocks, and MSN Weather. At the bottom of the Catalog Zone there is a list of zones into which the selected WebParts can be added.

One point of interest is that the MSN Weather WebPart appears on both the Page and Declarative catalogs. This is because the WebPart wasn't initially on the page but was added from the Declarative Catalog and later closed. Closing a WebPart is different from deleting it, because closure

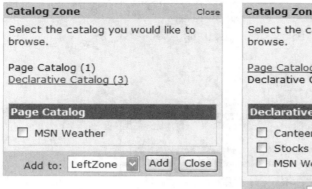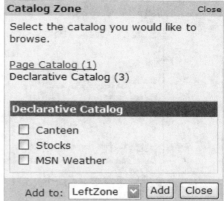

FIGURE 13.8: Displaying the Catalog of WebParts

just adds it to the Page Catalog, whereas deleting the WebPart completely removes it from the page (along with display of an appropriate warning).

Importing and Exporting WebParts

Another—but less frequently used—catalog is the Imported WebPart Catalog, which allows you to import WebPart declarations stored outside of the catalog. You declare an import catalog by use of the `ImportCatalogPart`, used alongside the `PageCatalogPart` and `DeclarativeCatalogPart`:

```
<asp:ImportCatalogPart ID="import" runat="server" />
```

Selecting the Imported WebPart Catalog (see Figure 13.8) allows you to browse the file system to find exported WebParts. These are XML files with a `.WebPart` suffix that define the properties of the part such as Title, whether minimizing is allowed, and so on.

Importing and exporting of WebParts is primarily used to copy WebParts between pages.

Editor Zones

The Editor zone allows properties and behavior of WebParts to be modified by the user, and is displayed when the `DisplayMode` of the `WebPartManager` is set to `WebPartManager.EditDisplayMode`. The Editor zone displays one

FIGURE 13.9: The Imported WebPart Catalog

or more Editor parts, each of which has a specific function; without any parts (see Figure 13.9), the Editor zone has no function (see Figure 13.10).

There are four Editor parts that can be used in any order that may or may not appear depending upon the capabilities of the WebPart being edited. Changes applied to settings in the Editor zone will be saved with the personalization and thus will persist across sessions. The act of personalization can change the styling of the WebPart being personalized. For example, the `SelectedPartChromeStyle` is applied when a part is being edited:

```
<SelectedPartChromeStyle BorderColor="#A7B756"
  BorderStyle="Dotted" BorderWidth="5px" />
```

This would place a dotted border around the WebPart being edited, making it clear which WebPart is selected.

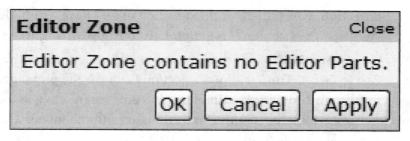

FIGURE 13.10: The Editor Zone (without editor parts)

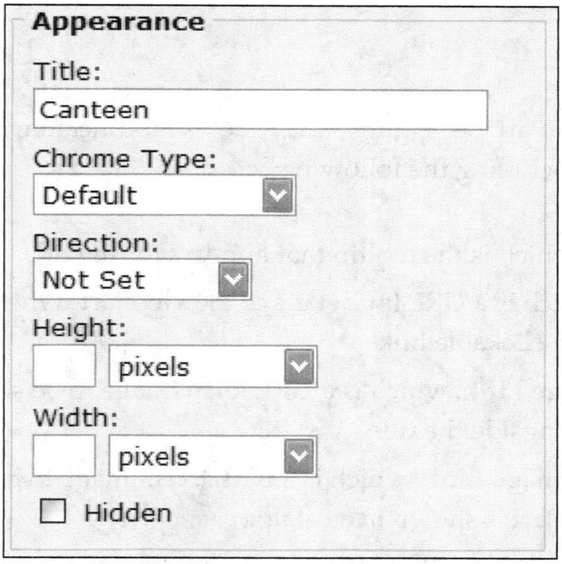

FIGURE 13.11: The Appearance Editor Part

AppearanceEditorPart

The Appearance Editor Part (see Figure 13.11) allows modification of the appearance of the WebPart, including the following:

- **Title**, which is the text appearing in the title bar
- **Chrome Type**, which is the titling and bordering. A drop-down list allows you to select from **Default, Title and Border, Title Only, Border Only, None**

- **Direction**, which dictates the direction of text flow within the WebPart. The list allows **Not Set, Left to Right,** or **Right to Left**

- **Height and Width**, which allow the height and width of the Web-Part to be set. The list allows selection from **pixels, picas, points, inches, millimeters, centimeters, percent, em** (relative to the parent element's font), **ex** (relative to the height of the character x of the parent element's font)

- **Hidden**, which allows the WebPart to be hidden when in display mode but visible when in edit mode

BehaviorEditorPart

The Behavior Editor Part (see Figure 13.12) allows modification of how the WebPart behaves, including the following:

- **Description**, which is the tooltip that appears for the title

- **Title Link**, which is a URL for details of the WebPart. When set, the Title becomes a clickable link

- **Title Icon Image Link**, which is a URL to an image to be shown in the title bar alongside the title

- **Catalog Icon Image Link**, which is a URL to an image to be shown when the WebPart is shown in a catalog

- **Help Link**, which is a URL for more help on the WebPart. When set, the Help link is shown in the verbs menu

- **Help Mode**, which defines how the help file is shown, either as a model form (Modal), a modeless form (Modeless), or by directly navigating to the file (Navigate)

- **Import Error Message**, which is the error message to show if an error occurred when importing the WebPart

- **Export Mode**, which defines if exporting is not allowed (Do not allow), or if it is allowed, whether all data (Export all data), or only non-sensitive data (Non-sensitive data only) is exported

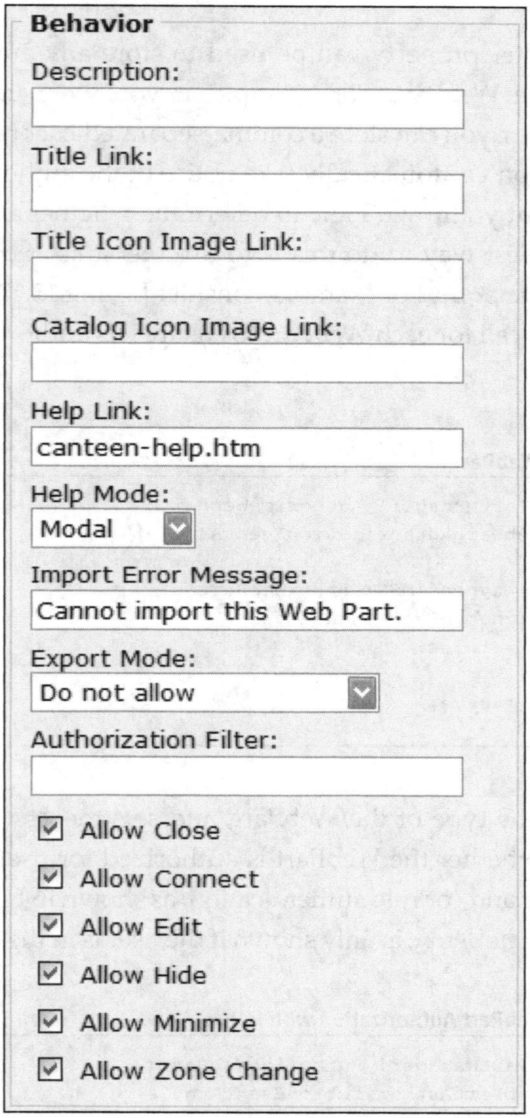

Behavior

Description:

Title Link:

Title Icon Image Link:

Catalog Icon Image Link:

Help Link:
canteen-help.htm

Help Mode:
Modal

Import Error Message:
Cannot import this Web Part.

Export Mode:
Do not allow

Authorization Filter:

☑ Allow Close

☑ Allow Connect

☑ Allow Edit

☑ Allow Hide

☑ Allow Minimize

☑ Allow Zone Change

FIGURE 13.12: The Behavior Editor Part

- **Authorization Filter**, which indicates the authorization for this WebPart. See the Authorization Filter section for more details. **Allow___ (Close, Connect, Edit, Hide, Minimize**, and **Zone Change)** indicate which verbs appear on the verbs menu and whether the WebPart can be moved between zones

Authorization Filter

The Authorization Filter property can be used to store any authorization information about the WebPart. For example, if you want to authorize WebParts based on roles, you can store a comma-separated list of role names. However, WebParts don't automatically take notice of the authorization, so you have to implement your own logic to determine whether a WebPart is authorized. The simplest way to do this is to use the `AuthorizeWebPart` event of the `WebPartManager`. For example, consider Listing 13.12, which the `WebPartManager` will call for each WebPart to ensure it is authorized for use on the page.

Listing 13.12. Authorizing WebParts

```
protected void WebPartManager1_AuthorizeWebPart(
   object sender, WebPartAuthorizationEventArgs e)
{
   Type msnWeather = typeof(MSNWeatherWebPart);
   if (e.Type.IsAssignableFrom(msnWeather))
     e.IsAuthorized = false;
   else
     e.IsAuthorized = true;
}
```

This code checks the type of the WebPart, and sets the `IsAuthorized` property to indicate whether the WebPart is authorized for use. You could combine this with user and/or role authentication, as shown in Listing 13.13, where the `MSNWeatherWebPart` is only shown if the user is in the `Admin` role.

Listing 13.13. Combining WebPart Authorization with Roles

```
protected void WebPartManager1_AuthorizeWebPart(
   object sender, WebPartAuthorizationEventArgs e)
{
   Type msnWeather = typeof(MSNWeatherWebPart);
   if (e.Type.IsAssignableFrom(msnWeather) &&
       !User.IsInRole("Admin"))
     e.IsAuthorized = false;
   else
     e.IsAuthorized = true;
}
```

Since this logic is applicable to the `WebPartManager`, you have two options if you want it across multiple pages. The first is to use Master Pages and place the `WebPartManager` and associated code in the Master Page. The second is to derive a class from `WebPartManager` and place the common authorization code in the derived class.

For the page catalog, the `DeclarativeCatalogPart` explicitly checks to see if each WebPart is authorized, and if not, the WebPart is not shown in the catalog. Because the `PageCatalog` only shows WebParts that have been included on the page, no unauthorized WebParts will be shown.

LayoutEditorPart

The Layout Editor Part (see Figure 13.13) defines which zone a WebPart appears in and whether the state of the part is normal or minimized. The Zone Index identifies the order of the WebPart within the zone, with 0 being the first WebPart.

PropertyGridEditorPart

The Property Grid Editor Part shows custom properties of WebParts and is used for exposing custom properties to users. For example, consider a weather WebPart that shows a forecast for a few days and displays this as a series of images in a table. You can offer the user a choice of whether the images are horizontally or vertically aligned. Within the WebPart, this would be defined as a public property, perhaps as an enumeration. Consider Listing 13.14, where the property is called `Orientation`, using the `Weather-Orientation` for the allowable options. To ensure this is exposed to the property grid, the `Personalizable` and `WebBrowseable` attributes are used.

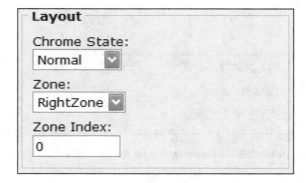

FIGURE 13.13: The Layout Editor Part

Listing 13.14. Exposing Custom Properties in WebParts

```
public enum WeatherOrientation
{
  Horizontal,
  Vertical
};

private WeatherOrientation _orientation =
  WeatherOrientation.Horizontal;

[Personalizable]
[WebBrowsable]
public WeatherOrientation Orientation
{
  get { return _orientation; }
  set { _orientation = value; }
}
```

When this WebPart is edited, the property grid (see Figure 13.14) shows custom properties, as a text box for scalar types, or as a list for enumerations. Changing the orientation changes how the WebPart displays its weather images, giving the user a chance to interact with the WebPart itself.

Connecting WebParts Together

We've used the example of a weather WebPart several times in this chapter, and in early examples this used a `ZipCode` property to state the location to display the weather for. A better solution would be to have the Zip Code supplied to the WebPart, perhaps by another WebPart. This is achieved by WebPart connections, where data can be supplied directly from one part to another.

FIGURE 13.14: Property Grid for the YahooWeatherWebPart

WebPart connection revolves around providers that supply data and consumers that use data. Both providers and consumers use a common interface to define the data being passed between them, and the WebPartManager manages the connection. Figure 13.15 shows the flow of data between the provider and consumer, and how the WebPartManager controls this.

The steps are:

1. The WebPartManager calls a method on the Provider.
2. The WebPartManager receives the provider interface.
3. The WebPartManager passes the interface to the Consumer.
4. The Consumer calls the Provider using the supplied interface.

Implementing WebPart Connections

Implementing connections requires an interface to define the data and for a Provider to implement that interface. The Consumer doesn't need to implement the interface but will require a reference to it, because it is the interface that is used to pass the data.

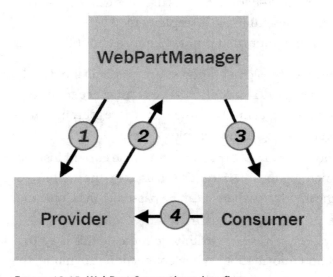

FIGURE 13.15: WebPart Connections data flow

Creating the Interface

The first part of implementing WebPart connections is to create an interface that defines the data. For example, the weather WebPart requires a Zip Code, the interface for which is defined in Listing 13.15.

Listing 13.15. The Zip Code Interface

```
public interface IZipCode
{
   string ZipCode { get; }
}
```

This simply defines a read-only property, `ZipCode`, which is the only piece of data needed. The interface can be more complex, containing properties and methods, providing a great deal of flexibility when connecting Web-Parts.

Implementing the Interface in the Provider

Within the provider, the interface is implemented to supply the data to consumers. In our example, the Contacts WebPart is a Provider and is also a user control. The code-behind for this user control is shown in Listing 13.16, where the `IZipCode` interface is implemented.

There are some important points to notice about this code:

- The interface implementation simply returns the details of a cell from a `DetailsView` control. If your interface requires more information, you simply implement those, perhaps more, properties, or even returning more complex types.

- A method, `ProvideIZipCode`, returns the current instance of the object implementing the interface. This is used by the `WebPartManager` to fetch the interface, where it can be passed to the Consumer.

- The `ProvideIZipCode` method is decorated with the `ConnectionProvider` attribute to indicate this is a Provider of connection information. When connections are made, the values defined in the attribute are used; the first value is the description, and the second is the name of the connection point—the connection point is a specific point within a Provider that provides a connection interface, and giving explicit names allows multiple connection points.

Listing 13.16. Creating the Provider

```
public partial class ch13_Contacts :
    System.Web.UI.UserControl, IWebPart, IZipCode
{
    #region IWebPart Members
    ...
    #endregion

    #region IZipCode Members

    public string ZipCode
    {
        get { return DetailsView1.Rows[10].Cells[1].Text; }
    }

    [ConnectionProvider("Zip Code", "ZipCodeProvider")]
    public IZipCode ProvideIZipCode()
    {
        return this;
    }

    #endregion
}
```

Using the Interface in the Consumer

Within the Consumer, the interface isn't implemented. Instead, a connection end point is defined that accepts an instance of the interface, as shown in Listing 13.17.

Listing 13.17. Consuming the Connection Interface

```
private IZipCode _provider;

[ConnectionConsumer("Zip Code", "ZipCodeConsumer",
    AllowsMultipleConnections=true)]
public void GetIZipCode(IZipCode provider)
{
    _provider = provider;
}
```

Here there is a method that takes a single parameter of type IZipCode—the interface. The WebPartManager receives the interface from the Provider and passes it to the Consumer using this method. In the example code, the interface is simply stored in a variable for later use (which we'll come to in a moment). The Consumer method is also decorated with an attribute, in this case the ConnectionConsumer attribute, the parameters of which are the description, the connection point name, and optionally, whether multiple connections can be made to this end point.

Listing 13.18 shows how the Consumer uses the interface from the Provider. First it is checked for a null value, which would indicate there is no connection in place. If the connection is in place, the property defined by the interface is accessed to fetch the data from the Provider; in this example it is used to format a query to the Yahoo weather RSS feed, which supplies a forecast for several days.

Listing 13.18. Using the Data from the Provider

```
if (_provider != null)
{
  string qry = string.Format(
    "http://xml.weather.yahoo.com/forecastrss?p={0}",
    _provider.ZipCode);
```

Once the interface and end points have been defined, you need to connect the WebParts together.

Connecting WebParts Together

Connections between WebParts can be static or dynamic. Static connections are defined by the page creator, while dynamic connections are created by the user at runtime. Static connections are created within the Static-Connections section of the WebPartManager, as shown in Listing 13.19.

The connection details are defined in four properties of the WebPart-Connection:

- ConsumerConnectionPointID, which is the name of the connection point on the Consumer. This is the name defined in the ConnectionConsumer attribute

- `ConsumerID`, which is the ID of the WebPart acting as the Consumer. In this example, it is the custom server control with the ID of `yWeatherWebPart`

- `ProviderConnectionPointID`, which is the name of the connection point on the Provider. This is the name defined in the `ConnectionProvider` attribute

- `ProviderID`, which is the ID of the WebPart acting as the Provider. In this example, it is the User Control with the ID of `Contacts1`

Listing 13.19. Creating Static Connections

```
<asp:WebPartManager ID="WebPartManager1" runat="server"
  Personalization-Enabled="true"
  OnAuthorizeWebPart="WebPartManager1_AuthorizeWebPart">
  <StaticConnections>
    <asp:WebPartConnection ID="connection1"
        ConsumerConnectionPointID="ZipCodeConsumer"
        ConsumerID="yWeatherWebPart"
        ProviderConnectionPointID="ZipCodeProvider"
        ProviderID="Contacts1"
        />
  </StaticConnections>
</asp:WebPartManager>
```

Because this connection is permanent, data will be supplied from the Provider to the Consumer as long as both parts are on the page. For example, consider Figure 13.16, which shows the Contacts and Weather WebParts, which are connected, even though it doesn't appear to be so. The reason is that the data provided is for the DetailsView, and no contact is currently selected.

If a contact is selected, data is available to be provided to the Consumer, so the weather details automatically show.

User-Initiated Connections

You can allow users to connect parts together or to disconnect WebParts (even statically created ones) by using a `ConnectionsZone`, as shown in Listing 13.20.

Listing 13.20. Declaring a ConnectionsZone

```
<asp:ConnectionsZone
  ID="ConnectionsZone1" runat="server" />
```

Figure 13.16: Connected WebParts (with no data selected)

When the `DisplayMode` of the page is set to `ConnectDisplayMode`, the Connect verb is added to the verbs for WebParts. Selecting this displays the `ConnectionsZone`, the contents of which depend upon the current connection state of the WebPart (see Figure 13.17). For a WebPart with no current connections, you would see a message indicating that no connections are present, with a link to create a connection. For example, Figure 13.18 shows the connection zone for a Provider that has no active connections.

For a WebPart with connections, you see the current connections (with an option to delete them), as well as the link to create connections, as shown in Figure 13.19. This shows the Contacts WebPart with a connection to the My Weather WebPart, sending the Zip Code (the description for the data being sent is taken from the `ConnectionProvider` attribute). For providers, the interface has the same layout but with the appropriate name changes (see Figure 13.20).

Whether on a Provider or Consumer, clicking Disconnect will remove the connection between the WebParts. Clicking the **Connect** link allows connection to a WebPart. For example, Figure 13.21 shows connecting from the Consumer—getting data from the Contacts WebPart, and Figure 13.22 shows the opposite, connecting from a Provider—sending data to the Weather WebPart.

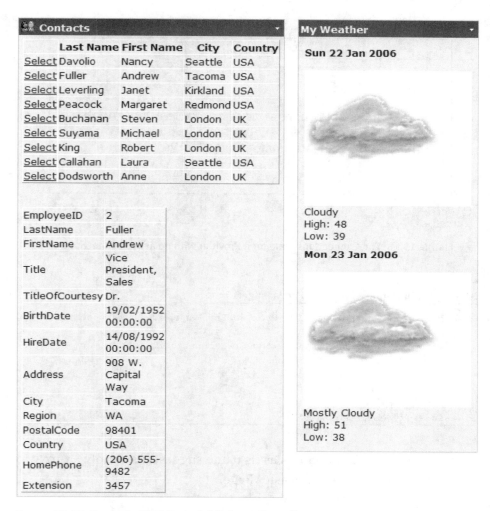

FIGURE 13.17: Connected WebParts (with data selected)

WebParts can be both Providers and Consumers, consuming or supplying data from a number of WebParts.

Connecting to WebParts in Master Pages

When using Master Pages, you will generally have the `WebPartManager` on the Master Page. If you wish to define connections between WebParts on the Master Page and the content page, then you need to use a `ProxyWebPart-Manager` on the content page, as shown in Listing 13.21.

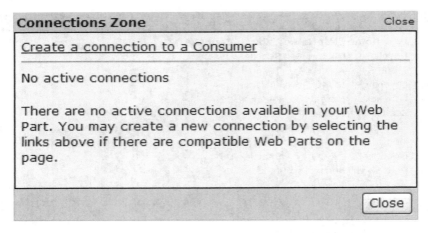

FIGURE 13.18: The Connections Zone for a Provider with no active connections

Listing 13.21. Declaring a ProxyWebPartManager

```
<asp:ProxyWebPartManager ID="ProxyWebPartManager1" runat="server">
  <StaticConnections>
    <asp:WebPartConnection ID="MyFirstConnection"
      ConsumerID="yWeatherWebPart"
      ProviderID="Contacts1">
    </asp:WebPartConnection>
  </StaticConnections>
</asp:ProxyWebPartManager>
```

The `ProxyWebPartManager`, as its name suggests, is simply a proxy to the `WebPartManager` on the Master Page.

Transformers

When connecting WebParts, you obviously aim for flexibility, and perhaps you want a WebPart to either provide or consume a variety of different data types. If writing your own WebParts, this is easy to achieve since you can add the types to the interface, but if using third-party WebParts, you may have to deal with data in formats you aren't expecting. The solution to this is to provide transformers, which transform data from one type to another.

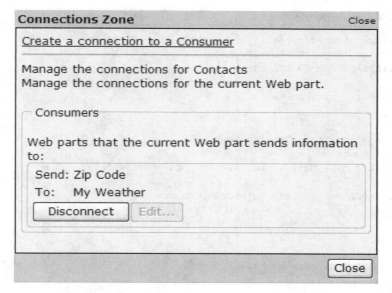

FIGURE 13.19: The Connections Zone for a Provider with active connections

A transformer is a class that converts data between types exposed by interfaces—the interfaces that Consumers and Providers use. For example, consider two WebParts that expose data via interfaces, one of which exposes integer data while the other exposes string data. By default, you would not be able to connect these, because the data types are incompatible. However, by creating a transformer, you can transform the data as it flows between the WebParts. To make this easy to understand, consider two WebParts, one that provides string data, and one that consumes integer data. While it is easy to convert between these two, the principles of a transformer are easier to understand with simple types, and the technique can be applied between any types. For example, consider Listing 13.22, which implements a `Web-PartTrasnformer`, converting data from a string provider to an integer consumer.

The transformer is identified by the `WebPartTransformer` attribute, which defines the type to convert from and the type to convert to. The class inherits from `WebPartTransformer` and implements the `IIntegerData`

Listing 13.22. A Sample Transformer

```
[WebPartTransformer(typeof(IStringData), typeof(IIntegerData))]
public class IntegerToStringTransformer :
  WebPartTransformer, IIntegerData
{
  IStringData _stringData;

  /// <summary>
  /// Transforms from IFoo to IBar
  /// </summary>
  public override object Transform(object providerData)
  {
    _stringData = (IStringData)providerData;
    return this;
  }


  #region IIntegerData Members

  public int IntegerData
  {
    get
    {
      if (_stringData.StringData != null)
      {
        try
        {
          return int.Parse(_stringData.StringData);
        }
        catch { }
      }
      return -1;
    }
  }

  #endregion
}
```

interface—the interface used by the consumer. The `Transform` method
provides access to the string data, and the implementation if the `IInte-
gerData` interface simply converts the data from this interface.

Before a transformer can be used, it must be defined in the `webParts`
`transformers` section of `web.config`. The type should be set to the full
type name of the transformer.

```
┌─────────────────────────────────────────────────────────────┐
│ Connections Zone                                       Close  │
│ ┌───────────────────────────────────────────────────────────┐│
│ │ Create a connection to a Provider                          ││
│ │                                                            ││
│ │ Manage the connections for My Weather                      ││
│ │ Manage the connections for the current Web part.           ││
│ │                                                            ││
│ │ ┌─Providers─────────────────────────────────────────────┐ ││
│ │ │                                                        │ ││
│ │ │ Web parts that the current Web part gets information    │ ││
│ │ │ from:                                                  │ ││
│ │ │ ┌────────────────────────────────────────────────────┐│ ││
│ │ │ │ Get:  Zip Code                                      ││ ││
│ │ │ │ From: Contacts                                      ││ ││
│ │ │ │ ┌──────────────┐ ┌─────────┐                        ││ ││
│ │ │ │ │ Disconnect   │ │ Edit... │                        ││ ││
│ │ │ │ └──────────────┘ └─────────┘                        ││ ││
│ │ │ └────────────────────────────────────────────────────┘│ ││
│ │ └───────────────────────────────────────────────────────┘ ││
│ │                                              ┌─────────┐   ││
│ │                                              │  Close  │   ││
│ │                                              └─────────┘   ││
│ └───────────────────────────────────────────────────────────┘│
└─────────────────────────────────────────────────────────────┘
```

FIGURE 13.20: Connections Zone for a Consumer with active connections

Listing 13.23. Configuring the Transformer

```
<webParts enableExport="true">
  <transformers>
    <add name="String to Integer Transformer"
      type="Sample.Web.UI.IntegerToStringTransformer"/>
  </transformers>
</webParts>
```

At runtime, the transformer is injected into the connection between WebParts, first by allowing the connection to take place (because the transformer converts between incompatible types) and then by providing the actual conversion process. The great point about this is that the technique can be used for converting data from third party WebParts without having to get the third party to expose (or consume) data in a form it doesn't

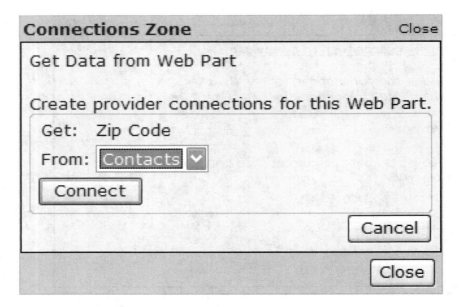

FIGURE 13.21: Connecting to a Provider

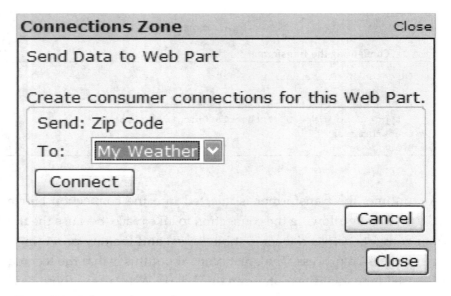

FIGURE 13.22: Connecting to a Consumer

require. You can write the transformer yourself, integrating previously incompatible WebParts.

SUMMARY

In this chapter we have examined the portal framework supported by WebParts in ASP.NET 2.0, an architecture that allows users to customize the look and feel of Web pages. We first looked at what WebParts and portals mean, seeing how WebParts provide concise portions of functionality for sites.

In looking at the framework, we started with the WebPartManager, the control that organizes WebParts on a page and manages how those WebParts can interact with users. We saw that you can provide simple menus to define what customization is allowed, and that authorization can be integrated with WebParts so that certain functionality can be removed for certain users or roles.

We then looked at what WebParts consist of, and that when placing them on a page you use distinct zones to define page areas. Because WebParts can be server controls or user controls, creating WebParts is extremely simple, and if complete control over the WebPart is required, a custom server control can be created. Whichever form of WebPart you use, you have control over how it looks by customizing the look and feel of the zone.

We then looked at the different zones that allow customization. The Catalog Zone allows closed WebParts to be added back into the page, or WebParts to be defined on a page, but not initially seen. The Editor Zone allows customization of the look and feel of WebParts, allowing properties such as the title, whether borders are shown, links for additional information or help, and custom WebPart properties to be changed.

The final topic saw how WebParts can be connected together, allowing data to flow between them. This allows the discrete WebParts to act together as a whole, making a page of WebParts indistinguishable from a page without WebParts. Because this is a more advanced topic, you have to write code to provide the definition of how WebParts connect and what data is available for transfer. We also saw that even if the connection points of WebParts use different data types, you can use transformers to convert between these data types.

Now it's time to look at making Web pages more accessible to a variety of different user types, from those with visual impairments to those with mobile devices or in different countries.

■ 14 ■
Usability, Accessibility, Mobile Devices, Localization

S O FAR, THIS BOOK has concentrated on the features of ASP.NET with respect to developing Web pages and Web applications that generate standard HTML output for the browser. In fact, ASP.NET automatically takes advantage of some of the features of modern browsers. For example, as you saw in earlier chapters, it generates client-side JavaScript code to implement the postback mechanism required by certain kinds of links and other interactive page content.

However, the actual HTML and other content sent to the client has not been something you have concentrated on, assuming that what ASP.NET generates is suitable for all types of browsers and all visitors. This is, unfortunately, not always the case. In most of your applications, you must consider the suitability of the output you generate in terms of both the technical capabilities of the user's browser and the limitations some users encounter when accessing the Web.

This chapter concentrates on the techniques for making your Web sites more suitable for all types of clients. It looks in general at the issues of:

- Detecting the browser's capabilities and providing alternative content
- Specifying extra information that makes your pages easier to use
- Adding features to support disabled users and specialist user agents

- Building pages that work on small-screen and mobile devices
- Building pages that support localization and multiple languages

In fact, the first two of these topics are important in that they provide general assistance to all users and should be a consideration in all the sites you build, regardless of your target audience.

Page Validation, Browser Capabilities, and Alternative Content

It is very easy to build your Web site in ASP.NET, perhaps using an IDE like Visual Studio, and test it only in your favorite browser. In fact, the built-in ASP.NET Web server and automatic launching of the pages in the default browser (Internet Explorer) does little to influence a change in this approach. However, this is a recipe for building browser-specific Web sites. It may even result in sites that are inaccessible to visitors using other browsers or specialist user agents.

It is true that there are only a few types of Web browsers in general use; at the time of writing this book, the bulk of hits on your pages are likely to be from Internet Explorer; Mozilla Firefox; any of a variety of Netscape browsers; and others such as Avant and Opera. All of these support the features required by ASP.NET, such as cookies (to provide support for ASP.NET sessions), client-side script (for link buttons, auto-postback, validation, etc.), and the standard set of HTML elements and CSS styles.

The best solution is to install as many of these browsers on your test system as you can (or run virtual machines) and test your pages in all of them. Doing this quickly reveals any issues that you must solve if you want to provide full support for all browser types. Also bear in mind that most browsers are available for different operating systems. The user may be running the browser on Unix or Linux, or on an Apple computer running a version of MAC-OS. While the browser manufacturers aim to provide the same appearance and enable the same behavior on different operating systems, this goal is not always achieved. The appearance of rendered output certainly varies considerably, so you should test your pages in these circumstances as well, if you can. If not, you may be able to solicit feedback and even screenshots from other users who have access to non-Microsoft environments.

You can obtain the latest browsers from these locations:

- Internet Explorer: **http://www.microsoft.com/windows/ie/**
- Mozilla Firefox: **http://www.mozilla.org/**
- Netscape: **http://browser.netscape.com/**
- Avant: **http://www.avantbrowser.com/**
- Opera: **http://opera.com/**

Validating Page Content

Visual Studio, by default, will check the content of your pages and show any issues by underlining the elements and attributes in Source view. This makes it easy to validate the content against a range of HTML and XHTML schemas. You can choose which level of conformance you require using the drop-down list in the Formatting toolbar. Figure 14.1 shows how, when you

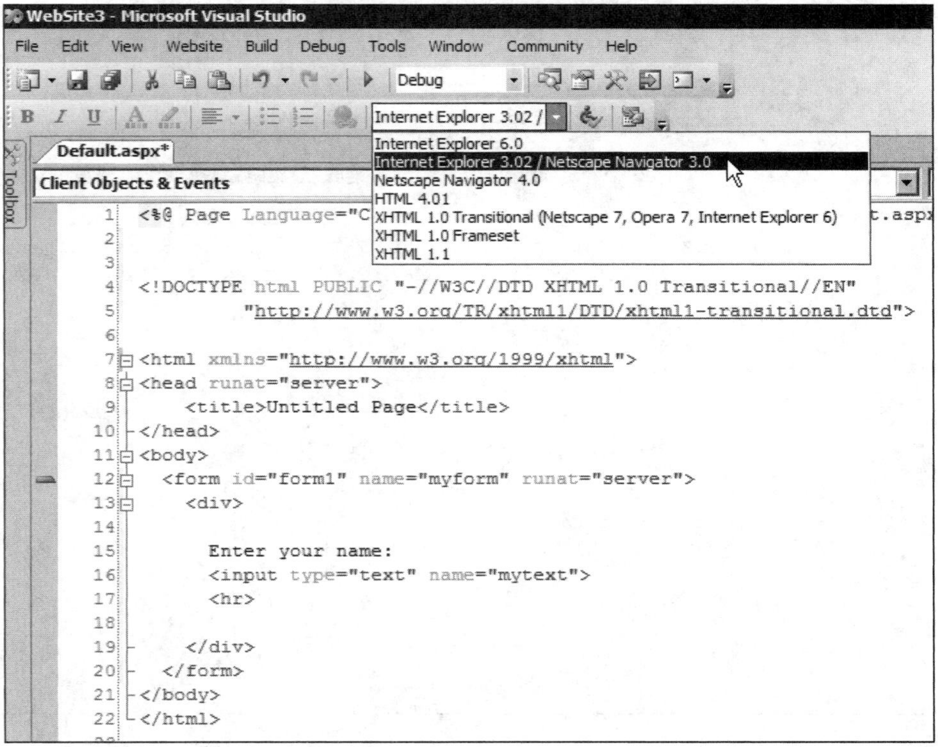

FIGURE 14.1: Validating HTML content against a legacy schema

select a legacy format such as HTML 3.2 for Internet Explorer and Netscape Navigator 3, content that is not valid against the current HTML 4.0 and XHTML schemas is acceptable—there are no warning underlines in the source code.

However, with the default schema, XHTML 1.0 Transitional, warning underlines appear in your HTML source (see Figure 14.2). This schema forces stricter element and attribute structure that more closely conforms to XHTML standards, but it still permits the use of certain HTML 4 attributes.

If you hover over the underlined elements and attributes, Visual Studio shows details of the validation failure and useful tips for fixing the problem. For example, in XHTML, a `<form>` element should not have the `name` attribute—as you can see in Figure 14.3. However, (not visible in this monochrome screenshot), this error is flagged as a warning rather than an error

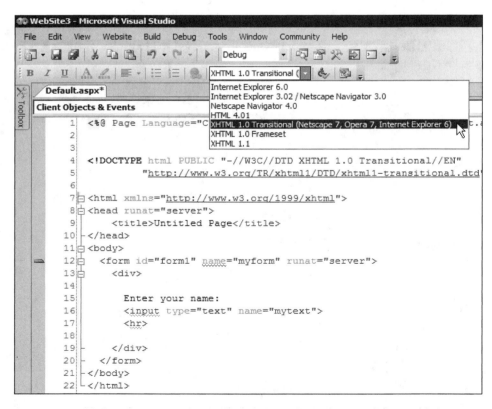

FIGURE 14.2: Validating HTML content against the default XHTML Transitional schema

```
<form id="form1" name="myform" runat="server">
  <div>
             Validation (XHTML 1.0 Transitional): Attribute 'name' is considered outdated. A newer construct is recommended.

    Enter your name:
    <input type="text" name="mytext">
    <hr>
```

FIGURE 14.3: A warning that the <form> element should not have the name attribute

(the underline is purple not red). In the XHTML 1.1 Strict schema, Visual Studio would flag it as an error.

Visual Studio flags other problems in the example as errors (with a red underline), and these must be fixed to make your page compatible with the selected schema. In Figure 14.4, you can see that the single-tag element for a horizontal rule must use the correct empty-element syntax of including a space and a closing backslash, as <hr /> to be considered valid. The same applies to the <input> element above it and to other elements such as <br />.

Other Validation Services

The Visual Studio editor does a good job of helping you write valid HTML; for example, it automatically adds the closing slashes for empty elements and forces you to use them on all ASP.NET Web Control declarations. It also performs some validation of other documents such as CSS stylesheets by providing pop-up lists of valid selector names and by checking the overall structure. However, if you prefer, you can use one of the many external validation services to check your pages and stylesheets.

```
    Enter your name:
    <input type="text" name="mytext">
    <hr>
         Validation (XHTML 1.0 Transitional): Empty elements such as 'hr' must end with />.
  </div>
```

FIGURE 14.4: An error indicating a missing closing slash in an empty element

> The W3C provides both CSS and HTML validation services, and a Web search will locate plenty of others. The W3C CSS stylesheet validation service is at http://jigsaw.w3.org/css-validator/, while the W3C HTML validation service is at http://validator.w3.org/.

XHTML Compliance

ASP.NET allows you to create pages that are compatible with the XHTML specification. While this book does not cover the XHTML standards, some of the effects of specifying the XHTML-compliant format for your pages affect not only the output rendered to the browser, but also the output from page templates. The major issues involved are the following:

- Client script tags render without the `language` attribute and with the `type` attribute.
- Hidden fields, such as those used by viewstate, render within a `div` element whose `display` attribute is set to `none`.
- Input elements render within a `block` element, and therefore there is a `div` element immediately inside the `form` element.
- The form `name` attribute only renders when the `W3CDomVersion`.`MajorVersion` property of the `BrowserCapabilities` class is greater than zero.
- Special characters (such as ampersands, apostrophes, and angle brackets) are encoded in both the attributes and the query strings rendered by controls.

Note, however, that some controls you use in ASP.NET do not always create output that is strictly in conformance with XHTML 1.1. This is because the `target` attribute used in hyperlinks is not valid in XHTML 1.1. The controls where you can set the `target` attribute, such as the `Hyperlink`, `BulletedList`, `ImageMap`, and `TreeView`, will produce XHTML 1.1 conforming output as long as you do not set properties such as `Target` that cause this attribute to appear.

Detecting Browser Capabilities

If you want to build pages that vary their content in some custom way depending on the type of browser each visitor is using, you must be able to detect the browser type or its capabilities within your code. ASP.NET automatically detects the browser type and provides output tailored to the current browser where possible. For example, a `Panel` control renders as a `<div>` for modern browsers, but as a single row, single column table for older browsers that may not support the `<div>` element.

You can hook into this browser detection mechanism, or influence the behavior of ASP.NET, in your pages. In Chapter 9, in the Specifying the Client Target section, you saw how you use the `ClientTarget` property of the `Page` class to specify behavior that overrides the default automatic browser detection process.

Browser Definitions

To detect the browser type, ASP.NET matches the USER-AGENT value sent to the server in the HTTP headers of a client request to a set of browser definition files stored in the `Browsers` subfolder of the main ASP.NET configuration folder. By default, this is:

```
\%WINDIR%\Microsoft.NET\Framework\v2.0.50727\CONFIG\Browsers\
```

The browser definition files follow the general format shown in Listing 14.1.

Listing 14.1. The General Format of a Browser Definition File

```
<browsers>
  <browser id="device-name" parentID="family-type-to-inherit-from">
    <identification>
      <!-- Specifies how to identify this browser -->
    </identification>
    <capture>
      <!-- Specifies additional HTTP header values to match -->
    </capture>
    <capabilities>
      <!-- Specifies capabilities values to set, for example -->
      <capability name="cookies" value="true" />
    </capabilities>
    <controlAdapters>
      <!-- Specifies control adapters to use for this browser -->
    </controlAdapters>
  </browser>
</browsers>
```

There is a file named `Default.browser` that defines the default values and capabilities for the base browser type, and there are files for the more common manufacturer-specific values (such as Internet Explorer and

Mozilla). The `id` and `parentId` attributes in each definition link them to each other, creating a hierarchy of inherited and version-specific settings relevant to each browser.

ASP.NET compiles all these files into a single compact representation when you install the Framework. If you update a definition, you can recompile them manually by running the `aspnet_regbrowsers.exe` utility installed along with the Framework. An interesting possibility arising from this is that automated updates to browser definitions will be much easier to implement and might even become part of the Framework update process in time.

> You can also place browser definition files in the special folder named `App_Browsers` within your application root folder. Also, any browser definitions within a `<browserCaps>` element in a `web.config` file are recognized and merged into the final set of definitions used by the Framework. However, ASP.NET ignores any definitions in the `machine.config` file.

The BrowserCapabilities Class

Although the implementation and operation of the device detection system in ASP.NET is automatic, you can use it in your code to find out about the current browser and change the behavior of your pages, if required. The current `Request` instance (an `HttpRequest`) exposes an instance of the `HttpBrowserCapabilities` class through its `Browser` property. This means that you can write code that interrogates the browser capabilities properties; for example, this code returns the browser name and major version number of the current browser:

```
String details = Request.Browser("Browser")
          + Request.Browser("MajorVersion");
```

There are over a hundred properties for the `HttpBrowserCapabilities` class. Some are not relevant for common tasks, but the majority are useful for detecting all kinds of capabilities. For example, you can detect if a browser supports cookies, frames, color, sound, scripting, and more. For a full list of the properties of the `HttpBrowserCapabilities` class, see http://msdn2.microsoft.com/en-us/library/system.web.httpbrowser capabilities_ members.aspx.

Browser-Specific Pages and Sites, and Client-Side Code Support

One point to bear in mind is that the `HttpBrowserCapabilities` class simply provides information based on the contents of the browser definition files. This means that, for features that the user can turn on and off in their browser, you may not always get accurate results.

For example, the user may have disabled client-side scripting in VBScript and/or JavaScript, turned off display of images, or disabled cookies. If you rely on these features in your pages, you must implement more intrusive detection methods yourself, or use an alternative browser detection scheme. Third-party tools are available to perform browser detection. A good example is BrowserHawk, which automatically updates its own browser definition files to provide accurate detection of new browser types and new versions. It also detects if the user has disabled a range of common browser features. You can find BrowserHawk at **http://www.cyscape.com/products/bhawk/**.

You can also create your own code to detect currently enabled capabilities such as cookies and client-side script. Code like this often relies on an initial page sent to the client (usually `Default.aspx`) that contains both a `<meta>` redirection directive and a client-side script redirection statement. Listing 14.2 shows the `<head>` section of a page containing a `<meta>` redirection directive to a page named `no-script.aspx` that causes the browser to load that page after three seconds. Below this is a client-side script section that contains a function to redirect the browser to the main page in your site. Finally, the opening `<body>` tag contains an `onload` attribute that causes the JavaScript function to execute and open the main site page when the `Default.aspx` page has finished loading:

```
<body onload="jumpScriptEnabled()">
```

If the user has disabled client-side scripting, the browser will load the `no-script.aspx` page, which can display a message indicating that client-side script is required for your site to work correctly. Alternatively, if you have a version of the site that works without client-side script, you could place this URL in the `<meta>` directive to redirect the user to that site. Another approach is to store a value in the user's session indicating that client-side script support is not available and then use this in your site pages to provide alternative features that do not rely on it.

Listing 14.2. Detecting if Client-Side JavaScript Is Enabled

```
<meta http-equiv="refresh" content="3;url=no-script.aspx" />
<script language="JavaScript">
<!--
function jumpScriptEnabled() {
// jump to page using client-side JavaScript - if jump not executed
// then client does not have scripting available or it is disabled
window.location.href = 'mainmenu.aspx';
}
//-->
</script>
```

It is also a good idea to include a `<noscript>` section in your page. Most browsers allow users to disable `<meta>` redirection, and some proxy servers can also prevent this. In these cases, when client-side script is disabled or unavailable, the browser automatically displays the contents of the `<noscript>` section, and you can use this to provide information and links to other sites.

Detecting Cookie Support

Most server-side programming environments depend on cookies to maintain a session for each user. Without this, some features of the ASP.NET framework and some server controls will fail to work correctly. In addition, if you store data in the user's session in your server-side code, you rely on cookie support in client browsers unless you take advantage of the cookieless session support feature in ASP.NET. Fortunately, in modern browsers, there are features that allow users to disable cookie support where it is undesirable (third-party cookies that originate in another site) but retain it for the current site.

However, you can quite easily detect if the current browser supports cookies by adding some simple code to your `Default.aspx` page. All this code has to do is set the value of a session variable, which you can then look for in subsequent pages. If it is not available, you know either that the user entered the site through another page or that the user does not have cookies enabled in his or her browser. Listing 14.3 shows a simple example that redirects the user to a page that requests enabling of cookies and that contains a link to the main site menu page. Alternatively, you could just redirect them to a version of your site that uses cookie-less sessions.

Listing 14.3. Detecting if Cookies Are Enabled

```
In Default.aspx:
<script runat="server">
Sub Page_Load()
  ' put value in session to check for cookie/session
  ' support by looking for it again in the next page
  Session("SessionCheck") = "OK"
End Sub
</script>

In your main site menu page:
<script runat="server">
Sub Page_Load()
  ' look for "sessions-enabled" cookie
  If CType(Session("SessionCheck"), String) > "OK" Then
    Response.Redirect("no-sessions.aspx")
    Response.End()
  End If
End Sub
</script>
```

The cookie-less session feature in ASP.NET uses URL-munging (inserting the session ID into the URL automatically on each page request) to keep track of individual users and maintain their sessions. To enable cookie-less session support, you use the `<sessionState>` element in the `<system.web>` section of `web.config` to specify that ASP.NET should use cookie-less sessions:

```
<sessionState cookieless="true" />
```

For more details, see the section Cookie-less Sessions and Cookie-less Forms Authentication in Chapter 11.

CSS Support Quirks

While, in general, the later versions of all the mainline browsers support all the features required by ASP.NET, there are cases where support for CSS varies between browsers. For example, Internet Explorer and Mozilla vary from the W3C recommendations for CSS support in a few small areas, while Opera does not behave the same way as these two browsers for issues such as dynamic element positioning.

The differences between the behavior of a browser and the standards or recommendations are often referred to as "quirks." You can change the way that Internet Explorer 6.0 and later, Opera 7.0 and later, and Mozilla behave using an appropriate DOCTYPE declaration at the start of your pages. These browsers take into account the MIME type (such as `"text/html"` or `"text/xml"`) that the server sends to the browser in the HTTP headers, and the document type declaration (DTD) and URL present in the DOCTYPE element.

If your page design or layout depends upon behavior caused by one or more of the quirks exposed by older browsers, you can specify this fact by omitting the DOCTYPE declaration or by using a DOCTYPE element and specifying a version of HTML prior to 4.0 or the transitional version of HTML 4.0 (a better solution):

```
<!DOCTYPE HTML PUBLIC "-//W3C//DTD HTML 3.2//EN">
<!DOCTYPE HTML PUBLIC "-//W3C//DTD HTML 4.0 Transitional//EN">
```

To trigger standards-compliant mode in modern browsers, you can use any of the following DOCTYPE elements:

```
<!DOCTYPE HTML PUBLIC "-//W3C//DTD HTML 4.0//EN">
<!DOCTYPE HTML PUBLIC "-//W3C//DTD HTML 4.0 Strict//EN">
<!DOCTYPE HTML PUBLIC "-//W3C//DTD HTML 4.0//EN"
                    "http://www.w3.org/TR/REC-html40/strict.dtd">
```

If your pages are XHTML compliant, you can indicate this by using the appropriate DOCTYPE. This triggers standards-compliant mode in all modern browsers:

```
<!DOCTYPE html PUBLIC "-//W3C//DTD XHTML Basic 1.0//EN"
                    "xhtml-basic10.dtd">
```

By default, Visual Studio automatically adds a DOCTYPE element to your pages that specifies partial XHTML compliance, using:

```
<!DOCTYPE html PUBLIC "-//W3C//DTD XHTML 1.0 Transitional//EN"
            "http://www.w3.org/TR/xhtml1/DTD/xhtml1-transitional.dtd">
```

For more information on the different modes, their effects in each browser, and the alternative ways that you can trigger each mode, see:

http://msdn.microsoft.com/library/en-us/dnie60/html/cssenhancements.asp

http://www.mozilla.org/docs/web-developer/quirks/doctypes.html

http://www.opera.com/docs/specs/doctype/

There is also a useful site called QuirksMode that provides side-by-side feature lists that show the differences between the modes in the mainstream browsers at:

http://www.quirksmode.org/css/quirksmode.html

Making Your Pages Easier to Use

As well as adhering to standards, you should create pages and sites that are easy to use. There are many examples on the Web of sites where you seem to go round in circles trying to locate information, or where links to other pages seem to be hidden until you realize that some non-standard form of hyperlink is in use. Other issues you will have come across include sites where simply reading the content is hard work, because each page follows a different design and structural layout, uses strange fonts and colors, or covers the page with floating windows and other random features.

A good Web site should follow consistent design, with consistent interactive element styles. This allows visitors to roam the site with ease, making the experience more enjoyable and relaxing. It also means that they can concentrate on the content and find what they want more easily. This does not mean that your site must be boring or look like every other site. It does mean using a consistent structure, layout, color scheme, and linking metaphor.

Overall Site and Page Design

There are recurrent themes in terms of layout in many Web sites. The menu bar at the top, list of links or other navigation features on the left, and text links at the bottom of every page may seem to limit creativity, and you can certainly use an entirely different layout if you prefer. However, visitors will immediately recognize the commonly used layout patterns, making it easier to use your site.

Also, consider your user's screen size and browser window size, which may not be the same. Some users like to use the browser maximized, while others prefer to open multiple windows that are smaller than the overall screen size. Some users have portrait-mode screens, while the majority use either standard or wide-screen mode. In addition, although screen resolutions continue to increase, the majority of users are still working at 1024 x 768, or even 800 x 600.

One effect of these varying screen resolutions is that, if you use CSS or HTML tables to position elements rather than relying on the natural flow provided by HTML, you should test your pages at lower screen resolutions and in non-maximized browser windows to ensure that doing so does not affect the layout, appearance, and readability of the content. Also, check that long lines do wrap correctly, particularly when using code-style or preformatted text elements such as `<code>` and `<pre>`.

Some Web sites attempt to solve the variable screen resolution problem by deciding on a specific width for the main content area and then centering that area on the page so that (on high-resolution screens) blank areas appear on either side. This means that they will usually work fine at 1024 pixels wide, but either wrap or overshoot the screen in lower resolutions while forcing additional scrolling on users of large resolution screens because the content is in a band down the center of the screen. However, because very long lines of text are hard to read, this approach does have its advantages.

In the end, the best way to decide on a layout is to browse plenty of sites to see what they do, how they work, and whether they provide the appearance and capabilities that you want for your site in terms of layout and overall page structure.

> Page layout and structure generally affect the browsing experience for disabled visitors even more than other users, as you will see later in this chapter.

Controls, Captions, Short-cut Keys, and Tab Order

In the next major section of this chapter, Supporting Disabled Users and Specialist User Agents, you will see recommendations on the positioning of text captions for interactive controls such as text boxes, list boxes, and radio buttons. However, one useful capability of HTML 4.0 and later, when building pages that use the various interactive form controls (such as lists, buttons, checkboxes, and text boxes), is to associate a text label with a control. This is one of the features of HTML and ASP.NET that you should aim to take advantage of in all your pages to provide behavior that is more consistent and that meets the needs of the maximum number of users.

Linking Captions to Interactive Controls

The `Label` control in ASP.NET exposes the `AssociatedControlID` property, which sets the `for` attribute in the `<span>` element that the `Label` control creates, and allows you to connect a label to an interactive element on a `<form>` in your page. For example, this declaration of a `Label` and `TextBox` control links the `Label` to the `TextBox` using the `AssociatedControlID` property of the `Label` control:

```
<asp:Label id="MyLabel" Text="Name" runat="server"
        AssociatedControlID="MyTextBox" />
<asp:TextBox id="MyTextBox" runat="server" />
```

In a normal graphical browser, this has no effect. However, it allows nonvisual user agents and specialist page readers to link them together and indicate to users what the control caption is when they navigate to the text box. For this reason alone, you should consider always using the `Label` control and setting the `AssociatedControlID` property.

You can also use the `Caption` property of controls that generate an HTML table, such as `Table`, `GridView`, and `Calendar`, to generate a caption that automatically links to the control (this creates a `<caption>` element within the `<table>` element).

Implementing Short-cut Keys

In most modern browsers, you can define a hot key or short-cut key for the control and then display this key in the associated label to make the form more like a traditional Windows executable application (you saw the `AccessKey` attribute used in Chapter 10 in association with the `Hyperlink` control). You set the `AccessKey` property for the `Label` to the key you want to act as the hot key. You can also indicate this key to the user by underlining it in the `Label` text:

```
<asp:Label id="MyLabel" Text="<u>N</u>ame" runat="server"
        AccessKey="N" AssociatedControlID="MyTextBox" />
<asp:TextBox id="MyTextBox" runat="server" />
```

Now, when the hot-key combination (in this case, Alt+N) is pressed, the focus moves to the `TextBox` control automatically. Likewise, you can set the `AccessKey` property of a control that creates an HTML table, such as the `GridView`, and underline a letter in the caption to indicate the short-cut key. You will see both of these techniques demonstrated in the example in the next major section of this chapter, Supporting Disabled Users and Specialist User Agents. However, you cannot use keys already defined for the various UI features of the browser. For example, you cannot use Alt+T in Internet Explorer, because it activates the **Tools** menu.

Setting the Tab Order

By default, the browser moves the input focus from one control to the next in the order they appear on screen, horizontally and then vertically, as you press the Tab key. If you use a table to lay out the controls in columns, the input focus moves across the rows and then down to the next row. However, you can control the tab order by setting the `TabIndex` property.

A value of zero (the default if not specified) indicates that the tab order is not set for this control. Other positive values define the order. When the user loads a page, the input focus is initially set to the address bar of the browser and then moves through the controls on the page in the order of their `TabIndex` values, starting with the lowest non-zero value. Afterwards, the input focus moves through the remaining controls in the order they appear in the page.

The `TabIndex` property is available for all the ASP.NET Web Controls, though it has no effect on controls that cannot receive the input focus. However, keep in mind that it applies to controls such as `Hyperlink` and `LinkButton` as well as the more usual text boxes, lists, and button controls. Again, you will see this technique demonstrated in the example in the next section of this chapter.

Supporting Disabled Users and Specialist User Agents

Web developers must increasingly consider the needs of users of non-graphical Web browsers, such as text-only browsers, Braille output devices, aural page readers, and other specialist user agents. There are also issues to consider such as the use of colors and small text for users who have less than perfect vision. Many governments require that their Web sites conform to certain accessibility guides: In the Unites States, Section 508 of the Rehabilitation Act covers this; in Canada, the Treasury Board sets standards; and in Australia, there is the Disability Discrimination Act. Many other countries also require adherence to certain standards.

> The best place to start when investigating issues of accessibility for your Web sites is the W3C Web Accessibility Initiative (WAI). An introduction to the issues, guidelines and techniques, and details of the ways you can evaluate accessibility are available at http://www.w3.org/WAI/.

General Techniques for Maximizing Accessibility

The major issues for maximizing the accessibility of your Web pages and Web sites concern navigation to each page and within each page, exposing content so that all users can read and comprehend it, and supporting visitors who do not use the traditional input devices such as a mouse. Special user agents and other types of Web access software designed for users with different types of disabilities depend on Web pages implementing some or all of the features presented in this section that make pages more easily accessible.

Navigation Accessibility Features

These recommendations help users to navigate from one page to another, and within individual pages:

- A consistent layout of the content and sections between pages makes it easier for users to navigate within the pages once they are familiar with the layout—for example, the position of menus, content, and links.

- "Skip to" links (described later in this section) placed at the start of the page allow users with the appropriate type of user agent to jump straight to the part of the page they require, without having to navigate through menus, links, and other non-content sections.

- Self-referring links (links that load the same page again) are confusing and you should avoid them if possible.

- A meaningful `<title>` element in every page allows users to quickly determine if the page and content are what they require.

- For HTML `<form>` controls, placing the caption for a textbox or list to the left of the control makes it easier for non-sighted users. Likewise, for a radio button or checkbox, placing the caption to the right of the control is the accepted standard. For complex forms, the `<label>` element can link a caption to a control through the `for` attribute.

- Hyperlinks should describe the target page and its contents instead of containing meaningless text such as "click here."

- Tables are easier to use if the main row identifier value appears first when reading from left to right (or right-to-left in languages where this is the default). The `<th>` element indicates to the user that this cell contains the identifying value for the row, and you can add a `scope` attribute to identify if the cell contains data that applies to the row (`scope="row"`) or to the column (`scope="col"`). The example in Chapter 8, Using the HTML Table Control, shows how you can add headers attributes to an HTML table. Later in this section, you will see an example that shows how you can achieve the same results with a `GridView` control.

Identifying Elements

These recommendations help users to identify individual elements within the page and make sense of the content if they cannot make use of the "default" view. For example, they can allow unsighted users to access an aural description of an image.

- All `<frame>` elements should include a `name` and a `title` attribute, and all interactive elements (such as `<a>`, `<input>`, `<select>`, and `<textarea>`) should contain a `title` attribute. These can provide extended descriptions of the content or target. For ASP.NET server controls, you set the `title` attribute using the `Tooltip` property.

- An `alt` attribute in every image element acts like a title by providing a brief but meaningful text description of the image. Where an image such as a spacer, bullet, or horizontal rule does not contribute to the meaning of the page, the attribute `alt=" "` (an empty string) indicates that it can be ignored. ASP.NET provides a `GenerateEmptyAlternateText` property for the appropriate elements, which creates an empty `alt` attribute.

- Every `<area>` definition within a client-side image map should include an `alt` attribute. You should avoid using server-side image maps, because most user agents cannot present them to the user in a meaningful way.

- The `longdesc` attribute for images is ideal for providing a link to a separate page that contains a more detailed description of the image or alternate content such as a sound file.

General Recommendations

The following recommendations provide general assistance to disabled users and users of non-standard user agents:

- The generic and standardized CSS font sizes, such as `"x-small"` and `"large"`, are preferable to fixed font sizes. This allows visitors to view an enlarged version of the font if required.

- Alternative text content is helpful for all non-text content. For elements such as `<object>` and `<applet>`, you can place text within the element tags and outside any contained elements such as `<param>`. Browsers and other user agents display this text when they do not or cannot load the object or applet.

- Content generated by client-side script is unlikely to be available in many text-based page readers, most of which cannot execute script. A `<noscript>` section is a useful way to provide alternative content in this case.

Evaluating and Testing Your Pages and Sites

Visual Studio contains features that allow you to check the accessibility of your Web pages. The Formatting toolbar contains a button that allows you to check the page against two of the common recommendations, the Web Content Accessibility Guidelines (WCAG) and Section 508 of the Rehabilitation Act (published by the United States Access Board). You can also display within the Error List window a checklist of topics that you should consider (see Figure 14.5).

> The Web Content Accessibility Guidelines are available from the W3C Web site at http://www.w3.org/TR/WAI-WEBCONTENT/. The Section 508 guidelines are at http://www.access-board.gov/508.htm.

Figure 14.6 shows the results of running the accessibility check on the page you saw at the start of this chapter when looking at HTML validation. While there are no errors, there are warnings about connecting control labels (such as the "Enter your name" caption) with the controls to which they relate. There is also a general suggestion about grouping controls to make them easier to use in specialist user agents.

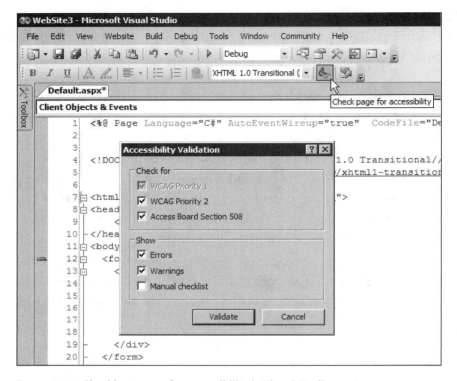

FIGURE 14.5: Checking a page for accessibility in Visual Studio

However, the best way to see how your pages and sites actually appear to disabled visitors and in alternative browsers is through testing them yourself. Try accessing your pages in a text-only browser such as Lynx. Also, try one of the "page reader" applications such as the IBM Home Page Reader. If you close your eyes or turn off your screen, can you navigate through your own site?

Error List

		Description	File	Line	Column	Project
⚠	1	WCAG 10.2 : Ensure that implicitly associated labels for form controls are properly positioned. The LABEL element must precede its control on the same line. If using one line for the control and one for the LABEL element, <label> must be in the line preceding its control.	Default.aspx	12		
⚠	2	WCAG 12.3 : Large blocks of information should be grouped so they are more manageable. If this form is large consider breaking it up using <legend> and <fieldset>.	Default.aspx	12		
⚠	3	WCAG 12.4 : Explicitly associate labels with form controls. Consider using <label> with the "for" attribute within your form.	Default.aspx	12		

0 Errors   ⚠ 3 Warnings   ⓘ 0 Messages

Error List
Ready

FIGURE 14.6: The results of an accessibility check on a simple page

The W3C provides a list of over 30 browsers, specialist user agents, tools and add-ins for disabled users at http://www.w3.org/WAI/References/Browsing. There is also a useful list of tools and resources for testing your pages at http://www.w3.org/WAI/ER/existingtools.html.

Accessibility Features in ASP.NET Controls

While the server controls provided with ASP.NET cannot provide all of the solutions for accessibility maximization (only good page design and implementation can do that), they do provide the following useful features:

- The `Caption` property, and the associated `CaptionAlign` property, can display a caption that describes a table. These properties apply to the `Calendar`, `DetailsView`, `FormView`, `GridView`, `Table`, `DataList`, and `DataGrid` controls.

- The `DescriptionUrl` property can provide nonvisual page readers with the URL of a page that contains more details of an image, perhaps in text or aural form that can be presented to the user in a way that can convey what the image contains or represents. This property applies to the `Image` control.

- The `GenerateEmptyAlternateText` property instructs a control to add the attribute `alt=" "` (an empty string) to the element(s) it generates. This attribute should be present on any image that does not contribute to the meaning or content of the page. Examples are graphical bullets, page divider images, or "blank" images used to align or position other elements. This property applies to the `Image`, `ImageButton`, and `ImageMap` controls.

- The `UseAccessibleHeader` property forces a control that displays a table to add the `scope` attribute to the header cells, which a nonvisual user agent can take advantage of to make it easier for the user to understand what the contents of a table mean. This property applies to the `Calendar`, `GridView`, `DataList`, and `DataGrid` controls.

- The `AssociatedHeaderCellID` property is an array of `String` values that link a table cell to one or more specific table header cells through their ID values. In tables that do not have a simple grid layout (in other words, tables that use column or row spans, or that identify individual rows with row headers), this allows nonvisual user agents to relate the data in the table with the correct headers. This property applies to the `TableCell` control.

* The `AccessibleHeaderText` property can specify text that explains what each column header means in more detail, without being visible in the normal output (and therefore not disturbing the layout of the table). This property applies to the controls that generate columns or rows in a `GridView` and `DetailsView` control, namely, `BoundField`, `AutoGeneratedField`, `ButtonField`, `CommandField`, `CheckBox-Field`, `HyperlinkField`, `ImageField`, and `TemplateField`.

Using Alternate Text and Long Descriptions

Other than text, the most common content on the Web is images. Most Web sites contain a large number of images, some that provide essential information, some that are just additional content, some that are there simply for decoration, and some that are used to control the spacing between elements or act as an alternative to standard list bullets and horizontal rules.

To a visually impaired user with a text-only browser or page reader, all of these images just get in the way. Such a user cannot tell what the image is, if it is important, and what it contains. Therefore, you should always follow the guidelines given earlier by providing alternate content and information about the images themselves.

This means using at least the `alt` attribute to identify and quantify the image. If it is a picture accompanying a description of, for example, a new type of spacecraft, it should carry an `alt` attribute that specifies something like "Photograph of the spacecraft during blast-off." Likewise, other types of non-accessible content should carry alternate text descriptors. While the user still cannot see the image, they at least know what it contains.

However, what do you do about those non-contributing images such as bullets and horizontal rules? In this case, you should add the attribute `alt=" "`, which indicates that the user can ignore the image altogether. The problem is that, with ASP.NET server controls, setting a property to an empty string means that the control will not render the relevant attribute. The answer is to use the `GenerateEmptyAlternateText` property. Setting it to `true` causes the control to generate the `alt=" "` attribute.

Listing 14.4 shows a simple declaration of three `Image` controls. The first sets the `AlternateText` property (which generates the `alt` attribute) to an empty string. The second omits the `AlternateText` property but sets the `GenerateEmptyAlternateText` property to `True`. The third sets the `AlternateText` property to a suitable string and adds the `DescriptionUrl` property. This property generates the `longdesc` attribute, which in this case points to a separate page that describes the image.

Listing 14.4. Declaring the Alt and Longdesc Attributes for an Image

```
<asp:Image id="img1" runat="server"
    ImageUrl="bullet.gif" ImageAlign="AbsMiddle"
    AlternateText="" />
Image with AlternateText=""

<asp:Image id="img2" runat="server"
    ImageUrl="bullet.gif" ImageAlign="AbsMiddle"
    GenerateEmptyAlternateText="True" />
Image with GenerateEmptyAlternateText="True"

<asp:Image id="Image1" runat="server"
    ImageUrl="bullet.gif" ImageAlign="AbsMiddle"
    AlternateText="Sample Bullet Image"
    DescriptionUrl="bullet.htm" />
Image with AlternateText="Sample Bullet Image"
and DescriptionUrl="bullet.htm"
```

Figure 14.7 shows the results of the code in Listing 14.4. You can see that in a normal graphical browser, they all look the same—only the text placed after each one is different. However, if you place your mouse pointer over the last one, you see the alternate text appear.

To see what difference the `alt` and `longdesc` attributes really make, you need to view the source of the rendered page in the browser (select **Source**

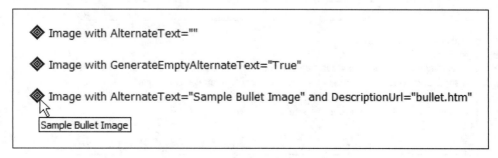

FIGURE 14.7: Using the alt and longdesc attributes for images

from the **View** menu). The first image has no `alt` attribute, because setting it to an empty string removes it from the element:

```
<img id="img1" src="bullet.gif" align="absmiddle"
    style="border-width:0px;" />
```

The second image has the empty `alt` attribute, as intended, created by setting the `GenerateEmptyAlternateText` property to `True`:

```
<img id="img2" src="bullet.gif" alt="" align="absmiddle"
    style="border-width:0px;" />
```

The third image contains the `alt` attribute specified in Listing 14.4, plus the `longdesc` attribute. A specialist page reader or text browser can expose the URL declared in this attribute (`"bullet.htm"`) as an optional link, or even fetch the content of the page and display it alongside the image or in some other suitable way:

```
<img id="Image1" src="bullet.gif" longdesc="bullet.htm"
    alt="Sample Bullet Image" align="absmiddle"
    style="border-width:0px;" />
```

The URL referenced in the `longdesc` attribute might be a sound file that describes the image, a link to another site that contains alternative content about the image, or a simple text file. In this example, the page `bullet.htm` is an HTML page that—when displayed in a normal Web browser—looks like Figure 14.8. A page reader or text browser will be able to present this as a text description of the image.

Implementing "D" Links and Alternative Content

You saw in the previous section how you can expose extra information to users by adding the `alt` and `longdesc` attribute to images and by providing

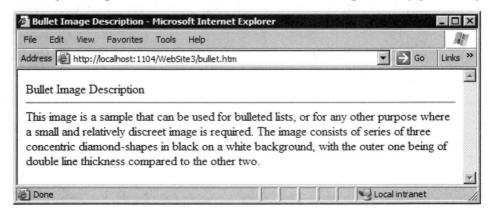

FIGURE 14.8: The contents of the alternative description declared in the longdesc attribute

alternate content for other elements. One of the other accepted ways to indicate that alternate content is available is through a "D" or "description" link. This is simply a hyperlink that displays the letter "d" or "D" next to the item for which you provide extra information and navigates to a page or resource containing that information.

The example you will see in a later section, An Example of an Accessible Page, shows a "D" link in use. While the link is usually visible to users of graphical browsers, you can hide it using the same approach you will see demonstrated for skip-to links in the next section. However, leaving it visible provides an indication to partially sighted or color-blind users, who may use a graphical browser with a large text size setting, so that they can see more information if they cannot completely comprehend the default content (for example, a chart using very fine or colored lines).

Implementing "Skip-to" Links

Users of graphical browsers, when faced with a complex Web Page, can generally tell quite easily which sections contain the content they want to view, and they can visually skip over other items such as menus, navigation bars, lists of links to other pages, and other non-relevant content. However, most specialist browsers or page readers present the content serially, starting at the top of the page and working through it. This means that the user may have to wade through the same non-relevant sections of content on every page load, including the menus, links, disclaimers, descriptions of the page heading images, and more. You can make it easier for these users in the following two ways:

- Implement skip-to links that allow them to skip over non-relevant content, and jump directly to the sections of the page they want to access. You will see this demonstrated in this section of the chapter.

- Use the positioning features of CSS to ensure that the main content section comes before the non-relevant sections in the source of the page. In graphical browsers that support CSS, users will see no difference. However, serial page readers will present the content first. One minor issue here is that, unless you add skip-to links that jump to the navigation sections, users may still find it hard to navigate the site.

Skip-to links are simply hyperlinks that are visible to page readers and text browsers, but may not be visible to users of graphical browsers (though they can be if you wish). The link points to an anchor element within the same page, located at the position of the corresponding content section. You can use more than one skip-to link in a page if this is appropriate, but you should limit the number to two or three for simplicity.

Some of the controls included in ASP.NET generate skip-to links, or—to be more accurate—skip-over links automatically. An example is the Menu control, which generates a link at the top of its output that allows users to skip over the control to an anchor located at the end of its output.

Listing 14.5 shows two skip-to links and the corresponding anchor elements located just before the related sections of the page. In this case, a range of techniques including <font> elements and CSS styles hide the links in graphical browsers. The image used in the hyperlinks is a single-pixel transparent GIF file. Beware of using the CSS display and visible selectors, because these may cause some specialist browsers to fail to display the links.

Listing 14.5. Skip-to Links for Aural Page Readers and Text-Only Browsers

```
<div style="position:absolute;height:0px;"><font size="1"
color=#ffffff">
<a href="#navigation"
   style="color:#ffffff;font-size:1px;text-decoration:none">
  <img width="1" height="1" hspace="0" vspace="0"
       src="images/_blnk.gif" border="0" style="height:0"
       alt="Skip to Navigation Links" />
</a>
<a href="#content"
   style="color:#ffffff;font-size:1px;text-decoration:none">
  <img width="1" height="1" hspace="0" vspace="0"
       src="images/_blnk.gif" border="0" style="height:0"
       alt="Skip to Main Content" />
</a>
</font></div>
 . . .
 . . . page header here  . . .
 . . .
<a name="navigation" />
 . . .
 . . . navigation links here  . . .
 . . .
<a name="content" />
 . . .
 . . . main page content here  . . .
 . . .
```

An Example of an Accessible Page

As an example of both "D" links and skip-to links, and providing alternative views of information, Figure 14.9 shows a Web page that displays a graphical chart. This page contains skip-to links, which you cannot see in a normal browser but which are visible in other browsers—as you will see later. Above the chart are option buttons that allow visitors to choose the viewing format for the information. By default, it is as a chart. Below the chart, you can see the "D" link that provides more information.

The example uses a separate class file that simply generates a `DataSet` containing the static information for this example by adding rows to a `DataTable`. A separate ASP.NET page creates the chart dynamically at runtime as a GIF image (you can see the text from the `alt` attribute in Figure 14.9). You will see how this page works in Chapter 15. Meanwhile, this chapter

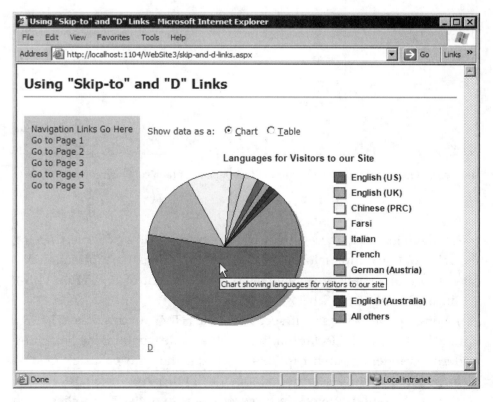

FIGURE 14.9: An example page that displays a chart viewed in a graphical browser

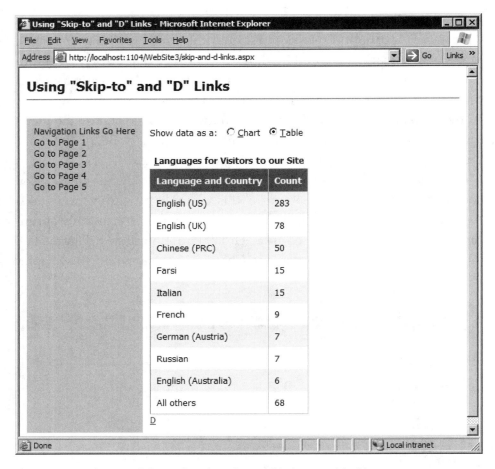

FIGURE 14.10: The same information viewed as a table in a graphical browser

concentrates just on the accessibility features built into this example. Clicking the **Table** option button reloads the page, and this time the information displays as an HTML table generated by a GridView control (see Figure 14.10). Again, a **"D"** link appears below the table.

Listing 14.6 shows the main sections of the HTML for this page. The two option buttons each declare an AccessKey and contain the matching underlined letters in their captions. They use the auto-postback mechanism, so that making a selection automatically displays the chart or table. However, this will not work in browsers that do not support client-side script, and so a submit button (with the caption **Go**) is added within a

`<noscript>` element. It will appear only if the browser does not support client-side scripting or if it is disabled.

Listing 14.6. The Main Page That Displays a Chart or a Table

```
<a name="content"/>
<span>Show data as a: </span>
<asp:RadioButton id="optShowChart" CssClass="body-text"
    GroupName="ShowAs" AutoPostBack="True" AccessKey="C"
    Text="<u>C</u>hart" Checked="True" runat="server" /> 
<asp:RadioButton id="optShowTable" CssClass="body-text"
    GroupName="ShowAs" AutoPostBack="True" AccessKey="T"
    Text="<u>T</u>able" runat="server" />  
<noscript>
  <!-- button to submit form if no client-side script -->
  <input type="submit" value="Go" />
</noscript>
<p />

<!-- placeholder to hold image of results -->
<asp:PlaceHolder id="ctlPlaceholder" runat="server" />

<!-- GridView to display results as a table -->
<asp:GridView id="grid1" EnableViewState="False" runat="server"
    UseAccessibleHeader="true" AccessKey="L"
    AutoGenerateColumns="False">
  <Columns>
    <asp:BoundField DataField="Language"
        HeaderText="Language and Country"
        AccessibleHeaderText="User langauge and country" />
    <asp:BoundField DataField="Count"
        HeaderText="Count"
        AccessibleHeaderText="Number of visitors" />
  </Columns>
</asp:GridView>

<!-- D link to more information page -->
<asp:HyperLink id="lnkD" runat="server" Text="D" AccessKey="D"
    ToolTip="Alternate Description"
    NavigateUrl="pie-describe.aspx" />
```

Following the option buttons is an ASP.NET `PlaceHolder` control. As you saw in Chapter 8, this control reserves a location within the control tree where you can insert other controls at runtime. After the `PlaceHolder` control is the `GridView` control that displays the HTML table. Finally, a `Hyperlink` control provides the "D" link to the page containing the alternative content. Notice that the code defines an `AccessKey` for both the

GridView and the Hyperlink, so that they are easily accessible to users who do not or cannot use a normal mouse.

To display the appropriate content, the Page_Load event handler, shown in Listing 14.7, detects the setting of the option buttons. If the **Chart** option is selected, the code creates a new Image control and sets the properties for the separate ASP.NET page that generates the GIF image of the chart, the value for the alt attribute, and the value for the longdesc attribute. Then it inserts the new Image into the PlaceHolder control.

If the **Table** option is selected, the code uses the GetDemoDataSet method of the separate class file to fetch a DataSet and binds it to the GridView control to display the information as an HTML table. It also populates the caption for the table and sets the AccessKey. Because the GridView has its viewstate disabled (the declaration contains the attribute EnableViewState="False"), it

Listing 14.7. The Page_Load Event Handler for the Accessible Example Page

```
protected void Page_Load(object sender, EventArgs e)
{
  // show table if client browser does not support color
  if (!Page.IsPostBack && !Request.Browser.IsColor)
  {
    optShowTable.Checked = true;
  }
  // see if we are generating a chart or a table
  if (optShowChart.Checked)
  {
    // insert new Image element for chart into page
    Image ctlImage = new Image();
    ctlImage.ImageUrl = "piechart.aspx";
    ctlImage.AlternateText = "Chart showing languages . . . ";
    ctlImage.DescriptionUrl = "pie-describe.aspx";
    ctlPlaceholder.Controls.Add(ctlImage);
  }
  else
  {
    // get table of the results using separate class method
    DemoLanguages dl = new DemoLanguages();
    grid1.DataSource = dl.GetDemoDataSet();
    grid1.DataBind();
    grid1.Caption = "<u>L</u>anguages for Visitors to our Site";
    grid1.AccessKey = "L";
  }
}
```

contains no data and no caption unless reset by this code. This means that it disappears when reloading the page to show a chart.

One other feature you can see in Listing 14.7 is that it attempts to provide the most appropriate information format automatically when the page first loads. The code in the `Page_Load` event handler uses the current `Http-BrowserCapabilities` instance (obtained from the `Browser` property of the current `Request`) to check if the current browser supports color. If it does not, or if does not support images at all, this property will be `false` and so the obvious course of action is to display a table and not a chart.

Clicking the **"D"** link in this example opens the alternative content page, which contains just a text description of the values in the chart/table shown in the previous page (see Figure 14.11). A link at the bottom of this page takes the user back to the previous page.

The code to create the alternative content for this page is simple, and (as you would expect) uses the same data source as the chart and table views. Listing 14.8 shows the `Page_Load` event handler for this page. It contains

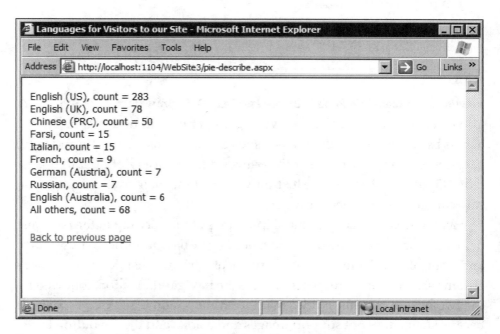

FIGURE 14.11: The alternative content page viewed in a graphical browser

a relatively generic routine that iterates through the rows in the `DataSet` table and builds up a `String` containing the data. It then inserts this into a `Label` control on the page. The final line of code sets the `NavigateUrl` property of the `Hyperlink` on this page to the URL of the referring page so that clicking it takes the user back to the previous page.

Listing 14.8. The Page_Load Event Handler in the Alternative Content Page

```
protected void Page_Load(object sender, EventArgs e)
{
  // get table of the results and display them
  DemoLanguages dl = new DemoLanguages();
  DataSet ds = dl.GetDemoDataSet();
  DataTable dt = ds.Tables[0];
  StringBuilder builder = new StringBuilder();
  foreach (DataRow row in ds.Tables[0].Rows)
  {
    builder.Append(row[0].ToString());
    builder.Append(", count = ");
    builder.Append(row[1].ToString() + "<br />");
  }
  lblOutput.Text = builder.ToString();

  // set "Back" link URL
  lnkBack.NavigateUrl = Request.UrlReferrer.ToString();
}
```

Viewing the Accessible Page Example in a Text-Only Browser

You can get a good idea of how your pages appear in non-graphical user agents by using a text-only browser such as Lynx. This is a simple and light, easy-to-use text-only browser that runs under a variety of operating systems. Figure 14.12 shows the text-only view of the main example page you saw earlier in a graphical browser.

Here, you can clearly see the skip-to links at the very top of the page just below the page title (the different colors Lynx uses to indicate hyperlinks and controls, and the current input focus, are not visible in the monochrome screenshots here). Then there is the navigation section, followed by the two option buttons. Notice that the **Table** option is selected by default because Lynx does not support images and colors, and the **Go** button is visible because Lynx does not support client-side script. At the end of the page is the "D" link for displaying the alternative view of the information.

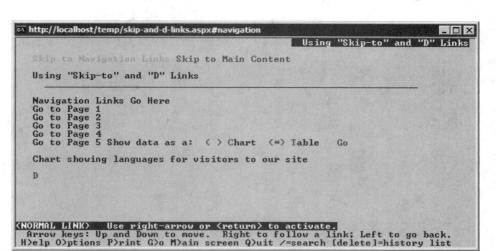

FIGURE 14.12: The example page skip-to links in a text-only browser

Lynx can display simple HTML tables, so selecting the **Go** link displays the information in a usable format (see Figure 14.13). Meanwhile, selecting the **"D"** link displays the text-only equivalent of the alternative content page (see Figure 14.14).

The home of the Lynx browser is http://lynx.browser.org/, and you can download a version for your operating system from http://lynx.isc.org/current/.

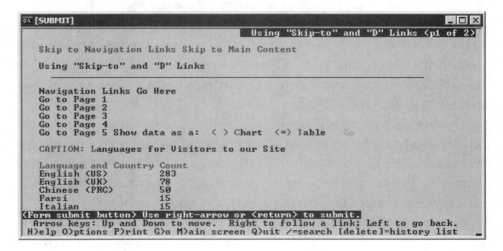

FIGURE 14.13: The table view of the data in a text-only browser

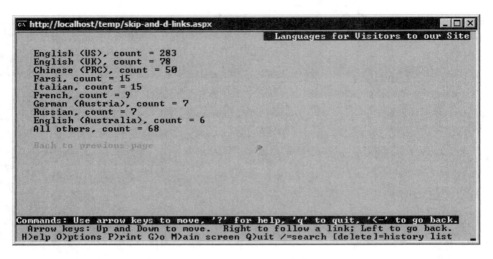

FIGURE 14.14: The alternative content page in a text-only browser

Maximizing Accessibility for HTML Tables

When a browser renders an HTML table, comprehending the information it contains is generally a matter of scanning the rows and columns and mentally relating them with the header descriptions for each row. Often the table is like a spreadsheet in design, where each cell value in the body relates to the description for the column and the row where it resides.

For most users, this just involves looking at the header and the left-hand row to locate the desired descriptions and then scanning down and across to the cell where they meet. However, for users of nonvisual browsers and user agents, this is hard to do. Their browser will usually iterate through the table row by row, and it is easy to lose track of the header descriptions that relate to each cell in the row.

To assist such users, HTML 4.0 includes the `headers` attribute for a table cell, which should be set to a list of the header cell ID values for the header and row description to which this cell relates. This way, the browser can extract the header and row descriptions as it iterates through the cells in each row and present them to the user in a suitable manner.

In Chapter 8 (in the example of using the `Table` control), you saw one solution—the use of the `AssociatedHeaderCellID` property of each cell in a table to link the cells with the relevant header cells. Listing 14.9 shows the HTML rendered to the browser to display the table. You can see the column and row `<th>` elements and the `headers` attributes on each `<td>` element, which relates the cells to the appropriate row and column headers.

Listing 14.9. An HTML Table Containing Headers Attributes

```
<table id="MyTable" rules="all" border="1">
  <tr>
    <th id="Header0">Header0</th>
    <th id="Header1">Header1</th>
    <th id="Header2">Header2</th>
  </tr>
  <tr>
    <th id="RowDesc0">RowDescription0</th>
    <td headers="Header1,RowDesc0">Row0 Col1</td>
    <td headers="Header2,RowDesc0">Row0 Col2</td>
  </tr>
  <tr>
    <th id="RowDesc1">RowDescription1</th>
    <td headers="Header1,RowDesc1">Row1 Col1</td>
    <td headers="Header2,RowDesc1">Row1 Col2</td>
  </tr>
  . . . more rows here . . .
  <tr>
    <td>Foot0</td>
    <td>Foot1</td>
    <td>Foot2</td>
  </tr>
</table>
```

Using Short-cut Keys, Tab Order, and Table Captions

The `AssociatedHeaderCellID` property you saw in the previous section only applies to the `TableCell` control. If you want to add `headers` attributes to the cells generated by a control such as the `GridView`, you must do so by handling events that occur as ASP.NET generates the rendered table. This example demonstrates this, the use of the associated `Label` controls and short-cut keys, and setting the tab order in a page.

Figure 14.15 shows the rendered page for this example. You can see that the captions for the three text boxes and the grid have underlined letters that correspond to the short-cut keys that move the input focus to them. What you cannot see is that there is also a short-cut key (Alt+S) for the **Show** button.

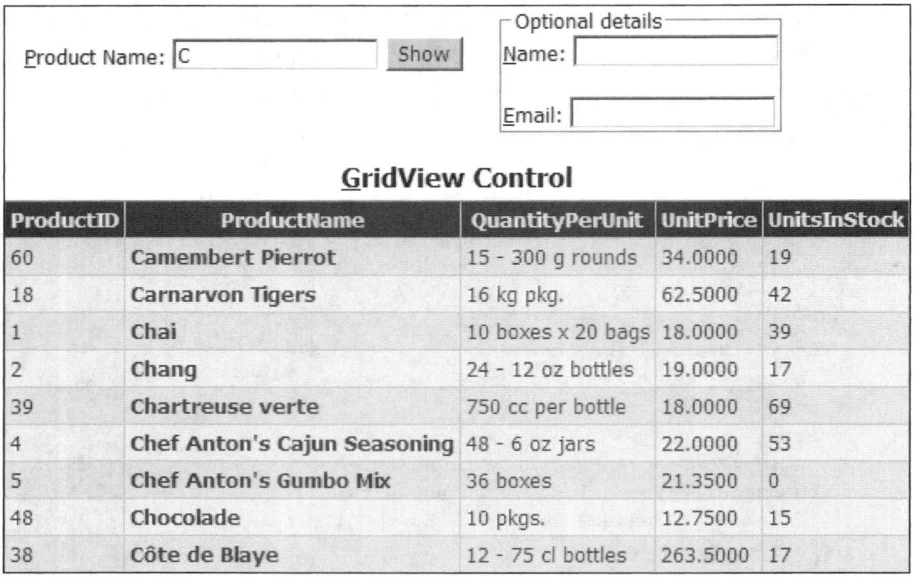

ProductID	ProductName	QuantityPerUnit	UnitPrice	UnitsInStock
60	Camembert Pierrot	15 - 300 g rounds	34.0000	19
18	Carnarvon Tigers	16 kg pkg.	62.5000	42
1	Chai	10 boxes x 20 bags	18.0000	39
2	Chang	24 - 12 oz bottles	19.0000	17
39	Chartreuse verte	750 cc per bottle	18.0000	69
4	Chef Anton's Cajun Seasoning	48 - 6 oz jars	22.0000	53
5	Chef Anton's Gumbo Mix	36 boxes	21.3500	0
48	Chocolade	10 pkgs.	12.7500	15
38	Côte de Blaye	12 - 75 cl bottles	263.5000	17

FIGURE 14.15: Demonstrating short-cut keys and GridView accessibility

You cannot underline text in a standard `Button` control, because the HTML elements (the `<u>` and `</u>` tags) simply display as text on the button. However, if you use the HTML-style `<button>` element, you can force Internet Explorer to display an underlined button caption:

```
<button id="mybutton" runat="server"><u>S</u>how</button>
```

The problem with this control is that it does not cause a postback, and so you must wire it up to a client-side function that calls the `submit` method of the form.

If you experiment with this page, you will see that you can move the input focus to any text box or the grid using the short-cut keys. You can also tab through the controls, in which case the order is the **Product Name** text box followed by the grid, and then back up to the **Name** and **Email** text boxes—an order different than the default tabbing order. Listing 14.10 shows the declarations of the `Label`, `TextBox`, and `Button` controls, each with the relevant `AccessKey` and `TabIndex` properties set.

Notice the grouping of the optional controls within a `Panel` control. Specifying the `GroupingText` property causes this control to generate an HTML `<fieldset>` and nested `<legend>` element, which is the recommended way to clarify the layout of complex forms for specialist user agents to better understand the contents.

Listing 14.10. The Declaration of the Label, TextBox, and Button Controls

```
<asp:Label id="lblProduct" runat="server"
           Text="<u>P</u>roduct Name:"
           AccessKey="P" AssociatedControlID="txtProduct"
           TabIndex="0" />
<asp:TextBox id="txtProduct" runat="server" Text="C"
             TabIndex="1" />
<asp:Button runat="server" id="btnGo" Text="Show"
            ToolTip="Start search for matching products"
            <TabIndex="2" AccessKey="S" /><p />

<asp:Panel GroupingText="Optional details" runat="server">
  <asp:Label id="lblName" Text="<u>N</u>ame:" runat="server"
             AccessKey="N" AssociatedControlID="txtName" />
  <asp:TextBox id="txtName" runat="server" TabIndex="4" />
  <br />
  <asp:Label id="lblEmail" Text="<u>E</u>mail:" runat="server"
             AccessKey="E" AssociatedControlID="txtEmail" />
  <asp:TextBox id="txtEmail" runat="server" TabIndex="5" />
</asp:Panel>
```

Listing 14.11 shows the HTML that the code in Listing 14.10 generates.
You can see the `accesskey` and `tabindex` attributes, and the `title` for the
submit button (you can also add `title` attributes to text boxes by setting
the `Tooltip` property of the `TextBox` control).

Listing 14.11. The HTML Generated by the Label, TextBox, and Button Controls

```
<label for="txtProduct" id="lblProduct"
       accesskey="P"><u>P</u>roduct Name:</label>
<input name="txtProduct" type="text" value="C" id="txtProduct"
       tabindex="1" />
<input type="submit" name="btnGo" value="Show" id="btnGo"
       accesskey="S" tabindex="2"
       title="Start search for matching products" />

<fieldset>
  <legend>
    Optional details
  </legend>
  <label for="txtName" id="lblName"
         accesskey="N"><u>N</u>ame:</label>
  <input name="txtName" type="text" id="txtName" tabindex="4" />
  <label for="txtEmail" id="lblEmail"
         accesskey="E"><u>E</u>mail:</label>
  <input name="txtEmail" type="text" id="txtEmail" tabindex="5" />
</fieldset>
```

The `GridView` control declaration for this example (see Listing 14.12) also contains some extra property settings that aid accessibility. The `Caption` property generates the caption above the grid, and the value used in this example causes underlining of the hotkey specified for the `AccessKey` property of the `GridView` (look back at Figure 14.15 to see the result). You can also see the `TabIndex` property set so that the grid gains the input focus before the two text boxes above it in the page. The declaration of each column is not relevant here, and so these are not visible in the listing.

Listing 14.12. The Declaration of the GridView Control

```
<asp:GridView id="MyGrid" runat="server"
    Caption="<u>G</u>ridView Control" CaptionAlign="Top"
    AccessKey="G" TabIndex="3"
    RowHeaderColumn="ProductName"
    UseAccessibleHeader="True"
    DataKeyNames="ProductID" DataSourceID="ds1"
    BorderWidth="1px" BorderColor="#E7E7FF" BorderStyle="None"
    BackColor="White" CellPadding="3" PagerSettings-Mode="Numeric"
    AutoGenerateColumns="False"
    OnRowDataBound="AddHeadersAttr">
    . . .
    . . .
</asp:GridView>
```

Adding Accessible Headers to a GridView Control

Notice in Listing 14.12 that the `RowHeaderColumn` property is set to the name of the column in the source rowset that contains the most useful and descriptive value from each row—the product description—and the `UseAccessibleHeader` property is set to `True`. These property settings will add some of the accessibility features to the generated grid.

The `RowHeaderColumn` property causes ASP.NET to generate a `<th>` element rather than a `<td>` element for the cells in this column of each row, making them appear in bold text in a graphical browser. More importantly, it means that a page reader or non-graphical user agent can tell which column contains the information most useful in describing each row to the user. The `UseAccessibleHeader` property causes ASP.NET to add the `scope` attributes to each column and row header, specifying whether the heading or value in that cell applies to the row or the column in which it is located.

However, these property settings do not provide the `headers` attributes in each cell like you saw with the `Table` control example in Chapter 8, but you can add them yourself using code. You can see in Listing 14.12 that the `OnRowDataBound` property specifies an event handler named `AddHeadersAttr` that runs as ASP.NET generates each row of the HTML table that represents the grid.

Listing 14.13 shows this event handler in full. The code checks to see what type of row ASP.NET is creating. For a header row, it adds to each cell an `id` attribute that contains the text "`ColumnHeader_`" and the name of the column. For the rows that form the body of the table, the code iterates through the cells in the row checking each one to see if it is a row header (a `<th>` element represented in the control tree as a `DataControlFieldHeaderCell` control) or a normal data cell (a `<td>` element represented in the control tree as a `DataControlFieldCell` control).

For row header cells, the code adds to the cell an `id` attribute containing the text "`RowHeader_`" and the value of the primary key of the row taken from the `DataKeys` collection of the `GridView` (the `DataKeyNames` property of the `GridView` control is set to the `ProductID` column, as shown in Listing 14.12). For data cells, the code generates a `headers` attribute on the cell that specifies the value of the `id` properties of the current column and row header cells.

Listing 14.14 shows a section of the HTML generated by this example. You can see the `accesskey` and `tabindex` attributes on the `<table>` element, and the nested `<caption>` element with its underlined letter. In the first row of the table are the column header cells, each with the `id` set to the value added by the code in the `AddHeadersAttr` event handler, and the `scope="col"` attribute added by setting the `RowHeaderColumn` and `UseAccessibleHeader` properties.

In the next row, the second cell is the row header (the product name) and again has an `id` attribute. The other four cells are data cells that contain the `headers` attribute with the appropriate column and row header `id` values. You can see from this how suitable page readers or text-only user agents can describe the cell to the user as they navigate through the table by reading out or displaying the contents of the column and row header cells.

Listing 14.13. The Code to Add the Headers Attributes to the GridView Control

```
protected void AddHeadersAttr(Object sender, GridViewRowEventArgs e)
{
  if (e.Row.RowType == DataControlRowType.Header)
  {
    // this is the column header row so add ID to each
    // column using column name. NOTE: cannot set ID property
    // because this includes the ID of all parent controls as well
    // for example "MyGrid_ctl1_3" instead of just "3"
    for (Int32 i = 0; i < e.Row.Cells.Count; i++)
    {
      e.Row.Cells[i].Attributes.Add("id",
          "ColumnHeader_" + MyGrid.Columns[i].HeaderText);
    }
  }
  else if (e.Row.RowType == DataControlRowType.DataRow)
  {
    // this is a data row
    for (Int32 i = 0; i < e.Row.Cells.Count; i++)
    {
      Object oCell = e.Row.Cells[i];
      if (oCell is DataControlFieldHeaderCell)
      {
        // this is the row header so add an ID using the ProductID
        DataControlFieldHeaderCell oHeaderCell
            = oCell as DataControlFieldHeaderCell;
        oHeaderCell.Attributes.Add("id", "RowHeader_"
            + MyGrid.DataKeys[e.Row.RowIndex].Value.ToString());
      }
      else
      {
        // this is a data cell so add appropriate headers attribute
        DataControlFieldCell oFieldCell
            = oCell as DataControlFieldCell;
        oFieldCell.Attributes.Add("headers", "ColumnHeader_"
            + MyGrid.Columns[i].HeaderText + ",RowHeader_"
            + MyGrid.DataKeys[e.Row.RowIndex].Value.ToString());
      }
    }
  }
}
```

If the text of the column headings (the `HeaderText` property) is not descriptive enough of the contents of a column, or if you omit the text in a particular column header for aesthetic reasons, you can provide a more descriptive explanation of the contents of the column. The `Accessible-HeaderText` property of the various column objects (such as `Bound-Field`, `HyperlinkField`, and `ButtonField`) sets the `abbr` attribute for the corresponding `<th>` element in the column header row, which is available to specialist user agents but is not visible in a graphical browser.

Listing 14.14. The HTML Generated by the Accessible GridView Control

```html
<table accesskey="G" tabindex="3" cellspacing="0" . . . >
  <caption align="Top"><u>G</u>ridView Control</caption>
  <tr style="color:#F7F7F7; . . . ">
    <th id="ColumnHeader_ProductID" scope="col">ProductID</th>
    <th id="ColumnHeader_ProductName" scope="col">ProductName</th>
    <th id="ColumnHeader_QuantityPerUnit"
        scope="col">QuantityPerUnit</th>
    <th id="ColumnHeader_UnitPrice" scope="col">UnitPrice</th>
    <th id="ColumnHeader_UnitsInStock" scope="col">UnitsInStock</th>
  </tr>
  <tr align="left" style="color:#4A3C8C; . . . ">
    <td headers="ColumnHeader_ProductID,RowHeader_60">60</td>
    <th id="RowHeader_60" scope="row">Camembert Pierrot</th>
    <td headers="ColumnHeader_QuantityPerUnit,RowHeader_60">15</td>
    <td headers="ColumnHeader_UnitPrice,RowHeader_60">34.0000</td>
    <td headers="ColumnHeader_UnitsInStock,RowHeader_60">19</td>
  </tr>
   . . .
   . . .
</table>
```

Building Pages for Small-Screen and Mobile Devices

In Chapter 10, you saw a brief mention of the ASP.NET Mobile Controls that are part of the standard ASP.NET installation. In this section, you will see more details of these controls and how you can use them to create pages and sites that work on a range of mobile devices.

Page Design and Device Support

As you discovered in Chapter 10, the controls from the `System.Web.UI.MobileControls` namespace automatically change the markup and output they create to suit the type of device accessing the page. They can produce a range of different markup types, including HTML, Wireless Markup Language (WML), and other special compact forms of HTML such as cHTML that are used by some mobile devices. So does this mean that you can now build pages and even complete Web sites or applications that will work on any device? The answer is "yes," but—in most cases—you probably will not want to.

The reason has to do with the design of the page and how well it matches the devices on which it will be viewed. Although 2.5G and 3G cellular phones are appearing that have increased bandwidth and screen size compared to older GPRS phones, the fundamental issues relate more to the actual rendered page size versus the available screen size and to the input devices available on the client.

For example, a common design for pages aimed at the traditional Web browser is multiple columns, separate navigation bars at the top or left, and a multitude of small text links or clickable images. This kind of page generally depends on the use of a mouse to navigate. On the latest cellular phones, there is generally no mouse, though there may be some kind of navigation pad. However, the majority of compact mobile phone devices can display only simple text, perhaps up to 20 characters per line over six lines, and may not even be able to display images.

So, while the mobile `Label`, `Command`, or `TextBox` control can modify its behavior to suit the device and the markup language required, there is no real possibility of designing the layout of the entire page so that it "works" (in the usability sense) on all devices. In addition, this is not the aim of the Mobile Controls. Instead, they allow you to build pages using the same techniques, tools, and programming model; but you will generally have to implement different versions of your Web applications to suit the different major categories of devices you want to support—probably one version for ordinary Web browsers and one version for mobile devices.

Creating Pages for Mobile Devices

Visual Studio provides excellent support for developing Web sites and Web pages aimed at mobile devices. When you create a new site, or add pages to an existing site, you can select a range of items specific to mobile device development. The Visual Studio Toolbox also contains the full range of mobile controls that are ready to drag and drop onto your pages just as when you are building ordinary HTML Web pages. Figure 14.16 shows a mobile page under construction in Visual Studio, and you can see the range of mobile controls in the Toolbox in this screenshot.

Notice that there is a major difference between a mobile page and an ordinary HTML page. Mobile pages allow you to add more than one server-side `<form>` to the page as long as you use the `Form` control from the **Mobile Web Forms** section of the Toolbox. This is because the way that mobile device pages work is quite different from normal HTML pages.

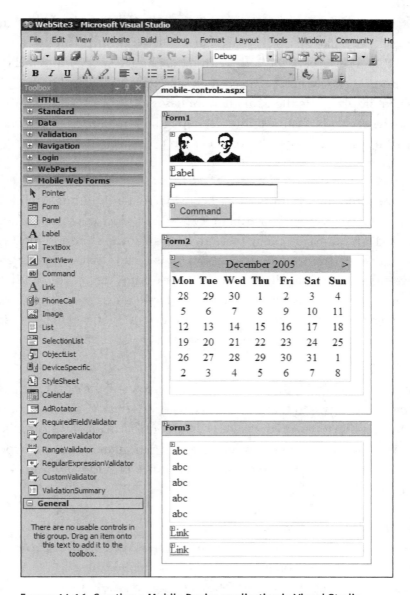

FIGURE 14.16: Creating a Mobile Device application in Visual Studio

Mobile devices generally have only limited memory capacity and processing power, as well as small screens, and so they work best when displaying only a few controls at a time. However, instead of creating multiple small pages, each with one screen of information, each mobile form acts as a single screen. In WML terminology, each form is a "card," and the set of screens that make up the mobile page is called (not surprisingly) a "deck."

You then use server-side code within the page to specify the card to display, and you can switch between them as required to display them in an order that implements the equivalent of navigating between separate Web pages. The server holds the entire deck (page) in memory and sends to the device the appropriate card (form) on each postback.

Issues to Consider with Mobile Device Web Forms

There are some important issues to consider when building Mobile Web Form pages. To conserve device memory, ASP.NET does not store `viewstate` in the card it sends to the client. Instead, it uses a key to store and retrieve the `viewstate` data from the user's session. This means that you must ensure that session support is available, and—because many devices do not support cookies—you will generally have to use cookie-less sessions for your mobile device pages. To enable cookie-less session support, you use the `<session-State>` element in the `<system.web>` section of `web.config`:

```
<sessionState cookieless="true" />
```

Because the client makes multiple requests to view the cards in a page as they navigate between them, it is worth storing data you need in a separate card (mobile form) on the page. All the controls in all of the cards on the page maintain their values as inter-card navigation takes place, so you can use this "extra" card to store values and just not provide any route for the user to view it.

The Mobile Web Forms Control Set

The comprehensive set of controls in the Mobile Web Forms control set provides all the features you are likely to need for building pages aimed at small-screen and mobile devices. The class `MobilePage` is the base class for all mobile pages, and it acts as the "deck." The basic form controls for displaying text and data, and collecting user input, are:

- `Form`. The container for controls within a mobile page that creates a single "card"
- `Label`. Displays read-only text output
- `TextBox`. Provides a normal single-line text box

- `TextView`. Displays large fields of text and can automatically page it as separate "screens" on the device.
- `Panel`. Provides a container for grouping, styling, and controlling pagination for the contained controls, and acts as a placeholder for dynamically inserting controls
- `Image`. Displays an image
- `Command`. Provides a link or button (depending on the device) to initiate a postback
- `Link`. Provides a hyperlink to another card (form) or a URL

There is also a set of list controls that work much like those in the Web Forms control set, supporting data binding as well as the use of the declarative `<asp:ListItem>` approach:

- `List`. Displays a read-only list of items
- `ObjectList`. Displays a list of data objects
- `SelectionList`. Displays a clickable or selectable list of items

There are some special controls for styling, generating rich output, or performing phone-specific tasks:

- `StyleSheet`. Stores and organizes styles for other controls
- `DeviceSpecific`. Displays sections of content, depending on a device filter
- `PhoneCall`. On suitable devices, can initiate a voice call
- `AdRotator`. Provides an advertisement rotation feature
- `Calendar`. Generates a date-picking feature for mobile devices

The mobile control set also includes a full set of validation controls that work in exactly the same way as the standard Web Forms equivalents:

- `CompareValidator`. Compares the values in two controls, or to a specific value
- `RangeValidator`. Determines if a control value falls within a specified range
- `RegularExpressionValidator`. Performs validation against a regular expression

- `RequiredFieldValidator`. Forces input to be provided for a control
- `CustomValidator`. Performs validation using a custom validation function
- `ValidationSummary`. Displays a summary of all the validation errors

All of these controls work in fundamentally the same way as the ASP.NET Web Forms equivalents, though with a limited number of properties—some specific to mobile devices. Writing code to manipulate the controls is just like writing ordinary Web Forms code, and you use event handlers and the postback and event-driven architecture of ASP.NET in just the same way.

Mobile Device Filters

Mobile device pages are usually simple and contain very little in the way of formatting or device-specific output beyond that created by the controls themselves. This is because, if you place an element such as a horizontal rule `<hr />` in a mobile page, it will be delivered to every device accessing the page. Many of the WML-based or other specialist devices will not recognize this element, and it will cause an error. Instead, you rely on the controls themselves to generate appropriate output.

However, this does not mean you cannot add some of your own device-specific output as long as you make sure that it is only sent to devices that recognize it. One way to do this is with device filters. You can define filters based on any of the properties exposed by the `HttpBrowserCapabilities` class, or the more specific `MobileDeviceCapabilties` class. For example, Listing 14.15 shows a `web.config` file that declares four device filters, using the `Browser` and `PreferredRenderingType` properties.

> When multiple browser definitions or device filters match the current client, the one that specifies the device with the most precision is chosen, though the settings specified in definitions from which this one inherits are also available if not overridden. For example, an Ericsson T86 phone will expose all the properties defined for a browser definition named `Ericsson T86` plus any that are not overridden here from a general definition aimed at all Ericsson devices, as well as any that are exposed from the `WmlBrowsers` definition.

Listing 14.16 shows one way you can use device filters like those declared in Listing 14.15. When delivering an image to a mobile device, you

Listing 14.15. A web.config file That Declares Device Filters for Different Device Types

```
<configuration>
<system.web>
  <deviceFilters>
    <filter name="IsIE" compare="Browser" argument="IE" />
    <filter name="IsHTML32" compare="PreferredRenderingType"
            argument="html32" />
    <filter name="IsWML11" compare="PreferredRenderingType"
            argument="wml11" />
    <filter name="IsWML12" compare="PreferredRenderingType"
            argument="wml12" />
  </deviceFilters>

  <sessionState cookieless="true" />

</system.web>
</configuration>
```

must ensure that it is of the correct format—most mobile phones that accept WML require a two-color image in the special WBMP format. The `Image` control in Listing 14.16 uses a `DeviceSpecific` control to select the correct image file at runtime, depending on the filter that applies to the current device. The `AlternateText` attribute specifies the text that the device will display if it does not support images.

Listing 14.16. Using a DeviceSpecific Control with the Device Filters

```
<mobile:Form runat="server" id="frmMain" styleReference="styMenu">
  <mobile:Image runat="server" id="myImages"
        AlternateText="Image cannot be displayed on this device.">
    <DeviceSpecific>
      <Choice Filter="IsWML11" ImageUrl="TheLogo.wbmp"/>
      <Choice Filter="IsWML12" ImageUrl="TheLogo.wbmp"/>
      <Choice ImageUrl="TheLogo.gif" Alignment="left" />
    </DeviceSpecific>
  </mobile:Image>
</mobile:Form>
```

Mobile Device Stylesheets

A second technique for adding device-specific content to the output is with a `StyleSheet` control. You declare one or more `<mobile:Style>` sections within the `StyleSheet` control, each identified by a unique `Name`. Within each `<mobile:Style>` section, you can use `DeviceSpecific` controls to specify the output depending on filters declared in your `web.config` file.

Listing 14.17 shows an example of this approach, which uses templates to add some bold text and a series of <font> elements to the head of every page and then closes the <font> element at the foot of every page when the client is a normal HTML-supporting device. For other devices, it just outputs the text "Dave and Al" within a standard <p> element, which all devices recognize.

Listing 14.17. A StyleSheet Control Containing Device-Specific Content

```
<mobile:Stylesheet ID="StyleSheet1" runat="server">
  <mobile:Style Name="styMenu">
    <DeviceSpecific>
      <Choice Filter="IsHTML32">
        <HeaderTemplate>
          <font face="Tahoma,Arial,sans-serif" size="4">
          <b>Welcome to the<br /><font color="#993333">
          - Dave and Al -</font><br />Mobile Web Site</b><p />
          </font><font face="Tahoma,Arial,sans-serif" size="2">
        </HeaderTemplate>
        <FooterTemplate>
          </font>
        </FooterTemplate>
      </Choice>
      <Choice>
        <HeaderTemplate>
          <p>Dave and Al</p>
        </HeaderTemplate>
      </Choice>
    </DeviceSpecific>
  </mobile:Style>
</mobile:Stylesheet>
```

You can then apply this stylesheet to any of the cards in the deck by specifying the Name of the stylesheet as the StyleReference attribute of the mobile form element that implements the card:

```
<mobile:Form runat="server" id="frmMain" StyleReference="styMenu">
  . . .
</mobile:Form>
```

A Simple Mobile Web Forms Example

As an introduction to the mobile controls, this simple example uses a selection of the controls to create an application with three cards or forms. Listing 14.18 shows the page directives that specify this is a mobile page and then import the required assembly. Visual Studio adds these automatically when you create a new Mobile Web Forms page.

Following this are the opening `<html>` and `<body>` tags, and the first form. By default, the first form is the one shown when you first load the page. This form contains an `Image` element with a nested `DeviceSpecific` element, as discussed earlier in this section, which sets the appropriate value for the `ImageUrl` property of the `Image` control. Following the `Image` are a `Label` and a `TextBox` control, and a `Command` with the caption **Next** that executes the server-side routine named `cmdName_Click`.

Listing 14.18. The Page Directives and the First Form in the Example

```
<%@ Page Language ="C#" AutoEventWireup="true"
    CodeFile="mobile-controls.aspx.cs" Inherits="mobile_controls" %>
<%@ Register Tagprefix="mobile" Namespace="System.Web.UI.Mobile Controls"
    Assembly="System.Web.Mobile" %>

<html xmlns="http://www.w3.org/1999/xhtml" >
<body>
  <mobile:Form ID="Form1" runat="server" StyleReference="styMenu">
    <mobile:Image ID="Image1" runat="server"
          AlternateText="Picture cannot be displayed">
      <DeviceSpecific>
        <Choice Filter="IsWML11" ImageUrl="TheLogo.wbmp" />
        <Choice Filter="IsWML12" ImageUrl="TheLogo.wbmp" />
        <Choice ImageUrl="TheLogo.gif" Alignment="Left" />
      </DeviceSpecific>
    </mobile:Image>
    <mobile:Label ID="Label1" runat="server">Your name:</mobile:Label>
    <mobile:TextBox ID="txtName" runat="server"></mobile:TextBox>
    <mobile:Command ID="cmdName" runat="server"
          OnClick="cmdName_Click">Next</mobile:Command>
  </mobile:Form>
```

The other two forms on the page, shown in Listing 14.19, contain a `Label` and `Calendar` control, and a `List` and two `Link` controls. Selecting a date in the `Calendar` will execute the server-side routine named `Calendar1_SelectionChanged`. The `List` control declaration is empty, because code will populate it at runtime. The first `Link` controls point to the first form (with the caption **Home**), by using the familiar URL syntax of a hash followed by the name of the target form as `#Form1`. The second `Link` control points to an external Web site. The page also contains the `StyleSheet` you saw in Listing 14.17.

Listing 14.19. The Remaining Two Forms and Stylesheet in the Example

```
<mobile:Form ID="Form2" runat="server">
  <mobile:Label ID="Label2" runat="server">Birth
        date:</mobile:Label>
  <mobile:Calendar ID="Calendar1" runat="server" Font-Size="Small"
        OnSelectionChanged="Calendar1_SelectionChanged">
  </mobile:Calendar>
</mobile:Form>

<mobile:Form ID="Form3" runat="server" OnActivate="Form3_Activate">
  <mobile:List ID="lstLanguages" runat="server">
  </mobile:List>
  <mobile:Link ID="lnkHome" runat="server"
        NavigateUrl="#Form1" SoftkeyLabel="Home">
    Home
  </mobile:Link>
  <mobile:Link ID="lnkDaveAndAl" runat="server"
            NavigateUrl="http://www.daveandal.net">
    Dave and Al
  </mobile:Link>
</mobile:Form>

<mobile:Stylesheet ID="StyleSheet1" runat="server">
  ... as shown in Listing 16 ...
</mobile:Stylesheet>

</body>
</html>
```

Listing 14.20 shows the complete server-side code for this example. The event handlers for the `TextBox` on the first form, and the `Calendar` on the second form, simply activate the next form by setting the `ActiveForm` property of the default `MobilePage` class. The final method handles the `Page_Load` event of the third form. As you can see, it uses the same class file as in the previous section on accessibility (An Example of an Accessible Page) to get a `DataSet` containing a list of languages and a count of the number of visitors for a fictitious Web site.

However, in small-screen devices, you often cannot display data in a table. One way around this is to concatenate the values in each row as single text strings and then display them in a suitable list control. In this example, the code adds a new column to the table in the `DataSet` and sets an expression for the column that combines the language name and the number of visitors into a text string. Then the code binds the `List` control to the table, specifying that it should display the contents of the new column (named `DisplayText`).

Listing 14.20. The Code for the Mobile Web Forms Example Page

```
protected void cmdName_Click(object sender, EventArgs e)
{
  ActiveForm = Form2;
}

protected void Calendar1_SelectionChanged(object sender, EventArgs e)
{
  ActiveForm = Form3;
}

protected void Form3_Activate(object sender, EventArgs e)
{
  // get table of the results and display them
  DemoLanguages dl = new DemoLanguages();
  DataSet ds = dl.GetDemoDataSet();
  DataTable dt = ds.Tables[0];
  dt.Columns.Add(new DataColumn("DisplayText",
      Type.GetType("System.String"), "Language + ' = ' + Count"));
  lstLanguages.DataSource = dt;
  lstLanguages.DataTextField = "DisplayText";
  lstLanguages.DataBind();
}
```

You can see the results of this example in Figure 14.17. A reduced-size Internet Explorer browser window gives you a good idea what the page will

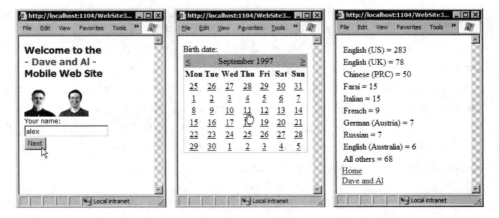

FIGURE 14.17: The application viewed in an HTML device, such as a Pocket PC

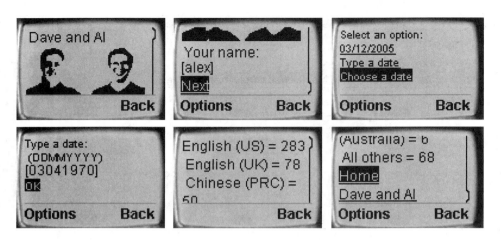

FIGURE 14.18: The same page viewed in a mobile phone emulator

look like in a Pocket PC device, and you can see that the content looks much the same as normal Web pages built as a Web Forms application.

However, if you view the same page in a mobile phone emulator, the result is very different (see Figure 14.18). The two-color image appears this time, and all navigation is through links. The behavior of a `TextBox` control is entirely different (depending on the device type), and the `Calendar` control uses a multistep process to collect the date, because it cannot display it as a table. Finally, the list of languages and visitors shows as a series of text strings, as created by the expression in the new column of the `DataTable`.

It is interesting to look at the code that the mobile controls actually create when the client is a WML-enabled device such as a mobile phone or emulator. The code varies depending on the type of device and the features it supports, but Listing 14.21 shows a typical example. Notice that the `<html>` and `<body>` elements in the original source of the page (required in Visual Studio) are automatically removed and replaced by the `<wml>` and `<card>` elements. You can also see that ASP.NET only sends the current card to the device, minimizing the memory requirements.

Listing 14.21. The WML Code Generated by the Page for a Mobile Phone

```
<?xml version="1.0"?>
<!DOCTYPE wml PUBLIC "-//WAPFORUM//DTD WML 1.1//EN"
          "http://www.wapforum.org/DTD/wml_1.1.xml">
<wml>
  <head>
    <meta http-equiv="Cache-Control" content="max-age=0"/>
  </head>
  <card>
    <do type="prev" label="Back">
      <prev/>
    </do>
    <p>
       Dave and Al
      <br/>
      <img src="TheLogo.wbmp" alt="Picture cannot be displayed"/>
      <br/>
       Your name:
      <br/>
      <input name="mcsvdvmpp0"/>
      <anchor title="Next">
        Next
        <go href="mobile-controls.aspx?__ufps=129306" method="post">
        <postfield name="__EVENTTARGET" value="cmdName"/>
        <postfield name="txtName" value="$(mcsvdvmpp0)"/>
      </go>
      </anchor>
    </p>
  </card>
</wml>
```

Mobile Browser Emulators

Visual Studio includes some device emulators that you can use to view your pages. However, the selection is limited to Pocket PC devices designed for use with the Compact Framework, and a few SmartPhone emulators. All of these expect to receive HTML, and so you will not see the output as it appears for WML devices. If you do not have a mobile device to test your pages, you can use one of several other emulators to simulate a mobile phone, including the following:

- Mobile Phone Simulator from OpenWave, available at http://developer.openwave.com/

- R380 WAP Emulator from Symbian, available at http://www.symbian.com/developer/
- Nokia Mobile Browser from Nokia, available at http://forum.nokia.com/
- SmartPhone Emulator from Yospace, available at http://www.yospace.com/

Using one of these emulators allows you easily to test how well your pages work on a WML-enabled device. Of course, mobile devices include PDAs and phones based on Windows Pocket PC. Although these devices feature a version of Internet Explorer, you still face the problems of a small screen size, so you need to adjust and test your pages accordingly. Find out more about Microsoft Mobile Support at http://www.microsoft.com/windowsmobile/.

Supporting Localization and Multiple Languages

Applications that support localization usually require some method for storing text strings and other content in multiple languages and formats. The usual approach is through resources stored within the project in the standard `.resx` file format. In ASP.NET, you can set up a page or an entire Web application for localization by specifying the resources it requires when you build it, and you can reference resources within an application in both declarative and programmatic ways.

ASP.NET has built-in support for identifying cultures, which define the language and other settings required for the localized output. You can declaratively define resource keys for controls, subobjects, and their properties without writing any code, and you can use page-level or application-level resources to localize an application without having to create and compile satellite assemblies. Finally, you can also use the new mechanism to enable inherent extensibility of resources by storing and retrieving resources from a database or in any other custom format.

In this section, you will see an overview of the code-free approach to localization and multiple culture-handling techniques before moving on to see how to use the new expression types, resource types, and attributes to localize a page—again, without writing any code.

Code-Free Localization

ASP.NET allows you to localize a Web application without writing any code. Microsoft provides built-in localization support within the .NET Framework and Visual Studio 2005. You can localize an application using a combination of implicit and/or explicit expressions as well as page-level and/or application-level resources. The following subsections explain these expression types and resource types with examples.

Using Implicit Expressions and Local Resources

The simplest way to apply localization is through implicit expressions. Visual Studio 2005 greatly simplifies the localization of a page using implicit expressions, page-level or local-level resources, and declarative programming. This gives you an automatic way of applying resources to control properties. Listing 14.22 shows a simple example of this approach with a page that contains a Button, a TextBox, and a Label.

Listing 14.22. A Simple Demonstration of Implicit Expressions

```
<%@Page Language="C#" %>
. . .
<asp:Button ID="Button1" runat="server" Text="English Button" />
<asp:TextBox ID="TextBox1" runat="server" Text="English TextBox" />
<asp:Label ID="Label1" runat="server" Text="English Label" />
```

You can create this page in Visual Studio 2005, switch to Design view, and click **Generate Local Resource** on the **Tools** menu. This writes a resource key into each control and into the Page directive, and adds the Culture and UICulture attributes as shown in Listing 14.23.

Listing 14.23. The Resource Keys Added to the Example Page

```
<%@Page Language="C" meta:resourceKey="PageResource1"
        Culture="auto" UICulture="auto" %>
. . .
<asp:Button ID="Button1" runat="server" Text="English Button"
     meta:resourcekey="Button1Resource1" />
<asp:TextBox ID="TextBox1" runat="server" Text="English TextBox"
     meta:resourcekey="TextBox1Resource1" />
<asp:Label ID="Label1" Runat="server" Text="English Label"
     meta:resourcekey="Label1Resource1" />
</asp:Label>
```

The `Page` directive and every server control now have a resource key indicated by the `meta:resourcekey` attribute. The combination of this attribute and the resource key is an implicit expression. The **Generate Local Resource** command performs several functions:

- It creates an `App_LocalResources` folder (if one does not already exist) to store page-specific resource files.
- It creates a culture-neutral resource file in this folder, using the page name with the extension `.resx`. This file contains the resource values for the keys declared in the page.

You can view the `.resx` file by double-clicking on it in the Solution Explorer window to open it in the RESX editor, as shown in Figure 14.19.

The `.resx` file contains a resource key and the corresponding value for each control property designated internally in the control as localizable. The Visual Studio designer uses the `design-time-only` attribute as a pointer for properties inserted into the `.resx` file. Note that this is not a runtime feature.

Each control can have different properties designated as localizable, although most text-based properties are marked localizable by default. As

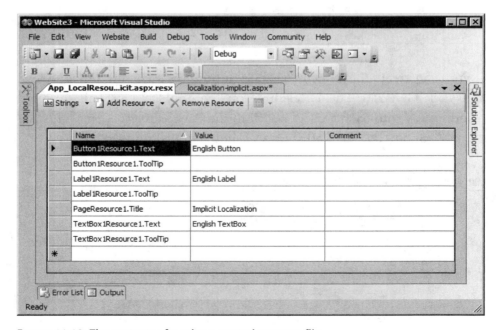

FIGURE 14.19: The contents of a culture-neutral resource file

you can see in Figure 14.19, the `Button` control properties such as `Text` and `ToolTip` are marked as localizable by default. The file also contains a key/value pair for the `Page` directive, which sets the page title. The RESX editor displays all `String`-type properties in the Strings category, and all other types (such as `Boolean`) in the categories available from the drop-down list at the top-left of the Resources Editor window.

You can now create a new resource file that contains resource values in the German culture. Change all occurrences of "English" to "German" in the **Value** column, and save the file with the `.de.resx` file extension (the string "de" is the standard abbreviation for German). Visual Studio adds the new file to the `App_LocalResources` folder and displays it in the Solution Explorer window. You now have two `.resx` files, one for German and the original one not marked with a language abbreviation. The unmarked file is the default, used for any browser requests that do not explicitly request German. In other words, it is the *neutral* culture, sometimes referred to as the *fallback* culture.

The `UICulture="auto"` attribute added to the page automatically by Visual Studio causes ASP.NET to read the culture information within the HTTP headers sent by the client browser. When accessed from a browser that indicates it is set up for the German culture, ASP.NET displays the German version of the page. You have localized a page without writing any code. At runtime, the ASP.NET compiles the `.resx` files and adds them to the assembly, and the Resource Manager performs the resource lookups to get the appropriate values. Figure 14.20 shows the result of running this page with the default culture.

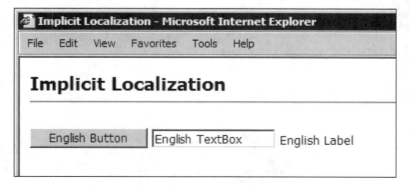

FIGURE 14.20: The result when opening the localized page under the default culture

To see how the culture-specific resources appear, you can set the culture for your browser accordingly. To set the browser culture to German:

1. In Microsoft Internet Explorer, choose **Internet Options** from the **Tools** menu.

2. In the **General** tab of the Internet Options dialog, click the **Languages** button.

3. Click **Add** in the Language Preference dialog, and select **German (Germany) [de]** from the list of languages.

4. Click **OK** to close the Add Language dialog.

5. Back in the Language Preference dialog, select **German (Germany) [de]** from the list of languages, and then click **Move Up**.

6. Click **OK** to close the Language Preference dialog.

7. Click **OK** to close the Internet Options dialog.

Once you set German as the browser culture, ASP.NET will automatically read resource information from the `.de.resx` file and display the German content (including the page title in the browser title bar), as shown in Figure 14.21. If you change the browser culture to any other language, the page will not find a corresponding `.resx` file and will revert to the culture-neutral `.resx` file (the English version).

FIGURE 14.21: The result when opening the localized page under the German culture

You can support more cultures by creating corresponding .resx files. You can then send these files to agencies or translators, along with a read-only version of the source Web page so that they can see the context for the text. After translation, you simply add the .resx files to the App_Local Resources folder and run the page under various browser settings to verify the localization.

◼ **NOTE**

Design view of a localized page always uses the culture-neutral resource file.

Using Explicit Expressions

In the previous section, you saw localization using implicit expressions. Another technique is to take advantage of explicit expressions. Expressions allow you to assign values declaratively to almost any property of a control or an object in a Web page. You can localize a control or an object on a per-property basis using the new expression syntax:

```
<%$ Resources: [NameSpace,] [ClassName.]ResourceKey %>
```

Explicit expressions are useful for localizing those properties not marked as localizable. For example, you can use an explicit expression to localize the BackColor property of a button. You must first define a color resource, which must be available in all appropriate resource files, including the culture-neutral resource file.

You should always add any resource key/value pair manually defined in a culture-specific resource file to the culture-neutral resource file as well.

You can edit the resource files in the built-in resource editor, or by right clicking on them and selecting **Open with**... and then **XML Editor**. Listing 14.24 shows part of the XML view, with a color resource named Mycolor added to the default and the German .resx files using the data and value elements. The color in the culture-neutral resource file is set to Red, and in the German file it is set to Yellow.

Listing 14.24. Additions to the Resource Files to Support a Color Resource

```
Default .resx file
. . .
  <data name="MyColor" xml:space="preserve">
    <value>Red</value>
  </data>
</root>

German .resx file
. . .
  <data name="MyColor" xml:space="preserve">
    <value>Yellow</value>
  </data>
</root>
```

Note that `MyColor` is of type `System.String`. ASP.NET automatically converts the string value to the destination type, as required. You can now use these resource files to change a color property of any control, depending on the current culture. In Visual Studio 2005, you can apply this resource using the Expressions dialog box shown in Figure 14.22. Open the Expressions dialog by clicking the **Expand (...)** button in the **Expressions**

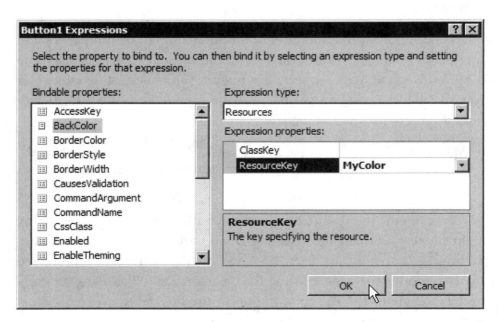

FIGURE 14.22: Setting the BackColor property using the Expressions dialog

box in the Properties window for `Button1`. A pink-colored icon in the Properties window indicates localized properties.

Clicking **OK** in the Expressions dialog creates an explicit expression that assigns the resource to the property you are editing:

```
<asp:Button ID="Button1" runat="server"
    BackColor="<%$ Resources: MyColor %>"
    Text="English Button"
    meta:resourceKey="Button1Resource1" />
```

This expression indicates that the `BackColor` property will use the `MyColor` resource. ASP.NET selects the exact value of the resource at runtime, depending on the culture setting of the user's browser. It converts the resource value to a value of type `System.Drawing.Color` as required by the property of the control.

As with implicit expressions, you can use explicit expressions without writing any code. Figure 14.23 displays the result under German culture after setting the `BackColor` property for the `TextBox` and `Label`.

Of course, you can type the explicit expression directly into the control declaration in Source view instead of using the Expressions dialog box. Expressions are not case sensitive.

Using Global Application Resources

Local resources are great for storing unique resource keys for individual Web pages. However, shared resources are best stored as global application resources. All application-level resources are stored in an `App_Global`

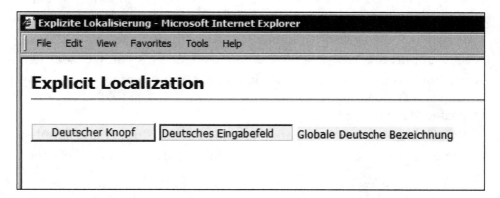

FIGURE 14.23: The results in the German culture when using an explicit expression

`Resources` folder at the Web application level. You can then use them by specifying the namespace and/or class name within the explicit expression syntax.

For example, you can use a shared resource called `MySharedKey` from the files named `MyResources.aspx` and `MyResources.de.aspx` (in a page that has culture resources defined) to set the `Text` property of a `Label` like this:

```
<asp:Label ID="Label1" runat="server"
    BackColor="<%$ Resources: MyColor%>"
    Text="<%$ Resources: MyResources, MySharedKey %>"
    meta:resourceKey="Label1Resource1" />
```

In this example, the `Text` property is set using an explicit expression. However, the expression uses an expanded syntax that includes the name of the resource file (`MyResources`), and the resource (`MySharedKey`). By using this expanded syntax, you can point a property to resources in an application resource file, which in turn allows you to access the same resource file from multiple pages.

You can use both implicit and explicit expressions together, as shown in the example just presented. In such cases, implicit expressions have higher precedence over explicit expressions. In other words, the .NET Framework will use the value of `Label1Resource1.Text` instead of `MySharedKey` to set the `Text` property.

To illustrate this, in the example code just presented, the text in the title bar and the `Tooltip` property of the label will use the local resource file, because this is where the `meta:resourceKey` attributes point. The `Back-Color` property will use the `MyColor` resource from the local resource file, and the `Text` property will use the `MySharedKey` value in the application-level resource file named `MyResources`. You can create as many culture-specific application resource files as you need, and (as you will see later) access both page-level and application-level resources programmatically.

Localizing Static Content

ASP.NET also supports localization of static text markup. This is simply a matter of enclosing the static content within an `<asp:Localize>` element:

```
<asp:Localize runat="server">This will be localized</asp:Localize>
While this will not.
```

After enclosing the text that you wish to localize in the `<asp:Localize>` element, you use the **Generate Local Resource** command in Visual Studio. It creates a resource key for the `<asp:Localize>` element, encodes the text enclosed by the `<asp:Localize>` element, and stores the result as the value for the resource key in the culture-neutral resource file for the page.

> You can work with the `<asp:Localize>` element only in Source view. This element can contain only static content, and not ASP.NET Web Controls. ASP.NET treats all content as static and pushes it into the resource file as it appears in the source of the page, so ASP.NET will not execute any server controls the `<asp:Localize>` element contains at runtime.

Figure 14.24 shows an example page that uses both local (page-level) and global (application-level) resources, and displays the culture name as well. You can get the culture name from the current thread using:

```
String culture = Thread.CurrentThread.CurrentUICulture.ToString();
```

Note that you must import the `System.Threading` namespace into your code file to be able to access the `Thread` class. In C#, you add this statement to your file:

```
using System.Threading;
```

Exempting Controls from Localization

If you do not want to localize a control or `Page` directive, you can set the `meta:localize` attribute to `false`:

```
<asp:Button ID="Button1" Runat="server"
            Text="Don't Localize Me!"
            meta:localize="false" />
```

The button will display the default text "Don't Localize Me!" for all cultures. When you use the Generate Local Resource command, no resource key is generated for controls with the meta:localize attribute set to false.

Hiding Controls at Runtime

In some cases, instead of localizing the properties of a control, you might simply want to hide the control altogether for some cultures. For example, perhaps your Web page contains a graphic that you want to show for some

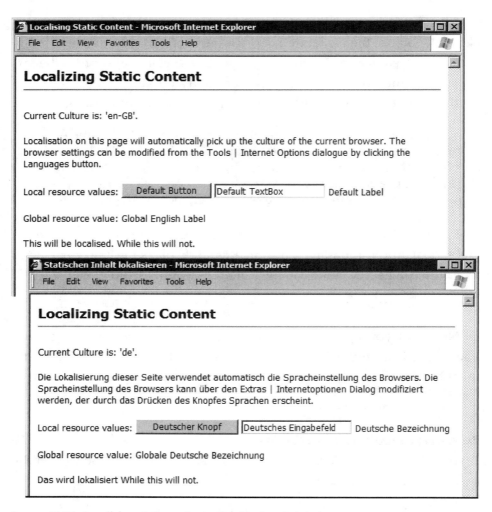

FIGURE 14.24: Localizing static content using local and global resources

cultures but not for others. To hide a control under a specific culture, you add a resource value for the control's `Visible` property and set it to `false`. In the first example, if you want to hide the text box for the German culture, you would add the key `TextBox1Resource1.Visible` with the value `false` to the `.de.resx` file. At runtime, ASP.NET will not include the `TextBox` control in the output for German culture requests, but will display it for all other cultures.

TABLE 14.1: Using the Different Expression and Resource Types

	Can Refer to Local Resources?	Can Refer to Global (Application) Resources?
Implicit expressions	Yes	No
Explicit expressions	Yes	Yes

What Expression Type to Use, and When?

In general, you should use implicit expressions to localize a control or object. The shortened notation allows you to declare the resource key at the control level, instead of having to define an expression for each property of the control. However, you can only use implicit expressions with local resources, meaning that you must have a set of .resx files for each page.

If you are using shared (application-level) resources, you must use explicit expressions to localize a property of a control or object. You can use either expression type with the Page directive, and you can use both implicit and explicit expressions for the same control, as you saw earlier. Such a combination might be useful for properties not localized by default. Table 14.1 shows how the different expression types behave with different resource types.

User-Selectable Localization

There may be times when you prefer your users to be able to select the locale for which they will view the site. Typical implementations have a page showing flags for the languages supported, and selecting the appropriate flag sets the culture. In ASP.NET, you can accomplish this by storing the selected culture as a property of the profile for each user (Chapter 12 describes the profile feature in ASP.NET).

Setting the culture as each page loads, or in a Master Page, is not possible. However, there is a solution: using one of the application events in Global.asax. Consider Listing 14.25, where the CurrentCulture and CurrentUICulture for the CurrentThread are set to a culture stored in the UserCulture property of the user's profile. If no profile is stored, the code sets a default value.

Listing 14.25. Setting Localization Using Code in Global.asax

```
<%@Application Language="C#" %>
<%@Import Namespace="System.Globalization" %>
<%@Import Namespace="System.Threading" %>

<script runat="server">
  protected void Application_PostAcquireRequestState(
                           object sender, EventArgs e)
  {
    CultureInfo ci = null;
    if (Profile.UserCulture != String.Empty)
    {
      ci = new CultureInfo(Profile.UserCulture);
    }
    else
    {
      ci = new CultureInfo("en-gb");
    }
    Thread.CurrentThread.CurrentCulture = ci;
    Thread.CurrentThread.CurrentUICulture = ci;
  }
</script>
```

However, there is a problem in that the culture is set before the page loads, and so any user interaction to change the culture setting will not take effect until the page reloads or the user loads a different page. One way that you can get around this is by adding the culture to the query string of a hyperlink, as shown in Listing 14.26.

Listing 14.26. The Flag Icons and Links to Select the Required Language

```
<asp:Hyperlink ID="Hyperlink1" runat="server"
    ImageUrl="images/en-us.gif" ToolTip="US Culture"
    NavigateUrl="localize-select.aspx?culture=en-us" />
<asp:Hyperlink ID="Hyperlink2" runat="server"
    ImageUrl="images/de-de.gif" ToolTip="German Culture"
    NavigateUrl="localize-select.aspx?culture=de-de" />
<asp:Hyperlink ID="Hyperlink3" runat="server"
    NavigateUrl="localize-select.aspx"
    Text="<%$ Resources: Hyperlink3.Text1 %>" />
```

Then, in the `Page_Load` event handler or in the event handler of a control that causes a postback with the new culture value, you can check if the user selected a language different from that in the user's current profile setting. If so, you can update the profile—making sure you do not attempt to set the `String` value it contains to `null`—and then reload the page using the `Response.Redirect` method (see Listing 14.27). This code also displays the current culture setting.

Listing 14.27. Setting the Profile Property Value and Reloading the Page

```
protected void Page_Load()
{
  String query = Request.QueryString["culture"];
  if (query == null)
  {
    query = String.Empty;
  }
  if (Profile.UserCulture != query)
  {
    // set profile value
    Profile.UserCulture = query;
    // reload page to pick up new culture
    Response.Redirect(Request.Url.ToString(), true);
  }
  lblCulture.Text = Thread.CurrentThread.CurrentUICulture.ToString();
}
```

An alternative approach, if you enable personalization for your site, is to set the culture using an HTTP module that executes before the page Load event occurs. This approach was used in Chapter 12 to set the theme for a page by extracting the user's selection from his or her current profile. As demonstrated in that chapter, in the section Using an HTTP Module to Set the Theme, you create a class that implements the IHttpModule interface and then add it to your web.config file so that ASP.NET executes it as part of the request process. In the module, you extract the selected culture from the profile and apply it to the page.

Figure 14.25 and Figure 14.26 show the example page, first with the US-English culture selected and then with the German culture selected.

Programmatic Access to Resources

Resources are not strongly typed, but you can access them programmatically through the Resource Manager or the methods named GetPage-ResourceObject and GetGlobalResourceObject. Listing 14.28 shows a simple example. Notice how you must create instances of the correct types before assigning them to the control properties, including a System.Drawing.Color instance to set the BackColor of the Button control.

Extensibility

Sources for resource keys and their values are not limited to the file-based .resx format. You can use the rich extensibility mechanism of ASP.NET to

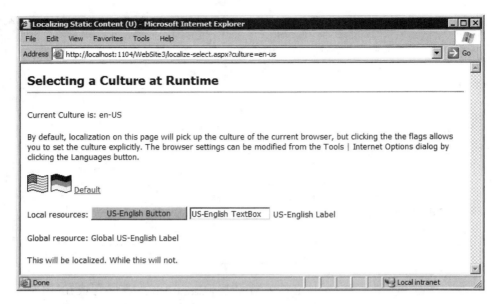

FIGURE 14.25: Selecting the US-English culture in the example page

store and retrieve the resource keys and their values from a database or any custom file format. Using a database makes it easier to centralize the resources for the application across many servers in a Web farm and to ensure central consistency.

FIGURE 14.26: Selecting the German culture in the example page

Listing 14.28. Accessing Local and Application-Level Resources Programmatically

```
protected void Page_Load(object sender, EventArgs e)
{
  Page.Title = GetLocalResourceObject("PageTitle").ToString();
  Button1.Text = GetLocalResourceObject("MyButtonText").ToString();
  String clrName = GetGlobalResourceObject("MyResources",
                                           "MyColor").ToString();
  Color clr = Color.FromName(clrName);
  Button1.BackColor = clr;
  TextBox1.Text = GetGlobalResourceObject(
              "MyResources", "MyTextBoxText").ToString();
}
```

Both the .NET Framework and Visual Studio 2005 support extensibility. You can read and write resource values from a custom source using the `ResourceProviderFactory` and `DesignTimeResourceProviderFactory` classes. For more details, see http://msdn2.microsoft.com/en-us/library/ 9b1d2yze.aspx and http://msdn2.microsoft.com/en-us/library/system. web.ui.design.designtimeresourceproviderfactory.aspx.

Web Resources

Along with their assemblies, control developers often have to supply additional static files such as stylesheets and images. With the new resources model in ASP.NET, you can embed these static files as resources within assemblies. You simply use the `WebResource` attribute from the `System. Web.UI` namespace, as shown in Listing 14.29.

Listing 14.29. Storing an Image As a Resource Within an Assembly

```
[assembly: WebResource("MyImage.gif", "image/gif")]
namespace MyDemoControls
{
  public class MyImageControl : WebControl
  {
    // over-ride creation of child controls
    protected override void CreateChildControls()
    {
      // create new Image element and set ImageUrl
      Image img = new Image();
      img.ImageUrl = this.Page.ClientScript.GetWebResourceUrl(
                  typeof(MyWebControl), "MyImage.gif");
      Controls.Add(img);
    }
  }
}
```

At compile time, you embed the resource into the assembly using:

```
csc /t:library /out:MyImageControl.dll
    /r:System.dll,System.web.dll
    /res:MyImage.gif,MyImage.gif
    MyImageControl.cs
```

The Web resources feature is not limited to just images. For example, to embed JavaScript for client-side support, you could add:

```
[assembly:WebResource("MyScript.js", "text/javascript", true)]
public class MyControl
{
  // control code here
}
```

The third parameter of this attribute indicates that ASP.NET should invoke the Web resource parser for this resource (which is not the default behavior). This ensures that the embedded resource will be valid when used by the client. ASP.NET pages, and controls such as the `TreeView`, use this technique to provide the images and JavaScript they require. You can also access embedded Web resources directly from within ASP.NET pages in code, like this:

```
img1.Image = Page.ClientScript.GetWebResourceUrl(
                 Type.GetType("MyControl"), "MyImage.gif")
```

We are grateful to Dietrich Birngruber for the assistance in the German translations used in this chapter.

SUMMARY

In this chapter, you have seen some of the issues that you should consider when building Web pages and Web applications so that they are accessible to the widest possible audience. You may consider some of these issues to be optional; for example, supporting multiple languages or targeting mobile devices. However, other issues are more important. Making sure your sites are accessible to disabled users is a mandatory requirement in many cases—especially for corporate or government sites that risk legal action if not properly accessible.

This chapter looked at a range of issues that fall under the general heading of "accessibility," both from the technical aspect of browser support and the physical standpoint of the user's capabilities. The first part of the chapter discussed the technical issues of detecting the capabilities of the browser and providing suitable content or information on the requirements to use the site. This included support for features such as client-side scripting and cookies. It also looked at how you can make your pages easier to use by taking advantage of alternate content, short-cut keys, tab order, and general design principles.

The final three sections of the chapter discussed specialist user agent requirements for your sites, breaking this down into categories. The first was how you can provide better support for disabled users, including techniques such as alternate content, provision of extra information within the pages for specialist user agents, and designing the site as a whole to make it easier to use. These are, of course, just extensions of the general techniques discussed in the first parts of the chapter.

The second of the three sections on accessibility showed how you can use a special set of controls that are part of ASP.NET to enable your pages to work correctly on the small-screen and mobile devices that are becoming ever more popular. These often require a special type of markup language as well as consideration of the overall page size, complexity, and navigation strategy you use.

Finally, the last section of the chapter looked briefly at the way you can build sites that support localization (sometimes confusingly referred to as globalization), by allowing users to choose the language for the site or by building your site with conversion to a different language as an installation option. As you saw, this involves more than just changing the text content of the pages.

Overall, you should now have a good grasp of the issues involved in building accessible Web sites and Web applications and be prepared to implement these features as you design and build your sites.

■ 15 ■
Using the Framework Classes

M OST OF THIS BOOK so far has concentrated, quite correctly, on the classes in the `System.Web` and associated namespaces of the .NET Framework. This is what you would expect, because it is here that the classes implementing ASP.NET reside. However, .NET provides a rich environment of managed code objects that you can use from code in your ASP.NET pages.

This makes many tasks much easier than in previous (and other) environments where you have to instantiate external components to be able to step outside the bounds of the intrinsic language capabilities. For example, in versions of ASP prior to ASP.NET, you often had to resort to registering COM objects of various kinds and then instantiating them within the process of your Web server.

Now, using the Framework classes, you benefit from the inherent flexibility, efficiency, and safety that managed code provides. There is no need to go across processing boundaries when calling other classes; and the features such as automatic garbage collection, integrated debugging capabilities, simple no-registration deployment, and compatible data and parameter types make using the Framework classes much easier.

In this chapter, you will see some of the ways you can use the classes in the namespaces outside of `System.Web`, including:

- Storing data with the `System.Collections` classes
- Reading, writing, and compressing data with the `System.IO` classes

- Creating graphics and images with the `System.Drawing` classes
- Accessing the Internet with the `System.Net` classes
- Sending e-mail with the `System.Net.Mail` classes
- Accessing Active Directory with the `System.DirectoryServices` classes
- Encrypting data with the `System.Security.Cryptography` classes

The chapter starts with a look at the example application provided for this chapter, which illustrates techniques related to all of the topics just presented.

The Example Application

Any one of the topics listed in the introduction to this chapter would, if covered in detail, fill a whole chapter on its own. The breadth of the .NET Class Library, and the number of classes in each namespace, can be intimidating until you begin to find your way around. The purpose of the example application, and this chapter as a whole, is to help you discover what features are available, how they are used, and where to look for more information when you need to perform tasks of greater complexity than those in the example application.

You will not see all the code in the example application listed in this chapter. Instead, you will see the important concepts described, along with the relevant sections of code. In addition, pointers will show you where to go to see the code in its entirety within the application source, and where to find out more details of the classes that it uses.

Figure 15.1 shows the application when you start it up. The best way to see it, and work with the code it contains, is to load the project from the `Ch15` subfolder of the example files into Visual Studio.

As you can see, the example allows you to create instances of seven different types of objects or select an existing file, perform up to three processes on that object, and then output it to one of four destinations. Throughout this chapter, you will see the way it works, what the results look like, and how the underlying code accomplishes these tasks.

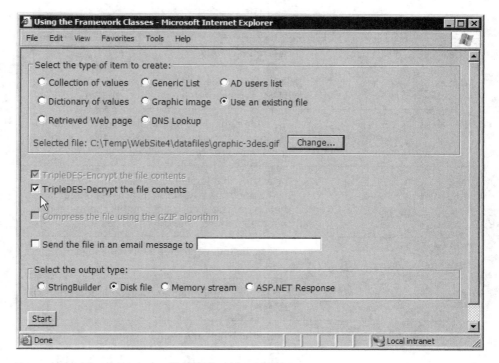

FIGURE 15.1: The example application for this chapter

There is a lot of code in the project. To help you find your way around, Table 15.1 contains a list and description of the main files.

Configuring the Example on Your Machine

At runtime, ASP.NET compiles the files in the `App_Code` folder automatically to take into account any edits you made to these files. However, before you run the example on your machine, there are a few setup tasks. First, open `default.aspx.cs` and edit the four `String` values near the top of the page to suit your machine and requirements (see Listing 15.1). These represent the URL of the Web page that the example will attempt to retrieve, and the URL for which it will attempt to retrieve the DNS entries. The final two values must be set to an e-mail address that is valid on your e-mail server or domain, so that the SMTP service or mail server will accept

TABLE 15.1: The Files in the Example Project

File Name and Location	Description
default.aspx	The interface file for the main page, containing the HTML, server controls, and other content.
default.aspx.cs	The code-behind file for the main page, containing the code that manages the main interface features and handles the interface events.
App_Code\ Ch15DataProcess.cs	A class file that implements the main processes in the application. It contains a series of methods that demonstrate each topic in this chapter and that the interface code calls as required.
App_Code\ PieChart.cs	A class file that generates a bitmap image of a pie chart.
App_Code\Point.cs	A class file that implements a generic collection of objects.
datafiles folder	The folder where the example generates its output files.
images folder	Two images used in the TreeView control you will see later in this chapter

and send your messages, and the name or IP address of the SMTP mail server to use.

Listing 15.1. The Configuration Values in default.aspx.cs

```
// specify these values to suit your requirements
String theWebPage = "http://your-own-site.com/";
String theDnsHost = "your-own-site.com";
String emailFromAddr = "from.you@your-own-site.com";
String smtpServerName = "your-smtp-server-name";
```

In fact, the classes in System.Net.Mail read SMTP configuration data from the <mailSettings> section of the web.config file. You can configure the default values here and remove the code that sets them from the example if you prefer. Listing 15.2 shows the syntax of the <mailSettings> section of web.config.

Listing 15.2. Configuring Your Mail Settings in web.config

```
<system.net>
  <mailSettings>
    <smtp from="from.you@your-own-site.com">
      <network host="your-smtp-server-name" port="25"
               userName="your-username" password="your-password"
               defaultCredentials="true" />
    </smtp>
  </mailSettings>
</system.net>
```

Using a Remote SMTP Server

The simplest setup is to use the local SMTP server on the machine where you are running the example (if it is Windows 2000 Server or Windows Server 2003). If you want to relay through a remote mail server, you should be sure to log on to your machine with an account that has relay permissions on the mail server.

You can specify credentials when you send e-mail messages if your account does not have permission to send e-mail through a remote SMTP server. Near to the end of the `SendEmailMessage` routine in the file `Ch15DataProcess.cs`, you can add code to generate a suitable `Network-Credential` instance, and replace the one used in the code. For sending messages under your default credentials, the code uses:

```
// add default credentials for accessing SMTP server
sender.Credentials = CredentialCache.DefaultNetworkCredentials;
```

Instead, the code shown in Listing 15.3 creates a new `Network-Credential`, adds it to a new `CredentialCache`, and then sets it on the `SmtpClient` that sends the message to the SMTP server. You specify the URL or server name of the target server, and the authentication method (such as "Basic" or "NTLM") that it requires. If needed, you can specify the domain in which the account resides as well, as shown in the listing.

Listing 15.3. Creating a NetworkCredential for the SMTP Server

```
NetworkCredential nc;
nc = new NetworkCredential(username, password [, domain]);
CredentialCache cc = new CredentialCache();
cc.Add(new Uri("your-smtp-server-url"),"auth-type", nc);
sender.Credentials = cc;
```

Setting Disk Access Permissions

The other task is to ensure that the account you are running the example under has read, write, and modify (change) permission for the `datafiles` subfolder where it will place its generated files. If you are running the example from within Visual Studio or VWD, you should set up permission for your own account. If you are running the example under IIS, you should set the permissions for the **ASPNET** and **NETWORK SERVICE** accounts.

The User Interface of the Example Application

As well as a demonstration of many techniques using the classes in the namespaces you saw listed at the start of this chapter, the example also shows how you can use two useful ASP.NET server controls—the `Multi-View` and `TreeView`. You saw the `TreeView` used in Chapter 10, but this example uses it in a different way by populating the nodes dynamically on demand.

Using the MultiView Control

As you run the example, it appears to consist of three different pages. The first, shown in Figure 15.1, contains the controls to select the operation(s) you wish to perform. The second page, shown in Figure 15.2, displays a list of the drives, folders, and files on your system. The third page, which you will see later, displays the results of the selected operation.

While these appear to be separate pages, they are in fact all just views of specific sections of a single page. The `MultiView` control allows you to define a series of sections in a page using `View` controls, and then activate one of these views dynamically at runtime. Listing 15.4 shows an outline of the code in the page `default.aspx`, and you can see the `MultiView` control and the three `View` controls (some of the content of each `View` control has been removed for clarity, but you can see it all by opening the page in Visual Studio or a text editor).

The `ActiveViewIndex` property of the `MultiView` control defines the `View` that will show when the page loads, with the `View` controls indexed from zero. The attribute `ActiveViewIndex="0"` you see in Listing 15.4 therefore means that the first view defined within the page will be visible

Listing 15.4. Using a MultiView Control to Display Separate Views of the Page content

```
<asp:MultiView ID="MultiView1" runat="server" ActiveViewIndex="0">

  <asp:View ID="view1" runat="server">
    <asp:Panel ID="Panel1" runat="server"
        GroupingText="Select the type of item to create:">
      ...
    <asp:Button ID="btnStart" runat="server" Text="Start"
        OnClick="btnStart_Click" />
  </asp:View>

  <asp:View ID="view2" runat="server">
    <asp:Panel ID="Panel3" runat="server"
        GroupingText="Select an existing file:">
      <div style="padding:5px">
        <asp:TreeView>
          ...
        </asp:TreeView>
      </div>
    </asp:Panel>
    <asp:Button ID="btnCancel" runat="server" Text="Cancel"
        OnClick="btnCancel_Click" />
  </asp:View>

  <asp:View ID="view3" runat="server">
    <asp:Panel ID="Panel4" runat="server"
        GroupingText="Result:">
      <div style="padding:5px">
        <asp:Label ID="lblResult" runat="server" />
        ...
      </div>
    </asp:Panel>
    <asp:Button ID="btnBack" runat="server" Text="Back"
        OnClick="btnCancel_Click" />
  </asp:View>

</asp:MultiView>
```

when the page loads for the first time. After that, the viewstate of the page will maintain the `ActiveViewIndex` value so that the same view displays until you change it.

In the example, code in an event handler that executes when clicking the **Use an existing file** option in the first view displays the page containing the `TreeView` control shown in Figure 15.2, using this code:

```
MultiView1.SetActiveView(view2);
```

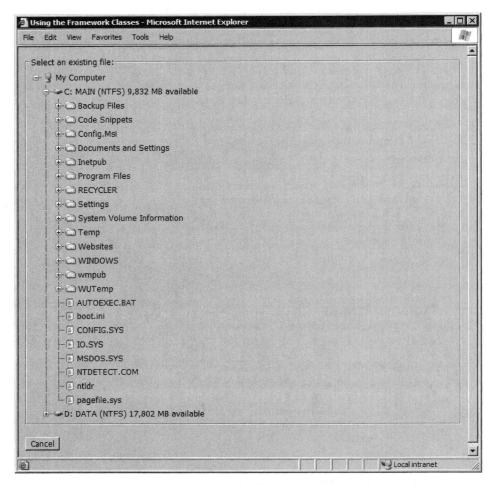

FIGURE 15.2: The second page of the example displays drive and file information using a TreeView control

In a similar way, clicking any file in the `TreeView` then executes an event handler that re-displays the first view, while clicking the **Start** button in the first view executes the selected process(es) and shows the third view containing the results. The code in the `btnCancel_Click` event handler, which buttons in the second and third views call, simply displays the first view again using:

```
MultiView1.SetActiveView(view1);
```

You can see that the `MultiView` is an extremely useful control for building pages that require separate "screens" as part of an overall process. In fact, it gives you the opportunity to build pages that work in a similar way to the `MobilePage` with its multiple sever-side `<form>` sections you saw in the previous chapter. The advantage is that ASP.NET automatically maintains the values in the controls in all views, irrespective of whether they are visible or not, making writing the code much simpler.

The downside is that this increases the viewstate of the page, and hence the amount of data that is sent back and forth over the network with each page request. It also, of course, increases the processing load on your server, though this is only likely to be noticeable in very large pages or very busy sites.

Styling and Dynamically Populating a TreeView Control

In Figure 15.2, you can see how the example uses a `TreeView` control to display the contents of your system's hard disk. This is a common way to view disk information, and one of the styles included with ASP.NET, which you can apply using the **Auto-Format** option in the task pane for the `TreeView` in design view, provides the appearance you see here. You can also apply it directly by setting the `ImageSet` property to "XPFileEx-plorer", as shown in Listing 15.5.

Listing 15.5. The TreeView Control Using the ImageSet That Generates a File Explorer

```
<asp:TreeView ID="treeDir" runat="server" ImageSet="XPFileExplorer"
    NodeIndent="15" ShowLines="True" ExpandDepth="1"
    PathSeparator="\" LeafNodeStyle-ChildNodesPadding="3"
    NodeStyle-Font-Size="X-Small" EnableClientScript="false"
    OnTreeNodePopulate="PopulateNode"
    OnSelectedNodeChanged="SelectNode">
  ...
</asp:TreeView>
```

Notice that the declaration in Listing 15.5 sets the attributes `Enable-ClientScript` and `OnTreeNodePopulate`. The code in the example populates the `TreeView` control dynamically, rather than using data binding as in earlier chapters. However, you must consider how the user will interact with the control, and how this may affect performance, when using any control that can potentially contain as much content as you see in Figure 15.2.

The example displays drive and file information, and experience of using some directory listing tools (especially over a network) will have shown that retrieving this information is not an instantaneous process. If you were to populate fully the `TreeView` with the contents of every drive and every folder when starting the application, and the user never activated that view, all that effort, processing cost, and delay would have been wasted. Even if you were to populate it only when activating this view (perhaps by handling the `Activated` event), users would still experience significant delays. In addition, the viewstate would be huge.

Far better is to populate only a small section at the root of the `TreeView` by default, and then populate each drive and subfolder only as the user opens it. This process, called **populate on demand,** is how Windows Explorer works. You must disable client-side script in the `TreeView` control so that the action of opening nodes in the tree causes a postback to the server. Then you handle the `OnTreeNodePopulate` event in your server-side code to populate each node as the user opens it by creating and adding `TreeNode` instances. You will see how the example page does this in the section Reading Drive, Folder, and File Information later in this chapter.

> You can implement populate-on-demand client-side by writing script that either stores all of the required data on the client at page load, or that fetches it in the background using callbacks as required. In this case, you would leave client-side scripting enabled on the control, and implement the required client-side event handlers. For more information, see: http://msdn.microsoft.com/library/en-us/dnvs05/html/ treeview. asp and http://www.dotnetjunkies.com/Article/E80EC96F-1C32-4855-85AE-9E30EECF13D7.dcik

Storing Data with the System.Collections Classes

The .NET Framework provides a rich set of classes you can use to store collections or sets of data. This includes the common approaches such as using an array, plus many specialist classes such as `ArrayList`, `HashTable`, `SortedList`, `Stack`, and `Queue`. While you can implement these kinds of collections using custom code, the built-in classes make it much easier by automatically handling issues such as increasing the size to accommodate new items, and providing methods for interacting with the contents. In this section, you will see come examples of using these classes.

The main collection classes are in the namespace System.Collections, while the System.Collections.Specialized namespace contains some more specialized types such as NameValueCollection and String-Collection. The generic collections classes, which allow you to create collections of specific or custom objects, are in the System.Collections. Generic namespace. You must ensure that you add a reference to the appropriate namespace to your project, and import these namespaces into your pages when you use these collection classes.

ArrayLists

Probably the most commonly used collection class is the ArrayList, which provides a way to store values of any type in a structure based on an array. It provides properties that indicate the capacity and current size; and a wide range of methods that allow you to resize the list; and add, remove, copy, and find items. For example, the code in Listing 15.6 (taken from the Get-Collection method of the Ch15DataProcess.cs file) shows how you can create and add String values to an ArrayList, then sort the list based on the default sorting order of the contents. You can also specify start and end indexes to sort sections of the ArrayList. If you store custom objects in the list, or want to sort it in a non-standard way, you can create a class that implements the IComparer interface and use this when sorting the contents.

Listing 15.6. Creating, Populating, and Sorting an ArrayList

```
// create an ArrayList and add some values
ArrayList theList = new ArrayList();
theList.Add("Horse");
theList.Add("Dog");
theList.Insert(0, "Hamster");
// sort the list contents
theList.Sort();
```

Listing 15.7 shows how you can clear all the items from an ArrayList, and then add items from another collection to the end. In this case, it is a Queue but it could be another `ArrayList` or other type of collection. To insert items in the middle of the `ArrayList`, you would use the `InsertRange` method.

This code also shows how you can find and remove items using the `Contains` method to see if it exists first, and then locating it using the `IndexOf` method and removing it with the `RemoveAt` method. There is also the `LastIndexOf` method for locating the last occurrence of an item, and the `Remove` method that removes the first instance of a specified item. Notice in the last line of Listing 15.7 how you can convert an `ArrayList` into a normal array, specifying the data type of the items for the array.

Listing 15.7. Clearing, Adding a Range, Searching, and Removing an Item from an ArrayList

```
theList.Clear();
theList.Add("Goat");
theList.AddRange(theQueue);
// remove an item after checking it is there
// using index (though "Remove" method would be
// easier as it takes the value and finds it)
if (theList.Contains("Pig"))
{
   theList.RemoveAt(theList.IndexOf("Pig"));
}
// get an Array from the ArrayList
Array theArray = theList.ToArray(Type.GetType("System.String"));
```

Stacks and Queues

The `GetCollection` method in the example application also demonstrates use of a `Stack` and `Queue` collection. A `Stack` provides a "last-in-first-out" (LIFO) collection where you `Push` an item onto the stack and the `Pop` it from the top of the stack, or `Peek` to see what the top item is without removing it. You can also query properties of the `Stack` class to see how many items it contains, clear the stack with the `Clear` method, and see if it contains an item using the `Contains` method.

The `Queue` collection provides a similar set of properties and methods to the `Stack`, but is a "first-in-first-out" (FIFO) collection. You add items to the end of the queue using the `Enqueue` method, and remove them from the front of the queue using the `Dequeue` method. Listing 15.8 shows how the example uses a `Stack` and a `Queue`, including creating them from an existing collection.

Listing 15.8. Using the Stack and Queue Classes

```
// create a Stack from the ArrayList and
// remove and add a value at top
Stack theStack = new Stack(theList);
String retrieved = theStack.Pop().ToString();
theStack.Push("Pig");
// create a Queue from the Stack and add
// at end the value popped from the Stack
Queue theQueue = new Queue(theStack);
theQueue.Enqueue(retrieved);
// remove a value from front of Queue
// add put back at end, and add new value
theQueue.Enqueue(theQueue.Dequeue());
theQueue.Enqueue("Cat");
```

Sorted Lists, HashTables, and Dictionary-Based collections

The collection classes you have seen so far are one-dimensional, in that they store what is, basically, a list of values. You can, however, create custom classes or objects and store these in a collection such as an `ArrayList`. Other collection types store values in dictionary form, where a key locates each entry. Examples of this are the `SortedList`, `HashTable`, `StringDictionary`, and `NameValueCollection`.

These types of collections provide access via a key value, and you can obtain a list of the keys or a list of the values from the `Keys` and `Values` properties of the collection, or (depending on the type of list) use methods such as `GetKey` and `GetValue` to retrieve items. There are also properties and methods such as `Clear`, `Add`, `Remove`, and `CopyTo` for examining or manipulating the contents of the collections.

ASP.NET uses the `NameValueCollection` class for tasks such as storing the name/value pairs in a query string, and is ideal where you want to be able to manipulate values using the key name. The `StringDictionary` class is a good way to manage a simple list of `String` values where a key identifies each one. The `HashTable` class uses a hash function to generate unique keys that identify values, and stores the values internally in a way that optimizes performance when searching for and retrieving values.

The `SortedList` class, meanwhile, is a more complex class that automatically maintains the contents sorted into the default order of the key values. This makes it ideal for situations where you need the items sorted at all times, and can considerably simplify your code. When you create a `SortedList` instance, you can—as with the `ArrayList`—provide a custom object that implements the `IComparer` interface to manage the sort order in a non-standard way.

The `SortedList` class also implements many more methods than the other `Dictionary`-based classes. For example, there are the `ContainsKey`, `ContainsValue`, `IndexOfKey`, and `IndexOfValue` methods for locating items, `GetByIndex` for retrieving items, and `RemoveAt` for removing an item—over and above the methods implemented by the other collection classes.

Listing 15.9 shows some of the ways you can use the `SortedList` class (this code is also contained in the `GetCollection` method of the `Ch15DataProcess.cs` file). It takes an `Array` of `String` values and inserts these into a new `SortedList` instance in the order they appear in the array. You cannot iterate over an `Array` using a `foreach` construct, and so the code demonstrates an alternative approach. You could use a `for` loop, and stop when it reaches the end of the array determined by the `Length` property. However, this example shows how you can create an **enumerator,** which works over many list types including the `SortedList`.

A call to the `GetEnumerator` method returns an instance of a class that implements the `IEnumerator` interface. This interface contains methods that allow you to iterate over the list, including the `MoveNext` method that returns `false` when it reaches the end of the list. At any point, the `Current` property of the enumerator returns a reference to the current item in the list.

The result of the code in Listing 15.9, combined with the previous blocks of code in this section of the chapter, creates a `StringBuilder` containing a list of animals in the variable `sourceString`. The example then displays this string in the third `View` control and makes it the active view, to give the result shown in Figure 15.3. You can see the original ordering of items

Listing 15.9. Using the SortedList Class

```
// create a SortedList and fill with the Array
SortedList theSortedList = new SortedList();
// Array does not support foreach so must create
// an enumerator and iterate the array with MoveNext
IEnumerator en = theArray.GetEnumerator();
Int32 index = 0;
while (en.MoveNext())
{
  // add the animal name as the key and a number
  // to indicate its original position in the list
  index++;
  theSortedList.Add(en.Current.ToString(), index);
}
// return the SortedList collection as a String
// use a StringBuilder to concatenate the values
StringBuilder builder = new StringBuilder();
foreach (String key in theSortedList.GetKeyList())
{
  builder.Append(key + " was added in position "
          + theSortedList[key].ToString() + "\n");
}
sourceString = builder.ToString();
return SourceFileType.Text;
```

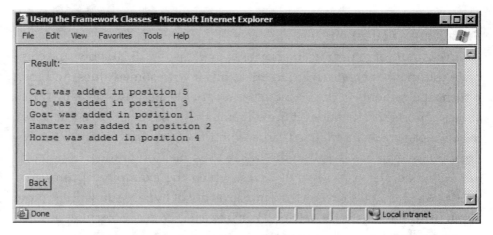

FIGURE 15.3: The result of creating a collection of values using several of the collection classes with the Framework

in the `ArrayList`, `Stack`, and `Queue` collections after adding and removing them. However, the `SortedList` automatically maintains the ordering based on the key value—which in this case is the name of the animal.

How the Example Returns Values

You can see that the value returned from the `GetCollection` method is a `String`, stored in the variable `sourceValue`. This variable, along with a variable named `sourceBytes`, is declared at the beginning of the `Click` event handler for the `Start` button (`btnStart_Click`). This event handler manages the selection of the function that generates the initial object, applies the selected process(es) to it, and then generates the type of output selected in the initial page of the example.

Depending on which type of item the example is creating, it stores the value either as a `String` or as a `Byte` array. A third variable named `sourceType` indicates which of the other two variables contains the result. The code sets this variable to one of the values from the `SourceFileType` enumeration that is declared in the `Ch15DataProcess.cs` file. Each routine in the `Ch15DataProcess.cs` file that creates a source item takes a reference to both the `Byte` array and the `String`, and returns a `SourceFileType` value to indicate the type of data created.

Serializing a Collection

As an example of returning an array of `Bytes`, Listing 15.10 shows the complete routine that creates a `HashTable`, fills it with some values, and then returns the contents in the `sourceBytes` variable. Because the `HashTable` class supports serialization (it implements the `ISerializable` interface), the code can create a serialized representation of the class using a `Binary-Formatter` instance. A call to the `Serialize` method of the `BinaryFor-matter` generates a `Stream` of bytes, which the example captures in a `MemoryStream` and then converts into an array of `Bytes`. You will see more about using streams in the section *"Working with Streams, StreamReaders, and StreamWriters"* later in this chapter.

If you select **Dictionary of values** as the source item type in the example page, and **Memory stream** as the output type, you will see the results of serializing the `HashTable` object—as shown in Figure 15.4.

Listing 15.10. The Routine to Create a HashTable Instance as an Array of Bytes

```
public static SourceFileType GetDictionary(
      ref Byte[] sourceBytes, ref String sourceString)
{
  try
  {
    // create and fill a HashTable with some values
    Hashtable theTable = new Hashtable();
    for (Int32 index = 0; index < 20; index++)
    {
      theTable.Add(index, "Item" + index.ToString());
    }
    // create a BinaryFormatter to serialize the contents
    IFormatter formatter = new BinaryFormatter();
    MemoryStream ms = new MemoryStream();
    formatter.Serialize(ms, theTable);
    ms.Position = 0;
    sourceBytes = new Byte[ms.Length];
    ms.Read(sourceBytes, 0, (Int32)ms.Length);
    return SourceFileType.Bytes;
  }
  catch (Exception ex)
  {
    throw ex;
  }
}
```

Remember to import the System.Runtime.Serialization and System.Runtime.Serialization.Formatters.Binary namespaces if you want to use the BinaryFormatter class as shown here.

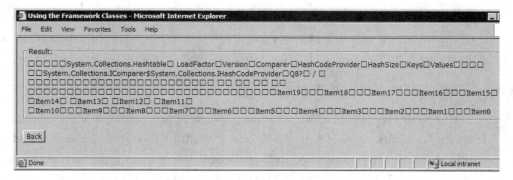

FIGURE 15.4: Serializing a HashTable instance and displaying the serialized contents

Generic Collections

One of the recent features added to both the C# and VB.NET languages is support for generics. You can use generics to define data structures that are type-safe, in other words will only accept instances of values and objects of a specific type, without having to actually specify the type when you build the structure. You then use generic syntax to create instances of these types that are specific to the required data type. For example, if you have a class that stores instances of some generic type, and you want to be able to use the class with different data types, you can declare it like this:

```
public class MyStructure<T>
{
    ... implementation here ...
}
```

You can then create an instance of this structure that works with integer values using:

```
MyStructure<Int32> theStruct = new MyStructure<Int32>();
```

If you then try and pass any item other than an `Int32` to the class, it will raise an exception as it is now specific to it the `Int32` data type. The result is that you can re-use code without having to generate different classes for each data type they must handle, while still getting type-safety checking performed when referencing the class and its methods. The equivalent syntax in VB.NET to declare a generic class is:

```
Public Class MyStructure(Of T)
    ... implementation here ...
End Class
```

You can then create an instance of this class in VB.NET for integer values using:

```
Dim theStruct As New MyStructure(Of Int32)()
```

The `System.Collections.Generic` namespace contains some useful classes for working with generic code including the generic `List` class (although you can use other collection classes as a basis for your own generic lists). Listing 15.11 shows the declaration of a very simple class called `Point` (in the file `Point.cs` of the example) that stores the X and Y coordinates of a point.

Listing 15.11. The Custom Point Class

```
using System;
using System.Runtime.Serialization;

[Serializable]
public class Point
{
  private Double m_x;
  private Double m_y;

  // constructor - takes X and Y values for new Point
  public Point(Double X, Double Y)
  {
    m_x = X;
    m_y = Y;
  }
}
```

The `GetGenericList` method of the file `Ch15DataProcess` uses the `Point` class when you select the **Generic List** option in the main page. The method code (shown in Listing 15.12) creates a new generic `List`, adds some new `Point` instances to it, then generates a serialized representation of the contents using a `BinaryFormatter`—as you saw in the previous section.

Listing 15.12. Generating a Serialized Representation of a Generic List

```
List<Point> points = new List<Point>();
points.Add(new Point(10, 10));
points.Add(new Point(20, 40));
points.Add(new Point(76, 0));
points.Add(new Point(104, 17));
points.Add(new Point(133, 200));
// create a BinaryFormatter to serialize the contents
IFormatter formatter = new BinaryFormatter();
MemoryStream ms = new MemoryStream();
formatter.Serialize(ms, points);
ms.Position = 0;
sourceBytes = new Byte[ms.Length];
ms.Read(sourceBytes, 0, (Int32)ms.Length);
return SourceFileType.Bytes;
```

For more information on generics in C#, see http://msdn.microsoft. com/library/default.asp?url=/library/en-us/dnvs05/html/csharp_ generics.asp and http://msdn.microsoft.com/msdnmag/issues/ 03/09/NET/default.aspx.

For VB.NET, take a look at http://msdn.microsoft.com/msdnmag/ issues/04/09/AdvancedBasics/ and http://msdn.microsoft.com/ library/en-us/dnhcvs04/html/vs04k1.asp

Reading, Writing, and Compressing Data with the System.IO Classes

After storing data in collections, the next most common tasks are to read and write data in a range of ways. This can include simply storing it in memory, accessing a stream of data from another object, or accessing the file system—in particular by reading and writing disk files. This section shows you some of the ways you can achieve all these tasks, as well as how you can compress data using classes built into the .NET Framework.

Working with Streams, StreamReaders, and StreamWriters

Many classes that handle data in .NET consume or expose it as a stream. A stream is just a series of data items read serially from the source object or to the target object. There is a base class `Stream` from which almost all stream-based classes in .NET are descended. The concrete classes you will use most often are the `MemoryStream`, `FileStream`, and perhaps the ASP.NET `Response.OutputStream`.

There are operations you can perform directly on a stream. For example, (as you saw in the previous section) you can capture output from a class such as the `BinaryFormatter` in a `MemoryStream`:

```
MemoryStream ms = new MemoryStream();
formatter.Serialize(ms, theTable);
```

Effectively, this just creates the `MemoryStream` over the output of the `Serialize` method and pushes the data into the stream. Then you can reset the "current position" pointer of the stream back to the start, and read values from it. The `Read` method of a stream takes a reference to a buffer array of `Bytes`, the starting index within the stream for reading, and the number of bytes to read. In the example that you saw earlier, the code creates a new

`Byte` array of the same length as the stream, and reads from zero to the length of the stream to capture all of it in the `Byte` array:

```
ms.Position = 0;
sourceBytes = new Byte[ms.Length];
ms.Read(sourceBytes, 0, (Int32)ms.Length);
```

The `MemoryStream` is a useful tool for acting as an intermediary between other objects. You can also create a `MemoryStream` and populate it from an array of `Bytes`, like this:

```
MemoryStream outStream = new MemoryStream(sourceBytes);
```

The `MemoryStream` can then act as input to another process or object that requires data in stream format. Like most streams, the `MemoryStream` exposes a series of properties and methods that provide information and allow you to manipulate the stream. The `CanRead`, `CanSeek`, and `CanWrite` properties provide information about the stream, and their values depend on how you create the stream and from what object it is populated. The `Capacity` and `Length` properties provide information about the maximum and the current size, while you can read and/or set the current position using the `Position` property.

The .NET Framework also provides classes you can use to read and write streams. The `StreamReader` and `StreamWriter` accept a stream as the input or output, and expose methods that make it easy to access the underlying stream. For example, the `StreamReader` exposes the `Peek`, `Read`, `ReadBlock`, `ReadLine`, and `ReadToEnd` methods for reading data from the stream. The `Peek` method reads a value without consuming it (without moving the current position pointer), while the `Read` and `Read-Block` methods read one or more values and move the current position pointer. The `ReadLine` method reads up to the next carriage return in a text stream, and the `ReadToEnd` method reads the remainder of the stream.

The `StreamWriter` class exposes the `Write` method in a range of over-loads for writing individual values to the stream, and the `WriteLine` method for writing a line of text followed by a carriage return. Both also expose the `Close` method, and it is important with all streams to close them when you have finished working with them—or take advantage of the `using` statement construct to automatically close and dispose of the stream reader/writer and underlying stream after use.

Most of the stream-based classes are in the `System.IO` namespace, which you must import into your pages in order to use them. Other classes in this namespace include the `BinaryReader` and `BinaryWriter` for reading primitive types from a stream, and the `BufferedStream` that you generally use in networking applications.

The example application uses a range of stream types, and the `Stream-Reader` class. For example, Listing 15.13 shows the code used to display the contents of a `MemoryStream` in the "results" part of the application. It first checks that it can read from the stream, then creates a `StreamReader` over the `MemoryStream` and ensures that the current position pointer of the `MemoryStream` is at the start of the stream. Then the code calls the `Read-ToEnd` method to get the contents as a `String` to display in a `Label` control. Notice that, if the selected input type was a Web page, the content is HTML-encoded for display. Otherwise, the browser will interpret the HTML tags in the result rather than displaying the string itself.

Listing 15.13. Using a StreamReader over a MemoryStream

```
if (outStream.CanRead)
{
  StreamReader reader = new StreamReader(outStream);
  outStream.Position = 0;
  String result = reader.ReadToEnd();
  if (sourceOption == "web")
  {
    // HTML-encode it for display
    result = Server.HtmlEncode(result);
  }
  lblResult.Text = result;
}
else
{
  lblResult.Text = "Cannot read from MemoryStream.";
}
outStream.Close();
```

You will also see a `StreamReader` used in the sections *"Reading Text and Binary Files from the File System"* and *"Retrieving Web Pages"* later in this chapter.

One other very useful class is the `Path` class, which exposes a series of static methods you can use to manipulate file paths and file names. For example, you can use the `GetDirectoryName`, `GetExtension`, `GetFileName`, `Get-FileNameWithoutExtension`, `GetPathRoot`, and `GetFullPath` methods to extract sections of an existing path and file name string. You can check if the name has an extension, and change it, using the `HasExtension` and `Change-Extension` methods. You can see if a path contains the root drive information using the `IsRooted` method. You can also combine parts of a path, automatically ensuring that the correct separator character is used, with the `Combine` method. Other methods of the `Path` class allow you to check for invalid characters in the file name and path, get a random or a temporary file name, and discover the path to use for temporary files.

Reading Drive, Folder, and File Information

Many Web-based applications require access to disk files and folders. The .NET Framework provides a rich set of features for working with the file system. These classes are all in the `System.IO` namespace, and the example demonstrates how you can use them to get listings of drives, files, and folders.

The main classes are the `DriveInfo`, `DirectoryInfo`, and `File-Info` classes; and the corresponding `Directory` and `File` classes. The "info" classes provide information about the corresponding object. For example, the `DriveInfo` class exposes properties such as `Name`, `Total-Size`, `TotalFreeSpace`, `AvailableFreeSpace`, `DriveFormat` (such as NTFS or FAT32), `DriveType` (such as local, removable, or network), `IsReady`, `RootDirectory`, and `VolumeLabel`. It also provides the static `GetDrives` method to get a list of all available drives.

The `DirectoryInfo` class provides information about a specific folder, including creation, last read, and last access times; the name and name extension; and the parent folder. You can also manipulate folders using methods such as `Delete`, `CreateSubdirectory`, and `MoveTo`. Finally, there are methods to get a list of files and folders within this folder.

The `FileInfo` class provides a similar set of properties and methods for getting information about a specific file; deleting or moving the file; and reading and setting the file attributes. In addition, there are methods to open, read, and write to the file, create a new file, and set encryption on the file.

While the `DirectoryInfo` and `FileInfo` classes reference specific instances of a folder or a file, the `Directory` and `File` classes provide a range of static methods for performing similar operations but require you to specify the target folder or file. This means that you do not have to navigate to the drive and folder tree and get a reference to the folder or file you want to manipulate or get information about. They also provide a few extra useful methods beyond the "info" classes.

For example, the `Directory` class provides the `GetCurrentDirectory` method that returns the current working directory of the application, and `GetDirectoryRoot` method that returns details of the volume and root folder for a specific path. Meanwhile, the `File` class provides the useful `ReadAllBytes`, `ReadAllLines`, and `ReadAllText` methods that read an entire file and then close it afterwards, and the `WriteAllBytes`, `WriteAll-Lines`, and `WriteAllText` methods to write data to a file, replacing any existing file, and then close it.

> Other commonly-used classes in the `System.IO` namespace include the `TextReader` and `TextWriter` classes, and the `StringReader` and `StringWriter` classes, which you can use to read and write to streams, files, and `String` instances.

Reading Drive Information

The example application provides a listing of all the local fixed drives on your system, and the contents of these drives, when you select the **Use an existing file** option in the main section of the page. The listing, shown in Figure 15.5, uses a `TreeView` control (as discussed in the section Styling and Dynamically Populating a TreeView Control, earlier in this chapter). While the basic style of the `TreeView` comes from the `XPFileExplorer` image set, applied with the **auto-format** option in Design view, one or two aspects are different in the example.

The image shown for each drive is a custom GIF image, located in the `images` subfolder, and any empty folders show with another custom image from the same location. In the latter case, this is a one-pixel-square transparent image accompanied by the text "(no files)." Without this, because the node is a leaf with no child nodes, the control will display an empty folder using the file icon instead of the folder icon.

The code to populate the `TreeView` control is in `default.aspx.cs`, and it first clears the control of any existing nodes before creating a root `TreeNode` instance with the name "My Computer" and the value "Root"

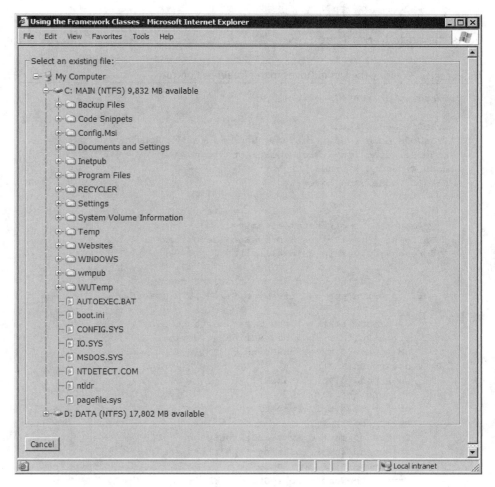

FIGURE 15.5: The drive, folder, and file listing in the example application

(see Listing 15.14). As the child nodes of this root node (the list of drives) will be visible by default, the SelectAction property of the new node is set so that clicking it has no effect, and the Expanded property is set to true. Then the code adds the new node to the TreeView.

Following this, you can see the code that uses the static GetDrives method of the DriveInfo class to get a list of all installed drives, then iterates through them. For each fixed, formatted, and available (ready) drive, the code creates a new node containing details of the drive. It then sets the ImageUrl to the custom image, specifies that clicking this node will cause a postback that executes the "populate on demand" event handler, and adds the node to the TreeView.

Listing 15.14. Creating the List of Drives in the TreeView Control

```csharp
private void CreateTreeView()
{
    treeDir.Nodes.Clear();
    TreeNode node = new TreeNode("My Computer", "Root");
    node.SelectAction = TreeNodeSelectAction.None;
    node.Expanded = true;
    treeDir.Nodes.Add(node);
    try
    {
        // get a list of installed drives
        DriveInfo[] allDrives = DriveInfo.GetDrives();
        foreach (DriveInfo d in allDrives)
        {
            // only include fixed drives that are ready
            if (d.DriveType == DriveType.Fixed && d.IsReady)
            {
                // create text for the TreeView to display
                StringBuilder sb = new StringBuilder();
                sb.Append(d.Name.Substring(0, 2));
                sb.Append(" ");
                sb.Append(d.VolumeLabel);
                sb.Append(" (");
                sb.Append(d.DriveFormat);
                sb.Append(") ");
                Double space = d.AvailableFreeSpace / 1024 / 1024;
                sb.Append(space.ToString("#,###,###,##0"));
                sb.Append(" MB available");
                String theName = sb.ToString();
                String theValue = d.Name;
                // add a node to the TreeView with "drive" image
                TreeNode child = new TreeNode(theName, theValue);
                child.ImageUrl = "images/drive.gif";
                // specify postback for populating child nodes
                child.SelectAction = TreeNodeSelectAction.Expand;
                child.PopulateOnDemand = true;
                node.ChildNodes.Add(child);
            }
        }
    }
    catch (Exception ex)
    {
        lblError.Text = "ERROR: " + ex.Message + "<p />";
    }
}
```

> Notice in Listing 15.14 that the value for each drive node is the name of the drive, such as "C:\". You will see later how, combined with the values of the folder and file nodes, this makes it easy to extract the full path and name of a selected folder or file.

Reading Folder and File Information

When the user clicks a drive node or a folder node in the TreeView, the PopulateNode event handler executes because the declaration in default. aspx specifies this as the OnTreeNodePopulate attribute of the TreeView. The PopulateNode event handler, shown in Listing 15.15, gets the value of the current path for the clicked node, and removes the string "Root" from the start of it. This works because the declaration of the TreeView also sets the PathSeparator property to the value "\", which means that the ValuePath of a node will return, for example, "Root\C:\\folder1\folder2".

By using the path to the current node to get a DirectoryInfo instance, and from this a FileSystemInfos collection (through the GetFileSystemInfos method of the DirectoryInfo class), the code can obtain a list of all folders and files within the current node and physical file system drive or folder.

Then it is just a matter of iterating through the contents of the FileSystemInfos collection examining each FileSystemInfo to see if it is a subfolder (in which case the actual type is a DirectoryInfo instance) or a file (a FileInfo instance). If it is a subfolder, the code creates a new TreeNode, sets the relevant properties so that it causes a postback that will populate its child nodes, and adds it as a child to the current node in the TreeView. For files, the code adds a new child node that is selectable, and which will therefore raise the server-side OnSelectedIndexChanged event of the TreeView control when clicked. Notice how the code ends by checking if any child nodes were created, and if not adding the "(no files)" leaf node as discussed earlier.

The final section of code concerned with the TreeView is the handler for the OnSelectedIndexChanged event, which the declaration in default.aspx sets to the event handler named SelectNode. This just has to extract the full path and file name, remove the leading "Root", and replace any double backslashes (such as will exist after the drive letter). Then it makes the Label control visible and shows the View control containing the TreeView control (see Listing 15.16).

Listing 15.15. Populating the TreeView Control on Demand after a Postback

```
protected void PopulateNode(Object sender, TreeNodeEventArgs e)
{
  // runs when a node should be populated with child nodes
  // get value path representing current file system path
  TreeNode node = e.Node;
  String valPath = node.ValuePath;
  if (valPath.Substring(0,4) == "Root")
  {
    // remove root folder value from value path
    valPath = valPath.Substring(5);
  }
  // set flag to create "no files" node
  Boolean noFiles = true;
  try
  {
    // get list of folders and files
    DirectoryInfo thisDir = new DirectoryInfo(valPath);
    FileSystemInfo[] infos = thisDir.GetFileSystemInfos();
    foreach (FileSystemInfo fsi in infos)
    {
      if (fsi is DirectoryInfo)
      {
        // this is a subfolder (directory) so add to the
        // TreeView specifying it will cause a postback
        // that will populate its child nodes
        TreeNode child = new TreeNode(fsi.Name);
        child.SelectAction = TreeNodeSelectAction.Expand;
        child.PopulateOnDemand = true;
        node.ChildNodes.Add(child);
      }
      else if (fsi is FileInfo)
      {
        // this is a file so add to the TreeView and make
        // it selectable so that a click can be detected
        TreeNode child = new TreeNode(fsi.Name);
        child.SelectAction = TreeNodeSelectAction.Select;
        node.ChildNodes.Add(child);
        noFiles = false;
      }
    }
  }
  catch (Exception ex)
  {
    lblError.Text = "ERROR: " + ex.Message + "<p />";
  }
  if (noFiles)
  {
    // add a "no files" empty node using blank image
```

```
    // file - prevents last subfolder showing as a file
    // image instead of a folder image after a postback
    TreeNode child = new TreeNode("(no files)", "");
    child.SelectAction = TreeNodeSelectAction.None;
    child.ImageUrl = "images/_blnk.gif";
    node.ChildNodes.Add(child);
  }
}
```

Writing Files to the File System

As you have seen in the descriptions of the `File` and `FileInfo` classes, there are several different ways you can create and write to disk files. The example contains simple routines that write both a text file and a binary file, demonstrating both approaches (see Listing 15.17). If the `sourceType` variable indicates that the input data is binary (an array of `Bytes`), the code creates a `FileStream` that writes directly to the file system, specifying the physical path to the disk file and the `Create` value from the `FileMode` enumeration so that it will overwrite any existing file with the same name. Then it creates a `BinaryWriter` over the `FileStream` and calls the `Write` method to write the contents of the `Byte` array named `sourceBytes` to the file, closing it afterwards.

Writing a text file is even easier. Still in Listing 15.17, you can see that the code simply creates a new `StreamWriter` pointing to the result of a call to the static `CreateText` method of the `File` class. This creates a text file, and the code then writes the contents of the `sourceString` variable to the file and closes it.

Listing 15.16. The Event Handler for the TreeView OnSelectedIndexChanged Event

```
protected void SelectNode(Object sender, EventArgs e)
{
  // get value path which, as declaration of TreeView uses
  // backslash as node separator, will be a valid file path
  // except for the "Root" node - so remove this first
  String valPath = treeDir.SelectedNode.ValuePath.Substring(5);
  // store path in Label and display view1, while
  // removing double backslashes in file path string
  lblFilePath.Text = valPath.Replace(@"\\", @"\");
  divFilePath.Visible = true;
  MultiView1.SetActiveView(view1);
}
```

Listing 15.17. Writing Text and Binary Files

```
String physicalPath = Server.MapPath(targetPath + targetFileName
                                      + targetFileExt);
if (sourceType == Ch15DataProcess.SourceFileType.Bytes)
{
  // create a binary file, replacing any existing file
  using (FileStream fs = new FileStream(physicalPath,
                                        FileMode.Create))
  {
    // create a BinaryWriter over the file stream
    using (BinaryWriter writer = new BinaryWriter(fs))
    {
      // write the array of bytes and close the file
      writer.Write(sourceBytes);
      writer.Close();
      fs.Close();
    }
  }
}
else
{
  // create a text file containing the string
  using (StreamWriter writer = File.CreateText(physicalPath))
  {
    writer.Write(sourceString);
    writer.Close();
  }
}
```

Of course, you can create files in other ways and write values to them individually rather than all in one step as shown in this example. You can create a text file, open a StreamWriter over it, and then write individual lines to it using the WriteLine method, or you can open a TextWriter and use its WriteLine method. Alternatively, for a binary file, you can use the Write method of the FileStream class or the Write method of the StreamWriter class.

Reading Text and Binary Files from the File System

Reading file contents is just as easy as writing them. The example page makes some assumptions about the file type from the file extension using the code shown in Listing 15.18—you can see the use of the static Path.GetExtension method here.

Listing 15.18. Deciding if the File Is a Text File or a Binary File

```
String fileExtension = Path.GetExtension(filePathAndName).ToLower();
String txtExtensions =
        ".txt.css.aspx.ascx.asax.xml.xsl.xsd.cs.vb.ini.log.bat";
if (txtExtensions.IndexOf(fileExtension) >= 0)
{
  // text file so return contents as a String
  ...
}
else
{
  // not a text file so return contents as Bytes
  // create a FileStream over the file
  ...
}
```

If the file is a text file, you can read the contents into a `String` using a single line of code:

```
sourceString = File.ReadAllText(filePathAndName);
```

Likewise, if it is a binary file, you can read all of the bytes from it into an array using:

```
sourceBytes = File.ReadAllBytes(filePathAndName);
```

You can also read individual lines and characters or all the content from a text or binary file by using the various "read" methods of the `StreamReader`, `BinaryReader`, or `FileStream` classes. In the example, the code uses a `BinaryReader` over a `FileStream`, as shown in Listing 15.19. Notice the `using` construct, which ensures that the classes correctly dispose of any unmanaged resources they use (important when dealing with the file system).

Because the `ReadBytes` method accepts only an `Int32` value for the buffer size, you must call it more than once for files larger than `Int32.MaxValue`. However, because this is over 2GB, you will probably find this situation occurs rarely.

Compressing Data

The .NET Framework in version 2.0 adds support for compressing files using the non-proprietary GZIP and Deflate algorithms. The example page allows you to apply GZIP compression to the source you select, as shown in Figure 15.6.

Listing 15.19. Reading a Binary File Using a BinaryReader and a FileStream

```
// create a FileStream over the file
using (FileStream fs = new FileStream(filePathAndName,
                           FileMode.Open, FileAccess.Read))
{
  // create a BinaryReader for the FileStream
  using (BinaryReader reader = new BinaryReader(fs))
  {
    // read the contents into the byte array
    // using statement will call Close and Dispose
    // though does no harm to include call to Close
    sourceBytes = new Byte[bytesToRead];
    Byte[] buffer = null;
    while (bytesToRead > Int32.MaxValue)
    {
      buffer = reader.ReadBytes(Int32.MaxValue);
      buffer.CopyTo(sourceBytes, sourceBytes.Length - bytesToRead);
      bytesToRead -= Int32.MaxValue;
    }
    buffer = reader.ReadBytes((Int32)bytesToRead);
    buffer.CopyTo(sourceBytes, sourceBytes.Length - bytesToRead);
    reader.Close();
    fs.Close();
  }
}
```

The result, if you choose to output to a file, is a link that you can use to open the file (see Figure 15.7).

However, if you want to "look inside" this file, or any other file of any type, remember that Visual Studio provides a binary editor. Right-click on the file in Solution Explorer, select **Open With**, and then choose **Binary Editor** (see Figure 15.8).

The code in the example that applies the compression to the file takes advantage of the GZipStream class from the System.IO.Compression namespace. You create a stream to receive the compressed data and then instantiate a GZipStream over this stream, setting the CompressionMode option (Compress or Decompress). The final parameter determines if the GZipStream will leave the output stream open after writing. Because the output stream in this example is a MemoryStream, this parameter is set to true so that the data is available afterwards. If you are writing to a file, you would use false for this parameter (see Listing 15.20).

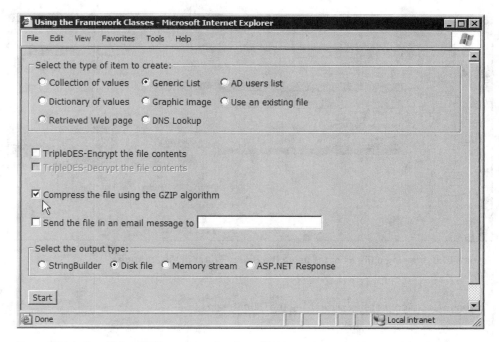

FIGURE 15.6: Specifying GZIP compression for a file

The next step is to call the `Write` method of the `GZipStream` class, specifying a buffer array (of `Bytes`) that contains the data to compress, the starting point within the array, and the number of bytes to compress. Once complete, the code retrieves the compressed data from the `MemoryStream` into another `Byte` array.

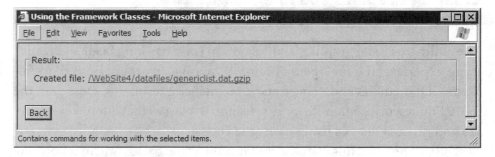

FIGURE 15.7: The result after compression, allowing you to access the new file

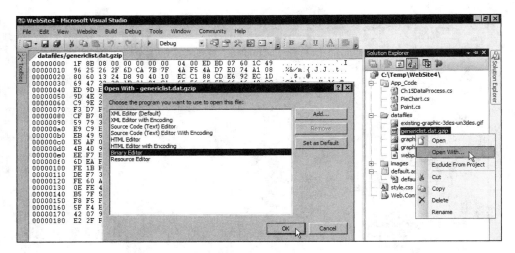

FIGURE 15.8: Viewing a file as bytes using the Binary Editor in Visual Studio

---

Listing 15.20. Compressing Data Using the GZipStream Class

```
// create a MemoryStream to receive the result of the process
MemoryStream ms = new MemoryStream();
// create a new GZipStream over the output stream
// final parameter indicates to leave stream open
GZipStream czs = new GZipStream(ms, CompressionMode.Compress, true);
// compress the input byte array to the MemoryStream
czs.Write(inBytes, 0, inBytes.Length);
// convert result in MemoryStream back to a byte array
Byte[] gzipBytes = new Byte[ms.Length];
ms.Position = 0;
ms.Read(gzipBytes, 0, gzipBytes.Length);
ms.Close();
```

Creating Graphics and Images with the System.Drawing Classes

The ability to create graphics and images in code has long been an area for more experienced developers because it involves working with the Windows GDI methods and using handles to manage resources. However, the .NET Framework contains a large selection of classes that allow you to create and process images using managed code.

The example for this chapter contains the same basic code that you saw in the previous chapter for creating a pie chart dynamically as a GIF image. If you select the **Graphics image** option in the example and write the output to a disk file, you can click the resulting link and see the newly created chart (see Figure 15.9).

The file PieChart.cs in the App_Code folder of the example creates this chart and returns the generated chart as a Bitmap object instance. As you can see in Listing 15.21, code in the GetImage method of the Ch15Data-Process.cs file then creates a new MemoryStream, saves the Bitmap to this in GIF image format, and reads the contents of the MemoryStream into an array of bytes.

Listing 15.21. Retrieving the Bitmap as a GIF Image into an Array of Bytes

```
// get instance of class that generates the chart
PieChart chart = new PieChart();
String caption = "Visitors to our Web site";
// create the pie chart
Bitmap result = chart.DrawPieChart(420, 250, caption);
// save it to a MemoryStream in GIF format
MemoryStream ms = new MemoryStream();
result.Save(ms, ImageFormat.Gif);
ms.Position = 0;
sourceBytes = new Byte[ms.Length];
ms.Read(sourceBytes, 0, (Int32)ms.Length);
return SourceFileType.Bytes;
```

Creating Images with the System.Drawing Classes

With a few exceptions, all of the commonly used classes concerned with image generation, manipulation, and processing are in the System.Drawing and System.Imaging namespaces. Other namespaces are System. Drawing.Design, which contains the classes to build custom toolbox items and editors; System.Drawing.Drawing2D, which contains the gradient brushes and specialist transformation classes; System.Drawing.Printing, which contains classes concerned with printing; and System.Drawing.Text, which contains classes for advanced rendering and access to lists of installed fonts.

We do not have room to list the entire code for the PieChart class used in the example application, but the following shows the general techniques you can use to create simple graphics such as that shown in Figure 15.9. You can open the file PieChart.cs to see the way that it builds the chart; all of the code is commented to help you follow it more easily. It creates a DataSet containing the values to chart, an array of colors for the pie segments, and

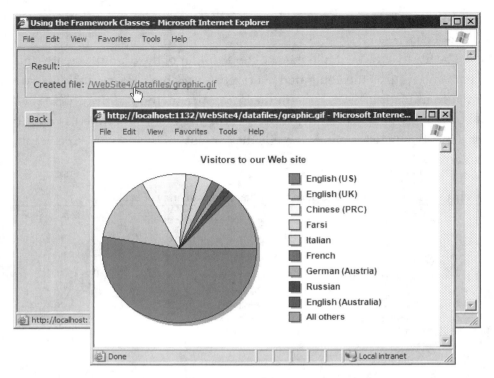

FIGURE 15.9: Creating a chart dynamically using the .NET Framework classes

then iterates through the rows in the `DataSet` table drawing the appropriate output for each one onto the `Bitmap`.

The basic technique for using the `System.Drawing` classes, as shown in the code extract in Listing 15.22, is to generate a new `Bitmap` or start with an existing `Bitmap`, create a `Graphics` object instance from it to act as the drawing agent, and then create brushes and pens to draw onto the `Bitmap`. Brushes come in different types—but for solid lines and area fills, the `SolidBrush` class is the obvious choice. To draw a shape such as a rectangle or ellipse, you can specify the bounding rectangle first and then draw the shape within this rectangle.

Listing 15.23 shows a section of the code that draws the individual pie slices onto the `Bitmap` for each value in the source data. It calculates the size of the slice in degrees from the value in this row, sets the color of the brush, and draws a pie segment; then it outlines it using a black pen to create a

Listing 15.22. An Extract of Code from the Example Page Creating a Bitmap and Drawing on It

```
// create a new bitmap
Bitmap bmap = new Bitmap(wid, high);

// create new graphics instance to draw on bitmap
Graphics gr = Graphics.FromImage(bmap);

// create a black pen for drawing lines and draw border
Pen pn = new Pen(Color.Black, 1);

// create a solid brush for the background and fill it
SolidBrush brsh = new SolidBrush(Color.White);
gr.FillRectangle(brsh, 0, 0, bmap.Width, bmap.Height);

// create rectangles for chart and shadow background
Rectangle pieRect = new Rectangle(0, topOffset, dia, dia);
Rectangle shadowRect = new Rectangle(5, topOffset + 5, dia, dia);

// create color for shadows to objects
Color cShadow = Color.FromArgb(153, 153, 153);

// set brush color and draw circle for shadow
brsh.Color = cShadow;
gr.FillEllipse(brsh, shadowRect);
...
```

crisper appearance at the edges. The code then updates the current end point within the pie (in degrees) and is ready to draw the next segment.

Listing 15.23. Drawing Pie Chart Segments into a Bitmap

```
...
// convert to number of degrees for this value
sliceDeg = (float)((sliceVal / totalVal) * 360);

// set brush color from array of colors
brsh.Color = colrs[rowIdx];

// draw filled pie slice and then outline in black
gr.FillPie(brsh, pieRect, sliceStart, sliceDeg);
gr.DrawPie(pn, pieRect, sliceStart, sliceDeg);

// save start position for next slice and increment row index
sliceStart += sliceDeg;
rowIdx += 1;
...
```

To write the text heading and caption, the code uses a `SolidBrush` and calls the `DrawString` method of the `Graphics` instance. A `RectangleF` structure (a rectangle that can have floating point values for its vertices) defines the area where the text will appear, and the code generates `Font` and `StringFormat` instances that specify the appearance and alignment of the text within the bounding rectangle.

Listing 15.24. Drawing Text onto a Bitmap

```
// create the rectangle to hold the text
RectangleF rectF = new RectangleF(iTop, iLeft, wid, high);

// create a Font instance for the text style
Font oFont = new Font("Arial", 12, FontStyle.Bold);

// create the format instance to define the format and style
StringFormat sFormat = new StringFormat();
// align to the left within the rectangle
sFormat.Alignment = StringAlignment.Near;
// center vertically within rectangle area
sFormat.LineAlignment = StringAlignment.Center;

// create a brush instance and draw the text
SolidBrush brsh = new SolidBrush(Color.FromName(clr));
gr.DrawString(sText, oFont, brsh, rectF, sFormat);
```

The example only shows a few of the basic techniques for using the `System.Drawing` classes. However, once you start to use them you will find that they are reasonably intuitive and easy to work with. In fact, it is surprising how you can quickly build quite complex images or draw on existing images. You may find these classes useful if, for example, you display pictures of products for sale on your site. You can dynamically draw "Sold Out" or "Special Offer" slogans directly onto the image at runtime.

Accessing the Internet with the System.Net Classes

Although not a common requirement, you sometime may need to access other resources on the Internet or a local network from within your ASP.NET code. This is easy using the wide range of classes in the `System.Net` namespace. While you can perform low-level network access through sockets in this way, the more common requirement is usually to be able to access another Web page. You may also want to, for example, look up the IP address for a specified host in a DNS server. This section looks at both of these topics.

> The next chapter looks at the topic of using and consuming another type of network resource—Web Services.

Retrieving Web Pages

Among the classes in the System.Net namespace are those that make it easy to send a request for a resource and then read the response. For HTTP requests, the classes you use are HttpWebRequest and HttpWebResponse. Other types are the base classes WebRequest and WebResponse, the FTP access classes FtpWebRequest and FtpWebReponse, and the classes FileWebRequest and FileWebResponse for accessing local files using the "file://" URI scheme.

Listing 15.25 shows the code the example page uses to fetch a Web page (the URL specified in the pageURL variable) from another site. The first stage consists of creating an HttpWebRequest instance using the static Create method of the WebRequest base class for the required URL. Then the code creates an HttpWebResponse instance over the return stream using the GetResponse method. The HttpWebResponse class exposes a series of properties, such as Status, that allow you to get information about the result of the request, as shown here.

To read the response, the code creates a StreamReader and initializes it by calling the GetResponseStream method. It can then extract the entire response as a String by calling the ReadToEnd method of the Stream-Reader. The example application uses this code in the GetWebPage method of the file Ch15DataProcess.cs.

The HttpWebRequest class (and the other request class types) expose properties that allow you to closely control the request by specifying any credentials required for access to the remote site, specifying the request method (POST, GET, HEAD), and selecting the proxy server to use (if any). You can also add and modify the HTTP headers, add cookies to the request, set referrer and accepted file type information, and manage redirection of the request.

The HttpWebResponse class allows you to access information about the responding server, the HTTP headers and cookies, the character set and encoding used, and the size and last modified date of the page.

Listing 15.25. Requesting and Receiving a Web Page

```
// create a Request object to request the page
HttpWebRequest req = (HttpWebRequest)WebRequest.Create(pageURL);
// create a Response object to receive the response
// by calling the GetResponse method of the Request
HttpWebResponse result = (HttpWebResponse)req.GetResponse();
StreamReader reader = null;
if (result.StatusCode == HttpStatusCode.OK)
{
  // response received, so read the stream
  reader = new StreamReader(result.GetResponseStream());
  sourceString = reader.ReadToEnd();
}
else
{
  sourceString = "Failed request, " + result.StatusDescription;
}
reader.Close();
result.Close();
```

Figure 15.10 shows the result of selecting the **Retrieved Web page** option in the example and sending the results to a disk file. When you open the disk file, which the example automatically allocates the .htm file extension, you see the page rendered almost as it would be if accessed directly in the

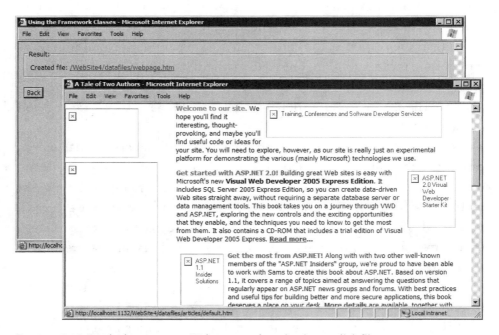

FIGURE 15.10: Retrieving a remote Web page and storing it as a disk file

browser. However, associated resources such as images do not appear, because these are not part of the request and response. A Web browser automatically reads the links to associated content when it loads the page and issues separate requests in exactly the same way to retrieve each of them for display.

To see what the returned content really looks like, select the **Memory stream output** option and repeat the request. As shown in Figure 15.11, the result is the source for the page as generated by the remote server.

From this short example, you should be able to see how easily you can build Web applications that request data behind the scenes or compile data from several Web-based sources.

Performing DNS Lookups

As a further example of accessing remote resources over the Internet, the code in Listing 15.26 shows how you can perform a DNS lookup on a specified domain. The `Dns` class in the `System.Net` namespace exposes the static `GetHostEntry` method that returns an instance of the `IPHostEntry` class.

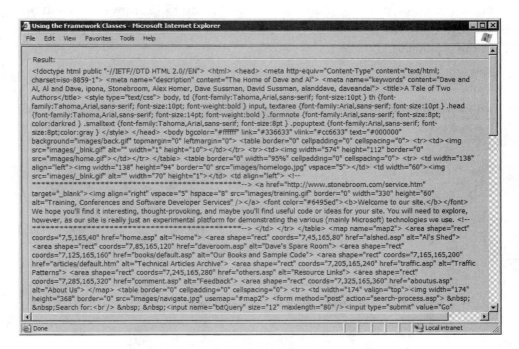

FIGURE 15.11: A remote retrieved Web page displayed as a stream of bytes

This class provides a collection of `IPAddress` instances in its `AddressList` property and a list of alias host names in its `Aliases` property.

Listing 15.26. Performing a DNS Lookup Using the System.net Classes

```
// perform the DNS request
IPHostEntry host = Dns.GetHostEntry(hostName);
StringBuilder builder = new StringBuilder();
builder.Append("Results of DNS lookup for '"
            + hostName + "'\n");
// iterate through the address list
foreach (IPAddress addr in host.AddressList)
{
  builder.Append("IPAddress = " + addr.ToString() + "\n");
}
// iterate through any list of aliases
foreach (String alias in host.Aliases)
{
  builder.Append("Alias = " + alias + "\n");
}
sourceString = builder.ToString();
```

The example page uses the code shown in Listing 15.26 in the `GetDNS-Lookup` method of `Ch15DataProcess.cs`. Figure 15.12 shows the result of a DNS lookup for "microsoft.com" (though the actual addresses are hidden in the screenshot).

FIGURE 15.12: The result of a DNS lookup for "microsoft.com"

Sending E-Mail with the System.Net.Mail Classes

One extremely useful and often-required feature in commercial and hobbyist Web sites is the ability to send e-mail automatically. The `System.Net.Mail` namespace contains all the classes you need for this, although `MailMessage`, `Attachment`, and `SmtpClient` are the ones you will use most often. The technique is to create an instance of the `MailMessage` class, set all the properties you require on this class, add any attachments you want to send, and then call the `Send` method of the `SmtpClient` class to generate the message and pass it to your mail server.

Sending Text and HTML E-Mail Messages

To send a text message, you use code like that shown in Listing 15.27. The "to" and "from" addresses are `String` values in this case, as are the `Subject` and `Body`. There are several overloads of the constructor for the `MailMessage` class, and you can set the `To` and `From` properties instead of providing them in the constructor. Other properties of the `MailMessage` class include `Cc`, `Bcc`, `ReplyTo`, `Priority`, and `DeliveryNotificationOptions`. If you use HTML for the body of the message, set the `IsBodyHtml` property to `true` to indicate this, ensuring that the recipient receives it as HTML.

Listing 15.27. Sending a Simple Text E-Mail Message

```
// create the email message
MailMessage msg = new MailMessage(emailFromAddr, emailToAddr);
msg.Subject = "Auto-generated by ASP.NET!";
// use the String passed to this routine as the message body
msg.Body = sourceString;
// specify the sender that will deliver the message using the
// local SMTP service. Alternatively can set up defaults in the
// <mailSettings> section of machine.config or web.config
SmtpClient sender = new SmtpClient(serverName);
// add default credentials for accessing SMTP server
sender.Credentials = CredentialCache.DefaultNetworkCredentials;
// send the message
sender.Send(msg);
```

For information on sending e-mail through a remote mail server that requires specific logon credentials, see the earlier section, Using a Remote SMTP Server.

You can also provide the e-mail addresses as instances of the `MailAddress` class instead of as a `String`. This class exposes the `DisplayName`, `Host`, and `User` properties as well as the `Address` (the e-mail address) property. Alternatively, you can use the standard format for a `String` e-mail address that contains a display name:

```
"Display name" email@domain.com
```

To use multiple e-mail addresses for a property, separate them with a semicolon.

Validating E-Mail Addresses

It is a good idea to validate any `String` e-mail addresses you use when sending messages automatically. An easy way is to use the `Regex` (regular expression) class from the `System.Text.RegularExpressions` namespace. Like all the other tasks you have met in this chapter, .NET makes it easy to use regular expressions—the hardest part is in understanding the actual expression. Listing 15.28 shows how the example application validates e-mail addresses you enter in the page, or the e-mail address you specify as the sender when you configure the application.

Listing 15.28. Validating E-Mail Addresses Using a Regular Expression

```
// validate the email addresses using a regular expression
Regex rx = new Regex(@"([a-zA-Z0-9_\-\.]+)@(([a-zA-Z0-9\-]+\.)+)"
                  + "([a-zA-Z0-9]{2,4})");
// test against the two email addresses
if (! rx.IsMatch(emailToAddr))
{
  throw new Exception("Email 'To' address is not valid.");
}
if (!rx.IsMatch(emailFromAddr))
{
  throw new Exception("Email 'From' address is not valid.");
}
```

Figure 15.13 shows the example page where the selected input is a collection of values (which, as you saw earlier, returns a small text string) and the option to e-mail the file to the specified recipient is enabled.

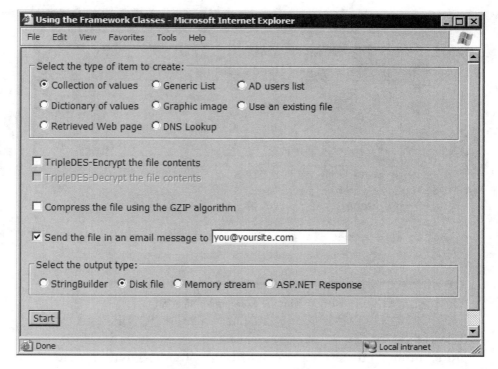

FIGURE 15.13: Sending a collection of values as an e-mail message as well as to a disk file

Figure 15.14 shows the e-mail after receipt. You can see the text string in the body and the subject that was—as it says—auto-generated by ASP.NET.

Sending E-Mail Messages with Text Attachments

Sending e-mails that have an attachment is more complex than sending simple text-only or HTML e-mails, but it is not difficult. The `Attachments` property of the `MailMessage` class can hold a collection of `Attachment` instances, each defining an attachment for the e-mail. The `Attachment` class has properties that define the name, encoding, and content type of the attachment. You can declare these values when you create an `Attachment` using one of the many constructors, or afterwards by setting the properties.

If the attachment is a file on disk, you simply specify the path and name file in the `Attachment` constructor, and optionally a `ContentType` (MIME type) value. If the attachment is a `String` value, you can use the static `CreateAttachmentFromString` method of the `Attachment` class to generate the attachment.

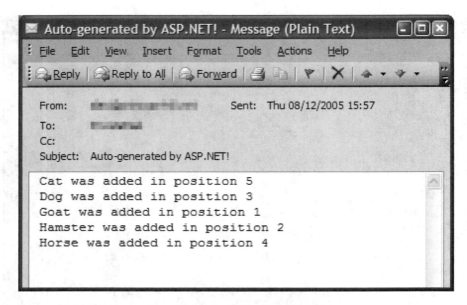

FIGURE 15.14: A text e-mail sent from the example application

You can also create attachments from a stream, which provides the flexibility required to generate binary attachments. In this case, you use one of the overloads of the `Attachment` class that accepts a stream. You can optionally provide the name of the file that the attachment represents and the MIME type.

Listing 15.29 summarizes the code used in the example to send text attachments. The `MediaTypeNames` class allows you to specify a whole range of MIME types, including `Text.Html` ("text/html"), `Text.Plain` ("text/text"), `Text.Xml` ("text/xml"), `Image.Gif` ("image/gif"), `Image.Jpeg` ("image/jpeg"), a whole range of `Application` types such as "application/zip," and more. After creating the attachment, the code uses the `Add` method of the `AttachmentCollection` class (exposed by the `Attachments` property of the `MailMessage` class) to add the attachment—before sending the message.

> Note that the `ContentType` and the `MediaTypeNames` classes are in the `System.Net.Mime` namespace, which you must import in order to use these classes.

Listing 15.29. Creating an E-Mail with a Text Attachment from a String

```
// specify the content type and file name
ContentType cType = new ContentType();
cType.MediaType = MediaTypeNames.Text.Plain;
cType.Name = fileName;
// create an attachment from the source String
attach = Attachment.CreateAttachmentFromString(sourceString, cType);
// create the email message
MailMessage msg = new MailMessage(emailFromAddr, emailToAddr);
msg.Subject = "Auto-generated by ASP.NET!";
// add the attachment to the message
msg.Attachments.Add(attach);
msg.Body = "Please find the attached file " + fileName;
SmtpClient sender = new SmtpClient(serverName);
sender.Credentials = CredentialCache.DefaultNetworkCredentials;
sender.Send(msg);
```

Sending E-Mail Messages with Binary Attachments

When sending a binary attachment that is not stored as a disk file, you must provide the content as a stream. The code in the example page, summarized in Listing 15.30, creates a `MemoryStream` over the array of `Bytes` that contains the data to send. After setting the current position pointer to the start of the file, the code creates a new `Attachment` using the `MemoryStream` and the proposed file name. The remainder of the code, as in Listing 15.29, adds the `Attachment` to the `MailMessage`, specifies the other details of the message, and sends it.

Listing 15.30. Creating an E-Mail with a Binary Attachment from a Byte Array

```
// get a stream over the array of bytes
MemoryStream outStream = new MemoryStream(sourceBytes);
outStream.Position = 0;
// create the attachment, specifying the file name to be
// used as part of the ContentType to identify the file
attach = new Attachment(outStream, fileName);
// create the email message
MailMessage msg = new MailMessage(emailFromAddr, emailToAddr);
msg.Subject = "Auto-generated by ASP.NET!";
// add the attachment to the message
msg.Attachments.Add(attach);
msg.Body = "Please find the attached file " + fileName;
SmtpClient sender = new SmtpClient(serverName);
sender.Credentials = CredentialCache.DefaultNetworkCredentials;
sender.Send(msg);
```

To see the whole process in action, Figure 15.15 shows selection of an existing file to be e-mailed to the specified address and output within the page using a `StringBuilder`.

Selecting the **Use an existing file** option in the page automatically displays a list of drives, and you can navigate to an existing file and select it. In Figure 15.16, a file containing the Web page retrieved earlier in this chapter is chosen.

Figure 15.17 shows the e-mail that the example generates. The existing file, a saved Web page, is attached to the message with the correct filename. Outlook also displays the filename using the appropriate icon. Double-clicking the file causes it to open in the browser just as you would expect.

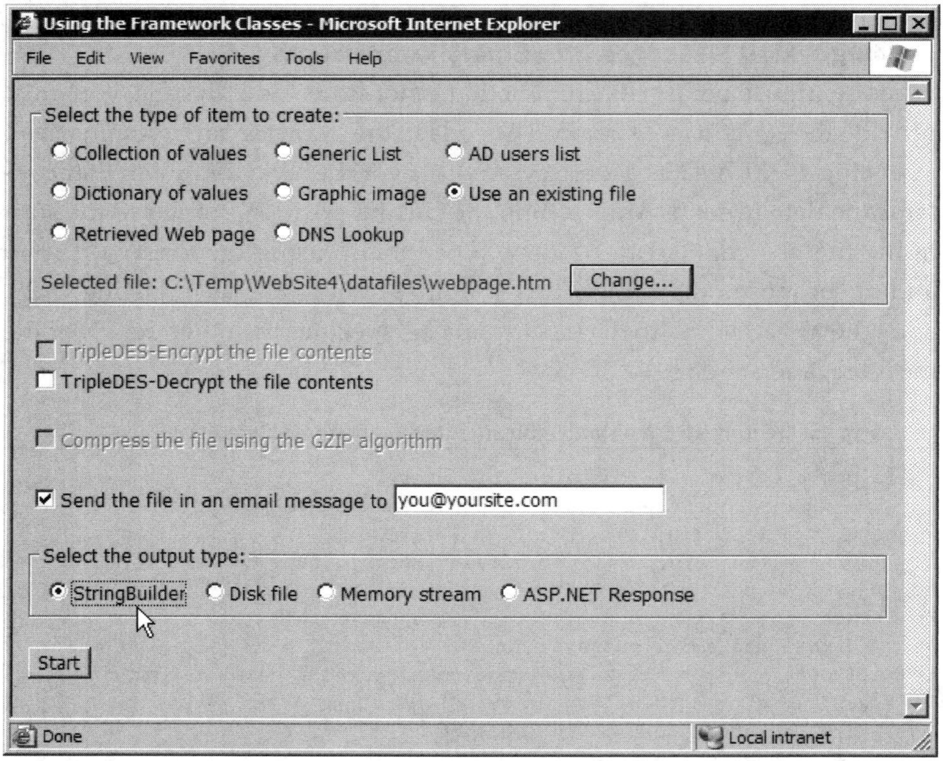

FIGURE 15.15: Selecting the options to send an existing file by e-mail

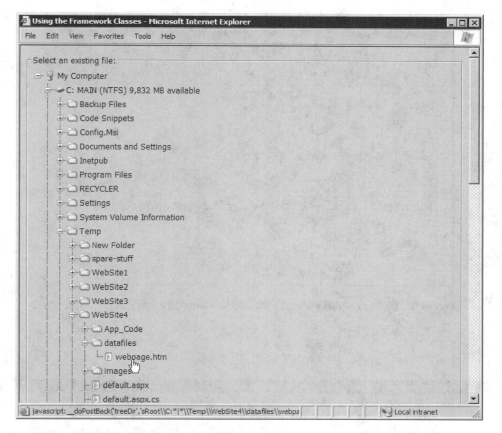

FIGURE 15.16: Selecting an existing file from disk

You can select a different source type in the main application page, for example, the **Graphic image** option (see Figure 15.18), so that the source is a dynamically generated array of bytes rather than an existing file.

Then send it as an e-mail attachment, open the e-mail in your e-mail client, and you will see the attached graphic file. Double-clicking this time opens the application designated for handling GIF files—in Figure 15.19, you can see that this is PaintShop Pro.

The latest version of PaintShop Pro is available for trial or purchase from the Corel® Corporation Web site at http://www.corel.com/.

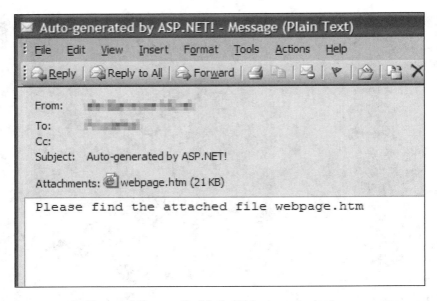

FIGURE 15.17: The resulting e-mail with the Web page attached

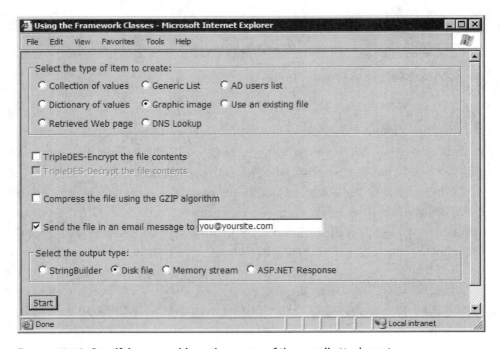

FIGURE 15.18: Specifying a graphic as the source of the e-mail attachment

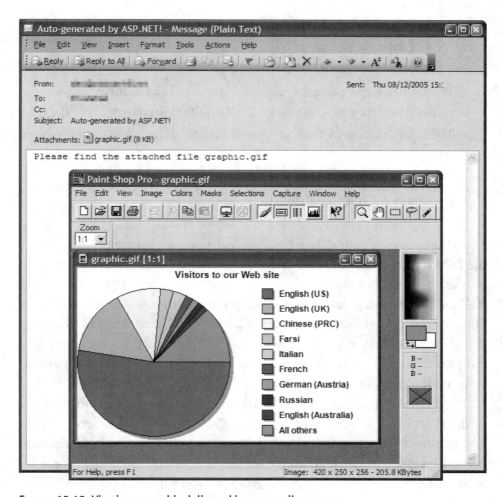

FIGURE 15.19: Viewing a graphic delivered in an e-mail message

Accessing Active Directory with the System.DirectoryServices Classes

If your Web server is a member of a Windows Active Directory-enabled domain, you may find that you need to be able to query (or even update) the directory from your ASP.NET code. This is most likely to be the case for intranet applications. Alternatively, you may wish to query other types of remote directory. The .NET Framework includes a series of classes in the

`System.DirectoryServices` namespace that provide access to directories using one of four protocols:

- The Lightweight Directory Access Protocol (LDAP) for Windows Active Directory or any other LDAP-enabled directory service
- The Internet Information Server (IIS) protocol for access to metabase information
- Novel Netware Directory Services (NDS)
- Windows NT internal protocol

In the example, you will see how you can use the most common of these, the LDAP protocol, to access Active Directory and get a list of values from one of the AD containers. However, for this to work, the account that ASP.NET is running under must have permission to access the Active Directory. If you are using Visual Studio or VWD, and running the page using the built-in Web server, you should find that it works. If not, try logging on to your machine with an account that has administrator permissions on the domain.

If you want to access Active Directory from an application running under IIS, you will most likely need to disable anonymous access to the application in Internet Services Manager, so that users must provide domain credentials when accessing the application. Be careful if you decide to allocate the anonymous IUSR account or ASPNET permissions within the directory, and restrict these permissions to the minimum required.

The main classes in the `System.DirectoryServices` namespace are the `DirectoryEntry`, which represents an individual item in a container within the directory; and `DirectorySearcher` and `SearchResult`, which you use to get a list of `DirectoryEntry` instances matching specific criteria. The starting point is to get a reference to the root of the directory. For this, you must specify the URI in the correct LDAP format. To access the local Active Directory, you require "LDAP://domain-name," for example:

```
DirectoryEntry root = new DirectoryEntry("LDAP://mydomain.com")
```

Note that the protocol definition (`"LDAP"`) **must** be uppercase.

You can then search for containers using the `DirectorySearcher` class, specifying the node to start the search from and the query that selects a container or value:

```
DirectorySearcher searcher = new DirectorySearcher(root, "CN=Users")
SearchResult result = searcher.FindOne();
```

The result of a call to the `FindOne` method of the `DirectorySearcher` is a single `SearchResult` instance, while the result of a call to the `FindAll` method is a `SearchResultCollection` capable of containing more than one `SearchResult`. Each `SearchResult` exposes the path of the item it found and a set of properties for that item. If you want to access the item itself, perhaps to perform more searches starting from here, you use the `GetDirectoryEntry` method of the `SearchResult`.

This is, of course, only a very brief overview of the capabilities of the `System.DirectoryServices` classes, but it is enough to demonstrate how useful they are.

Getting a List of Users

The `GetADUserList` method in the `Ch15DataProcess.cs` file returns a `String` value that is a list of the users found in the "Users" container of Active Directory within the local domain. Listing 15.31 shows the code used in the example. You can see that it first calls the static `GetCurrent-Domain` method to get the local AD domain name, accesses the root of the Active Directory hierarchy for this domain, and then uses a `Directory-Searcher` from this point to find the first container with "CN=Users" in its name.

This is the `Users` container, and so the code can get a reference to the "live" node in Active Directory for this entry and iterate through all the child nodes (the users). The `Name` property of each contains the LDAP protocol identifier, as `"CN=username"`, so the code removes this to leave just the name.

Listing 15.31. Listing Users from Active Directory

```
StringBuilder builder = new StringBuilder();
// get reference to current Active Directory domain
// and display domain name
Domain theDomain = Domain.GetCurrentDomain();
String domainName = theDomain.Name;
builder.Append("List of Active Directory Users for Domain '"
               + domainName + "'\n");
// get root entry in AD for this domain
using (DirectoryEntry root = new DirectoryEntry("LDAP://"
                                              + domainName))
{
  // search AD for child directory path with container CN=Users
  using (DirectorySearcher searcher = new DirectorySearcher(root,
                                              "CN=Users"))
  {
    // just return first match (only one such path should exist)
    SearchResult result = searcher.FindOne();
    if (result == null)
    {
      builder.Append("No 'CN=Users' entry found.");
    }
    else
    {
      // get the directory entry for the CN=Users path
      using (DirectoryEntry entry = result.GetDirectoryEntry())
      {
        // iterate through all the child entries (the users)
        foreach (DirectoryEntry child in entry.Children)
        {
          String userEntry = child.Name;
          // remove leading "CN=" from returned name
          builder.Append(userEntry.Substring(
                    userEntry.IndexOf("=") + 1) + "\n");
        }
      }
    }
  }
}
sourceString = builder.ToString();
```

Figure 15.20 shows the result. You can see that it detects the domain name automatically and finds a complete list of users (some of which are hidden here).

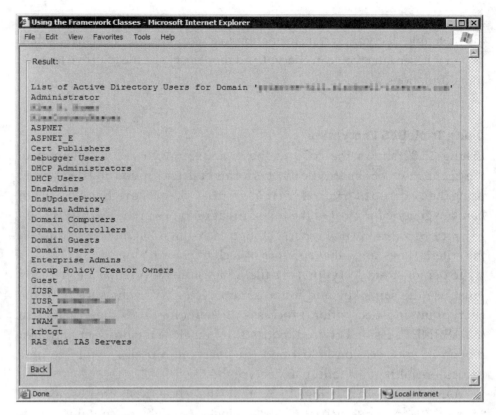

FIGURE 15.20: A list of users obtained from Active Directory

Encrypting Data with the System.Security.Cryptography Classes

The final topic for this chapter is a very brief excursion into the world of encryption. Within the .NET Framework are a series of classes that provide support for all kinds of encryption. However, the main set of classes is in the `System.Security.Cryptography` namespace. Here you will find classes that support all kinds of ciphers, codes, and transforms—including DES, TripleDES, SHA, MD5, RSA, Base64, and more.

While many programmers tend to shy away from this topic due to its complexity and specialist requirements, it is worth seeing an example of how you can use one of the classes here. The example page allows you to perform a TripleDES encryption transformation to the data when you generate it and the matching decryption transformation to an existing file. This means that, as you will see later, you can encrypt and then decrypt a file to prove that the transformations work.

Using TripleDES Encryption

Listing 15.32 shows the code in the `TransformToFrom3DES` method of the `Ch15DataProcess.cs` file that performs both encryption and decryption using the `TripleDESCryptoServiceProvider` class. The techniques shown here are generic for most of the transformation types in the `System.Security.Cryptography` namespace, though each differs slightly depending on the criteria, keys, and other specifics of each transformation.

To demonstrate decryption of a file, and restore the original file, the code must use the same key and initialization vector (IV) values for both the encryption and decryption processes. It therefore saves these values in the ASP.NET session between requests. If you close the browser and then reopen it, your session is lost and the decryption process will use new values—resulting in a failure to decrypt the file.

You can see in Listing 15.32 that the code first creates a new `TripleDESCryptoServiceProvider` instance, which contains auto-generated random key and IV values. Then it looks in the session for an existing key value, and if found, retrieves this and the corresponding IV and applies them to the `TripleDESCryptoServiceProvider`.

The `CryptoAPITransform` class performs the actual transformation, and so the code next creates an instance of this from the `TripleDESCryptoServiceProvider`, using the key and IV values it exposes. Most of the different types of transformation for the various cryptography providers use the `CryptoAPITransform` class in this way.

An individual transformation is limited to `Int32.MaxValue` bytes (around 2GB), and the `CryptoAPITransform` class exposes two methods that you use to perform larger transformations. The `TransformBlock` method allows you to transform blocks of data and store each set of results in the appropriate position of a `Byte` array. The last transformation uses the `TransformFinalBlock` method to transform any remaining data and add it to the end of the result array. However, in the example, the code assumes that the data is less than `Int32.MaxValue` and just uses the `Transform-FinalBlock` method.

Listing 15.32. Performing TripleDES Transformations

```
// create TripleDESCryptoServiceProvider instance
TripleDESCryptoServiceProvider provider
                = new TripleDESCryptoServiceProvider();
// get existing key and IV from session if available
HttpContext context = HttpContext.Current;
String keyString = (String)context.Session["3DESKey"];
if (keyString != null && keyString.Length > 0)
{
  provider.Key = Encoding.Unicode.GetBytes(keyString);
  provider.IV = Encoding.Unicode.GetBytes(
                      (String)context.Session["3DESIV"]);
}
else
{
  // save the key and IV in session
  context.Session["3DESKey"]
        = Encoding.Unicode.GetString(provider.Key);
  context.Session["3DESIV"]
        = Encoding.Unicode.GetString(provider.IV);
}
// create encryption transformer using key and initialization
// vector from TripleDESCryptoServiceProvider
CryptoAPITransform transform = null;
// check the encrypt parameter to this method to
// see if it should encrypt or decrypt the data
if (encrypt)
{
  transform = provider.CreateEncryptor(provider.Key, provider.IV)
            as CryptoAPITransform;
}
else
{
  transform = provider.CreateDecryptor(provider.Key, provider.IV)
            as CryptoAPITransform;
}
// transform the source array of bytes to a new array
// assumes that the source is less than Int32.MaxValue
// if larger, must use TransformBlock method first
Byte[] transformedBytes = transform.TransformFinalBlock(
                      sourceBytes, 0, sourceBytes.Length);
```

Figure 15.21 shows how you can see a TripleDES encryption using the example page. Select the **Graphic image** option as the source, turn on the

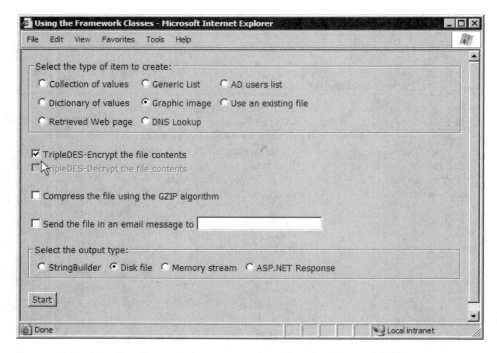

FIGURE 15.21: Selecting the options to encrypt the source data into a disk file

encryption option, and select **Disk file** as the output. Then click **Start** to create the encrypted disk file.

After creating the file, go back to the initial page and select **Use an existing file** and enable decryption as shown in Figure 15.22. Then click **Start** to perform the decryption.

Once complete, you can open the resulting file, which has been encrypted and then decrypted (see Figure 15.23). If you wish, open the original file (`graphic.gif`), the encrypted file (`graphic-3des.gif`), and the decrypted file (`graphic-3des-un3des.gif`) in the binary editor in Visual Studio (see Figure 15.8 earlier in this chapter) to view the binary content and confirm that encryption took place.

Note that the TripleDES process may not work properly on small files, such as the text files generated by the other input options in the example page.

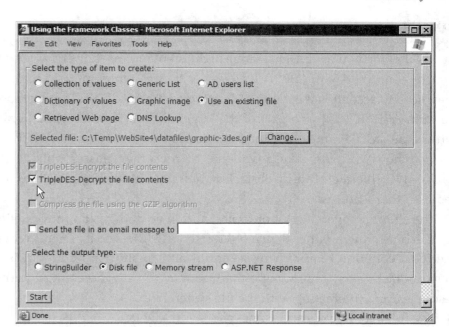

FIGURE 15.22: Selecting the options to decrypt the file just created

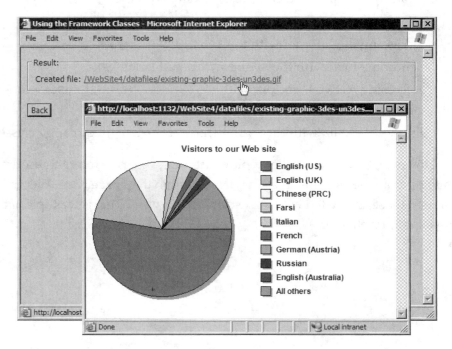

FIGURE 15.23: Viewing the decrypted image file

SUMMARY

In this chapter, you have seen a range of different topics—none of which are directly concerned with ASP.NET. However, they all represent tasks that you may need to accomplish in your Web sites and other ASP.NET applications. Because ASP.NET is just a part of the large and full-featured class library within the .NET Framework, the boundaries between what ASP.NET can do and how you can take advantage of the other classes outside the System.Web hierarchy are no obstacle to building complex applications that require other features.

The chapter covered a lot of topics, and in so doing is an introduction to each one of them rather than a full reference. However, it aimed to cover the most common requirement scenarios and to show how easy it is to perform tasks such as sending e-mail from a Web site, accessing Internet resources, and interacting with the file system.

The full list of topics and namespaces you saw is:

- Storing data with the System.Collections classes
- Reading, writing, and compressing data with the System.IO classes
- Creating graphics and images with the System.Drawing classes
- Accessing the Internet with the System.Net classes
- Sending e-mail with the System.Net.Mail classes
- Accessing Active Directory with the System.DirectoryServices classes
- Encrypting data with the System.Security.Cryptography classes

However, there is one other topic concerning access to Internet resources missing from the list. This concerns classes within the System.Web hierarchy, namely, those associated with the use of Web Services. That is the topic of the next and final chapter.

■ 16 ■
Web Services

F OR THE FINAL CHAPTER in the book we're going to be looking at extending the reach of your applications by allowing them to communicate with other applications. The reasons for this communication can be just pulling data from a feed, such as stock prices or weather details, or integrating data into a business application, such as placing orders remotely. Integrating business applications allows you to work with other organizations, either using their services or providing services for them to use, and to work with distributed applications, perhaps with remote offices, or with multiple machines in a single office.

In this chapter we're going to look at how you can incorporate Web Services into your applications, whether that's by exposing them for others to use or using those exposed by others. In particular we will cover:

- How Web Services can be used to communicate between applications
- How to create Web Services for use by other applications
- How to use Web Services supplied by other applications
- How to customize the transfer of data

There will also be a brief look at some new and future areas of Web Services.

Web Services

Historically, Web Services have always been a fringe technology, almost a solution without a problem. Look deeper into application communication, though, and you will realize that there was a problem: Communication between applications was hard. Distributed applications often required complex configuration, were tightly coupled, and used proprietary protocols and data types. Windows applications couldn't communicate with open source applications, at least not without a great deal of work.

Two applications that are communicating need to talk the same language, so a common protocol is required. The protocol needs to use a platform-independent language for data and for describing the data being exchanged. There also needs to be a way to describe the interfaces of the Web Service so that clients can find out what the entry points are. All of these problems are easily solvable and have evolved into a set of standards for use by all application types and platforms. If you are following standards development, the transfer of data takes place in XML format over HTTP, which allows Web Services to easily communicate—within existing architectures and without requiring configuration of firewalls and routers to open additional ports.

Standards and Interoperability

The use of standards has been a key point in the wider adoption of Web Services. Building services for your own use means you can use any protocol, but as soon as you need to extend your application, commonality becomes a requirement. Current standards in use are the following:

- HTTP, which is the transport protocol, typically using TCP port 80, although other ports can be used
- XML and XML Schema, which are the data format and data description languages used
- Namespaces, which uniquely identify resources on the Web
- SOAP, which stands for Simple Object Access Protocol, the protocol that defines how Web Services communicate. SOAP describes a simple XML package for sending messages
- WSDL, which is Web Services Description Language that describes the operations a Web Service can perform, the schema for each message, and the end point (URL) of the service

- WS-I, which is the Web Service Interoperability organization, an industry body that promotes interoperability between Web Services. WS-I's deliverables include Profiles, which define the base capabilities supported by a Web Service
- UDDI, which stands for Universal Description, Discovery, and Integration, and provides a way to find Web Services

There are a variety of other standards, some not in widespread use, but these are the core ones. In many cases, you won't need to know anything about them in depth, because Visual Studio 2005 and ASP.NET abstract them away from you.

Creating Web Services

Creating a Web Service in Visual Studio 2005 is as simple as picking the Web Service template when adding a new item. If you don't use code behind, then you will have a file created containing the code shown in Listing 16.1. There are several important points to notice about the created file:

- The file suffix is ASMX, as opposed to ASPX for ASP.NET pages
- The use of the `WebService` page directive, to indicate that this is a Web Service
- The inclusion of namespaces `System.Web.Services` and `System.Web.Services.Protocols`
- The use of attributes on the class and methods

We'll be describing these attributes in more detail as we go through the section.

If you use code behind, then two files are created. The first is the ASMX file, which consists only of the `WebService` directive. The second is a class file in the `App_Code` folder, containing the code for the server. This is the same code as shown in Listing 16.1, with the addition of a public constructor. It is important to note that because Web Services provide program-to-program communication, there is no user interface; the ASMX file is simply the ASP.NET way of exposing the underlying code. ASP.NET can generate a user interface for Web Services, but this isn't a part of the Web Service itself. You'll see how one is created, and how it can be controlled, a little later.

Listing 16.1. The Default Web Service Code

```
<%@ WebService Language="C#" Class="WebService" %>

using System;
using System.Web;
using System.Web.Services;
using System.Web.Services.Protocols;

[WebService(Namespace = "http://tempuri.org/")]
[WebServiceBinding(ConformsTo = WsiProfiles.BasicProfile1_1)]
public class WebService  : System.Web.Services.WebService {

    [WebMethod]
    public string HelloWorld() {
        return "Hello World";
    }

}
```

What you put into the Web Service is simply the methods you wish to expose. For example, the default code template contains a method called HelloWorld that returns a string. You can have both methods that return data and methods that accept data, much as you do in existing code. For example, consider Listing 16.2, which shows two simple methods, the first to fetch the shippers from the **Northwind** database, the second to insert a new shipper.

Listing 16.2. Web Service Methods that Return and Accept Data

```
[WebMethod]
public DataSet GetShippers()
{
  DataSet ds = new DataSet();
  ds.Merge(ShipperDataLayer.GetShippers());
  return ds;
}

[WebMethod]
public int InsertShipper(string CompanyName, string Phone)
{
  int ShipperID = -1;

  ShipperDataLayer.Insert(CompanyName, Phone, ref ShipperID);

  return ShipperID;
}
```

The only thing that differentiates these methods from other methods is that they are attributed, to indicate they are exposable as methods of a Web Service. The methods can be used internally, without making a Web Service call, so you can have a single method serve two purposes. You may, however, wish to abstract the Web Service interface so that changes to the underlying data or business classes do not affect the exposed Web Service methods. Web Service methods should be instance methods, and not static.

Web Service Attributes

There are several areas where attributes can be used in Web Services, some of which will be covered in the Data Transfer section later in the chapter. The minimum requirement is for the class and methods to have attributes. For the class, you use two attributes, the first of which is `WebService`, which indicates that this class is a Web Service. There are three properties of the `WebService` attribute:

- `Description`, a textual description of the service
- `Name`, the name of the Web Service, which defaults to the class name
- `Namespace`, the unique identifier for the service, often the company Web site URL. Namespaces in Web Services aren't the same thing as namespaces in code files

For example:

```
[WebService(Namespace = "http://northwind.org/services/",
   Description = "Web Services supplied by Northwind Traders")]
public class WebService  : System.Web.Services.WebService {
```

The `WebServiceBinding` defines the set of operations supported by the Web Service. The supported properties are:

- `ConformsTo`, used to specify that the Web Service will conform to a known set of standards, in this case those defined by the WS-I Basic 1.1 standard, which defines things such as the supported version of XML, XML Schema, UDDI, and so on. The only supported conformance claim at the current time is `WsiProfiles.BasicProfile1_1`, which indicates WS-I 1.1 Basic conformance. Note that this uses SOAP 1.1, and not SOAP 1.2, because SOAP 1.2 is not part of the WS-I Basic Profile 1.1

- `EmitConformanceClaims`, which defines whether or not document elements are emitted in the WSDL, indicating that the service conforms to WS-I Basic Profile 1.1

- `Location`, which defines the location for the binding of the Web Service and defaults to the URL of the service

- `Name`, which defines the name of the binding and defaults to the name of the service with `Soap` appended

- `Namespace`, which defines the namespace for the binding

For example:

```
[WebService(Namespace = "http://northwind.org/services/")]
[WebServiceBinding(ConformsTo = WsiProfiles.BasicProfile1_1,
  EmitConformanceClaims = true)]
public class WebService  : System.Web.Services.WebService {
```

For Web methods, you use the `WebMethod` on each method that you wish to expose. The Web Service can use other methods internally, but if they are not attributed they won't be exposed outside of the class. The `WebMethod` attribute has six properties:

- `BufferResponse`, which enables buffering of responses. The default value of `true` ensures that the results are sent in one step to the client

- `CacheDuration`, which is the number of seconds for which to cache the results of the method call. The default value of `0` indicates no caching. Methods with parameters will be cached based upon the parameter value

- `Description`, which is a textual description of the Web Service

- `EnableSession`, which enables session state for the method. The default value is `false`

- `MessageName`, which is a unique name for the method that is useful when you have overloaded methods. However, overloaded methods are not valid for the WS-I Basic Profile, even when using different message names, so you should use unique methods if conformance is required. If conformance is not an issue, then you can change the `ConformsTo` property of the `WebService` attribute to `WsiProfiles.None`

- `TransactionOption`, which indicates whether or not the method participates in a root level transaction—that is, whether it starts a transaction (transactions cannot be started by another application and flow into the Web Service). The value can be one of the `TransactionOption` values, but these behave slightly differently than normal. A Web method either does not participate in a transaction (where you would use `Disabled`, `NotSupported`, or `Supported`), or it does participate in a transaction (and you use `Required` or `RequiresNew`)

For example:

```
[WebMethod(CacheDuration = 60,
   Description = "Returns all of the Shippers")]
public DataSet GetShippers()
```

Testing Web Services

You can test your Web Services by navigating to the ASMX file. For example, consider Figure 16.1, which shows the results of navigating to the Northwind Web Service shown in Listing 16.2. Since Web Services have no user interface, ASP.NET has an HTTP Handler that accepts requests for the ASMX file and dynamically generates a help page. The figure shows the two methods within the Web Service and contains a lengthy description about the default namespace. This description is present because the namespace has been left at the default created by Visual Studio 2005, which is `http://tempura.org/`. If you change the namespace, perhaps to `http://northwind.org/services/`, then the description disappears and you only see the supported operations.

To test the methods in the Web Service, you can click them; you'll then see details about the method, such as the protocols supported, and a button to test the method.

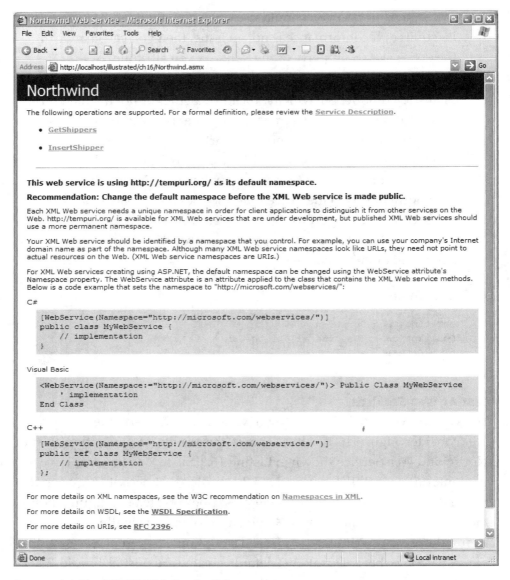

FIGURE 16.1: The ASP.NET Web Service Help page

Testing a Method that Returns Data

For a method that has no parameters, you see something like Figure 16.2, with an **Invoke** button to invoke the Web Service method. The content underneath this button describes the request and response formats for SOAP 1.1, SOAP 1.2, and HTTP POST.

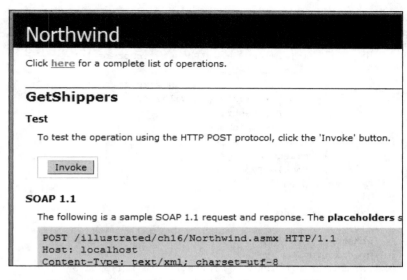

FIGURE 16.2: Testing a Web Service method without parameters

Clicking the **Invoke** button will run the Web Service, which will return the XML results. For the GetShippers method, the results are shown here. You can see that there is an inline schema as well as the data, which allows consumers of the data to understand the data structure.

```xml
<?xml version="1.0" encoding="utf-8"?>
<DataTable xmlns="http://northwind.org/services/">
  <xs:schema id="NewDataSet" xmlns=""
    xmlns:xs="http://www.w3.org/2001/XMLSchema"
    xmlns:msdata="urn:schemas-microsoft-com:xml-msdata">
    <xs:element name="NewDataSet" msdata:IsDataSet="true"
      msdata:MainDataTable="Shippers"
      msdata:UseCurrentLocale="true">
      <xs:complexType>
        <xs:choice minOccurs="0" maxOccurs="unbounded">
          <xs:element name="Shippers">
            <xs:complexType>
              <xs:sequence>
                <xs:element name="ShipperID"
                  msdata:ReadOnly="true"
                  msdata:AutoIncrement="true" type="xs:int" />
                <xs:element name="CompanyName">
                  <xs:simpleType>
                    <xs:restriction base="xs:string">
                      <xs:maxLength value="40" />
```

```
            </xs:restriction>
          </xs:simpleType>
        </xs:element>
        <xs:element name="Phone" minOccurs="0">
          <xs:simpleType>
            <xs:restriction base="xs:string">
              <xs:maxLength value="24" />
            </xs:restriction>
          </xs:simpleType>
        </xs:element>
      </xs:sequence>
    </xs:complexType>
  </xs:element>
  </xs:choice>
  </xs:complexType>
  </xs:element>
</xs:schema>
<diffgr:diffgram
  xmlns:msdata="urn:schemas-microsoft-com:xml-msdata"
  xmlns:diffgr="urn:schemas-microsoft-com:xml-diffgram-v1">
  <DocumentElement xmlns="">
    <Shippers diffgr:id="Shippers1" msdata:rowOrder="0">
      <ShipperID>1</ShipperID>
      <CompanyName>Speedy Express</CompanyName>
      <Phone>(503) 555-9831</Phone>
    </Shippers>
    <Shippers diffgr:id="Shippers2" msdata:rowOrder="1">
      <ShipperID>2</ShipperID>
      <CompanyName>United Package</CompanyName>
      <Phone>(503) 555-3199</Phone>
    </Shippers>
    <Shippers diffgr:id="Shippers3" msdata:rowOrder="2">
      <ShipperID>3</ShipperID>
      <CompanyName>Federal Shipping</CompanyName>
      <Phone>(503) 555-9931</Phone>
    </Shippers>
  </DocumentElement>
  </diffgr:diffgram>
</DataTable>
```

Testing a Method that Accepts Data

For a method with parameters, a form allowing entry for the parameter values is dynamically generated. The parameter values will be passed to the Web Service method when the **Invoke** button is clicked.

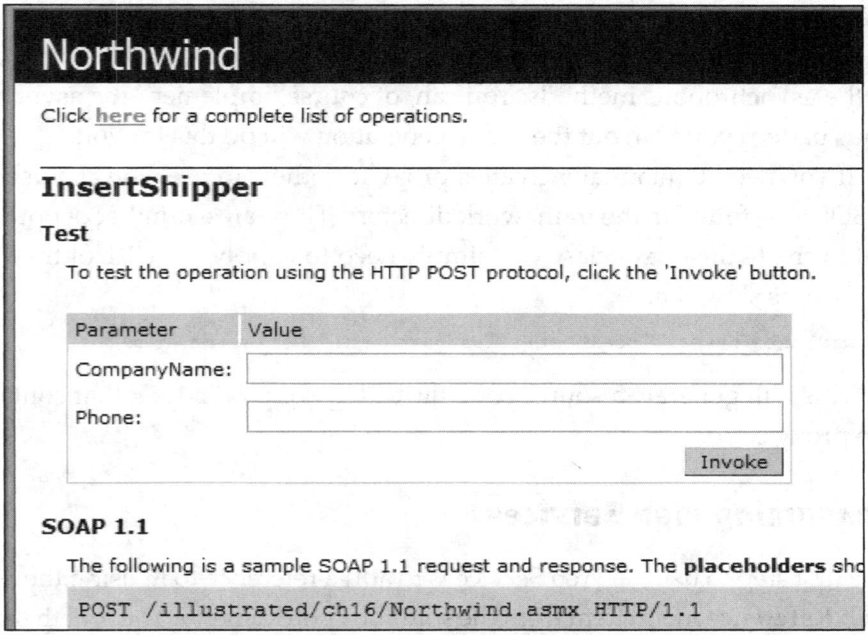

FIGURE 16.3: Testing a Web Service method with parameters

Caching and State

Caching within Web Services can be achieved using the methods described in Chapter 6, and should be done at the data layer or service layer, depending upon your needs. SQL Server notifications cannot be used, because they require an open connection, but this is no loss since one of the main points of Web Services is to provide loosely coupled applications. Notifications are designed for tightly coupled systems.

Although Web Services are stateless, they do have access to the Application and Session objects for state storage and are able to access the HTTP context to use the Cache object.

Creating Asynchronous Web Services

In Chapter 5 you saw that asynchronous operation can improve the performance of Web sites, and this is true in Web Services, especially remote ones. Web Services can be accessed locally without having to create a Web Reference in Visual Studio 2005, but this only gives you access to the methods exposed by the service, or the base class, `WebService`. If you use the Add Web Reference to add a reference, then a proxy class is created for you that gives you access to the asynchronous methods. You can, of course, implement the asynchronous pattern yourself, but the proxy generation will do this for you.

If you need to manually create a proxy for others to use, you can use the WSDL tool, found in the framework directory. There are a number of options, but to create the proxy class you simply need to supply the URL of the Web Service, as shown here:

```
wsdl.exe http://localhost/illustrated/ch16/Northwind.asmx
```

This will generate a source code file called `Northwind.cs` that contains the proxy code.

Consuming Web Services

The first step to using a Web Service is to add a reference to it, using the **Add Web Reference** menu item from the solution context menu. You will then see the **Add Web Reference** dialog (see Figure 16.4) that allows you to browse to the URL of the service. Once you click the **Go** button, the service will

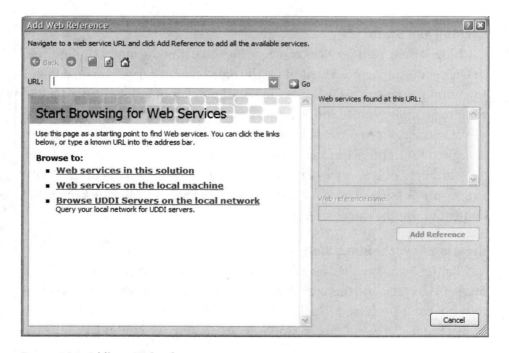

FIGURE 16.4: Adding a Web reference

be examined for Web methods (that is, those with a `WebMethod` attribute), which will be displayed in the lower part of the window. You then give the Web reference a name (which becomes the name the Web Service will have when it is added to the solution) and click the **Add Reference** button (see Figure 16.5).

Once the reference is added, you can access it like any other type. For example, Listing 16.3 shows how to instantiate a Web Service and call a method. In this case, the `GetShippers` method, which returns a `DataSet`, is used as the source of data for a grid.

Listing 16.3. Using a Web Service Synchronously

```
localhostNorthwind.Northwind nws =
  new localhostNorthwind.Northwind();
GridView1.DataSource = nws.GetShippers();
GridView1.DataBind();
```

Listing 16.4 shows that passing parameters to a Web Service is exactly like any other method call; here, the `InsertShipper` method is called, passing in the values of two TextBox fields.

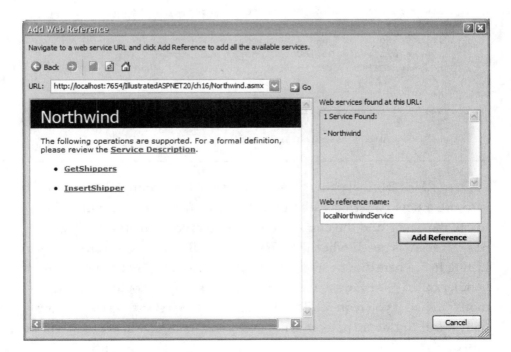

FIGURE 16.5: Naming the Web reference

Listing 16.4. Passing Parameters to a Web Service

```
localhostNorthwind.Northwind nws =
  new localhostNorthwind.Northwind();
int ShipperID = nws.InsertShipper(
  ShipperNameTextBox.Text, PhoneNumberTextBox.Text);
ShipperIDLabel.Text = "ShipperID = " & ShipperID.ToString();
```

Calling Web Services Asynchronously

When calling Web Services, you are generally calling another machine, often over the Internet, and are therefore dealing with a relatively slow service (compared to standard method calls, which are in-process). Because of this, you should consider the asynchronous pattern to call Web Services.

In ASP.NET 1.1, you had to use the `Begin` and `End` methods created by the proxy, as shown in Listing 16.5. You call the `Begin` method, passing in a callback, the method to be run when the Web Service finishes.

Listing 16.5. The Asynchronous Pattern in ASP.NET 1.1

```
private System.IAsyncResult _asyncResult;

private void Page_Load(object sender, System.EventArgs e)
{
  localhost.Northwind nws = new localhost.Northwind();
  _asyncResult = nws.BeginGetShippers(_name,
    new AsyncCallback(WriteResult), null);
}

private void WriteResult(IAsyncResult result)
{
  DataSet result = _service.EndGetShippers(result);
}
```

In ASP.NET 2.0, that pattern is supported, but the recommended approach is to use a new pattern, as seen in Listing 16.6. You use the `Async` method to call the event, and the `Completed` event to process the results. The `Completed` event is raised when the Web Service call is done. You can see this in Listing 16.5, where the `GetShippersCompleted` event is hooked into an event handler called `_service_GetShippersComplete` (you could use an anonymous method if you require). The Web Service is then started asynchronously with a call to `GetShippersAsync`, and when complete the event will be raised.

Within the event, the second parameter contains a property called `Result`, which is the actual result of the Web Service call, and in the code this is simply used as a data source for a grid.

Listing 16.6. Using a Web Service Asynchronously

```
private localhostNorthwind.Northwind _service;

protected void Button2_Click(object sender, EventArgs e)
{
  _service = new localhostNorthwind.Northwind();
  _service.GetShippersCompleted +=
    new localhostNorthwind.GetShippersCompletedEventHandler(
    _service_GetShippersComplete);
  _service.GetShippersAsync();
}

void _service_GetShippersComplete(object sender,
    localhostNorthwind.GetShippersCompletedEventArgs e)
{
  GridView1.DataSource = e.Result;
  GridView1.DataBind();
}
```

This is a much simpler and more intuitive pattern for dealing with Web Services asynchronously.

Handling Errors

You handle errors from Web Services in the same manner as other code, by using exceptions. You generally only deal with network exceptions (for example, the service was unavailable) or SOAP exceptions. You can use the `SoapException` (in the `System.Web.Services.Protocols` namespace) to detect specific problems, or `WebException` (in the `System.Net` namespace) for network problems, as seen in Listing 16.7.

The `WebException` will deal with network problems, such as a 401 error, while the `SoapException` will be used for exceptions within the Web Service. With `SoapException` you don't have access to an inner exception (it will be `null`), because it's an XML SOAP packet you receive back from the Web Service, rather than a local exception object. You do, however, have access to the message, stack trace, help links, and so on, just like other exceptions. If you raise exceptions within Web Service code, these will be wrapped in a `SoapException`.

Listing 16.7. Trapping SOAP Exceptions

```
try
{
  localhostNorthwind.Northwind nws =
    new localhostNorthwind.Northwind();
  int ShipperID = nws.InsertShipper(
    ShipperNameTextBox.Text, PhoneNumberTextBox.Text);
  ShipperIDLabel.Text = "ShipperID = " + ShipperID.ToString();
}
catch (SoapException soapex)
{
  MessagLabel.Text = "SOAP Exception" +
    soapex.ToString();
}
catch (WebException webex)
{
}
```

Controlling How Data Is Transferred in Web Services

When data is returned from a Web Service call, it is serialized into XML, meaning that you can only return native types, or types that know how to serialize themselves (such as the `DataSet`). If you have a strongly typed business layer, and you wish to return this as the result of a Web method, the first thing you need to do is make sure that the class has a parameterless constructor—otherwise it cannot be serialized.

Next, you must make sure that all properties you wish to serialize are read-write, because read-only properties are ignored during serialization, as are methods. Consider Listing 16.8, which shows a simple class for use in a Web Service.

Listing 16.8. The Shipper Class

```
public class Shipper
{
  private int _id;
  private string _companyName;
  private string _phone;

  public Shipper()
  {
  }

  public Shipper(int id, string companyName, string phone)
```

```
    {
      _id = id;
      _companyName = companyName;
      _phone = phone;
    }

    public int ID
    {
      get { return _id; }
      set { _id = value; }
    }

    public string CompanyName
    {
      get { return _companyName; }
      set { _companyName = value; }
    }

    public string Phone
    {
      get { return _phone; }
      set { _phone = value; }
    }
  }
```

When an instance of this class is returned from a Web Service, the XML contains an element for each property, as seen in Listing 16.9.

Listing 16.9. The Serialized Shipper Class

```
<?xml version="1.0" encoding="utf-8"?>
<Shipper xmlns:xsi="http://www.w3.org/2001/XMLSchema-instance"
  xmlns:xsd="http://www.w3.org/2001/XMLSchema"
  xmlns="http://aspnetillustrated.org/services/">
  <ID>5</ID>
  <CompanyName>Tortoise Inc</CompanyName>
  <Phone>555 123 1234</Phone>
</Shipper>
```

Customizing Serialization

You can change the way the XML is generated by attributing the class and properties. For example, consider Listing 16.10. The class has an XmlRoot attribute, which defines the name of the root element. The ID property has the XmlAttribute attribute, specifying the AttributeName, which will make the property become an XML attribute on the parent element. The Phone property has the XmlElement attribute, specifying the ElementName and that it can contain a null value.

Listing 16.10. The Shipper Class Attributed for Serialization

```
[XmlRoot("RegionalShipper")]
public class Shipper
{
  private int _id;
  private string _companyName;
  private string _phone;

  public Shipper()
  {
  }

  public Shipper(int id, string companyName, string phone)
  {
    _id = id;
    _companyName = companyName;
    _phone = phone;
  }

  [XmlAttribute(AttributeName = "ShipperID")]
  public int ID
  {
    get { return _id; }
    set { _id = value; }
  }

  public string CompanyName
  {
    get { return _companyName; }
    set { _companyName = value; }
  }

  [XmlElement(ElementName = "PhoneNumber",
    IsNullable = true)]
  public string Phone
  {
    get { return _phone; }
    set { _phone = value; }
  }
}
```

When the Shipper class is returned from a Web Service, the custom attributes are taken into account, resulting in the XML shown in Listing 16.11.

Serializing Collections

Collections are serialized to structured XML, with the parent element having a default name of ArrayOfClass, where Class is the name of the class being

Listing 16.11. The Serialized Shipper Class with Customized Serialization

```xml
<?xml version="1.0" encoding="utf-8"?>
<RegionalShipper
  xmlns:xsi="http://www.w3.org/2001/XMLSchema-instance"
  xmlns:xsd="http://www.w3.org/2001/XMLSchema"
  ShipperID="5"
  xmlns="http://aspnetillustrated.org/services/">
  <CompanyName>Tortoise Inc</CompanyName>
  <PhoneNumber>555 123 1234</PhoneNumber>
</RegionalShipper>
```

serialized. For example, Listing 16.12 shows the results of a Web Service that returns a generic list of Shipper objects (`List<Shipper>`).

Listing 16.12. A Serialized Collection

```xml
<?xml version="1.0" encoding="utf-8"?>
<ArrayOfShipper xmlns:xsi="http://www.w3.org/2001/XMLSchema-instance"
  xmlns:xsd="http://www.w3.org/2001/XMLSchema"
  xmlns="http://aspnetillustrated.org/services/">
  <Shipper ShipperID="1">
    <CompanyName>Speedy Express</CompanyName>
    <PhoneNumber>(503) 555-9831</PhoneNumber>
  </Shipper>
  <Shipper ShipperID="2">
    <CompanyName>United Package</CompanyName>
    <PhoneNumber>(503) 555-3199</PhoneNumber>
  </Shipper>
  <Shipper ShipperID="3">
    <CompanyName>Federal Shipping</CompanyName>
    <PhoneNumber>(503) 555-9931</PhoneNumber>
  </Shipper>
</ArrayOfShipper>
```

You can control the top element by adding an additional attribute to the Web method. For example, Listing 16.13 shows that you can specify the name of the element returned.

Listing 16.13. Specifying the Returned Element Name

```csharp
[WebMethod]
[return: XmlElement("Shippers")]
public List<Shipper> GetShippers()
```

The top-level element would no longer be `ArrayOfShipper`, but `Shippers`. Note that this only seems to affect SOAP requests, and not HTTP POST requests, which the Web Service Help Page uses. You can tell this by examining the WSDL or the sample output on the help page.

You can also use the `XmlElement` attribute to remove a layer of indirection from within the generated XML. For example, consider the class in Listing 16.14, which is a collection of Shipper objects.

Listing 16.14. The ShipperCollection Class

```
public class ShipperCollection
{
  private List<Shipper> _items;

  public ShipperCollection()
  {
    _items = new List<Shipper>();
  }

  public List<Shipper> Items
  {
    get { return _items; }
    set { _items = value; }
  }
}
```

Listing 16.15 shows that the results of the `ShipperCollection` class is returned from a Web method, and you can see that there is a redundant `Items` element.

Listing 16.15. The ShipperCollection Class Serialized

```
<?xml version="1.0" encoding="utf-8"?>
<ShipperCollection
  xmlns:xsi="http://www.w3.org/2001/XMLSchema-instance"
  xmlns:xsd="http://www.w3.org/2001/XMLSchema"
  xmlns="http://aspnetillustrated.org/services/">
  <Items>
    <Shipper ShipperID="1">
      <CompanyName>Speedy Express</CompanyName>
      <PhoneNumber>(503) 555-9831</PhoneNumber>
    </Shipper>
    <Shipper ShipperID="2">
      <CompanyName>United Package</CompanyName>
      <PhoneNumber>(503) 555-3199</PhoneNumber>
    </Shipper>
```

```
  <Shipper ShipperID="3">
    <CompanyName>Federal Shipping</CompanyName>
    <PhoneNumber>(503) 555-9931</PhoneNumber>
  </Shipper>
  <Shipper ShipperID="14">
    <CompanyName>Tortoise Couriers</CompanyName>
    <PhoneNumber>12555 123 456</PhoneNumber>
  </Shipper>
  <Shipper ShipperID="15">
    <CompanyName>Tortopoise Inc</CompanyName>
    <PhoneNumber>555 123 1234</PhoneNumber>
  </Shipper>
  </Items>
</ShipperCollection>
```

The `ShipperCollection` is the root element, with the `Items` property having an element, and then each `Shipper` an element of its own. To remove the redundant `Items` element, you can use the `XmlElement` attribute on the `Items` property in the collection (Listing 16.16), resulting in the `Shipper` elements becoming a child of the `ShipperCollection`.

Listing 16.16. Attributing the Collection

```
[XmlElement(ElementName = "Shipper")]
public List<Shipper> Items
```

Collections and arrays within classes can also be controlled with a variety of attributes such as `XmlArray` and `XmlArrayItem` to dictate how the array and items should be serialized.

Manual Serialization

By default, ASP.NET will perform the serialization and schema creation for you, but you can do this yourself, if necessary, by implementing `IXmlSerializable`. For example, consider Listing 16.17, which implements this interface. Unlike ASP.NET 1.*x*, you don't use the `GetSchema` method to define the schema; instead, you specify the method that supplies the schema with the `XmlSchemaProvider` attribute on the class. The `ReadXml` and `WriteXml` methods perform the actual serialization.

Listing 16.17. Manually Serializing Classes

```
[XmlSchemaProvider("CustomShipperSchema")]
public class CustomShipper : IXmlSerializable
{
  // standard properties and methods

  public static XmlQualifiedName
    CustomShipperSchema(XmlSchemaSet set)
  {
    XmlSchema s = new XmlSchema();
    s.Id = "Test";
    s.TargetNamespace = "urn:types-nw-com";

    XmlSchemaComplexType t = new XmlSchemaComplexType();
    t.Name = "CustomShipper";

    XmlSchemaElement shipper = new XmlSchemaElement();
    shipper.Name = "shipper";
    XmlSchemaElement id = new XmlSchemaElement();
    id.Name = "id";
    id.Parent = shipper;
    XmlSchemaElement name = new XmlSchemaElement();
    name.Name = "shipperName";
    name.Parent = shipper;
    XmlSchemaElement phone = new XmlSchemaElement();
    phone.Name = "phone";
    phone.Parent = shipper;

    XmlQualifiedName n = new
      XmlQualifiedName(t.Name, s.TargetNamespace);
    shipper.SchemaTypeName = n;

    s.Items.Add(t);
    s.Items.Add(shipper);

    set.Add(s);

    return n;
  }

  // this is not used in v 2.0 of the framework
  // instead the method defined by the attribute sets the schema
  public XmlSchema GetSchema()
  {
      return null;
  }

  public void  ReadXml(XmlReader reader)
  {
    XmlNodeType type = reader.MoveToContent();
```

```
    if (type == XmlNodeType.Element &&
      reader.LocalName == "shipper")
    {
      reader.ReadToDescendant("id");
      _id = int.Parse(reader.Value);
      reader.ReadToNextSibling("shipperName");
      _companyName = reader.Value;
      reader.ReadToNextSibling("phone");
      _phone = reader.Value;
    }
  }

  public void  WriteXml(XmlWriter writer)
  {
    writer.WriteStartElement("shipper", "urn:nw-com");
    writer.WriteElementString("id", _id.ToString());
    writer.WriteElementString("shipperName", _companyName);
    writer.WriteElementString("phone", _phone);
    writer.WriteEndElement();
  }
```

This technique gives you complete control over the schema generated, and exactly what is serialized, and can be useful in interoperability scenarios.

Web Service Enhancements

Many Web Services provide simple sets of data, but the true value of them lies in tying together applications, a way of providing loosely coupled services for distributed processing. To take Web Services from the simple method call to integral parts of enterprise applications, they need additional features. For example, how do you secure Web Services so that only authorized users can access them? Or how can you ensure that data in messages is secure? Or how can you route messages through third-party gateways?

Some of these issues are solvable with the current framework; security and encryption, for example, can be done in a number of ways, often requiring custom code. Web Service Enhancements (WSE) provides standard solutions to these issues. Now in version 3, WSE is a collection of industry-standard specifications, including WS-Security, WS-Addressing, and WS-Policy. The design goals of WSE 3 are to:

- Build secure Web Services easily, to provide secure end-to-end messaging, allowing messages to remain secure when routed through third parties.

- Simplify development, providing easy construction of service-oriented applications.
- Provide for future-proofing and interoperability, allowing existing Web Services to work with Microsoft's long-term vision of service-based architectures, Windows Communication Foundation (WCF), code-named Indigo.

With smaller Web sites, Web Services often don't require many WSE features, but the enterprise space is a different arena altogether. For example, consider a tiered system, where the client machine makes a Web Service call for a payment to a payment server. The message contains details of the payment, which are duly authorized, and the message is then forwarded to back-end services for processing and logging. There are two important points here, starting with message routing, with the message being routed through the payment server; WSE allows messages to pass through different servers on its route to its final destination. The back-end server receives the routed message, but how does it know that this is a valid message, or that the payment server hasn't been compromised? Because of WSE, the routing server can add signed headers to the message to guarantee the authenticity of the message. The second issue is security, where you may only want to have part of the message encrypted—perhaps some of the client details that the routing server shouldn't have access to. Wire-based encryption, such as HTTPS, doesn't provide the capability for partial message encryption, so WSE performs this at the protocol level.

WSE provides five main security profiles:

- Username over transport, where transport level security is used, such as HTTPS. Client authentication is performed against an authorization store such as Active Directory or SQL Server
- Username for certificates, where an X.509 certificate is used for security, and client authentication is the same as for username over transport

- Anonymous for certificate, where an X.509 certificate is used for security, and the client is anonymous
- Mutual certificates, where the client and server exchange X.509 certificates used to secure the data
- Kerberos, where the client and server are within a Windows domain

Which you use depends upon your scenario, but the ease and flexibility of WSE 3 makes writing secure Web Services far easier than in previous incarnations of WSE.

This book isn't the forum for an in depth discussion on WSE, so for more details visit the MSDN WSE page at **http://msdn.microsoft.com/webservices/ webservices/building/wse/**, where you'll also be able to download the WSE 3.0 Toolkit.

The WSE 3.0 Toolkit

The WSE 3.0 Toolkit is a free download and add-on to the .NET 2.0 Framework, providing base functionality as well as tool support. Once installed, you can configure the application by using the **WSE Settings 3.0** option from the application context menu, or manually with configuration files. Configuration and use of WSE 3.0 is based around policies that can be applied to Web Services, clients, and proxies. A policy defines the assertions required for each component of the Web Service.

You can set the policy using the configuration tool (see Figure 16.6). When you add a policy, the WSE Security Settings Wizard allows you to pick what you are securing and the security method (see Figure 16.7). The wizard also allows you to specify how the message is to be protected (see Figure 16.8). There are additional steps allowing you to explicitly declare users and roles authorized to access the Web Service.

Once the policy is defined, you need to configure the service code, starting with an attribute on the class, as shown in Listing 16.18; the value of the parameter to the `Policy` attribute is the name of the policy (creating using the **Add** button on Figure 16.6).

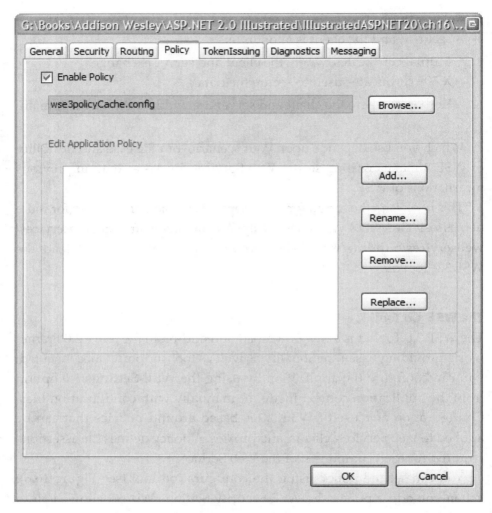

FIGURE 16.6: WSE policy configuration

Listing 16.18. Adding the Policy to the Web Service

```
[WebService(Namespace = "http://tempuri.org/")]
[WebServiceBinding(ConformsTo = WsiProfiles.BasicProfile1_1)]
[Policy("usernameTokenSecurity")]
public class Service : System.Web.Services.WebService
```

By default, authentication is performed against Active Directory, and all you have to do in your code is to extract the security token and authorize

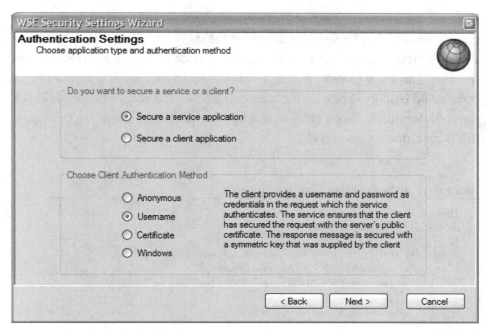

FIGURE 16.7: Selecting the application type and authentication method

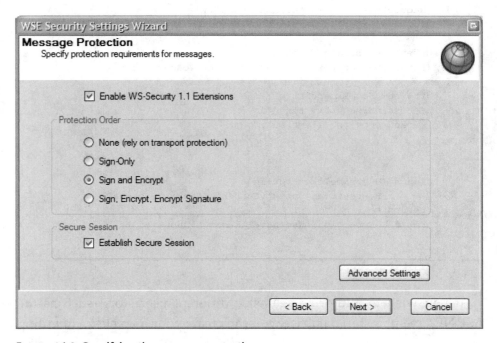

FIGURE 16.8: Specifying the message protection

the user, as shown in Listing 16.19. `GetUsernameToken` extracts the `User nameToken` (a WSE 3 object that identifies the user) from the security tokens of the SOAP request. This token is then used to check the username passed from the client, and if it doesn't match a valid user, an exception is thrown. This code could equally check for the user being in a valid role or have this check done declaratively. Since WSE authorizes the user against Active Directory, this is an authentication check.

Listing 16.19. Authorizing Users in a Web Service

```
[WebMethod]
public string HelloWorld()
{
  UsernameToken token = GetUsernameToken();
  if (token.Username != @"domain\user")
    throw new UnauthorizedAccessException("no way Jose");

    return "Hello World";
}

private UsernameToken GetUsernameToken()
{
  if (RequestSoapContext.Current == null)
    throw new Exception("Only SOAP requests are permitted.");

  // Make sure there's a token
  if (RequestSoapContext.Current.Security.Tokens.Count == 0)
  {
    throw new SoapException(
      "Missing security token",
      SoapException.ClientFaultCode);
  }
  else
  {
    foreach (UsernameToken tok in
             RequestSoapContext.Current.Security.Tokens)
      return tok;
    throw new Exception("UsernameToken not supplied");
  }
}
```

If you wish to authorize against a different user store, such as the ASP.NET membership database, you can create your own class, inheriting from UsernameTokenManager, and overriding the Authenticate Token method, which returns the password for the given user (Listing 16.20).

Listing 16.20. Authorizing Against the ASP.NET Membership Store

```
public class AuthenticationManager : UsernameTokenManager
{
  protected override string AuthenticateToken(UsernameToken token)
  {
    MembershipUser user = Membership.GetUser(token.Username);
    return u.GetPassword();
  }
}
```

On the client application, you perform a similar configuration process, running the WE Security Wizard to define the same rules as for the server. To call the secured Web Service, you create a UsernameToken with the credentials for the user, and use the SetClientCredential method to set the token on the proxy. You then define the policy and call the secured method (Listing 16.21).

Listing 16.21. Calling the Secured Web Service

```
localhost.ServiceWse proxy = new localhost.ServiceWse();
UsernameToken token =
  new UsernameToken(TextBox1.Text, TextBox2.Text,
  PasswordOption.SendPlainText);

proxy.SetClientCredential(token);

proxy.SetPolicy("usernameTokenSecurity");

Label1.Text = proxy.HelloWorld();
```

This is obviously only the simplest of cases, and WSE provides configuration and code for signing and encrypting messages that is just as easy. More detail is outside the scope of this chapter and would be enough content for a book in its own right. For more details, you should consult the WSE 3.0 Quick-Start Samples and documentation that is supplied with the toolkit, as well the GotDotNet Web Server Security Project (http://www.gotdotnet.com/codegallery/codegallery.aspx?id=67f659f6-9457-4860-80ff-0535dffed5e6), and the Microsoft Patterns and Practices Guide for patterns in secure Web Services, which is a free PDF download from the same site.

The Future of Web Services

WSE 3.0, in many ways, is only a stepping stone to the future platform for service-oriented applications, which is Windows Communication Framework (WCF), code-named Indigo. WCF takes a similar view in that service-based communication should be easy, and is aimed at bringing us into the era of Service Oriented Programming. Service Oriented Programming (SOP) has four key tenets:

- Boundaries are explicit. Developers will opt in to exposing, defining, and consuming public-facing services.
- Services are autonomous. Services are consumers, and are independently versioned, deployed, operated, and secured.
- Share schema and contract, not classes. Data never include behavior; objects with data and behavior are local to applications.
- Compatibility based upon protocol. Capabilities and requirements are represented by a unique public name.

WCF is backward-compatible with existing Web Service technologies and can be implemented with a few simple attributes. In fact, it's possible to take an existing ASP.NET Web Service and expose it to both existing clients and WCF clients with only a few attributes and configuration. At the time of writing, WCF is available as a Technology Preview, but it does have a GO Live license, so you can use it in your code right now. You can find more information, and links to the download, at http://www.window communication.net/.

SUMMARY

This chapter has been a brief look at Web Services and how they can be used to extend the reach of applications. This is already happening, with organizations such as Amazon.com having Web Services allowing access to its catalog and purchasing system, giving third parties the opportunity to integrate their users' experience with that of Amazon.com.

We started the chapter with a quick description of the protocols used in Web Services, before moving on to see how Web Services can easily be created and exposed from ASP.NET applications. You saw that even though Web Services have no user interface, ASP.NET dynamically creates a help page allowing you to both examine the SOAP packets used to communicate with the service and test the service.

You then saw how to use Web Services, seeing that once a reference to the service has been established, the service appears like any other class, with callable methods. You saw that the proxy object created by Visual Studio 2005 supports both synchronous and asynchronous calls, with the latter providing a simple event that is raised when the service call has completed. This eases the use of asynchronous services, providing increased performance for consumers.

You then saw how you can control the data serialization process, looking at simple schemes such as attributing the types in classes, and manually serializing the class and providing your own schema. This technique gives you more control over the layout of the XML and schema, which is useful when dealing with fixed schemas already in existence.

Finally, you saw how the Web Services Enhancements provide a simple toolkit for adding security to Web Services. Although this is an additional download, it integrates with Visual Studio 2005, providing a declarative way of stating security policies to use with Web Services. WSE is also an established standard, with wide third-party support, aiding interoperability.

This book has covered a lot of ground, and we hope that you've found it useful. We've endeavored to live up to the 'illustrated' title, showing practical topics and common scenarios. We've also provided links for you to further expand your knowledge, should a particular topic prove more interesting. While it would have been great to cover more topics in more detail, ASP.NET has become so large that this really isn't possible in a single book. ASP.NET 2.0 was a major upgrade to the technology, and improvements are still happening. Since ASP.NET 2.0 was released, several Visual Studio add-ins have been supplied by the ASP.NET team, and client-side scripting technologies are showing signs of a revival that will see even more exciting additions to the product. Keep an eye on the ASP.NET web site at http://www.asp.net/ for all the cool news.

Index

G

Microsoft .NET Development Series

.NET Framework Standard Library Annotated Reference

Volume 1: Base Class Library and Extended Numerics Library

Brad Abrams

0321154894

.NET Framework Standard Library Annotated Reference

Volume 2: Networking Library, Reflection Library and XML Library

Brad Abrams
Tamara Abrams

0321194454

.NET Web Services

Architecture and Implementation

Keith Ballinger

0321113594

A First Look at SQL Server 2005 for Developers

Bob Beauchemin
Niels Berglund
Dan Sullivan

0321180593

Visual Studio Tools for Office

Using C# with Excel, Word, Outlook, and InfoPath

Eric Carter
Eric Lippert

0321334884

Visual Studio Tools for Office

Using Visual Basic 2005 with Excel, Word, Outlook, and InfoPath

Eric Carter
Eric Lippert

0321411757

Graphics Programming with GDI+

Mahesh Chand

0321160770

Framework Design Guidelines

Conventions, Idioms, and Patterns for Reusable .NET Libraries

Krzysztof Cwalina
Brad Abrams

0321246756

Enterprise Services with the .NET Framework

Developing Distributed Business Solutions with .NET Enterprise Services

Christian Nagel

032124673X

Data Binding with Windows Forms 2.0

Programming Smart Client Data Applications with .NET

Brian Noyes

032126892X

Essential ASP.NET

with Examples in C#

Fritz Onion

0201760401

Windows Forms Programming in Visual Basic .NET

Chris Sells
Justin Gehtland

0321125193

The Visual Basic .NET Programming Language

Paul Vick

0321169514

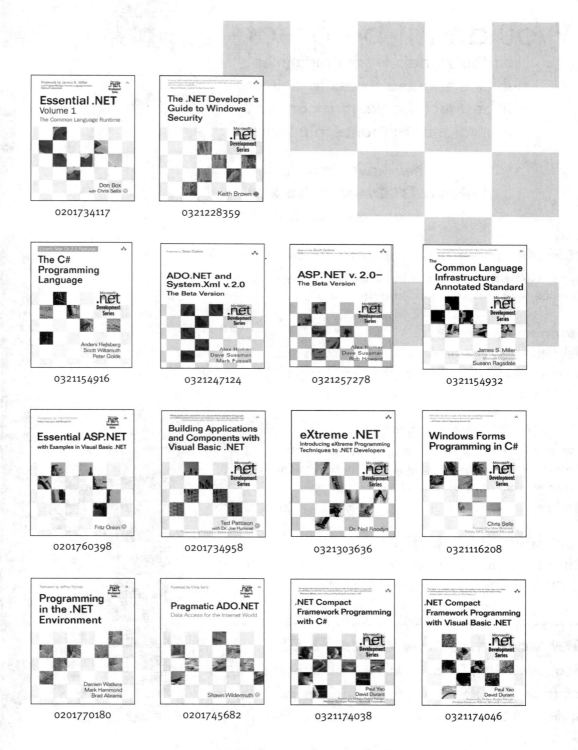

Essential .NET
Volume 1
The Common Language Runtime

Don Box
with Chris Sells

0201734117

The .NET Developer's Guide to Windows Security

Keith Brown

0321228359

The C# Programming Language

Anders Hejlsberg
Scott Wiltamuth
Peter Golde

0321154916

ADO.NET and System.Xml v. 2.0
The Beta Version

Alex Homer
Dave Sussman
Mark Fussell

0321247124

ASP.NET v. 2.0—
The Beta Version

Alex Homer
Dave Sussman
Rob Howard

0321257278

Common Language Infrastructure Annotated Standard

James S. Miller
Susann Ragsdale

0321154932

Essential ASP.NET
with Examples in Visual Basic .NET

Fritz Onion

0201760398

Building Applications and Components with Visual Basic .NET

Ted Pattison
with Dr. Joe Hummel

0201734958

eXtreme .NET
Introducing eXtreme Programming Techniques to .NET Developers

Dr. Neil Roodyn

0321303636

Windows Forms Programming in C#

Chris Sells

0321116208

Programming in the .NET Environment

Damien Watkins
Mark Hammond
Brad Abrams

0201770180

Pragmatic ADO.NET
Data Access for the Internet World

Shawn Wildermuth

0201745682

.NET Compact Framework Programming with C#

Paul Yao
David Durant

0321174038

.NET Compact Framework Programming with Visual Basic .NET

Paul Yao
David Durant

0321174046

For more information go to www.awprofessional.com/msdotnetseries/

THIS BOOK IS SAFARI ENABLED

INCLUDES FREE 45-DAY ACCESS TO THE ONLINE EDITION

The Safari® Enabled icon on the cover of your favorite technology book means the book is available through Safari Bookshelf. When you buy this book, you get free access to the online edition for 45 days.

Safari Bookshelf is an electronic reference library that lets you easily search thousands of technical books, find code samples, download chapters, and access technical information whenever and wherever you need it.

TO GAIN 45-DAY SAFARI ENABLED ACCESS TO THIS BOOK:

- Go to **http://www.awprofessional.com/safarienabled**
- Complete the brief registration form
- Enter the coupon code found in the front of this book on the "Copyright" page

If you have difficulty registering on Safari Bookshelf or accessing the online edition, please e-mail customer-service@safaribooksonline.com.

Addison
Wesley